FUNDAMENTALS OF

GENERAL

PSYCHOLOGY

By

JOHN FREDERICK DASHIELL

Kenan Professor of Psychology
The University of North Carolina

HOUGHTON MIFFLIN COMPANY

BOSTON · NEW YORK · CHICAGO · DALLAS · ATLANTA · SAN FRANCISCO

𝕿𝖍𝖊 𝕽𝖎𝖛𝖊𝖗𝖘𝖎𝖉𝖊 𝕻𝖗𝖊𝖘𝖘 𝕮𝖆𝖒𝖇𝖗𝖎𝖉𝖌𝖊

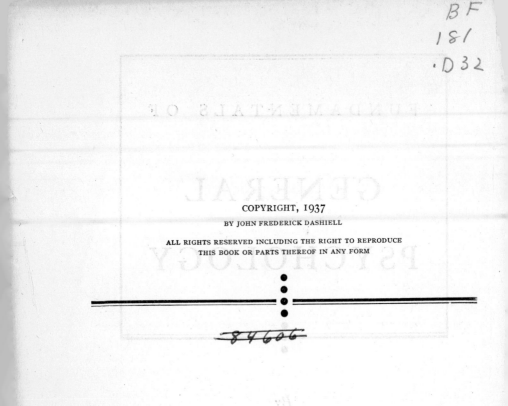

COPYRIGHT, 1937

BY JOHN FREDERICK DASHIELL

The Riverside Press

CAMBRIDGE · MASSACHUSETTS

PRINTED IN THE U.S.A.

TO THE MEMORY OF
JOHN WILLIAM DASHIELL
AND
FANNIE SOPHIA MYERS DASHIELL

PREFACE

THE present work is in a sense a revision of the author's *Fundamentals of Objective Psychology* published in 1928; but it is also a clear advance over that work, sufficient to warrant a new title. Much water has flowed under the bridge since the older manuscript was completed in 1927. New fields of research have led to mines of new factual material. New facts, in their turn, have demanded strikingly new and fruitful characterizations and interpretations. Certainly the psychology of today is enormously richer because of the developments of the decade. Objectivism (behaviorism) may fairly be said to have accomplished its mission of restoring the equilibrium of a science of human nature that had gone exclusively mind-gazing with the extreme post-Wundtian introspectionists. On the other hand, the ultra-simple and flinty concepts of the molecular behaviorism have been liberalized by a number of independent developments that have somehow combined to enrich the picture of genus *Homo sapiens*. More adequate observations of the phenomena of ontogenetic development have brought the principle of maturation back to its former importance and have provided for it an experimental substructure formerly lacking in the speculations of recapitulative and functional psychologies. The formerly unappreciated Gestaltist aspects of visual perception have led to a re-examination of other fields as well and the routing out of deceptively simple atomisms wherever they may be lurking. The masses of detailed clinical accounts accumulated by the psychoanalysts and near-psychoanalysts have, by their sheer weight, forced the psychologists to realize that their first concern is, after all, not with an abstract man but with people. The actual complexities of neural functioning which have come to light recently have served to discredit the use of neurons and of reflex arcs as complete explanatory bases of behavior. From many different laboratories, clinics, and surveys have come protests that *l'homme machine* is not a machine but a motivated organism and is to be interpreted by principles of life as well as by principles of mechanism. There have come, moreover, the belated reminders that man is not a biological but a bio-social organism and is a product of cultural determinants as much as of protoplasmic. Quite recently the vector and topological descriptive methods have re-emphasized the fact that behavior is not something residing in the organism but must be handled, from first to last, as unique organism-environment relationships. All these and other yeasts have been leavening the loaf. What the immature student and the thoughtless layman realize all too little is that, like newer concepts in physics or any other field of science, each advance does not destroy the older view but amplifies it.

A word on pedagogical assumptions. The teaching of beginning courses in psychology today in America may be said to vary — even vacillate — between two extremes. The student-centric view, as I will style it, emphasizes the humanizing of all studies so that they will arise naturally out of queries expressing the curiosity of the student; and psychology especially is thought by many as the opportunity to help the student in his orientation and practical problems. The science-centric view, *per contra*, is the more established one in which the interest of the student is assumed and in which all emphasis is placed on the presentation of the subject-matter as a field of human endeavor and as a body of knowledge. The author cannot escape the conviction that both aims are realizable by the competent teacher; that psychology can be taught on just as dignified a plane as any other field of natural science (which is not realized on many campuses, it must be confessed) with as great a stress on facts and on methodology in lecture and laboratory; and that, human nature being about the most interesting thing in all the world, the study thereof ought to be approachable from the direction of intrinsic human — I had almost written humane — problems. That the author has succeeded well in doing both in the present textbook he would be the last to suppose; but he will say that he has consistently kept before him the ideal of incorporating both by persistently stating leading psychological problems and then suggesting careful appraising of the evidence.

The order of topics and chapters is not to be considered rigid in any sense at all, and it is to be expected that the individual teacher will adopt an order to suit best his own presentations. He will also omit sections or perhaps even whole chapters which he feels unnecessary for his particular purpose.

I wish to acknowledge my debt to my colleague, Dr. A. G. Bayroff, who has read the entire manuscript, and whose criticisms and advice throughout the work have been of very great value in technical, in theoretical, and in pedagogical matters. I am indebted also to my colleagues, Mr. D. D. Wickens and Mr. D. K. Spelt, for detailed and most helpful criticisms of certain chapters. For reading one or more chapters and for special advice I owe much to others of my colleagues — Dr. English Bagby, Dr. Harry W. Crane, Mr. Wallace Nygard, and Mrs. Carol H. Nygard, and also to Dr. D. K. Adams of Duke University and Professor Hermon W. Martin of Emory University.

CONTENTS

CONTENTS

Chapter III. THE HEREDITARY BACKGROUND

Chapter IV. INDIVIDUAL DEVELOPMENT

Chapter V. THE BASES OF MOTIVATION

Chapter VI. SOME PERSONAL PROBLEMS
IN MOTIVATION

Chapter VII. EMOTION

Chapter VIII. MOTOR FUNCTIONS

Chapter IX. SENSORY FUNCTIONS

Chapter X. NEURAL ORGANIZATION OF BEHAVIOR

Chapter XI. STATISTICAL METHODS

Chapter XII. SET AND ATTENDING

Chapter XIII. INTELLIGENT BEHAVIOR

Chapter XIV. FUNDAMENTALS OF LEARNING

Chapter XV. CONDITIONS OF LEARNING

Chapter XVI. PERCEIVING

Chapter XVII. SOCIAL BEHAVIOR

Chapter XVIII. LANGUAGE HABITS

Chapter XIX. THINKING

Chapter XX. PERSONALITY

Chapter XXI. CONDITIONS OF EFFICIENCY

Chapter XXII. CONCLUDING ORIENTATION

ILLUSTRATIONS

CHAPTER I

INTRODUCTION

SOME SAMPLE PSYCHOLOGICAL PROBLEMS

1. Learning an Occupation. Some thirty years ago a practical problem of human efficiency attracted the attention of two investigators. Between the novice at telegraphy and the finished operator, they observed, the differences are truly enormous. The former must note down each letter sound as it comes. The latter, on the contrary, can often "copy behind" as much as ten or twenty words, letting the instrument tick off a long series of dots and dashes before he begins to copy on his typewriter. He can, at the same time, get the sense of the message, keep the run of its grammatical structure, punctuate and capitalize if desired, even catch errors in words transmitted and call the sender's attention to them. External disturbances, furthermore, have a very great effect upon inexperienced telegraphers, but affect the experienced ones very little. "It is not uncommon to see an operator doing a large amount of important work in a small room where half a dozen sets of instruments are working, trainmen running in and out, talking excitedly and asking questions, engines moving by the window, and trucks running noisily by on the platform. Yet the operator works ahead, calmly and rapidly, and even briefly answers questions addressed to him." [1] Emotional disturbances, also, such as fear, anger, joy, excitement, or the presence of a critical audience on the wire, have little effect on the trained dispatcher other than to facilitate his work, whereas the novice under such conditions perspires profusely and sends "rattled" messages that attract the attention of all the operators on the line.

Now, asked Harter, the telegrapher, and Bryan, the psychologist, how do such profound differences come about? How does it happen that a man can with practice alter so enormously his efficiency in an occupation? That people could learn to do such things as telegraphing had always, of course, been known; but *how* they learned and *why* they learned — what factors or causes helped and

---

[1] *Psychological Review*, 1897, **4**, p. 31.

hindered their learning — were questions that had been virtually ignored so far as any exact knowledge was concerned. The human being somehow did learn, and that was practically the end of the matter. These investigators, however, set about studying the problem in an experimental way. First, they discovered that there were important differences between different individuals — in the way they spaced their dots and dashes, their letter spaces and word spaces — differences that were constant enough to be characteristic of the individuals. Then they found that the progress of the learning by each operator could be accurately tabulated and graphically represented in "learning curves." (See Figure 95, page 369.) To make such tabulations the investigators kept a careful count of the number and length of the practice periods, divided the whole learning series into equal time-units, and then found how fast and also how accurately a given individual did his sending and his receiving over the wire, in each of the time-units. Certain striking features they found here: how the typical person practicing on the use of a code would show rapid improvement at first, would then slow down, then speed up again at certain intervals. (These features we shall take up in due time in the present book.) Finally, these investigators discovered that they could secure data on more subjective and personal sides of the learning: how a man's enjoyment of the work fluctuates, when and why he makes more intense efforts, and the like. These were found to be important factors in the learner's progress.

Research of this nature has thrown light on a large variety of learning tasks such as using a radio code, reading a foreign language, driving an automobile, mastering a musical instrument. The moral is clear: the relation of a man to his work need not always be the hit-or-miss matter that it has hitherto been. When one faces the opportunity or the necessity of acquiring some new technique or some new field of knowledge, he can know in advance something of what his progress is likely to be, what the best ways of practicing are, and what devices will help or hinder him. And, most important, he can know this more precisely than the "practical man" of everyday experience because he can rely upon experimentally determined and statistically analyzed facts.

2. Memorizing. As far back in human culture as educational procedures have been traced, learning by rote, "by heart," has been one of the tasks set before the young. Chinese schools have, from ancient times, required the memorization of the sacred Books and Classics.   But neither by philosopher nor by schoolman was memorizing thought of as a *natural phenomenon*, a phenomenon to which precise scientific methods could be applied.   Certain aphorisms were common coin ("he that learns quickly forgets quickly," "old people forget the things they last learned," and so forth); but such propositions were of the vague, indefinite sort so commonly derived from rough observations of striking cases.   In the 1880's, however, Ebbinghaus demonstrated by experimental investigations that the memorizing performance of a human being was a natural event in a natural world, that it could be measured by accurate technique and the data given quantitative presentation. He devised homogeneous learning material in the form of nonsense syllables and arranged them in series; and he then memorized each series by reading it over and over until he could reproduce it as a whole without error.   The number of readings required he then took as a quantitative measure of the efficiency of the learning. Then, by rigorously controlling the experimental conditions under which the learning proceeded, and by checking and evaluating all possible sources of error, Ebbinghaus was able to derive rules and formulas concerning the various sorts of factors that influence a person's efficiency in acquiring and retaining memory material. He proved that the rate at which a person acquires and forgets is dependent in certain precise amounts upon such conditions as the length of the series to be learned, the kind of material, continued practice even after the subject matter was learned, and relations between different parts of the subject matter.   And these rules and formulas had an exactness rivaling those of the physical sciences.

"Cause and effect," that is, a relation of dependence of one variable or factor on another, applies to these higher psychological processes of man as truly as they do to his circulatory and digestive processes or to the outcome of mixtures of chemical substances in a test tube.   "Mental" processes could be measured!

3. The Personal Factor in Scientific Observations.   Psychological methods have been applied not only to problems of occupation, industry, business, and daily life, but also to the work of scientists themselves.   In the year 1795 the director of the Greenwich Observatory dismissed his assistant because, as the director thought, the man had been making false observations of star transits.   The method involved was this: the astronomer directed a telescope equipped with a "hair line" to a point in the sky where a star was expected to appear; he set a clock to striking seconds, and at the exact moment that he saw the star cross the hair line he noted the number of the coinciding stroke heard or the distance from the nearest stroke.   Now the assistant at Greenwich had been making records of star transits about 0.8 of a second later than the director; and because this minute disparity was sufficient to disturb mathematical calculations of relative star positions, the man lost his place. But his reputation was saved some years later when several of the most noted astronomers found that the readings of no one of them agreed with those of any of the others in these time determinations; nor, for that matter, did any one man's reading always agree perfectly with his own readings made at other times.   With all the nicety of adjustment of their telescopes and all the exactitude of their mathematical formulas, these scientists realized that they had failed to take account of another set of factors entering into the measurements — the "personal equation," they called it.   But they were natural scientists, and instead of considering this "personal equation" something mysterious, unfathomable, from outside the province of science, they and the physiologists promptly undertook to determine its fundamental characteristics by experiment.

They found it possible to duplicate in the psychological laboratory the essential conditions which obtained in the recording of star transits.   How quickly, and with how constant a quickness, can a person X take note of and record a flash of light, a snap of sound, a brief touch on the skin?   What was needed, of course, was apparatus for providing the signal (flash, snap, etc.), apparatus by which the person or "subject" could make his response, and — most delicate of all — apparatus that would record both signal and response so precisely that the time interval between the two could be determined in thousandths of a second.   Simple as an experiment of this sort may sound, the work soon came to demand exhaustive and detailed planning of apparatus and of technique.   When a subject presses a key, for instance, he may do this simple act in so many different ways that detailed instructions are demanded from the start.   As a consequence, we have a voluminous literature on human "reaction times" and the various modifying factors upon which they depend.   The accurate measuring of the interval in such small units with no loss of time in getting the registering apparatus started and no loss in getting it stopped, has called for much mechanical ingenuity; so that today there are at least six different general types of "chronoscopes" based on as many radically different engineering principles.   (One is shown in Figure 10, page 46.)   Not only in connection with scientific research but in its practical applications is the measuring of a man's reaction time significant.   It is of recognized importance in highway motoring, airway flying, home-run hitting, and in hundreds of kinds of machine-tending jobs in industry.

4. Human Errors are Calculable.   Another aspect of the "personal equation" has received much attention.   If each and every observer shows some variations in his reactions, what about this variability itself?   We cannot hope to reduce it to zero; but we can see whether there is any constancy in the way the variations or "errors" occur.   "To err is human"; but is this a counsel of hopelessness?   The scientist, who holds to the faith that everything that happens, no matter how small, must have its causes, its explanation, has turned his scrutinizing eye upon this "erring," and knows that if it is "human" it is a natural phenomenon and subject to natural laws.   Examination of human variability assumed a statistical form.   What is John Doe's average score?   Then how widely does he vary from this average from trial to trial?   What is the average of these variations?   When he varies in one direction on one kind of performance, does he vary in the same way on another; and if so, can we therefore say that the two kinds of performances vary together and must be somehow related?   These are but a few beginning queries.   The employment of statistical procedures for analyzing human beings has gone on apace, so that today no psychologist would presume to investigate and to deliver opinions without being prepared to put his findings into statistical order.   Such things as slide rules and logarithmic tables are necessary not only for the measurement of land and strengths of materials but also for the measurement of human abilities and human organization.

5. Unearthing the Deeper Habit-Systems.   Men have always been interested in the play of their ideas and of their words; and ever since Aristotle they have busied themselves with laws to describe the order in which they occur.   But this was all speculation, concerned principally with working out the more purely logical and superficial relations in man's thinking in general.   Early in the 1880's, however, Francis Galton hit upon a way of dragging to light the subtle germinating principles that account for the actual trains of thinking, and of revealing the personal peculiarities of different individuals in this regard.   To others fell the opportunity to develop the method, particularly to the Swiss psychiatrist, Jung.   He would give to his subject or patient a list of words, one at a time, to each of which the patient was instructed to answer with the very first word that "came to him."   By making up a long list of "stimulus-words" chosen from a very wide range, Jung was able, he thought, through careful and thorough analysis of the responses, literally to "read his patient's thoughts."   That is, he could observe how thinking-reactions were linked together, and hence could judge how they would be likely to function in this or that concrete situation. For example, a mother and her daughter revealed highly similar thinking habits, as appears in the accompanying table.   As later investigators have shown, most people do their thinking along conventional and customary "grooves": their word-responses to the same stimulus-words are pretty much the same.   But some there are who reveal their originality and occasionally their maladjustments by responding with words not so ordinarily given.

Other aspects of the human personality were brought to light. Jung included in his lists many critical words that were calculated to arouse the patient's emotions, particularly if they centered about certain objects and experiences.   When a patient gave to one of these words a long-delayed response, or a far-fetched response, or no response at all, Jung concluded that the thing which the word named had some special personal significance for the patient; and

FREE WORD-ASSOCIATION TEST WITH TWO SUBJECTS *

STIMULUS WORD	MOTHER'S RESPONSE	DAUGHTER'S RESPONSE
Angel	innocent	innocent
Haughty	bad boy	bad boy
Stalk	leek's stalk	stalks for soup
Dance	couple	gentleman and lady
Lake	much water	great
Lamp	burns bright	gives light
Rich	king	king
New	dress	dress
Law	God's command	Moses
Great	God	father
Brother	loves me	love
Fire	great pain	painful

* From Jung, C. G. *Studies in Word-Association* (trans. by Eder). Dodd, Mead & Co., 1919.

that with an exhaustive examination of this sort the patient's emotional habits could be analyzed.

The word-association technique has become highly standardized today. It furnishes an interesting contrast to our third example of psychological research in that no instrument more elaborate than a stop-watch is required, and further in the fact that it is a probing device that becomes an invaluable tool in the hands of the clinical investigator as he studies each of his patients by himself, with the desire to understand him better.

Thus we see that even the most subtle and most intricate operations of a person's make-up can with patience be laid bare by employing standardized technique similar to that used in the objective and impersonal experiments of natural science.

With these few examples of concrete inquiry before us, let us turn to consider a number of more general questions about psychology.

VARIOUS AVENUES TO HUMAN NATURE

Three Avenues. Knowledge and understanding of human nature may be acquired in various ways. One is the direct way of *everyday practical experience*. The kindergarten child has embarked upon this road as he comes into contact with playmates and work mates and must respond appropriately to their presence. And where is the adult man or woman who does not rate himself a good judge of people about him, with plenty of ability to "see them through and through"? And so the day-to-day contact with one's fellows furnishes the opportunity — even necessity — to learn better and better how to get on with them: whom to approach and whom to avoid, and, for that matter, when to approach and when to avoid. And so skillful may the intelligent person become that he is much more often right than wrong in anticipating what his fellow is likely to do. (The truth of the matter is that he is usually unaware of just how he comes to make his judgments, and he is likely to attribute his own shrewdness to wrong things — but this we shall look into later.)

Another avenue of approach to human nature is the indirect route through *literature and other fine arts*, and through *history and biography*. Human beings are observed at second- or third-hand, and, though lacking in the concreteness of those encountered in the flesh, their correct understanding is presumably furthered by the interpretations of the writer. The interpretations may be offered in astonishing variety of forms, from the detailed analysis of particular people by a Dostoievski or a Henry James to the revelations of one's own inner springs by a Wordsworth or a Poe. This indirect avenue to knowledge of man is celebrated to excess in Pope's lines:

> When first young Maro in his boundless mind
> A work t'outlast immortal Rome designed ...
> Perhaps he seemed above the critic's law,
> And but from nature's fountains scorned to draw.
> But ... Nature and Homer were, he found, the same ...
> Learn hence for ancient rules a just esteem;
> To copy nature is to copy them.

The most direct and definite route to a knowledge of man is that furnished by the *methods of natural science*, namely, *observation* and *experimentation* with *statistical* refinements. Consider how man's grasp upon the world of living and non-living things has changed from the guessed-at, hit-or-miss, rule-of-thumb character of so-called practical knowledge picked up in daily life or received as the wisdom of the elders and the ancients, to the astonishingly precise knowledge of natural objects and processes that renders their activities and behavior so predictable that engineering and medicine are made possible. Historically, in the development of Western culture, scientific methods came to be recognized as a kit of intellectual tools invaluable for getting at the facts; and man came to realize the distinct advantage of addressing nature in a detached and impersonal manner. And so with regard to man himself. Putting aside our prides and prejudices, what are the discoverable facts about him? Modern psychology was born from this emphasis upon the application of scientific methods to the actions of man.

The reader should not become confused. Not just any opinion or information about man and his behavior is "psychology," even though it may claim to be such in newspaper advertisements and wood-pulp magazines; and not everyone who knows his fellowman usefully and adequately is a "psychologist." To call an effective salesman "a good psychologist" or a rabble-rousing political speech "good psychology," is as loose language as to call a successful farmer a good botanist or a trainer for a dog-and-pony show a good zoologist. Properly speaking, then, the name "psychology" is limited to those interests in human behavior that take the form of true scientific inquiry.

Scientific Psychology Serves Human Values. Let us think of the natural sciences as fields in which men apply a certain special technique to gain a better control of things, so that those things can be used more effectually to meet man's wants and make life better, more lovable, and more ideal. Then we can see that a study of the sciences does not at all threaten any humanistic values; and the study of man as an objective thing does not challenge any of the goods of human life. But if we can by such study get at what actually causes, influences, and determines man's behavior we can then control man better, or control the things that can make him happy. The study of habit making and habit breaking may be carried on without considering whether the habits are good or bad. But when we know something about habit making and breaking, we can apply that pure-science knowledge to the problem of developing good character in man instead of bad. Having determined just what conditions will produce a given result in the behavior of a person, we are able to create with some accuracy certain types of behavior by setting up the conditions which have been demonstrated to produce this behavior. None other than a great painter, Leonardo, said: "Those who are enamoured of practice without science are like a pilot who goes into a ship without rudder or compass and never has any certainty where he is going. Practice should always be based upon a sound knowledge of theory." Certainly his own thorough study of scientific subjects did not limit his appreciation and creation of beauty.

Different Attitudes Toward the Same Subject. It is one of those commonplaces so easily forgotten that no scientist is a scientist every minute of his day. When the anatomist sits down to his beefsteak he is addressing himself not to a piece of anatomy, but to appetizing food. When the chemist spreads butter on his toast he is assuredly not manipulating atoms or electrons, nor "glycerides of oleic, stearic, palmitic, butyric, caproic, caprylic, capric, and myristic acids." Consider the astronomer gazing at a sunset. What he is regarding is not a certain refraction of ether vibrations due to a certain spatial relationship of the astronomical sun to the planet called the earth. A physicist attending a symphony concert is most certainly not occupying himself with the length, amplitude, and composition of the waves of sound that are being produced by the scrapings and blowings of instruments on the stage. He listens to the sounds as music, and as music he judges them. This total difference of attitude that occurs with the donning and the doffing of a laboratory apron is well illustrated in the work of the surgeon. The fact that proper surgical treatment is not an affair between friends, but a scientific matter, is shown by the laws in certain states that prohibit a physician's performing major operations on his own near relatives.

Anything can be looked at from different points of view. Let us take that thing that we call man. If you are an economist, you will look at man as a producer and consumer, and on the ratio between these two things you will estimate his value to the world. If you are a salesman, you will see man as a prospective buyer: that is the way you form your judgment of him, and that is the way you treat him. If you are a teacher, man is a something that can learn. The way in which he is likely to learn, what stimuli you can apply to make the learning more effective, interests you. You do not care what he produces in economic goods. If you are a religionist or a moralist, the man is a soul to be saved. Suppose you are an artist, and take an artist's attitude toward man — he is then a body to be sculptured or painted. As a chemist you will regard him as an enormously complex combination of oxygen, carbon, and hydrogen, plus nitrogen, sodium, and other elements. If you are a politician, you will see him only as a ballot-marker. If you are a zoologist or a physician you will look upon this man as a specimen of *homo sapiens*, or as a vast complex of tissues, which get out of order easily; and you will not care whether he is one of society's producers, learns well or ill, beats his wife, is an ensemble of good lines and curves, or is a straight Republican. Such an object as a particular human being may stand in a great number of separate and mutually unrelated systems of study. We insist, then, that the description and analysis of our psychological object, a man, in terms of physical processes and material mechanisms, does not imply at all any lessening of man's dignity as viewed from other angles. Psychology challenges no poetical, ethical, religious, social, romantic, or other humanistic conception of his life and destiny. It is merely another way of looking at man. And, in fact, the humanitarians of any field should look to it with confidence for the methods of study and the factual findings that it can yield them.

SCIENTIFIC METHODS USED IN PSYCHOLOGY

Experimental Method. To come to closer grips with our subject: what are the particular methods especially employed in psychology? "Scientific method" is after all a rather broad term, for astronomers, physicists, naturalists, physiologists, and anthropologists, to name a few, use different techniques appropriate to their several kinds of materials. Psychological research may be said to proceed with two principal types of observation. The one to which most of the advancement in the last century is to be attributed is experimentation. (This method is best shown in the first three sample psychological problems at the beginning of the chapter.)

The student will recognize one of the simplest and clearest examples of experimentation from his knowledge of the chemical laboratory. There the experimenter holds by his left hand a glass test tube containing an accurately known and accurately measured substance. Into this he introduces one drop of another accurately known and measured substance. What happens is noted as precisely as possible. He introduces more drops. Or he applies a flame to raise the temperature ten degrees. What happens? Whatever does happen is assumed to be dependent upon the change of conditions which he has specifically controlled.

So in other experimental lines. In an ideal experiment a bit of soil, a new clover, a frog, a child, or an adult, is brought into a laboratory, where *all the conditions and surroundings are set by the experimenter* and where he has instruments for *carefully introducing changes in some one of those conditions.* He can observe if and when anything "happens" in the soil, clover, frog, child, or adult, when the change in the condition is introduced. He can change one condition after another; and after an exhaustive trying of many he will be in a position to say positively with which condition the happening in the soil, clover, frog, child, or adult is associated. Having controlled all other factors and having observed factor x to be the one with which the phenomenon is invariably related, he calls the factor x an *independent variable* and the phenomenon a *dependent variable.*[1]
He — and all who read his report — has now gotten a purchase on that phenomenon; he knows what (in a popular sense) "causes" it, and can produce it at will. It is predictable. It is under control.

---

[1] These terms are rough equivalents of "cause" and "effect," but are preferable because less misleading.

Example from an infra-human species. An illustration of control
secured in very high degree is furnished us in the case of the negative
geotropism of the young white rat, which varies with the factors
introduced into the experiment. (See Figure 1.) (1) Practically
invariably, if tested before its eyes are open, this animal, like a number of others similarly studied, will climb upward when on a vertical
or sloping ground. What is more, the steeper the incline the sharper
the upward turning. Repeated experimental studies of this phenomenon have led to a mathematical formulation of it.

$$\theta = K \log \sin \alpha$$

in which θ is the angle of turning by the animal, α is the angle of
inclination of the plane, and K is a constant whose value depends
upon the animal species (in this case the rat). ("Log" and "sin"
the student should recognize from trigonometry, but understanding
their meaning is not necessary to our purpose here.) Our phrase

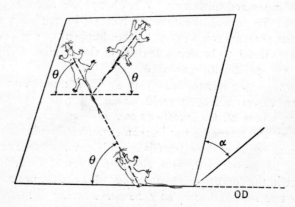

FIGURE 1. A CASE OF HIGHLY PREDICTABLE BEHAVIOR: RELATION
BETWEEN INCLINE OF SURFACE AND TURNING OF ANIMAL

The level plane on which the animal was in progress in the direction *OD* is inclined through
the angle α, resulting in the animal's turning upward through the angle θ. This highly definite
relation of dependence of turning on incline is well shown in the data:

α	θ	α	θ
15°	32.6°	40°	69.8°
20°	44.5°	50°	77.9°
25°	52.9°	60°	84.7°
30°	57.4°	70°	88.3°

(Adapted from Crozier, W. J., and Pincus, G., The Geotropic Conduct of Young Rats,
J. Gen. Physiol., 1926–27, **10**, 259.)

above, the steeper the incline the sharper the turning, is now restated in the equation with a high degree of mathematical precision.

But as we introduce more factors, more complications and more variations arise. (2) If while the rat is moving on the incline, and simultaneous with its movement, a light falls upon the rat from one side only, its course tends to be directed away from it. (3) If the light continues, the animal gradually becomes adapted to it so that it turns away from the light less and less. (4) If another light is set up at 180° from the first, the animal is directed along a mid-line. (5) Suppose adrenalin is injected into the organism: it moves faster, the angle of turning is increased, and the whole general performance is more variable. (6) When the rat's eyes have opened (at about two weeks' age), a highly significant further modification appears in its behavior: no longer does it react simply to the direction of the light rays but it will run for a dark place seen at a distance. We could continue to introduce other variations in the conditions and to complicate the resulting behavior-phenomena beyond all possibility of mathematical formulation in our present stage of knowledge.

If now we knew adult human beings so well that we could predict with similar precision exactly what one would do on this, that, and another occasion, the science of psychology would be complete. But *men are incredibly more complex* than infant rats. They are subject to a vastly greater variety of influences, and they have available a vastly richer repertoire of reactions. This, however, is a counsel of caution, not of despair. Substantial advances have been made and are being made; and the field of psychology can furnish very many statements with sufficiently substantial approximations to accuracy to render them highly important not only to serve as foundations for further psychological research but to be applied to practical problems of education, industry, the professions, and daily life.

Clinical Method. The ideal for performing a good experiment is to bring to light or to prove or disprove some principle of interpretation concerning natural (human) phenomena, a principle that promises to hold as a *general truth for mankind in general*. But an experimental analysis, though it is certainly the final touchstone, is not always feasible or possible. Many a psychological principle comes to light in examination of impaired or disordered functioning, such as lapses of memory, color blindness, stuttering, disordered and excessive emotional seizures, or inability to learn. All such personal peculiarities have great scientific value, for they bring to light what might in the general run of men be passed unnoticed. A colored tenant farmer when asked whether the used car he had recently acquired had a certain kind of engine-part answered simply, "Ah dunno. It ain't never broke down yit." So with our knowledge of the human make-up: it grows in part out of our studies of *particular cases of deficiency or impairment*. Such data for a science of human beings cannot often be obtained by the direct methods that are available to him who works on tadpoles and crayfishes, on metals, alkaloids, and electric batteries. A man cannot be locked indefinitely in a cabinet, fed unknown substances, be dismembered and decerebrated. The psychologist cannot, of course, produce disordered cases experimentally; he can only report cases that turn up in the schoolroom, playground, home, or hospital, giving them intensive examination in his clinic, and reporting them to the scientific world.

For another reason, also, clinical methods are important in psychology. We are not interested simply in mankind in general: we are oftentimes *interested in this particular man*, John Doe, *in his individuality* and all his idiosyncrasies. We may want to study him not as a type but for his own sake, oftentimes to advise or to help him (to correct a speech defect, to get a job, to overcome a persistent worry, or to do better studying). We then take a clinical interest in him. (The fifth sample problem at the beginning of the present chapter is largely clinical.)

Statistical Method. In some of the sample problems in psychology with which this chapter opened, the quantitative emphasis was surely indicated. In the third one, for instance, the fallibility of human observations has furnished a rich field of investigation. But what of the psychologist himself? If the observer whom he is observing makes errors (shows variabiiity), does not he himself make errors in the very act of observing him? More generally, does it not follow that all psychological data — like all physical and other scientific data — are subject to error, that is, show some degree of variability? True, and hence the preoccupation of the more exact natural sciences with statistics.

Consider also, as we have pointed out earlier, the enormous complexity and multiplicity of varying factors that contribute to a psychological phenomenon. It is no wonder that the same experiment has to be run in long series, and that check experiments have to be set up. And now, once a long series of data are assembled —

as, in the third example, several hundred reaction times from the same subject under the same conditions — the next procedure is their interpretation.   Here the experimentalist must turn statistician: he must *apply special mathematical techniques to analyze his mass of data* in order to find exactly *what he can and cannot safely conclude.*   In summary, the direct observational methods of clinical and experimental investigations must be supplemented by statistical analyzing.

DIRECTIONS OF PSYCHOLOGICAL APPROACH

Objective and Subjective.   One feature of psychological investigation that contrasts it sharply with any other natural science is the fact that it can approach its subject-matter, the human being, both by way of the observations made by experimenter or clinician and also in many cases by way of observations the subject-matter can make on itself.   Many of the phenomena we are to include in our survey are events occurring in a person which (*a*) can be noted and reported best by other people — a public approach, while some (*b*) can be noted and reported best by the person himself — a strictly private approach.   The emotions of a woman whose car is stalled momentarily on the railroad track before an approaching train can be observed in two ways: we can hear screams and see her frantic gesticulations and wasted motions; and she could afterward relate how "her heart was in her mouth" and the world spun around her.   In one who is paying rapt attention we can note the tensed muscles and immobile posture; and he could himself report how he thought of nothing else in his absorption.   In a street car we see a passenger reading the advertisement cards; he on his part would be able to tell us what they meant to him.   The approach from the public side is known as the *objective* or *behavioristic* approach, that from the strictly private is called the *subjective* or *introspective* approach.

Illustrations.   It should be obvious that whether an objective experiment or subjective experiment is to be performed depends upon the nature of the problem raised and the kind of answer sought. Is the progression to a climax in Berlioz' *Hungarian March* as personally thrilling as the old Russian hymn motive in Tchaikowski's *Marche Slav?*   Is the Japanese method of flower decoration as effective a method of balance as the familiar Occidental way?   What is the precise difference between an itch and a tickle?   Just when is a pain teasingly pleasant?   How far back into your early childhood can you recall episodes?   Were your emotions more vivid then than now?   Can you recall the lapping sounds of breakers on the beach?   Or the buoying effect of an ocean swell that lifts you off your feet?   For such questions we employ the subjective approach, for we are asking questions that only the subject can answer.   Of course we have no way of checking up directly on his answer, and so we treat it with the proper respectful caution.   But we can check up on his verbal descriptions by asking whether or not they correspond with those offered by other subjects concerning their own private experiences.   If these experiences of our subject are what we are after, then, the answer is at hand, and has been found by using the subjective approach.

Now let us suppose we are concerned with, say, the differentiation between itching and tickling.   How will our subject *act* when touched lightly with a sharp bristle and how will he act when stroked lightly with a soft brush?   This we can see for ourselves. Does he promptly scratch the spot or does he laugh and pull away? We could use a motion-picture camera, or construct a mechanism of levers with cords attached to the subject, or use other devices to take permanent records of just how he acts.   This time we would be using the objective approach.   Many phenomena of man are matters which can be best investigated in objective ways.   Does X walk in his sleep?   Is he awkward in his handling of things?   Does negativism (contrariness) usually appear before the age of three years?   Is an infant of one year capable of jealousy?   Are the child's first notions of animals specific in reference or general?   Is the moron capable of earning a living?   Does the depth of one's sleep decrease gradually through the night?   Is the dementia praecox patient ever hilarious?   And — since animals really come into psychology's purview — does the dog learn more rapidly than the cat?   Do apes display a primitive sympathy?

It is apparent, then, that *it is the nature of the problem and the kind of answer which we are seeking that determine the direction of approach.*

We must consider that there are many problems and answers that refuse to be classed as subjective or objective in any narrow sense.

(*A*) Suppose it is remarked that John Doe is a man of "good judgment."   Here is a trait that psychologists should be able to check and eventually be able to measure. But is his good judgment a matter of Doe's feelings, ideas, and the like? No. We might be so critical as to believe that Doe's experiences on the subject are not valid evidence. On the other hand, is his good judgment describable as the way in which his vocal cords operate or his gesticulating hand is moved by compensatory muscular flexions and extensions? No.

(B) Suppose one is investigating in home or nursery-school the conditions under which "jealousy" arises. Does he set about it by inferring this or that about how the child is feeling — whether he is experiencing a vivid love thrill colored by a tinge of resentment? Reports of observers show the contrary to be true. On the other hand, does the psychologist try to set down a detailed description of finger movements, lip curlings, and eyelid twitches?

(C) The time-honored method for studying "memory" consists of having a subject read through a list of items one-by-one, then having him attempt to reproduce the list. In such an investigation, what are the essential data? They are not descriptions of what "passed before the subject's consciousness," nor an account of the sensations or thoughts or feelings he had undergone. Nor do they consist of reports on how his eyeballs moved or his vocal cords tightened or relaxed or whether his voice maintained its levels of pitch and loudness.

(D) Let us now try a simple demonstration of the free word-association technique on the reader himself. Let him prepare himself to respond as quickly as possible by naming the opposite to each of the following words: "hot," "summer," "hard," "white," "fast." Now, what is the nature of the data to be obtained from this exercise? It consists of the printed stimulus-words and the subvocally pronounced response-words, plus the general reading context, the reader's willingness to co-operate, and so forth. But what of the psychological process being tested? Did the reader observe just how the reading of each word led to his answer? Can he, that is, introspectively recall any conscious process of germination and fruition? At the same time, he is not interested in the specific muscular adjustments of his vocal apparatus in the subvocal acts of saying the words; they are not the point at issue.

Now to summarize. A man's "good judgment," his "jealousy," his "memory," his "thought associations" may be uncovered and even measured by experimentally controlled processes or performances, but they cannot be considered as things purely "mental" nor purely "bodily." They are *capacities*, *abilities*, *aptitudes*, *propensities*, *proclivities*.

Throughout the present book, therefore, we shall present the data furnished by recent research, whether it has been obtained by observing others or by observing oneself. As a matter of simple fact, most of the research is of the former, the objective, sort; but we shall not scruple at including relevant observations made subjectively.

PSYCHOLOGY AND THE STUDENT

Not Prescriptions but Perspectives to be Sought Here. The reader is warned not to expect of this book — nor of any other text-book — explicit prescriptions. He should not hope to find here rules that are specific and that will fit this, that, or the other concrete personal situation that may confront him. Faced with a particular problem, he need not expect to find the answer ready-made on page such-and-such. Let him but consider any other field of practice, and he will recognize the importance first of developing the sounder points of view and equipping oneself with established principles and laws in general form. He is the one who must make the applications to specific cases. In medicine, for instance, the student well knows that he must master fields of information containing vast arrays of facts that he probably will never directly use in the form in which he studies them. In law and in engineering it is likewise. The student does not undergo a training in the memorization of judicial or mathematical formulations that he can later apply blindly. He is expected to carry away a training and perspective that will fit him to analyze better and that will enable him to think about and to bring into sharper focus the concrete problems that are to be brought to him. The value of a man of long and thorough professional training or of the man of many years of intensive business experience lies not so much in his memory for explicit rules or for particular experiences but in the richness and adequacy of his general point of view, in his background, and in the perspective he brings to bear on problems. That is what has always been meant by "wisdom."

The reader, therefore, is not to suppose that his problems all have their answers between these covers, and that all he needs is an index to direct him to them. First, last, and all the time, an intelligent person will find that in the conduct of his daily affairs he must apply his own judgment. Even were we to depart from the high road from which we can survey general psychology, and take one of the practical by-paths, such as, "how to study effectively" or "how to improve your memory" or "how to develop your personality," the reader would still find that he is forced to pick and choose, to judge for himself how far to apply this and that fact or rule to his particular case.

Both Facts and Methods are Important. Two things are needed to develop perspectives. One is a substantial knowledge of factual material ranging all the way from concrete particularized findings in a narrowly circumscribed area to broad hypotheses, theories, and laws. Now, in the course of such a survey, a reader will frequently catch himself saying, "But why this fact and that theory? What value are they to me?" It cannot be said too frequently nor too emphatically that it is precisely out of the soil of particular facts and theories that adequate viewpoints grow.

The other need is for acquaintance with the methods of investigation. It is possible that the reader may never find himself in the future in a position to use the brass instruments of the psychological laboratory, but there are certain to be times innumerable when in his contacts with people and their opinions he will do well to keep in mind the ideals and general methodology of science as applied to man's behavior.

Above all, he should develop and preserve a keen appreciation of what is and what is not to be used as *evidence*. As the historian must learn to use documentary evidence and as the jurist must learn to sift testamentary evidence, so the scientist must be trained to evaluate factual evidence. Of all fields of fact no one is a richer hunting ground for the quack and the fly-by-night charlatan than the psychological.

Some False Popular Opinions:

That one's character can be read from the shape of his head. This, the notion of "phrenology," is one of the most persistent of all the non-scientific beliefs. There has never been brought forward any scientific evidence for it whatever. Moreover, certain supposedly scientific beliefs, some in psychology and some in anatomy, that had led zealots to jump to this broad claim, have long ago been thoroughly exploded. We shall have more to say on this in Chapter X.

That one's character can be read from the shape of his face. "Physiognomy," as it is called, enjoys no more respectable status than does the view last mentioned and for the same reasons. It has never been actually demonstrated that the prominence of the nose and the chin, the width of the cheek bones, or other purely structural details, have any relationship to one's emotional or intellectual characteristics. This is saying nothing about one's habits of facial expression: about these the question is unsettled in psychological quarters, and the topic will be taken up in Chapter XVII.

That blondes and brunettes are different in psychological traits. Typical of the best controlled experiments on this line is that in which 374 blondes and brunettes were rated by 94 competent adults with respect to each of the traits given in a much-advertised "system of character analysis" (Blackford's) as belonging to people of those two physical types. In the results it was clear that blondes had been assigned "brunette" traits as often as had the brunettes; and vice versa. Indeed, only 63 per cent of the blondes showed what the author of the system claims blondes to have "everywhere and always."

The same results in substance were secured when sales managers in some forty national organizations rated their highly successful salesmen [3].[1]

That combinations of physical traits reveal one's personality. In another experiment ten subjects were used from each of three national fraternities or sororities. These subjects were rated by associates in their own organizations, and were rated also by casual observers, on the following traits: Sound judgment, Intellectual capacity, Frankness, Will power, Ability to make friends, Leadership, Originality, and Impulsiveness. The experimenters also carefully measured a great number of dimensions of head, face, and body that are held to be indicative of those traits according to certain well-known "systems of character reading." Their results showed that the ratings by the different close associates agreed well, and that the ratings by the casual observers agreed well, but that there was practically no agreement between the former and the latter. As for the results of the physical measurements made in accordance with the "systems," these agreed neither with the ratings of the close associates, nor with those of the casual observers, nor did they

---

[1] Numbers in brackets indicate references at the end of the chapter.

agree with the claims set forth in the "systems" themselves. Their statistical reliability was a flat 0.000.

That child prodigies are freakish and turn out poorly. Here again has developed in popular discourse an absolutely false opinion. Children found to be remarkable in their ability in earlier years, are as a matter of fact slightly more sociable, better looking, and more well-rounded than the average; and they maintain their superiority throughout life. This point is to be elaborated later (in Chapter XIII).

That the beautiful are "dumb." The inference from the preceding paragraph holds: if there is any difference in intelligence it is slightly in favor of the better-appearing individuals. In a study of over a thousand British geniuses a very large proportion of them were referred to by their biographers as having been notably handsome, comely, or imposing [1]. Of course, other factors are at work in daily life: those particularly unfortunate in physical appearance are somewhat spurred to make more of their "brains"; those especially beautiful or handsome may get distracted away from serious work by this social asset. But in their "raw" potentialities, the difference, if there be any, does not lie in the popularly assumed direction.

That opposites attract each other. A study has been made in England on the similarities and dissimilarities of married couples, with respect to such traits as height, span of arms, length of forearm, color of eyes, and longevity. Surprising as it may be, and contrary though it is to popular opinion, it was found that husband and wife are more alike, even in such traits as these, than are first cousins [4].

Now, what are the reasons for the development of such firmly held opinions? One is the *verbal fallacy.* For example, a person with a fine-textured skin is said to be "interested in the finer details of his work," also to be a man of "fine ideals."

But a more common fallacy, observable on many of the border lines of psychology, is that of the *dramatic instance.* A certain aggressive person has a large nose; *ergo,* aggressive persons have large noses. Some intellectual persons we know have high foreheads, and we conclude that the popular notion of high brows is correct. Washington had eyes well distanced: such eyes in a neighbor's head must betoken sagacity. A few striking instances tend to be remembered, while the abundance of negative cases are forgotten. Belief in prophetic dreams, mind transference, reasoning on the part of pet dogs, and a vast array of pseudo-psychological "facts," have the same fallacious basis as the rule that potatoes are best planted in time of full moon, or that if one sits in a chair facing a certain picture or window he will have better fortune at a game of bridge.

Cicero protested against this lack of logic: "I am extremely surprised, that though people have wit enough to give no credit to a notorious liar, even when he speaks the truth, they still, if one single dream has turned out true, do not so much distrust one single case because of the numbers of instances in which they have been found false, as think multitudes of dreams established because of the ascertained truth of this one."

If the study of psychology does no more than to make the reader forever critical of claims put forward for short-cut psychological gold-bricks and for the pet notions current in popular discourse about him — if it does no more than train him to insist upon *evidence* rather than anecdotes — psychology will have fulfilled one of its missions.

An Impersonal Attitude to be Cultivated.   When a pet dog with a broken leg snaps at his master who tends him, the master does not cuff him for it, but he recognizes the specific cause for the behavior and seeks to remove or ease it.   Now, this is the very attitude a scientist takes toward his subject-matter, and is therefore the attitude encouraged in psychology.   A human being is looked upon as an object of inquiry, and as a possible object of advice, help, or treatment.   It has taken the intelligent civilized world centuries to reach this point of view.   Criminal behavior, for one thing, is only today becoming recognized by a very few advanced authorities as a problem for scientific inquiry, in which the criminal's activities are recognized as having their own causes in the conditions of his home, neighborhood, health, and other factors. On this view it is perfectly obvious that the elimination of criminal sorts of behavior is to be sought by eliminating its manifold causes.

So with those unfortunates called the "insane."   They are not properly the objects of resentment nor of amusement: they are results of causal factors.   No longer do we send them to "asylums" (which means places of refuge), but to "hospitals."   They are ill.

Now, it is a harder thing to do, but this same attitude of impersonal, unprejudiced, dispassionate consideration is called for every day.   When a man or woman in our circle of friends or relatives shows outbursts of rage or torrents of tears, obnoxious positiveness of manner or despicable cringing, the most intelligent way of reacting is not that of resentment or of scorn with epithets of "wicked" or "silly," but that of unemotional inquiry into the causes of this behavior.   We should stand outside the sphere of his behavior, and seek to understand the reasons for it.

If our survey of human and sub-human behavior in this book can inculcate more of that inquiring and understanding attitude, a major goal will have been attained.

REFERENCES

1. Ellis, H.   *A Study of British Genius.*   Houghton Mifflin, 1926.

2. Gilliland, A. R.   A Study of the Superstitions of College Students. *J. Abnorm. & Soc. Psychol.*, 1930, **24,** 472–79.

3. Paterson, D. G.   Personality and Physique, in Harris, J. A., *et al.   The Measurement of Man.*   Univ. Minnesota Press, 1930.

4. Pearson, K.   Assortative Mating in Man.   *Biometrika*, 1903, **2,** 481–98.

5. Warren, H. C. (ed.)   *Dictionary of Psychology.*   Houghton Mifflin, 1934.

CHAPTER II

GENERAL CHARACTERISTICS OF BEHAVIOR

THE BIOLOGICAL APPROACH

MAN is an animal — a living organism. This is one of the most important things for the reader to keep in mind if he does not want to lose his bearings while making a survey of the principles of human behavior. To be sure, a man's ways of living and acting are superior in complexity and in refinement to those of any of the humbler forms of life: he can build fifty-story skyscrapers, he can determine the chemical composition of the star Arcturus, and he can produce artistic forms like the *Fifth Symphony*. Yet it remains true that all these capacities are most adequately viewed as only vast complications of animal traits. The species *Homo sapiens* is moved by what are in essence the same forces both without and within as are the lower animate forms, and he expresses his energies in the same general types of actions and action-tendencies. The differences are only differences of degree, however much the superficial appearances may suggest total differences of kind. Human psychology, in a word, is rooted in living protoplasm, and it is not to be explained totally apart from its antecedent biological history.

We are now ready to inquire: (1) What are some of the most general and fundamental marks or characteristics of human (and other animal) behavior? Again (2) what is their significance for understanding the human problems that are called "psychological"? The outstanding characteristics of behavior will be best seen and their significance best appreciated if we note some different types or kinds of behaving.

SPONTANEOUS EXCESS ACTIVITY

Everyday Examples. Consider a basketful of young kittens or a litter of pups. Their activity seems inexhaustible. At first they are a squirming mass of living bodies. Some days later they roll, romp, strike, somersault, and furnish all in all a picture of reckless abandon and *joie de vivre*, expending an enormous amount of energy that apparently has no importance in their lives.   Monkeys, with never a need to satisfy, will persist in meddling, chattering, "monkeying," annoying each other and sometimes their spectators, showing nothing so much as a superabundance of animal spirits.

Consider in like manner the human infant.   If only he be healthy, well fed, and comfortable, he will furnish a similar picture.   Lay him upon his back and, without offering on your part any special sight or sound to arouse or direct him, watch his activities.   He will set up a continual mild performance of waving the arms, working the fingers, kicking and hitching the legs, twisting the head, working muscles of cheeks and eyelids, gurgling, cooing.   Note that his actions are not called forth by any special outside agencies: he is not reaching or kicking on account of any particular thing, nor are his vocal sounds made for your or anyone's attention.   Note, further, that the movements and vocalizations are not definite and organized, but are random, aimless, and undirected.

Or, consider the adult man.   To be sure, much of his day's living is occupied with answering the manifold demands made upon him by his material and social surroundings; but in odd moments of the busiest day he may be observed drumming on his desk, whistling, clearing his throat, walking about aimlessly, glancing absently out the window, balancing and rocking back and forth on his chair. Still better, see him after hours, when the external demands relax: he grows more spontaneous and careless, reads the comic strips, pencils a cross-word puzzle, gets out his violin, goes for a walk to nowhere in particular, or restlessly tramps the house.   The central fact is that he does not relapse into mere immobility (unless it be to sleep), for when the urgencies of his surroundings relax it may even be as if a damper and restraint has been removed.

This spontaneous activity is primarily the expression of the metabolism of the organism.   The human body is an energy exchange.   The processes of life are both the up-building (assimilative or anabolic) and the down-wearing (destructive or katabolic). Energy is continually being taken into the body with food and drink and the inspired air; and energy is released in activities of diverse sorts, especially in the work done by the muscles in moving the bodily members.   Even in those cases when a specific sound or sight or contact does excite a definite act in a direct way, examination will reveal a middle term, the release of some internal energy. The external agency, such as a bright light, an electric current, a taste of sugar, or a painful burn primarily effects a liberation of energy that is stored up in nerve, muscle, gland, and other tissues; and this energy liberation takes the outwardly observable forms of bodily movement.

We may draw the conclusion that not all of a man's activity is excited directly from without.   A man is not a football, not the sport of incidental and accidental forces.   His conduct is the expression of his own internal energies.   It is they that impel him. Nor should the word "internal" here be given any mystical flavor. There is nothing sacrosanct or inscrutable about the energies that are generated by processes occurring in heart, lungs, blood vessels, intestines, striped muscles, or nerve fibers.   They are simply products of physical and physiological operations.

Importance of Actiyity in Development.   From the developmental viewpoint these spontaneous and excessive activities are recognized as especially marking the earlier stages of an individual's life.   Living, then, is predominantly activity.   With the months and years of increasing age the movements of the child and adult are seen to grow more organized and precise and become more directly responsive to the particular things about him.   Instead of aimlessly working his fingers, he takes more definite grasp of his rattle, of his spoon, of a pencil, of a surgical instrument.   Instead of merely waving his feet about, he comes to walk and run, to kick a football, to operate a sewing machine or a pipe organ.   Instead of babbling sounds, he voices words and sentences of ever more subtle and abstract meanings.   His energies, we may say, become increasingly channeled.

Just how these developmental changes come about is one of our primary concerns in psychology.   Experience as such has much to do with it, we are ready to say; and many detailed problems of incidental learning as well as formal tuition are bound to be raised. But the maturing and natural changing of the child as he grows to manhood must have much to do with it also, we would suppose.   It is natural, therefore, for us to inquire about the manner and rate of maturing of different human functions.

ORGANIZED ROUTINE ACTIVITIES

Examples.   In contrast with the sort of human behavior we have just been describing, much of a man's activity shows more organiza-

tion and definiteness, more co-ordination of movements in concerted performances that take place smoothly and connectedly.   A
person's skills and "knowledges," his acts of eating and walking and
talking, of posting entries and operating calculating machines, or
sweeping and dishwashing, are organized and mechanized performances that make up most of his daily living.   These are habits and
may be thought of as tools in the individual's possession.

Now, much of this routine sort of activity goes on without
special excitations and guidance from without.   In extreme cases
the activities seem to continue themselves once they get started.
Suppose at the sound of a class bell a student gathers his books and
papers and starts a walk across the campus: the bell need not continue to ring and the student need not continually remind himself
of bell or bell's significance to produce a continuation of his walking behavior.   The performance is so well established that it maintains itself, subject only to slight cues like the occasional sights of
the brick walkway, of other people moving this way or that, of doorways, and the like.   The student may start whistling a late dance
tune, and once started may continue without being able to tell you
later what it was he was whistling.   In a study period he may busy
himself with copying important definitions or rules from a reference
work; even though he puts much attention on the substance of the
definition or the rule, the writing act itself operates as a smooth-
running performance, and, so far as his fingers are concerned, the
student is little more than an automaton.   When his cigarette or his
pipe is in his mouth, he peacefully draws and puffs and draws in a
well-co-ordinated and timed performance that is more than a random
display of energy, yet represents no forced labor, crisis, nor emergency.   He is pursuing the even tenor of his way.

So large a part do these integrated and smooth-running forms of
activity play in everybody's daily life, and so large a part of education is given to the forming of such habits and skills and "knowledges," that many questions naturally present themselves to us.
What are these integrated forms of behavior?   How do they arise?
What conditions help and hinder them?   These are problems upon
which much careful scientific work has been done, work which we
shall want to review in later chapters.   For the present, however,
since we want first to get an overview of human-animal behavior,
we must turn to an aspect still more central and important.

READJUSTIVE BEHAVIOR

The Most Significant Aspect of Behavior.   We turn now to that aspect of human and animal behavior which will be for us most illuminating in bringing out those aspects of life that are of most psychological interest.   After all, man's living is not completely described — nor even well described — merely as spontaneous activity or overflow of energy: such a bubbling up of vitality while undirected and unharnessed would get him nowhere.   Nor is it well described merely as a set of semi-automatic acts that run themselves off like a job lot of mechanisms operating in grooved ways: such invariable kinds of behavior would make man only a machine from which the very heart and spark of life were missing.   Living things, whether plant or lower animal or man himself, are not like steam boilers full of raw energy nor like the contrivances of gear-wheels and pulley-belts which they drive.   If living is anything, it is dramatic: and the most significant and interesting things about life are those episodes in which the demand is for some novel mode of activity, some readjustment of one's behavior to meet the requirements of new or unusual situations.   As he grows from puling infancy to manhood's estate, the human being is faced day by day with new conditions, changes of material surroundings, new groups of human faces; and it is a truism that his mental development is shown in how he meets these ever-changing circumstances by remolding and reshaping his own reactions to them.   We must now inquire about the characteristics of this readjustive aspect of so much of human and animal behavior.   For our illustrations we shall use more scientific ones, that is, ones gained from experimental and clinical studies.

Illustrations.

Examples from animal behavior.   Let us start with a very simple animal form, the one-celled *Oxytricha*.   Suppose we were to examine a number of specimens under a microscope.   (See Figure 2.)   They will be seen to swim about in their glass trough with no particular preference as to directions.   But let one end of the trough be gradually heated.   The animals in this heated end now become very active as they dart hastily this way and that — an access of energy is visible.   As the temperature **rises** they give the avoiding reaction peculiar to these and related forms — darting backward and turning a little to the right, before dashing forward again. Whenever a specimen passes into the warmer end of the water or comes into contact with the glass sides it responds quickly with this avoiding reaction. It will be seen to dash forward, back up and turn, dash forward, back up and turn, and so on for a succession of interrupted excursions; until, chancing to make its forward dash into a cooler medium, it ceases to make the avoiding response but continues on its way. In brief, when this animal moves into the heated water it shows *increased* and *varied activity*.

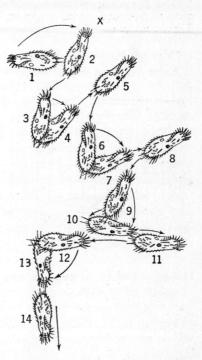

FIGURE 2. AN ANIMAL IN HOT WATER: REACTION OF OXYTRICHA TO HEAT

The slide is heated at the end *X*. An animal in the position *1* reacts as is indicated by the arrows: repeatedly moving backward, turning to the right, and moving forward, thus occupying successively the positions *1–14*. When it finally becomes directed away from the heat, as at *13–14*, it ceases to change its direction of movement, but continues in a straight line ahead, thus reaching a cooler region. (From Jennings, H. S., *Behavior of the Lower Organisms.* 1906. By permission of The Macmillan Company, publishers.)

One of the early studies of mammals was that made by Small on white rats. He placed in the animal's cage a box covered with wire mesh, having as its only opening a hole cut in the floor (Figure 3). The box was raised on pegs and banked with sawdust on all sides up to the level of the floor. Food was placed conspicuously inside the box and two hungry rats were allowed to attack the problem of finding a way to the food.

They crawled all over the box, and went round and round it monotonously. Sniffed continually. After an hour of persevering effort they began to get discouraged, their movements becoming haphazard and indifferent. One gave up and returned to the nest. The other, more frisky, soon began scratching about instinctively. The hole thus accidentally dug happened to be in the right place. The rat immediately poked its nose into the new opening, which was not large enough to admit its head. It then ran away as if frightened, but soon returned, sniffed cautiously at the hole, dug away more sawdust, and then scampered away again. These acts were repeated several times, till a large opening was made. The rat then entered cautiously, snatched a piece of food, and carried it into its hiding place in the corner of the cage. Time, 1 hr. 30 m.   [8]

Once again, increased and varied activity.

Examples from infant behavior.   As with lower animals, so with man. Observations to be made in any nursery are supported by scientific studies of babies under laboratory conditions in showing the same characteristics of emergency-meeting behavior. Suppose a baby is subjected to the annoyance of having an examiner's finger pressing constantly upon his chin. No longer is his behavior characterized by healthy overflow and playlike activity. His actions now take on a more jerky and vigorous character; his hands and arms are thrown about in an irregular manner, striking the offending finger occasionally but only by chance. In one careful study it

FIGURE 3. VARIED ACTIVITY OF THE HUNGRY RAT

Under the combined stimulation of internal hunger and externally seen-and-smelled food the animal strives to reach the food inside the box. To succeed it must dig through sawdust at the proper place to find the entrance. (Small, W. S., *Am. J. Psychol.,* 1900, *11.*)

was found that no infant below 21 hours of age made an immediate successful movement of defense against the irritating object; and even at the later ages the average number of ill-directed movements remained high. (Cf. Figure 4.) Throughout the series of trials the babies succeeded in hitting and brushing away the offending stimulus only after persisting in varied movements of arms and hands.

The same behavior appears when the maladjustment of the organism is less of the *negative avoiding* sort and more of the *positive seeking* sort. As everyone knows, babies — and rats and men as well — will react not only to things that threaten them but also to things that are of no particular value for weal or woe, but which simply attract attention. The young child will roll his eyeballs to fix his regard on a point of light, will rotate his head toward any

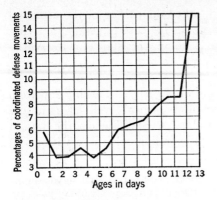

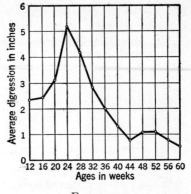

FIGURE 4

AGE CHANGES IN THE FREQUENCY OF
CO-ORDINATED DEFENSE MOVE-
MENTS

At each age period, the percentage of times
that each infant reacted to the stimulus with
the movement in question is averaged for all
the infants of that age. A co-ordinated defense movement was one in which both the
infant's hands or arms were brought up into
contact with the offending object.

(From Sherman, M., Sherman, I., and Flory,
C. D., *Comp. Psychol. Monog.*, 1936, **12**, No.
59.)

FIGURE 5

THE RANDOM CHARACTER OF EARLY
REACHING (POSITIVE) MOVE-
MENTS IN INFANTS

The average amount of digression of the
hand to the right or to the left of the most
direct line of movement toward the seen
object is plotted for successive ages of infants. (Halverson, H. M., *J. Genet. Psychol.*,
1933, **43**, 16.) These two figures show supplementary aspects of development of behavior. Figure 4 shows fixating of adjustive movements whereas this shows eliminating of non-adjustive movements

sharp clear sound, will reach toward a rattle box shaken in his field
of view. But at first he will not do these things in any precise
manner; on the contrary, he will make crude, spasmodic, jerky
movements in divers directions and extents. Here again the
evidence from a controlled study is pertinent. An infant seated in a
small Morris chair and supported with a canvas belt was placed
before a table, and on this a pellet was placed at a constant distance
from the table edge. This pellet attracted the subject's attention,
and he responded by making hand and arm movements in its
direction so that he eventually grasped it. But only eventually, for
in the earlier instances the arm movements were anything but well
directed, some of them averaging a digression of 5 inches out of line.
Figure 5 brings out two facts in this connection. For one thing, it is
clear from the general drop of the curve that it takes some weeks of
age before a baby can make fairly well directed movements toward
the pellet. At the same time, the initial rise of the curve is due not
to a decreasing accuracy of the reaching movements but to an in-

creasing participation of muscles other than those of the arm that pull the arm out of line, that is, to an increase of general activity. Here again at each age there is some persistence, with variations, until by chance [1] the appropriate movements happen to be made.[2]

Examples from emotional adjustment problems. Turning now from experimental studies on these simple biological levels let us note a few examples of readjustment on more advanced levels, the data in these cases being in the form of the individuals' observations on themselves as found in the clinical literature.

When unoccupied [reported one], I often lapse into periods of daydreaming in which I fix things up as I would have them be. Scarcely a day passes in which I do not indulge in daydreaming. This habit began when I was very young. My associates were older than I and enjoyed much more freedom of action. When I was thwarted or restrained from participating in certain group activities I indulged in daydreaming. In my fancy I could be whatever age I desired. Consequently the daydream began to furnish for me a mode of escape from actual life situations.

At the age of nine [reported another] I went to school with one of my brothers who on the way used to thrash me a great deal. I could not defend myself and so came home crying several times. That year one of my aunts stayed with us. When my brother would thwart my acts or desires I would go into a temper tantrum and cry for a long time. My aunt sympathized with me a great deal and rebuked my brother for striking me. My aunt's sympathetic intercession increased my temper tantrums. Every time I wanted something I would go into tantrums, and generally received what I wanted. I soon discovered that this was an effective method of getting what I wanted.

[A third case.] When I received my first report with a D in chemistry, I was bitterly disappointed because I was really trying to master the material. I tried harder and resolved to surpass the rest of the class. But I failed miserably and again received a D. My failure in chemistry threw me into utter despair, and I was fully convinced of my inferiority, but, while I regularly cut the chemistry classes I did my best to make up for the inferiority feeling for failing to get chemistry by overworking in my favorite studies, foreign languages and history.[3]

In such clinical cases as these we can readily make out the maladjusted individual struggling this way and that against some impediment or obstacle until some way out of it all happens to pre-

[1] In this chapter the word "chance" is not to be taken in its extreme meaning as equivalent to "completely uncaused," but in the more familiar meaning of "cause or causes not apparent." It may here be added that later we are to learn that the *degree* of randomness is a highly significant and differentiating feature of the behavior of different organisms and different persons. (Cf. esp. pages 376 ff.)

[2] These two examples of infant behavior are further described in Chapter IV.

[3] From Wallin, J. E. W. *Personality Maladjustments and Mental Hygiene.* McGraw-Hill, 1935.

sent itself to him, and by seizing upon it he establishes a more favorable equilibrium.

Example from reasoning. The same thing is true for man's more theoretical and intellectual inquiries as for the more personal and practical difficulties of his life. Even his highest rational processes are but tools and methods for straightening out tangles, be they ever so abstract and ever so non-practical in character. One example from a well-known experiment will perhaps suffice to exhibit this general readjustive character; and we can leave the details of thinking processes to a later chapter of the book.

The rôle played by thought processes when a person is working to solve a mechanical puzzle has been investigated. A wooden or wire puzzle was placed in a subject's hands, and a study made of his procedure in solving the puzzle by watching and recording visible movements and by obtaining indirect evidence from his verbal reports.

Of the latter, two examples may be chosen for our use here. They were the narratives furnished by one subject to describe his own procedure in attacking two of the puzzles. The reader may not be able to follow the details in all their concreteness, yet the method will become obvious. First, the "wire maze" puzzle. "Considerable uncontrolled manipulation was indulged in [the subject said], but the ring was not gotten off in such manipulation. The random movement seems, however, in some way to have suggested a new way of looking at the puzzle, and the latter ended in its solution. The manipulation resulting in success was here the testing of a definite hypothesis." Next, the subject later took up the "six-piece cross" puzzle (cf. Figure 6). The manner in which he eventually found his way to a solution is well indicated by his own words as he thought aloud:

Six pieces! No doubt it is a triaxial construction like the other one. [He here classified the pieces.] None have grooves on opposite faces. Does this mean that the pairs must face each other, i.e., have grooves toward each other, as in the other puzzle? ... Which are the pairs? ... The pieces can be arranged in order according to the amount cut out, and perhaps this gives the clue to the order in which they have to be put in. For if, as is certain, the piece with the least cut out has to be the last to go in, may it not be that the piece with the most cut out has to be the first, because it will allow the most to be put in after it itself is in position? I suppose that it is not, however, the amount cut out of a single piece but of the pair that counts ... Any pair that you choose must be either mates or at right angles. This

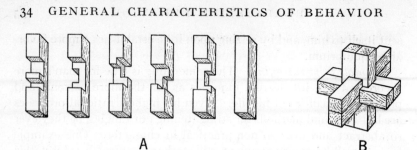

A   B

FIGURE 6. A SIX-PIECE-CROSS PUZZLE

A, the pieces to be assembled.   *B*, the result after the puzzle is solved.

ought to be of some help for if this is settled for only two bars, the field of experimentation would be narrowed.   The two that are alike cannot form a pair, for . . .   Therefore, the two that are alike must cross at right angles. Here's a third which cannot be a pair for either of the like ones, and thus I have one of each pair.   Now I'll look among the remaining two (excluding the plain bar) for one which would be the mate of one of the like ones.   This is not such plain sailing, as the "judgment" is involved, but I can judge largely by the space left.   One of the selections promises well.   Follow it up; here's the conclusion [6].

Here are two cases of thinking.   In the former, the subject made many overt movements of hands and fingers, but to no purpose, until through chance fumblings a new aspect of the puzzle was turned up, and this was followed out to a successful solution.   In the latter case, the subject made his trials in the form of guesses or hypotheses.   The situation first aroused in him some preliminary ways of looking at it, and these in turn awakened some thinking reactions as hypotheses to be tried out.   "Six pieces . . . triaxial"; "none have grooves on opposite faces . . . must face each other?" — and so on.   Certain thought acts tended to lead to overt movements and manipulations but were restrained or inhibited, until finally one of them "promised well" and was uninhibited.   This possibility took an overt form as the correct construction was begun with the fingers.   In both cases we can see how the subject used implicit thinking acts to do duty for overt manual acts.   The student is likely to have questions about some of the details, which must be postponed until later in the book.   He can discern, however, two familiar characters about the thinker's behavior.   (1) Faced with a puzzle he goes into action.   (2) The solving process itself is one of try-try-again methods, on this track or on that, until by some stroke of luck the adequate procedure is found.

Principles Discernible in Readjustive Behavior. The foregoing examples of readjustment, taken from sub-human and human life, should furnish us material for an analysis. What salient principles are to be discerned? A diagram should be helpful. (Figure 7.)

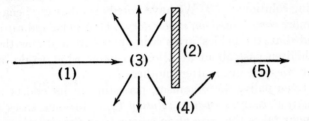

FIGURE 7. A DIAGRAM TO REPRESENT CARDINAL FEATURES IN READJUSTIVE BEHAVIOR

(Explanation in text.)

I. For one thing, some sort of *maladjustment of the organism to its particular environment* is a *sine qua non.* The Oxytricha could not live normally in hot water; the rat was hungry and could not get at the food; the baby was subjected to a hindering and annoying pressure, or he was attracted by a stimulus-object not readily within his grasp; the troubled children and adult were restrained from group play or from a high-school grade or from other desires; the would-be solver was challenged by the puzzle. Something was wrong in every case, some thwarting (*2*) of the normal processes of the individual (*1*). Now, in some instances, the disturbing factors appear to be agents outside the organism (extra-organic), as the heated water or the pressure-on-chin, while in other instances they seem to be intra-organic, as in the case of the rat's hunger or the human being's worries. If we take a broader viewpoint, however, it will be clear that the maladjustment is an organism-environment fact, not just the one or the other; and the behavior formula becomes, as the psychologist Lewin prefers to write it: $B = f(PE)$, that is, the behavior is a function of *both* the person *and* the environment in dynamic interrelation. Or, to put it another way, the environment acts upon the person, and he acts upon the environment at the same time. The behavior is obviously a result of this dynamic interaction.

II. In this condition of being maladjusted the living organism gets into action (*3*).   (*A*) For one thing, as we have already seen, it displays *persistent activity*, an *increase of vigor* and liveliness. The one-celled animal and the rat become more lively and vigorous in their running hither and yon, the infants in their hand and arm movements, the children and the adult in their worrying, the thinker in seeking solutions.   (*B*) We have noted also that the behavior becomes more *varied, random, exploratory*.   Oxytricha and rat run this way and that, the babies' arms swing now here and now there, the older children cast about at a loss to know what to do, and the reasoner tries one guess after another.

III. Eventually, the organism, persisting in its efforts to right the situation, *chances upon a solution* (*4*).   In some cases this readjustment takes the form of an escape from the situation; that is, the animal or person avoids the unfavorable and distressing factor. In other cases it takes more the form of remaking or remolding the situation.   But it is immaterial whether the change be one of the individual to fit his conditions of life more adequately or a change of the conditions to fit the individual.   There is a restoration of the optimal *relationship*; and the individual is said to be *readjusted* (*5*).

Adjustment a Form of Regulation.   The readjustive aspect of behavior of people and animals will be better interpreted and appreciated if seen against the background of a broader biological concept, that of "regulation."   All living organisms tend to maintain their normal structures and functions, that is, to maintain a physiological unity and harmony in spite of changes of environmental or even of internal conditions.

Men exposed to heat of 250 degrees F. will show no increase of their internal body temperature; and on the other hand, animals exposed continuously to cold of 30 degrees below zero show no decrease; and thus an internal temperature is maintained which is essential to normal functioning.   The situation is similar if the unusual condition be of internal origin.   The heat that is produced by very vigorous muscular exercise during twenty minutes would coagulate albuminous substances of the body to the consistency of a hard-boiled egg; but such a calamity is avoided by dissipation of the heat through profuse perspiration, shift of the blood to the skin for radiation, and other channels.   The active muscles produce as a by-product enough lactic acid to neutralize all the alkali in the blood; but other agencies appear and prevent that disaster.   When the skin is broken and the blood leaks out, substances in the blood itself produce a clotting that plugs the leak; and a profound alteration of the circulatory system appears in the constriction of peripheral blood vessels that reduces the flow in the leaking part [1].   A dog fed a starchy diet will produce digestive juices rich in the enzymes that digest starch, while if put under a meat diet it will produce juices rich in protein-digesting substances. If poison be injected into a guinea pig, the guinea pig will produce substances to neutralize this poison.

On simpler biological levels we have cruder changes that are made to maintain organismic integrity. A starfish that has lost an arm proceeds to regenerate it. A fragment cut out from any part of a polyp will reconstruct itself and grow to a complete individual. So too, the cells appearing after first division of the egg in many animal species will, if separated, develop into two perfect individuals.

Coming closer to phenomena called psychological, we have the organism maintaining its stocks of nutriment and water through the operation of appetites of hunger and thirst, which in turn arouse movements of the whole body toward sources of the needed materials.

Through all animal life, then, an outstanding characteristic runs — from clipped polyp to blood-clotting, to hungry foraging, to social evasions — *the tendency of the organism to maintain its normality against internal or external disrupting agencies*. When this takes the form of alterations made by man or animal in his relations to physical and social surroundings the phenomena are called psychological.

Concluding Note. A moment's consideration by the reader will make it clear that to describe a person's life activities under three different headings, as we have done in this chapter, is emphatically not to imply a hard-and-fast division of those activities into three distinct and independent kinds. When he is reading or writing, he is likely also to be tapping his foot, scratching his head, snuffling or grunting; and it may be hard to decide whether those undirected movements are the expression of superabundant energy or of the excitement and overflow born of an emergency. Certain it is that the behavior of man or beast varies by all degrees between the two poles of unorganized, scattered, overflow activity and the smooth-running performance of well-practiced routine motions. In this continued story of organization the spotlight of psychological interest plays upon those frequent dramatic episodes we have called readjustments.

THE ANALYSIS OF BEHAVIOR

The Reason for Analysis. In the preceding sections we have noted certain general features of behavior of human beings when considered as whole organisms or persons. This is the viewpoint of man that is naturally most interesting and most truly "human."

It is the viewpoint from which we shall take our departure, to which we shall return from time to time throughout our psychological survey, and with which we shall ultimately conclude and summarize.   Our interest — to put it succinctly — is, first and last, in persons.

It is going to be necessary, however, to supplement this consideration of the entire man with more analytic approaches.   One's primary interest in alarm clocks or automobiles is in their total performances, and "good" or "poor" clocks or automobiles are those that run well or badly; yet no adequate understanding or control of them can be had without taking them apart to note their details of operation.   One's interest in his pet dog or in his human playmate or friend is in a like manner centered on their total performances; but again no very sound and solid understanding of them can be had without knowing something of their details of bodily constitution and functioning.   We must apply to the field of psychology the same technique of analysis that has meant so much to all modern scientific study.   The ways in which a person lives and moves and has his being must be resolved into their constituent parts or units.   After that we shall appreciate better his nature as a whole.

What are the simplest possible divisions of human activity? One person withdraws his hand laid inadvertently on a hot radiator; another operates his motor car through dense traffic with admirable ease; another reaches a high note in his operatic aria without perceptible effort or strain; another falls in love and neglects his business or his studies; still another sees ghosts in a haunted house.   In all these performances it should be possible to disentangle component acts.

Through the discussion of the preceding sections there runs a biological dualism.   On the one hand is the *organism*, on the other the *environment*, the two being in complex interaction.   Let us consider some aspects of this matter.   If the organism is to make a living, it must be *sensitive* to conditions about it, to food, to poison, to the opposite sex, to enemy, to friend.   On the other hand, it must be able to *react* to the stimulations of such conditions — positively to the food, to the sex (under certain social conditions), to the friend; negatively to the poison, to the sex (under other conditions), to the enemy.   Thirdly, it is obvious that the reaction must be *appropriate* to the stimulation.   The differentiation of these two general sorts of processes, stimulation and response, and especially the adequacy of the one to the other, blocks out a large part of the investigative work of the psychologist. If we could always say with complete assurance that, given a certain stimulus, such as a friend *A*, a person *B* would be certain to respond in a definitely predictable way, or if we could be absolutely sure that when a person acts in a particular manner this is due to his being stimulated and controlled by such and such stimulus-conditions, then knowledge of human nature would be ideally complete. What further could be asked, for either theoretical or practical purposes? Much psychological inquiry, then, is cast in the form of *stimulation-leading-to-response.*

A First Step in Analysis: The Single Episode. It would be absurdly hopeless to make a complete list of all the stimulations that have played upon an individual throughout his past days and years or to make an exhaustive catalogue of his reactions throughout all that time. To be sure, the developmental story is of high importance, for a person is certainly in part the expression of his earlier years and experiences; and in some succeeding chapters we are going to pursue that biographical interpretation. But we must begin our simplification of the phenomena we are to study; and the most natural way is to start with a particular episode or event. To get ahead with our examination and analysis we are to suppose a person's total behavior-stream to be cut across during some particular moment or short period of time.

Consider a chauffeur at a street crossing. What is to be seen? On the stimulus side, he is being bombarded through the eye with uncounted lights and shadows and colors from other cars, pedestrians, a traffic policeman, and his own dashboard, through the ear with tones and noises of many degrees of loudness, suddenness, and of pitch, emanating from his passengers, from other cars and from his own. Stimulations reach him through the skin of hands and feet with manifold pressures of pedals, steering wheel, and gear shift; through the skin of back and legs from cushions on which he is sitting, through the nose from odors of gas exhausts and perhaps burning rubber or oil; and internally from his posturing and moving legs and arms, eyes and throat. On the reaction side, the picture is equally baffling in complexity. Five fingers grasp the gear shift while five others hold the wheel, one foot pushes in the clutch pedal as the other presses the brake, eyes and head move right and left to scan the traffic conditions, vocal organs keep up a conversation with a passenger, and supporting it all is the steadily maintained set of compensatory pulls by trunk muscles that keep the body sitting up erect. An enormous tangle of incoming and outgoing processes, though out of it all emerges a total behavior that is somehow integrated and adequate.

A Second Step in Analysis: The Sensori-Motor Arc. In the example just furnished, such an array and concourse of processes occurring at the same time cannot be effectively studied until broken up further. The total behavior is too much to handle. It must be formally simplified by the isolation of parts for preliminary treatment, so that, later on, we can better understand the whole. Specifically, our method must be to analyze further by directing attention to some particular detail of the stimulation in which we happen to be interested, and to that particular detail of the response with which, more than anything else, it appears to be connected.

Consider the case of Mr. X who is entering the station just as the conductor is heard calling, "All aboard!" He catches his breath, his eyelids and his head jerk up, and his heart stops and then palpitates as his legs quicken their movements. Perchance our belated passenger sees a friend and calls out briefly, "Hello there, Joe!" Perchance also a cinder enters his eye, to cause his eyelids to close forcibly with an accompaniment of a copious flow of tears. Here in this brief moment of Mr. X's life a number of different behavior acts can be differentiated and re-stated as stimuli and responses, $S \longrightarrow R$'s. Cinder in eye $\longrightarrow$ lid closing and tears flowing: almost a complete story within itself, having no significant connection with preceding or simultaneous happenings. Sight of friend $\longrightarrow$ crying a greeting: a fairly complete event, too, though clearly having backward and even forward implications. Hearing "All aboard!" $\longrightarrow$ arrest of breathing, jerking head, palpitation of heart: not at all complete in itself, for it is not the sound as sound but as a learned signal that constitutes the stimulus; and the excited response is certainly related to the whole physical surroundings as well as to the general "set" or intention established in the passenger, namely, to board that train.

Each of these cases, now, might be diagrammed as the operating of a given sensori-motor arc. The arrow, in each of our descriptions, could be expanded and divided into afferent and efferent pathways connecting through nerve centers. Indeed, a vast amount of psy-

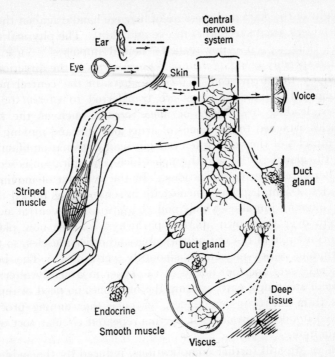

FIGURE 8. DIFFERENT TYPES OF END ORGANS INVOLVED IN DIFFERENT
FORMS OF STIMULATION-AND-RESPONSE

Afferent or sensory nerves are represented by broken lines, efferent or motor nerves by continuous lines. (The different lines of this figure should be traced out in connection with the
analyses of examples in the text.)

chological writing has been done in terms of such arcs, and they have
been referred to frequently as the "units of behavior." A grave
danger lurks therein, however, for it would certainly be untrue to
assume that by merely bunching together a number of such processes you get typical total behavior-patterns. This will be more
obvious as we go further. With this caution, then, let us proceed
a bit further with our analysis.

A Third Step in Analysis: Receptors, Connectors, Effectors.
Such accounts as these may be schematized and still further analyzed by use of Figure 8. (Let the reader carefully trace the proper
lines on this figure as he reads the following paragraphs.) The cry
"All aboard!" falls upon the ear, which is a sensitized part of the
body surface called a *receptor* or *sense organ*. Other *stimuli* such

as sight of the train and pressure of luggage handle against the palm and fingers, excite receptors in eye and skin.   The physical excitations thus set up — now called "neural impulses" — are transmitted speedily along *afferent* or *sensory nerves* in the direction indicated by the arrowhead to *nerve centers* in the central nervous system.   Here the impulses are transferred to *efferent* or *motor nerves*, leading to *effectors* or *motor organs*, such as the striped muscles attached to the bones of arms and legs and moving them, the muscles of the voice when one gives an exclamation of surprise, and the glands of the skin through which a perspiration is secreted.

There are other complications.   In the very act of moving, the muscles of arm, leg, and voice excite in sense organs buried therein new afferent impulses which pour back into the central nervous system over their own afferent pathways.   These now play the important rôle of re-exciting the same and other muscles, so that a continuous series of acts is smoothly performed.   The belated passenger sets one foot ahead of the other in a neatly alternating order of steppings, each exciting the next one: no need of repeated calls from the train announcer, for once the running process is started it takes care of itself by this repeated circular sort of self-stimulation.

There are still further complications, induced by the suddenness of the call.   When the passenger is startled, his "heart stops then palpitates," the stomach is temporarily arrested in its digestive work, and the processes of other organs are suddenly altered.   This we can trace back to an overflow of neural impulses from the central nervous system, out over other efferent nerves to (mostly) smooth muscle effectors and to glands in those organs.   At the same time some excitation of endocrine or ductless glands occurs, the secretion from these glands changing the blood stream in important ways.

Finally, let us note that this emotional reaction of being startled has important bearings upon our passenger's overt behavior.   From the disturbed internal organs and tissues there are returned still other afferent impulses; and these — as well as the change in the blood stream just mentioned — have a marked effect upon the startled man's overt acts — he steps more lively and his whole demeanor is more energetic.   By the same token, if he were to receive a very different sort of emotionally loaded stimulus, such as the sound and sight of the departing train and of the slamming gate, the effect of the deep visceral changes on his outwardly visible behavior would be quite the opposite: he slumps down and the muscles of his legs may refuse to carry him.

The reader may feel that we have neglected one important feature of the man's behavior. Why does he continue to make for the train in spite of all these other stimuli? Obviously he is set for the train — oriented toward it. Now this does not imply any process in him alien to those we have been discussing, but only a complication of them. "Goal-seeking," "intent," whatever terms we care to apply to this phenomenon, it remains a phenomenon of stimulus-response processes. The only new feature introduced into the story is the longitudinal feature, the temporal patterning and interrelationships of his activities. The set for boarding the train was established much earlier than the moment when we saw the man entering the station; and so the continuity and consistency in what he does is to be understood in terms of earlier reactions that determine his later reactions. But we must postpone development of these points to Chapters V and XII.

To Summarize: The process of stimulation is one that may involve any or all of three general sorts of receptors: those affected by agencies from outside the body — in the eye, the ear, the nose, the tongue, the skin; those affected by movements of muscles; and those affected by changes in the deeper-seated viscera. The process of response may involve any of four kinds of effectors: the striped muscles of skeletal movement, that is, overt behavior; the smooth musculature of the internal organs; the duct glands of alimentary canal and of the outside of the body; and the endocrine or ductless glands that secrete directly into the blood.

When all of these have been canvassed and listed it still remains true that the most important phases of the whole process of behavior lie in the central nervous system. How does it happen that certain modes of stimulation awaken certain manners of response and not others? The answer is plain: it all depends on the central switchboard; the system of connections and re-connections there is the heart of the story.

A Warning. By this time the reader should be free from certain common misunderstandings of the phrase "stimulus and response," or $S \longrightarrow R$. Since we will use these concepts repeatedly throughout our study of human beings and their ways of acting, it will be imperative that he keep in mind certain principles, as follows:

A response may be vocal in nature.

A response may be emotional in nature.

A response may be a maintained posture or set of the body or of a limb.

A response may be inhibitory rather than excitatory.

Many stimuli are internal stimuli.

Many $S \longrightarrow R$'s are connected in series.

General conditions of the organism modify the $S \longrightarrow R$.

A given $S \longrightarrow R$ is a part of a whole activity-pattern, and gets its final interpretation in terms of that pattern.

(It would make a valuable exercise for the reader to identify illustrations for each of these from examination of the two cases of behavior given above.)

REACTION TIMES

Introduction. The general principle of $S \longrightarrow R$ is nowhere better demonstrated than in the reaction time experiments [2, 5, 9]. In these, emphasis is laid upon precise control of the S presented, care is exercised to limit the R to some one predetermined type, and the relations between the two are measured in a quantitative fashion. A brief survey, therefore, of that type of experimental work should be helpful at this point in making more definite and concrete the terms of the $S \longrightarrow R$ formula, in its simplest forms. This is one of the pioneer forms of experimental research in psychology. It grew out of the fact that astronomers had come to realize that they, the astronomers, could not keep their own individual selves out of their most exact observations, and further that this "personal equation" as they called it was itself a legitimate and promising object of scientific investigation. (See above, pp. 3–5.)

How long does it take a person to react to an external stimulus, that is, how much time is required for a complete $S \longrightarrow R$ function to operate? Do individuals differ in this regard? Does the time required differ for different kinds of functions, different $S \longrightarrow R$'s? Is the time dependent upon any incidental factors that can be identified?

Apparatus. The experimental set-up may be fairly simple for demonstrations or for giving preliminary acquaintance. One form is shown in Figure 9. For research work, when greater precision in marking the exact time interval is a desideratum, as well as more control over the stimuli and the responses to be used, much more

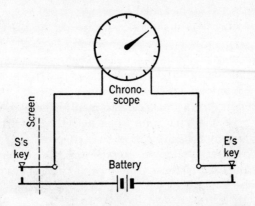

FIGURE 9. A SIMPLE REACTION TIME ARRANGEMENT

The subject, *S*, is first instructed to hold down (close) his key; then when he hears the experimenter, *E*, snap his key down, he is to release his own key as quickly as possible. During the brief interval between the closing of *E*'s key and the opening of *S*'s key, the circuit is closed, and electricity generated at the battery operates the clock-like chronoscope and its dial hand. The length of the interval can then be read off in terms of the distance the dial hand has traveled.

elaborate arrangements are called for. One of these appears in Figure 10. Ordinarily the reaction time is read in thousandths of a second, or "milliseconds" (ms.).

For the student of physics it may be of interest to mention that several different physical principles have been utilized for the construction of chronoscopes: the pendulum, clockwork (spring-driven or weight-driven), the galvanometer (amount of deflection indicating the interval the circuit is closed), the impulse counter (driven by interrupted current), and the synchronous motor (shown in Figure 10).

Simple Reactions. It has been abundantly shown that the time required for a person to make a simple response to a simple stimulus, such as closing or opening a key at a click sound, will vary for that same person in ways that depend upon manifold incidental factors. An interesting factor is that of the sense organ being stimulated. If we pool the published findings of various investigators, we see that simple responses to auditory stimuli vary from 120 ms. to 180 ms.; to visual stimuli from 150 ms. to 225 ms.; to tactual pressure, from 130 ms. to 185 ms. Reactions to warmth and cold, to pain stimuli, to tastes, and to smells have not been so thoroughly studied, but they tend to be much slower. Paradoxically enough from a broad biological viewpoint, the reaction time to pain is notoriously long.

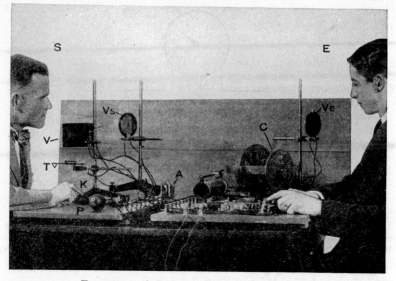

FIGURE 10. A DUNLAP CHRONOSCOPE OUTFIT

C, the chronoscope. Experimenter, *E*, has under control a variety of stimuli: simple auditory (telegraph sounder), *A*; tactual (hard rubber point operated by electromagnet), *T*; simple visual (lamp in box), *V*; complex visual (two different colored lamps in same box); auditory speech (*E* speaking at voice key), *Ve*. (Voice keys are delicate diaphragms, often of foil, which when made to vibrate at a sound temporarily break an electric circuit.) To these the subject, *S*, can react with any of several response keys: a pneumatic bulb, *P*; a simple telegraph key wired either for release or for pressure, *K*; and a voice key for vocal response, *Vs*.

A second outstanding variable is the intensity of the stimulus. It has been shown that, when the intensity of the stimulation is progressively increased (that is, light is brighter, sound louder, touch heavier) progressive decreases in the time of reaction are obtained.

Factors of the person concerned are of equal importance. Practice ordinarily shortens the reaction times and also makes them less variable. Fatigue has the opposite effects, lengthening them and making them more variable. Concentration of the reactor's energies upon the task in hand tends to shorten the times. In this connection, an interesting difference has been repeatedly exhibited between the times taken when the reactor is concentrating especially upon the reaction he is to make (called the "muscular" reaction) and when he is concentrating carefully upon the stimulus that is about to appear (the "sensorial" reaction); for the former is so uniformly the shorter that it is easily brought out in classroom demonstrations with untrained subjects.

The effect of drugs on the simple R–T have been investigated. Alcohol is generally found to lengthen the time of simple reactions and to make them more variable and irregular, though this depends much upon the dosage. Caffeine consistently decreases the average time and the variability. Opiates usually lengthen the time. Other drugs, such as those absorbed in tobacco smoking, have been investigated, but with no consistency of results.

Atmospheric conditions — temperature and humidity — as well as the varieties of emotional conditions in which the reactor happens to be, undoubtedly have important effects, also, but investigations have not been decisive in analyzing them.

With age changes, changes in average reaction times are found to be correlated. Through childhood, increasing maturity goes with increased quickness and decreased variability; while in later maturity and old age the opposite changes tend to be found.

A *practical application* of the reaction time technique is to be found in vocational selection for jobs that call for quick acting in definite ways when certain conditions suddenly arise. The examinations of applicants for such jobs as chauffeur and motorman often include a test of quickness of response in applying brakes when a picture of a child is flashed on a screen or one particular light out of several is thrown on.

Complex Reactions. The situations of daily life as well as of the scientific laboratory usually call for more complicated kinds of quick performance than is represented by the simple reaction time. In order to measure the time required for a man to make more complex reactions, several types of complication of the apparatus and setting have been developed. The subject may be instructed that he will see either of two lights (at *V* in Figure 10), a white or a green, and is to give his response, that is, release or press his key, as soon as he can discriminate or recognize just which one it is. This is usually called the *discrimination* reaction. Or, he may be provided with two keys, and be instructed to react with his right hand if the light be white, with the left if it be green. This is the *choice* reaction. Again, he may be told that a certain type of material is to be presented (such as colors or printed words), and that he is to call out the name of the specific stimulus when it appears. This *perceptual* reaction, as it is sometimes called, is more complex than a choice reaction for the reason that the reactor does not know more than that the stimulus is to be of a certain type or class, and he is required to respond to only one out of five, or ten, or even more. By this technique some curious facts about reading were exhibited long ago by Cattell. He found that perceptual reaction furnished a delicate test of familiarity with a language, in that the reactor requires a few thousandths of a second more to give the German names to pictures or objects than to give the French if he be a Frenchman bred though having a good reading knowledge of German; and quite the reverse if he be a native German who reads French even with ease.

Word-Association Reactions. With voice keys (*Ve* and *Vs* in Figure 10) it is possible to measure the time of word-associations. The reactor is told that he will hear a spoken word and is to respond by speaking aloud the very first word that is aroused on his part regardless of what it is. As contrasted with this *free* association, there is much use made of *controlled* associations. For example, the subject may be told to be prepared to respond with the opposite of whatever word he hears; he may be told to give a subordinate word, as when to "animal" he answers "horse"; or to be prepared for a noun-subject and to give a verb, as when to "dog" he answers "barks." This is probably the form of reaction time measurement most widely useful to psychology; and we shall have much to say about it in later connections. (Also see above, pp. 5–7.)

Serial Reactions. In many occupational situations the demand is for quickness of a more sustained or repetitive sort. A workman feeding a rotating machine may be called upon to make movements not at top speed all at once but at high speed again and again. In other situations the task is to add rapidly and continuously or read lines and pages of words or musical notations. This capacity to make repetitive responses in rapid time is not the same as the capacity to make one single one. Measurements of the two show little if any correlation. It seems that something more than a "quickness" or "speed" element is involved in the former, something in the way of "persistence" or "constancy" or even (in everyday parlance) "stick-to-it-iveness."

REFERENCES

1. Cannon, W. B. *The Wisdom of the Body.* Norton, 1932.
2. Garrett, H. E. *Great Experiments in Psychology.* Century, 1930. Chap. 9.
3. Halverson, H. M. The Acquisition of Skill in Infancy. *J. Genet. Psychol.,* 1933, **43**, 3–48.
4. Jennings, H. S. *Behavior of the Lower Organisms.* Macmillan, 1906.
5. Ladd, G. T., and Woodworth, R. S. *Elements of Physiological Psychology.* Scribners, 1911. Part II, Chap. VI.
6. Ruger, H. A. The Psychology of Efficiency, *Arch. Psychol.,* 1910, No. 15.
7. Sherman, M., Sherman, I. C., and Flory, C. D. Infant Behavior, *Comp. Psychol. Monog.,* 1936, **12**, No. 59.
8. Small, W. S. Experimental Study of the Mental Processes of the Rat. *Am. J. Psychol.,* 1900, **11**, 133–65.
9. Titchener, E. B. *A Text-Book of Psychology.* Macmillan, 1910. Pp. 428–47.
10. Wallin, J. E. W. *Personality Maladjustments and Mental Hygiene.* McGraw-Hill, 1935.

CHAPTER III
THE HEREDITARY BACKGROUND

INTRODUCTION

A Question of Interest and Importance. No problems are of more vital importance to man than are those concerning his immediate biological background and its significance in his affairs. No questions are more persistently interesting, either; for they furnish a perennial source of discussion in almost any informal gathering of thoughtful people, and personal opinions thereon are likely to crop out in spoken form on almost any occasion where the behavior of a newspaper character is in question, whether he be noted or notorious.

"Is the criminal born or made?" This is no merely academic question. If we act on the assumption that he is born with a make-up fatally determining him to a criminal career, there can be little choice in the way of public policy other than to segregate him permanently for the duration of his life or perhaps even to relieve him of that life altogether. If, on the contrary, we judge that the crimes he has committed spring not from some original and ineradicable taint but are the consequences of faulty habits and unworthy ideals acquired from family or neighborhood gang or school associates, then our faces are set in quite a different direction, and our duty a double one, that of trying to re-train and reform him in a very different sort of social setting, and at the same time to break up or change that original family-gang-school combination of causes so that no more such products may appear as its fruits. (Meanwhile, there are many different sorts of crimes, and it must be realized that the explanation of one may not be valid for another.) And so the study of criminology, with all its weighty import for the future of society, inevitably revolves in no small measure about the heredity-environment controversy.

Is "insanity" a trait that is inborn or does one acquire it, perhaps as he might acquire any more strictly physical disease? What more agitating question than this? Suppose our answer be that it is inborn: the procedure indicated is, for the man himself, isolation and protection, and for the sake of his possible descendants, prevention of his procreation. Suppose, however, we answer that this illness of his has no hereditary basis but is brought on solely by excessively trying conditions of life: there is indicated, for him, treatment of remedial aim, and for others, a prevention of recurrence of those conditions.

Is a genius what he is because genius will out, or because he has had most fortunate and favorable opportunities? And even when a man's brilliance is reflected in brilliant relatives and ancestry, is this evidence that he possesses his share of a family stock of brilliance, or is it evidence that with the cultural heritage and opportunities afforded him by them he has been stimulated to unusual development of what talents he had? A practical turn this question takes is, what is our educational hope? Is it a hope that by setting up rigorous courses of study and examination we can select the better-endowed, or is it the hope that by the very processes of training we can strengthen and equip the individual? Phrased differently: What is the significance of the academic diploma? Does it indicate that the holder had the raw material, was of the stuff, to get over the high hurdles; or does it signify that he is now equipped and informed; or both?

Our Limited Mode of Treatment. Any attack upon this general problem in a book devoted primarily to psychology would necessarily be limited by space. What we can best hope to do is, first, to grasp the few most fundamental biological concepts of evolution and genetics, without undue attention to details; and, second, to make a brief survey of the more psychological evidences that have bearing on the issues.

Even in his inquiries on specifically psychological lines, the student will find himself assuming one or another set of more basic biological notions. It is expedient, then, that he be properly oriented, that his assumptions be critically examined and solidly grounded. With this objective, it is the plan of the first part of this chapter to present in the briefest possible compass the outstanding concepts relevant to the general problem. No pretence of completeness of detail, of argument, nor of evidence is made. But the student who understands these few matters will be unquestionably set in the right direction.

OUTSTANDING CONCEPTS OF EVOLUTION

The Non-Inheritance of Acquired Traits. First, for a superstition.   It is believed by many persons that the fetus may be profoundly influenced by specific changes of the mother during pregnancy, even psychological states.   One hears tales of how de-
formities of certain infants were so caused: how, for example, a baby
is born with imperfect spine because shortly before his birth his
mother was frightened by a squirming snake, or how another baby
has a baboon-like face and head that can only be explained by the
fact that while he was being carried *in utero* his mother was terrified
by a circus monkey.   Such cases of *prenatal marking* turn out upon
logical analysis to be based on unwarranted reasoning backward
(the fallacy of *post hoc, ergo propter hoc*), when one is all-too-likely to
find what he is looking for.   What is more fatal to such notions is
that they do violence to the well-established fact that the fetus is not
truly a part of the mother organism.   Its nervous system develops
from the first as a totally independent one.   Even its circulatory
system is to some extent independent of the mother's, what transfer
there is from one to the other of oxygen, nutriment, waste products,
etc., being effected only by diffusion through separating arterial
membranes.   There is only a chemical interchange, then; and it is
inconceivable and impossible that the mother's seeing of a physical
object could determine the conformation of the fetal organism.

Less a superstition perhaps, but with little better status scientifically today is the claim made by the naturalist *Lamarck* about 1800
that the evolutionary change of a species is attributable to the transmission from one generation to the next of those variations in the
former that resulted from use or disuse.   The giraffe, it was asserted,
is in modern times a long-necked, long-legged animal because its
ancestors have for many generations stretched themselves to feed on
the foliage of trees, and the contemporary animal inherits the
stretched-out condition.   In similar vein, one hears it said that the
children in a given mill-town do poorly in their school work and are
low in intelligence generally for the reason that their parents and
grandparents had had no schooling; that is, that the children are
born with poorly exercised or poorly trained raw material.

Now, it is fair to say that from Lamarck's day to the present no
single thoroughly established demonstration has ever been furnished
for this view that the characteristics acquired by an individual in its

lifetime are transmitted biologically to its offspring and thus produce evolutionary changes. One after another, claims for such proof have turned out to be false alarms; and the reasonable position for the psychologist to take is simply that until some criticism-proof evidence is furnished one cannot assume the operation of any such processes. "The fathers have eaten sour grapes, and the children's teeth are set on edge. . . . Ye shall not have occasion any more to use this proverb." The reader would do well to bear in mind such everyday observations as the following. A war veteran who has lost an arm, marries: his children are not born one-armed; or, as it has been crudely expressed, "Wooden legs do not run in families even though wooden heads may." The child of a literary man must learn the A, B, C's all over again; the child of a mathematician must in his own turn be taught that 2 and 2 make 4.

The principle of the non-transmission of acquired traits is most clearly brought out in the principles enunciated by *Weismann* a century later. A distinction was drawn between those cells that form the *germ* or reproductive plasm in an individual organism and those cells that go to form his body or *soma*. As is well known, the fertilized ovum from which the individual develops goes through elaborate stages of cell-division and cell-differentiation, some of the differentiated cells becoming skeletal tissue, some neural, some epithelial, and so on. One type retains the peculiar characteristics of the reproductive cells and furnishes the material from which the next generation is to spring. The processes of living and learning that the individual organism goes through involve changes in the somatic plasm — his blood and sinew and brain and bone — but it is not from these that the next generation springs, rather *from the germ plasm alone.* (Cf. Figure 11.) Playing a piano keyboard, calculating profits and losses, scanning poetry, reading a cook book, repairing automobile engines, and all the divers and sundry learned activities of the father or mother would be the functioning only of various somatic cells and not of the germ cells at all; and it follows that the latter, being unaffected, will not transmit to offspring any of these acquisitions. The child may be "a chip off the old block," but the "block" is the germ plasm and not the parent's somatic plasm. Indeed the germ plasm is not individually the parent's own, for he is but the carrier or trustee thereof. When both parent and offspring, then, show the traits of eminent musicians or of excellent mathematicians, or when they show similar awkwardness of gait or

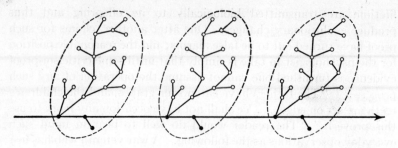

FIGURE 11. THE CONTINUITY OF THE GERM PLASM

A diagram to represent the principle of Weismann.   Each individual in the line of descent
develops from a single ovum.   The germ plasm, represented by a succession of dividing germ
cells (solid black dots), is continuous from generation to generation.   Each individual (in a
broken-line oval) develops from one of these germ cells, his body or soma being built up by the
differentiation of somatic cells (circles).   But these somatic cells are not continuous from
generation to generation; and the child is descended not from the parent's soma but only from
his germ plasm.   (For simplicity's sake the contribution of the other parent to each child is not
shown, but it is the same in principle.)

cleverness of fingers, or resemble each other in excitability or in
temperamental irascibility, the reason lies not in what has happened
to the parent's body in the course of his individual experience and is
then passed on, but rather in the characteristics of the stock from
which the two have sprung.

Natural Selection.   A question now presents itself forcibly.   If it
be granted that evolutionary changes in a line do not come about by
the summation of the somatic modifications of the individuals in that
line, how then are the evolutionary changes possible at all?   The
first clear-cut answer appeared in Darwin's *Origin of Species* in 1859.
Nature, he said in essence, operates as does the stock breeder.
Starting with a given population, the breeder selects those individuals that show most of those traits in which he is interested, keeps
them for breeding purposes, and by dint of repetition of this artificial
selection changes gradually the character of his stock.

Now let the rôle of selector be played by the natural conditions of
life as they favor the survival of some individuals and lead to the
early death of others.   The process of *natural selection* will follow
the same logic, and may be stated in five steps.

(1) *Overproduction.*   More individuals are born into a given
environment than can possibly survive, on account of limitations of
food, ground-space, and other necessary conditions.

(2) *Variation.*   No two individuals are ever born exactly alike.

"As alike as two peas" becomes a senseless expression as soon as one examines the peas with a lens or a delicate balance. If the leaves of one and the same tree or the individuals in one litter of guinea pigs or the left middle finger of all grown children in a large human family be carefully measured for length, it will be discovered that no two are precisely identical. Most such measurements will cluster about an average with fewer and fewer to be found toward the extremes; as is shown in the parent generation, P, and (better) in the two strains of the last generation, $F\ 8$, in Figure 12.

(3) *Competition.* In consequence of the overproduction of individuals some kind of struggle for existence occurs, not simply a tooth-and-nail combat of each against his fellows, but a peaceful enough rivalry for food and space, or a competition of speed or of protective coloring in escaping enemies, or even a competition in resistance to disease and other decimating agencies.

(4) *Selection.* In consequence of the variations among the competing individuals or groups some of them are better equipped for meeting the peculiar demands of the living conditions than are others; and hence it is they who show the so-called "survival of the fittest." (It is not necessarily the most pugnacious nor the best armed that survive: it is often the ones best protected against cold or heat, most immune to certain diseases, most cared for by parent, or most socially organized.)

(5) *Transmission.* Those individuals or groups that survive become the parents of the next generation; and — since they carry germ cells that differ slightly from those of the non-survivors — they establish the new average about which that next generation is to vary. Given a sufficient number of generations appearing under identical life conditions and these small shifts in the average of the stock will become summated to furnish marked alterations in the breed amounting even to changes of species. This, then, furnishes the answer to our question stated in an earlier paragraph: the materials by which evolutionary changes are made possible are the *selected natural variations.*

What at first appears a clear-cut demonstration of this general story is furnished in an investigation of a psychological trait (intelligence or learning ability) in a common laboratory animal, as shown in Figure 12. In that case it is perfectly certain for one thing that the traits of "brightness" and of "dullness" characterizing the two strains of rats produced by the eighth filial generation are not the

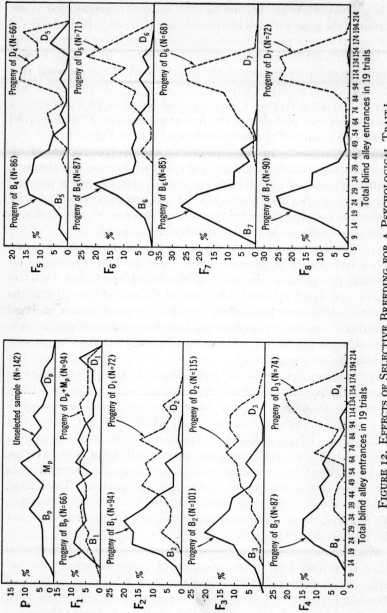

FIGURE 12. EFFECTS OF SELECTIVE BREEDING FOR A PSYCHOLOGICAL TRAIT [1]

[1] See note at foot of page 57.

results of the maze training actually given their ancestors but of the selecting based on the test results.

Mutations. Nowadays, an important amplification of these principles has been generally accepted. The minute variations which Darwin stressed turn out to be for the most part actually not inheritable. The production of apparently new strains, as in the breeding of "bright" and "dull" rats, may be only the isolation of different strains that composed the original population; and the emphasis has shifted to the suddenly appearing variations known as *mutations.* According to *De Vries* (1901) species have arisen not by the very gradual accumulation of very small individual differences (which are somatic only) but by jumps through sudden transformations (which are due to changes in the germ plasm). And these mutations are then transmitted to descendants. Black sheep, albino rats and guinea pigs and many other animals, mule-footed pigs, six-fingered hands and six-toed feet in man, are a few of the more striking sorts of mutations. Though more or less sudden in appearance, the mutations may yet be so small that they are masked by the effect of the somatic modifications and are to be detected only by special experiments.

Natural selection, therefore, is to be considered as at least in part a selection of mutations, large or small. Why or how mutations originate — of this very little is known. But, in any case, they are germinal variations; and to a brief study of the latter we now turn.

THE MECHANISMS OF HEREDITY

Mendelism. The first clear-cut indications of the part played by the germ plasm in determining inheritable characteristics appeared in an old neglected paper by the Austrian monk, Gregor Mendel, rediscovered in 1900, in which are set forth the results of some epoch-

---

Note to Figure 12, page 56. The 142 individuals of the original parental stock, *P*, were tested for their ability to learn the correct pathway through a maze of pathways (shown in Figure 93, p. 367). Their scores were distributed in a long curve showing the percentages of the group that entered 5, 9, 14, 19, 24, etc., blind alleys of the maze in the course of 19 trials. It will be seen that their scores were much scattered among the bright, B_p, the median, M_p, and the dull, D_p, animals.

Individuals of the next or filial generation, F_1, were likewise tested for maze learning. The scores of those that were progeny of the original bright rats, and the scores of the progeny of the original median and dull rats, were separated and plotted, forming scattered curves but with a slight divergence.

This procedure of separating the progeny of the bright and the dull as a result of maze tests was repeated for eight filial generations, producing — or separating — two distinct strains.

This is an example of artificial selection of natural variants.

(From Tryon, R. C., chapter in *Comparative Psychology* (Moss, ed.). Prentice-Hall, 1934.)

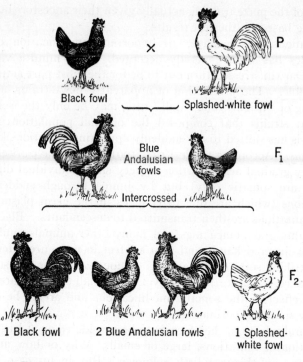

Black fowl   ×   Splashed-white fowl   P

Blue Andalusian fowls   F₁

Intercrossed

1 Black fowl   2 Blue Andalusian fowls   1 Splashed-white fowl   F₂

FIGURE 13. A CROSS-BREEDING OF PURE BLOODS

P, the parental generation. *F₁*, the first filial generation, in which all individuals are alike, of a bluish-black color. *F₂*, the second filial generation, derived by mating *F₁* individuals with each other. Segregation is here shown, the pure black, the hybrid, and the pure white appearing in the average ratios 1 : 2 : 1.

making experiments. Although he worked with the garden pea, his findings are more quickly grasped from description of another experiment. (Figure 13.) When a certain black fowl is crossed with a white one, the *hybrid* offspring, the *F₁* generation, turn out to be all blue Andalusians. But if these hybrid blues be interbred with each other, their offspring, the *F₂* generation, will consist of different colored fowls in definite ratios: ¼ black, ½ blue, ¼ white. Further breeding will show that the blacks alone or the whites alone will breed true (i.e., will have only descendants like themselves) throughout later generations, while the blue Andalusians will continue to produce in the above-mentioned ratios. The black and the white individuals will breed true because each carries the germ units for black, or for white, twice present, but the blues will not breed true, since each carries one black and one white unit. Crossing of the blues with the blacks or the whites will give offspring that follow equally definite ratios.

Frequently one of a pair of units is called *dominant* to the other, which is called *recessive*. They are so named because in the hybrid organism developed from both kinds only the former trait will appear in its bodily make-up, though not in its germ plasm. Example: the offspring of gray and white mice will all be gray, though in the second filial generation the white will appear in its usual ratio of $\frac{1}{4}$ against a $\frac{3}{4}$ for gray. From such phenomena Mendel framed his law of *segregation*, that the different determiners for any given trait in the germ-cells of a hybrid *remain separate units*, and in a second filial generation may become separated to produce individuals of distinct characters.

A further aspect of the matter appears when we consider more than one character of a plant or animal organism. For instance, at one stage of his experimentation on the fruit-fly, Morgan crossed white-eyed yellow-winged flies with red-eyed gray-winged ones. It was found that in the filial generations a given color of eye did not inevitably go with any given color of wing: the four mathematically possible combinations of either eye-color with either wing-color all being represented. (Cf. Figure 14.) Findings of this general type had led Mendel to his *law of independent recombination*, namely, that the segregations of the different kinds of units are independent of each other in greater or less degree.

The Theory of Genes. Morgan has been carrying on controlled matings of the fruit-fly (*Drosophila melanogaster*), and under these experimental conditions has produced over ten million of these organisms. He has noted with care many of the anatomical characteristics of each parent and of each individual of the progeny, generation by generation, such as the wing-color, eye-color, body-stripings. His analysis has led to the theory of the gene [9, 10].

In summary, it is as follows. The inherited characteristics of an individual are to be referred to special factors called genes, existing within the germinal plasm from which the individual springs. These genes are much too small to be seen through the microscope, and their existence therefore is only inferred; but the inferences are grounded on facts as substantial as those from which the chemist's invisible atoms or the physicist's electrons are inferred. Ordinarily the genes exist in pairs; and the many pairs are held together in certain linkage groups. Now, when the male and female germ-cells *mature* and are growing ready for the function of reproduction, the members of each pair of genes separate so that a given germ-cell contains only one set of genes. When male and female germ-cells unite in *fertilization* the different linked-up sets of genes recombine to form the full complement of genes in the somatic (non-germ) cell of the new individual. Finally, in the recombination of linked genes from male and female cells, some of the gene-pairs get exchanged or crossed over, and this crossing-over as traced out in the results of matings furnishes evidence from which can be deduced the relative positions of the genes within the germ-cell.

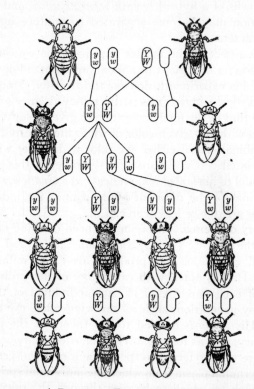

FIGURE 14. A BREEDING EXPERIMENT WITH DROSOPHILA

A white-eyed yellow-winged female is crossed with a red-eyed gray-winged male. The pairs of figures represent the pairs of chromosomes concerned in these traits, and, located in them, the genes determining them. *Y*, determiner for gray wing, *y*, yellow wing; *W*, for red eye, *w*, white eye. (The knobbed figure represents a chromosome which is concerned in sex determination.) (From Morgan, T. H., *The Physical Basis of Heredity.* J. B. Lippincott Company, 1919.)

But what about the more precise basis for these genes? The student of the biology of human nature will want to go deeper, to have pointed out the exact physical structures involved. Not content with locating the bases of genetic phenomena only generally in the germ plasm, he will want to find their specific mechanisms.

The Cell, Chromosomes, and Genes. Let us approach the matter now from another direction, that of knowledge of the germ cell and its changes. The typical living cell consists of a nucleus, which contains irregular, faint clumps of *chromatin*, and the surrounding cytoplasm, in which is found a *centrosome* just outside the nucleus. In ordinary growth, cells multiply to form large tissues and organisms by dividing. This division process involves the aforementioned structures in a series of progressive changes. Now, in that particular form of cell-division called *fertilization*, that is, where an egg or *ovum* (female cell) is fertilized by a sperm or *spermatozoön* (male cell) — to bring about the beginnings of a totally new organism from this combination of cells of two distinct parents — in that form of division something like the same procession of changes occurs, even though differently initiated and with different end-results.

Consider Figure 15. When the ovum is penetrated by the sperm the chromatin in the nuclei of both becomes rearranged into rods or other-shaped bodies known as *chromosomes*, which have previously been reduced to half their usual number when maturing in preparation for this reproductive function. The nuclei of the two cells draw together until their chromosomes lie about an equator with centrosomes marking the poles. The chromosomes then split lengthwise into pairs, and the two halves travel the one toward one pole, the other toward the other pole; so that about each pole will lie one chromosome from each of the pairs, hence *one from each parent cell*. Since the division of the mass is longitudinal each of the two newly formed cells has a full normal set of chromosomes, while keeping the arrangement of the genes constant save in the case of cross-overs.

Let us hope that it is now apparent to the reader that these known and visible facts about cell fertilization fit the gene version of Mendelism peculiarly well. He will be prepared even for the news that Morgan has been able actually to map out the location of many of the genes of the fruit-fly in its chromosomes, the distance of different genes from each other being computed from their degree of "linkage" in "crossing-over." *The laws of inheritance are, then, the rules*

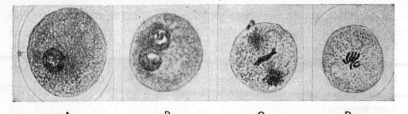

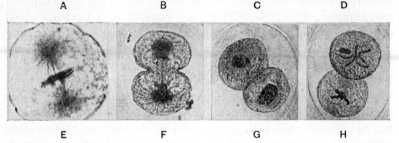

FIGURE 15. FERTILIZATION, ILLUSTRATED FROM A LOWER ANIMAL FORM

Showing the fertilized egg of the round-worm, Ascaris, which possesses two pairs of chromosomes. (Micro-photographs.) *A*, Immature (unfertilized) ovum with nucleus in "resting" phase. (Spermatozoön within left margin?) *B*, Fertilization has just occurred. The nuclei of egg and sperm are approaching each other; the chromosomes have begun to appear (spireme stage). *C*, Side view of the equatorial plate stage. The spindle appears, with the centrosomes at its ends; the chromosomes have arranged themselves round the equator. *D*, End view of the same stage. The four chromosomes (of this animal form) are clearly visible. *E*, Side view of a slightly later stage. The chromosomes have now split longitudinally. *F*, The two new sets of chromosomes have moved apart to the two centrosomes; the cell is deeply constricted. *G*, Two-cell stage. The egg has completely divided; in either cell the chromosomes have joined up to form a "resting" nucleus. *H*, Beginning of a second cleavage in each daughter cell. One cell is turned so that the four chromosomes have again appeared.

E is more greatly magnified than the others.

(From Haldane, J. B. S., and Huxley, J., *Animal Biology*. Oxford University Press, 1907.)

of the distribution and redistribution of the parts of the chromosomes of the male and female germ cells and the genes resident therein.

Some Fallacies. From the foregoing presentation many a reader may be led to assume that there is one gene for stature, one for eye-color, one for feeble-mindedness, another for normal-mindedness, and so on. The assumption is not borne out, however. In *Drosophila*, for example, over fifty genes cooperate to produce so simple a feature as the red eye-color, that is, if any of the fifty be missing the red color does not appear. Hundreds of genes produce the straight wing; and other characters are similarly complex in their genetic basis.

A second error is to infer that the range of variation of a stock is limited by the total number of possible recombinations of the genes as found in it. On an earlier page we have touched on the phenomenon of "mutations"; and we should now round out our notion of heredity by tying up that concept with the conception of the genes. Genes themselves may mutate, may be so changed in their intricate chemical character as to give rise to new mutant individuals. Finally, natural selection re-enters here, as an explanation of why such mutant individuals seldom survive and the stock maintains its general character without change through years and generations.

Another fallacy would be to assume that the genetic story for any given mating is always one and the same regardless of the surrounding conditions: that what sort of organism is to be born is invariably and precisely determined by the genes. Contrary evidence may be had in plenty from the fruit-fly experiments. Some of the flies inherit a tendency to produce supernumerary legs, that is, if hatched and raised in a low temperature; but if kept warm enough this abnormality does not appear. Others will show an abnormality of joints and of abdominal shape if kept in the usual moist air, but not if hatched out and raised in dry air. Or, consider another animal, the Mexican axolotl. This salamander normally retains its gills throughout life, living in the water, where it lays eggs and produces its young. These characteristics are transmitted to its offspring. But if it be subjected to certain changed temperature conditions the gills disappear, the body grows less large, is slenderer, and the animal comes out on land to remain there. The offspring as long as they are kept under the same conditions become land animals for generation after generation. Clearly, the sort of organism that is to develop from a given germinal start depends not simply on the genes themselves but also upon the conditions under which they work. Even here, then, in this fundamental and rock-bottom stage of the individual's development we find reminders aplenty that a fruit-fly or a salamander or, for that matter, a human genius or a human idiot, is certainly not simply "born" but is in some degree, at least, "made" [8].

EXPERIMENTAL AND STATISTICAL METHODS WITH HUMAN BEINGS

In the geneticists' experimental work on simpler animal forms, it was possible absolutely to control either the matings or the environmental conditions. To refer once more to the *Drosophila* investigations, it will be recalled that most of them were carried on as experiments in which the environment was held constant while the matings were varied, but a few identical matings were secured with varied temperature or other environmental condition. Such experimentally ideal arrangements have been approximated in a new series of investigations on man, wherein heredity has been held constant while environment was varied or else environment held constant while heredity was varied [14]. Meanwhile, the development of more accurate instruments for the measurement of some psychological capacities has naturally been of great importance.

Heredity Varied; Environment Constant.   Where should we look
to find individuals with a common heredity?   In children of the
same parents, of course — called *siblings*.   Among siblings we
would suppose a more common genetic identity between twins, and
especially between "identical" twins.   *"Fraternal" twins*, originating from different egg cells, fertilized by different sperm cells,
would share a less common heredity than *identical twins*, which
come from the same egg fertilized by one sperm.   Distinguishing
between fraternal and identical twins is largely a matter of inference
from degrees of resemblance in many bodily characteristics.   Similarity of palm and skin patterns is considered the best indication.
Corresponding hands of identical twins often show closer resemblance than the two hands of either one person [11].

To measure the effect of heredity in a comparison, say, between
identical and fraternal twins, the procedure is to compare the
measured likeness between pairs of individuals of the first type with
the measured likeness between pairs of the second; if the likeness in
the former case is higher (closer) this difference is ascribable to their
more common genetic base (assuming that in cases of all pairs the
two persons were reared in the same home).

When a number of intelligence and educational tests were administered to pairs of twins in school and to related and unrelated children in an orphanage, and were compared also with data from other
studies, a descending order of psychological resemblances appeared
among the different types of paired individuals that paralleled strikingly the decreasing degrees of closeness in genetic origin.   The
data are summarized in the accompanying table where the degrees

INTELLECTUAL RESEMBLANCE AMONG GROUPS EXHIBITING DIFFERENT
DEGREES OF GENETIC RELATIONSHIP [1]

Group	r =
Identical twins	.90
Fraternal like-sexed twins	.82
Fraternal like- and unlike-sexed twins	.70
Fraternal unlike-sexed twins	.59
Siblings	.50
Parent-child	.31
Cousins	.27
Grandparent-grandchild	.16
Unrelated children	.00

[1] From Wingfield, A. H. *Twins and Orphans: The Inheritance of Intelligence.*   J. M. Dent Co.
1928.

of psychological resemblance are stated in terms of coefficients of correlation.[1] From such results we are safe in concluding that there is something in the constitution of the human being upon which *general intelligence* depends and which is inherited. More practically put, we should be warranted in expecting higher ability and better performance in school work, and in occupations calling for the same sort of natural gifts, from the children or other relatives of people already known to be able. And the closer the blood relationship, the more definite the expectation.[2]

What about other psychological traits? Are such things as capacities for motor performances also laid down in a person's genetic constitution? To get at this matter, boy twins of high school age, including practically an equal number of fraternals and identicals, were given practice and tests calling on a variety of particular hand skills. The next table shows us the results in terms of the average values of r on each test for each group of pairs, combined

RESEMBLANCE IN MOTOR SKILLS BETWEEN FRATERNAL TWINS AND IDENTICAL TWINS, AND COMPARED WITH RESEMBLANCES IN OTHER TRAITS [3]

		Fraternal	Identical
This investigation	Pursuit rotor	.51	.95
46 fraternal pairs	Steadiness	.43	.83
47 identical pairs	Speed drill	.56	.82
	Spool packing	.44	.71
	Card sorting	.39	.85
From Holzinger	Tapping ability	.43	.78
52 fraternal pairs	Binet mental age	.67	.95
50 identical pairs	Height	.65	.93
	Weight	.63	.92
	Head length	.58	.91
	Head breadth	.55	.89
	Cephalic index	58	.90

[1] The coefficient of correlation is an index of the degree to which the various measurements in one group resemble those in a related group. Suppose in the above case one of the members of each pair is put into one group, and the other member of each pair is put into a second group. If the various members of the first group make scores that are the same as their partners in the second group, it is said that there is a perfect correspondence, represented by the value, $r = 1.00$. If, however, the members of the second group make scores that show no correspondence at all to the scores of their partners in the first group, then this value is $r = .00$. Finally, the degree of correspondence may vary, of course, from perfect to none at all, and the values of r, therefore, may vary from 1.00 to .00. For fuller explanation, see below, Chapter XI.

[2] Here and elsewhere the student will remind himself of the dangers arising from "errors of sampling": statements like the above are truer when many cases are under consideration than when there are only one or a few. They may not hold for individual cases. Cf. Chapter XI.

[3] From McNemar, Q. Twin Resemblances in Motor Skills, and the Effect of Practice Thereon J. Genet. Psychol., 1933, **42**, 70–97.

with results of another investigation on other than motor traits. There can be no question about it: twins coming from the same egg and sperm show very high resemblance (around .90) in matters of *motor abilities* as well as of *physique*, much higher than do those twins arising from separate eggs and sperms (around .50). Again and on other sides we see that the genetic basis from which a man has sprung is of tremendous importance in determining his achievements.

Environment Varied; Heredity Constant.

Studies of identical twins reared apart. A highly interesting method of holding heredity practically constant and letting environmental differences do their worst, is to take cases of identical twins that have been reared apart in different social and material living conditions. Some ten cases are on recent record. The environments for most of the pairs were strikingly different. "A," for example, had been adopted into a large family living in a crowded middle class section in London and had suffered deprivations during the war, while her twin "O" was early brought to Canada as an only child in a family of good social standing in a small town. "E" was kept at home to do housework for an illiterate mother, while "G" had studied in a convent, academy, and normal school. "Ada" and "Ida" had both suffered childhood hardships in their different homes of adoption; but the former had later lived an unhappy married life in cities, while the latter's married life was placidly spent on a farm. "Raymond" was adopted by a well-to-do physician in a large city, "Richard" by a truck driver. In spite of such disparities of social and cultural opportunity and of nutritional and hygienic surroundings, some rather striking resemblances appeared when the pairs were brought together for observation — the resemblances extending not only to details of *physique* but also to measurable *emotional-temperamental attitudes* and *interests*, to *intellectual capacities*, and even to items in their *disease histories*. And, where differences between the two were at all prominent, the more favorable difference was not always to the child that had had the more favorable environment [11].

Such a finding — stated in this general form — is not at all surprising. But we would want to know more. We would want answers to the persistent question, How do these resemblances compare with those of other types of pairs (fraternals, siblings, unrelated)? Only a little data of this kind is available. If we ask about their intelligence, the accompanying table furnishes us a very

DIFFERENCE IN INTELLIGENCE TEST SCORES BETWEEN IDENTICAL TWINS
REARED APART, COMPARED WITH DIFFERENCES FOR OTHER PAIRS

	Average difference in I.Q.	Range of differences in I.Q.
10 identicals reared apart	7.7	0–17
50 identicals reared together	5.3	0–20
50 fraternals reared together	9.9	0–43
Same individuals on test-retest	6.8	0–53

little meat in the form of I.Q. scores.[1] From such data little can be safely concluded. The reader will be able to discern a certain trend; but he will also be aware that the figures are small and probably unreliable. As is true of many pioneer intellectual interests, the matter is a "problem for future research."

Studies of foster children. The weight to be attached to environmental factors in bending the twig and so modifying its later development may be checked by observing the results of the placing of children of equivalent heritage in different grades of private homes. If environment is a heavy factor those adopted into good homes obviously should reveal higher capacities than those adopted into poor homes [4, 5].

In one study the heredity factor was made more constant by dividing the children into the legitimate and the illegitimate before the difference of foster home was calculated. It was found when intelligence measurements were made, the average I.Q. of legitimate children placed in superior homes was 101, while that of those in inferior homes was 89; and for the illegitimate placed in superior homes, 109, in inferior, 96. These are averages of groups of children taken apparently without respect to their relationship to each other. Another way of rendering the heredity factor more constant, was by comparing pairs of siblings where one of each pair had been adopted into a better home than was his sib. In I.Q. measurements, again, the scores were found to be: for the siblings in better homes, 95, for those in poorer, 86.

In both the foregoing studies a further point was considered. Surely, if environment has influence in shaping the child, we would expect this influence to be the more manifest the younger the child is when the environment begins to operate on him. Dividing the

[1] For the meaning of this score see Chapter XIII. It is based upon standardized tests of "general intelligence," and is an index of the individual's relative "brightness." An I.Q. of 100 means that he is at the average point of the population of his age, higher and lower scores mean that he is "brighter" or "duller" than the average.

groups accordingly into those adopted at an earlier age and those adopted at a later, it was found in the first-mentioned study that the younger-adopted averaged I.Q. 96, the older-adopted, 88; and similarly in the second-mentioned study, the younger-adopted averaged 95, the older-adopted, 86.

So far as *general intelligence* measurements go, then, the home *environment contributes its share*, and the younger and more plastic the individual, the greater its share. This leaves us in a somewhat unsatisfied state, it must be confessed. The above figures have significance for us only if the I.Q. is an index of something rather fundamental and is not a mere measure of information. We are also left unsatisfied by the lack of knowledge about how other psychological capacities and traits have fared in the different family environments.

SOME CONCLUSIONS FOR THE PSYCHOLOGIST

Can We Change Fundamental Human Nature? Is the human stock improvable? To this question a categorical answer is returnable. Yes; but only *by selection*. There are very many selective agencies in human society, war being undeniably the worst of all. Meanwhile, *eugenic* investigations and programs primarily concerned with the gaining of ever more accurate knowledge of which human traits are inheritable and what the best means are for their selection and transmission are constantly being carried on.

Another side of the same principle is that much that is "human" is certainly transmissible by "*social inheritance*," by the familiar process of handing down through family life, education, religion, and other institutional channels. This is "culture" in its technical meaning; this type of change is the subject matter of history, for since man became man on the earth, the changes that have come about are far less changes in human nature and are far more changes in his material things and his institutions. Physically and intellectually, says Osborn, we are probably no whit superior to the men of twenty-five thousand years ago.

Which is the More Important, Nature or Nurture? Surely, if we have learned anything from our survey of biological principles and of experimental and statistical studies, it is that such a question is naïve in the extreme. So stated, it belongs with all those easy and vague generalizations that become the bane of intelligent discourse, and from which scientific knowledge in particular works away toward ever more definite and particularized fact.   It represents a mental vacuum to be avoided.   It is weak because too general. Restated in a more promising way, it becomes: "In the production of the psychological trait X, does nature or nurture contribute the more?"   From the evidences furnished by studies in the latter half of the present chapter, we would be justified in substituting a few explicit values for X and in rendering a provisional answer.   In the cases of genius, feeble-mindedness, the middle levels of intelligence, some forms of insanity, motor abilities, and apparently also certain emotional-temperamental traits, the contributions of heredity are heavy.   And it is only fair to assume that in cases of many other traits where there is close dependence upon details of bodily structure, the weight of heredity would be equally considerable.   But observe that these are *general capacities;* they are not specific details of performance.   Particular *skills, knowledges, likes-dislikes* must await the opportunity and practice which are afforded by environment.   Who will attempt to say how much of the expert bookkeeper's efficiency is a matter of general capacity and how much a matter of learning, or what part of a writer's art is ascribable to his experience and what to his native talent?

Aristotle said, "the nature of a man is not what he is born as, but what he is born for"; and a psychologist has recently remarked, "heredity determines what one can do, environment what he does do."   As suggested in Figure 16, the psychograph of a man, if by some miracle he were allowed and encouraged to develop every inborn talent to its utmost, would be quite a different picture from that allowed by any actualities of life.

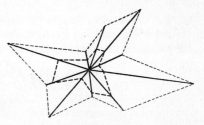

FIGURE 16.   HEREDITARY POSSIBILITIES AND REALIZED ACTUALITIES

Let each radiating solid line represent by its total length the ultimate possible development of a psychological capacity under environmental circumstances 100 per cent optimal and favorable.   The light dotted lines then furnish a profile of what the man *might* have become (in the various alternative directions, for he could not have developed in all).   The heavy broken lines outline him as his actual environmental conditions have permitted him to develop.

Not Heredity versus Environment but Development, is the Object of Our Inquiries.   But all this is perhaps too simple.   Heredity does not stop its work at the individual's birth, providing him with a *tabula rasa* to be inscribed upon by the stylus of experience which is now in exclusive operation.   In the mammals, to be sure, there is an early period in which the conditions surrounding the organism are almost completely uninfluenceable because it lies protected in the mother's body; and we have become accustomed to calling "inherited" those characteristics that are determined before it leaves that isolated state, and "acquired" all those determined later.   No conception could be more erroneous.   As a matter of established biological fact, what is going on from the moment of fertilization to the moment of the individual's death is an astonishingly complex interaction of the protoplasmic material and its *milieux*.

At fertilization of the ovum the genes interact, not merely with each other, but with the cytoplasm, with food substances and oxygen in cytoplasm and fluids surrounding the cell, and also with products of chemical activities occurring in neighboring cells.   In some lower animal forms, the first cell fission is into two cells which usually produce the right and left halves of the body; but if they be separated — an environmental influence — each will proceed to develop into an entire animal.   Still later, when by proliferation the organism has reached the gastrula stage, there appears at the "front" tip a differentiating influence that spreads from cell to cell, bringing on the gradual specialization of cells into spinal cord, brain, eye, ear, and skin; but if this tip end be cut loose and rotated about, the differentiating influence creeps through from the same origin, but in the new direction, so that cells originally to become eye may now become midbrain or ear or skin.   The fact that two-headed or cyclopean or misshapen monsters are producible experimentally in very many growing animals simply by omitting certain ingredients in the water, is perhaps familiar to the reader, as is also the fact that within more developed organisms, transplantations assume new structures and functions. Finally, may be mentioned the important researches of Child on physiological gradients, in which he has demonstrated that the foundation for an organism's permanent structure is first determined by external energies that establish accelerated metabolic activity in a particular region of a body, which then by induction sets up gradations of lesser activity in adjacent parts of the body.

At every step, then, it is the *intricate interplay of the protoplasmic unit* (gene, cell, organ, or organism) *with its surrounding conditions* that determines what the next stage shall be.   It is the *intrinsic factors interacting subtly with extrinsic factors*, and in so complicated a way that what may be regarded as intrinsic from the point of view of a larger unit (such as an organ) must be regarded as extrinsic to a smaller contained unit (as a cell).

This, be it noted, is a profoundly significant viewpoint for psychology. Instead of debating whether walking, for instance, is entirely "instinctive" or is entirely "learned" we will do better to observe it as *a succession of stages.* Even such a process as remembering is nowadays coming to be treated not simply as a function of practice but as a function of growth as well. *No longer obsessed with an obligation to sort the phenomena of human psychology into the purely hereditary and the purely environmental, we shall be freer to study the actualities of development in an empirical and factual way.* We now turn to development in the individual.

REFERENCES

1. Castle, W. E. *Genetics and Eugenics.* Harvard Univ. Press, 4th ed. 1931.

2. Child, C. M. *Physiological Foundations of Behavior.* Holt, 1924.

3. Darwin, Ch. *The Origin of Species.* 1859.

4. Freeman, F. N. The Effect of Environment on Intelligence. *School and Soc.,* 1930, **31,** 623–32.

5. Freeman, F. N., Holzinger, K. J., and Mitchell, B. C. The Influence of Environment on the Intelligence, School Achievement, and Conduct of Foster Children. *27th Yearbook, Nat. Soc. Study of Educ.,* Pt. I, 1928.

6. Galton, F. *Hereditary Genius.* Macmillan, 1869.

7. Geddes, P., and Thompson, J. A. *Evolution.* Holt, 1911.

8. Jennings, H. S. *Biological Basis of Human Nature.* Norton, 1930.

9. Morgan, T. H. *The Theory of the Gene.* Yale Univ. Press, 1928.

10. Morgan, T. H., Sturtevant, A. H., Muller, H. J., and Bridges, C. B. *The Mechanism of Mendelian Heredity.* Holt, 1915.

11. Newman, H. H. *Jour. of Heredity.* 1929, **20,** 49–64, 97–104, 153–66; 1931, **22,** 41–50; 1932, **23,** 2–18; 1933, **24,** 209–14. *Jour. Genetics,* 1931, **23,** 415–46.

12. Schwesinger, G. C. *Heredity and Environment.* Macmillan, 1933.

13. Weismann, A. *The Evolution Theory* (trans. by Thomson). London, 1904.

14. Whipple, G. M. (ed.). *27th Yearbook, Nat. Soc. Study of Educ.* Nature and Nurture. I. Their Influence on Intelligence. II. Their Influence upon Achievement. Bloomington: Public School Pub. Co., 1928.

15. Wingfield, A. H. *Twins and Orphans: The Inheritance of Intelligence.* London: Dent, 1928.

CHAPTER IV

INDIVIDUAL DEVELOPMENT

INTRODUCTION

To THE modern way of thinking it is almost axiomatic that to understand a given occurrence or phenomenon properly one must take account of its genesis. Social events have their roots in history; and biological facts find their rationale based on their developmental past. This is emphatically true of psychological phenomena. No comprehension of an individual person can be at all adequate unless there be some knowledge of his individual past; and in general, no solid science of human adult behavior can claim anything like competence unless it be based upon the available data and principles of human development. In the present chapter, then, we will try to get a running start for our later tasks of understanding man in the fullness of adult stature and the complexity of his ripened capacities, by noting the more outstanding things that characterize him in his earlier stages.

No contrast is more vivid than that presented by the adult and his own infancy. The family album, with its amusing repository of photographs of one and the same person, taken at widely separated ages from long dresses to long dresses again, merely hints at the remarkable changes that occur without after all changing the individual's personal identity. And who has not, as he gazed musingly at the face and form of a babe in arms, speculated as to just what were its potentialities, what would be its later actualities, and what would be the story of the changes to be wrought? Popular thinking seems not, however, to have resolved the matter into specific questions; and we shall find our own queries shaped much by the outcomes of investigative research.

INDIVIDUAL DEVELOPMENT IN SOME LOWER ANIMALS

Introduction. Since humankind is but a species of the animal kingdom, we may here — as in so many places in a psychological survey — block out best the main problems and the main theories that bear upon them, by taking note of contemporary research on development in some infra-human forms. It would be rash to attempt to present here a complete picture of development in all the phyla and genera of animal life — such a task belongs to Animal Behavior as a special field. We will content ourselves with studying three or four fields of research that have yielded most fruitful interpretative light on individual development (ontogenesis) of human beings.

Individuation of Specific Movements out of Mass Activity. Psychologists have caught a fruitful lead from Coghill's studies on the development of the tadpole of the salamander *Amblystoma punctatum*. (Cf. Figure 17.) When first hatched this creature reacts to stimulation only by a gross bending of the whole body to right or to left, the limbs simply dragging along as merely dependent ap pendages. At later periods, however, out of this movement of the whole organism as a simple kind of unit there emerge independent movements of the legs bending at the shoulders, then of the fore joints of those legs bending at the elbows, and still later independent foot and even independent toe movements. In time the salamander shows in its swimming, walking, and prey-catching an enormous repertoire of individuated movements of local members of its body. What was originally a *total pattern* of swimming, for instance, becomes

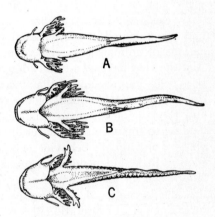

FIGURE 17. EARLY STAGES IN THE DEVELOPMENT OF BEHAVIOR IN A SALAMANDER

A. Ventral view of *Amblystoma punctatum.* The fore limbs moved slightly when the trunk moved, but they failed to respond to repeated local stimulations. (The fore limbs are short processes to be seen just behind the gills.)

B. The same, later. The fore limbs made slight movements in response to direct stimulation, but these were accompanied by slight movements of the trunk.

C. The same, a day or two later. The fore limbs now respond to direct stimulation without any perceptible action of the trunk.

(From Coghill, G. E., *Anatomy and the Problem of Behavior.* 1929. By permission of The Macmillan Company, publishers.)

expanded; and, by a process of individuation, partial patterns and reflexes become separated in some degree from the unitary total;

and the behavior, though retaining its essential character as locomotion, becomes more and more elaborate and complex. Instead of just a general bending aside of the forward part of the trunk there is to be seen in the more advanced stages a turning of the head, supported by forward and backward strokes of the limbs, the auxiliary team play of the feet and toes, and so on. Generalized, this conception of the matter takes the form of the statement that the changes which occur in individual development are essentially a differentiation of more and more details within the whole.

Independent Reflexes at the Beginnings of Behavior. The foregoing view has excited a large stir partly because it contravened so flatly the age-old reflex theory. As early as 1855 Herbert Spencer had promulgated the celebrated dictum that the more complex actions of animals were really but combinations of reflex actions. And the view has had a tremendous vogue up till recent years, owing both to its happy simplicity and to the powerful influence on American psychological thought of the Russian reflexologists, Bekhterev and Pavlov (of whom we shall have much to say later). Those holding to this viewpoint naturally conceived the primordial beginnings of an animal's behavior as being the joining of the diverse and sundry little independent reflexes that were its first repertoire. *Integration* (or joining together) of discrete movements *into patterns* was the keynote. Conceived in this extreme degree, the whole reflexological interpretation has lost ground considerably; and to think of the first movements of rat or chick or chimpanzee as consisting only of so many discrete simple actions is today rated as naïve.

The Coghill view, however, is a swing to the other extreme; and of late a *via media* is suggested in the work of several investigators who have come to see great limitations in his formulations [9, and especially 5]. In the fetus of the guinea pig, for instance, they discern not only the massive activities but also many of simple reflex type.

Their work was as follows. After transection of the spinal cord of a mother guinea pig had rendered her insensitive and immobile at the abdominal level, an incision was made in the uterus. She was kept partly immersed in a saline bath solution, so permitting the fetus, now exposed through the incision, to remain connected with the maternal organism by the umbilical cord. Under these conditions a variety of contact and other stimulations were applied, in

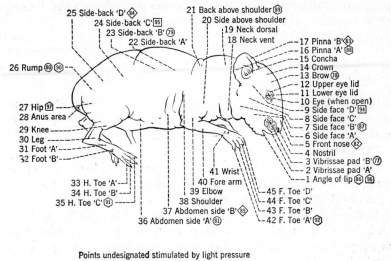

25 Side-back 'D' Ⓧ
24 Side-back 'C' ⬜95
23 Side-back 'B' Ⓧ79
22 Side-back 'A'

21 Back above shoulder Ⓧ89
20 Side above shoulder
19 Neck dorsal
18 Neck vent

26 Rump Ⓧ80 Ⓧ90

27 Hip Ⓧ97
28 Anus area
29 Knee
30 Leg
31 Foot 'A'
32 Foot 'B'

--17 Pinna 'B' Ⓧ
--16 Pinna 'A' Ⓧ88
--15 Concha
--14 Crown
--13 Brow Ⓧ78
--12 Upper eye lid
--11 Lower eye lid
--10 Eye (when open)
--9 Side face 'D' ⬜94
--8 Side face 'C'
--7 Side face 'B' Ⓧ87
--6 Side face 'A'
--5 Front nose Ⓧ82
--4 Nostril
--3 Vibrissae pad 'B' Ⓧ77
--2 Vibrissae pad 'A'
--1 Angle of lip Ⓧ86 Ⓧ96

33 H. Toe 'A'
34 H. Toe 'B'
35 H. Toe 'C' Ⓧ91

41 Wrist
40 Fore arm
39 Elbow
38 Shoulder
37 Abdomen side 'B' Ⓧ85
36 Abdomen side 'A' Ⓧ81

45 F. Toe 'D'
44 F. Toe 'C'
43 F. Toe 'B'
42 F. Toe 'A' Ⓧ92

Points undesignated stimulated by light pressure
Points noted by ◯ stimulated by needle
Points noted by ◇ stimulated by single break shock
Points noted by ⬠ stimulated by faradic current
Points noted by ⬜ stimulated by warm and cool

In late fetuses rotation (101); Post-rotation (102); Passive flexion
of limbs·fore (103)·hind (104); and righting responses noted

Points noted by ⬠ stimulated by pressure, etc. after high cervical section

FIGURE 18. RECEPTOR AREAS STIMULATED IN THE FETAL GUINEA PIG

The points used for experimental stimulation are indicated on a diagram of a late fetus.
Only the lateral view is presented. Dorsal and ventral views which show 30 additional points
are not reproduced in this figure. (From Carmichael, L., An Experimental Study in the Pre-
natal Guinea-Pig, etc. *Genet. Psychol. Monog.*, 1934, **16**, Nos. 5–6.)

a systematic fashion, to many predetermined spots on the fetal body.
Figure 18 shows many of these, and records of the responses were
obtained in shorthand notes and motion pictures.

The first activity to appear consisted of movements that were
aroused by unknown stimulation (so-called "spontaneous" behavior). But as the experimenters repeated their round of systematic explorations of the receptor areas, they noted an enormous
variety of responses ranging from the simplest movement of a single
joint to rather complex combinations.

Area 5. *Front nose.* Stimulation here brought out raising of a forepaw,
not repeated for 7 days. Then also a wink of the still closed eyelids. At

various times there appeared wrinkling of vibrissae pad, an eye wink, pinna reflexes, mouth, tongue, lip, jaw movements.

Areas 16, 17. *Pinna.* First to be aroused, lateral flexion of trunk. Later more limb and trunk movements, some of the former definitely touching the stimulated spot. Most characteristic, a contraction of the whole pinna or a bit of it around the point touched. Eye wink often elicited.

In this manner varying segments of activity were obtainable at all stages of fetal life: which amplifies and corrects the Coghill generalization mentioned a few paragraphs above.

The Control of the Patterning.

The rôle of extrinsic factors. The Chinese psychologist, Kuo [16], has made the point that, after all, for the understanding of how an organism develops it is not of great concern to decide whether the earliest embryonic movements are massive and involve the body as a whole or are merely independent reflexes. In either case their importance lies in the fact that they are the raw material out of which the various response systems of postnatal life become organized. According to him, the more fundamental problem really is, *What are the causal factors directing the integration and differentiation and reintegration* of such basic materials as they become organized into temporal patterns of behavior?

With this query in mind Kuo made exhaustive studies on some three thousand embryo chicks. He chipped away some of the egg shell and coated the exposed membranes with vaseline to make them transparent. Then he noted with care the character of movements made from time to time. He was especially attentive to other changes occurring within the egg at the same times, both to the changes in the structure of the organism and to those in the character of the immediate surroundings, the yolk sac, shell wall, etc. Here are typical coincidences of activity-change and structural change that he noted.

(a) On about the fifth day of incubation, the head movements change from bending toward the breast and lifting to a circular kind of side turning; but on this day and after it is to be noted that the head has become relatively very heavy though the neck is quite small, and the difficulty of raising it straight up is a sufficient reason for its side turning. (b) On about the eighth day of life, the fore limbs, which have been moving headward-tailward, now show sidewise flapping movements, which a day or two later disappear; but note that these alterations in activity coincide with the appearance of a wing-like structure in the fore limbs and with such elongation as to crowd them against the shell wall. (c) On about the twelfth day, the trunk movements of bending and straightening, and lateral twisting disappear, and are replaced by jerkings and wrigglings; but at this time the organism is so increased in length that there is insufficient space within the shell for any but the latter types of body movements.

From an array of such coincidences between changes of activity on the one hand and alterations of body structure and of embryonic surroundings on the other, the deduction seemed a safe one that the former are determined by the latter.   The way in which behavior becomes organized, even in the embryonic stages, is not merely the inevitable coming to full bloom of some intrinsic pattern that was somehow implicit and hidden in the earlier stages.   It is also in some degree a result of incidental extrinsic factors.

It would be easy to exaggerate this view into the extreme notion that all is acquired, nothing is constitutional, and that since the effective factors that are involved in making a person what he is are those that direct his learning, then psychologists should devote their time to the phenomena of habit-acquisition, with a confidence that if only we could control a man's opportunities and his ways of acquiring habits we could mould his behavior into any desired form.

The rôle of intrinsic factors.   Evidence that the view just outlined is an exaggeration, however, can be had from many sources.   One of the best known is the work of Carmichael with salamander's and frog's eggs [6].   Embryo forms were placed in a chloretone solution, which inhibits any overt activity but does not hinder growth. Meanwhile a control group were allowed to live in the normal way in fresh water.   Several days after the latter had developed free swimming movements, the drugged and inert animals were also placed in fresh water.   As soon as the effect of the anesthetic had worn off, these animals were swimming and darting about as freely and naturally as were the controls.   Evidently, the appearance of a form of behavior typical to the species *did not wait upon exercise* or practice but matured quite irrespectively thereof.

The Problems Now Defined.   This brief survey of a few of the many studies on embryonic development in subhuman forms need not lead us to definite generalizations: it will have served us well if it has focused our attention on the most central issues to be raised in our study of the ontogenesis of the human species.   The first two investigations reported have precipitated into the clear the problem: *Is "individuation" or "integration" the keyword in individual development?*   That is, do the growing organism's ways of acting appear by differentiation out of total massive behavior (the *organismic* view), or are they established by the joining together of independent movements (the *reflexological* view)?   In addition to this query which concerns more, let us say, the mechanics of the matter, these two types of investigation have brought to the fore a more causative and dynamic question. *Is "maturation" or is "practice" the keyword for explaining the development of behavior?* That is, are the forms which an individual's behavior assumes the result of unfolding of characters that were implicit and intrinsic in him (the *preformistic* view) or are they determined by the incidental play of extra-organic and extrinsic forces (the *epigenetic* view)?

No critical reader, it is safe to say, will have concluded this section with his mind ready to adopt either extreme position on either question.   Will the facts of man's development order themselves along these directions and lead us to a generalization, a generalization that can be carried with us in our further studies of human psychology?

DEVELOPMENT IN THE HUMAN FETUS AND NEWBORN

Different Conceptions of the Child.   (I) At certain times in history, and notably in the eighteenth century, the child was regarded as merely an *adult in miniature*, a pint-size edition of what he would later become.   It had to be admitted, of course, that in infancy he was incapable of speaking, of walking, and of sexual reproduction, but in a general way no great qua'itative differences were supposed to hold.   Such a view has long since been stamped as grossly untrue.   On the side of physique, the differences between baby and adult in proportion of various parts are well known; and the reader has himself probably often noticed that head and eyes in the baby are much larger in proportion to the rest of him than is the case in youths and adults.   Consider the different rates of growth of other parts.   The musculature is said to increase in mass some 48 times, the skeleton 26, the lungs 20, the liver 14, the heart 13, while the spinal cord increases only 7 times, the brain less than 4, and the eye less than 2.   What a monstrosity the infant would become if all his parts grew at equal pace!   Now, if this be the story of his physical development, it is natural to infer that in the development of his behavior, too, the person changes in the relative importance of different phases, so that maturity in conduct means something quite different from infant activities on a larger scale. This inference is abundantly justified by the facts, as we shall see.

(II) A second view is to the effect that the infant is primarily a *bundle of reflexes*. On this view, his behavior consists of a great number of specific, independent, simple reactions to stimuli. As he develops into child and on into man these separate action-units become joined together more and more completely and complexly. One of the best studies leading to this conception is that conducted by Mrs. Blanton (working with J. B. Watson) [1] in a psychological laboratory attached to the maternity ward of Johns Hopkins Hospital. The following highly condensed notes will suggest the type of observations she obtained when she subjected her subjects to a variety of stimulating conditions.

Reactions of respiratory apparatus. *Sneezing* was the earliest reflex noted, appearing in one case even before the birth cry. *Crying* usually had to be artificially stimulated at birth in order to establish breathing — by rubbing, slapping, or immersion. Its nature varied from individual to individual. *Hiccoughing* was noted as early as at six hours of age. Twice *yawning* was noted within five minutes after birth.

Reactions of eyes, face, and head. An inequality of *eye movements* was not uncommon, the two eyeballs not always turning together in perfect unison. Fixation upon a bright light was common soon after birth. Following a slowly moving object that reflected light — a hand, a nurse's costume, a sunlight spot on wall paper past which the baby was being carried — was noted at later dates. *Tears* were not shed by many infants until many days of age; and *smiling* was also delayed. Ability to *hold up the head* when the trunk was supported in a sitting position was observed at varying ages, from 2 to 15 days. Nearly all subjects (4 to 29 days of age) gave some definite response to light rattling *sounds* of paper, some turning the head and eyes directly to the sound (localizing). *Sucking* appeared invariably at the first test. But readiness in *swallowing* was not so certain. The *cheek reflex* (turning the head toward a tap on the cheek) and *lip* and *tongue* adjustments for nursing were elicited soon after birth.

Reactions of arms and hands, legs and feet. The *grasping* reflex (reflex closure of fingers over a rod put in contact with the palm) was highly definite, and but little influenced by other bodily activities and conditions occurring simultaneously. Two infants in whom life was almost extinct clung tenaciously to the rod. *Spreading of fingers* was observed in a few cases. Kicking and, to a lesser extent, *moving of arms* were practically continuous during the waking hours of some infants; and much stretching of fingers, toes, arms, legs, arching of trunk, and so on, followed removal of clothing. *Pain stimuli* at a toe (needle prick to draw blood) excited kicking movements of the other foot; at a finger (lancing), vigorous arm movements and lusty crying. Very light pin pricks at the wrists elicited minor movements of the hands. To *cold* certain clear responses were obtained: a drop of alcohol on the lower half of the abdomen aroused kicking — if on the left side of the abdomen, by the left leg, if on the right side, by the right leg. No *preferential* use of either hand was clearly noted.

Studies of this type have been made by others, and they are indeed interesting and valuable, as showing the infant to be equipped with many local response-units. But do they go far enough? Do they furnish a well-rounded picture of the babe in arms?

(III) Beside this reflexological view of infancy, another (which had developed from the work of Coghill *et al.*) has been set up that is quite its antithesis. Originally infant behavior is a *mass activity*, which then goes through a gradual process of *individuation of specific movements*. From the general and unspecialized motions of the organismic body-mass, there gradually emerge more and more independent actions of hand, of foot, of voice, and so on. It happens that no competent empirical investigation of infancy and childhood has wound up with this extreme interpretation; and for illustration of it we shall have to depend upon some studies reported in the next section wherein it is accorded a very important, though not an exclusive, rôle.

Between these two opposed views just mentioned, there is today some controversy; and we will do well to make a brief survey of the experimental evidence. This we should take seriously, too, for many times through our survey of the field of psychology we will find ourselves returning to the question: is development from parts to whole, or from whole to parts, or does development involve them both?

Experimental Studies of Fetal Behavior. Minkowski, a Swiss surgeon, had the unusual opportunities of observing seventeen immature human fetuses that had to be removed from their mothers by Caesarian section to preserve the lives of the latter [18]. Placed in a saline solution at slightly-above-body temperature, the immature organisms were kept alive long enough to permit some behavior observations. Some of the typical ones are worth describing.

"One does not observe," Minkowski writes, "isolated reflexes limited to the member stimulated, but movements that irradiate to other members, to the head and trunk, and that are extremely variable." When he lightly applied a brush or pencil to one foot, this brought out not only a flexion of the foot touched but also a variety of movements (flexing or extending) in the other leg and in the arms, often also in head and trunk, varying from one case to another, and even in the same case varying from one application of the stimulus to another. In one case the touching of a hand aroused, besides flexion of the arms, repeated movements of the mouth, which opened and closed with a simultaneous retraction of the head. "It can be said that in general every part of the skin can serve as a stimulable zone for quite variable motor reactions, near or remote, having a tendency to spread more or less generally over the whole fetal organism. With the older organisms (2–5 months) the motor phenomena externally aroused become somewhat more constant and their tendency to irradiate to other members is a little less pronounced."

By stimulating deeper-lying receptive organs other movements could be elicited. If the head was turned to one side, so as to stimulate certain neck muscles through forced changes of their position, there generally occurred a movement of the arm toward which the head was turned and often one of the other arm, movements which persisted as long as the head was kept turned. Here again it was noted that the great variability of the responses appeared to be somewhat reduced in the older fetuses. Again, when the whole fetus was passively displaced in space, as from a vertical to a horizontal position or the reverse, there appeared symmetrical movements of both hands or both feet or of all four, promptly occurring upon the passive displacement and as promptly ceasing ["compensatory movements"]. Once again, however, variability was a striking character of the behavior, for responses to the same bodily displacement may begin "with flexion or extension, with adduction or abduction, by a rotation inward or outward."

These features of behavior — *irradiation, variability,* and *age changes* — serve now to round out the characterizations of fetal behavior in other species as presented in a preceding section of this chapter.

Experimental Studies of Behavior of the Newborn. Intensive researches have been conducted in recent years on the subject of our present inquiries. Of these the work done by a group at Ohio State University under the inspiration of Weiss represents well the development of technique in this field in America. If observations are to be made of just how the baby acts and reacts and to what, why not put him under precisely controllable conditions? Therefore, a special apparatus was built for the double purpose of providing well-controlled stimuli and of securing permanent records of any movements or changes of posture the subject might make.

The baby was placed in a cabinet consisting essentially of a large box, 3 ft. × 4½ ft. × 5 ft., with windows through which the experimenter and his assistant could observe the infant. (See Figure 19.) Heater, thermostat, and humidifier assured a constant air environment. The infant was laid upon a "stabilimeter," consisting of a light platform on roller bearings, and so constructed that whenever the infant moved, the platform wobbled and the motions were transmitted along strings to two recording pens tracing lines on a traveling strip of paper. On this same strip other marks and notations were made by the two observers as they sat at the windows. Thus the paper furnished continuous records that were automatically and personally taken of the infant's activities.

When the infant was unstimulated from without, the most striking characteristic it exhibited was the great amount of energy expended in the course of such mass activities as when the body squirmed, twisted, and rolled, the back arched, the hips swayed, the head rolled from side to side, arms and feet slashed about and kicked, hands and feet and fingers and toes were in continuous movement, sucking and

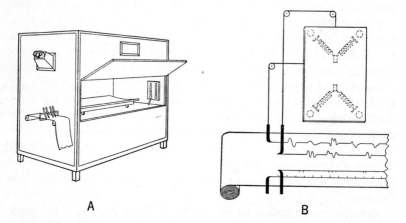

A   B

FIGURE 19. APPARATUS FOR CONTROLLED OBSERVATIONS ON INFANTS

A. The cabinet. The stabilimeter and air-controlling devices are seen through the opened door. Two windows in the walls offer opportunity to watch the infant. A motor-driven continuous strip of paper takes the ink records.

B. The stabilimeter rests on ball bearings and is held in place by four light springs. Any motions imparted to the stabilimeter by movements of the baby are transmitted to two of the recording devices on which pens are mounted. The other pens are operated by an observer and by a time-marker.

(Adapted from Pratt, Nelson and Sun.)

smacking and loud crying were heard — all of these movements occurring as components of *mass activity* of the body generally and not as strictly local acts [14]. This was characteristic of the "unstimulated" baby. But are we to assume that it was entirely unstimulated? On the contrary, its activity was greatest during evident hunger, bowel evacuating, intestinal disturbances, regurgitation, and sometimes micturition; and it was concluded that this mass behavior was therefore *initiated by internal (organic) stimulations.*

The reader can afford to dwell for a moment on this picture. The newborn is distinctly active. And his activity is not that of a marionette-baby with head and limbs bobbing up and down under the manipulation of outside agencies. Quite the contrary: he is an active energy-transforming organism in which the raw materials of food, oxygen, and the like get most intricately worked over inside him, and furnish the energy which eventually finds its outlet largely in the form of overt muscular activity. Enormous energies stored up within, physiological processes going on without any guidance from without, and on occasions these energies and processes overflowing, as it were, into skeletal muscle activities — this is the truer picture of the baby.

Some specific movements there were, to be sure. There was a flexing of a knee or elbow, an extension of the legs, a short roll of the head, and other localized bits of activity. But they fell into no integrated patterns, if we except sucking and one or two more.

When the infant is under external stimulation, we might expect to find more of the localized kinds of response. To test for this, other experimenters [20] carefully applied particular forms of stimuli to the newborn as it lay in the cabinet. Lights were flashed, white and colored; sounds were made with snapper or electric bell; taste substances were dropped on the tongue; temperature cylinders were applied to the skin; pressures were applied to the soles of the feet and to the face; and its nose was held or its arms restrained. Now, if the baby be a bundle of reflexes, we would expect under such circumstances definite eyeball and eyelid responses to the lights with very little accompaniment of movements elsewhere, definite head-turnings to the sounds, tongue movements and swallowings to the tastes, whiffings to the odors, and the like. In actual fact, however, the reactions of the baby were for the most part of general sorts.

Stimulation of almost any group of receptors by almost any kind of stimulus will lead to a response in almost any part of the organism. *The reaction tends, however, to manifest itself most strongly in that part of the organism which is stimulated,* and from there *spreads out with decreasing frequency and intensity* to the other segments of the body [the phenomenon of "irradiation"]. . . . The newborn infant is equipped with quite a number of reflexes, but the degree of their specificity and their significance seem to have been unduly exaggerated. For the most part these reflexes are vegetative in character, and even the others are in no way peculiar to human beings.

Mass Actions Not Always Chaotic and Formless. The reader should be warned against a possible misunderstanding fostered by some of the language we have employed and particularly by the quotation just used. The massive activities of the newborn are not entirely amorphous, and the reaction appearing at one moment and under one set of conditions may differ recognizably from that of another. Indeed, fifteen or more responses have been differentiated [10] in each of which practically all movement systems of the entire body participate. What distinguishes each one from the others is its general patterning, its characteristic combination of the component movements. This the reader can readily see if he considers such illustrations as sneezing, shivering, being startled, the sleeping position, and vigorous crying.

Behavior of the Newborn is Adjustive in Some Degree. It is time to correct a possible error in our perspective. The reader may have gained the impression that in such investigations as those mentioned in the foregoing paragraphs the psychologist looks upon the baby's behavior in so purely descriptive a manner that he gives no interpretative thought to it at all, that psychological observation is nothing but an enumeration of actions and reactions much after the manner of the happy child on Christmas Day who explores the various mechanisms with which her new doll is equipped — squeaking "mama" and "papa," closing its eyes when laid down, retaining graceful positions in which its arms have been placed, taking steplike movements of its legs when dragged along, and the rest. This would be an error. It is psychologically important not only to know something of the repertoire of mechanisms of the newborn, but also to appraise their adjustive significance. Psychology is concerned with not a mere inventory of stimuli and movements, but some appreciation of their value or lack of value to the organism and its biological needs. Or, to translate freely a remark by the Viennese child psychologist, Charlotte Bühler [3]:

In what are we really interested when we take an inventory of the baby's activities?   It is the success or failure of his efforts to reach *objectives*.   The relationship of his activity and the outcome, *the effect of his successes or failures upon the situation*, these are the main factors of psychological interest. We should keep a record which would include changes that are brought about in the object or the situation as results of the child's reactions.

A good example is to be had by watching the defense movements that an infant makes when his arms or head are held in restraint or when *pressure is applied to his chin*.   One study will serve as an illustration [21].   The infant to be examined was placed on his back and a nurse gently held his head in mid-position.   The examiner applied an accurately measured pressure of 750 grams for the constant period of 30 seconds; and the movements made by both arms were noted, those that produced some contacts with the pressure apparatus being recorded as truly defensive.   Records were secured from subjects ranging from just-born to 13 days of age, and plotted as in Figure 4, to be found on page 31.   By inspection of the figure we can see that very few combined co-ordinated defense movements appeared before the sixth day, but after that there was rather steady increase of efficiency with age.

And now for an example of positively directed adjustive behavior. In the Ohio State University studies one of the more definite forms of response was found to be *sucking*.   It was operative from the very first, though the changes then passed through are noteworthy. On the sensory side, a variety of stimuli would call it forth — temperature at the skin, odors including ammonia, any taste including quinine, even some simple noises — but eventually the stimuli became so *differentiated* that of all these only the sweet taste continued to be effective.   On the motor side, what was at first a very loose conjunction of many reaction-bits — turning head when cheek was touched, opening of mouth, sucking movements of lips, and swallowing — became in time a well-fused and smooth-working *co-ordination*.   In brief, the effective stimulus became more and more specific and the appropriate response became more and more organized [15].

In these cases a point of cardinal significance is the fact that there was some adequacy from the very first.   The newborn is not a totally, helpless individual, but reveals some forms of adaptive response to unfavorable and to favorable agents applied to him.   However tender the age of the baby, then, he is always and ever an *adjustive living organism* and his overt behavior is as truly *regulative* (cf. Chapter II) as are the more hidden processes of heart-beat, breathing, digesting, excreting, temperature-maintenance, and the like. To call him only a complicated array of mechanisms, mechanisms that have no particular rhyme or reason in his life-economy, is as libelous to the baby himself as it would be considered insulting by his parents.

Vegetative Processes. In the foregoing summary of the native behavior equipment of very young babies our interest has been in motor mechanisms or reactions of more or less overt types. Are babies as helpless on the "inside" as on the "outside"? Are their various visceral and organic functions as poorly organized?

Not at all. Respiration, once it is established in the newborn, operates with fair rhythmic regularity and smoothness. The beating of the heart ever since about the third or fourth week of fetal life has been continuing almost automatically. The blood has been circulating through the fetal mass, performing its functions of inter-relating the different parts chemically and nutritively. Bowel movements may sometimes occur previous to delivery; and digestion — with all its complexity of glandular and muscular processes — waits only upon the intake of food. For months before his birth the baby has been living — orderly and co-ordinated processes have been going on within him. (Of course the co-ordinations of physiological functions are not by any means perfect, and we must recognize that most of the concern of mother, nurse, and pediatrician during the first days and months is a concern over the establishing of efficiently regular digestion and other complicated visceral processes.) "Our viscera know how to live," it has been said, but "our motor mechanism does not know how to carry to the viscera the things we must have to live on. And we are infants-in-arms until our motor mechanism learns to perform that service for us."

General Behavior Traits. We have been confining ourselves to the inborn patterns of response. That, however, is not the whole story of original human nature, even from the standpoint of mechanisms. Individuals may differ in their mechanisms in very general ways which are evident enough in their everyday activities as well as in a few experimental studies. Jack may *react more quickly* than Jim, not to this special stimulus or to that, but to many or to most things. Alice may be more *graceful* in her movements than Elsie, whether it be in striking piano keys, dancing, tying a new scarf, or embroidering. One person may more quickly *learn* new ways of doing things, or may *retain* longer the skill to do them; another may, by virtue of greater general muscular power and *strength*, be able to do the "impossible." We must proceed warily in the description of general traits (for dealing in generalities about people is a besetting sin), but it cannot be seriously doubted that the human reactive equipment as a whole possesses certain characteristics independent of, and more general than, particular sensori-motor arcs or groups of arcs.

DEVELOPMENT IN THE INFANT AND THE CHILD

How do the Basic Behavior-Patterns Appear? The typical human being is at this stage of our survey barely launched on the high seas of life. From his maternal haven he has issued; and we have been taking stock of his equipment and general fitness and seaworthiness. Or to change the figure, the newborn baby's overt activities are largely raw material; and henceforth our interest will be devoted more to the processes by which this material becomes worked up into serviceable and effective ways of meeting the demands of living in this world of benignant and malignant things and people.

We shall want to know: (1) what are the important stages in the development of each behavior-pattern; and (2) whether in each case the order of development is the same for different children. The caterpillar must pass through the pupa stage before becoming a butterfly, and the frog's egg must hatch a tadpole before a frog appears; and though such changes can be altered in their speed by thyroxin and other drugs, no stage is skipped. By analogy, shall we expect the development of activities in the human species to pass through regular stages?

The Developmental Sequence.

(*A*) *Locomotion.* Nothing is so commonly regarded as marking the graduation from mere infancy to early childhood as the beginning of walking. It is one of the great milestones of achievement in the individual's life. It is rightly hailed with enthusiasm by his cheering family, and it has emotional consequences even for himself. Now, an age-old debate is whether a baby learns to walk, as he learns so many other acts, or "just naturally comes" to walk; that is, whether practice and habit-forming or maturing and growth is the decisive group of factors.   As in all debates about matters of fact, the proper procedure is to adjourn from the hall of debate to the laboratory and clinic of direct and unprejudiced observation. Naturally, when the topic is so universally interesting, we should expect to find that many competent scientific observers for a half-century have analyzed the onset of locomotion; but as their findings are adequately represented by the most recent thoroughgoing study, which moreover brings out additional interpretations, it will be sensible for us to confine our attention to the last-named.

Twenty-five babies were systematically and repeatedly examined in their own homes over a two-year period by experts from the Minnesota Institute of Child Welfare; and the dates of appearance of many sorts of behavior-items, large and small, were noted and checked [22].   To make a long story very brief, a fairly definite order of development was found, one motor achievement preceding the next and that the next.   The major items of this developmental motor sequence are set forth in their proper order and the approximate ages of their appearance in Figure 20.

The conclusion is that the developing of walking in the young child as well as that of many other forms of gross overt behavior shows itself to be a *regular developmental sequence*.   And its very inevitableness points to the operation of intrinsic determining factors in the processes of growth itself, that is, *maturation*.   As the infant grows he takes on new activities, performs new stunts, not as skilled acts which had to be learned, but as acts that simply emerge upon appropriate stimulation as soon as the underlying body mechanisms have reached the necessary point of growth.

A curious thing about it all is that oftentimes the emergence of a new co-ordination may be a fairly sudden affair.   Preyer, writing fifty years ago, and many a biographer of babies since have observed how, once a baby has taken his first step or two without aid, he may promptly launch out on long trips around and around the room and through the house.   On the basis of his now-sufficiently-matured muscular and nervous capacities, he has "caught the knack" of it all by having struck just the right co-ordination; and this brief achievement in turn appears to operate as an emotional facilitation, if one may judge by the excited facial and vocal manifestations that now accompany the locomotor activity.

(B) Manipulation.   Another direction in which the growing infant manifests increasing interest and increasing achievements is

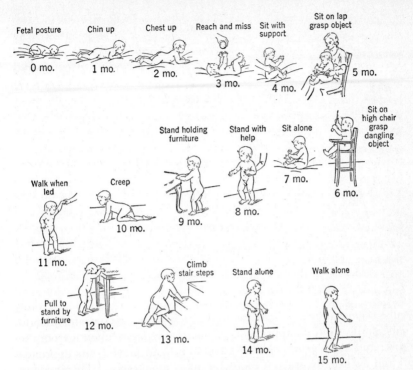

Fetal posture 0 mo. Chin up 1 mo. Chest up 2 mo. Reach and miss 3 mo. Sit with support 4 mo. Sit on lap grasp object 5 mo.

Stand holding furniture 9 mo. Stand with help 8 mo. Sit alone 7 mo. Sit on high chair grasp dangling object 6 mo.

Walk when led 11 mo. Creep 10 mo.

Pull to stand by furniture 12 mo. Climb stair steps 13 mo. Stand alone 14 mo. Walk alone 15 mo.

FIGURE 20. THE GENERAL DEVELOPMENTAL MOTOR SEQUENCE

Some of the outstanding items in the behavior of the infant are represented in their order of emergence. The ages given are only approximate: the items are not equally spaced in time, and different infants differ considerably in the general rate of development, though not in the order of the items. (From Shirley, M. M., *The First Two Years.* Univ. Minnesota Press, 1933.)

in handling his toys and other objects. Though it is an activity that has always interested his adult spectators, it has not until recent years come into its share of detailed scientific analysis. So complicated and swift is the baby's reaching-and-handling that the components of it all and the story of their co-ordination had to await the motion-picture technique of recording. At the Yale clinic this has been elaborated along with many other devices for rigorously standardizing the situation in which the baby is placed and for recording accurately the responses that he makes. Under such careful scrutiny the process of how a child reaches for and takes hold of a block placed on a table before him was broken down into some fairly clearly distinguishable stages [13]. The mere sight of the

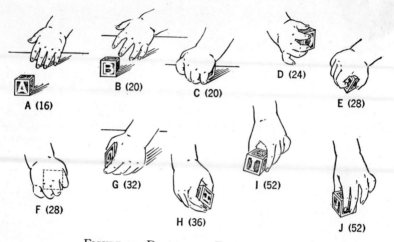

FIGURE 21. DEVELOPING TYPES OF GRASP

Different patterns of prehension, and the approximate ages (in weeks) at which they appear. (From Halverson, H. M., An Experimental Study of Prehension in Infants, *Genet. Psychol. Monog.*, 1931, **10**, Nos. 2–3.

cube seems sufficient stimulus to excite in him activity which is unmistakably bent on apprehending it: his eyes fixate upon it from the first, and as he grows older his arm and hand movements approach it and eventually grasp it more and more effectively. This increase of effectiveness in the seizing will be worth our attention for the light it throws on a general problem of development, the one raised some pages back as to whether the development of behavior is one of differentiation or of integration. Infants of various ages, at four-week intervals, were presented with the cube at a particular spot on the table before them. (Cf. Figure 21.)

(A) At the earliest tested age, 16 weeks, the typical infant fails to make contact with the cube, though he is clearly regarding it. (B) Contact will be made sometimes at 20 weeks; (C) and the grasping will be in the form of a primitive squeeze. (D) At 24 weeks the block is often corralled or swept in by a looping movement of the arm. Later (E) it is seized by a paw-like downward movement, the fingers curling about it with the thumb simply paralleling the fingers. (F) Then the thumb comes to be placed on the opposite side from the fingers — the beginning of thumb-opposition that is so important in nearly all performances of the human hand. (G) A further advance appears when only the radial (thumb side) of the palm is put in contact with the cube, and only the thumb and first two fingers are used. (H) Later, only the tips of thumb and finger are used. (I) This is much more delicately done by a child several weeks older; and (*J*) eventually he can reach for and seize the cube without resting the hand on the table.

In this account there is again to be seen a lawful sequence of behavior-items, but the sequence is not so much a supplanting as a changing; and as one method of grasping shades into the next higher, something of a double process is discernible. For instance, in (*F*) there is an individuation of the thumb, a differentiation of its action, so that instead of continuing to be just another finger it plays an individual rôle. But it is not an isolated rôle. It is now playing in co-ordinated team-work with the fingers. *Both individuation and integration,* then.

The Method of Co-Twin Control. When perusing accounts such as the foregoing the reader may at times be suspicious that after all training may have entered into the story more than is stated. It is reassuring, then, to turn to another method adopted at the same clinic for determining whether or not maturation does play the major rôle. A pair of presumably identical twins aged 46 weeks were given differential experience. Twin *T* was given training daily in stacking blocks and in climbing stairs while Twin *C*, to serve as a control, was given no training of either sort. After *T* had had the practice for 6 weeks, her performance was compared with that of *C*. A day-by-day analysis of her work had shown the usual stages and advances; yet when tested at the 52nd week of age, *C*, with no training at all, was her equal in the cube work and not greatly inferior in the stair-climbing. Moreover, after 2 weeks of practice at this age, *C* was able to surpass *T's* performance in the latter task. Evidently enough, to be most effective training must be introduced at the proper stage of maturation. (Such indeed is the conclusion drawn by some half-dozen other investigators who have repeated this kind of work.) [12]

(*C*) *Vocalization.* The examples of infant and child behavior which we have been examining in this section of the chapter have been of the manual-pedal, or better, skeletal, class in which smaller or larger segments of the body are moved through space by the moving of jointed parts of the skeleton. But some of the most significant human functions are not skeletal in that larger sense. For instance, sound production with the voice. We shall give the development of vocal and verbal powers only a brief introduction here, leaving a somewhat fuller treatment to the chapter on language behavior.

The initial repertoire of sounds in the newborn is scanty, consisting of little but crying. With days and weeks of age, however, an increasing number of sounds are at his disposal. These are not put at his disposal by the environing adults, for he seems not to imitate others at all in these early months, but have their genesis in a growing vocal apparatus that becomes gradually more versatile.

A conclusive experiment on this point is one that extended the procedure of co-twin control to language acquisition, employing the same identical twins mentioned in a preceding paragraph [23]. Twin T was given intensive training in naming common objects for a period of 5 weeks, beginning when she was 84 weeks old and continuing through her 88th week. Twin C was given the same course of training for 4 weeks, beginning at her 89th. When the achievements of the two were compared for equivalent learning trials — but an age disparity of 5 weeks — the superiority of C was quite marked. She learned the same words more quickly. The difference of five weeks' time in which to mature further was a critical point. This is not to deny that language learning is learning, but it does emphasize the fact that learning is by no means the whole story, and that it must be built upon the substructure of organic growth.

Further, we can anticipate that a thorough analysis of the process of language acquisition will illustrate again the double process of differentiation of the various sounds and integration of them into new sound-combinations.

(*D*) *Other Behavior Categories.* We have been taking note of some general principles of individual development as brought out and supported by experimental research concerning three of the more easily identifiable types of human behavior in its early stages. Is it legitimate to conclude that such principles hold in general, that is, that they are applicable to all or at least to most other lines of behavior-change with age? A text attempting a survey of the whole field of psychology cannot, of course, go into the complete account of ontogenesis; and the author will have to assume the responsibility of summarizing current research in very sketchy fashion in this place, leaving more explicit presentation to later treatments of specific topics.

As to the *emotional* behavior of the newborn there is some agreement that it is apparently undifferentiated, being only a general kind of excitement or other unpatterned and indefinite organic condition. As the baby matures, more recognizable and differentiable emotions make their appearance, though not in a well-established sequence; and possibly experiential factors are as potent here as are those of inner maturing. The most striking of all emotional changes is that often found in adolescence. If this is to be explained as due directly to the physiological changes of that period (as claimed in Hall's classic pronouncements, though denied by some), it is emphatic evidence of a maturation effect on emotional life.

In his *social* aspects, the human being starts at zero. He takes no notice of the person who tends him, and only after some weeks does he respond to him in particular. Later on he reacts differently to familiar and to strange, and in time to differentiate a threatening mien from a kindly one. Meanwhile he comes to notice other children; and by stages through the early years he becomes able to play with two, three, four, and more children. A curious incident is the occurrence at certain age levels of negativistic attitudes in the child. These are commonly reported for the age of two to four years, and again for early adolescence; but they are not well understood.

In the *perceptual* and *thoughtful* guidance of his behavior the infant manifests developmental stages so definitely that they have been precisely worked out for the average child in the average environment, and cast into normative scales by which the rate of development of particular individuals may be measured — the well-known intelligence tests.

SUMMARY AND ORIENTATION

Formulations. 1. From the first, both more specific and more mass activities are present in the developing individual, the latter preponderating in the early stages and to some degree falling into very roughly discriminable types.

2. The materials for development are furnished by individuation of specific acts out of mass activity, and by the emergence of new items (usually in a regular sequence).

3. Maturation (and learning also) involves the twofold process of differentiation and integration.

4. Some traits emerge not gradually but suddenly.

5. The intrinsic factors of maturation are more important for laying down the skeleton of the individual's psychological make-up; the extrinsic factors of habit-forming are important for refined skills and for the detailed adjustments to environmental demands.

Maturation is Supplemented by Learning. Frequently in the preceding pages maturation and practice or learning have been treated as if opposed. In the developing of the individual they are really supplementary aspects, the one referring to inner growth processes more or less inevitable and self-regulative, the other referring to contacts between the organism and his environment and the readjustment of the organism's behavior forced thereby. Like figures in a drama, however, they play into each other's rôles, and each depends upon the other.

A girl about ten years old was found near Châlons in 1731. Several unsuccessful attempts were made to capture her and she baffled her pursuers by the agility with which she moved among the branches of trees. She could not utter a word, and her yells and howls are described as terrifying. She was extremely skillful in catching fowl and rabbits, which she skinned with her nails in a twinkling and greedily devoured raw.[1]

Human, this girl, and — as found out afterward when she was reared in convents and became quite educated — with all the fundamental traits and capacities of other girls. The difference? A matter of cultural opportunity, of learning.

The technical treatment of learning on its own account will be assigned to two special chapters. Meanwhile, there are certain concrete aspects of the human person to which we should now turn.

REFERENCES

1. Blanton, M. G. The Behavior of the Human Infant During the First Thirty Days of Life. *Psychol. Rev.*, 1917, **24**, 456–83.
2. Bridgman, C. S., and Carmichael, L. An Experimental Study of the Onset of Behavior in the Fetal Guinea Pig. *J. Genet. Psychol.*, 1935, **47**, 247–67.
3. Bühler, Ch. *The First Year of Life* (trans. by Greenberg and Ripin). John Day, 1930.
4. Carmichael, L. An Experimental Study in the Pre-Natal Guinea-Pig of the Origin and Development of Reflexes, etc. *Genet. Psychol. Monog.*, 1934, **16**, 339–491.
5. Carmichael, L. Origin and Prenatal Growth of Behavior. Chap. 2 of *Handbook of Child Psychology*, 2d edition, Clark Univ. Press, 1933.
6. Carmichael, L. The Development of Behavior in Vertebrates Experimentally Removed from the Influence of External Stimulation. *Psychol. Rev.*, 1926, **33**, 51–58.
7. Child, C. M. *Physiological Foundations of Behavior.* Holt, 1924.

[1] From Briffault, R. *The Mothers.* New York: Macmillan, 1927. By permission of the publishers.

8. Coghill, G. E. *Anatomy and the Problem of Behavior.* Macmillan, 1929.

9. Coronios, J. D. Development of Behavior in the Fetal Cat. *Genet. Psychol. Monog.*, 1933, **14**, No. 4.

10. Dennis, W. A Description and Classification of the Responses of the Newborn Infant. *Psychol. Bull.*, 1934, **31**, 5–22.

11. Gesell, A., and Thompson, H. *Infant Behavior: Its Genesis and Growth.* McGraw-Hill, 1934.

12. Gesell, A., and Thompson, H. Learning and Growth in Identical Infant Twins. *Genet. Psychol. Monog.*, 1929, **6**, No. 1.

13. Halverson, H. M. An Experimental Study of Prehension in Infants by Means of Systematic Cinema Records. *Genet. Psychol. Monog.*, 1931, **10**, Nos. 2–3.

14. Irwin, O. C. The Amount and Nature of Activities of Newborn Infants Under Constant External Stimulating Conditions During the First Ten Days of Life. *Genet. Psychol. Monog.*, 1930, **8**, No. 1.

15. Jensen, K. Differential Reactions to Taste and Temperature Stimuli in Newborn Infants. *Genet. Psychol. Monog.*, 1932, **12**, nos. 5–6.

16. Kuo, Z. Y. Ontogeny of Embryonic Behavior in Aves. V. *Psychol. Rev.*, 1932, **39**, 499–515.

17. McGraw, Myrtle. *Growth: Johnny and Jimmy.* Appleton-Century, 1935.

18. Minkowski, M. Sur les mouvements, etc. *Rev. Neur.*, 1921, **37**, 1105–18, 1235–50. Or, Zur Entwicklungsgeschichte, etc. *Schweizer Archiv. für Neurol. u. Psychiat.*, 1923, **13**, 475–514.

19. Murchison, C. (ed.) *A Handbook of Child Psychology.* Clark Univ. Press, 2d ed., 1933.

20. Pratt, K. C., Nelson, A. K., and Sun, K. H. The Behavior of the Newborn Infant. *Ohio State Univ. Contrib. to Psy.*, 1930, No. 10, 235 pp.

21. Sherman, M., Sherman, I., and Flory, C. D. Infant Behavior. *Comp. Psychol. Monog.*, 1936, **12**, No. 59.

22. Shirley, M. M. *The First Two Years.* I. Postural and Locomotor Development, 1931; II. Intellectual Development, 1933; III. Personality Manifestations, 1933. Univ. Minnesota Press.

23. Strayer, L. C. Language and Growth, etc. *Genet. Psychol. Monog.*, 1930, **8**, No. 3.

CHAPTER V

THE BASES OF MOTIVATION

INTRODUCTION

A Practical Problem.   It is the day of the big game.   Shouted salutations.   Noise.   Bustle.   Automobiles.   Crowds.   More crowds.   The varsity team, collectively and individually, may now be pretty accurately rated — at least by sports-writing experts — as to its muscular power and speed and stamina and as to its alertness and athletic prowess and canniness.   And the opposing team has been as thoroughly analyzed.   What, then, is awaited by the spectators, arriving by thousands on their special trains?   When two opposing forces are well known and measured, what remains but to make a mathematical calculation and settle it all on paper? But, you answer truly, no one can know absolutely every detail of ability in every player concerned and the totals can be only the roughest approximations.   Then there are the elements of chance, the "breaks," that may lead to unexpected results: a wind, a pool of water, an injured thumb on the hand of the receiving quarterback. But still another factor enters into this opposition of human forces. Why the brass band?   Why the talks by the coaches in the dressing-room?   Why the banner-waving and lusty cheering in the stands? In the language of the mass meeting on the night before, it means "pep" in the players.   Now what, psychologically, is the source of this "pep"?

Again, why do men work?   Theoretical writers on economic topics are frequently devoting themselves to variations of this theme.   Is there some unidentifiable "instinct of industry," some "instinct of workmanship"; is it because their recurring pangs of hunger force them to earn the wherewithal to buy bread; is it because they fear being called "bums"?   In his considerations of producing and consuming agents the economist does well to raise such questions as why men work, and why labor and skill are more easily recruited for one type of industry than for another, why men like to buy this thing and not that, and so create demands and markets.   And it is just as legitimate to ask why a given man will not work.

A Scotland Yard detective, when asked his opinion about a poorly investigated murder case which recently figured prominently in American newspapers, remarked: "I would first seek to establish the motive. After that I could know in what direction to look for my man."

Courts of law in modern times make distinctions between motives such as were unknown to primitive justice. The *lex talionis*, "an eye for an eye," has lost its validity — except for lynching parties or for that private form of retaliation known as the "unwritten law." Killing by accident is no longer to be avenged in the same way as killing by deliberate intent. We now speak of murder in the first degree, in the second degree, manslaughter, and accidental homicide, and the progress of legal philosophy may be measured by the progress in recognizing finer and finer distinctions in man's motives.

The technique of teaching no longer assumes that a pupil is a learner and then concerns itself only with that which is to be presented to him. It recognizes that good teaching presupposes a "will to learn," a disposition on the pupil's part to seek instruction — in a word, motivation. What was once secured largely through a generous use of the rod is now being sought through incentives of a less negative and less crude type. The pupil must somehow be made interested, not by urging from behind, but by the exploitation of interests already actively at work in his behavior.

Such concrete incidents and problems bring to light the fundamental need of a scientific knowledge not alone of how a man acts and just which things he does but of *why* he gets into action and why he does the things he does. Not only the machinery of the organism but also the way it is energized and operated are pertinent psychological problems. This distinction is, however, not to be taken as a final one, for surely one thing we have learned in our survey is that the human being, like any other living organism, is not in the last analysis a truly inert machine to be set into operation by the application of a power source more or less distinct from itself. Mechanical analogies fit life processes very imperfectly! Nevertheless, even though the distinction between a mechanism and the way it is energized is a difference of emphases more than of entities, it will advance our purposes if we make use of it, and for the present emphasize the dynamic aspect of human life and conduct.

External Stimuli Function Principally as Releases. One source of energy for organic activity is, of course, external stimulation.

The electromagnetic and air vibrations producing sight and hearing, the chemical agencies affecting smell and taste receptors, the changes of temperature and the impact of physical masses at the skin surface are all readily recognized as moving forces in human behavior. If you would see a man get into action touch him with a needle point or sound an auto horn behind him, call him by name, slap him on the back, announce a circus parade or a fashion parade, call out the word "fire." Among the conditions that activate human nature we could list, then, all those classes of stimuli we shall canvass in Chapter IX.

But even in the crude illustrations just offered it does not need much discernment to note that the extra-organic (exteroceptive) stimulations tell by no means the whole story. Human nature is not a football. It is not immediately and solely subject to the actions of external forces alone.[1] Rather, these *exteroceptive stimuli serve mainly to release, to touch off, the energies* stored and systematized within that extremely complex balanced mass we call a living organism.

To be sure, there are numerous types of reaction that are dependent only in a minor degree upon intra-organic conditions and to a major degree upon the direct, unequivocal result of exteroceptive stimulation. The knee jerk and the pupillary reflex are examples of this order. They are to be described and explained more in terms of their immediate stimuli than in terms of the chemical disequilibrium of the whole organism or of the inadequacy of a specific organ or tissue. However, such relatively unmotivated responses play only the rôle of supernumeraries on life's stage. Eyelid twitchings and finger jerks, necessary as they are to the behavior of man, have no central part in determining in what way or with what energy a person will act.

Let us make sure of our orientation again. In an earlier chapter of this book we saw from concrete examples that it is of the essence of animal and human behavior to seek or to maintain optimal conditions for one's self so that one's intra-organic processes will be adequately furthered. The key to man and to subhuman forms is to be sought more in the enormously complex energy exchanges

---

[1] This is one reason for a common misunderstanding of a scientific psychology that seeks to know man in terms of cause-and-effect relationships. It is a very superficial view of the science that characterizes it as making man into a robot, a puppet, a marionette, acting out his whole drama of life merely in response to external promptings. But it is equally as impossible and absurd to suppose that the only alternative is to assume mysterious agencies, entities, *daemons* implanted in man's nature and operating him.

going on within him than in the fortuitous play of outside energies working upon him. You can lead a horse to water, but the sight of water will not be an effective stimulus unless he is thirsty; in that case an untethered horse will lead himself to the trough. A mate does not excite the pigeon or the frog to sexual advances except when the latter is in a certain physiological state. It is even said that a lion must be hungry to attack a peaceful and unaggressive man. Is the child hungry? Then and only then will he approach the food. Is he tired? The bed now invites him as it did not while he was in the flush of play. It is when he is cold that the warm radiator can attract him, when he is in pain that he runs to his nurse. *The primary drives to persistent forms of animal and human conduct are tissue-conditions, local and general, within the organism giving rise to stimulations exciting the organism to overt activity.* A man's interests and desires may become ever so elaborate, refined, socialized, sublimated, idealistic; but the raw basis from which they are developed is found in the phenomena of living matter.

Organismic Regulation the Fundamental Fact. On earlier pages it has been pointed out that human and animal behavior are best understood and appreciated as a manifestation of the tendency of all living organisms to be self-regulatory. This rather obvious but very profound biological fact is so clearly the appropriate conception from which we should begin our pursuit of animal motives that we should review it.

Investigation of the functional activities of organisms, particularly the higher animals and man, could not proceed very far without becoming aware of the existence of various mechanisms and processes which serve to control, order and adjust the various activities to varying conditions in such manner as to maintain the physiological unity and harmony of the organism in the changing environment to which it is subjected. Through such mechanisms and processes the activities of organisms are "regulated" within certain limits, and physiologists have very naturally come to call them regulatory mechanisms and processes. We know more or less concerning many such mechanisms in organisms; e.g., the mechanism of the regulation of heat production and heat loss in the warm-blooded animals, of respiration, of blood flow and blood volume, of neutrality in the blood and tissues, of blood sugar, of the heart beat, of various digestive functions, of various internal secretions, of the transport of water, salts and carbohydrates in plants, and so on....

Even the simpler organisms behave, in general, in ways that favor their maintenance. In the absence of food, activities appear which tend to provide it. Motile [1] forms in a region of insufficient oxygen attempt to escape.

[1] Capable of moving from place to place.

Forms normally living in darkness or weak light tend to move away from strong light, those needing light move from darkness or weak light into stronger. All such reactions are not only physiologically speaking equilibrations, but are also regulations in the stricter sense that they are useful.[1]

To the activities that are obviously of quite immediate and direct utility and value to the organism are to be added those that are apparently useless and purposeless. Most animals expend far more energy than is necessary to keep themselves fed, warm, and out of harm's way, and the "animal spirits" as expressed in frolicsome activities that are not productive of shelter and food are the rule rather than the exception. In other words, much of the activity of dog and guinea pig and ape and child is "spontaneous," instead of being obviously directed from without; and general playfulness and superfluous movement often are taken as serviceable indices to one's physical vigor.

THE ENERGETICS OF ACTIVITY

The Question of Energy Sources. It would be quite foolhardy to attempt to work out all the sources in the living body whence come the energies that take the form of overt movements. It would presuppose an exhaustive knowledge of physiological chemistry, for one thing, and of the particular rôle played by each type of organic tissue and cell in the inconceivably intricate drama of the metabolic transformations of the energies from the raw intake of food, air, and other supplies, into the energies which reappear in motor and excretory activities. This transformation is a drama that has numerous intermediate scenes, as energy a is transformed into b, that into c, that into d, and so on, so that each step interlocks with and is interdependent upon other simultaneous steps throughout the organism as a whole. We will recognize to begin with, then, that any person or animal is in some measure in general activity every minute of his life.

On the other hand, investigable problems aplenty present themselves in the fact that the level of any person's or animal's activity varies from day to day and hour to hour and that these variations are correlated with discoverable conditions in identifiable parts or tissues of the body. Szymanski in Vienna, and later Richter and his

---

[1] From Child, C. M., *Physiological Foundations of Behavior*. Henry Holt & Co., 1924. The student should re-read pp. 36 f., above.

students at Hopkins, have made the approach by first charting the periods of relative activity and inactivity in many animals from the simplest insects to human infants and adults. The principal types of recording methods used were the revolving drum and the stationary tambour-mounted cage. (*A*) The *revolving drum cage* is shown in Figure 22. It consists of the "squirrel cage" type of enclosure that will revolve when an animal "runs" it, the revolutions being automatically registered by a counter, so that after a given interval of time the amount of the animal's activity (running) during the interval can be read off the counter. Usually this wheel opens into a stationary nesting and feeding cage. (*B*) The *tambour-mounted cage* is usually triangular in floor-plan, each corner resting on a rubber-covered air chamber or tambour which is in pneumatic connection with a recording device attached to a smoked drum kymograph. Any movement of the enclosed animal changes the pressures on the three tambours and is automatically registered on the kymograph. If an independent marker be connected with a circuit-making clock, the time

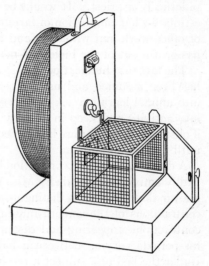

FIGURE 22. THE REVOLVING
ACTIVITY CAGE

The active animal enters the wheel-shaped cage and spins it by running. Each revolution in either direction is automatically registered by a cyclometer. When inactive the animal rests, eats, sleeps in the smaller cage.

of each movement and the total amount of activity in a given interval can be read off directly from the kymograph. An adaptation of this idea to the human subject appears in Figure 23.

Hunger. The values of eating have always been to a degree a measure of other values in the life of man. "I would rather do that than eat" is a colloquial expression of this fact. A formal meeting of people who are called together for even a serious purpose is generally incomplete without a dinner or banquet to celebrate the occasion. Love feasts and communions solidify religious association. A motion picture of epic dimensions ("Grass") has vividly presented the true story of a whole tribe of fifty thousand people who were forced annually to migrate over glaciers and precipices and across dangerous rivers, with great losses of livestock and human life and incredible personal sufferings — all for the sake of obtaining grass.   With another Asiatic tribe, dependent solely upon their milk supply for food, the buffalo is a sacred animal, the dairy building their nearest approach to a temple, and the dairyman practically a priest.   It would be an instructive exercise to try to estimate what proportion of farming and milling, of transportation, of office work and wholesale and retail counter service in America has grown out of the biological need of something to eat.

The fact that hunger operates as a drive [1] to increase overt activity has been assumed and used experimentally in nearly all research into animal learning.   A genuinely hungry rat or monkey will get into activity and keep in activity until its hunger is satisfied, and if obstacles to hunger are interposed it will show exploratory activity until it surmounts them.

A direct study of the connection between hunger drive and general bodily activity was made by Miss Wada.   From earlier work it was known that hunger, as distinguished from appetite, is traceable to contractions of the smooth musculature of the stomach walls, the contractions appearing and disappearing in rhythmic alternations for periods varying between a half-hour and an hour and a half. Under the bed of a subject a receiving tambour was arranged with the rubber diaphragm connected to the under surface of the bed by a spiral spring and made so sensitive that every overt bodily movement of the subject, even the moving of a finger, affected the tambour.   By way of a rubber tubing the movements were communicated to a recording tambour and pointer placed in another room, and were traced on a long paper kymograph.   A simultaneous record of stomach contractions (hunger) was made with an inflated

[1] Certain terms in the psychology of motivation are given varying uses by contemporary authorities.   For the sake of clarity in our own discussion let us adhere to the following meanings.   By a *drive* let us understand a certain organ or tissue condition by which an animal is set into activity. An *incentive* then will refer to the object or situation toward or away from which the drive-originated activity is impelled.   Examples: hunger-driven behavior is, or comes to be, directed toward a food-incentive; pain-driven behavior is, or comes to be, directed away from a hot-wire-incentive.   The word *motive* we shall employ throughout our treatment in its widest sense, to cover every form of impulsion, from the simplest physiological drive to the most elaborated, sophisticated, and intellectualized ideal.   Similarly, "motivated" will be used with breadth of meaning.   *Desire* is best applied to those motives and their objectives of which the individual is well aware, as when one says he is thirsty and desires a drink or says he desires to graduate at the next Commencement. The term *interest* is used when the emphasis is upon a motive as predisposing its possessor to pay attention to a certain thing or class of things, as an interest in Chinese porcelains, in politics, or in pig-raising.

balloon communicating with a recording manometer, much like the one shown in Figure 23. By comparing the two lines traced upon the kymograph record, Miss Wada was able to show that both during sleep and during a quiet waking state (that of reading a book) there was a very close correlation between the rhythmic occurrences of hunger and the rhythmic occurrences of gross striped [1] muscular activity. (Cf. Figure 24.) Further, by awakening sleeping subjects at different times she obtained some evidence of a greater tendency to dreaming during the hunger contraction periods; and by testing waking subjects at various intervals, with a hand dynamometer and with intelligence tests, she found that hunger apparently facilitated both gross reactions and the finer thinking reactions. [2]

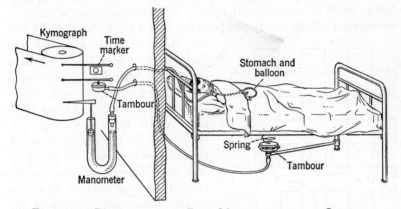

FIGURE 23. REGISTRATION OF BODY MOVEMENTS AND OF STOMACH
CONTRACTIONS

Any slight movement of the sleeper affects the spring and the receiving tambour under the bed, and, by pneumatic connection, operates a recording tambour with its writing lever bearing on the kymograph drum. Stomach contractions compress the rubber balloon swallowed by the subject. These compressions are pneumatically transmitted to a manometer with its writing point. A time marker is also mounted (at the top) on the drum.

(NOTES: A "tambour" is a metal air-chamber with top covered by a rubber diaphragm. It has a single inlet-outlet for tube connection. In the receiving type, varying external pressures on the diaphragm are transmitted as varying pressures through the connecting tube. Conversely, in the recording type variations in air pressure in the connecting tube raise and lower the diaphragm and the writing-lever resting upon it. A "manometer" is a U-tube partially filled with liquid. One arm of it is connected by air through the tubing with the balloon or other receiving apparatus; the other arm contains a cork float upon which is mounted a rod and writing-point. Changes of air pressure in the connecting tube displace the liquid and so raise and lower the writing-point. "Time markers" are of several types, one being an enclosed clockwork operating a pointer once per second. (Redrawn from Wada, T., *Arch. Psychol.*, 1922, no. 57.)

---

[1] Striped muscles are the skeletal muscles usually attached at one end to a fixed part of the body and at the other end to a movable member.

[2] The writer has devised a simple method of demonstrating hunger as a drive to excess exploratory

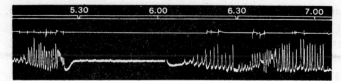

Time
Bodily movements
Stomach contractions

FIGURE 24. CORRESPONDENCE BETWEEN THE PERIODS OF HUNGER CONTRACTIONS AND THE PERIODS OF OVERT BODILY MOVEMENTS

A sample kymograph record. Upper line: time indicated by half-hour breaks. Middle line: bodily movements indicated by vertical departures from the horizontal level. Lower line: stomach contractions shown as tonus in the long level tracing, as hunger contractions in the pronounced vertical records. (Wada, T., *Arch. Psychol.*, no. 57.)

How does hunger (stomach contractions) and how does general bodily need of nourishment operate to produce excess activity of the striped muscles? It has been suggested by Richter that when the chemical equilibrium of the body is disturbed by a nutritive deficiency, chemical products of the deficiency may directly affect the stomach (which is known to be sensitive to chemical stimulation), setting up in the empty stomach the hunger contractions which in turn send afferent impulses to the central nervous system to excite greater tonus and activity in the striped muscles.

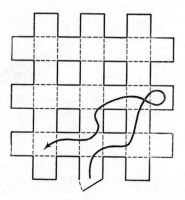

FIGURE 25. EXPLORATORY MAZE

Heavy lines show the walls, broken lines the squares marked off on the floor, the heavy curved line a sample record. The wandering path taken by a rat was recorded by tracing on a printed copy of the floor plan, thus showing the number of squares entered and the number and variety of turns made. (From Dashiell, J. F., A Quantitative Demonstration of Animal Drive, *J. Comp. Psychol.*, 1925, **5**.)

Sex Urge. Food and sex are among the great interests of the individual and of society. These may work out in various secondary forms, but the ground patterns of man's life are determined largely by these two elemental forces. This is, of course, an oversimplification of the story of the motivating of man's behavior; but it may be said that whereas the need

activity in the white rat. A maze was laid out on a plan allowing the animal to run about through many criss-crossing alleys. The floor was marked off lightly into squares; and the animal's total activity in a given time was counted in terms of the number of squares entered. (See Figure 25.) Hungry rats were found to average a distinctly greater number of squares entered than rats that had been recently fed, the average being 42.9 as against 26.7.

of food, when extreme, may become most imperious, the urge to mating has played the most dramatic part in human history and is notorious for its power often to drive men through all barriers of individual inhibitions and of social taboos.   On account of the formidable, impelling character of this bodily urge on the one hand, and of the complicated restrictions that have become established by society concerning the means of its satisfaction on the other, this is nowadays recognized as the greatest of all sources of maladjustment of human beings to their social environments. Freud, indeed, once held it to be the one and only drive of importance in the genesis of mental disorders.

This organic urge arises from a condition in the sex apparatus. Wang used a revolving cage and counter and confirmed earlier observations that the adult female albino rat showed rhythmic changes in the amount of general bodily activity in cycles of about four days' length. What drives a female rat, he asked, to show such regular cyclic changes of overt behavior?   By microscopic examination of the epithelium of the reproductive tract he then confirmed earlier findings that the periods of oestrus (heat) occurred in cycles of the same duration as the changes of the epithelium.   (Cf. Figure 26.) Moreover, he was able to show not only that these two kinds of cycles were coincident, but that any interruption of the oestrous rhythm by pregnancy and lactation or by removal of the ovaries resulted in an interruption of the cycles of gross activity.   Thus it

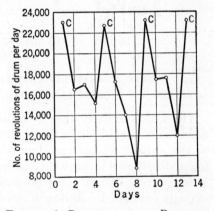

FIGURE 26. CORRESPONDENCE BETWEEN OESTROUS RHYTHM AND CYCLES OF GENERAL BODILY ACTIVITY IN A FEMALE RAT

Encircled dots indicate examinations made of reproductive tract, those marked C being those at which were found cornified epithelial cells, indicative of "heat."   The vertical distance of each dot represents the total amount of general bodily activity of the animal on the day on which the examination was made.   (Wang, G. H., Comp. Psychol. Monog., 2, no. 6.)

was proved that the hypertonicity and hyperactivity of the animal was excited by stimulations of intra-organic origin (in the sex apparatus) when it was in certain physiological conditions.

The male rat does not show the same rhythmic phases in his sex life; yet the dependence of his excess overt activity in large measure upon stimulations from the sex apparatus was demonstrated clearly. It is a familiar fact that if castrated the male of any domestic animal is less aggressive and less restless; and in Richter's laboratory the point was put on the same level of scientific evidence as was the activation of the female. (See Figure 27.)

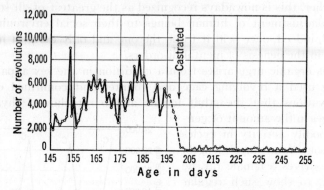

FIGURE 27. EFFECT OF CASTRATION ON GENERAL ACTIVITY

(From Richter, C. P., Animal Behavior and Internal Drives, *Quar. Rev. Biol.*, 1927, **2**, no. 3.)

The excess activity that is set up as the result of the afferent neural currents arising in the sex apparatus is by no means limited to the striped musculature but is evident also in effectors to be found distributed through the viscera. The tension, in other words, is not merely one of overt posturings and restlessness: it is also strongly emotional. And such emotional conditions are themselves in turn important in the energizing of the individual.

The part played in sex behavior by external stimuli is originally very minor and secondary to the intra-organic; but early in the biography of an organism the whole pattern of emotion becomes conditioned to (excitable by) the sight, smell, touch, or other form of stimulation from mates, so that these external kinds of excitation later come to have an increasingly important share in the arousing of the sex drive.

Temperature Maintenance. The two drives described above at length are distinctly intra-organic, and their dependence upon organism-environment adjustment is an indirect one. Not so with some others, as, for instance, the regulatory maintenance of body temperature in human beings.

Summer and winter this is so effectively operated that a variation of only two or three degrees from the normal 98.6° F. is considered a symptom of illness. In part, this great mechanism is a function of the *skin*. The processes of combustion in the body liberate an enormous amount of heat, only a fraction of which is necessary to keep up the level required for the organism's metabolic functions. The remainder is released mainly through the skin surface to the outside. Sometimes the rate of release becomes excessive, owing to the chill of a disease within or to a frigid air temperature without; sometimes it becomes insufficient, owing to a raging fever within or to a torrid temperature without. In either case the condition at the skin operates as a stimulus that sets up afferent neural impulses passing into and through the connecting system and out to striped muscles and other effectors, occasioning a change in activity that will be continued until either the organism's production of heat has been readjusted or the environment has been changed to a more equable one.

The amount of general initiative shown in man's behavior varies with this relation of his internal heat production to his external conditions. The torrid heat belt about the earth, extending from about 30° north latitude to about 30° south, is notorious for not producing important advances in the arts of living or in the sciences, literatures, or fine arts, while at the same time the frigidity of Arctic and Antarctic zones is directly responsible for a poverty of cultural development in those regions. The particular directions assumed by activity that is prompted by unfavorable skin conditions are in the first place the seeking and fashioning of clothing and shelter. When the roving savages of the Andaman Islands retreat before severe weather to the seashore and there each hollows out a hole in the sand under some overhanging cliff, a beginning has been made in the direction of shelter construction, which we see elaborated by other men into actions and occupations centering about the production and transportation of fuel and of building materials.

It is interesting to note that the gregarious form of life among some animals at least is undoubtedly an outgrowth of reactions motivated by unfavorable skin conditions: their original "sociability" is a huddling together of individuals who have been restlessly moving about until the warmth of each other's bodies furnished enough heat to allow the organisms to come to rest — as is easily observed in the nestling together of very young animals.

It has furthermore been found [8] that all the phases of nest-building have in common the one feature that they can be understood as functions of the heat-regulating mechanism of the body. Nest-building increases in low external temperatures, and when the internal body temperature decreases before puberty, during the dioestrous interval, pregnancy, or starvation. It decreases when the environmental conditions are warmer, and also when the body temperature increases as in oestrus.

For experimental measurement of the driving function of skin temperature conditions we may turn to a study of an invertebrate form, the water-mite. Agar placed specimens of these Hydrachnids (spiderlike forms living in water) in tubes of water kept at different constant temperatures. Each tube was marked off into five longitudinal sections, named A, B, C, D, E; and the locomotor activity of each animal was recorded in terms of the sections entered. The optimal temperature for this organism lies between 12.5° and 22.5° C. Figure 28 presents partial records of the same organism when placed in tubes kept at four different temperatures. It will be observed that in the tube maintained at 12.5° C. the animal after its admission near section A typically followed the tube through its full length until forced to turn, whereupon it followed it again through its length, and so on continuously. In a tube of the lower temperature, 6.5°, the animal moved through the length of the tube fewer times, such excursions being frequently interrupted by unforced reversals. In a tube at 32°, the animal again frequently turned about face; and in one at 37°, its reversals were so frequent that it did not once traverse the whole tube. At optimal temperatures, then, this organism is active but in a routine straightaway manner; whereas at abnormally low and abnormally high temperatures its behavior shows *variability* in high degree. The variability in the behavior increases in direct proportion to the degree of lack of balance between internal and external temperature conditions. (Let the reader be clear on one point: action of the animal is not determined by external heat as such or by cold as such in a direct or simple reflex fashion, but by the conditions of energy exchange in the skin tissues.)

In the operation of each of these three motivations (hunger, sex urge, and temperature-maintenance) we can now see that *the fundamental part of the drive is to be traced to certain tissue conditions of the organism that set up afferent neural impulses passing to and*

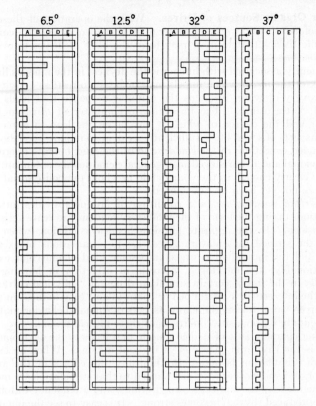

FIGURE 28. SCHEMATIC REPRESENTATION OF THE MOVEMENTS OF THE
SAME HYDRACHNID IN TUBES KEPT AT DIFFERENT CONSTANT
TEMPERATURES

Arrowheads indicate places of introduction of the animal into the tubes, at top of figure, and
the continuous lines show directions of locomotion thereafter from section to section (*A*, *B*, etc.,
of the tube. The graphic records include most of the total runs at the two lower temperatures,
less of the run at 32 and only the first small part of that at 37. (From Agar, W. E., *J. Comp.
Psychol.*, 1927, **7**.)

through nerve centers and out to effectors, the visceral often included,
exciting them to excess activity; and that the adequate external stimulus, such as food or mate serves here as a trigger or release for
directing some of the reactions by providing the necessary environmental opportunity for their full appearance (leading to the elimination of the exciting condition in the tissue and to a subsidence of the
drive). "Excess activity," moreover, may be in the form of *more
vigorous* movements or in the form of *greater variation* in movements.

Other Organic Sources of Drives. With the operation of these three drives before us we may sketchily refer to other inadequacies in the condition of organic tissues that form or may form the basis of drives to overt behavior.

Frequently associated with hunger is the dryness in the mucous lining of the back of the *throat* which impels man or beast to restless activity until the discovery of water awakens the drinking response that leads to the removal of the cause. The importunate character of *thirst* in human behavior and the degree to which it has taken the lead in determining certain aspects of social life is sufficiently evident to require no elaboration.

Distended conditions of the *bladder* and of the *colon* operate to stimulate the individual and if unrelieved may generate emotional excitement. This is shown clearly enough in the young child in whom the polite social inhibitions have not yet been well developed.

The *striped musculature* in a condition of fatigue provides automatic stimulations taking the form of the inhibitory tendency to cease activity, to rest, to sleep. In the opposite physico-chemical condition (when one is rested) the striped musculature gives rise to stimulations of excitatory nature, and the individual is urged into some kind of muscular exercise. Unquestionably, the developed interests in athletics, in hunting or in tramping, in the use of certain stimulant drugs, in "physical culture," as well as the interests in a restful bed or chair, in an "easy living," in the use of sedatives, are a few of the many aspects of human behavior motivated fundamentally by opposite conditions of these muscle tissues.

Another characteristic of striped muscle that leads to the development of a drive is the rhythmic character of its contractions. When an external source of stimulation is acting rhythmically the efforts of the auditor, spectator, or hand worker to adjust himself to that stimulation are modified and influenced by the subject's own rhythms, and a tendency to follow an easily reproduced rhythm becomes strong. It is easy to see the importance of this as a component of the human interest in dancing, music, and poetry. Incidentally it is to be noted that rhythmic activity appears to have emotion-arousing value — at least if it is intense and long maintained — as is shown in the arts just mentioned, and is so dramatically exhibited in war dances, in whirling dervishes, and in camp-meeting oratory, when excitement mounts to a veritable frenzy.

Then there are the *respiratory* and *circulatory* systems. Smothering or suffocating promptly excites most vigorous skeletal movements, especially extensor thrusts, and the subject frequently develops emotional excitement of the rage type. Accelerated or retarded blood circulation, whether directly affecting receptors or not, plays a central part in the activity of other processes that furnish drives — digestion, overt muscular exertion, heat elimination, and so on.

It needs no demonstration here to show that the *skin* is so loaded with receptors that, when it is subjected to injury, violent defensive reactions are at once set up. Avoidance of pain stimulation has motivated not a little of the social submissiveness of the slave, of the prisoner of war, of the convict in the turpentine camp, of the suspect in a back room at the police station, of the school child, and of the younger brother. In case the pain condition is persistent or intense, the motor effects include extensive visceral disturbances which may lead to powerful emotional outbursts, as in the pet dog that, when his foot is caught in a trap, snaps at his own master, or the child with a cut finger who alternately cries in .terror and berates his nurse. Both the rage and the fear types of excitement are to be observed in man or beast under such circumstances.

Very different conditions at the skin may arouse quite an opposite form of behavior. Skin that is mildly stroked and patted, and thus probably facilitated in its blood circulation and in other normal metabolic processes, gives rise to energy changes which as afferent impulses excite inhibitory motor innervations, leading to muscular relaxation. The effect of this on young and old is marked, and such manipulation has been used to quiet the restless baby, to bring sleep to an uneasy adult, and as a form of therapy for a definitely "nervous" patient. At particular points of the skin are to be noted special *sensitive zones* where gentle stimulations have special effects that are more excitatory but still of a general, positive, seeking type. For a good example the well known tickling response will serve us. A light scratching on the soles of the feet or a firm rubbing of the skin over the ribs awakens laughter and wriggling movements of body and limbs. A variety of responses clearly belonging to the same category may be elicited at lips, armpits, nipples, and other sensitive zones, in the form of smiling, gurgling, arching of back, and squirming. All such behavior involves emotional components, but at present we know little about them in detail.

Probably the reactions of *sensory apparatus* should be included here. Nearly all the receptors have associated motor tissues. Consider the eye and its three pairs of muscles to rotate the eyeball, its sphincter muscle to regulate the size of the pupil, and its ciliary muscle to adjust the lens for distances. Consider also the receptors of the skin: they may not have muscular tissues so completely identifiable as integral parts of the sense organ, but for them much the same part is played by the skeletal muscles that move exploring fingers over and around objects. The tendency of the eyes to be turned to a light, of the ears to be cocked in the direction of a sound, of the fingers to move about a mildly stimulating object, of the tongue to expose itself to a sapid substance — all such simple receptor-adjusting tendencies are strikingly evident in infancy. Such reflex adjustments seem to be set up partly as an expression of the metabolism of the receptors, for they give place to stimulus-avoiding reflexes whenever the light or noise or other external agency becomes excessively intense. It is possible that in these phenomena we have the core of the very attention-giving that, apart from any other drive to exploratory movement, is at the basis of the type of behavior called "curiosity."

Endocrine Participation in Energizing the Organism. In the preceding pages we have been uncovering and identifying those tissues and organs in a person's or an animal's body whence arise the forms of energy that expend themselves in a fairly direct manner as

outward bodily activity on his part.   In each case the tissue
demand sets up afferent neural impulses which in turn excite efferent
neural impulses to the muscles and so set the individual into action.
But all is not so simple.   The energy transformations that go on in
the metabolic processes of living are bewilderingly complex; and
back of the local exciting of afferent impulses are energizing phenomena of even more diffuse sorts.

Take the endocrines or ductless glands.   Later we shall want to
go into their particular functions, at least as they bear on psychological problems, but for the present it is sufficient to note how they
contribute through their special secretions to the general energizing
of the body.   Figure 29 presents some of the evidence in clear-cut
fashion.   After rats had been running the revolving cage shown in
Figure 22, one was deprived of its pituitary gland, the other of its
adrenal glands.   The effect in each case on the activity level is decided.   Both the glands named were playing their obscure but
crucial parts in working up the energy to make the animals physically active.

The effect of drugs is an interesting subject for inquiry at this

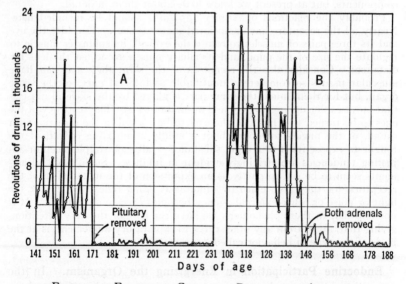

FIGURE 29. ENDOCRINE GLANDS IN RELATION TO ACTIVITY

   A. The effect produced on a rat's running activity by loss of the pituitary gland.   B. The
effect produced by loss of the adrenal glands. (From Richter, C. P., *Amer. J. Orthopsychiat.*,
1932, **2,** p. 347.)

point; but as they come into the picture only through artificial dosing, their consideration is best postponed until Chapter XXI.

Emotional Participation in the Energizing. It is likely that the reader is ready to remonstrate: If it is activity we are interested in, why not go where we find it highest — in a person or animal who "rips and tears and screams and rares"? Why not take him when he is excited? And an opportune reminder it is, for one of the commonest of everyday observations is that never is a man's behavior so vigorous as when he is "worked up." It is then that he slams doors instead of quietly closing them in his usual manner. It is then that his words are loud-spoken or even replaced by cries and screams. He runs, not like a rabbit but like a frightened rabbit; he charges, not like a bull but like a maddened bull. And much so-called "practical psychology" is devoted to exploiting the motivational efficiency of using goad and gadfly, caffeine and heroin, rest and air cures. The ancients recognized well enough these energizing effects. *Quamlibet infirmas adjuvat ira manus* (anger assists the hands however weak); *furor arma ministrat* (rage supplies weapons); and *pedibus timor addidit alas* (fear gave wings to his feet).

But there is another well-recognized type of effect that one's emotional conditions may have on his outward behavior.

> Desponding fear, of feeble fancies full,
> Weak and unmanly, loosens every power.

The paralyzing effect of some fears that flesh is heir to, the enormous weighting down of him that is beset by grief, the slothfulness that peaceful comfort often breeds — such cases can be multiplied a hundredfold. A stomach distended with a heavy dinner, a skin submitted to a warm bath, a severely injured skin or other tissue, a fatigued muscle — each in its own way is likely to set up visceral changes that produce some emotional inhibition or depression of overt behavior.

We must, then, bring into line with our survey of energetics those more diffuse conditions of a person's viscera that lead not only to increased vigor in his overt activity but also to sluggishness and quiescence; that is, *emotional re-enforcement* and *emotional inhibition*. In Figure 30 an attempt is made to suggest the manner in which these emotional segments of a man's total response play an important intermediate rôle between the original stimulus and the

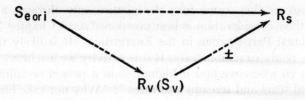

FIGURE 30. THE PART PLAYED BY EMOTIONAL EXCITEMENT OR
DEPRESSION IN THE ENERGIZING OF OVERT BEHAVIOR
(Explanation in text.)

skeletal segments of the response that is made. A stimulus, external or internal ($S_{e \, or \, i}$), may excite not only the more overt response segments involving skeletal musculature (R_s) but also visceral response segments of smooth musculature and glands (R_v). These visceral changes may in turn set up stimulations (S_v) that strengthen (+) or weaken (−) the overt response. For example, pain ($S_{e \, or \, i}$) excites withdrawal movements (R_s) but also at times rage excitement (R_v), which in turn re-enforces (S_v+) the withdrawing movements. Receipt of bad news (S_e) evokes not only such actions as talking and writing (R_s) but also grieving (a depressed visceral condition, R_v), which in turn slows down and weakens (S_v−) the overt talking and writing. The effect of visceral conditions upon overt behavior is not always exercised over neural pathways but is sometimes a more direct chemical effect through the blood stream. This will be discussed later.

As Spinoza wrote in 1665, "by emotion we mean the modifications of the body by which the body's power of acting is increased or diminished, assisted or restrained, and also the consciousness of these modifications." But further description and analysis at this point is unwise. The emotional phases of human life are so subtle, so complex, so variable, that nothing would do but for us to devote a special chapter to the topic.

THE DIRECTING AND CHANNELING OF ACTIVITY

The Problem Stated.   We have traced the original sources of the motivation and energizing of human behavior back to tissue demands in the organism. Energies generated within take the outward expression of motor activity, activity which is partly guided by the exteroceptive stimulations received from the world about. But if all human ideals and aspirations, plans, and purposes be sprung originally from such protoplasmic soil, what can have been the processes of their growth?[1]   At first blush it would seem a far cry from sensitive zones to filial devotion, from glandular secretion to romantic poetry, from circulatory changes to activity in politics, from sense organ reflexes to a planned tour of Europe.

Juxtaposed in this bald manner, such extremes taken from the whole range of interests of humankind may seem utterly foreign to each other; but between them lie all manner of intermediate degrees. And especially, if we read the genetic story of the child's development and witness the appearance of the crudest and most primitive wants years before "honor" or "loyalty" or "charitable giving" or "professional ambition" can have any meaning at all for him, we are prepared to find that the most basic and immediate wants of the child-animal become progressively modified little by little into the mature and sophisticated interests and aims of civilized manhood.

Is Spontaneous Activity at First Undirected and Non-Specific? To begin at the beginning of this biographical story, let us ask: On the very first occasion does the hunger-activated person or animal show a specific excitation of his eating mechanisms and specific activation toward food; does the sex-driven one display rudiments of sex acts specifically and attention toward sex objects; does the "uncomfortable" organism make specific avoiding responses and direct itself definitely away from the source of the annoyance?   So the problem is in reality a double one.   *Even when a person's activity is traceable back to an identifiable appetite (drive), (a) does it consist of just those movements and acts especially appropriate to relieving (terminating) the appetite; and (b) is it directed primarily toward those environmental objects especially significant in this relief?*

The issue may be made clearer by sketching the two most extreme views in answer to these questions, an ultraconservative and a radical one.   According to an historic conception of "instincts," any man or animal when under a given urge or drive was predisposed (in advance of any experience) (*a*) to go through the appropriate movements, and (*b*) to seek out and select appropriate objects; for ex-

---

[1] It would be a gratuitous inference, as unfair as it would be illogical, to conclude that this tracing back of human values to origins in "mere matter" amounts to a debasing of those values.   It would be fully as rational to urge that the argument demonstrates rather the essential ideality and spiritual potentiality of "material substance" and of natural processes.   Surely, to profess to despise matter is today no more than mediaevalism — or else affectation.

ample, if hungry he "naturally" started salivating, licking his chops, exciting gastric secretions, and went about looking for food and food alone.   This is the operation of "the feeding instinct," as it used to be called.[1]   According to another and equally extreme view, that of the environmentalists, (*a*) every man or animal displays only random and general movements of restlessness, regardless of the particular inner impulsion under which he is operating, and (*b*) he is headed toward no one thing in particular; for example, if hungry the child at first only squalls and wriggles — no differently from the way he would squall and wriggle if a pin were sticking into him or colic were assailing him within — and the sight or smell of food would no more orient his graspings and kickings than would the sound of another baby's crying or the play of a light beam on the ceiling.   This "leftist" view assigns the all-important lead in the drama of life to experience and learning.   To take for our illustration again the hungry organism: in the course of its excited threshings about, it may chance to come in contact with food, and in the course of its manipulations it may chance to get it into his mouth, and the re-flexes there and throughout the alimentary canal will then do the rest, resulting in an easing and reduction of the drive; then after a few such incidents the organism will learn to go more directly to the food and to help himself to it with more proper feeding movements.

These are the two extreme factions of opinion.   Are we to choose the one, the other, or neither?   Of course, for literary or for philosophical purposes we might be moved to a decision that suits our temperament and our notion of the fitness of things; but for scientific purposes, we must see what the available evi-dence indicates.

Evidence from Human and Infra-Human Actions.   On a preced-ing page (85) it has been related that a form of activity that would presumably be a specific "expression" of hunger, namely sucking, was discovered in the newborn infant to be really a common avenue of outward-bound energy released by a wide variety of conditions

---

[1] Much of the discussion of "instinct" has been vitiated by a confusion.   At one time the term has been used with reference to a pattern of activity (for example, walking, manipulation), at an-other with reference to the motivation of activity (for example, curiosity, pugnacity, parental love), and perhaps most frequently, in a way both descriptive and explanatory.   The classic notion of "instincts" as God-given faculties mysteriously implanted in animals to guide them aright has given place to inquiries of more scientific types; but contemporary discussions are remarkable for the amount of misunderstanding and confusion traceable to the vagueness of this one term.   Ber-nard found in the literature 849 separate types of "instinct," which he was able to condense to 325 irreducible ones.   As Bohn puts it, "Qu'est-ce que l'instinct?   Un mot"; or even as Condillac says, "L'instinct n'est rien."

set up by external stimulation.   These included the effects of warmth applied to the skin, all odors used including ammonia, all tastes used including quinine, and even the noises of a can and bells; and in another study, pulling the hair and pinching the toe [6].   It was by no means a specific response excited exclusively by hunger (a); and the baby's responses were certainly not directed to food in any differentiated way (b).

Another relevant observation is one forming part of a research to be described on a later page (174).   There are many who are willing to assert that each of the kinds of bodily needs that set up crying in a baby can be distinguished by the kind of cry that is set up.   Sherman [15] put this to an experimental test.   He allowed advanced psychological and medical students and nurses-in-training to hear very young babies crying, but without informing them as to the cause in each case, and asking them to judge as to this.   The results, as the reader can perceive from the accompanying table, show a surprising inability to differentiate the cries arising from the

CONDITIONS GIVING RISE TO CRYING

THE JUDGMENTS	HUNGER	BEING DROPPED	BEING RESTRAINED	BEING STUCK WITH NEEDLE
"Hunger"	6	2	2	5
"Pain"	0	3	5	5
"Colic"	4	7	3	2
"Fear"	3	1	4	0
"Anger"	2	6	2	1
"Irritation" and "Discomfort"	0	1	3	2
"Sleepiness"	2	2	0	0

different conditions.   On the vocal side at least, the general overt explosion of energy that occurs when a very young baby is hungry or in pain, or disturbed by other means well known to excite him, is not a specific pattern of response (at least it is undifferentiable by observers). [1]   It is a general avenue of outflow.   (We should add that, from other studies, it seems to be true that with infants a few

[1] It would seem obvious that since there are two distinct human factors involved here — the baby and the judge — it is important that one of them be eliminated.   This Klein and Gray have done by employing an oscillograph (cf. p. 207) to make physical records of the patterns of sound. Their preliminary data points in the direction of distinguishable vocal patterns in the infants' reactions to hunger, to fear-arousing, and to rage-arousing situations.   (From a private communication.)

weeks older — these were 3–7 days — it becomes fairly easy for nurses and mothers to distinguish the cries issuing from different bodily conditions. Whether the difference is a matter of maturing or of learning, we need not at this point consider.)

If we turn from the human species to other forms we find weighty evidence in the other pan of the scales. Of all the forms and sorts of bodily appetite it might be presumed that the sexual is the one most likely to point the organism toward its appropriate goal-objects and to awaken the particular behavior-pattern most adequate and suitable. This is, in fact, what has been found for white rats, both male and female: when one reaches the age of puberty it finds or is receptive to an appropriate member of the opposite sex, and its whole new pattern of activity is well integrated in such a degree that no previous experience is at all necessary for the complete performance [16].

Something the same was found true also of nest-building by the same animal. The parturient (pregnant) female rat manifests a strong nest-building tendency that is closely associated with her organic condition. The seizing of paper strips and other building supplies laid available to her and the constructing of her character-istic type of nest appear to be activated primarily by some not well-known physiological factors within her body at the time rather than by stimuli from her external surroundings [18].

If now we turn back in the direction of higher forms, on the road to man, these pictures of clear-cut directing of an animal's moti-vated activity by the kind of drive that is operative show less definitely. The rise of sexual activities in young chimpanzees and monkeys has much less definiteness than is seen in rats. A variety of elementary acts of a quite variable nature — acts that are fre-quently observed as parts of other organized series of responses, by the way — are only gradually organized into the sort of copulatory response usual in adults, and only by degrees become directed to members of the opposite sex and to those that are receptive. More-over, this organizing or integrating seems to come about more as a result of the animals' random play experiences than as a result predetermined by any particular internal physiological factor; that is, learning rather than maturing [1, 12].

In this connection, it will be of interest to note that Freud styles the human child "polymorphous perverse," that is, one in whom sexual interests are likely to assume a very great variety of forms and tendencies: there is little or nothing predetermined about it. While not constituting evidence of experimental character, this observation by a deep student of human motivation is worth attention.

Summary and Interpretation. In attempting an interpretation of this let us fall back on the helpful concept that the evolution of higher and higher forms of life — and within the order Mammalia the evolutionary change toward man — is marked by the universal characteristic of increasing plasticity. Motivated behavior becomes ever more variable and plastic; so that *in human behavior* we may assume *a minimum of internal steer and a maximum of capacity to change and modify the directions* of one's interests, even of the most basic sort.

Some Stages in the Development of Directions. Assuming, as we have just done, a minimum of any steering done by the manifold metabolic changes in the human organism that provide it its propelling energy, we face the problem: how does that organism then acquire those particular lines of motivated conduct, those special avenues of interest, that come to mark off one person from another in increasing degree, and make him ultimately a man of vested interests, of focalized ambitions, of partisan friendships and allegiances?

Our knowledge on this score is incomplete, at least so far as scientifically recorded evidences go, and we must construct the story of what occurs by inferences from observations incidental to the studies of development of behavior patterns in the early infant, and interpret them in accordance with well-known phenomena of learning in adults. But first, in order the better to follow the formal analysis about to be made, the reader should be advised of two well-established characteristics of learning. (I) *When in the course of its random activities a child (or other organism) happens to do something that produces a better adjustment (such as removing an irritant or obtaining a bit of food), upon later occasions it will tend to repeat this act more and more directly and effectively.* This is known as the "trial-and-error" character. (II) *When a child (or other organism) is making a definite response to a particular stimulus any frequently accompanying stimulus is likely to be responded to in the same way.* This is known as the "conditioned response" character. Now, without attempting until Chapter XIV to go behind the scenes to scrutinize these principles, the reader should bear them in mind through the paragraphs and pages that lie immediately ahead.[1]

Stage I.   In the arousing of an organism's activity an external stimulus acquires increasing potency.

It is a matter of general observation that the human infant feeds when and only when he is hungry: offer him food when he is sated and he will refuse it in no uncertain manner.   But it is equally well observed that a few months or years later the same individual will be likely to eat whenever an orange or a stick of favorite candy be presented to him, even though he may have just confessed to being "full."   And in adult behavior certain foods (desserts) are reserved for the end of the meal on account of their potency to appeal to a diner even after the intra-organic drive of hunger has become inoperative.   Precisely the same observations are valid for the drinking type of response.

Well-rested musculature, supported by tonic conditions of respiratory and circulatory organ systems, induces in any healthy baby the random slashing and kicking and finger working that is called "play"; while a condition of even mild fatigue in the striped muscles, or a condition of preoccupation of the circulation with the digesting and assimilating of a stomachful of milk leads to a prompt falling off to sleep.   But observe the same individual when he has become a three-year-old child: under the stimulating conditions of other children around him, of dolls and tin soldiers and picture books, his "play" activities may be continued far beyond bedtime.   Like the puppy that has learned to frisk about, not merely as a consequence of abundant "animal spirits" but as a response to the frisking of other puppies, the child may now "play until he drops."

When an infant is released from skin irritation by a pricking pin or twisted clothing, reflex behavior appears, such as smiling, gurgling, accelerated free movements of the limbs, and doubtless visceral conditions of the smooth-running sort.   Now if the mother frequently is the agent that brings about this release from irritation, in time a mere sight of her face will suffice to excite this well-being type of behavior.   And the mother has become a stimulus to some of the reactions that enter into that pattern of behavior called "filial love."

---

[1] Two notable attempts to solve the problem of this section have been made by Troland [20] and by Holt [4].   The present writer is of the opinion that they can be reduced in essence to the trial-and-error and the conditioned response descriptions of learning, and have not furnished interpretations basically different from the statement in the present pages, which was originally written prior to their publication.   They should, however, be read by the interested student.

Like most subhuman species, man in a "state of nature" would presumably exhibit special interest in persons of the opposite sex only under the solicitation of sex drive within himself. But in actual life, nothing is more striking than the potency of eligible or receptive possible mates to excite at least mild or amused interest on his part, even under conditions of quiescence or atrophy of his sex glands.

In summary: Behavior that at first was little more than an expression of internally generated energies becomes attached to external environmental conditions, even to the point of being arousable by them in absence of the primary tissue demand.

Stage II. Once a given mode of behavior has become excitable by a certain external object or situation, it may become excitable by other associated objects as well. For one extra-organic stimulus a new extra-organic stimulus may be substituted.

The baby who has acquired the habit of eating when offered fruit or candy, even in absence of hunger, will rapidly develop interest in the fruit or candy store, in doing this or that to earn the tidbits, in pennies that will procure them, in uncles who furnish the pennies.

The child who plays not only when rested but whenever play-things and playfellows are about him comes also to react with enthusiasm to sight of a toy store, to organized games, to recess or play periods at school, and so on almost *ad infinitum*.

After coming to welcome the sight of mother or nurse or other solicitous attendant, a child will react in a welcoming spirit to in-numerable things associated with her: her voice in the other room, her dress, nurse's "beau," Mother's Day, etc.

Sex interest furnishes our most extreme example of substitution of stimuli. The conditions of civilization serve to enhance the exciting value of sights, odors, sounds, pictures, music, articles of clothing, and all sorts of things in any way connected with the original personal sex object. The astonishingly complex and subtle ramifica-tions of these networks of associated and induced interests furnishes much of the raw material for psychoanalysis.

These substitutions, of course, come to be literally countless within two or three years; and they become so refined and complex that it is small wonder that we are frequently at a loss to identify the original drives underlying a given line of motivated conduct. Even in simpler social cultures than our own the "reason why" with regard to a man's behavior may not be at all easily analyzed.   In the following speech attributed to a Sandwich Islander, the various lines of interest expressed — crude though they be — are already far too sophisticated, far too removed, to be readily reduced to this or that organic craving.

"With such a pearl," exclaimed Falea, "with such a pearl I would be a king!   I could go anywhere and have anything.   I could visit the white men's ports and ride their ships, and white men would wait on me.   I could have a pink silk shirt, and a gold chain, and rings, and shoes — big yellow shoes.   I could have a music-box and bottles of scent and sweet-scented oil, and neckties and a Jew's-harp, and a watch with a bell in it, and a green umbrella, and three kinds of tinned meat for breakfast."

Stage III.   Words and other symbols come to play the same stimulus rôle as the things they represent.

The Islander's speech brings out also the point that in the elaboration and refinement of motives and interests verbal symbols often are used to replace concrete things.   The mere sound of "candy" is a potent substitute for the object named, and a child will set store by such mere symbols as wholeheartedly as his parents would to the typed marks on a telegram.   Names for toys and games, learning the rules for games, counting out the players, or talking of riddles and puzzles, call a child into action as well as do "Let's go swimming" or "Come play ball!"

We hardly need to multiply illustrations on this point.   Through many of the later chapters we shall meet the phenomenon of word-replacing-thing and shall make an analysis of this symbolic behavior.[1]

Illustrations.   Rested musculature, in the absence of other strong internal or external stimuli, will awaken movement-play, which in infancy appears in finger-play.   Taking this as one example of primitive drive let us note some further developments that have appeared with different children in different situations, as noted by the writer.   (Consult Figure 31.)

George, who found prominent among his toys building-blocks and mechanical erector sets, developed manual activity interest in constructing miniature bridges, houses, and then in making new building supplies and new toys.   This interest, strengthened and

---

[1] A dramatic case will be found in Figure 43, p. 187, where it is shown that the profound emotional disturbance occasioned in a Belgian woman in a London laboratory during the Great War when she heard the noises of a German air raid occurred also on another day when she heard only the word "bombs" from the experimenter.

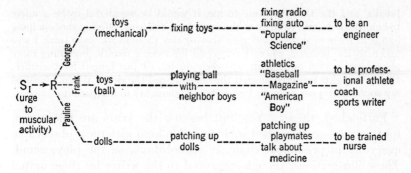

FIGURE 31. FROM BIOLOGICAL URGE TO OCCUPATIONAL IDEAL

A few selected steps in the development of interests out of one arbitrarily chosen tissue demand. The divergence of lines of development is due to differences in environmental opportunities and no doubt also to intrinsic differences in the three personalities. Further explanation is given in the text.

fixated, appeared in a later absorption in tearing up and reassembling old alarm clocks and various gadgets about the house, and when permitted, in tinkering with the radio and the automobile. His reading turned to the popular science magazines. Eventually this determined his choice of the engineering profession.

Frank, playing much with balls and toys that call for romping activity, soon was looking to the day when he could play ball with the neighbor boys, then on to the day when he would participate in high-school athletics. The interest being high, it came to show itself in its verbalized form: always it was the sporting page and the athletic magazines that he read by preference. And when the time for choosing a calling approached he was already oriented in a general way: he was going to be a coach or athlete or sports writer.

Pauline, with dolls as her infant toys, chanced a few times to glue a broken arm or sew up a sawdust leak. The process of patching up, performed with gratifying results, became an established interest; and soon she was wrapping Susan's finger or dropping iodine on Jane's cut toe. Now she began to prick up her ears when conversations turned to medicine; and by her high-school days she had already begun planning for the training of a nurse.

In a study of interest-autobiographies one appeared that corresponds closely to the last case.

"As I advanced in the primary grades," reported a young woman, "I took to dolls. I enjoyed treating them for sickness, bandaging their wounds and breaks, and the thought came to me, it would be wonderful to be a nurse to help the sick, relieve them of their pain and suffering, offering them helping hands in their weakness; and after sharing this thought for some time, I was taken to the hospital where I remained for over a month, becoming more acquainted with a nurse's life and their duties. I just longed for their life; all my thoughts centered around the hospital and the sick. When I finished my sophomore year at high, I revealed my thoughts to my parents." [1]

Farfetched, these? Yes, but because the years are telescoped, for the processes described are identical in kind with those observable everyday in pre-school clinic, in school days, on the playground. These illustrations, though suggested to the writer by three actual children he has observed, suffer by appearing too sketchy. Instead of five or six periods and crucial incidents there are literally thousands in any child's development. For another thing, they suffer by appearing too selected; for at any one of the periods named other basic drives play a part. The number of environmental factors in operation is certainly legion, and the chances of interests sprouting in other directions is high indeed. But it is hoped that the illustrations will clothe the three psychological stages with some helpful concreteness.

The Socializing of Human Motives. Man is a social animal. Far more than is true for any subhuman forms his activity is the resultant not simply of organic factors and of non-personal environmental agencies but also — and especially — of social factors. The debt of an adult man to his fellow men for the particular constitution of his habits, his attitudes, and his behavior generally is incalculable. A baby is born into a world of persons, and from the moment he draws breath he is almost constantly surrounded by them throughout his life. We may postpone detailed analysis of how individuals interact in psychological ways until a later chapter; but in the discussion of an individual's motivation, the personal factors in his environment cannot be neglected.

The personal factors are indeed implicated in the satisfying of the very earliest organic wants. The baby's first breath usually waits upon a spanking or other form of vigorous skin stimulation administered by an attendant. The relieving of his hunger and thirst, the protecting of his delicate skin from cold, depend upon the ministrations of others. As the infant becomes a child, and the child a youth and an adult, most of the habits and attitudes he

[1] From Fryer, D. *The Measurement of Interests.* Holt, 1931. P. 377. By permission of the publishers.

acquires in their greater and greater complexity are ways of behaving toward the people around him.

One source of influence from other human beings lies in their administration of rewards and punishments. If the individual acts in a way to awaken anger in another person he suffers punishment for his conduct (he receives stimuli forcing him into avoiding reactions); if he acts in a way that happens to conform to the motives of another he earns a reward (he receives stimuli leading him into further positive reactions). In this manner the course of his career is being constantly steered by the reactions of other people toward whatever he does; and by the time he is in his teens or his twenties nearly his whole stock of attitudes and habits will bear evidence to these social controls. He wears clothing — clothing of certain cuts and fabrics. He uses knife, fork, and spoon in the process of eating. Upon meeting with an object that would satisfy a want but that happens to be in the possession of another he does not plunge in and seize it: he approaches the owner and offers him pay. In a word, he is in large measure "socialized."

The socialization of an individual is not confined to the inculcating of particular habits of action toward particular people or things: it takes the form also of shaping his general habits of social demeanor. Much browbeating and bullying of a person, or much exaggerated solicitude and "babying," are likely to develop in him a tendency to excessive humility and self-abasement before others (an exaggerated reaction-to-punishment). By the same token, servile or cringing attendance upon him, or a too ready compliance with his demands, may develop in him an overweening pride and a self-assertive demeanor (an exaggerated reaction-to-reward). More fortunate than either of these extremes is that degree of sensitiveness to social approval inculcated by the individual's frequent reliance upon the good-will of his fellows, which secures effective co-operation between him and them. He knows how to get along with them without "rubbing them the wrong way" or compromising his own self-respect. He is socially well-adjusted.

Habituation Operates as a Quasi-Motive. There is one phenomenon underlying all the established trends of life which deserves special mention; for in any practical consideration of why people do this or that, it must be reckoned with. It operates as a determining factor of such weight as almost to seem a force in itself. "The accustomed routine of life," Bain said long ago, "leads to a craving almost of the nature of appetite. As the time comes round for each stated occupation, there is a tendency or bent to proceed with that occupation, and an uneasiness at being restrained. Our appetites, properly so called, may have their times of recurrence determined by our customary periods of gratifying them." And a century earlier, Reid said, "I conceive it to be a part of our constitution that what we have been accustomed to do, we acquire not only a facility, but a proneness to do on like occasions." This "force of habit," then (note the popular expression), is responsible often for the direction which a man's energies may take. It is this, says James in an oft-quoted passage, that "prevents the hardest and most repulsive walks of life from being deserted by those brought up to tread therein. It keeps the fisherman and the deck-hand at sea through the winter; it holds the miner in his darkness, and nails the countryman to his log-cabin and his lonely farm through all the months of snow."

The interruption or thwarting of a routine manner of conduct frequently acts upon the individual like a positive irritant. He may struggle and slue about until he is enabled to fall back into that habitual performance, not because the old way secures any more effective satisfaction of his fundamental drives than striking out boldly in some new way would secure, but, apparently, because it entails less expenditure of energies.[1] The promoter of a new commodity in the market soon learns how great a resistance on the part of the public must be overcome by him: no matter how healthful, cheap, convenient, and attractive the new article may be, prospective purchasers will show a pronounced tendency to continue to buy the old familiar ones. A convict who has spent nearly his whole lifetime in prison may, upon release, beg to be readmitted. Workwomen in a garment-making shop have been known to go on strike when ordered to make some slight alteration in the pattern by which they have long been working. The archives of anthropology are full of instances in which the taboos of a savage or civilized group are plainly based not upon the practical value of a given procedure but upon its sanctification by custom. With many peoples, indeed, the equivalent word for taboo denotes any departure from custom. The habit of wearing clothing, which originated from needs of skin

[1] This is a rather general explanation; but little more can be said appropriately here. Why a routine activity is performed with greater ease and facility and is energy-conserving for the organism involves some profound biological questions. An approach to some of them is to be offered in the more technical study of learning in a subsequent chapter.

protection or from the sense organ stimulating value of decoration, has attained the status of a compulsive custom. With a modern man, that which he and his parents and ancestors have always done and have been used to doing determines in large measure his judgments of right and wrong — ethically, esthetically, religiously, economically, and socially.

ATTITUDES

Their Definition and General Importance. An experiment will give us our direction. Groups of students, after having given their rank-order preferences for sixteen English and American authors (Barrie, Conrad, Hardy, Whitman, Wilder, and others), were given several weeks later sixteen mimeographed passages, all actually from Stevenson's writings but each ascribed to one of the authors in the list mentioned, with instructions to rank them in the order of their literary merit. In no case was the deception suspected; and — except those few who stated that they had intentionally ignored the authors' names — they made judgments as to the pure merit of the passages which conformed in a definite degree to their previously expressed rankings of the supposed authors, with an average correlation of + .46. Writing attributed to a favorite author was rated high, while that attributed to a less-favored author was judged lower in the scale. It is clear that these students were unconsciously prejudiced. They prejudged under the influence of established predispositions that each individual had toward certain classes of named stimuli, authors [14]. Properly speaking, these are "attitudes."

A well-known playwright and producer for years resorted to the device of bringing in the American flag toward the end of the first act of nearly every play staged by him. The explanation is obvious enough; any typical American audience is made up of individuals who have long-established tendencies to react with enthusiasm whenever the Stars and Stripes are publicly displayed, and such behavior enkindled during the presentation of a play will have an important effect upon the responses of the audience to the play itself. The producer was capitalizing an attitude. For an honor system to operate effectively on a college campus the individual student must be strongly disposed to react with extreme disfavor to any infringement of a certain code of rules on the part of another or of himself. The students must possess the proper attitudes builded upon practice and precept repeatedly and vividly. Observance of Mother's Day is a mode of affirming and strengthening those permanent emotional tendencies that may be called the attitude of filial respect and love. A slighting remark about Kansas or California or Virginia is altogether likely to awaken characteristic vigorous behavior on the part of a native of the particular State: he has a deep-rooted propensity to display such behavior. So it is with the attitudes readily developed with reference to Santa Claus and Christmas and the Fourth of July, one's own church or lodge or political party, one's rival in business or in love. All such objects are what they are because of the attitudes built into the persons concerned with them.

In the longitudinal or biographical view of how people's motives become established along particular grooves, this concept of "attitude," which is coming much to the forefront of social and personality psychology, is a most helpful one. The meanings with which this word has been used in psychology are several, and here, as in so many other places, the student must be on guard against confusing a technical psychological meaning with literary and popular usages of the same word. The term "attitude" is nowadays being applied in a technical way to *an enduring acquired predisposition to react in a characteristic way, usually favorably or unfavorably, toward a given type of person, object, situation, or ideal.*[1]

The significance of attitudes, as of habits, in human life is tremendous. The organization of emotional reactions into habitual forms of activity furnishes stability in human behavior and human social relations, and molds into regular and constant modes of behavior a man's ways of loving and hating, his likes and dislikes in foods, dress, automobiles, and fiction, his loyalties and his cynicisms. His neighbors, family, office force, and club members can deal with him to some purpose because they know what he is likely to do on almost any given occasion. Character training, whether broadly or narrowly conceived, is a process of training desirable attitudes so that socially valuable rather than harmful behavior will be aroused by "whatsoever things are true, whatsoever things are honest, whatsoever things are just."

---

[1] The reader will find the term employed in psychological literature as referring also to what later we shall describe as "postural responses"; but these have reference not to enduring but to quite temporary ways in which a person gets set. (To be treated in Chapter XII.) For the sake of clarity we shall insist on the distinction, and use "attitudes" only for the more enduring predispositions.

A great simplification of the psychology of motivation is afforded by this concept. The "prejudices" of all kinds that form the very warp of a person's whole make-up are attitudes. The "complexes" discovered by the psychoanalysts are really attitudes that happen to operate pathologically. It is indeed surprising how much attempts at describing emotional behavior are simplified by recognizing the fact that emotional reactions become habitually attached to the stimuli that chance to excite them and thereafter tend to have the right of way whenever those stimuli reappear.

How Attitudes are Learned. Since attitudes are acquired enduring functions of the individual, they would seem at first to come under the head of "habits," if the latter term be loosely used; but more precisely, a person's "habits" refers to his responses toward more specific stimuli, responses that are more automatic and less obviously related to his interests and motives. The automobile driver reveals an imposing equipment of particular skills as he manipulates his engine and machinery through traffic (habits); and at the same time he reveals partisan *pro* and *con* tendencies when he "speaks his mind" about the dangers of speeding, too many "drunks" on the road, men who blow their horns with hideous blatancy, the alertness of the highway commission, or the impressive body styles in the new year's cars.

Like a habit, a person's attitude toward an object is an acquired one. (a) It may be a *residuum of many somewhat similar responses*, a result of cumulative experience operating by both individuation and integration. This is shown in the attitude toward honesty, which develops only gradually out of many specific cases of acting honestly, and even in later childhood has not yet become well generalized and unified [3] (see pp. 592 ff. below). Such was found to be the case of many atheists who had reached their convictions gradually after months of reflections upon their readings in history and science [21]. (b) Or the attitude may have been formed and fixated after *one dramatic experience*. This is true of a celebrated case in which an intense fright at a locomotive engine suffered by a child of two years who had wandered near the forbidden tracks, established in him a lifelong dread of locomotives, which had become for him avenging gods; and this in spite of his insight and better judgment [10]. (c) Or again, the attitude may have been *adopted ready-made*, taken over from people about. This is illustrated by the white child who himself has no prejudice or dislike toward

Negroes until after he has seen and heard people poke fun at the polysyllabic utterances, the shuffling gait, or the superstitions of Sambo [9].

Analysis of the learning process as a phenomenon in its own right must be postponed until a later chapter. But we may well pause a moment to recognize a certain continuity of discussion in our topics. The reader will discern in the formation of many if not all attitudes the operation of two principles described in previous sections — *socialization* and *habituation*. The individual person is subtly influenced by the expressed feelings and opinions of his fellow men. The moldings thus given to his responses tend by their habitual character to predetermine his behavior on later occasions. This double process will be aptly illustrated in the topic to follow.

Social Stereotypes as an Extreme Form of Attitudes. We have seen that many of the prejudices of which an individual person is seized and possessed are clearly social in their origin and maintenance. A notable example is that of racial prejudices. Now, these have been found so uniform in various parts of the country and so strong even where members of the races concerned have never been met with that they must be set down not as reactions based on actual experiences but reactions merely toward race-names. They are "social stereotypes," that is, they are *socially standardized* predispositions to respond with acceptance or aversion *toward certain names or labels*, having become established in the individual more or less uncritically (often unknowingly) after the patterns of people about him. If a man has heard the mere names "Republican" or "Negro" or "bloated bondholder" or "communist" used often enough in one consistent prejudiced and partisan way, he will be a remarkable man indeed if he does not soon get rooted within him reaction-tendencies toward such labels, and of such strength that thereafter, upon meeting a Republican or Negro or capitalist or communist he will unthinkingly and as a matter of course treat that individual according to his preconceived pattern.

As we shall see upon closer analysis of emotional behavior in a chapter to follow, one can learn to become afraid or unafraid of this object or that if one's associates are afraid or are unafraid; moreover one will then come to show the same response to the mere name and mention of the thing. What is more, one learns to become afraid of, or resentful toward, or enthusiastic about, mere symbols, names, tags, applied to things one has never seen nor expects to see, if only the other people he meets daily and the printed matter he reads daily reveal that kind of fear or resentment or enthusiasm, for early in life he has established the habit of doing much as other people do.

If we will but stop for a moment to ponder the extraordinary degree in which the social life of man is permeated and shot through with his responses to emblems, shibboleths, hackneyed phrases, and epithets, without benefit of first-hand acquaintance and cool-headed analysis of men and issues actually involved, we shall understand the avid interest of the social psychologist and the sociologist in the psychology of attitudes.

Some Attitudes in College Life.   It is at once apparent that an investigator could not get a person's attitudes directly under his analytical gaze but must depend upon their outward manifestations in the way in which he acts or the way he talks.   The former would make a hopelessly long task and one impossible to standardize. But his verbally expressed opinions can be standardized by having him respond in certain alternative set ways to a set list of questions bearing upon the objects of the attitude.

In one extensive research of this sort the answers of over four thousand students in one university concerning their individual opinions on various phases of college studies and college life were obtained anonymously.   On the question of "cribbing" or cheating, varying proportions of the student group admitted to cheating in varying degrees of frequency.   Of more interest here is the divergence of opinion on the ethics of cheating as expressed by the admitted cheaters and by the non-cheaters, as summarized in the accompanying table.

ATTITUDES OF CHEATERS AND NON-CHEATERS ON THE ETHICS
OF CHEATING[1]

	NON-CHEATERS	EXTREME CHEATERS
1. Cheating is as bad as lying	52%	6%
2. It shows a defect of character	10	0
3. It is unfair but not immoral	20	16
4. Honesty desirable but unattainable	9	29
5. Cheating is the only way to gain one's rights	8	29
6. It is merely playing the game between teacher and student	1	16
7. Student should take all he can get	0	3

[1] From Katz, D., and Allport, F. H. *Students' Attitudes.* Craftsman Press, 1931.

Interesting sidelights on the attitudes encouraged by (or leading to) fraternity membership were obtained in this research. Over two-thirds of those who were fraternity members were classed "as institutionalists" after stating their belief that the "active personnel changes from year to year but the fraternity goes on" as a sort of super-individual entity; the other third were "individualists" who stated each that his fraternity was nothing more than a group of individuals. Now it turned out that this line of cleavage ran through many other attitudes. Somewhat more of the "individualists" (a) laid emphasis upon athletics for all students instead of varsity teams, (b) thought that a poor athletic season impaired the university's reputation and merit, (c) thought that professors should have freedom of expression in the classroom, and the editor freedom in the student's paper, and (d) were more willing to admit to fellow-membership certain student types (those of unconventional morals, Bolshevists, Turks, Hindus, anarchists, and others). The attitude of independence would seem from this to be general in character: an individualist in one situation is likely to be an individualist in another, at least as far as his expressed opinions indicate.

THE MEASURING OF MOTIVES

The Obstruction Method. A type of animal research that may turn out to be adaptable with modifications to the measuring of human motives employs the method of obstruction. An animal is separated from the incentive object (water, food, mate, young, or strange box) by a difficult but not impassable barrier such as an electric grid; and the intensity of the animal's drive at that time is measured in terms of the amount of obstruction, such as the strength of electric current used, which the animal is willing to overcome in obtaining access to the incentive. (See Figure 32.) The method is, in spite of certain criticisms, highly promising, and is certainly ingenious. It permits the measuring of an animal drive in terms of the number of times the average subject would cross the electrified grid of a standard strength in a standard interval of 20 minutes. To illustrate: in a study of thirst, a hundred white rats were segregated into groups and tested after being deprived of water 1, 2, 4, and 6 days respectively. On the test the animal was allowed a sip of water after each crossing before it was removed again to the entrance chamber. The greatest average number of crossings was after

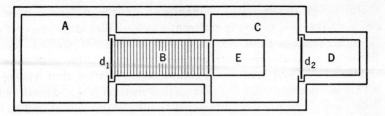

FIGURE 32. THE OBSTRUCTION BOX

An apparatus for the measuring of different animal drives. The subject is introduced into the compartment A, and after the door d_1 is raised it must cross an electric grid in the obstruction compartment B, in order to reach the release plate E that operates the door d_2 giving it access to the incentive stimulus (food, female, water, young, strange maze, etc.) in D.

1 day of water-deprivation, namely 20; while the other tests were: after 2 days, 16 crossings, after 4 days, 13, and after 6 days, 7. The last shows a rapidly weakening intensity of thirst [24].

After rats had been tested in this manner for intensity of several other drives, the results were contrasted by comparing the greatest average score (crossings) for each drive respectively. It would appear from the accompanying table that thirst, hunger, and sex rank in that order, with the maternal drive the highest of all and the exploratory definitely the weakest.

MAXIMUM NUMBER OF CROSSINGS MADE (AT ANY PERIOD) UNDER
VARIOUS DRIVES

DRIVES TESTED	MAXIMUM No. OF CROSSINGS
(males)	
Thirst	21.1
Hunger	19.1
Sex	13.5
Exploratory	6.0
(females)	
Maternal	22.4
Thirst	19.7
Hunger	19.0
Sex	14.1

No doubt, particular numerical values like these must be viewed with caution; but in any case we have in this series of experiments a mode of attack that may prove suggestive for procedures with human subjects. "How much is he willing to pay for it?" is a frequently used measure of a man's motive or interest; and it explains the historical development of money as a common denominator of different people's values in different lines. "Would he prefer it to the other kind of thing (home site, toilet soap, oil painting, vacation)?" is a query arising in innumerable practical life situations.

There is, indeed, a study of childhood motivation that has some points in common with the obstruction method [11]. School children were given work requirements (multiplication) that had to be met before a reward (chocolate bar) was granted. This requirement was systematically increased for each child up to the point where no children earned the reward; then it was systematically decreased to the point where nearly everyone earned it.[1] The maximal incentive value for each subject was the highest work score he turned in. That, calculated on the basis of his work when under no incentive, was "the price he was willing to pay," and amounted on the average to an increase of 52 per cent.

"Methods of Impression." Probably the oldest formal method of determining a person's attitude (likes and dislikes) is that of presenting to him a number of incentives (stimuli) for his choice. In Fechner's original procedure, known as the *Method of Paired Comparisons*, the experimenter displays the materials two at a time, and records the subject's indicated preference between them. When each stimulus has been paired once with every other one, a totaling of the number of preferences given to each furnishes the final order of the subject's choices. In the *Method of Order of Merit*, the subject is supplied with the whole set of materials; and he is to arrange them in a sequence or row to show which one he prefers most, which he likes next most, and so on down to the one least preferred or most disliked. Simple though the procedures seem, many errors and pitfalls of carelessness need to be guarded against in either; and perhaps, indeed, their great merit lies in the fact that they are adaptations of methods in everyday use from time immemorial but now rigorously standardized and purified of many of the sources of error that creep into the judging of babies, prize hogs, needlework, jellies, and bathing beauties. All in all it can be said that they have justified themselves by their useful employment in several psychological fields, especially in esthetics (see pp. 475 ff.) and in the comparative study of advertising appeals.

In connection with the "Methods of Impression" one frequently

---

[1] This will be recognized as a method first developed in psychophysical measurements. Cf. pp. 254 ff.

sees mention of the "Methods of Expression." These, however, are more fitly taken up in our more intensive study of Emotion in the chapter to follow.

The Vocational Interest Blank. A person's interests in a wide range of things can be identified and measured by a technique that has been especially well developed in connection with occupational diagnosis and advice. It consists of an elaborate set of questions bearing upon a great number of specific situations. The examinee is instructed to indicate in each case whether he likes a given thing, or dislikes it, or is indifferent to it. For example, Strong [17] has different lists of items such as the following, concerning occupations, amusements, school subjects, peculiarities of people, and general activities.

Draw a circle around one of the symbols after each item below:

Being a floorwalker	L(like)	?	D(dislike)
Being a farmer	L	?	D
Playing golf	L	?	D
Attending symphony concerts	L	?	D
Reading *New Republic*	L	?	D
Cowboy movies	L	?	D
Studying geography	L	?	D
Studying algebra	L	?	D
Repairing a clock	L	?	D
Acting as cheer leader	L	?	D
Looking at shop windows	L	?	D
People with gold teeth	L	?	D
Religious people	L	?	D

If the examiner wants to know whether or not his subject has the interests presumably fitting him for the engineering profession, his responses on the blank are compared with the responses previously obtained for many successful engineers by means of a specially scored reference stencil. If the subject's interest fitness for ministerial or medical or legal or life insurance or any of twenty-odd other occupations is in question, his responses are checked against the scores made by successful men in each.

This is by no means the whole story of vocational fitness, of course, for what one likes may not well indicate what he can really do. See, for instance, pp. 356 f. below.

Attitude Scales. The questionnaire method of soliciting opinions has been standardized by Thurstone who applied one of the procedures long known to psychophysics (see p. 254) to the construction of a scale. A wide variety of statements of opinion on the matter in question is sorted by each of many judges into eleven piles of estimated equal steps. Those statements having small scatters (that is, assigned by most judges to the same pile, with few assignments to others) are retained and given scale-values corresponding to their piles. Then when used by a subject whose opinions are being sought, he checks those statements with which he agrees and his score is the mean scale-value of these checked items [19].

For instance, in a study of prohibition a few statements used, and their scale-values when scored were:

It is absolutely immaterial whether we have prohibition or not (5.5)
The 18th Amendment should be repealed (10.2)
Possession of intoxicating liquor in any form should subject the individual to punishment (1.4)
Prohibition should come as a result of education, not legislation (6.4)

Scales have been worked out for the measurement of attitudes on a number of social topics — birth control, communism, prohibition, evolution, God, war, the Chinese, the Germans, and the Negro; and others are in rapid production. These are available for the comparison of different groups of subjects in order to discover the attitude-forming influences of various factors. For example, to ascertain the effect of a single motion picture on children's attitude toward Chinese, children of two towns were given an attitude test

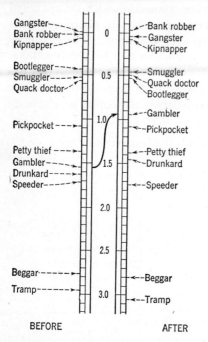

FIGURE 33. SHIFT OF ATTITUDE AS THE EFFECT OF A MOTION PICTURE

To the left and to the right are scaled various "crimes" on the basis of children's opinions (secured by the Method of Paired Comparisons) registered before and after seeing the film, *Street of Chance*, which depicted the life of a gambler in unfavorable light. Note that all other "crimes" were given again much the same scale-values while "gambler" came to be judged more severely. (From Thurstone, L. L., *J. Soc. Psychol.*, 1931, 2, 298.)

on the Chinese; then a week later while those of one town were shown a film picturing Chinese culture in a favorable light those of the other were shown one that had been criticized as being unfavorable; and finally the attitude test was again administered to all. The results showed that the attitudes of the children were changed in opposite directions in the two towns, toward the more favorable and the less favorable respectively.

For another study somewhat similar see Figure 33.

REFERENCES

1. Bingham, H. C. Sex Development in Apes. *Comp. Psychol. Monog.*, 1928, **5**, No. 1.

2. Fryer, D. *The Measurement of Interests.* Holt, 1931.

3. Hartshorne, H., and May, M. A., *et al. Studies in the Nature of Character. I: Studies in Deceit.* Macmillan, 1928–30.

4. Holt, E. B. *Animal Drive and the Learning Process.* Holt, 1931.

5. Hurlock, E. B. The Psychology of Incentives. *J. Soc. Psychol.*, 1931, **2**, 261–90.

6. Jensen, K. Differential Reactions to Taste and Temperature Stimuli in Newborn Infants. *Genet. Psychol. Monog.*, 1932, **12**, Nos. 5–6.

7. Katz, D., and Allport, F. H. *Students' Attitudes.* Craftsman Press, 1931.

8. Kinder, E. F. A Study of the Nest-Building Activity of the Albino Rat. *J. Exper. Zoöl.*, 1927, **47**, 117–61.

9. Lasker, B. *Race Attitudes in Children.* Holt, 1929.

10. Leonard, W. E. *The Locomotive-God.* Century, 1927.

11. Leuba, C. J. A Preliminary Experiment to Quantify an Incentive and its Effects. *J. Abnor. & Soc. Psychol.*, 1930, **25**, 275–88.

12. Maslow, A. H. The Rôle of Dominance in the Social and Sexual Behavior of Infra-Human Primates, II. *J. Genet. Psychol.*, 1936, **48**, 310–38.

13. Richter, C. P. Animal Behavior and Internal Drives. *Quar. Rev. Biol.*, 1927, **2**, 307–43.

14. Sherif, M. An Experimental Study of Stereotypes. *J. Abnor. & Soc. Psychol.*, 1935, **29**, 371–75.

15. Sherman, M. The Differentiation of Emotional Responses in Infants, II. *J. Comp. Psychol.*, 1927, **7**, 335–51.

16. Stone, C. P. The Congenital Sexual Behavior of the Young Male Albino Rat. *J. Comp. Psychol.*, 1922, **2**, 95–153. The Initial Copulatory Response of Female Rats, etc. *J. Comp. Psychol.*, 1926, **6**, 73–83.

17. Strong, E. K. *Vocational Interest Blank.* Stanford Univ. Press.

18. Sturman-Hulbe, M., and Stone, C. P. Maternal Behavior in the Albino Rat. *J. Comp. Psychol.*, 1929, **9**, 203–37.

19. Thurstone, L. L., and Chave, E. J. *The Measurement of Attitude.* Univ. Chicago Press, 1929.
20. Troland, L. T. *Fundamentals of Human Motivation.* Van Nostrand, 1928.
21. Vetter, G. B., and Green, M. Personality and Group Factors in the Making of Atheists. *J. Abnor. & Soc. Psychol.*, 1932, **27**, 179–94.
22. Wada, T. Experimental Study of Hunger in its Relation to Activity. *Arch. Psychol.*, 1922, No. 57.
23. Wang, G. H. The Relation Between "Spontaneous" Activity and Oestrous Cycle in the White Rat. *Comp. Psychol. Monog.*, 1923, No. 6.
24. Warden, C. J., *et al.* *Animal Motivation.* Columbia Univ. Press, 1931.
25. Young, P. T. *Motivation of Behavior.* Wiley, 1936.

CHAPTER VI

SOME PERSONAL PROBLEMS IN MOTIVATION

REACTIONS TO FRUSTRATION OF DOMINANT MOTIVES

Readjustive Behavior Again. In our review of the nature and the development of motives in the preceding chapter we have given but little consideration to the consequences incurred when a highly motivated person meets obstructions. Yet when all is said, it is the behavior characterizing people when their basic drives find no relief, when their desires are in danger of non-realization, when their interests go unsatisfied, when their hopes and ambitions are challenged — it is their behavior then that makes human life human. This has been given artistic expression in the drama and in literature generally. From Greek tragedy to modern, much of the high interest lies in the baffling toils of circumstance in which an individual is caught and the never quite extinct spirit of dogged endeavor. Off the stage as well, the most interesting episodes of life, and in a psychological sense often the most important, are those in which man faces a situation that frustrates or even destroys his values without utterly destroying him.

The definitely moral situations, which have so preoccupied the life and thinking of a large proportion of North Europeans, fall clearly within the category of situations of frustration. A moral crisis occurs when a neighbor's doll or wagon arouses in a child to an intense degree the primitive and naïve tendency to appropriate it, but at the same time arouses the negative reaction of leaving the coveted thing alone, or of saying, "I mustn't take things that don't belong to me without asking: that would be stealing." It is a moral crisis again when a woman hesitates between retailing a fresh piece of unconfirmed gossip and refusing to do anyone wanton harm; or when a man is in a dilemma between making the solicited contribution to a worthy enterprise and keeping the funds for extra pocket-money.

There is, of course, nothing new here. We have repeatedly in preceding chapters referred to the behavior of man or beast when he meets some sort of obstruction to his progress. In Chapter II, in fact, we made this readjustive behavior a corner stone of our psychology. We saw there that in a situation where the organism is maladjusted by reason of non-optimal relations with its environment, it displays activity that is both persistent and variable, until by good fortune it may find a way out of the perplexity. But the story as so briefly told calls for elaboration; and in the present place it is fitting for us to examine more narrowly into what happens when the motive under which a person is operating is a powerful or well-organized one and when the way out of the difficulty is exceedingly hard to find or is heavily beset with difficulties. Under such conditions some of the most fascinating sorts of behavior appear.

The life of children and the life of infrahuman animals is each replete with examples of readjustive behavior, and a selection of some simple presentations should help to prepare us for the more complicated pictures of adults.

Basic Types of Crises. Lewin [4] has made a simple descriptive analysis of crises in child life by using his notion of "valences," which is a term borrowed from chemistry and extended to mean the attracting or the repelling power of an object according to the needs of the organism.[1] A simple valence is shown when an infant

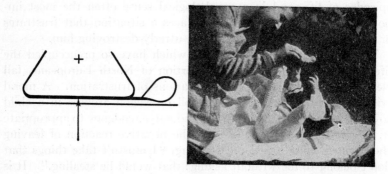

FIGURE 34. AN ILLUSTRATION OF POSITIVE VALENCE

(From Lewin, K. *A Dynamic Theory of Personality*, p. 82. McGraw-Hill, 1935.)

---

[1] This notion of valence is in line with a growing recognition that a psychological phenomenon is neither organic only nor environmental only but rather is an organism-environment relationship; and relationships exist and operate just as truly as do isolated objects. "Drive" and "incentive," for example, are two end-terms of this relationship or "valence." Again, the notion of "tropism," as referred to in Chapter I, is not that of something residing simply in the animal itself nor having its locus in the heat-source or earth-source or other phase of the surroundings toward which the animal turns. Also, in the inorganic world, consider what is meant by "gravitation." It is not a "force" but a relationship between the masses of two or more bodies.

is offered a doll, as shown in Figure 34. But obstructions to valence and conflicting valences, too, play a large rôle in child life; and these are divisible into three basic types. (See Figure 35.)

(*A*) The child may stand between two positive valences, such as between going on a picnic and staying home to play with his play-mates. Unlike the fabled case of Buridan's ass that starved to death between two stacks of hay, this is a labile equilibrium, rather than a stable equilibrium, and one of the valences is sure to out-pull the other. The child is sure to do the one thing or the other — go to the picnic or stay and play. Such situations are usually simply resolved.

(*B*) The child may find himself between two negative valences, such as when threatened by punishment to do a task he is reluctant to do. Again such situations usually resolve themselves, through the greater repelling of one of the forces. Sometimes, however, the simultaneous and contrary repulsions drive the child off at a tangent, and, as Lewin puts it, he goes out of the field. He runs away from his difficulties. Now, as we shall shortly see, this human tendency to resolve a difficulty by simply running away from it, by utilizing any avenue of escape that one may chance upon instead of remaining on the scene to work it out, this human propensity is at the bottom of so many private personal problems of life that it may fairly be called one of the most ominous weaknesses that flesh is heir to. But more on that later.

(*C*) The child may be caught between two oppositely directed forces, of which one is attracting, the other repelling in character. He wants to stroke an uncertain-looking dog, let us say, or to eat a forbidden cake. The negative valence assumes the character of a barrier, much as if the dog were behind a fence or the cake on too high a shelf. Here again a common resort is that of flight. The child may physically leave the room or psychologically leave the situation by playing with something else present. Often, he withdraws only temporarily; he does not completely "pass up" the forbidden incentive, and returns to the situation again and again. Ultimately, he may yield to the temptation; he may put it behind him once and for all, refusing ever to consider it again; or he may remain for an indefinite period persistently vacillating between turning his back on the incentive and returning to have another look at it. This form of behavior, also, the reader will recognize as significant in one's private adjustments to life's prob-

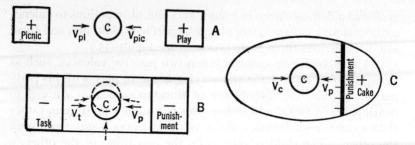

FIGURE 35. TYPES OF CONFLICT SITUATIONS

In each case the child, C, is involved in valences that attract or repel in contrary directions, as indicated by the arrowheads.

A. The child by his very nature and by the nature of the incentives is attracted in both directions.

B. He is repelled in both directions. Sometimes the repulsions together force him off in a third direction.

C. He is attracted toward the incentive-object but repelled by a (social or non-social) barrier. (From Lewin, K., *A Dynamic Theory of Personality*, McGraw-Hill, 1935.)

lems, especially those of an ethical sort. Still another solution appears at times when the circumstances permit — making a detour. The alert person may discern a roundabout way, and by circling the obstruction attain the objective. The detour need not be — and usually is not — a physical traveling-around, but may be a subtler business of utilizing other people (as when the child persuades another child to obtain the cake for him on a fifty-fifty basis) or of reformulating the obstruction or the incentive (as when a lawyer advises his client on how the statute might be interpreted or how he could rename or rephrase his objectives). This reformulating, by the way, is another tendency of humankind that grows to excess. Consider the language of diplomacy and political campaigns as well as the excuses given by the person who constantly deceives himself as to why he does this or that.

Some Disruption of Behavior may be Produced. The conditions by which a strong urge is thwarted may become so critical that a delicately balanced nervous system may be sorely tried and behavior thrown entirely out of gear in explosive manifestations. This is true even of the dog [7]. Dogs have been trained (that is, "conditioned," see Chapter XIV) to react positively (by preparatory feeding actions, as salivating) whenever they saw a circle of light, which preceded a feeding, but never when they saw an ellipse of light, which preceded no feeding at all. The original dimensions of the ellipse were in the ratio 2:1. After this discrimination had been well established the experimenter changed the ellipse signal by stages to make it more like the circle, until a point was reached (the ratio 9:8) when the task of discriminating became too difficult. The animal no longer could tell through any extended series which was the feeding signal. What is more, curious symptoms were suddenly displayed. The hitherto quiet and businesslike dog began to squeal and howl, to wriggle about, to bite and tear at the tubes and the strappings. And only after laborious retraining with the original pair of signals was anything like equilibrium restored in the distraught organism's behavior. This, significantly, has been called a *neurosis*; and it affords us some reflection on the fundamental meaning of neurotic behavior in man.

Morbidly Resolved Crises as Illustrated in Hysteria. M., a young man who had been a dancer and acrobat in a circus, enlisted in the army long after the World War. Here he found the discipline rigid, his duties irksome, and his experiences monotonous. He longed for the travel, excitement, attention, and opportunity for exhibition enjoyed in his former life. The situation became quite intolerable, but to leave meant that he would be treated as a deserter. A hysterical reaction resulted which was prompted by two conflicting motives, the one to conform to the requirements of military life, the other to secure escape from a hated situation. The hysterical reaction consisted of a dissociation of the conscious sensory and motor functions of his lower extremities, and it provided a solution which permitted him to gain his own end of obtaining immunity from unpleasant experiences and tasks, and at the same time enabled him to maintain his self-respect. On arrival at the mental hospital to which he was transferred he could neither walk nor stand, and his legs were anesthetic to even vigorous prickings by a pin. At the same time he displayed a significant attitude of satisfaction with his disabilities although as far as he was consciously aware they were complete and incurable. His lack of concern is to be explained by the fact that the penalty was less than the gain, although one must not conclude that this weighing of advantages and disadvantages was at all a matter of conscious reflection. A few months later the man was discharged from the army on a surgeon's certificate of disability. Soon the suspended motor and sensory functions began to return. Persistent efforts to walk gradually met with success and in another three months he left the hospital practically well.[1]

The record files of clinical psychologists and of psychiatrists are full of cases of which this is typical.[2] On its face this case of the

[1] From Noyes, A. P. *Modern Clinical Psychiatry*. W. B. Saunders Company, 1934. P. 395. Reprinted by permission.
[2] The evidence for much that is to be presented on the following pages is of clinical character. Accordingly the reader will not expect to find the various principles demonstrated by clean-cut

acrobat possesses elements of the bizarre, and, to the man of the street, it is a bit incredible.   But by virtue of this very unusualness and exaggeration of the "normal" it ought to do us some service by throwing into prominence the salient features of the topic before us.

Note first that the man's paralysis and anesthesia had utility for him, that the incapacities furnished a way around his difficulties, a solution.   This is not accident.   In this as in other hysterical cases, the very type of disorder and the particular times of its waxing and waning put it beyond peradventure of a doubt into the class of *an adjustive device.*   Or, as commonly stated, it was *wish fulfilling.*   Considered in the light of Figure 35, *B*, the hysterical disabilities furnished a way of flight out of the psychological field where the repulsion from military routine and that from the ignominy and discipline meted out to him who disobeys, combined to make an intolerable situation.

How explain?   Applying our Figure 7 on p. 35 to the present instance we have Figure 36.   Here the powerful motive to get away from army life ran into the obstacle of another motive not to incur penalties.   The distraught man may have displayed excess

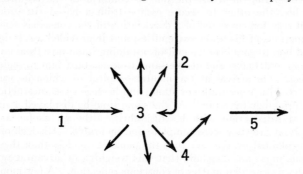

FIGURE 36. A DIAGRAM TO REPRESENT A CONFLICT OF MOTIVES

Compare directly with Figure 7 representing readjustive behavior in general.   Here instead of the motivated organism running into an obstruction in the more literal sense, one of its powerful motives (1) runs into conflict with another motive (2), and a crisis arises (3), in which here again "persistent activity" that is "varied and exploratory" leads perchance to a "solution" (4), that restores "favorable relationship," a "readjustment" (5).   Compare also the three examples on page 32 ff.

laboratory experiments where most extraneous factors are eliminated.   The clinician works with people as he finds them living their lives in the midst of things; and he cannot perform experimental tests on all the insights he gains into his patients' motivations.   On the other hand, the broadness of his purview of observation is advantageous: he can relate and interpret widely scattered incidents and details so as to bring them under common simplifying principles.

activity in the form of worried excitement, and it is certain that he cast about, whether deliberately or not, in search of some graceful escape. At length the sensory and motor paralyses were hit upon; and by this device he was able to detour the barrier and attain the objective toward which he had been so impelled.

We are not to suppose that this solution was concocted deliberately and with clear intent. We dare not accuse him of malingering (intentional feigning). So far as he was aware his illness was genuine and real. From knowledge of other cases, however, we may hypothetically reconstruct the antecedents to this illness. We may suppose that in his unhappy quandary he chanced to see or hear or read about or recall a case of a paralytic. It is possible that he deliberately said to himself, "What a lucky fellow: *he's* not in the army!" And with a nervously unstable person that would be enough: some fine morning he would simply awaken to find himself lame. Doubtless the reader is about to say: "But that is impossible on two accounts. How could a 'thought' work if he wasn't thinking it? And anyhow, how could a 'thought' lame the body?" That, however, is no more mysterious than are those many mechanisms of self-regulation we have noted elsewhere (pp. 36 ff., 99 ff.) which occur on the purely physiological level. The soldier's incapacity is *as if* he had planned it so; but likewise the quick production of sweat which cools the skin when the body temperature is raised a fraction of a degree is *as if* it were intentional and planned.

(Here is as good a place as any for the reader to get clearly in mind the important fact that the motivation of behavior is more fundamental and deep-seated than conscious intent. Purposes and conscious desires are not necessary for the appearance of adaptive behavior, but *out of adaptive behavior* in the developing child as in the evolving animal forms, *gradually and sporadically there appear purposes and conscious desires.*)

We could follow this avenue on out into the major psychoses ("insanities"). We could interpret many kinds and cases as the unhappy fixation of wrong modes of adjustment to personal difficulties: the "flight into reality" of the excited manic, the "withdrawal from reality" of the seclusive schizophrenic, the hopelessly fixated "rationalizing" by the deluded paranoid — these and many other central characteristics of psychotic individuals are solutions once chanced upon and now fatefully set.[1]   However, in a first survey of psychology we are not interested in abnormal people on their own account; and we shall take the other avenue back to the normal, hoping that having seen exaggerations of the mentally ill we can better recognize the motivation-trends of the mentally sound.

Some Methods of Resolving Crises Found in Everyday Life:

(A) By Compensating.   When a person finds a powerful motive thwarted by circumstances, he may hit upon and fixate (without being fully aware of it) a way of making up for this or *compensating* by *over-reacting in some other* (often the very opposite) *line of behavior.*   This is particularly likely to happen if the conflict arises from a persistent attitude of one's own inferiority, for this attitude operates as a barrier to many of the lines of activity he would otherwise follow out.   An infamous Western desperado who had terrorized the population of several states with his deeds of outlawry was at length apprehended; but when he was brought in he proved to be a puny, undersized man with an utterly insignificant bearing, and in the language of an officer, "He was too d—— scared to talk." Now, a psychiatrist who investigated the case learned that the boyhood history of the man had been one of physical inferiority leading to persistent tormenting and teasing by other boys until at last he hit upon the procedure of turning into a "bad man" as a release from the conflict between the motive to be a he-man among men and the social contempt that obstructed it.

The writer knew the case of a college student who, having been partially incapacitated from a childhood illness of infantile paralysis, was known for his recklessly fast driving, and had a history of accidents terminated only by one in which he and two other students met their death, speeding over a hill and around a curve.   There is Bagby's case of the student whose enormous ears made him the object of looks and comments wherever he went.   He cast about for a solution of the problem: (*a*) he tried wearing his hair long, only to find another similar problem then on his hands; (*b*) he tried picking his associates only from those who were sympathetic, but he continued to run the gauntlet of uncomplimentary looks from strangers; finally (*c*) happening once to hear strains of distant music unheard by others the inspiration came to him that the very size

---

[1] Some psychoses have a purely organic basis in structural changes in the nervous system, and hence are not "psychogenic" as are those mentioned.

of his ears gave him an acute sense for small tonal differences. Thereupon he took up the serious study of music and actually became an excellent teacher of singing. Thus he was readjusted [1].

Adler, who is responsible for the notion of "inferiority complex" leading to overcompensation, attributed the attitude mainly to the realization of physical inferiorities; but others have broadened this causal basis. For illustration, a basic and ineradicable timidity is surprisingly often the true psychological *daemon* at work in the person who is boisterous, in the woman who is haughty and apparently so "self-conceited," in the man who speaks much and often in his declamatory fashion, especially in public assemblies. And everyone knows that many a bully is at heart a coward. At the same time, it is truly surprising that so few people prepare themselves to find in the man of unctuous flattery or the woman of saccharine gushiness a fundamental core of meanness, petulance, and pugnacity.

Let us hasten to be reminded that compensatory behavior does not necessarily lead to deceptive or to socially maladjustive conduct. Consider the above case of the man with enlarged ears. Consider the case of the Greek orator Demosthenes and his pebbles, and that of the strenuous Theodore Roosevelt, who had been a physical weakling. The Great War gave opportunities for many a disgraced pariah, many a hopelessly unsuccessful business aspirant, and many another who was "down on his luck" to work out his personal salvation by offsetting all that when throwing his baffled energies into a stupendous task "for home, for country, and for God." [1] All this is clearer if we bear in mind that "methods of substitute satisfaction," as they are often called, are primarily psychological phenomena: it is only incidentally that they become objects of ethical judging.

(B) **Resolving Crises by Rationalizing.** Often a frustrated motive gets release when its possessor happens to find a way of verbally describing it in such manner as to weaken the antagonism, or, less abstractly, when he (often unawares) concocts plausible though false reasons for his attitudes or actions. He is "rationalizing," or, in colloquial language, he is "fooling himself with his alibis." The behavior is certainly very common. The business world knows many a Babbitt who talks endlessly of Service. If the train conductor overlooks a passenger's ticket, the man does not call the

---

[1] See also the third case given on p. 32 above.

conductor's attention to it; and the conflict between this particular expression of his money-saving tendencies and his more highly socialized tendencies to honorable dealing is weakened by such remarks as "This railroad is making too much money, anyhow," or, "I don't wish to embarrass the conductor." In international relations the pronunciamentos put forth to justify the action adopted by prince or premier are all too often couched in language tending to weaken opposition between the aims that are behind the actual procedures set up and the aims maintained by intelligent citizens, as, for example, establishing a "protectorate," "making the world safe for democracy," carrying the "white man's burden," "protecting" three thousand nationals with an intervention army of twenty thousand. A father goes to the circus "to take the boy"; a girl eats all the candy without sharing it with her younger brother because "it isn't good for him"; a boy fails in his arithmetic and grammar because "he has a poor teacher in those subjects"; a man drinks liquor because "one can't refuse a friend under such circumstances." It is too cynical to say, as has been said, that all systems of philosophy "are nothing more than unconscious apologies for our faults — a gigantic scaffolding to hide the philosophers' own sins," but certain it is that the resolving of conflicts between antagonistic desires or ideals all too often takes this form of deceiving one's self by a rephrasing of the true motive-causes at work. Polonius's admonition, "To thine own self be true," is more often disregarded than observed:

Rationalizing, as we have described it, is nothing at which to be surprised. For one thing, strict logic, thoroughly rational reasoning, is exceptional in human life. Man is often styled the "rational animal"; but, like the references to Lincoln or Washington as the typical American, the phrase reveals an ideal more than an actual fact. And note that, even so, man is called an animal. From the broad biological viewpoint intellectual processes, the capacities of thinking have gradually evolved or emerged as forms of behavior that have utility for the organism employing them. They supplement his cruder brute force ways of responding to this thing and that more effectively than would sharper claws or more powerful arms, and serve him as instruments of unlimited power. Desires have not arisen out of intellect, but intellect out of desires. Of this much more in the later chapters of our book. But here let it be realized that thinking is a way of adjusting, that it is motivated; and we can expect to find the operations of "pure thought" directed by very human motives, conscious and unconscious.

Some modes of adjusting to situations in which one's dominant motive is frustrated, though called by other names are really forms of rationalizing. There is *projecting*, the process in which one attributes to other people the very motive which is influencing him but which for social reasons he disowns. A psychoanalyst has recently asserted that the warlike attitudes so world-wide today are in part a result of the constant imputing to the other fellow and hence the other nation that very belligerency one actually would find working within himself did he but look closely and critically enough. The egotistical child finds other children about him so egotistical that he can scarcely bear with them. The coward likes to assume cowardice in others; hence he is a potential bully. What has been heartlessly called "old maid's insanity" — but is not always limited to women — is that familiar delusion that every second person of the other sex who happens to look at one is ready to fall in love. And rare indeed is the motorist so fair in judgment that in case of collision he is not readier to blame his brakes or the other driver than himself. So common is this penchant for projecting one's own weakness into other people that there is much truth in the remark that whenever you encounter a surprisingly intense prejudice concerning some human shortcoming you can look first for that shortcoming or a related one in the prejudiced person himself. The fool hath said in his heart, "all men are liars": then we should be on our guard against his own dishonesty.

There is the *sour grapes* device by which the unattainable objectives turn into undesirable ones and thus change their motive power, so that the crisis ends. Riches are only a source of evil, and it is the poor who are the blessed. The jilted lover now sees a hundred failings in his erstwhile sweetheart. Doubtless here is one root of the popular error that is to be mentioned in several places in this book — the opinion that he who is superior in one regard must be inferior in another: that the student of high scholarship in one line must surely be poor in others or at least be poor in athletics or campus politics; that the infant prodigy is certain to be physically unfit; that the beautiful are dumb. Even the most profound attitudes of humankind may be dictated by this mode of thinking. Instead of meeting the difficulties that life presents, the Buddhist, the Stoic, the Mohammedan dervish, and the ascetic Christian flee the field of contest and take refuge in revilings of the flesh and contemplations either of utter Nothingness in Nirvana or of bliss that is to be distinctly unearthly.

(C) **Resolving Crises by Daydreaming.** The last point leads us to another major way of meeting the frustrations of one dominant urge by another. As we are to see later, the function of imaginary representation is one of incalculable importance to the human being who must anticipate the morrow; and the fertility of his capacity so to imagine is an important determiner of the effectiveness of his thinking. The unimaginative person is the humdrum bore who can contribute nothing to general discourse nor save himself from the treadmill of routine. But what concerns us here especially is that imagining furnishes an avenue on which one temporarily escapes the literalness of the day's drab events. It is here that not only religion but fiction, poetry, and the drama have much of their *raison d'être*. They afford temporary surcease and refreshment from the actualities of life, and so have a function that, even from the narrowest bread-and-butter practical considerations, is wholesome and valuable.

A danger lurks, however. If one would only return from his moments in the clouds refreshed and strengthened for tackling the problems actually at hand, or if he would bring down with him a new project or an inspiration to be tried, the adjustive value of it all would be immense and indisputable. But many a day-dream has been used only as an escape-mechanism, the air castles as a city of refuge from the responsibilities of everyday life. The evils of *phantasy-forming*, as it is called, are recognized by all clinicians, and for them has great significance in two types of cases especially. In one it is a symptom of a fixed habit of withdrawing into oneself before all unpleasantness, all thwartings of one's interests, a habit that grows to such proportions that its possessor comes to spend most of his day in the non-real, and even comes to lose appreciation for the difference between non-real and real. That way madness lies — madness in which the victim becomes more and more inaccessible to others. Another type of phantasy viewed with concern by the clinical expert is that in which "dangers bring fears and fears more dangers bring"; for out of the social baffling of this or that primary urge may grow a mounting dread and suspicion of everyone. That way, too, madness lies — a madness in which delusions may steel their possessor to violent deeds against others or oneself.

(D) **Resolving Crises by Repressing.** In many of the everyday illustrations given on the preceding pages as well as in more severe cases like that of the hysteric, the reader will have noticed that the true motive at work in the person is one of which he is not clearly or not at all aware. It has undergone a certain type of forgetting. Yet it has not been rendered wholly ineffective but continues to energize and to direct conduct and thinking, as we have seen. It is repressed. Sometimes this repressing goes to pathological limits, as the following two cases will show.

A man suffered from a phobia [uncontrollable fear] of being grasped from behind, the disturbance appearing early in childhood and persisting to his fifty-fifth year. When walking on the street he was under a compulsion to look back over his shoulder at intervals to see if he was closely followed. In social gatherings he arranged to have his chair against the wall. It was impossible for him to enter crowded places or to attend the theater. . . . He could give absolutely no explanation of the origin of his fear. In his fifty-fifth year he returned to the town in which he had spent his childhood. After inspecting his old home, he went to the corner grocery and found that his old boyhood friend was still behind the counter. He introduced himself and they began to reminisce. Finally the grocer said this, "I want to tell you something that occurred when you were a boy. You used to go by this store on errands, and when you passed you often took a handful of peanuts from the stand in front. One day I saw you coming and hid behind a barrel. Just as you put your hand in the pile of peanuts, I jumped out and grabbed you from behind. You screamed and fell fainting on the sidewalk." The episode was remembered and the phobia, after a period of readjustment, disappeared [1].

In the famous "bell tower" case of Prince's, a woman had a phobia for towers and church steeples, especially those in which bells might ring. She was utterly unable to explain it. But while she was in a condition of hypnosis (a condition resembling sleep in which the subject is highly suggestible and sometimes shows unusual recall) some memories of an incident in her childhood were brought out. In her abstracted state she wrote: "G—— M—— church and my father, took my mother to Bi—— where she died, and we went to Br—— and they cut my mother. I prayed and cried all the time that she would live, and the church bells were always ringing and I hated them." She wept during this writing. After becoming fully awake she was able to reconstruct a substantial part of the story, under guiding questions from the examiner. Her mother had once undergone a major surgical operation, the outcome of which was fatal; and the overly conscientious daughter who feared she had not given her every care in the nursing was meanwhile in a protracted agony of mixed grief and remorse —— "and the church bells were always ringing." Now, this later recall of the full story did not at first

shake the phobia. It persisted until Prince had finally succeeded in per-
suading the woman that her childhood attentions to her mother had actually
been most devoted and that the fatal outcome was due to a sequence of
causes quite out of her control.

In both cases the traumatic (injury-producing) experience was
one not only intensely emotional but also involving some sense of
guilt, that is, some *dread* of it based upon early socialized behavior.

In the last remark is found the key to the clinician's interpretation
of pathological repression. It is "protective forgetting," or, more
broadly, it is a form of adjustive response to an object of fear —
not now in the physical surroundings but in the self-condemning
attitude. It is avoided by being forgotten. The phobias in the
two cases just presented simply represent the patients' avoidance
of those stimuli that might occasion recall of the original episodes,
with their dreaded attitude of self-condemnation. The very operation of the phobias eloquently testifies to the continued functioning in some fashion of the repressed experiences. They were "forgotten" yet remained as motivating factors in behavior.

How is this possible? Two well-established psychological principles are involved.

(1) Much as a person withdraws from a painful physical stimulus,
so also he can in some instances "withdraw" from a painful memory,
that is, he can actively *forget* it. The process is probably some form
of *inhibition*, that is, a sidetracking of one function by another —
as when a dog that is scratching himself with his right hind leg,
upon receiving a pain stimulus at the left foot stops scratching to
use the right foot for standing while the left is sharply retracted,
or as when a child about to reach for a piece of forbidden cake is
restrained by voice or sight or memory of the forbidding adult.

(2) If a process is inhibited from overt expression or even if it is
kept from the subject's awareness, the process is not thereby necessarily rendered inert. Many phases of human psychology present
illustrations of this general truth. A person is unaware of just how
he performs this and that act of skill and indeed may be quite
unable to perform it if he pays attention to the processes involved.
Most people are unaware of the motives urging them toward their
dominant interests. Most striking of all is the fact that, as we shall
see later on, productive thinking processes can go on while a person
is attending to something quite different, or while he is actually
sleeping. Like these and other phenomena, then, a repressed or

actively forgotten motive may continue to be active and responsive to organic or to environmental stimuli.[1] And consequently, the crisis still exists.[2]

A Word of Caution. These and other ways of finding substitute avenues of satisfaction furnish to the skilled clinician helpful concepts in unraveling the difficulties of his patients and uncovering motivation sources of which the patients themselves are hardly or not at all aware. But they have also caught the imagination of the non-technically trained public; and not only in the recent wave of debunking biographies but also in the everyday conversations about everyday third parties it has become a sort of "highbrow" gossiping. It is an "indoor sport" that is pleasant and easy and at the same time has about it a flavor of subtlety and profundity. But it is dangerous if too carelessly tried. The chances of unfair personal judgments are great indeed, and this not simply because of lack of training but also because interpreting everybody else's behavior in terms of methods of substitute satisfaction may itself become a mode of substitute satisfaction.

Perhaps, after all, the principal profit from the foregoing survey lies not in our learning the specific devices resorted to by people in resolving crises. The real value is more likely to be gained through developing a wholesome respect for the complexity of motives at work in anyone of higher mental complexity than the moron. Whether introspectively or objectively sought out, the reasons for a man's conduct are difficult to analyze.

Assimilating the Source of Frustration. In our brief survey of some outstanding methods that people chance upon to secure indirect satisfaction for their thwarted motives, we have found that in very many cases these methods are used in inadvisable ways: The satisfactions secured are temporary or illusory or half-way. Or the readjustments may cause further complications in one's relationships toward other people. Paths of indirection are so often insecure and treacherous. A general formula for the maintenance of a balanced perspective on self and world, for the preserva-

---

[1] In the strict psychoanalytic usage this is the meaning of a "complex," that is, an emotional attitude which though repressed still influences thought and action.

[2] Let the reader be warned against a certain manner of misrepresenting these facts of unconscious functioning: they do not point to the working of a Subconscious Mind, nor even of a Subconscious or the Unconscious. Such notions are (a) needless. Moreover they are (b) burdensome, for, far from explaining anything, they themselves need explanation. Often, in fact, they are used as (c) a last refuge of ignorance. Historically they (d) hark back to the pre-scientific mode of thought in which human actions are explained by the operations of daemons residing within.

tion of robust mental health, might be phrased informally as follows:

Meet and recognize your difficulties as they arise. Face the music; do not dodge or run away. Like a fully rational adult human being do not regress to childish or "small" ways of acting; do not simply grow emotional, but looking the problems fully in the face apply intelligence and rational analysis to the whole matter. As in any other of life's emergencies, "don't be a big baby, but use your head." This is often not so easy as it sounds; and one may need to consult with a psychological adviser. But his or her aid would be directed to helping you to do just this; the aid would not solve the problem for you. You must save your own soul.

> Therein the patient
> Must minister to himself.

This attitude will help one to *assimilate* the difficulty. The term has one root in sociology. It is illustrated by the process of Americanization of an immigrant, a process in which the foreign individual goes through a certain amount of conflict until he learns how to get along with others and comes to adopt their attitudes. The same thing happens with the fraternity or lodge initiate, the religious neophyte, the newly hired member of a construction gang or steamship crew. By analogy, we may speak of a material or social situation that blocks one's motivated behavior as being a foreign element that needs assimilation into his personal systems of attitudes and habits. Unless thoroughly thought through and made consistent with his other dominant motives, it will be like the grain of sand within the oyster's shell, a source of irritation and disturbance to the whole organism.

EXCESSIVE EMOTIONALITY

Importance of "Controlling" Emotional Excitement. It will already have struck the reader perhaps that when people in crises fall back upon various inadequate devices of substitute satisfaction (such as we have reviewed), they frequently display enormous emotional tension; and aside from its ending their bafflement, an adequate solution of their problems means a reduction of this tension. The importance of excessive emotional conditions deserves a few words on its own account.

Crile has roughly likened the effect of emotion upon the body mechanism to that produced on an automobile mechanism when its engine is kept running at high speed while the vehicle stands stationary. It is a matter of common observation that while emotional excitement of sthenic types, such as rage, fear, love, joy, tends to re-enforce the activity of striped muscles, it is at the expense of some disrupting of the more delicate integrations: "it will lend wings to one's feet and power to his arm, but it will impair his judgment and thinking." (A convincing laboratory demonstration of this general point is to be reported later, on pp. 378 ff.) Stage fright is an excellent illustration here. The conduct of a man in a lynching mob, or of a woman in a bargain-counter crush, or of a child in a fire panic, serve as further examples. Every boxer knows this principle in his own way: learning not to get angry at any cost is as important as skill in blocking and jabbing and punching, for once he grows enraged, the skillful co-ordinations trained into him break down, and he fights not wisely but too well and leaves fatally unprotected his most vulnerable spots.

> When anger rushes, unrestrain'd, to action,
> Like a hot steed, it stumbles on its way:
> The man of thought strikes deepest, and strikes safest.

For much the same reason, love is proverbially held to be blind; a scientific seeking of fact for fact's sake must be divorced from personal prejudices; a court must tolerate no excitement on the part of the audience that might be communicated to the jurors. "He that is slow to anger is better than the mighty; and he that ruleth his spirit than he that taketh a city." [1]

To counteract the tendency to emotional tension the recipe is, in formulation at least, simple. Visceral reactions are like other reactions; if they are not to be aroused, either the *stimulus* (situation) must be *removed or its character altered*, or *another stimulus* must be provided to *set up a different activity* to divert the individual's energies. A well-controlled case of altering the stimulus is to be reported on pp. 177 ff. in which the negative fear-arousing character of a rabbit stimulus became changed to a positive play-arousing character, by the judicious employment of a positive food-eating response.

Work has been called a savior of the soul; and certainly many everyday observations prove the aptness of the phrase. Any occu-

---

[1] This contrast between the emotional aspects of behavior and the intellectual aspects which can exert controlling influences thereover, has received a physiological interpretation that goes far to support the claims and the exhortations of Buddha and Confucius and all the moralists of history. The control of the emotions by the intellect is the control of hypothalamic-centered visceral activities by cerebral inhibitory influence. (See pp. 170 ff., 276 f.)

pation that provides a series of stimuli that arouse appropriate activity by the worker, particularly if the activity called for be absorbing, will serve to relieve his tensions by setting up a different (antagonistic) activity. A man of the writer's acquaintance developed pronounced emotional reaction, amounting almost to despair, upon the death of his mother; but he was at the time faced by the task of finishing a piece of research leading to the master's degree — toward which he had organized a powerful attitude — and the urgency of that work-demand sufficed to keep him on his problem enough hours of the day to weaken in some degree the intensity of the grief. But the work motive need not be of the highly sentimental (emotional) sort: the oft-repeated duties of a daily job, when they have acquired habit-arousing potency, will serve to direct some of the individual's total activity, and to that degree will save him from emotional excesses. In order that the work may be effective in this strain-reducing function, it must either (a) elicit much interested (motivated) attention or (b) provide for vigorous grosser behavior. The former we have illustrated; the latter is shown in many familiar devices. The solicitations of recurring sex drives and the attendant emotions are partly overcome by a strenuous participation in athletics; a mounting rage is "worked off" satisfactorily at the wood pile; whereas a fear that is prevented from taking the overt form of a use of fists or heels becomes all the more intense as a visceral disturbance. It is because of this that release through performing one's occupation is often valuable.

An Extreme Case of Emotional Disruption. The fear type of visceral excitement (which includes "worry" and "anxiety") is one of the most disrupting. We have had two illustrations in which the "worry" was based on some self-accusatory attitude (pp. 151 f.). Let us conclude this section with one in which the latter was apparently not present, but which forms in some ways the most impressive case in all psychological literature.

We come back to the common story of a young girl twenty years old, called Irene, whom despair, caused by her mother's death, has made ill. We must remember that this woman's death has been very moving and dramatic. The poor woman, who had reached the last stage of consumption, lived alone with her daughter in a poor garret. Death came slowly, with suffocation, blood-vomiting and all its frightful procession of symptoms. The girl struggled hopelessly against the impossible. She watched her mother during sixty nights, working at her sewing-machine to earn a few pennies necessary to sustain their lives. After the mother's death she tried to revive the corpse, to call the breath back again; then as she put the limbs upright, the body fell to the floor and it took infinite exertion to lift it again into the bed. You may picture to yourself all that frightful scene. Some time after the funeral, curious and impressive symptoms began. . . .

The crises last for hours, and they show an elaborate dramatic performance, for no actress could rehearse those lugubrious scenes with such perfection. The young girl has the singular habit of acting again all the events that took place at her mother's death, without forgetting the least detail. Sometimes she only speaks, relating all that happened with great volubility, putting questions and answers in turn, or asking questions only, and seeming to listen for the answer; sometimes she only sees the sight, looking with frightened face and staring on the various scenes, and acting according to what she sees. At other times, she combines all hallucinations, words, and acts, and seems to play a very singular drama. When, in her drama, death has taken place, she carries on the same idea, and makes everything ready for her own suicide. She discusses it aloud, seems to speak with her mother, to receive advice from her; she fancies she will try to be run over by a locomotive. That detail is also a recollection of a real event of her life. She fancies she is on the way, stretches herself out on the floor of the room, waiting for death, with mingled dread and impatience. She poses, and wears on her face expressions really worthy of admiration, which remain fixed during several minutes. The train arrives before her staring eyes, she utters a terrible shriek, and falls back motionless, as if she were dead. She soon gets up and begins acting over again one of the preceding scenes. . . .

Let us watch her during the intervals of her fits, during the period in which she seems to be normal; we shall soon notice that even at that time she is different from what she was before. Her relatives, when she was conveyed to the hospital, said to us: "She has grown callous and insensible, she has soon forgotten her mother's death, and does not seem to remember her illness." That remark seems amazing; it is, however, true that this young girl is unable to tell us what brought about her illness, for the good reason that she has quite forgotten the dramatic event that happened three months ago. "I know very well that my mother must be dead," she says, "since I have been told so several times, since I see her no more, and since I am in mourning; but I really feel astonished at it. When did she die? What did she die from? Was I not by her to take care of her? There is something I do not understand. Why, loving her as I did, do I not feel more sorrow for her death? I can't grieve; I feel as if her absence were nothing to me, as if she were traveling, and would soon come back." The same thing happens if you put to her questions about any of the events that happened during those three months before her mother's death. If you ask her about the illness, the mishaps, the nightly staying up, anxieties about money, the quarrels with her drunken father — all these things have quite vanished from her mind.[1]

[1] From Janet, P. *The Major Symptoms of Hysteria.* The Macmillan Co., 1907. By permission of the publishers.

MORALE

The Supreme Importance of Morale. It can fairly be said that
the problem of problems in the motivating of human beings is in
the establishing and maintaining of their morale. It is, as Hall
called it, the supreme standard of life and conduct [3]. It may not
be easily analyzed, yet nothing is more conspicuous by its presence
or by its lack. In great competitive fields where masses of men
must move with both energy and skill it comes to the forefront of
recognized necessities. Every athletic coach knows what it means.
It is that which every year or so brings about amazing upsets in
which a group of men, beaten perhaps in every previous game
of the season, gird their loins and in the desperateness of "everything to gain, nothing to lose" overtake and overthrow their
much-touted bitter rivals. Every business or industrial administrator knows what it means; for without it a demoralized force or
company of men shows impairment of individual efficiency and loss
of inter-individual co-ordination. A worker will not give to his
work all his energies, nor will he work steadfastly and persistently,
nor will he give his job that extra unpaid-for personal interest and
thought. The product then suffers in quality not less than in
quantity. The term "morale" has not been precisely defined;
though everyone knows in a way when the term is appropriately
applied. We can, nevertheless, posit certain marks by which the
person of high morale is distinguished from the demoralized one.
His activity shows a *greater amount* of energy expenditure in *more
tenacious* ways, that are *constructive* and *concerted*. And the activity is supported by an *emotional* condition of sthenic, or *re-
enforcing*, type (variously named "zest," "élan," "hope," "confidence").

Factors in Morale as Illustrated in Army Organization. The
building up and maintaining of morale in an army was recognized
as a problem of capital importance by both antagonists in the
Great War. Foch is said to have written: "Ninety thousand
conquered men retire before ninety thousand conquering men
only because they have had enough, because they no longer believe
in victory, because they are demoralized — at the end of their
moral resistance"; and Napoleon before him had said: "In war, the
morale is to the physical as three is to one." As Colonel Munson
points out: "The stirring painting, 'The Spirit of '76' depicts no

material strength or physical power, but expresses the mental harmony, conviction, and determination which brought success to the Colonial Army."

The methods and agencies for developing military morale in the recent war were many and complicated; but running through them all was a recognition of certain factors that cause proper motivation in the soldier. (1) For one thing the maintenance of the individual's *physical health* was, of course, important not only to keep him able-bodied but also to keep him emotionally fit, for most illness and disease tends to the asthenic, weakening, rather than the sthenic visceral activities. The medical and sanitary corps of the American army were concerned not only with the wounded and sick, but with the prevention of sickness and of its effect upon fighting spirit.

(2) A second principle, never so well recognized before, is that "Thrice armed is he who hath his quarrel just." The individual recruit must "see something in it," must "have conviction in the justice of his cause," must *"idealize* it," must be given some special incentive — all of which amounts in more technical language to the fundamental truth that one's action will be enormously reenforced in intensity and in persistence if it is aroused by some well-organized attitude. Let him identify another human being, at whom he is instructed to fire or charge, as "an enemy of my country" or "the slayer of my pal," and he will proceed with real avidity. (It must be admitted that this substitution of one response for another by the device of rephrasing the stimulus is by no means easy, as was evidenced by the fraternizing between enemy private soldiers in the American Civil War, the Great War, and no doubt in all conflicts between people who have some identity of cultural and racial ideals.) Religious activities in the army, as well as propaganda furthered by the government among both the civil population and the military, served this end of adding special incentives in the form of what is called idealizing.

(3) A *confidence* in one's cause, assurance that it will, or at least can, ultimately prevail is another essential to morale. "Nothing succeeds like success," and a fighting spirit is fed by victories, even though they be insignificant victories. In the Great War certain attacks by the French upon Chemin des Dames and Mort Homme were prepared with utmost care to ensure successes in order to improve the soldiers' morale; and an offensive launched against a

prominent German salient on the Marne was undertaken not so much for the ground that was to be regained as in the expectation of some sort of victory that would check the fear and depression spreading among the troops.   The change of fortunes in the last year of the great conflict was in part a matter of change in confidence in the outcome; for, once one side could see no prospect whatever of success, the war was over.   Both line officers and propaganda agencies were concerned with the development of confidence.

(4) Finally, the importance of *recreation* was brought to the forefront.   Athletic games, vaudeville and picture shows, mass singing, were deliberately provided and encouraged by military authorities. Army recreation officers were appointed from without and within the personnel of line officers.   Ever since the time of Aristotle it has been a problem to know how to explain in technical terms just why recreational and relaxational activities cause heightened morale in the day's heavy occupations, and today we have a choice of theories; but the fact is incontestable, and in some dim fashion it is put into operation universally.

Morale in Other Applied Lines.   We can see the same principles of morale building in education in the intelligent handling of school children.   Medical inspection and treatment have convincingly shown the effect upon the pupil's work of dental decay, adenoids, and malnutrition (1).   Moral, patriotic, and religious instruction and discussions of future occupations and the responsibilities of citizenship are much resorted to (2).   And this is done not simply to build into the child the socially approved patterns of attitudes and emotional habits, but also to "fire" him by directing his reading, writing, and arithmetic toward objectives for which he can easily form emotional attachments.   The effect of special incentives, because they operate both to motivate the child's learning and to help develop the attitude of confidence in his school work (3), has long been a part of pedagogical doctrine and practical procedure. In a later chapter we shall see experimental verification of a few of these special incentives.   Recreational activities have been specially encouraged; playground supervision, for example, is being undertaken as a part of school routine (4).

Consider how the industrial world today has become aware not only of the problems of machines and materials but also of the problems of men.   Special personnel offices and programs are the order of the day; and to keep the worker effectively motivated is a primary desire. The maintenance of his health is sought through the provision of rigidly sanitary buildings and working conditions, and prompt medical aid (1). The emotionally deadening effect of the repetitious work in modern machine industry have been offset in different ways: prizes are awarded for valuable suggestions as to improvement in the conduct of the business; a "work change bureau" sees to the transfer of workmen from one kind of job to another as soon as the monotony of the first begins to affect their emotional attitude; changes are made in the jobs themselves so that the individuals are left some liberty in planning or directing them (2). In keeping with this is the encouragement of confidence in an employee's own work by offering him bonuses for improved output, and by promoting capable men so that some of the blindness is taken out of blind-alley jobs (3). Finally, welfare work with its reading rooms, gymnasiums, and athletic grounds, and the shortening of the working day, have combined to motivate the worker by obtaining for him outside recreations (4).

If principles such as these are effective for the other person, they should be applicable as well to oneself. When the student, the business or professional man, or the housekeeper, finds himself "going stale," losing that eager readiness to prosecute a task effectively, let him look to several possible factors. Let him look to his health: insufficient sleep or a deranged digestive system often put surprisingly heavy drags upon one's effectiveness (1). Let him inquire into the nature of the work itself: has he lost his perspective upon it so that his "wagon" is no longer "hitched to a star"; that is to say, so that the work is no longer capable of arousing those attitudes built up about some more distant objective (2)? Or is the trouble to be found in his own emotional conditions at the time: some fear or worry that tends to inhibit rather than to re-enforce the desired activity? He should remember the famous golf champion who ascribed some of his success to the fact that he always played each shot by itself: any previous error or slip was in the dead past and was not allowed to excite unfavorable visceral disturbances now (3). Finally, we all know that not least important for the person who has lost the proper zest for his work is the query as to whether he has maintained a proper balance between it and his recreations and hobbies. "All work and no play makes Jack a dull boy"; and wise is the person who has learned by experience just how to proportion the two most effectively in his own particular case (4).

A point of detail that the reader will find helpful is the following. When one's interest in and zeal for a work task is low, but the work is such as will clearly demand attentiveness and interest, he will be wise to begin by way of some related easy routine work that will occupy him for a while; for once in the routine, his interests in the whole business will gradually assert themselves. Any activity is interesting and absorbing once you really get into it.

More Knowledge of Emotions Needed. In the preceding chapter and especially in the present one we have been making abundant references to the emotional phases of a man's behavior, particularly as they affect the adequacy of his general conduct toward other people and toward the turns in his own individual fortunes. But we must dig deeper. We must obtain a more precise knowledge of what emotional behavior is, and, so far as possible, return to the laboratory for experimentally verifiable facts. For a topic of such richness and complexity nothing but a special chapter would be adequate.

REFERENCES

1. Bagby, E. *The Psychology of Personality.* Holt, 1928.
2. Groves, E. R., and Blanchard, P. *Introduction to Mental Hygiene.* Holt, 1930.
3. Hall, G. S. *Morale.* Appleton, 1920.
4. Lewin, K. *A Dynamic Theory of Personality.* McGraw-Hill, 1935.
5. Morgan, J. J. B. *The Psychology of Abnormal People.* Longmans, 1928.
6. Noyes, A. P. *Modern Clinical Psychiatry.* Saunders, 1934.
7. Pavlov, I. P. *Lectures on Conditioned Reflexes.* International Publishers, 1928.
8. Pressey, L. C. *Some College Students and Their Problems.* Ohio State Univ. Press, 1929.
9. Shaffer, L. F. *The Psychology of Adjustment.* Houghton Mifflin, 1936.
10. Wallin, J. E. W. *Personality Maladjustments and Mental Hygiene.* McGraw-Hill, 1935.

CHAPTER VII

EMOTION

THE GENERAL NATURE OF EMOTION

A Preliminary Description. The term "emotion" is derived from the Latin *emovere*, which means "to shake," "to stir up"; and through all the literature of the emotions, technical and popular, this note is frequently sounded. Yet a moment's reflection will assure us that the term is also used to refer to the very opposite of being shaken or stirred up. Observe a person at the end of a perfect day when peace and contentment rule; or think of the substantial satisfaction of one who contemplates his labor well begun, or the serenity of demeanor of him who anticipates a hereafter with the blessed saints, or the smiles and pats and gentle movements of the adult watching the antics of a child. Both the stirring up and the quieting down, then, are meant by our word "emotion."

These alterations not only in the patterning of a person's reactions toward people and things about him but also in their vigor and their smoothness are to be traced, as we have seen in the preceding chapter,[1] not so much to the stimulating circumstances in an immediately direct way, but to diffuse conditions of the organism, conditions that are themselves often reactions to the external stimuli.

What is the essential nature of those phases of a person's life we call "emotional"? It may now be formulated. *The changes of diffuse internal conditions in his organism (through external or internal stimuli) act indirectly (neurally) or directly (chemically) upon his organs of overt response. As a result his behavior toward things and people is strengthened and accelerated or is weakened and retarded. He is typically aware of these internal conditions, and may report them verbally as feelings of "pleasantness," "happiness," "anger," "reproach," and so on.*

To give this complicated- and abstract-looking statement more concreteness, we may use Figure 37. Suppose an external stimulus (a burglar, a comic actor, or an insulting gesture) arouses afferent neural impulses (as indicated by heavy line) which, upon being

---

[1] In this connection the student should not fail to reread pp. 113 ff., and consult Figure 30.

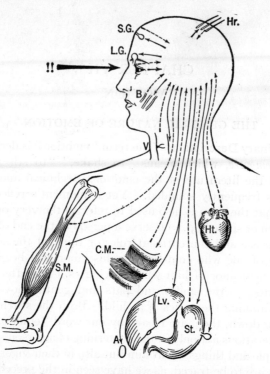

FIGURE 37. SOME OF THE REACTIONS IN EMOTIONAL BEHAVIOR

(Explanation in the text.)   Heavy continuous lines, the original stimulation.   Light continuous lines, the efferent pathways to the various organs.   Broken lines, the afferent pathways
leading from the various organs back into the central nervous system.   *Omitted*, lines to indicate efferent pathways by which the inpouring impulses from the various organs pass out again,
especially to striped muscles at work in the overt activities toward environmental objects.
(From Dashiell, J. F., *Psychol. Rev.*, 1925, **32**.)

conveyed to the central nervous system (not shown), pass out by
efferent neural pathways (continuous lines) to many different effectors.   Motor changes (excitatory or inhibitory) are then produced —
in the lachrymal glands, *LG*, resulting perhaps in tears; in the sweat
glands, *SG*, producing the "cold sweat" or the wet brow; in the
position of the hair, *Hr*, when one "bristles up" (this is associated
with "gooseflesh"); in the arterial blood vessels, *B*, producing the
blanching or the flushing of the skin, as well as grosser changes in
general blood supply; in the striped muscles of overt activity, *SM*,
showing as strained and accelerated, or as depressed and sluggish,
movement; in the heart muscle, *Ht*, producing faster or slower pulse,

and (along with B) heightened or reduced blood pressure; in smooth muscles and glands of the stomach and intestines, St, furthering or arresting digestion; in certain ductless glands, as the adrenal bodies, A, and the liver, Lv, their secretions altering the contents of the blood stream and so affecting other organs and the overt activity of the striped muscles; in the striped muscles of the chest, CM, with accelerated or retarded, shallower or more profound, breathing; in the striped muscles of the larynx, V, producing screaming or other cries.   All these and many more motor reactions go to make up the picture of behavior we call emotional.

Two important aspects of emotion remain to be added to this figure.   (1) The afferent impulses traveling the broken-line pathways do not, of course, stop in the central nervous system but pass through it and out to skeletal muscles especially.[1]   The burglar is run from or is attacked; the comedian is laughed at; the insulter is thrashed.

(2) Also it seems that what the individual experiences as his emotional "rage," "fear," or "joy," is based upon these afferent currents from the viscera, just as his experiencing of things seen or smelled or heard is based upon afferent currents over optic, olfactory, or auditory nerves.   (Cf. Chapter IX.)   A person's emotional feelings obviously could not be represented on such a diagram.[2]

So far our description has been couched in generalities.   To give more definiteness to it all, let us turn to experimental work on lower animals in which some clean-cut and precise results have been obtained.

Stomach Changes in Emotion.   A child of the writer's, when some two and a half years old, faced his first Santa Claus with trembling lip and widened eyes, but answered the latter's questions and showed him to the fireplace.   When asked later if he had been frightened, the child answered, "No, I wasn't scared, but my stomach was scared!"   That the digestive organs play their part in much emotional behavior has been recognized from ancient times by old and young.   Let us note some experimental proofs.

---

[1] The reader need not be confused by the lines that run to and from the skeletal muscles. The fact is that the skeletal muscles (a) play a part in the original emotional response, and (b) are also subject to re-enforcement and inhibition in consequence of that response.

[2] It would be a valuable exercise for the student to bethink himself of different kinds of emotion-arousing situations; then, for each situation, to try to determine precisely how each organ would participate in the emotional response that would be aroused.   He could get data by noting what other people do, as well as how his own organs seem to operate as he can consciously sense them. Finally, he could trace the effect of the emotional changes upon the overt behavior toward the situation.

The activity of the gastric glands of animals under different conditions has been studied by means of the surgical technique of tying off a part of the stomach wall to form a side pouch with an opening at the surface of the body, and so allowing direct measurement of the secretions. In one investigation upon the dog, a cat was brought into the room, whereupon the former flew into a great fury. After the cat was withdrawn and the dog had apparently been pacified, it was given its usual feeding for five minutes, but the stomach's glandular secretion was found strikingly reduced from a normal 67 cc. to only 9 cc. The same phenomenon occurred in a small boy who on account of a blocked oesophagus was fed by a tube direct to the stomach: whenever he had grown angry, the food that was given a little later aroused no flow of the glandular secretions.

The activity of the gastric muscles has been observed by the use of a different technique. A cat is fed bismuth (opaque to X-rays) mixed with its food, and X-rays are sent through the abdomen and projected upon a fluoroscopic screen. The normal movement of the stomach in digestion is then observable as a slow succession of peristaltic waves. Now in this experiment some cats were found to grow restive and excited when first fastened into their holders, and when having the nose and mouth held. On such occasions the stomach contractions were seen in the fluoroscope to be totally arrested — sometimes for more than an hour.

Secretion of Adrenin in Emotion. One of the most detailed studies of an integral part of emotional reaction is Cannon's series of researches on the activity of the adrenal glands [7]. (For these glands see pp. 217 f. below.) First let us look at some circumstantial evidence. After the final and most exciting football game of the 1913 season, twenty-five members of the Harvard squad were given urinalysis. Twelve players showed the condition of glycosuria, that is, the abnormal presence of sugar in the urine, due to an excessive amount (0.2 to 0.3 per cent) in the blood forcing some of it past the barrier set up by the kidneys. That this was not the result of muscular activity on the gridiron was indicated by the fact that five of these twelve men had been substitutes sitting on the bench throughout the contest, and also by the fact that tests made upon an excited spectator revealed marked glycosuria just after the game but none on the following day. College examinations have played their part, too, as stimuli to the excess production of sugar in the blood: of 34 medical students tested, 1 showed glycosuria just before an examination, and 7 showed it just after; of 36 students at a woman's college who showed no glycosuria before an examination, 6 showed the symptom immediately after.

Now, glycosuria is in part an indirect effect of excess adrenal secretion into the blood; and as such it is one detail in one of the most interesting stories illustrating the place of certain types of emotion in the regulative functions of the human organism.

When a cat is stimulated by the furious barking of a dog, by the bindings of a laboratory animal-holder, or by an induction shock, excited behavior that is called *fear*, *rage*, or *pain* is manifested. As a part of this behavior the adrenal glands are excited to increased secretion of their peculiar hormone, adrenin, and the effects of this hormone are widespread. (A) When carried to the liver, adrenin excites the latter to release some of its store of sugar into the blood, which is then distributed widely, especially to the striped muscles. Now since sugar is a form of energy that is readily available for muscle tissue an excess supply in circulation aids the processes of muscular activity and of muscular repair. (B) But the effect of adrenin is also more direct: it counteracts fatigue in the muscle tissue, and it does this much more quickly than does resting. (C) Adrenin acts upon smooth musculature of the digestive apparatus and of different segments of the circulatory system to effect a shift of the bulk of the blood away from the abdominal viscera and into the brain, lungs, heart, and the active striped muscles. (D) Associated with this shift of blood volume is a constriction of the small arteries. This fact, taken with the one next following, accounts for the heightened blood pressure that forms a part of strong emotional reactions. (E) Adrenin acts directly upon the heart to augment its beat both in rate and in amplitude; and upon the musculature of the bronchioles it produces relaxation and so a dilating of those air passages. (F) Finally, the adrenal secretion affects the blood itself in such a way as to hasten its coagulation upon exposure.

How can these various secondary effects of the reaction of the adrenals in emotional behavior be given a consistent interpretation in terms of our descriptions in earlier chapters of an-animal-adjusting-to-its-environment? Cannon has offered us an interpretation. Those conditions that excite in an organism rage or fear or the pain reaction or fleeing or fighting are emergencies. To meet them adequately the organism is called upon for expenditure of power and for endurance far beyond its usual capacities. It must go on a war footing. The excitation of all these changes by the sight or sound, smell or touch of the dangerous agency may be looked upon, then, as an elaborate re-enforcing reaction, preparing for, facilitating, maintaining the vigorous overt activity of the struggling animal or man. If the reader will glance again over details *A–E*, their significance and value to the attacking or fleeing animal or caveman will become apparent enough. Such re-enforced activity is seen also in the most civilized and refined man. He may as a child have learned habits of inhibitory control of his natural outbursts of clawing and biting, screaming and dodging and running. But the more implicit reactions are there.

A point of clinical interest is worth mentioning here. It is well known that "nervous indigestion" appears in people who are inclined to much worrying; and if we remember that worrying is a variety of fearing its causal relation to the digestive disturbance should be obvious.

Emotion as Experience. It is safe to say that the first and primary reason for interest in the emotional characteristics of behavior is that they mean so much in the modification of what the other fellow or what oneself does or is going to do. When the boss is "mad" the office force must appear quiet and industrious; when the opponent is "rattled" the moment for supreme concerted attack is at hand; if one's sweetheart is sullen it is no occasion for levity and carelessness; and any three-year-old knows the immense practical importance to himself of adults' impatient moods or their merriment. Indeed the most important lesson of life is learning how to make allowance for the emotionally modified actions of other people. And of oneself. Who has not been astonished at his own conduct when, in that so-accurate phrase, he is beside himself? Who has not been chagrined at his own timidity or fear that paralyzes practical execution and public performance?

At the same time there is no denying the fact that the study of emotions springs also from popular interest in how they "feel." Long before one has reached the stage of appreciating music intellectually as an art-form he welcomes the agreeable thrills it awakens in him. Poetry is above all a language of emotional experience, and one reads it with an interest in "tasting" the moods and nuances of feeling intended by the poet. Practical life recognizes the desirability of increasing the number of occasions that will set up certain emotional experiences and reducing those that set up others.   In the case of certain neurasthenics, esthetes, *bons vivants*, and indeed in certain classic philosophies of living, these emotional expressions become morbidly overemphasized.

Where, then, do these experiences that the emotional person can report come into our story?   A hint has been given on preceding pages, but only a hint; and as serious students of psychology we must take notice of a controversial matter that for many years now has had the psychological world by the ears.

The James-Lange Theory and its Critics.   In the 1880's James, the American psychologist, and Lange, a Danish physician, almost simultaneously formulated anew a conception of how one's awareness of emotion is related to his emotional organic changes.   As James phrased it: "*The bodily changes follow directly the perception of the exciting fact, and our feeling of the same changes as they occur IS the emotion*"; or, as we might rephrase it: The exciting stimulus reflexly arouses bodily changes, and the sensory experiencing of these changes due to returning afferent impulses furnishes the emotional tone to the whole experience.

Almost any reader will be inclined to arise and challenge this. He will say: "But our everyday observation is that we first feel the anger or dread or love, and *then* after that have the bodily changes. That is why these changes, especially those visible in face and gesture and voice, are called 'expressions' of the emotion-as-felt." On the other hand, not all popular thought has been as represented. Consider such expressions as "bowels of compassion," "men of his kidney," the still less elegant "man of guts."   There is the answer to the question whether life is worth living that says that "it depends upon the liver."   Or even "absinthe makes the heart grow fonder" is an example of this type.   In any case, untrained observations furnish no final evidence; and they are exceedingly untrustworthy here, for whether the experienced feeling or the organic changes come first is a matter of a split second,[1] too short an interval for reliably noting which is horse and which is cart.   Moreover, when trained introspectionists analyze just what it is they are aware of when emotional they find they have sensory experiences with origins indubitably in organic or visceral receptors together with

---

[1] Motion pictures of the "startle" response to the sound of a pistol shot have shown that the whole response-pattern may come and go completely in less than a half-second [13].

others (kinesthetic) originating in contracted muscles.   An example
or two will make this clear.

"I received a telephone call and was told of my election to Phi Beta Kappa.
"My mind seemed to be a 'blank,' that is, there seemed to be no ideas
present, at least at first.   Then there were kinesthetic and organic sensations
in head as blood seemed to rush to head.   I was hot all over and hands were
moist — great emotion of joy.   Organic sensations in chest, breathed fast,
then it seemed as though I must say something to somebody.   Want to
'burst' with such an emotion of joy and as always, I couldn't keep it to myself.   Head became cooler and I tried to reason with myself in terms of
snatchy verbal ideas to see that I must calm down a little.   Left my hair-
dresser and felt so good that I wanted to run.   Exhilaration and still also joy."
After a vigorous scolding another subject reported:
"Feeling of warmth arises in entire body.   Biting of lips; rapid beating
of heart; quivering in 'pit of stomach.'   The warmth sensations give prickly
feeling in face.   Then quivering in arms.   I dug nails into palms of hands.
Breathing came faster.   Perspiration felt in palms of hand and under knees;
also soles of feet were moist.   Face twitched as blood came up.   So angry
that I was ready to hit E." [1]

Attacks upon the James-Lange theory still continue, however.   Cannon
opposes it on clinical and experimental grounds [6].   For one example he
cites Dana's case of the woman who, having sustained a broken neck, lost
completely all sensations in her skin and all deep sensitivity from the neck
down, yet continued to show emotions of grief, joy, displeasure, and affection, with no change in her personality or character.   He also cites Mara-
ñon's reports of subjects who had received injections of adrenin.   From
our discussion a page or two above we would expect that excessive amounts
of this hormone in the blood would, by bringing about certain visceral
changes, be the occasion for the experiencing of excited emotions.   Some subjects did indeed have full-fledged emotional experiences; but many reported
feeling only as if they were "going to have" such experiences, and some said
they had none.   (It must be borne in mind, however, that this secretion is
not claimed to be the only condition of emotion, so that the last-named evidence is not decisive.)
To follow Cannon's theory we would have to modify our Figure 37 by
locating the central neural connections more explicitly in the hypothalamus
and the cerebral cortex (which are both to be described in Chapter X).   Figure 38 puts this in a nutshell.   It will be noted that the afferent currents supplied to the cerebrum, and responsible for the emotional feeling, are represented as arising not in the bodily organs but in the hypothalamus.   This
is the heart of the opposition to the James-Lange view.

In regard to this controversy there is this much to be said.
Whether the James-Lange theory be ultimately established, or
modified, or rejected lock, stock, and barrel, is from our point of

---

[1] From Ruckmick, C. A.   *The Psychology of Feeling and Emotion.*   McGraw-Hill, 1936.

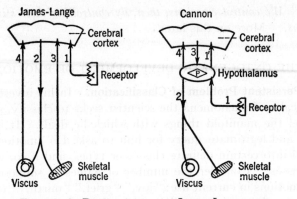

FIGURE 38. DIAGRAMS OF THE JAMES-LANGE AND
THE HYPOTHALAMIC THEORIES

The connecting lines represent neural pathways, with arrowheads to indicate directions of propagation. *P* signifies the existence of a patterning of neural connections not drawn in with lines.

According to the James-Lange theory: When an emotion-arousing object stimulates the external receptor, the afferent impulses propagated to the cerebral cortex on 1 set up there efferent impulses which pass on 2 to the visceral and skeletal organs of response; changes there excite afferent impulses back to the cerebrum on 3 and 4, determining the emotional experience [and further overt behavior].

According to Cannon's version of the hypothalamic theory: The afferent impulses from the original stimulation at the external receptor are propagated on 1 to the hypothalamus; there they are relayed over 1' to the cerebrum; but they also arouse in the hypothalamus a co-ordinated pattern of impulses that include (*a*) sensory ones ascending over 4 to the cortex, there determining the emotional experience, and (*b*) motor ones descending over 2 to the visceral and skeletal organs of response; these patterned responses being subject to inhibitory control by impulses descending to the hypothalamus from the cortex on 3.

(From Cannon, W. B., *Psychol. Rev.*, 1931, **38.**)

view an academic and almost purely a technical question. On any practical view there are two points about emotion that are far more significant. One is that, as hinted in Figure 38, *3*, the cerebrum exercises inhibitory control over the hypothalamus, so that the *effects of experience* that operate through the former *have much to do with the controlling of emotional outbursts*. This point on the behavior side has already been emphasized in the preceding chapter; on the physiological side it will be mentioned again in Chapter X. A second point is that in any case emotional experiences, just like emotional organic changes, are set up *as a consequence of stimulation*. An appropriate exciting stimulus must be provided to instate them. One does not kindle a process of raging or sorrowing or rejoicing or being jealous except by first placing before oneself — actually or imaginatively or in words — something that is likely to arouse that process. *We control emotions, then, by controlling their stimulating conditions.* More on this later.

THE ONTOGENETIC DEVELOPMENT OF EMOTION

The Persistent Problem of Classification. In his investigations of any realm of phenomena the scientist seeks to classify, sort out, and label the manifold things with which he deals. It is an inevitable and legitimate query for him to ask: Do emotional reactions fall into certain definite classes or types, and if so, what are these classes? Consider the number of names of supposedly different emotions in current use: "joy," "grief," "mirth," "ecstasy," "restiveness," "exuberance," "wonder," "fear," "disgust," "detestation," "timidity," "shame," "awe," "tenderness," "coyness," "love," "lust," "jealousy," "pride," "exultation," "remorse," "dread," "anxiety" — and on and on through a list of interminable length. For centuries thinkers have been describing and comparing the behavior supposedly referred to by such names, and much ingenuity was shown in matching them, to discover differences and identities. In fact, the multiplication of such classificatory descriptions led James to exclaim that he "should as lief read verbal descriptions of the shapes of the rocks on a New Hampshire farm as toil through them again." Emotions have been divided into the "strong" and the "weak," the "pleasant" and the "unpleasant," those "slowly arising" and those "suddenly arising," "egoistic" and "altruistic," the "sensuous" and the "intellectual," "subjective" and "objective," "sthenic" and "esthenic." By other writers they have been divided into large genera with their several species and varieties, for example, the "defensive" genus, including fear, disgust, timidity, awe, shame; the "social" group of affection, cordiality, pity, gratitude, admiration, scorn, suspicion, revenge; the "aggressive" genus of envy, anger, hatred, exultation, pride. There seem to be as many different groupings as there are writers who have attempted the classificatory task.

The genetic avenue of approach to this question seems to offer promise; and without more ado we turn to the history of the development of emotion. The issues that present themselves are essentially those raised in Chapter IV, and the theoretical possibilities much the same.

Some Changes Observed. First for some observational data.

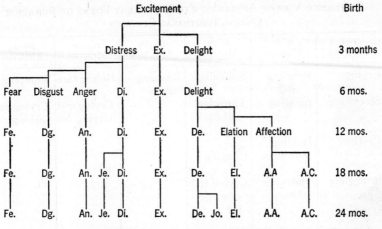

FIGURE 39. APPROXIMATE AGES AT WHICH VARIOUS EMOTIONS BECOME
DIFFERENTIATED IN THE FIRST TWO YEARS

Je, jealousy; *Jo*, joy; *A.A.*, affection for adults; *A.C.*, affection for children.   (From Bridges,
K. M. B., *Child Development*, 1932.)

Bridges [5], in the course of observations on over sixty infants daily
through three or four months, found that in the newborn there is
probably only one kind of emotion, a general and undifferentiated
agitation or "excitement." In the early days of infancy "distressed" and "delighted excitement" become differentiated from
general "excitement." Then distress becomes differentiated into
the "angry," the "disgusted," the "fearful," and other simple
types of emotion; from "delight" the specific forms of "elation" and
"affection" split off. Note the differentiations, and the age dates
thereof, suggested in Figure 39. In another Canadian laboratory
observations were recorded at less frequent intervals over a longer
period. The table shows the results described more concretely in
terms of what the babies did at successive age periods rather than
what emotion-names seemed to apply.

These studies set the problem for us neatly. No one would deny
that in the development of the individual an increasing specialization and refinement of emotions is what occurs, and that the adult
shows emotions of which the baby is surely not capable. But is it,
as the first-mentioned observer concluded, that "emotional behavior
and development are very much determined by particular events
and experiences and the routine of living," or is the emphasis to be

DIFFERENT AGES OF APPEARANCE OF DIFFERENT FORMS OF BEHAVIOR DURING EMOTIONAL EPISODES [1]

1-4 Months	4-8 Months	8-12 Months	12-16 Months	16-20 Months	20-24 Months
Crying	Refusing and resisting	Stiffening	Running away	Hiding face	Slumping
Screaming		Throwing self back		Crying and saying No	Crying and asking
Restless	Holding out arms	Clinging			
Struggling	Throwing things	Crying and attempting			
Starting	Crying and Calling				

[1] From Blatz, W. E., and Millichamp, D. A. *The Development of Emotion in the Infant*, p. 19. Univ. Toronto Press, 1935.

placed more, as the latter observers say, on the fact that "the genetic sequence of the forms of behavior follows a definite pattern, and follows the genetic sequence of developing motor and mental capacity"? That is to say, is the important factor experience or maturation?

Are There Emotional Patterns in Advance of Learning? There have been those who have asserted that the chaotic and purely general character of emotion processes in the newborn is complete. Their claims are based on observations incidental to some experiments that have been mentioned in previous chapters (pp. 82 ff., 116 ff.), also [22], when the experimenters themselves or their picked judges were unable to sort and label the different infantile kicks, clutchings, grunts, mouth twitchings, and the like into consistent classes with emotion names. Whatever finally be the answer on this particular point about the newborn there is striking evidence that within the first year of life differentiating and patterning go on apace.

In one interesting research college students were shown some photographs of the emotional reactions of a ten-months-old baby; and they were instructed in each case to judge which out of several possible situations was the one that had evoked the reaction. On the average, the photographs and the situations were correctly matched in 47 per cent of the judgments, nearly 6 times the percentage to be expected by chance. Now, since the subject of the photographs was only ten months old it seemed doubtful that the reaction-patterns could have been picked up in any important degree from other people; and it was concluded that however greatly an adult's emotional expressions may be inhibited, modified, and feigned for social reasons, there is nevertheless a core of native reaction-patterns that appear too early to be explained by training or experience [11].

Still more interesting evidence that the visible patterns in emotional behavior are unlearned has been furnished by the same investigator when she noted and photographed the behavior of a child totally deaf and blind from birth. For instance, when the child after much struggling had managed to free a doll that was tangled in her dress, she threw herself back in her chair, raising both hands in an attitude of apparent delight or triumph, and gave forth peals of laughter. Then the doll was clasped caressingly in both hands and the laughter quieted into a smile as of pleased satisfaction. In her other reactions, too, the child showed striking fidelity to the classic descriptions of emotional behavior [10].

Emotions are Subject to Training. There is the other side to the biographical story. If mental development be considered a fabric for which the innate endowments and intrinsic maturing furnish the warp, then habit-forming through social experience contributes the woof. Watson's epoch-making conditioning experiment is the measure of all others here [23].

A child eleven months of age was selected for the subject in conditioning the fear response. The child had been reared almost from birth in a hospital environment and showed no fear reaction to such stimuli as a white rat, a rabbit, a dog, a monkey, masks, cotton wool, burning papers. Practically everything was reached for when brought near to him. The fear pattern of behavior was, however, excitable by the sound of a steel bar struck sharply just behind him. For the procedure and results let us follow the experimenters' notes.

Eleven months, three days. 1. White rat suddenly taken from the basket and presented to Albert. He began to reach for rat with left hand. Just as his hand touched the animal the bar was struck immediately behind his head. The infant jumped violently and fell forward, burying his face in the mattress. He did not cry, however. 2. Just as the right hand touched the rat, the bar was again struck. Again the infant jumped violently, fell forward, and began to whimper. In order not to disturb the child too seriously no further tests were given for one week.

Eleven months, ten days. 1. Rat presented suddenly without sound. There was steady fixation but no tendency at first to reach for it. The rat was then placed nearer, whereupon tentative reaching movements began with the right hand. When the rat nosed the infant's left hand, the hand was immediately withdrawn. He started to reach for the head of the animal with the forefinger of the left hand, but withdrew it suddenly before contact. It is thus seen that the two joint stimulations given the previous week were not without effect. He was tested with his blocks immediately afterward to see if they shared in the process of conditioning. He began immediately to pick them up, dropping them, pounding them, and so on. In the remainder of the tests the blocks were given frequently to quiet him and to test his general emotional state. They were always removed from sight when the process of conditioning was under way. 2. Joint stimulation with rat and sound. Started, then fell over immediately to right side. No crying. 3. Joint stimulation. Fell to right side and rested upon hands, with head turned away from rat. No crying. 4. Joint stimulation. Same reaction. 5. Rat suddenly presented alone. Puckered face, whimpered and withdrew body sharply to the left. 6. Joint stimulation. Fell over immediately to right side and began to whimper. 7. Joint stimulation. Started violently and cried, but did not fall over. 8. Rat alone. *The instant the rat was shown the baby began to cry. Almost instantly he turned sharply to the left, fell over on left side, raised himself on all fours, and began to crawl away so rapidly that he was caught with difficulty before reaching the edge of the table.*

The attachment of the fearing response to the white-rat stimulus operated, moreover, as an attachment to several other objects that formerly did not operate as stimuli to this response. A rabbit, a dog, a sealskin coat, cotton wool, a hairy mask, were all reacted to violently. A lack of specificity of the $S \longrightarrow R$ relation was thus demonstrated, the R excited by a certain specific S being also excitable by many other S's having certain visual stimulus qualities in common with it.

Finally, it is important to note that the conditioned reaction persisted over a full month's interval, although in not quite its original intensity.

Many Fears are Acquired. One corollary from the above experiments has extremely practical bearings. If a child is afraid that "the goblins'll git" him, that is evidence enough that a misguided parent or ignorant nursemaid, thoughtless teacher or bullying brother, has been trying to control him by deliberately attaching his fear response to such words as those, as well as to darkness, to the attic, to the big policeman, to the old black man, and has then been calling up such stimuli to cow him into submission when obedience was not promptly forthcoming. It may be well to develop in the boy or girl caution in crossing a busy street or with reference to contagious diseases or any of the many conditions and situations of life in which danger actually lurks; but the cultivating of such attachments to essentially harmless and even nonexistent things is indefensible. As a matter merely of physical hygiene it is to be remembered that fear, like rage or any other emergency type of emotion, is antagonistic to the healthy body-developing processes of the organism. And when the reactions become so violent as to turn into "tantrums," grave consequences may be entailed to the poise and nervous equilibrium and even to the sanity of the man or woman in the making. Of this, however, more is to be said later.

Retraining an Emotional Response. If, then, a child's fears may be a serious and even a dangerous factor in his development, psychology, after having shown definitely how fears can be built up, bears the obligation of showing how they can be eliminated. Mrs. M. C. Jones made experimental attacks upon this problem by trying out several different procedures, as follows. (1) Mere disuse — will the fear die out? (2) Verbal appeal — will talking about the thing cure the fear? (3) Negative adaptation — will he get used to it? (4) Repression — will ridicule help? (5) Distraction — will diverting the attention reduce the fear tendency? (6) Reconditioning — will associating the feared object with some much-liked thing help? (7) Social imitation — will the sight of others handling the object with no fear reduce one's own? Her subjects were chosen from the inmates of a children's institution where they were so carefully attended that no emotional stimuli of the sorts in question would be encountered. Those were chosen who manifested, however, emotional responses developed prior to entry into the institution.

Only the last two of the methods were found effective. A child with fear attachments to white rats, rabbits, furs, feathers, frogs, fish, and mechanical toys, was used as one of the subjects. A rabbit was selected as the stimulus from which the fear response was to be detached, and a positive, playful attitude (generally during feeding) was selected for the response that it was hoped could be attached. The child was seated in a high chair and given food which he liked. The experimenter brought the rabbit in a wire cage as close as possible without exciting a negative reaction. Gradually, in trial after trial the animal was brought closer until finally the fear was

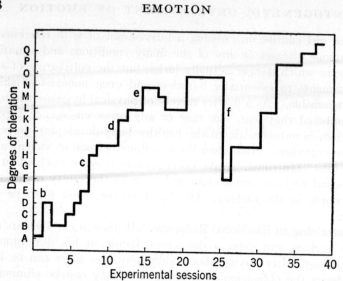

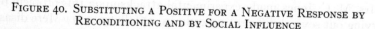

FIGURE 40. SUBSTITUTING A POSITIVE FOR A NEGATIVE RESPONSE BY
RECONDITIONING AND BY SOCIAL INFLUENCE

(The degrees of toleration are not equal units, nor are the experimental sessions equally spaced in time.) At *b* and *e* positive responses were facilitated by the presence of another child who played with the rabbit; at *c* and *d*, by the presence of an admired adult. At *f* the child had received a slight scratch while carrying the animal to its cage. (Jones, M. C., *Ped. Sem.*, 1924, **31**.)

The degrees of toleration represented on the Y axis follow:

A. Rabbit in cage anywhere in room excites fear.
B.   "   "   " 12 feet away is tolerated.
C.   "   "   " 4 "   "   "   "
D.   "   "   " 3 "   "   "   "
E.   "   "   " close by is tolerated.
F.   "   free in room   "   "
G.   "   held by experimenter is touched.
H.   "   free in room is touched.
I.   "   defied by spitting at, throwing at, by imitating it.
J.   "   allowed on tray of high chair.
K. Boy squats in defenseless position beside rabbit.
L. Helps experimenter carry rabbit to cage.
M. Holds rabbit on lap.
N. Stays alone in room with rabbit.
O. Allows rabbit in play pen with him.
P. Fondles rabbit affectionately.
Q. Lets rabbit nibble his fingers.

eliminated: to the rabbit stimulus the positive reaction became conditioned. The change is graphed in Figure 40.

As Mrs. Jones says, this method requires delicate and judicious handling. Two sensori-motor connections are being dealt with:

$S_{food} \rightarrow R_{positive}$ and $S_{rabbit} \rightarrow R_{negative}$; and it is easy to see that an incautious and precipitate experimenter might, instead of forming the new connection $S_{rabbit} \rightarrow R_{positive}$, actually form the undesirable one, $S_{food} \rightarrow R_{negative}$. It was necessary not to bring the rabbit too near at first.

The effectiveness of social factors is also illustrated in the figure. The handling of the feared objects by others or the mere presence of others in whom one has confidence had reassuring effects.

A survey of methods used by parents has brought out the efficacy of also helping the child to develop ways of dealing with feared objects, as playing games incidentally involving the dark room or closet, learning how to work a dreaded mechanical dog, and like forms of assimilation [15].

Concluding View. Everybody speaks of "fear," "rage," "disgust," "love," and "sorrow," as if he were referring to distinct patterns of emotional behavior. What is the justification? Are there such natural, biological emotions? What is the ontogenetic evidence? Despite the fact that the emotional phases in the infant, like the rest of his behavior, are notoriously unorganized and confusing to observe, the weight of the evidence supports the assumption that there is some *intrinsic predisposition to react emotionally in more and more differentiated ways*, ways that appear by a process of maturation. At the same time, the *experiences* of the human being, *especially with other people, exercise important directing and redirecting effects* upon his "emoting," so that things, persons, and situations acquire, lose, or change their emotion-arousing values.

So much for the longitudinal view. The problem of emotional specificity is to be attacked also from a cross-sectional viewpoint. In adults, that is to say, can we find characteristic combinations of organic changes that make up emotional pattern-reactions specific for the different emotions of "anger," "fear," "grief," and so on? For example: when a person is "angry" is his digestion always retarded, his breathing more rapid and deeper, his fingers clenched, his pulse accelerated, and so on for the rest of a whole detailed picture? When he is "fearful" is his digestion always retarded, his breathing more rapid but shallower, his fingers loose, his pulse slowed, and so on? Is the visceral picture an invariable one and a distinct one for each emotion? It goes without saying that unaided eye-observation will not suffice: most of the organs participating are hidden away inside a person and their workings must be brought to the surface by special apparatus.

METHODS OF INVESTIGATING EMOTIONS

Instrumental Techniques

Historical. Descriptive analysis of "what an emotion feels like" and just how and how much one "feels different" from another has been an indoor recreation of philosophers for centuries. We have paid our respects to this procedure indirectly as it bore on the question of classification. The only substantial outcome of this unaided introspective approach seems to be the almost universal acceptance of a continuous range of variation in all conscious experiences, which extend in all degrees from extreme *pleasantness* to extreme *unpleasantness*, called their *affective tone*. As the reader is perusing this page, his awareness of page and print and the topic and problem being discussed is tinged — we hope — with a mild pleasantness or agreeableness such as one ordinarily experiences when interested in an intellectual topic; and as he follows the argument to a definite conclusion or as he comes upon an interesting figure or concrete illustration, the pleasantness is somewhat intensified. On the other hand, in case the argument offers tough sledding and is otherwise "dry," he may feel a tinge of unpleasantness or disagreeableness. Obviously, an unexpected grade of "A," and an equally unexpected grade of "F," are likely to arouse in him complex kinds of awareness colored with more intense pleasantness and unpleasantness respectively.

Introspection, however, has not gone unaided; and a great volume of experimental work employing laboratory instrumentation has been devoted to discovering just what bodily changes are correlated with this scale of affective tone. The two great organic systems most studied in this connection are the respiratory and the circulatory. From a great array of researches that have appeared since about 1900 it will suffice us to select a few leading ones and summarize them in the accompanying table. Detailed inspection of the table certainly brings to light one fact: Experimentation has failed to establish any stable or consistent differences between those respiratory and circulatory changes that are occurring in a person when he is feeling "pleasant" and those that are occurring when he is feeling "unpleasant." How interpret this? Undoubtedly there are false assumptions in regard both to the stimuli and to the responses in lumping together in this manner researches conducted by different men with different ultimate objectives. What these

METHODS OF INVESTIGATING EMOTIONS 181

CHANGES INVOLVED IN EMOTIONAL CONDITIONS DIVIDED INTO THE "PLEASANT" (DENOTED BY P) AND THE "UNPLEASANT" (U) [1]

	RESPIRATION		CIRCULATION		
	Rate	Depth	Pulse Rate	Blood Pressure	Blood Volume
Mosso...............					P−
Lehmann..............			P− U+	P+ U−	P+ U−
Binet................	P+ U+	P+ U+	P+ U+		P− U−
Külpe................			U−		
Gent................			P± U+	P+ U−	P+ U−
Zoneff and Meumann...	P+ U−	P− U+	P− U+		
Angell and Thompson...	No consistent changes.		No consistent changes.		P− U−
Shepard..............			P− U−	P− U−	P− U−
Stevens..............	P− U−		P− U−		
Eng.................	P+ U−	P− U+	P− U+	P+ U−	P+ U−

[1] From Dashiell, J. F. *Psychol. Rev.*, 1928, **35**, 323, with additions.

false assumptions are will appear incidentally as we go further into the matter; but our table will serve as a premonitory warning not to expect unequivocal results too quickly nor with unstandardized technique. It can fairly be said that the experimental study of emotion is the most baffling and tricky that the psychological laboratory knows.

Skeletal, Respiratory, and Circulatory Changes.

> Some strange commotion
> Is in his brain: he bites his lip, and starts;
> Stops on a sudden, looks upon the ground,
> Then lays his finger on his temple; straight
> Springs out into fast gait; then stops again,
> Strikes his breast hard; and anon he casts
> His eye against the moon: in most strange postures
> We have seen him set himself.

We have been emphasizing the point of view that the significance of emotional changes lies, in the very first place, in the ways they modify overt behavior, that is to say, the functioning of the **skeletal musculature.** Changes in tonicity or *tension* and in *steadiness* have been studied by instrumentation to be described elsewhere (pp. 323–27, 569 ff.) in a variety of psychological settings. For more specifically emotional studies, a rubber bulb or a receiving tambour [1] is placed under the subject's fingers of one or both hands, so that any changes of finger-pressure or of steadiness are communicated through tubing to a recording tambour and inscribed upon a drum.

There is the story of the Austrian card shark who boasted that he was able to tell by watching an opponent whether or not he was bluffing. He watched the opponent's breathing. And everyday speech is full of "sighs of relief," startled catchings of breath, and the like. Changes in the functioning of the **respiratory system** appear as alterations of **rate** of breathing and alterations of depth or **amplitude.** These are usually recorded graphically on a kymograph drum by tambour connection with some form of *pneumograph.* A simple type is the Sumner, shown in Figure 41. The presence of emotional excitement during attempts to deceive has been brought out ingeniously in laboratory experiments in which the subject was instructed to answer questions either truthfully or falsely as he chose [2]. The recorded breathing curves were analyzed and the relative durations of inspirations and expirations expressed by the ratio I/E, as follows.

> True: I/E before answering > I/E after answering
> False: I/E before answering < I/E after answering.

Another card-player story is that of an expert who was able to hide his feelings from all opponents save one who had noticed that a blood vessel in his forehead was always slightly enlarged when he was under the strain of bluffing. Erisistratus, of the third or fourth century B.C., asked to diagnose the illness of the King's son, upon observing an acceleration of his heart beat whenever a certain beautiful maiden entered the room promptly diagnosed the complaint as that of love. In fact, the very word "heart" is used less often in its literal than in its metaphorical sense as an organ of emotion. Involvements of the circulatory system in emotion are betrayed in at least four ways, for each of which a type of apparatus has been devised. The **pulse rate** is recorded with a *sphygmograph* (sphygmo = pulse), which in its most common forms is an arrangement of a receiving tambour which fits snugly over the artery at the wrist or at the neck. Changes in pressure on the rubber by the pulse

---

[1] Tambours, manometer, and time marker are described in connection with Figure 23, p. 103. The descriptions should be read again at this point, as these instruments will be referred to frequently.

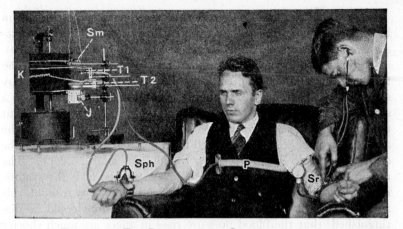

FIGURE 41. THE PNEUMOGRAPH, SPHYGMOGRAPH, AND
SPHYGMOMANOMETER, WITH RECORDING DEVICES

The model of *pneumograph* here shown (Sumner), *P*, consists of a coiled spring in a sealed rubber tube strapped snugly about the chest. Movements of inspiration and expiration stretch and relax the tube, drawing or driving the air in the small tube that connects with a recording tambour. The recording *tambour*, *T2*, is a metal chamber covered with a rubber diaphragm, across which lies a free-moving pointer. Air on entering the chamber pushes the diaphragm and pointer upward and on leaving draws them downward (inscribing the third line). The model of *sphygmograph* shown (Mackenzie), *Sph*, is a cone-shaped tambour, the rubber diaphragm of which is fitted closely over an artery, so that beats there are pneumatically conveyed through a tube to a second recording tambour, *T1* (inscribing the second line). The pointers of the recording tambours bear against smoked paper mounted upon the revolving drum of a *kymograph*, *K*, operated by clock work. Simultaneous tracings are made by a *signal marker, SM*, operating electrically to indicate points when a stimulus is given (top line), and by a *time marker* (Jacquet model shown), *J*, indicating seconds (bottom line). The model of *sphygmomanometer* shown (Tycos), *Sr*, is a silk-covered rubber bag wrapped about the upper arm and inflated by a bulb (held in examiner's left hand). The air pressure is registered on a dial slung in front and connected to the bag by a tube.

beat are transmitted to a recording tambour which inscribes them on the drum as waves. One is shown in the figure.

> Thou tremblest; and the whiteness in thy cheek
> Is apter than thy tongue to tell thy errand.

The distribution of the blood to different parts of the body is well-known to be subject to alterations in emotional stress. The volume of blood being sent into a particular member of the body, such as arm, hand, or finger, is registered by a *plethysmograph* (plethysmo= enlargement), which is a liquid-filled chamber enclosing the member in question and connected also with a recording tambour. This instrument will also bring out the pulse. See Figure 42.

More important than either of the preceding are the changes in **blood pressure** level. These are revealed through the *sphygmo-manometer* (sphygmo + manometer, see p. 103). This instrument, in common use in medical examinations, consists of a rubber bag that is bound about the upper arm and inflated, and is connected by air tubing to a mercury manometer with a millimeter scale, or to a spring and dial. When by inflation of the bag the pressure about the arm is sufficient to overcome the blood pressure within the artery, the pulse will be prevented from passing, which point can be determined by feeling the pulse or by applying a stethoscope. The reading on the manometer or dial taken at this point is the systolic blood pressure. It has been claimed [20] that by use of this apparatus the anger, the fear, and the sex emotions could be distinguished: that the blood pressure rises in anger are much shorter and more abrupt than those in fear, though they do not reach so high a level; and that with sex emotion there is a distinct drop. This needs confirmation by others.

To get records of the **heart contractions** in a more direct way one would use a *cardiograph*. An older form was little more than a sphygmograph placed on the chest just over the heart. The more modern form is an electrical setup that employs the string galvanometer, an instrument that registers extremely delicate electrical changes. The poles of the electric circuit are placed at points on the surface of the body selected so that currents operating between them will pass through the body near the heart, and, since muscular activity is accompanied by electrical changes,[1] will be affected by the heart-muscle contractions. This form of cardiograph was used as part of an investigation into the effects on a person when he was suddenly and unexpectedly dropped backward in a falling chair (which was caught by a door check) [3]. In all the subjects there was (*a*) an immediate and abrupt speeding up of the heart, followed by a retardation. There was (*b*) an immediate increase in the force of the heart's contraction which lasted several minutes. There was also (*c*) a marked disturbance of the rhythm with which the heart normally beats. Meanwhile, we might add, there were characteristic changes in breathing as shown by a pneumograph.

The Galvanic Skin Response. Over forty years ago it was noticed that if two points on the human skin are connected with a sensitive galvanometer, a deflection of the latter will reveal the passage of an

---

[1] See below pp. 205 ff.

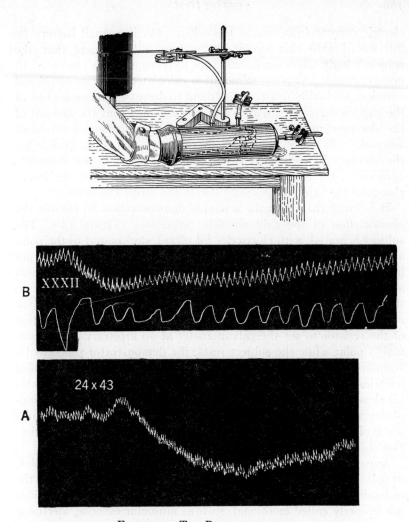

FIGURE 42. THE PLETHYSMOGRAPH

Above is shown in operation a plethysmograph for hand and forearm. The water which, with the hand and arm, fills the metal cylinder, also fills rubber tube and tambour. Increase or decrease in volume of the hand and forearm resulting from vasodilatation or vasoconstriction drives the water toward or draws it from the tambour, and so works the recording lever up or down.

Below, *A*, a plethysmographic tracing obtained from a subject just before and just after being assigned a problem in subvocal arithmetic. The great drop in general level is the result of vasoconstriction in the member; the rhythmic fluctuations are due to respiratory changes; and the very abrupt rises and falls indicate heart beats. (From Howell, *Text-Book of Physiology*, Saunders, 1936.) *B*, plethysmographic and pneumographic tracings from a subject just before and during the time he was thinking of a friend's illness. (From Angell and Thompson, *Psychol. Rev.*, 1899, **6**.)

electric current from one to the other.   Or, if a small battery be
introduced into this circuit, deflections will indicate that the
subject's body offers some resistance to passage of the current.   If,
now, the subject is given stimulation calculated to excite emotional
reaction, his bodily resistance is found to decrease: the excursions of
the galvanometer are greater, and it is assumed that the amount of
the decrease measures the amount of the emotional excitement
aroused.   (As to the precise bodily process which is responsible for
the changes in resistance to the current, there is not complete
agreement, though most authorities have located it in the sweat
glands of the skin and possibly also in the striped muscles.)

It is quite easy to make a simple demonstration to exhibit the
phenomenon of the galvanic skin response.   (Figure 43.)   The
subject is seated, with electrodes (of nickel, say) bound to the palm
and back of a hand, or his two hands or two fingers of one hand are
immersed in separate water receptacles.   Wires are used to connect
a light battery, a resistor, and a fairly sensitive galvanometer to
the electrodes in such a way as to place battery, resistor, galvanometer, and subject all in one electric circuit.   After manipulation
of the resistor to set the galvanometer at an arbitrary zero ("normal") point while the subject rests, the demonstrator proceeds by
stimulating the subject with emotional stimuli (noises, embarrassing
questions, jokes, revolting pictures, small animals in his hand or on
his chest, and so on), and by noting from time to time the readings
of the galvanometer on its scale (projected on a wall).   If the results
are typical, the galvanometer will be seen to make a definite deflection shortly after each time the subject was emotional.

Apparently simple!   On the other hand, it is exceedingly complex,
at least if anything like research is intended.   For one thing, the
resistance at the skin is decreased by a number of bodily conditions
not properly called emotional, such as muscular exercise, alertness,
deep breathing, concentration on an intellectual problem, and a
number of others.   In fact, authorities do not agree as to what
psychological processes the technique measures best, though the
majority believe that under carefully controlled conditions its
employment for studying emotional behavior is warranted.

On the side of the instrumentation the pitfalls are many.   First, as to the
electrodes.   The ever-threatening polarization (counteracting currents that
get set up through dissociation of materials present) has driven research
workers to adopt a variety of kinds of electrodes — zinc with kaolin paste,

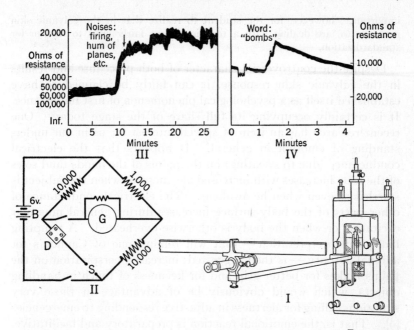

FIGURE 43. THE GALVANOMETRIC MEASUREMENT OF EMOTIONAL REACTION

I, a commonly used form of galvanometer. The amount of current passing through the instrument determines the position of a moving coil hung within the case; and riding on the latter is a small mirror that reflects numbers from the horizontal scale in front into the telescope.   (For very delicate researches the Einthoven string galvanometer is often used.)

II, one arrangement of connections (Wheatstone bridge) for the study of emotion: *S*, the human subject under observation; *G*, galvanometer; *B*, battery; *D*, dial resistance; other resistances shown as coils and indicated in ohms.

III, record of changes in resistance in a subject during an air raid over London by enemy planes.   Beginning at the tenth minute of the observations she heard the noise of warning maroons, of humming aeroplanes, and of gunfire, which continued for some time.

IV, record of changes when the same subject was given the word "bombs," no noises as in *III* being present.   Note that a mere word has assumed effectiveness as an emotional stimulus.   (The records in *III* and *IV* were obtained by photographic recording of the positions of a light beam reflected by the mirror of the galvanometer upon a traveling film.)   (*III* and *IV* from Waller, A. D.   *Nature*, 1921, **107**, 185, and *Proc. Roy. Soc. of London, B*, 1917, **90**, 217.)

calomel, salt solution in clay tube in bath of zinc sulphate, are but a few. Again, as to the circuit: shall the direct current from a battery be used, or a form of alternating current; and shall subject, battery, and galvanometer be placed in one single circuit, or shall a secondary circuit be employed, or a Wheatstone bridge?   Finally, as to the recording instrument: different types of galvanometers are in use, even the extremely delicate string galvanometer, and indeed some have replaced the galvanometer entirely with an electron vacuum tube.   This is no place for us to go into these details.   It is of some importance, however, for the student to realize that in the galvanic skin response we are dealing with a technique that fairly cries to heaven for standardization.

Despite the controversial character of both procedure and results in the galvanic skin response, it can fairly be claimed to have established itself as a psychological phenomenon of first importance. It is certainly occupying its full share of the stage today.   One recent research has an item of special interest for us in our understanding of emotion in general.   It appears that the electrical conductance (due to sweating) on the palms of the hands (and soles of the feet) increases with increased alertness, as when the subject is startled or even when he awakens.   The electrical conductance of other parts of the body-surface increases during general muscular excitation or when the body is otherwise overheated.   A tempting biological interpretation — that will remind one of Cannon's for adrenal activity — is then suggested: increased perspiration on the palms makes for better grip and for keenness of touch in handling objects, which would obviously be of advantage in those very situations calling for alertness in adjustive responding to emergencies [9].   That is, the emotional reaction is preparatory and facilitative.

Word-Association Technique.   A method of bringing to light emotional responses that has had rather better success than the use of instrumentation — though it has usually been employed along with some form of the latter — is that of the free word-association. Instructions are given to the subject in somewhat the following manner: "I am going to say a word aloud; as soon as you have heard it I want you to respond by speaking out the first word that then occurs to you, just as quickly as you possibly can — no matter what the word may be.   Suppose that I were to say 'table' and you were to start at once to say 'chair,' or that I were to say 'hot' and you say 'cold' or you say 'summer.'   I have a list of words that I will use, one at a time."   The experimenter keeps accurate record of each stimulus word, of the subject's response word, and of the exact time interval between the two, as measured by a fifth-second stop watch or by a chronoscope started and stopped with voice keys.   (Cf. Figure 10.)   In some experiments he may go over the whole list a second time.

If, as was suggested in the preceding chapter, many words may come to operate as substitute stimuli, the subject in this experiment may be expected to react emotionally to certain of the words and not to others. (Cf. Figure 43, III and IV.) The problem then arises, how is the experimenter to know when his subject is so reacting and when he is not? He may often exhibit telltale changes in posture, breathing, circulation, etc.; but how is the experimenter to know from the character of the subject's *verbal* responses?

In the usual employment of the experiment the matter is not simple; for the subject under examination shows inhibitory processes at work, as is found with the normal or neurotic person who is unwilling to divulge secrets of his past immoral history, or with the criminal subject who is trying to conceal all knowledge of the crime in question. In such cases, the presence of emotional disturbance in response to certain stimulus words, especially in connection with a fear of exposure through his verbal reactions, may lead to a disturbing of his otherwise smoothly running word reactions and produce symptoms readily recognized by the skilled operator.

Among the symptoms or *diagnostic signs* of emotionally disturbed word associations the following have been included by workers in this field:

(1) An overlong reaction time in giving the word
(2) Extremely short reaction time
(3) No response whatever
(4) Repetition of the stimulus word itself
(5) Repetition of a response word used previously
(6) Strange and apparently senseless reactions
(7) Apparent misunderstanding of the stimulus word
(8) On a later retrial with the same stimulus, a defective reproduction of the word response given the first time [8, 12]

No one of these symptoms is used by itself as indicative of emotion.

In this technique — just as in the employing of instrumentation to register changes in blood pressure, respiration, and so forth — it must be said that we are not provided with a method of determining very precisely which emotional reaction pattern is in activity at a given time, but we are enabled to know when some kind is occurring, and also to know with what stimuli or situations the emotional responses of the subject are bound up. And the last-mentioned advantage is one of enormous practical utility, in assisting an examiner to get at crucial points ("suppressed complexes") of habit-forming in the individual's past history, as well as to find out some of his present emotional quirks.

Facial Reactions.   In everyday life the emotional reactions in a person are often revealed by his facial expressions, by his vocal utterances, and by his bodily posture; and the motion-picture industry has done much to exploit and to standardize these supposedly telltale signs into stereotypes.   Only the first named has been given any careful laboratory analysis.   First, we must keep in mind the distinction between the fidelity of A's facial expression to his inner condition, and the capacity of B to judge A's expression correctly.   The latter aspect of the matter has had much experimental attention, which is to be reviewed in Chapter XVII, for it is primarily a social capacity; but the former aspect has received less.

Landis [17] gave to college students a variety of stimuli that aroused definite emotional disturbances in them, and secretly photographed them meanwhile.   Upon comparing the names of the emotions reported by the subjects with the pictured patterns of their facial reactions he found very little correspondence.   He suggested, therefore, that facial expressions in adults are not reliable indices of the emotional processes occurring, but instead are conventionalized reactions of the face — "social expressions," much like the polite words and other affectations of the socially experienced person.

Combined Methods.   In our hasty survey of the leading techniques for objective study of emotion we have not been careful to note the fact that as a matter of actual history no one technique has yielded wholly satisfactory results when used alone — not even blood pressure, the galvanic response, and word-association.   Need we be surprised?   Emotion is a state of widespread bodily response, and how "emotion" differs from a non-emotional state or how "emotions" differ from each other is not a matter of this particular organ or that one but depends upon *the total pattern of responses*.   It might have been surmised in advance that success in bringing a man's emotional condition out where others could observe it would be better assured if several methods were used together.   And such has proved to be true in a number of lines of research.   We must take space for one which possesses additional features worth noting.

The most dramatic successes have been scored by use of the misnamed "lie detector" [1] in the hands of Larson [18], working in California and Illinois.   Using in combination a special form of sphygmomanometer that produced continuous records, a pneumo-

---

[1] What it detects is not lying but a type of emotion commonly appearing when one is lying.

graph, and a modified word-association method as well as direct questioning, he has produced striking results in leading men to confess who were guilty of various misdemeanors and crimes, from bootlegging to murder, and in helping clearly to free innocent accused.   His achievements have been acknowledged even by hard-boiled police.   It is important to bear in mind, however, that Larson is both a physician and a criminologist; and no one with insufficient knowledge of physiology or of the criminal should expect to duplicate his accomplishments.   *The apparatus is by no means fool-proof.*   It is significant, also, that he had less striking success in artificial laboratory setups of deception: this may have either of two explanations, that the laboratory emotions were too artificially aroused, or that some of Larson's success with criminals was due to nonexperimental factors residing in his skill as an expert in handling and questioning criminals.

Laboratory conditions can, of course, be made realistic in some ways; and we shall close this section with a note on one study in which an unexpected pistol shot, electric shock, and pin prick were effective enough.   The particular criterion of disturbance was: do the organic processes in question show *more irregular rhythm* immediately after the stimulation?   Records for the 25 seconds following a stimulus were compared with those for a resting 25-second period.   Each of these records was expressed not in terms of change in the average or the general level, but in terms of the irregularity or variability — by the mean deviation (cf. p. 297). The observations taken were on the galvanic skin response, pulse rate and amplitude, respiration rate and amplitude, and I/E ratio. Results were positive: on all six tests the mean deviation was increased.   (Cf. Figure 44.)

The last-mentioned study is representative of the present status of the experimental psychology of emotion.   Other researches can be found [1] by the interested student in which two, three, or more of the sort of techniques we have reviewed were successfully employed in bringing to light organic disturbances of emotional character.   But in one and all, the best results were obtained by *sudden unexpected stimulation* — as in Blatz's falling chair and Caster's electric shock or pistol shot — and those responses most unequivocally registered were various species of one genus, what is nowadays called "startle."

[1] By Bayley, Darrow, Gaskill, Landis, Skaggs, and others.

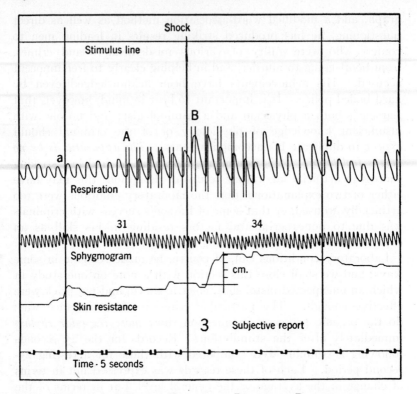

FIGURE 44. A SAMPLE KYMOGRAPH RECORD OF DISTURBANCES
FOLLOWING A SHOCK STIMULUS

The time line shows 5-sec. breaks, and the long vertical lines drawn later mark the 25-sec.
periods preceding and following the stimulation. Inspection of the curves during the after-
period will reveal irregularities as follows. Respiration tracing (from a pneumograph): in rate
of breathing (read from cycle to cycle), in amplitude or depth of breathing (read from top to
bottom of each cycle), and in I/E ratio (determined by measuring the distances between vertical
lines drawn through the highest and lowest points of five cycles before and after the stimulation).
Pulse tracing (from a sphygmograph): in rate of pulse beat (cycle to cycle) and in amplitude of
pulse (top to bottom of cycles). Galvanic skin response tracing. in levels of resistance (vertically
measured). The figure 3 indicates that the subject reported the intensity of his experience as
"moderate" — 3 on a five-point scale. (From Caster, J. E., Emotional Reactions to Strong
Stimuli, *J. Gen. Psychol.*, 1930, **4**, 131–153.)

The Present Status. We return to a problem that has been
recurring throughout our survey of emotion. What about the
specificity of patterns, the distinctiveness of "hope," "dread,"
"joy," "grief," and the rest as behavior-totals? With the help of
laboratory instruments can we "tell them apart"? We cannot.

It is not the *kind* of disturbance but the mere *fact* of disturbance that is brought to light by instrumentation.   But let us get the correct perspective on this.   It does not necessarily point to the futility of the objective experimental approach, the breakdown of brass instrument psychology.   Nor does it indicate that bodily disturbances are not really the core of emotional response.   What it does in all probability show is that emotional patterns — such as truly exist — are most highly variable in their details.   Results obtained by introspection point to the same conclusion.   We are led then to the view rather widely expressed today that such distinctions as those between the emotions of "fear," "rage," and "love" are not really drawn on the basis of their respective stimuli as such, nor of their respective reactions as such.   Rather these distinctions between emotions are based on *their gross behavior results — the character of the back action upon the stimulus in each case.*   "Fear," for example, is a protective response tending to avoid the stimulus; "rage," a protective response tending to destroy the stimulus; and "love," a response tending to continue and get more of the stimulus.

On the credit side of the account we have had some clear demonstrations of the usefulness of apparatus for bringing out for observation (a) *suppressed general excitement* aroused by critical situations, and (b) the *"startle" component* to be found in many emotional conditions.

REFERENCES

1. Beebe-Center, J. G.   *The Psychology of Pleasantness and Unpleasantness.*   Van Nostrand, 1932.
2. Benussi, V.   Die Atmungssymptome der Lüge.   *Arch. f. d. Ges. Psychol.*, 1914, **31**, 244–73.
3. Blatz, W. E.   The Cardiac, Respiratory, and Electrical Phenomena Involved in the Emotion of Fear.   *J. Exper. Psychol.*, 1925, **8**, 109–32.
4. Blatz, W. E., and Millichamp, D. A.   The Development of Emotion in the Infant.   *Univ. Toronto Studies: Child Dev. Series*, No. 4, 1935.
5. Bridges, K. M. B.   Emotional Development in Early Infancy.   *Ch. Devel.*, 1932, **3**, 324–41.
6. Cannon, W. B.   Again the James-Lange and the Thalamic Theories of Emotion.   *Psychol. Rev.*, 1931, **38**, 281–95.
7. Cannon, W. B.   *Bodily Changes in Pain, Hunger, Fear, and Rage* (2d ed.).   Appleton, 1929.

8. Crosland, H. R.   The Psychological Methods of Word-Association and Reaction-Time as Tests of Deception.   *Univ. Ore. Publ., Psychol. Ser.*, 1929, **1**, 104.

9. Darrow, C. W.   The Galvanic Skin Reflex (Sweating) and Blood-Pressure as Preparatory and Facilitative Functions.   *Psychol. Bull.*, 1936, **33**, 73–94.

10. Goodenough, F. L.   Expression of the Emotions in a Blind-Deaf Child.   *J. Abnor. & Soc. Psychol.*, 1932, **27**, 328–33.

11. Goodenough, F. L.   The Expression of Emotions in Infancy.   *Ch. Devel.*, 1931, **2**, 96–101.

12. Hull, C. L., and Lugoff, L. S.   Complex Signs in Diagnostic Free Association.   *J. Exper. Psychol.*, 1921, **4**, 111–36.

13. Hunt, W. A., and Landis, C.   The Overt Behavior Pattern in Startle.   *J. Exper. Psychol.*, 1936, **19**, 309–15.

14. James, W.   *Principles of Psychology.*   Vol. II, chap. xxv.   Holt, 1890.

15. Jersild, A. T., and Holmes, F. B.   Methods of Overcoming Children's Fears.   *J. of Psychol.*, 1935, **1**, 75–104.

16. Jones, M. C.   Emotional Development, in *Handbook of Child Psychology* (2d ed.).   Clark Univ. Press, 1933.

17. Landis, C.   Studies of Emotional Reactions.   *J. Comp. Psychol.*, 1924, **4**, 447–509.

18. Larson, J. A.   *Lying and Its Detection.*   Univ. Chicago Press, 1932.

19. Luria, A. R.   *The Nature of Human Conflicts* (trans. by Gantt).   Liveright, 1932.

20. Marston, W. M.   Sex Characteristics of Systolic Blood Pressure Behavior.   *J. Exper. Psychol.*, 1923, **6**, 387–419.

21. Ruckmick, C. A.   *The Psychology of Feeling and Emotion.*   McGraw-Hill, 1936.

22. Sherman, M.   The Differentiation of Emotional Responses in Infants.   *J. Comp. Psychol.*, 1927, **7**, 265–84; 1928, **8**, 385–94.

23. Watson, J. B., and Rayner, R.   Conditioned Emotional Reactions.   *J. Exper. Psychol.*, 1920, **3**, 1–14.

CHAPTER VIII
MOTOR FUNCTIONS

INTRODUCTION TO THE THREE FOLLOWING CHAPTERS

WE HAVE been studying the behavior of human (and sub-human) beings as total organisms. At times we have analyzed conduct into some simpler components, even down to reflex arcs; but our eye has been on the person (or animal) as a whole — integrated, self-regulatory, and in contact and interaction with his environment at many points. He has developed from a single cell, and his growth has been the growth of a body with delicately inter-dependent parts. His activities have been the activities concerned with the adjustment of his whole self to conditions of life.

Such a viewpoint too rigidly maintained may lead to vagueness, however, and we need to know more precisely how the particular parts work. We shall, therefore, carry out an analysis suggested in Chapter II, and give attention in turn to the functioning of the particular motor mechanisms, the particular sensory mechanisms, and the main types of neural or organizing mechanisms.

When this survey is completed we shall return to the viewpoint of a man-as-a-whole, and proceed to consider the more elaborate and refined developments of his behavior throughout the remainder of the book.

INTRODUCTION TO THE MOTOR FUNCTIONS

Psychology, we have said, is primarily the scientific study of human nature. Human nature, we have said, is primarily a question of how the human being behaves. And now behavior in its first intention, so to speak, is a matter of activities. The first things we can know about any person, before we can go into analysis of his deeper-lying possibilities and potentialities, are the ways and manners in which he acts. In the preceding chapters it should have become evident that a psychological interest in prediction and control is one involving, first of all, inquiries as to how, when, and why a man does this or that, acts thus and so, desires, seeks, accepts, rejects — in a word, why he moves.

Psychological study of the motorist, for example, naturally begins with a survey of just how he does things with feet and hands: the way he pushes in this pedal, pulls out that dashboard lever, turns this large wheel, throws that gear-shift lever, and turns head and eyeballs sharply this way and that. So with the business man at his desk: we may see him reach over and pull out a file of papers, riffle through them with fingers and thumb, lay one flat on his desk, seize a pen and make ink marks with it, press a call-button, make sounds by using his voice, and all the while be moving his eyeballs (and even the head in which they are rotating) left-right-up-down in a bewilderingly rapid and continual play of excursions. To be sure, all such activities are but the resultants of energies playing upon motorist or business man as well as of complicated energy-changes that have been going on within the body, and they are but a small part of the whole story; yet if we are to begin we may as well begin here with these more observable phenomena, and work our way backward to the processes that precede and determine them.

Activities of these sorts are primarily the functioning of striped muscles. These are the tissues at work in eating, walking, listening, sewing, talking — in fact in nearly all the activities of a person that are externally observable. It behooves us then to learn the barest essentials of striped muscle processes, first in the gross, then in somewhat finer detail.

THE STRIPED MUSCLES

Their Distribution and Arrangement. The striped muscles constitute from a third to a half of the total mass of the organism; there are over six hundred of them all told. Their function of moving a part of the body is typically performed by pulling on levers. The bony skeleton furnishes a framework, consisting mainly of systems of levers upon which the body is hung and stretched; and it is by the manipulation of these levers by the muscles attached to them with tendons that the body changes its positions and postures.

An Example. Every boy knows the biceps because he has felt it dozens of times to estimate his growing strength. It is located just above the elbow and to the front of the humerus bone of the upper arm, and it plays the simple but enormously important rôle of raising the lower arm. That performance may be part and parcel of behavior processes of a very wide range: the lower arm may come up sharply at the buzzing sound of a mosquito, or it may snap up in a military salute; it may go up in response to a barked command out of the darkness to "stick 'em up!" or it may be making the first movement of manipulating a cocktail shaker; it may be the preliminary to striking a piano keyboard, or it may only be a transference of a spoonful of oatmeal to the mouth. But, whatever the variety of dramatic and undramatic total performances in which it participates as a segment, the raising of the arm is one and the same mechanism when it is considered locally and in isolation. Let us analyze this with the aid of Figure 45.

The upraising of the forearm and hand is accomplished by the contracting of the biceps muscle. This round, spindle-shaped mass has its attachment at one end to a bone of the shoulder, the scapula, and at the other to the radius of the forearm. Upon shortening, it draws forearm and hand toward the shoulder. The elbow joint and, to a lesser extent, the shoulder joint, serve as the fulcrum.

The conditions that can excite this contraction are several: a sharp blow, a sudden stretch, certain chemicals, electricity, a sudden temperature change; but the normal excitation is a neural

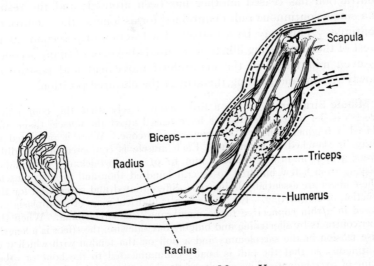

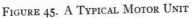

FIGURE 45. A TYPICAL MOTOR UNIT

The two muscle-groups, biceps and triceps, operate the lower arm as a lever with the elbow serving as the fulcrum. Their modes of innervation and reciprocal action are described in the text.

impulse received via motor (efferent) nerve fibers from the central
nervous system — and coming originally, we will remember, from
receptors somewhere. The energy changes in the nerve serve to
excite energy changes in the muscle. In the figure this *innervation*,
as it is called, of the biceps is indicated by a line running to it
and bearing a + sign.

The Nature of Contraction. The story of a simple phasic
(periodic) contraction includes first a "latent" period, which is
the interval between the time the neural impulse is received and
the beginning of contraction; then comes a contraction which is
at first slow, then rapid, then slow; finally a relaxation appears.
The duration of latent period of contraction, and of relaxation, is
in each case a matter of hundredths of a second, the whole operation frequently occupying less than one tenth of a second. However, the simple twitch type of muscle contraction is the exception
rather than the rule. Barring a few extremely simple reflex actions,
the excitations received via motor nerves are multiple rather than
simple. They appear at a rate varying greatly for different fibers,
but average around fifty per second. They reach the muscle
fibers in a succession or volley, which is so rapid that before one
contraction has ceased another has been aroused; and the result
is a single continuous pull maintained for as long as the excitations
continue. This may be a matter of a fraction of a second, as in
most of the arm-raising illustrations used above, or of many seconds
or even minutes as in the maintained movement and posture of
slowly raising and holding the arm in the elevated position.

Minute Structure. To see a little more closely what this contraction
process is, let us assume that we have teased apart the muscle tissue and
placed a fragment under a low-power microscope. What is presented to
vision is sketched in Figure 46. Each muscle is composed of threadlike
fibers, 3 to 4 cm. in length and .1 mm. to .01 mm. in thickness, the number
varying from a few hundred to several hundred thousand in each muscle.
These fibers are essentially living cells differentiated and specialized for the
function of contracting. Each fiber is a cylindrical mass of protoplasm enclosed in a thin connective tissue membrane, the sarcolemma. When the
fiber contracts by shortening and bulging out sidewise, the effect is a lengthwise tension in the sarcolemma and a pull on the tendon with which it is
continuous, so that the pull is finally communicated to the bone or other
point of attachment. The simultaneous shortening of hundreds or thousands of these fine fibers may produce a pull of great power on the part of
the whole muscle.

As suggested in the figure, the muscle fiber presents a striated appearance,

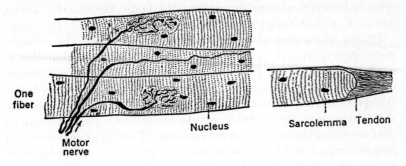

FIGURE 46. FIBERS OF STRIPED MUSCLE HIGHLY MAGNIFIED

Note the striated appearance, the many nuclei, the sarcolemma, continuous with the tendon, and the motor nerve, with its end plates.

with light and dim bands alternating. During the phase of shortening in contraction, some of the protoplasmic material in the light bands is imbibed into the substance of the dim bands; and in the phase of lengthening in relaxation the imbibed material passes back into the light band. So much can be described. But precisely of what this change consists in more detailed terms has not been made out with certainty. One thing is clear: during the contracting, important chemical changes occur. Glycogen and oxygen disappear, while carbon dioxide, lactic acid, and water are produced. Heat also is liberated and an electrical change has been observed.

The "all-or-none" principle is found to hold in the operation of the individual muscle fiber. It contracts either to its fullest extent or not at all. It follows, then, that the intensity of the pull exerted by the muscle as a whole is dependent not upon the intensity of neural excitation per fiber but upon the number of different fibers excited.

Antagonistic Relations of Musculature. To return to our example of the biceps, this muscle when it shortens to draw up the forearm is not merely pulling up a dead weight; it is pulling against the triceps (see Figure 45 again). The latter muscle is found to the back of the humerus bone; and because it is attached by tendons to bones at the shoulder (humerus and scapula) and to the ulna, it operates to pull the lower arm in the downward direction. The biceps, then, tends to flex the arm, the triceps to extend it. Thus the upward sweep of the hand is often arrested at some given point, as in a salute or in lifting a glass to the mouth; this stoppage is made more definite by the timely innervation of the triceps — over the efferent nerve supply indicated in the figure by another "+." This antagonistic arrangement of the muscle systems is common enough throughout the body; the muscles are so paired as to check and control each other.

During the easier sweeping movements, however, the antagonistic muscle may be in relaxation. It is to be noted that this is not a purely negative phenomenon: it is the result of a different innervation process, an inhibitory one. When the biceps is being thrown into sharp contraction and the arm is being raised quickly, the triceps may be receiving neural impulses of another sort, so that its relaxation is a genuine response. This reciprocal innervation of antagonistic muscle groups by excitatory and inhibitory neural impulses simultaneously is a phenomenon found very widespread.

Many movements, of course, are not simple one-way affairs: they may consist of up-and-down or back-and-forth alternations of directions. Tapping the foot, walking, swaying the body forward and back, shaking the head, and numerous others appear in a person's behavior every day. Typical of them is the process of shaking a bottle or a test-tube. In the latter performance, the oscillation consists of an alternation of upward-downward-upward, etc., movements; and it is plain enough that the neuro-muscular story is one that may be condensed into such form as: biceps + and triceps −, biceps − and triceps +, biceps + and triceps −, etc.

One connecting link is necessary to this story. How does it come about that toward the end of one excursion the muscles then receive innervations the effect of which is the reverse of those just preceding? We must now recognize a further muscle and nerve relationship, one of the sensory or receptive type. In and on the muscle fiber there lie also the sensitive ends (receptors) of *afferent* nerves. (Not shown in Figures 45 and 46 but to be seen in Figure 56, p. 232.) These are to be discussed later; but it is essential at this point to understand that when a muscle is thrown into contraction, this change of the condition in the muscle tissue, as well as in the tendinous tissue to which it is attached, is an adequate stimulus to excite sensitive nerve beginnings that are found there and in the joints, and so to generate neural impulses running away from the moving member and toward the nervous centers. Bearing in mind these two kinds of innervations, the efferent and the afferent, it should now be simple to understand how a movable member can by its own movements elicit still further movements by circular reflexes via the nerve centers. An upstroke of the forearm itself furnishes neural stimulation leading to a downstroke, the downward movement arouses impulses leading to an upstroke, and so the story may go on.

Tonic Contractions. So much for some of the simpler types of movement in the forearm (or other movable segment of the body). There are other types. There is, for example, the holding of a certain half-way position assumed as in tonic contractions. So far we have been occupied with *phasic* contractions, as they are sometimes called, contractions that are more or less prompt and that usually result in a pronounced movement in space. But of equal importance in understanding a man's behavior are his less noticeable *tonic* activities, which are of mild intensity and long sustained. It is false to suppose that when a muscle shortens under excitation what occurs is an awakening from a completely inert and flaccid state. Quite the contrary. The movement elicited is superimposed upon, or is merely the intensification of, the previously existing tonus. It is impossible to say in very precise terms what this phenomenon is (cf. *infra*, pp. 339 f.). At any rate, it is certainly directly dependent upon innervation of some kind coming over motor nerves from nerve centers, for if the nerves be cut the muscle becomes longer and more flaccid, and loses its tone.

From the centers these impulses can be traced back to afferent origins in receptors. Typical are (1) the receptors associated with muscle-tendon-joint apparatus (mentioned in a preceding paragraph), the afferent impulses from which serve to re-excite the same apparatus. This may be shown negatively by cutting the efferent fibers from the leg of a frog without cutting the afferent ones, which produces marked loss of tone of the musculature of that leg. Important also are (2) receptors in the labyrinth of the ear (pp. 234 ff.), which are important for the maintenance of upright posture in sitting or standing. It is also clear that the degree of muscle tone at a given time may be dependent upon still other afferent sources of neural impulses. The vigor displayed by men in cold weather, and again by men emotionally aroused, suggests (3) cutaneous sense organs and (4) others operating in complicated ways through the higher centers.

The rôle of the phenomenon of tonicity in determining human behavior is tremendous and should not be overlooked. (1) For one thing, gross *postural reactions* are maintained by tonic contractions. Aiming at a target, listening to a lecturer, computing at the accountant's desk, feeding any industrial machine — all such performances depend upon the supporting tonus of muscles in legs, trunk, and neck. (2) Again, a general tonus makes for excitability or irritability in the muscles of the whole body so that upon receipt of any definite stimulation one's reactions are more prompt and more intense than they would be otherwise.   It is a condition of readiness, *alertness*.   With muscles on the *qui vive* a man responds the more quickly and vigorously; as, for example, after he has been aroused from his drowsiness by a cold shower bath, or after the football coach has warned him to "be on his toes."

(3) So much for functions of tonicity in the muscles in general. The degree of tonicity, however, waxes and wanes in different ways for *different groups of muscles;* and this differential character is of fundamental importance to the understanding of some psychological phenomena.   On an earlier page it was stated that simple reaction time is shorter when the subject's energies are concentrated (when "he attends") upon the R he is to make than when they are concentrated upon the S he is to receive.   The difference can probably be described physiologically as a difference in the particular coordinated muscle group that is maintained in higher tone — whether these be muscles about to be used in the R, or the muscles co-operating in the attitude of listening for the S.   (This difference, of course, is one to be traced back through the nervous centers to a difference in receptor stimulations, such as the heard sounds, "Prepare yourself for the movement," or, "Look out especially for the signal.")   Further elaboration of this principle may be postponed until we discuss the phenomena of set in Chapter XII.

Co-ordinations of Muscles.   Suppose the reader at this moment were to reach for a pencil lying eighteen inches from this book.   His "hand reaches for it," he might say.   But on examination it is clear that an enormous number of muscles are sharing in this act.   The angle at the elbow widens: biceps and triceps co-operate.   The upper arm is raised from the shoulder: the massive deltoid plays the principal part.   The fingers are extended, all five of them: each being pulled by its own combination of muscles in the forearm. The trunk of the body shares in the reaction by leaning forward: a great number of separate muscles are involved.   The head is tilted upward on its cervical axis: this is done by a concerted shortening of several back muscles.   The eyes turn toward the object: a delicate co-ordination of the six muscles of each eyeball takes place.   Other muscle movements, also, could be mentioned.   This is team work.

The advantages secured to the organism by this co-ordinating of its muscles may be reduced to three: *strength, speed*, and accuracy or *precision*. That a combination of pulls may make a stronger total pull is readily enough seen; but in many cases the particular combination that will give the maximum power is not evident to the worker, and he is likely to continue lifting loads from the ground with the musculature of his back instead of with that of his legs, or a man will sing *forte* with an extravagant expenditure of breathing efforts. Somewhat the same general point is true with respect to speed. The speediest boxer is by no means the one with the most excessive strength, but the one who has the nicest organization of pulls by one muscle and another in forearm, upper arm, shoulder, trunk, and legs, all of which require great precision in timing. As for precision or accuracy in performance, it too is essentially a matter of economy. He who can lay a brick with six or eight co-ordinated movements in succession instead of the fifteen or eighteen of his fellows is the skillful worker. So likewise is he who can let one circular motion do what two angular ones had done. Precision is also a matter of balance. When one undertakes to drink a glass of water, too strong use of the deltoid will toss the water over the head, too strong use of the pronators will empty it on the floor, too strong use of the elbow flexors will strike the glass against the face.

The study of precisely what combinations of movements make for efficiency in motor activity is of universal interest, supporting on the one hand the highly paid athletic coaches and on the other the highly analytic "motion study" experts.

Laboratory technique for measuring these three characteristics — strength, speed, and precision — includes the use of such apparatus as that shown in Figure 47.

Another important factor in general motor efficiency is muscular *exercise*. If left unused, a muscle rapidly weakens and may even waste away; this is often seen when a muscle is not used because of infantile paralysis. Aside from the many and widespread effects throughout the body (on respiration, heart action, circulation, digestion, and peristalsis, heat production, and the like) adequate — not excessive — exercise of the striped muscles is a *sine qua non* of effective work by the muscles themselves. This point, however, important as it is, needs less repetition and elaboration in the twentieth century than it needed in the hothouse eighteenth and Victorian nineteenth.

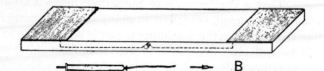

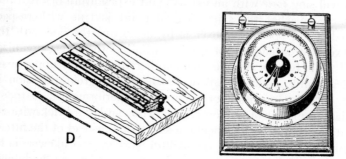

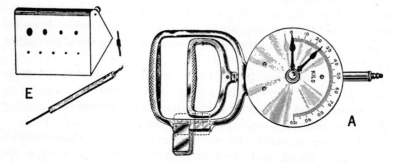

FIGURE 47. APPARATUS USED FOR MEASURING MOTOR EFFICIENCY

The Smedley spring dynamometer (A) is used for testing *strength* of hand grip. In gripping, the fingers pull upon the stirrup which is held by a stout spring. The tapping board (B) consists of a brass plate to be wired in circuit with a battery, the stylus shown with it, and a recording device such as the dial instrument shown (C) which registers "makes" of the circuit; and the *speed* with which the hand taps the stylus to the plate is recorded in terms of contacts or "makes." *Precision* of movement is tested also with an open circuit arrangement, by mechanically recording the number of contacts of a stylus being guided between two metal strips (D), or of a stylus inserted and held free within a small hole cut in a metal plate (E).

THE DETECTION OF ACTIVITIES OF MUSCLES

Introduction. When we are observing a human being we are noting what he is doing, what his actions and postures are; and in a sense this resolves itself into what his muscles are doing. Now, a great deal of muscular activity goes on in so minimal a way that it cannot be observed by ordinary methods. It is implicit. Particularly is this true of activity during functions of much psychological interest such as "paying attention," "thinking hard," and the like. Without instrumentation, with only naked-eye methods, we should be forced to remain in a state of ignorance analogous to that of the physiologist and zoologist before the microscope was discovered or that of the astronomer before Galileo discovered the telescope. Accordingly the development of techniques for bringing out into the open the obscure and the minute processes occurring in human behavior must be recognized as of first importance. They are of many types.

For the immediate present we will confine ourselves to a technique that is designed to detect and measure one of the most delicate phenomena. (Since this phenomenon is found in neural as well as in muscular tissue, we may find it convenient to refer to the former at places in the discussion that follows, even though more specific descriptions of neural tissue and their general functions must be delayed till a subsequent chapter.)

General Nature of Action Potentials. It has long been known that whenever a muscle is thrown into contraction (or thickens) or whenever neural impulses pass over a nerve, a wavelike electrical change ("action current") passes through the tissue concerned. Suppose, for instance, that an isolated muscle or nerve fiber be stimulated near one end, as shown in Figure 48. A wave of excitation in the form of a difference of potential that is negative with respect to the rest of the fiber will pass from the stimulated point along the fiber. This is learned simply by attaching electrodes from a galvanometer at points a and b. At the instant A, when the excitation passes point a, a current will be revealed by the galvanometer in the direction indicated by the arrow α; at instant B, when the excitation passes point b, a current of opposite direction β will be revealed. A permanent and continuous record can be obtained photographically. Let a beam of light be reflected from the mirror of the galvanometer upon a traveling film, so that a deflection caused

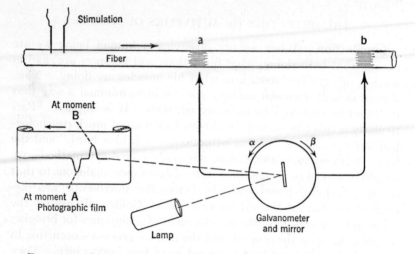

FIGURE 48. ARRANGEMENT FOR REGISTERING ELECTRICAL POTENTIALS
FROM AN ACTIVE MUSCLE OR NERVE FIBER

The simple galvanometer here indicated is ordinarily replaced by more sensitive instruments.
Explanation is given in the text.

by a current flowing in the α direction will be recorded as a drop in
the light beam and therefore in the light-line on the film, and a deflection of opposite β direction will be recorded as a rise in the beam and
in the line.   Then the successive passing of points a and b on the
muscle (or nerve) fiber by a single wave of excitation of that tissue
will appear as a diphasic tracing on the film.   If desired, a time line
can be produced by a regularly oscillating light beam from another
source playing upon the upper part of the film; and a measurement
of the time relations involved is in this manner rendered easy.

In this description we have assumed that the tissue being studied
is a single fiber (cell).   As a matter of fact, the studies made in
psychological laboratories have been upon muscle masses or nerve
trunks, consisting of many, even hundreds of distinct fibers.   Since
it is certain that different fibers may differ greatly in their characteristic manners of energy propagation (in frequency and in intensity),
the wave form along a bundle of fibers will vary in its complexity
with the number of fibers composing the trunk.   For example,
when a pianist is striking his keys, any action current "picked up"
from the contracting triceps participating in the movement will be
a complex one.

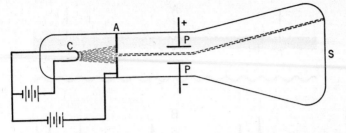

FIGURE 49. ESSENTIALS OF THE CATHODE RAY OSCILLOGRAPH

C, the cathode. *A*, the anode. *P*, *P*, the plates, in circuit through amplifying systems with the electrodes on the body. *S*, the screen upon which the deflected beam of electrons traces a picture of the electric potentials operating through the plates, making them visible as waves. A camera, mounted to face this screen, will take permanent records of the waves, (still or motion picture). (From Henney, K., *Radio Engineering Handbook*. McGraw-Hill, 1933.)

For simplicity's sake, in presenting the general notion of action currents we have mentioned the use of the ordinary mirror galvanometer. In practice, however, the moving parts of that instrument have too much inertia for prompt and delicate responsiveness to very rapid oscillatory changes of potential. Even the much more sensitive *string galvanometer* is often replaced with the *cathode ray oscillograph*.

The general physical principles of the latter instrument are similar to those of the ordinary radio or electron tube. (See Figure 49.) Some of the electrons flying off a hot cathode pass through an aperture of the anode, and form a stream that falls upon a screen at the end of the tube. On its way this stream passes between two pairs of plates, one pair horizontal and one vertical; and the changing states of the electrical field created by these plates deflect the stream in various ways. To these plates the action potentials from the muscle or nerve are communicated (after being very greatly amplified). In this way, any change of electrical potential in the tissue deflects the stream of rays as they play upon the screen. The wave form is visible to the eye, and can be photographed. (See Figure 50.)

We shall have several later occasions to refer to the phenomenon of action potentials.

THE SMOOTH MUSCLES

Their General Rôle. The behavior of a man toward the people and objects about him is not limited to activities involving his striped musculature only. When the motorist sees a child dart suddenly across his path, what he does then is not completely described as slamming in clutch and brake pedals, sudden throwing of his steering wheel over to one side, and the like, for there are also

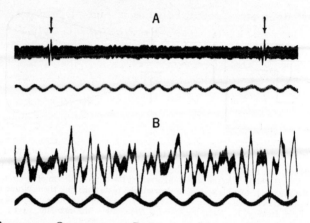

FIGURE 50. OSCILLOGRAPH RECORDS OF MUSCLE CONTRACTIONS

A. A slight contraction of a single motor unit (a group of muscle fibers innervated by a single nerve fiber). The electrodes were hypodermic needles inserted through to the muscle. The rate of the discharges was about 9 times per second, of which 2 are shown.

B. A contraction of a muscle as a whole. The electrodes were placed on the skin surface over the muscle mass. Many motor units were discharging asynchronously, the total frequency being some 400 to 500 per second.

In both *A* and *B* the time is indicated in 1/100 second by the wavy line.

(By the courtesy of Dr. L. E. Travis.)

a catching of breath, a sudden pallor, and soon a "cold sweat," a dry mouth, a loss of appetite. Similarly for the man in ordinary fighting array: his pugnacity appears not simply in the clenching of fists and swinging of arms but as well in the widening of his eyes and dilatation of their pupils, in the reddening of his face and neck, in certain noticeable bristling of his hair, perhaps in "tears of helpless rage." Certainly these phenomena are of sufficiently deep psychological concern to interest us in the mechanisms at work. As in the preceding section, we must here limit attention to the end-segments, the effectors. In such components of human behavior as we found in the startled or angry man, there is a striking participation of smooth muscles, duct glands, and ductless glands. We will take them up in that order.

It is not only in the exciting, dramatic moments of emergency in life that these effectors are at work. The process of living is a process of continuous internal functions — circulation, digestion, excretion, and the like — and the outward conduct and performances of the most staid individual in his most staid moments are intimately dependent upon these internal operations.

Distribution and General Function of Smooth Muscles. Smooth muscles are to be found in the walls of the so-called hollow viscera of the body — such as the arteries and veins, the esophagus, stomach, and intestines, the passages and ducts of the genital and urinary organs, the bronchi, and the ducts of certain glands, and also in the skin in connection with the hairs.

Generally speaking, these muscles are disposed in the hollow organs in two typical ways, longitudinal and circular. Figure 51, right, shows circular muscle tissue *b* in a cross-section of an artery. Its contracting and relaxing produce constriction and dilation of the blood vessel, thereby decreasing or increasing the "bore" of the blood vessel. This muscular control of the diameters of the different blood vessels in the whole body results in a control of the direction in which the excess supplies of blood are sent — to striped muscles and to lungs, to digestive apparatus, to sex apparatus, to brain, to skin, and so forth; and this phase has prime importance in the mechanics of the body machine. On the left of the figure is shown a longitudinal section of one wall of the small intestine, with its circular muscle *cm*, operating much as that of the artery to control the internal diameter of the intestinal canal; also longitudi-

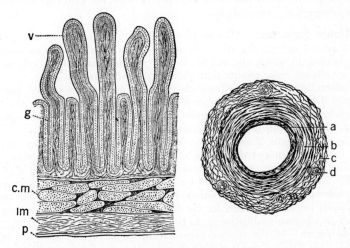

FIGURE 51. SMOOTH MUSCLE TISSUES

On right: cross-section of an artery, showing smooth inner coat, *a*, muscular layer, *b*, and outer connective tissue coat, *c*. On left: longitudinal section of one wall of small intestine, showing villi, *v*, and glands, *g*, of mucous membrane; circular muscle bundles (in cross-sections), *cm*; longitudinal muscle fibers, *lm*; outer coat or peritoneum, *p*.

nal muscle *lm*, which by contraction draws together adjacent sections of the canal, thus shortening it locally.

The circular and longitudinal musculatures play co-operative rôles in the process of peristalsis by which food is moved along in the alimentary canal. While a horse is drinking, the peristaltic movement of its esophagus may be plainly seen along its neck. A half-inch or so of the longitudinal muscle contracts, pulling the next lower part of the canal up over a lump of the contents; the circular fibers next contract, squeezing the material a short way along the tube; then the fibers next below repeat the process; and thus the contents are forced along in a wavelike motion. In the stomach section of the alimentary canal this activity is complicated by the addition of oblique muscles which help to churn the contents, and by sphincter muscles at the two ends, which shut off esophagus and intestine during the churning.

Sphincter muscles are of the circular type, and are found at various openings, such as those of the bladder, the rectum, the iris of the eye, and a few glands, such as the sweat glands.

In general, the smooth type of muscle tissue is to be found intimately involved in the maintenance — and in the disturbances — of vital processes of the more vegetative sort, for example, alimentation, excretion, circulation.

Minute Structure. Microscopically, smooth muscle tissue is composed of elongated spindle-shaped cells, united to form in most cases muscular membranes, in which the cell-fibrils may be continuous from cell to cell. These cells are more minute than those of striped muscles.

Contraction. The smooth muscle responds, as does the striped, not only to neural impulses but also to artificial conditions, including various drugs which have differential effects upon the musculature of different organs — ergot, digitalis, epinephrin, ipecac, and so forth.

The contractions of smooth muscles may be characterized as less prompt and more independent than those of striped muscle. A single *phasic* contraction may occupy several seconds, the whole movement being slow and gentle. *Tonus* may be continued for long periods, even after the severing of the motor nerve supply. Variations in this tonic activity in different organs may spell health or sickness for the body, and, in turn, adequacy or inadequacy in a person's adjustments to the world about him.

The Heart. In the cardiac musculature we have an organ not falling readily into either of the foregoing classes. It is a striped muscle in appearance, but a smooth muscle in function. The cardiac muscle is even more independent of motor nerve stimulation than is smooth muscle; the contractions being self-stimulated and only accelerated or retarded by the nerve impulses delivered to the heart.

THE DUCT GLANDS

The Essential Nature of Glands. Glands are important organs of response, whether in the smooth-running placidity of an easy-going day, in the precipitant haste of excitement, or in the lethargic heaviness of depression.

Glandular tissue is built out of cells that have become specialized for the function of secreting or excreting. Every cell in the body may be thought of as making constant exchange with the blood and lymph stream. The latter acts as a common carrier, transporting nutritive and other substances to the cell and bearing away the waste and other products given back by the cell. The secreting cell (1) receives certain substances from the blood, (2) remanufactures them, or at least isolates parts of them, and (3) delivers these products to other tissues for which they are useful, either by reshipment *via* the blood and lymph stream (as in ductless glands), or by direct transmission through a duct (as in duct glands). The excreting cell performs much the same function, except that its products are for elimination from the organism, being waste products of cells throughout the body.

Distribution and General Function of Duct Glands. A duct gland of simple type is represented in Figure 52. The hollow chambers, or alveoli, are lined with the secreting type of cells, that receive their raw material from the blood capillaries and exude their products into the chambers, from which they are conveyed by the duct to some opening at a surface, as the skin or the mucous lining.

At this point we need hardly do more than enumerate the more important duct glands. Along the alimentary canal many are to be found. There are three pairs of *salivary* glands supplying the mouth, and many *gastric* glands found in the walls of the stomach; there are those in the walls of the *intestines* providing the intestinal juices, and there are the large *liver*, and the *pancreas*. The combined function of these glands is primarily that of digestion of food, but it includes lubrication of the alimentary canal for the onward movement of its contents, and also elimination of waste products from the blood. On the outside of the body several different duct glands are to be observed. The *lachrymals* furnish liquid for the eye; the *sweat* and the *sebaceous* (oily) glands serve for conditioning the skin, excreting waste products from the body, and regulating

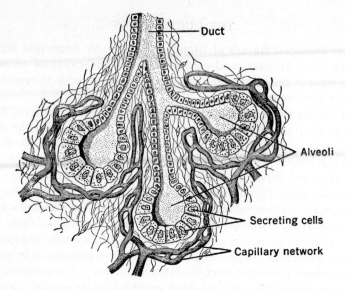

FIGURE 52. A SIMPLE DUCT GLAND, WITH CONNECTIVE TISSUE AND
BLOOD VESSELS

(From Hough, T., Sedgwick, W. T., and Waddell, J. A. *The Human Mechanism.*
Ginn and Co., 2d revised ed., 1929.)

the temperature; the *kidneys* are perhaps the greatest excretory
organs in the body; the *sex* glands serve for reproduction.

But these are functions having special reference to the internal
metabolism of the body. In what ways are the duct glands involved
in the story of man-and-his-environment? By way of anticipation
let the reader consider the rôles played by one or another of these
duct glands in some types of human behavior. (*A*) They act as
organs of direct response when, for instance, the sight of an audience
causes a dry mouth in the amateur actor, or when sounds of a burglar
downstairs occasion the householder's cold sweat, or when the
receipt of a telegram marked with the warning star arouses tears.
(*B*) They act as occasions or sources of self-stimulation when the
dyspeptic writes a *Sartor Resartus* or when the sex-urge impels to
mating. (*C*) In addition, glands often play a considerable part in
social behavior; for tears shed in another's presence are well calculated to stimulate the latter to some kind of response.

THE DUCTLESS (ENDOCRINE) GLANDS

Introduction. An outstanding trait of the human (and infra-human) organism is the mutual dependence within it of part on part, so that, far from being a mere agglomeration, it manifests some approximation to unity; it is an individual. Much of the character of a person's behavior toward the things and the people about him depends upon the degree to which this organization into individuality is achieved. Integration is a key word in psychology.

How is this interconnection of organ with organ secured? First, mechanically: through mere juxtaposition and also through connective tissues; second — and this is more striking — through chemical agencies. But the quickest in action is the neural interconnection; and when in later chapters we analyze the behavior of a man we shall have occasion constantly to keep in mind the "integrative action of the nervous system." For the present, however, our attention should be given to the chemical interconnection. The chemistry of the human body is just beginning to be understood in all its enormous complexity. Latter-day discoveries of the importance to life of the different vitamins, of the maintenance of proper acid-alkaline balance, of the necessity of supplying minute amounts of calcium, iodine, and so on, when certain glandular organs are defective — these and many other examples of insight are giving us some realization of how astonishingly subtle are the chemical interrelations of this *milieu interne.* The human being is an organism balanced chemically upon a knife edge. Let this equilibrium be ever so slightly disturbed and the result may be fatal. Should he escape death, he may bear the marks in a misshapen skeleton, he may be an idiot charge upon the community, or he may be a permanent hospital patient with fits of depression giving way to manic excitement and overactivity.

The ductless or endocrine glands — our fourth type of effector end-organ — are vitally involved in this story. Their functioning is so strikingly connected with normality or abnormality in human behavior that writers of fiction have not been slow to seize upon them as dramatic material. And there are some writers with more technical aims who have let their anticipations outrun scientific assurance. We must therefore proceed with circumspection in attempting any generalizations in this field. The reader will do well to be cautious.

The endocrines are glands having no special outlet. Each is well supplied with motor nerves, mostly from the autonomic division. Their remanufactured products are placed back in the blood and lymph stream, and conveyed over the body. These products are called "hormones," or better, "autacoid (remedial) substances" (Schäfer), and are very complicated chemically. The general locations of the different endocrines are sketched in Figure 53.

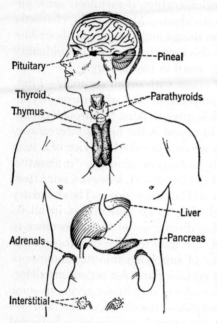

Pineal

Pituitary

Thyroid

Parathyroids

Thymus

Liver

Adrenals

Pancreas

Interstitial

FIGURE 53. A SKETCH TO SHOW THE GENERAL LOCATIONS OF THE PRINCIPAL DUCTLESS GLANDS

The Thyroid Gland. The most definite information about the effects of internal secretions on human physique and human behavior is that obtained from investigations of the thyroid. This organ consists of two lobes, one on either side of the windpipe, connected by a narrow neck, the whole gland averaging about 5 cm. by 6 cm., but varying greatly.

It has been known for many years that atrophy, or wasting away, of this gland in the young is responsible for the conditions of arrest both in physical growth and in the development of behavior known as *cretinism*. The victim of the disease makes a characteristic dwarflike picture: he is stunted in height, but obese, with protruding abdomen; the head is short and broad; the skin is dry and scaly, loose and wrinkled; sex organs fail of normal development; the hair is dry, coarse, and brittle. (Cf. Figure 54.) But what interests us more in a psychological way is the general sluggishness in the patient's activity toward things about him, and a sluggishness in development of this overt behavior as the child grows older. His apathetic facial expression suggests well this deficiency in intelligence, which is frequently so grave as to be classed as idiocy. His emotional life is almost colorless. Such unfortunates are absolutely

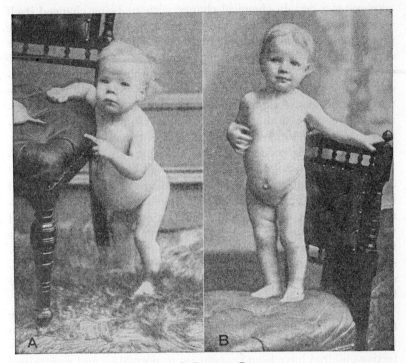

FIGURE 54. A CASE OF CRETINISM

A, at the age of two years and eight months.   *B*, the same, after four months' treatment with thyroid powder.   (From Nicholson, H. O.   *Arch. Pediat.*, 1900, **17**.)

incapable of meeting the demands of life around them; they cannot take care of themselves and must be placed in special institutions. Every large colony for the feeble-minded has its cretins.

Atrophy of the thyroid tissue in the adult produces much the same effects (*myxedema*).   Loss of hair, puffy dry skin, with fatty masses evident in places, brittle nails, and other structural changes accompany a deterioration in behavior traits.   The person appears slow of movement and lacks interest in things around him.   He is frequently emotionally depressed, and in adapting himself to situations he is sluggish and inefficient, owing to his faulty memory and his retarded thinking — a condition that sometimes leads to delusions and other psychotic (= "insane") disturbances.

How is this compound effect to be understood?   A key notion is that the thyroid's hormone is a "catalyzer" — a substance that accelerates a certain chemical change without being changed itself — and that this facilitates the chemical breaking-down of waste products of metabolism throughout the body so that they can be eliminated (at the kidneys, lungs, and skin). If this breaking-down process be arrested, then the waste products cannot be properly eliminated from the organism; they will serve only to clog the normal processes of the whole living machine. With this key concept the reader is in a position to understand each of the above-mentioned disturbances in physique and in behavior.

So much for hypofunctioning of the thyroid. Marked hypertrophy or overdevelopment may give rise to "exophthalmic goiter."[1] Among the manifestations of the latter are: rapid heart beat and high blood pressure, protrusion of the eyeballs, precocious development of the sex characteristics, elongation of the skeleton; and withal a "nervous" excitability and busyness of general conduct that knows no rest nor relaxation. At times the patient is low-spirited and tearful, at others cheerful and smiling, but always resents being thwarted or contradicted. This condition also may become exaggerated to psychotic proportions.

Medical treatment in cases of hypothyroidism has assumed the form of feeding the patient with thyroid tissue or extract taken from other animals; and sometimes with fair success. Many defective children have been brought up to normal — and maintained there when the feeding was kept up (Figure 54.) Myxedema patients may show almost as dramatic a change under the treatment. This, however, has not been true of anything like 100 per cent of the cases.

The Parathyroid Glands. Four small bodies about the size of peas are found upon the thyroid, and have been called accordingly parathyroids, though they have nothing to do with the thyroid's activity. Their secretion is important to bones and teeth. Their removal produces muscular tremors, spasms, agonizing cramps; and the patient is likely to develop maniacal excitement and rage seizures. Under treatment with parathyroid extract a striking reformation of his temperament and deportment is often brought about.

The Thymus Gland. The thymus gland is found in the upper thorax. It is relatively large in infancy and largest at puberty,

[1] This is not the most common form of goiter (colloid goiter), which is of less significance, medically or psychologically.

probably undergoing degeneration thereafter. Concerning its functions there is much disagreement; it may not even be a gland. But one opinion inclines to the view that it may secrete a hormone that helps to hold in check the otherwise premature development of the sex glands and the body characteristics secondary to them (described a few pages below).

The Pineal Body. This small organ is a part of the brain structures (cf. Figure 71, p. 280). In childhood it has a glandular structure which is gradually lost with the approach of puberty. It is supposed to produce a hormone inhibitory toward the sex glands, similar to that mentioned in connection with the thymus.

The Adrenal Glands. These two organs are located one on each of the kidneys — with which they have nothing to do. Each is a compound of an internal "medulla" and an enclosing "cortex" of different structure, and they should be treated as two distinct endocrines.

The secretion of the *cortex* seems to influence all the cells of the body. When it fails, the individual grows weak, restless, irritable, and unco-operative; then when it is artificially supplied it brings about a restoration of his enthusiasm and energy. See also Figure 29, *B*, p. 112. There is indication that it is closely associated with the activity of the sex glands. Whether this relation is one of cause or one of effect is uncertain, but the former is more probable, for overactivity when involved in a tumor makes for pronounced masculine sexual development. The active substance is "cortin."

The secretion of the *medulla* has been prepared synthetically and is called "epinephrin" or "adrenin." Its effects upon various tissues of the body assume much psychological importance and have attracted attention. In general it may be said to play an important part in a man's behavior when in emergencies prompt and vigorous activity is called for. In several ways that are too detailed for us to follow it serves to support the muscles called upon for action: by stimulating the liver to release some of its stored sugar into the blood-stream for transportation to the muscles; by speeding up the heart beat and at the same time raising the blood pressure; by reducing the activity of the smooth muscles of the stomach and intestines and so slowing down digestion. The effect of these and other changes associated with them is that the person can react more vigorously and with much more endurance; his digestive and certain other vegetative processes may be stopped, but his outward conduct is more emphatic; for example, his run is faster, his fist hits harder. The significance of this change in the demeanor of a man we have already considered as a phase of his emotional reaction (Chapter VII).

The Pituitary Body. The pituitary body (also called *hypophysis*) is really composed of two independent bodies, an "anterior" and a "posterior" lobe. The whole structure is about the size of a very large pea and fits into a small pocket in the bony floor of the cranium in the very center of the head. Though connected with the brain stalk, it has nothing to do with brain functions. It is important in the activation of the body, as we have seen in Figure 29, *A*, p. 112.

The *anterior lobe* has, in general, an important relationship to the nutritive condition of the body during growth, particularly of the skeletal structures. Its hormone seems to promote the growth of the bones and connective tissues. If this secretion is excessive in early life the result may be *gigantism*, with elongated skeleton and massive bones in the extremities. An individual thus developed often finds his way into museums and circuses. If this hypersecreting takes place after maturity the long bones do not become longer, and the stature is not increased, but the shape of the face gradually changes (*acromegaly*). The bony ridges over the eyes become more pronounced, the nose is more prominent, the chin projects, and in general an increased ruggedness of the features approaches the facial look of the gorilla, or, better, the type identified in literature with Punch and other court jesters. Incidentally there may be good reason for depicting jesters with such a face, for not infrequently the accelerated reactions of the acromegalic may make him a sharp-witted, interesting companion.

From the *posterior lobe* and its *pars intermedia* is secreted a hormone — possibly one, possibly four — that affects the activity of the smooth muscles much as does adrenin, though not exactly. The blood pressure is heightened, the heart rate slowed, and the contractions in the intestines, the bladder, and especially the uterus are increased. The extract pituitrin has well-known use as a tonic for the uterine muscles in childbirth. Thus the tonus of smooth muscles, so necessary to the life functions, is maintained by the posterior lobe; its atrophy produces sluggishness in these functions.

It seems also as though the pituitary in one or both of its lobes exercises a stimulating effect upon the development of the sex glands and the related secondary characteristics.   Hyperpituitarism acts as a cause of precocious sexual maturity, hypopituitarism as a cause of sexual infantilism.

As to more psychological traits: hypopituitarism may make of one a drowsy, forgetful, unambitious person, apparently "neurasthenic."   Excess of secretion, on the contrary, may make him irritable, distrustful, "psychasthenic."

The Sex Glands, or Gonads.   The sex glands proper are duct glands necessary for the function of reproduction.   The female glands produce the ova, or eggs, and the male glands produce the spermatozoa; and the union of these two different kinds of cells is the process of fertilization, which is necessary before segmentation and development of the new individual life can take place.   It has long been known that in some way the development of the sex apparatus is essential to the appearance in the individual of the secondary sex characteristics; and this was formerly supposed to be a function of these duct glands acting also as internally secreting organs.   But it has now become established — certainly for the male — that the development of the secondary characteristics is a function of other kinds of glandular tissues — the *interstitial* cells of Leydig in the male, the *corpus luteum* in the female, neither of these being reproductive glands proper, but neighboring tissue.   (The interstitial bodies lie imbedded about the sex glands in the testicle; the corpus luteum, or Graafian follicle, is the structure in the ovary from which the ova arise and periodically escape.)

The *secondary sex characteristics* include many traits of physique and of activity that differentiate man and woman.   There are the well-known differences in height and weight.   Male and female differ also in body shape or contours, the former showing more angularity and the latter more curved lines.   They differ in voice. The distribution of hair on the body, including the beard, and the development of mammary glands are further contrasting traits. Differences in characteristics of a more psychological nature have hardly been made out.   There *may* be some differences in the fundamental nature of striped muscle-skeleton co-ordinations; and there *may* be inborn emotional and temperamental differences.   On the other hand, in the traits involving fine implicit habit formations and activities — "memory," "intelligence," "reasoning capacity," and the like — no differences are demonstrable at all.   The whole question of innate sex differences is complicated by the fact that the childhood training of boy and of girl is in marked contrast, so that it is almost impossible at present to rule out the effects of environment in the explanation of why Jack and Jill behave so differently on certain occasions. To say, for instance, that woman has more of an "instinct of tender care" and man more of a "pugnacious instinct" is nonsense, as is also the assertion that the one "uses his reason" while the other "uses her intuition." This matter will receive our attention again in Chapter XX.

The normal development of the secondary sex characteristics dates from puberty and is traceable to the hormone of the interstitial cells (also called the "puberty gland") or of the corpus luteum. Experimental work on animals other than man has usually taken the form of transplanting testes from one body to another (in which case the sex glands proper usually atrophy and the interstitial cells multiply); or it has assumed the form of injecting either of two not thoroughly understood extracts of the corpus luteum (*theelin* and *progestin*) into males or into immature or aged females. Steinach and others report remarkable results. When castrated male guinea pigs or rats had grafted within them the ovaries from females, their usual secondary male characteristics failed to appear and the genital organs remained infantile, while various characteristics of the female made their appearance in both physique and behavior. On the other hand, the transplanting of male interstitial tissue into ovariectomized (spayed) females produced animals that looked and acted decidedly more like males than like females. In spite of these striking results upon other animals, and in spite of certain over-advertised results with humans, we are far from having definite knowledge of how — by operative or other technique — to control the development of sex traits or to secure "rejuvenescence." Here popular fiction-making tends to obscure fact.

One thing certain is that the gonads have much to do with motivating the organism. This has already been shown in Figures 26 and 27.

The Pancreas. Besides acting as a duct gland concerned with digestion, the pancreas acts also as an endocrine organ through the internal secretions of the small islets of Langerhans found scattered through the body of the organ. The *insulin* secreted by these islets has lately played a dramatic rôle in the medical treatment of diabetes mellitus.

The Liver. The liver, too, has endocrine functions. (1) It transforms nitrogenous waste products in the blood into urea for excretion at the kidneys. (2) It also serves as a stabilizer of the sugar content of the blood: it changes the sugar absorbed into the blood from digested food into glycogen, which is stored up in the liver; this glycogen is later transformed back into sugar, which is returned to the bloodstream on demand. This demand is occasioned by a change in the acid-alkali character of the blood, or by an increased amount of adrenin. In either case the function ultimately fulfilled is the supplying of readily available energy to working muscles. We have considered this as an important phase of emotional behavior in Chapter VII. Fighting and fearing both involve these changes, and unless we know something of the changes, we cannot fully understand fighting and fearing. (3) An extract from the liver has been prepared that may be used to reduce blood pressure and so remove a Damoclean sword from over the head of the aging person.

Interdependence of the Endocrines. We have surveyed these ductless glands one by one. The qualifying words, "it seems," "probably," "may be," so frequently used in describing the functions of a given gland, should serve to remind us that these many different endocrines really act in an interlocking way. We might almost refer to them collectively as "the endocrine system," so intimate is their interdependence, in stimulating one another, controlling one another, compensating for one another. Consider these examples: (1) The atrophy of the ovaries after the menopause leaves the thyroid without its former counterbalance and a hyperthyroid condition ensues; this awakens overactivity of the adrenals with a train of symptoms. (2) Hyperthyroidism may be traceable to underactivity of the pituitary or to overactivity of the adrenals. (3) The pancreas opposes the pituitary, and the adrenals oppose the pancreas. (4) The development of the sex glands we have seen to be possibly advanced or held in check by the pituitary, the pineal, the thymus, the adrenal cortex, the thyroid. Balances and counterbalances! When we consider this amazing complexity of interrelations and bear in mind the technical difficulties involved in experimental work on such delicate structures and substances, we do not wonder that endocrinology is a much-delayed branch of knowledge, important though it is to the understanding of man and the reasons for his behavior.

In general, we may say that knowledge of the operations of ductless glands is important in several ways to a psychological analysis of human nature. (1) These glands are of prime importance in the general *development* both of physique and of behavior. (2) They have great influence upon the person's general *efficiency* at a given time. This includes (a) proper interaction of organ with organ inside the body, and (b) adequate support of overt reactions toward people and things outside. (3) They play significant rôles in *emotional* behavior. It should not surprise us, then, to learn that many forms of nervous and mental disorders are now being treated with glandular extracts.

And now a general word to the reader. A consideration of even these sketchy accounts of how a person's intellectual, emotional, and physical development depends upon these bodily factors as causes, how his temperamental characteristics and behavior toward people about him are to a large extent the outcome of his physical conditions, should help to induct the reader into the scientific and impersonal attitude toward his fellow-man.

REFERENCES

1. Dunlap, K. *Outline of Psychobiology.* Johns Hopkins Univ. Press, 1914.
2. Evans, C. L. *Recent Advances in Physiology.* Blakiston, 4th ed. 1930. Chs. VI–VIII.
3. Freeman, W. Personality and the Endocrines; a Study Based Upon 1400 Quantitative Necropsies. *Annals Intern. Med.*, 1935, 9, 444–450.
4. Gasser, H. S., and Newcomer, H. S. Physiological Action Currents in the Phrenic Nerve. An Application of the Thermionic Vacuum Tube to Nerve Physiology. *Am. J. Physiol.*, 1921, 57, 1–26.
5. Hoskins, R. G. *The Tides of Life.* Norton, 1933.
6. Howell, W. H. *Text-book of Physiology.* Saunders (13th ed.), 1936.
7. Jacobson, E., and Carlson, A. J. The Influence of Relaxation upon the Knee Jerk. *Am. J. Physiol.*, 1925, 73, 324–28.
8. Max, L. W. An Experimental Study of the Motor Theory of Consciousness. I. History and Critique. *J. Gen. Psychol.*, 1934, 11, 112–25. II. Method and Apparatus. *J. Gen. Psychol.*, 1935, 13, 159–75. III. Action-Current Responses in Deaf-Mutes during Sleep, Sensory Stimulation, and Dreams. *J. Comp. Psychol.*, 1935, 19, 469–86.
9. Timme, W. *Lectures on Endocrinology.* Hoeber, 1924.

CHAPTER IX
SENSORY FUNCTIONS

SENSITIVITY IN GENERAL

The Importance of Studying Sensory Phenomena. There can be no expression without impression, no response without stimulation. A man does nothing, is not active, in any manner involving the effectors studied in the last chapter, unless in some way he is being influenced by energy-changes occurring inside or outside of him which play upon his receptors — provided we except a few cases of smooth muscle and gland excitation by hormones. The student interested in the phenomena of human nature and in their prediction and control must have some definite knowledge as to how men are sensitive to influences: to what kinds of forces or influences they are sensitive; at what degrees of intensity; and at what places on or in the body the influences must be applied. Many are the practical questions that turn upon such facts. What are the most effective colors for switch lights and street-crossing signals? Can all men see them equally well? What is the best form of illumination for a factory? How fine a difference can the average pilot detect in the directions of the motion of his airplane when it is enveloped in clouds? Do different pilots vary much in this regard, and can such variations be measured and tested? How good an "ear" and what kind of "ear" must one have to become a successful violinist? What are the essentials of a good musical tone? Just what is the nature of the difference of tones which proceed from various string, wood-wind, and brass instruments? In what way does the rolling of a ship excite nausea? When one is learning to operate a typewriter, what controls the speed and accuracy of the strokes? Why is the touch method of typing recommended? In learning to hold a billiard cue or a fencing foil precisely right, what receptors are involved? To put all this in a nutshell: no attempt systematically to understand the hows and whys of human behavior can be successful unless consideration be given to *the paramount rôle of stimulation in the initiating and in the controlling of behavior.*

A second reason for the study of human sensitivity presents itself as soon as we recognize the other centuries-old motive for psychological study — the analysis of one's own personal and private conscious experience. It is a fact that the great majority of thoroughgoing inquiries into the nature of consciousness have been highly analytical in character, and have discovered as the basis of consciousness sensations of one sort or another. One's awareness of an object perceived or of an event imagined or dreamed, the feelings of his emotional responses, and even the processes of thinking as he is conscious of them — all are held to be reducible to the primordial sensory experiences of particular colors, tastes, sounds, pressures, strains, and the like. This analysis of one's consciousness while for the most part exceedingly difficult for the untrained, is well typified by some fairly easy and common analyses attempted by the average man. He may, for example, examine the experience he calls the taste produced by his lemonade to determine whether it has sourness enough or sweet-ness enough, or he may examine the taste of his breakfast cereal to see whether the sweet-ness and the salt-ness of the taste are properly balanced. To summarize: any systematic study of psychology from the introspective point of approach must recognize *the central importance of sensations* (that is, the individual's awarenesses occasioned by stimulations) *in the analysis of consciousness.*

In keeping with the aims of this book as announced in the first chapter, we shall, for the most part, approach the sensory processes in the objective rather than the subjective manner, though supplementing the former with the latter at a few points. Putting it more simply: our primary inquiry will be to see how our hypothetical subject reacts to the various forms of stimulation which we bring to bear upon him and what differences in his actions are explainable by the changes of stimulation; but we shall now and then amplify this account by asking him, "How does it 'feel' or appear?"

A more general reason for including sensitivity in our survey of psychology lies in the fact that this division of psychology has probably been more thoroughly worked out in its details than any other; and it would be an unfair introduction to the field if we did not give the reader some acquaintance with some of these details.

A Classification of Receptors.   The facts of stimulation and sensitivity are so many and diverse that we will do well to block out the phenomena by a preliminary classification.

A Classification of the Receptors and their Stimuli

STIMULI	RECEPTORS	CLASSES
I. *Energy changes in environment*	*Exteroceptors*	
light	in eye	visual
sound	in ear (cochlea)	auditory
heat (and cold)	in skin	cutaneous
pressure	in skin	cutaneous
chemicals	in nose	olfactory
chemicals	in tongue	gustatory
II. *Changes in position and movement of organism*	*Proprioceptors*	
of parts	in muscle, tendon, joint	kinesthetic
of whole	in ear (canals and vestibule)	static
III. *General organic conditions, especially of alimentary canal and other viscera*	*Interoceptors*	
emptiness or distention of a viscus, chemical substance, etc., etc.	in linings of alimentary canal and in other deep tissues	organic
IV. *Conditions tending to do immediate injury.*	*Nociceptors*	
	in skin	pain
	in nearly all important organs, deep and superficial	pain

This is far from a completely clear-cut set of divisions. The fourth division includes not only excitation of certain specific receptors found in the skin, but also excitation in intense degree applied to the structures in which most of the other receptors are found. We know as yet too little about all the stimulating conditions in the third class. This ignorance is the result, for one thing, of a relatively great difficulty in experimental analysis; for while in the laboratory it is a comparatively easy matter to control whatever light or sound stimuli are to be allowed to fall upon the eye or ear, it is quite another thing to attempt similarly to manipulate the normal stimuli that play upon receptive areas in the soft organs of the bodily interior.

The stimuli here listed are the usual or *adequate stimuli* for the respective receptors. In many cases the latter are excitable by other kinds of agencies or conditions. For instance, when the eyeball is poked with the finger, the eye may be affected as if by a light; and electricity applied to the eye, ear, tongue, or skin will be seen, heard, tasted, or felt.

The Relative Nature of a Stimulus. In order to function as a stimulus an agent must play upon a receptor not in absolutely constant manner but with some change or contrast. For example, it is not only the absolute intensity of the agent, but its contrast with accompanying or with immediately preceding agents that makes it effective in exciting a receptor. To affect hearing, for instance, a sound must be louder or softer, higher or lower, or in some other way different from other sounds preceding or accompanying it. To be seen, an object must differ from its surroundings and background. The converse of this principle is strikingly demonstrated in the camouflage of war vessels and in the protective coloration of a chameleon or a flat fish, which, by changing their coloration and pattern to correspond to those of their background of tree trunk or ocean bottom, escape the vision of predatory animals.

Associated with this point is the phenomenon of *sensory adaptation*. After continuous stimulation of a given receptor the stimulating agent progressively becomes less effective and may ultimately have no effect at all. This is true of most classes of sensation, ranging from smell and from temperature sense, in which it is strikingly shown, to pain, in which it is hardly observable. The nose, as is well known, becomes rapidly inexcitable by the same odor if the odor is long continued; the skin receptors of cold become inexcitable after the bather is once well in the pool.

CUTANEOUS SENSITIVITY [1]

Stimuli and Receptors. It is natural to begin our analysis of sense organs with those operating at the general surface of the body. These are relatively simple and are rather generally distributed. The skin is affected by temperature and pressure changes.

---

[1] The presentation of the different classes of sensitivity in the following pages will not follow strictly the order appearing in the table given above. Simple but well analyzed classes will be presented first, and the most complex will be reserved for treatment last.

Let us follow a typical experiment. A small area of the skin is marked off with boundary and cross lines, and a variety of stimuli are then applied systematically to the whole area point by point. If a dull-pointed brass cylinder of the temperature 37° to 40° C be placed in contact with the skin, it will in some places produce characteristic experiences and responses on the part of the subject: if properly instructed, he will say "warm" when it touches these points. These warm spots are relatively sparsely distributed. Now let a cooled cylinder of 12° to 15° C be applied in the same manner of exploration, and other places on the skin will be found to be affected — the "cold spots." There are on the average about 13 cold and 2 warm spots to a square centimeter area. Next if we apply with gentle pressure a round wooden point we will succeed in obtaining verbal reactions from the subject throughout most of the area — he will be experiencing "touch" or pressure — and invariably so if we touch a hair or the skin just to the "windward" side of a hair. Finally, if we employ a rather stiff and sharply pointed bristle we will find that all parts of the area — with rarely an exception — will be sensitive to the pricking in a way that, if intensified, will evoke reflex retraction movements, and our subject will report *pain*. A sample map of the sensitivities in a small area (from the volar surface of the forearm) as determined by this exploring is given in Figure 55. In this diagram points where application of *warm* stimulus elicits response are indicated with *dots*; where application of *cold* elicits response, with *circles*; where *pressure fails* to elicit response, with *crosses*. The application of pain stimulus was effective throughout this area.

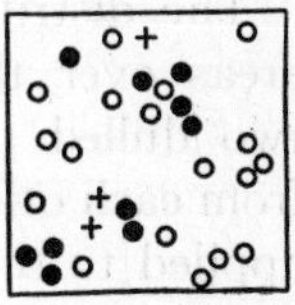

FIGURE 55.
(Explanation in text.)

It is now obvious that within the same kind of sensitivity (here, the cutaneous) different sensory functions may be included. The so-called "sense of touch" is not a single and simple capacity but a multiple one. On the structural side we would infer that within the skin there must be not one but several kinds of receptors, each selectively sensitive to its own peculiar type of agent — warmth, cold, pressure, or pain. On dissection of the skin several different kinds of minute structures are found which are closely associated with the afferent endings of neurones and are in consequence supposed to be the receptors in question. Recent critical work [3] has, however, thrown so much doubt upon the traditionally accepted list of skin receptors that we shall not take space to expand this topic.

Some Special Phenomena.   It is not to be assumed, of course, that by ordinary agents only one receptor will be excited at a time. More commonly, many receptors of the same and of different types are aroused.   The fact is well shown in the way immersion in water baths of different temperatures is found to excite different combinations of receptors and different qualities of experienced "feels." This is brought out in detail in the accompanying table.   There the reader should note how at different degrees of temperature three kinds of receptors are excited in varying combinations and degrees, giving rise to experiences of qualitatively different character.

Temperature in centigrade	Receptors excited	How experienced
Below 10	Cold and pain	"Biting cold"
15–30	Cold	"Cold"
35–42	Warm	"Warm"
46–50	Warm and cold	"Hot"
Above 50	Warm, cold, and pain	"Burning hot"

The distribution of sense organs varies greatly in the different areas over the body.   A two-point esthesiometer, consisting of two dulled points of hard rubber, fixed at adjustable distances from each other and so placed on a handle as to be easily and lightly applied to the skin, is used to determine *spatial thresholds* of pressure, that is, the minimal distances that must separate two points before the subject can perceive them as distinct points.   Some of these thresholds are:

Tip of tongue	1 mm.
Tip of finger	2
Outer surface of lip	5
Palm	8
Forehead	22
Back of hand	30
Along spine	60

A well-known phenomenon of cutaneous sensitivity is the rapid *adaptation* of the temperature end organs.   Suppose three vessels of water be provided at the temperatures 20°, 40°, and 30° C, respectively exciting the cold receptors, the warm receptors, and neither (the "physiological zero").   Let the left hand be held in the 20° bath and the right in the 40° bath for one minute, and it will be found not only that the excitation of the cold and of the warmth receptors gradually disappears, but also that when both hands are plunged into the "neutral" water at 30° the left (previously in cold) shows stimulation of its warm receptors and the right (previously in warm) stimulation of its cold. Thus it is the change of temperature that is effective.

GUSTATORY SENSITIVITY

Stimuli and Receptors. In order to act upon the organism as a *taste*, a substance must be in liquid, or at least soluble, form and must be brought into contact with the "taste buds" located principally in the mucous membrane of the tongue and to a lesser degree on the soft palate and the lining of the pharynx. The taste buds on the tongue are embedded in some of the papillae (protuberances visible to the eye). In each of these buds the dendrite end of an afferent nerve is in close connection with hair cells, the hairy ends of which project out into the mouth cavity and are exposed to the substances there. The process of receptor stimulation is, then, excitation of some energy change in the hair cells caused by a substance having taste, consequent excitation of the nerve ending, and the transmission of this excitation along the afferent nerve to the central nervous system.

The sense of taste is, like the sensitivity of the skin, a multiple function; it is possible to classify all taste stimuli into the four groups *sweet*, *salt*, *sour*, and *bitter*, and their many combinations. Sensitivity to sweet substances is greatest near the tip of the tongue, to sour along the sides, and to bitter toward the back, while that to salty substances is more generally distributed.

The technique for the experimental investigation of taste is relatively simple. With camel's hair brushes or with pipettes simple sapid liquids (liquids having taste, such as solutions of sugar and of common salt, tartaric acid, quinine hydrochlorate) are applied to individual papillae or to areas of the tongue, and the subject's verbal responses are noted. Care must be exercised to eliminate disturbing factors, particularly those other classes of stimulation mentioned in the preceding paragraph.

Some Special Phenomena. Some adaptation of the receptors may be observed. After continued eating of candy or syrupy food, a child may declare that a more mildly sweet food is not sweet at all; and salty ham becomes less salty with successive bites.

Contrast effects are also present. A sweet stimulation of subliminal intensity (that is, too weak to be effective) on one side of the tongue may be rendered supraliminal by the simultaneous application of a sour stimulus on the other side. The same heightened effect is seen when the sour and the sweet stimuli are applied successively. Similar contrasts are obtained between sour and salt, and between salt and sweet.

An outstanding fact about taste in everyday life is that it is commonly confused with other modes of stimulation. In the process of eating, food stimulates the tongue as a cutaneous surface and ordinarily stimulates the olfactory receptors in the nasal passages in a marked degree, so that the effect of such things as hot coffee or iced lemonade is by no means an effect on taste alone.[1] For that matter, a person's preferences in foods may be traceable even to kinesthetic or to auditory stimulation, as when a salad or a pie crust is pronounced crisp.

OLFACTORY SENSITIVITY

Stimuli and Receptors. To furnish olfactory stimulation to an organism an agent must be in the form of, or must produce, gaseous particles which, when brought into direct contact with the olfactory membrane in the nose, will chemically excite it. This special membrane is of very limited area, not so large as a dime, and is to be found in the upper part of the left and right nasal passages. The receptors proper are simple, consisting of afferent nerve cells with dendrites running out to the surface of the mucous lining and bearing fine hairs that project into the air of the nasal passage. We have seen that there are different kinds of cutaneous and gustatory receptors; whether there are different kinds of olfactory receptors cannot at the present be determined, for point-by-point exploration is virtually impossible on account of the well-nigh inaccessible position of the olfactory membranes.

Some Special Phenomena. With the double olfactometer two kinds of odorous substances can be presented at the same time. This instrument consists (*a*) of two glass tubes curved at one end for insertion into the nostrils, and (*b*) over each a larger tube, lined on the inside with the odorous material and sliding smoothly so

---

[1] An instructive demonstration is to have a blindfolded subject hold his nose well closed, and then to lay upon his tongue (not to be chewed) a small bit of onion and one of apple alternately, to see if he can discriminate between them.

that the amount of the material exposed by it to the air that is being drawn into the smaller tube and into the nostril is adjustable. One result of the simultaneous presentation of two odors is that each may cancel or *neutralize* the effect of the other, as occurs with iodoform and Peru balsam. This principle has been hit upon in the practical employment of deodorants, as when carbolic acid is used to neutralize the odor of gangrene. On the other hand, two odors may *fuse* and form a new kind of stimulation, as do xylol and turpentine. Many synthetic perfumes illustrate this phenomenon. If presented in succession, the second odor may be enhanced by the first, showing the contrast effect familiar in other classes of sense.

Adaptation is nowhere better shown than in olfactory sensations. After continued presentation most odors show diminishing stimulus value down to total abolition; and simple laboratory tests with such substances as iodine, heliotrope, and camphor may show this to occur within from one to six minutes. In everyday life the phenomenon is common indeed. We may recoil on first entering the foul atmosphere of an overcrowded auditorium or a fish market or a dissecting room, but inevitably, if we remain a while, the odor will become ineffective.

Reactions Aroused. The primary biological function of taste and smell is, of course, that of inspecting substances about to be taken into the digestive and respiratory tracts. The connection of these two senses with those tracts is so intimate that a strong, foul odor may upset and even reverse some of the normal processes of digestion, while another odor may powerfully facilitate them. It is true, moreover, particularly in the case of smell, that peculiarly intimate sensory-motor connections exist with other internal organs as well and thus awaken emotional reactions. Advertisers of perfumes make much of this in the descriptive names they apply, as, for instance, "*toujours fidèle*," "seductive," "indiscreet," "*toujours moi*," "*l'heure romantique*," "irresistible," "confession," and the like. And everyone has noticed the peculiar vividness with which a flower scent has recalled for him the past experience of a love or a funeral or even of a job in a manufacturing plant.

KINESTHETIC SENSITIVITY

Stimuli and Receptors. Of all the classes of sensitivity the kinesthetic (from the Greek *kinesi* — movement) is the most fundamental and the most necessary to man or animal. Man is an organism whose behavior includes the simultaneous and successive functioning of an enormous number of different action units; therefore if his behavior is to show organization and consistency, he must be so equipped that these action units can reciprocally affect one another. A contraction of a muscle at one place must in some way influence the contraction or relaxation of another muscle at some other place.

The *muscles*, *tendons*, and *joint surfaces* are supplied with afferent nerve endings originating in receptor structures that are not well known in detail. (Cf. Figure 56.) As a muscle contracts or relaxes, the receptors in the muscle tissue are naturally affected and,

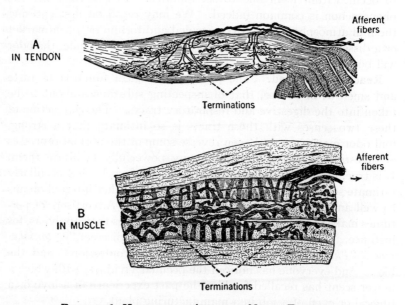

FIGURE 56. KINESTHETIC AFFERENT NERVE ENDINGS

A, in tendon. The tendinous bundle near the point of attachment of muscle fibers splits up into spindles, and among these the finely divided nerve branches ramify and end in plate-like expansions. *B*, in muscle. The muscle tissue is divided into many spindles, and the nerve branches wind around these spirally and circularly, and end in plate-like expansions. (After Huber and DeWitt, and Ruffini.)

since the muscle pulls upon its tendinous connections, the receptors located in it are likewise affected. If movement occurs, the change of position of one member with reference to another to which it is joined (as forearm to upper arm at the elbow) produces a change in the location and amount of pressures at the surfaces of the joint, thus affecting receptors there also.

Importance to Behavior. The manner in which the contraction of one muscle plays a part in determining the contraction of another is illustrated in so simple a performance as tapping the finger or waving the hand: *the muscular contraction that produces one movement furnishes the necessary stimulation for exciting the muscular contraction that results in the reciprocal or the next movement.* Very different members may be so connected, as in walking, when the contractions in the left leg in the forward swing of the foot lead to the alternately succeeding contractions in the right. This is shown in a negative way in tabes dorsalis, sometimes called locomotor ataxia, where the diseased condition of the spinal cord blocks the afferent impulses arising from a moving leg; without this source of renewed stimulation and control the movement of the other leg is seriously handicapped, and a reeling, staggering gait is the well-known result. (Cf. Figure 69, p. 272.) Or again, consider the case of K——, who at eight years of age could neither dress nor feed herself, could not walk without stumbling nor go through any motor performances in a way normal to her age. All her movements were guided by visual instead of kinesthetic stimulation; and when a large collar was put about her neck obstructing her view of her feet she would refuse to climb or descend stairs and would fall if she attempted to walk. Now, during many months of her infancy she had been seriously ill and bed-fast, and had been prevented from developing the normal kinesthetic-motor functions; she had tried to control all hand and foot movements by watching them. It was only after being slowly re-trained with a blindfold that she developed full normal control of her dressing, walking, handwriting, and other motor activities.

Stimulation of the kinesthetic receptors may take place not only when there is observable movement but also whenever the muscle-tendon-joint apparatus is thrown into a condition of tension. The object against which an arm, head, or leg is pushing may be immovable, but the motor apparatus in play is doing work, so that its receptors are affected and set up their afferent neural impulses.

Tension in a muscle may stimulate the same muscle, as when an increased pull on the fingers holding a bucket or rope excites an increased condition of contraction to counteract it. Variations in the degree of tonus (cf. pp. 201 f.) that is present in the general musculature of the body, from great strain to relaxation, give rise to variations in kinesthetic impulses sent toward the central nervous system and eventually out again to the effectors; and in this way the amount of motor activity already in process in the body has important effects upon the amount of activity to be shown subsequently. In passing, the reader should note that kinesthetic functions are not limited to those members of the body involved in grosser movements, but are essentially involved in such finer adjustments as those of the eye muscles in reading, in seeing objects as distant, and those of the laryngeal muscles in speaking aloud or to one's self. To these we will return at several points later.

In spite of the downright importance of kinesthetic sensitivity, relatively little experimentation has been done in this field, except for the *lifted-weights experiment.* In this experiment the question is raised: how fine a difference between two weights can be detected by simple "hefting" between thumb and finger? The blindfold subject is given in irregular order two weights to be lifted, one of a Constant value (for example, 100 gr.) the other of Varying values above or below the Constant. The Variable is increased and decreased through carefully planned series: and the whole series of judgments by the subjects are totaled and compared to find just how much heavier (or lighter) the Variable had to be in order to be discriminated. One consistent outcome of several decades of work is the conclusion that the heavier the Constant weight, the greater must be the difference between it and the Variable; so that acuteness here is a relative matter — an instance of the Weber-Fechner law, to be discussed later.

STATIC SENSITIVITY

Stimuli and Receptors. Closely associated with the kinesthetic receptors are those of the semicircular canals and the vestibule of the ear. The internal ear (see Figure 57) is a tortuous cavity in the temporal bone, divisible into a central portion, the *vestibule;* an upper portion, the *semicircular canals;* and a lower portion, the

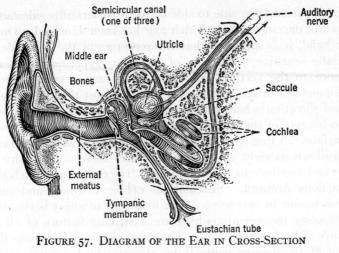

FIGURE 57. DIAGRAM OF THE EAR IN CROSS-SECTION
(Explanations in text.)

cochlea.[1] Within this bony labyrinth lies a membranous labyrinth, roughly following the general structure of canals and of cochlea, but dividing into two large sacs in the vestibule, which are called the utricle and the saccule. On the inner walls of the canals and also of the utricle and the saccule lie cells with hairlets projecting into the liquid that is within the membranous labyrinth. About the base of these hair cells arise the afferent nerve fibers.

The immediate stimulus acting upon the hair cells consists of varying pressures of the liquid when it is disturbed by a movement of the head. By the familiar principle of inertia, when a bucket containing water is suddenly spun around or when it is jerked in any direction, the water itself shows a lag and exerts a reverse pressure on anything projecting from the wall of the bucket into the water. The same thing occurs in the canals and vestibule, where the suddenly displaced liquid presses against the highly sensitive hair-bearing cells. That the receptor cells of the semicircular canals are specially affected by *rotary* movements of the head is suggested by their peculiar arrangement — the three canals of each ear approximating the three planes of space. The relation of the canals to rotary movements can be demonstrated. If one pair of the canals in the ear of a pigeon is destroyed, the bird keeps

[1] The cochlea is quite distinct in function from the other two parts. In it are located the receptors for hearing.

moving its head from side to side or turns somersaults sideward or backward, depending upon which pair has been damaged. On the other hand, it is supposed that the receptors of the vestibule are especially sensitive to changes of *rectilinear* type, especially with reference to the vertical (gravity). Deaf-mutes with imperfect development of utricle and saccule cannot adjust themselves to the vertical direction when swimming in deep water, and may even drown because of the absence of cues to guide their strokes toward the surface. A frog with the vestibule removed is as likely to swim upside down as right side up. It is easy to see, then, why the canals and vestibule have been dubbed "the compass of the body."

Reactions Aroused. Stimulations of the vestibule and canals effect behavior in two ways. The first type of effect is the reflex *compensatory* movements, which are a striking feature of all disturbance of body orientation. The reader will find a curious illustration of these movements if he observes birds standing upon slightly swaying wires. With the backward and forward swings of the wire the bird will gently thrust its head forward and backward so that, when he is observed against a background, his head remains stationary. These compensatory movements have been investigated with the rotating-chair technique by Dunlap and his students, and by Dodge. When the chair begins to turn to the left and as long as the rate of turning is being increased, a subject seated in the chair with his eyes closed will show alternating movements of the eyeballs: a slow turning or drift backward toward the right, frequently corrected by quick movements in the forward direction. Along with this there is a twisting of the trunk and a lateral straining in the legs. The subject will report, "I'm turning left." Once a constant speed of rotation is reached, these motor readjustments decrease gradually to passivity (the adaptation phenomenon); and he will report, "Not turning at all!" Finally, upon a slowing down of the rotation, precisely the reverse compensatory movements are set up, which gradually subside after a complete stop, the subject meanwhile reporting, "Now turning right!"

Secondly, afferent impulses from the canals and vestibule play a highly significant part in the maintenance of *muscular tonus*. The pigeon already referred to with injured semicircular canals displays, in addition to its faulty spatial adjustments, enfeeblement of general behavior: its flying is weak, its legs do not remain rigid, its whole attitude is drooping and listless. The knockout blow so

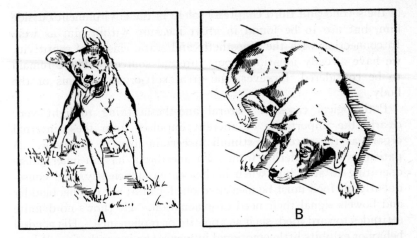

FIGURE 58. BEHAVIOR CHANGES FOLLOWING INJURY TO STATIC RECEPTORS

A. A dog after recovery from an operation in which the semicircular canals and vestibule of the right side were destroyed. The subject fails to make appropriate compensatory movements to right the head position.

B. A dog after recovery from an operation in which canals and vestibule of both sides were destroyed. The subject shows loss of muscular tonus over the whole body.

(From Wilson, J. G., and Pike, F. H. *Philosophical Transactions of the Royal Society*, Series B, vol. 203, 1912, 127–160.)

well known to the boxer is one given to the jaw bone, imparting such a shock to the inner ear that its afferent functions are temporarily abolished; and, lacking this source of stimulation, the muscles of the previously vigorous athlete lose their tone, becoming inert and paralyzed as he lies, a mere lump, upon the floor.

The subject himself is seldom keenly aware of the static functions, but in unusual cases of disturbance he can report them; for example, when in an elevator operated with unaccustomed speed, when balancing himself on the hind legs of a chair, when dizzy from digestive upset or eyestrain, or when seasick.

The essential part that these two functions play in human and animal behavior is evident from Figure 58, in which are shown the serious alterations produced when they are abolished.

ORGANIC SENSITIVITY

Its General Importance. The original sources of the energies that set an animal or a man into action are not (as we have seen in the second and third chapters) solely in the environment outside him, but are to be found in great measure within him as well. In connection with the kinesthetic and static classes of sensitivity we have already identified some internal sources. There remain to be considered, however, the great soft-organ systems of the body.

Pathological cases of visceral anesthesia bring to light very clearly the importance of afferent impulses from these internal organs as the necessary stimuli in certain lines of behavior. A patient who is suffering from such anesthesia has no inner gauge operating to stop him when he has eaten sufficiently, and consequently his food must be measured out for him; nor can his bladder and bowels signal their need of evacuation. He shows no definite attitudes toward food, such as appetite or repugnance. His general behavior exhibits little emotional influence; he is apathetic. Whatever the time-beating mechanisms within him may be, they are now ineffective as controls of his reactions, for he cannot time his day's activities except by the clock, nor can he correctly judge whether on waking he has slept one hour or ten.

It must be admitted at the outset, however, that very little can be definitely stated concerning the receptor mechanisms involved. (1) For one reason, they are so difficult or often impossible of access that experimental control of the application of stimuli is frequently out of the question. (2) Since the normal processes of digestion, circulation, and so forth are somewhat constant and regular, they seldom provide any sudden and pronounced changes of stimulus to the local receptors, such as the external world provides for eye or ear, nose or skin.

Different Forms of Organic Sensitivity. Two forms of organic sensitivity have been satisfactorily determined. *Thirst* is found to arise from the mucous lining at the back of the throat, and to be set up when that membrane reaches a condition of dryness. The thirst stimulations disappear whenever the membrane is sufficiently moistened, either by the introduction of water into the system through drinking or injection, or by the local application of an acid, such as citric acid. *Hunger* (which is not to be confused with appetite for particular foods) has been traced to vigorous rhythmic contractions of the walls of the empty stomach. The subjects of an experiment swallowed soft balloons attached by rubber tubing to recording devices, and these were inflated in the stomach so that movements of the latter would be pneumatically conveyed to the recording instruments. (Cf. Figure 23.) During the first three to five days of a fast, the hunger contractions became gradually weaker until they practically disappeared.

For hunger and thirst, then, the local tissue-conditions would lead us to assume that no type of stimulation or of receptor exists other than those already described for other senses. Thirst appears to be a form of cutaneous sensitivity, hunger of muscular. It is reasonable to suppose that none of the forms of organic sensitivity involves the functioning of any unique type of receptor.

On account of the scantiness of our information we can only roughly classify the rich number of different sources of afferent impulses. Nausea is probably associated with a reversal of the peristalsis (cf. p. 210) of the *digestive* tract. From the *respiratory* system arises suffocation. From the *circulatory* arises heart panic, and so forth. From the *sex apparatus* arises sex appetite in its various phases. From the *distention* of many *hollow organs*, stomach, colon, bladder, and others, arise impulses akin to kinesthetic or cutaneous pressure. From tonic conditions of the *smooth musculature* itself probably come afferent streams of impulses having much influence upon the general attitudes and energy of the body. From many, but not all, tissues and organs arise impulses of the nociceptive, or *pain*, type.

From these few notes it may be gathered that very much of the motivation of a person — what makes him "go" — is traceable to these organic afferent impulses. Already we have seen (in Chapters II and V) that the typical situation for setting an organism into activity is one in which environmental conditions are unfavorable to its internal needs. We are now in a better position to see that these unsatisfied internal needs set up stimulations, which arouse efferent impulses to the active organs, muscles and glands.

AUDITORY SENSITIVITY

Stimuli and Receptors. Hearing is a result of stimulation by vibrations of air, typically, but also by other material media, such as the bones of the head, water, and so forth; and these vibrations may fall between the extreme limits of frequency of 20 and 20,000 cycles per second.

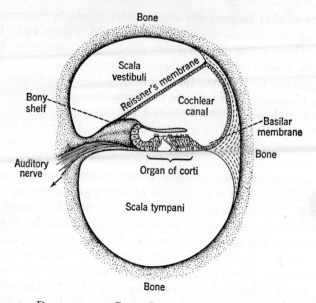

FIGURE 59. DIAGRAM OF A CROSS-SECTION OF A COIL OF THE COCHLEA
(Explanation in text.)

Diagrams of the ear are offered in Figures 57 and 59. Vibrations of the air passing up the canal called the external meatus set into vibration the tympanic membrane or eardrum. By means of the system of levers formed by the three small bones of the middle ear the vibrations of the eardrum are transmitted to a membrane stretched across a window of the inner ear, thus communicating the oscillations to the liquid filling the cavities of the inner ear, including the cochlea. The cochlea is a tapering cavity winding spirally through the bone for two and a half turns, and longitudinally divided into canals by a bony shelf and membranes. Along one of these canals (the cochlear) stretches the basilar membrane bearing the organ of Corti and its hair cells, about which are to be found the dendrites of afferent nerve fibers. It is supposed that vibrations of the liquid of the inner ear and the cochlear canal excite these hair cells in some indirect manner, and that these in turn set up the chemical changes in the nerve endings, which, as neural impulses, take an afferent course along the auditory nerve to the brain — thence, of course, to pass out along efferent nerves to effectors.

Theories of the Auditory Mechanism. Much speculation has been devoted to the question of precisely what mechanisms in the cochlea make possible differential responses to the ten thousand different pitches of sound heard; and a variety of hypotheses have been advanced. Helmholtz's theory is historically the most famous. The basilar membrane, he pointed out, contains transverse fibers which vary in their mechanical properties in a continuous way, so as to give a progressive tuning from high to low, like the strings of a piano. Assuming the principle of sympathetic vibration, Helmholtz supposed that each particular vibration of the liquid of the cochlear canal sets into oscillation some particular region of fibers of the basilar membrane, and this in turn excites the hair cells in the immediate neighborhood and the afferent nerve endings there.

To this a theory has recently been added concerning the method of neural conduction along the afferent (auditory) nerve. It is well known that a given nerve fiber has its refractory period, so that when stimulated, let us say, by the bending of the hair cell with which it is connected, the fiber transmits an impulse and then remains inactive for a time (in thousandths of a second) until it becomes again excitable; and the alternation of excitable and refractory phases sets up in the fiber a rhythm of conduction faster than which it cannot conduct. Now, the wave-frequency of a high tone is known to exceed the frequency at which any single nerve fiber can conduct. How, then, can the auditory nerve transmit to the central nervous system the effects of such high tones? But the auditory nerve is composed of a very great number of individual fibers; and like a drummer who beats a tattoo with both hands alternately, producing a total effect twice as rapid as the beat of either hand alone, so the composite nerve can with its individual fibers conduct a variety of impulses of different frequencies but so spaced as to reproduce in the central nervous system a total effect duplicating the complex stimulation impressed upon the sense-organ end [13].

In this connection a curious fact was brought to light. When electrical action potentials (cf. pp. 205 ff.) were led off by wires from the auditory nerve of an anesthetized cat and conducted to a distant room it became possible to hear from an amplifier stationed there a faithful report of all the sounds occurring in the room in which the cat was placed, even conversation [14].

Defects of Hearing. Any impairment of functioning of any of the several links in the conduction of vibrations from air to nerve — eardrum, chain of bones, window, cochlear canal, organ of Corti — will of course produce *deafness*. Most commonly the trouble lies in the middle ear, where blocking of the Eustachian tube prevents the equalization of air pressure on the two sides of the eardrum, or where there is hardening or destruction of the three small bones, and hearing is reduced for all ranges of pitch. With old age many people grow more hard of hearing, especially for tones high in pitch.

It is important that defective hearing be early recognized, for

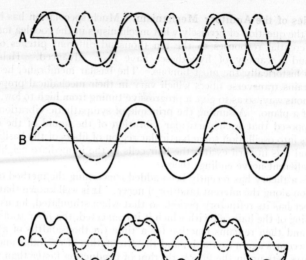

FIGURE 60. VARIATIONS IN WAVE FORMATION

In *A*, the continuous line represents a greater wave length and lower frequency than the broken line. In *B*, the continuous line represents a wave of greater amplitude. In *C*, the continuous line represents a complex wave that can be analyzed into two wave frequencies as represented by the broken lines.

this alone is often the only cause of some school children's poor responses to instructions and even inattentiveness — behavior that is too often supposed to be due to general mental dullness.

Three Variables in Sound Stimulation. Vibrations of air may differ from one another in *frequency* or *length*, in *amplitude* or *intensity*, and in *purity* or *composition*. (Cf. Figure 60.) The ability of a person to react appropriately to different sounds depends in the first instance upon a capacity to distinguish between them in terms of the above variables. Distinctions based on variations of frequency are known as *pitch* differences; those based on variations of amplitude as *loudness* differences; those based on variations of wave composition, as *timbre*.[1] The sounds employed in music are organized in terms of pitch differences in order to make melody. Changes in loudness (coupled with changes of time relations) furnish variations in emphasis and accent. Variations in timbre provided by the different kinds of instru-

---

[1] These relationships hold only within certain limits. Thus with great increase of loudness some tones may be heard with altered pitch or with altered timbre [4].

ments of a symphony orchestra — strings, wood winds, brass — and even by the individual pieces within each of these choirs, give opportunity for musical effects that are interesting and important to the concertgoer.   In learning to adjust his behavior to the human voices about him a child quickly learns the differences between high note and low, loud voice and soft, his nurse's voice and his sister's.

The wave composition, which we have said determines the timbre of a tone, is analyzable into the *fundamental*, by which its assigned pitch is established, and its *overtones*.   Resonant bodies vibrate in parts as well as in wholes.   A stretched metal string, for instance, when plucked will vibrate not only in its whole length but also in two segments, in three, in four, and so on.   (This can be demonstrated easily by damping a full-sounding string at its half-way point, third-way, quarter-way, and so forth.)   The whole tone from such a string has a complex makeup of one (fundamental) tone determined by the string's length, plus others (overtones) corresponding to vibration rates that are simple multiples of the rate of the fundamental.

When air vibrations are non-periodic and irregular or are less than two full vibrations, they produce *noises* rather than *tones*. The vast majority of sounds ordinarily heard are of this character: the pattering of rain and the hissing of wind, the puffs of an engine and the rattle of wheels, the rustle of a newspaper and the clatter of dishes, and all the wide range of rumbles and sputters and snaps and pops.

Some Interrelations of Sound Stimulation.   If two tones that are nearly identical in pitch are sounded together, there will be a pronounced *beat* or swell in loudness occurring at regular intervals, with as many beats per second as the difference in number between the cycles of one tone and those of the other.   Two forks set at 435 and 437, for example, would produce two beats per second.   This is purely a physical, not a physiological, effect, and is due to alternate reinforcement and interference between the two lengths of air waves, as they occur in the same and in opposite phases.

If the two original tones sounded together are more widely separated in pitch, they may set up in the hearing apparatus excitations similar to those producible by additional sound stimuli of other frequencies.   These are called *combination* tones.

Quite the most elaborate and complex uses for which man has organized sound stimuli are in music; and one of the knottiest psychological problems in the musical field is concerned with the fundamental nature of *consonance*. In those simultaneous and successive pitch patterns that are called harmonies and melodies the frequencies of the component tones turn out to be related to each other in certain mathematical ratios. The octave, for instance, shows the following ratios of vibration frequency to C:

C	D	E	F	G	A	B	C_2
1	9/8	5/4	4/3	3/2	5/3	15/8	2

With the insertion of intermediate tones, still other intervals are provided. Some of these intervals are much employed and preferred in music because they produce harmony or consonance, and certain others are actually avoided because they produce dissonance. Precisely what is the basis of consonance and dissonance? Many persons have sought to identify it in terms of some physical characteristic of the sound waves produced. The matter is controversial, and too technical for us here. But whatever the physical basis for these musical preferences of man may be, it is certain that the part played by *habituation* is great. Moore has experimentally demonstrated that a person may be trained to regard as consonant certain intervals between tones that do not readily fuse, especially the "sevenths"; and that such clean fusions as the "octave," the "third," and the "fifth" come to have low musical value for experienced auditors. Getting used to certain intervals certainly has an influence upon one's preferences among tone-combinations, as is evident when we compare European music with Chinese, the classical German school with the ultramodern Russian, or the hearing of an untrained child with that of a seasoned concertgoer.

VISUAL SENSITIVITY

The Stimuli. The energies that fall upon the visual apparatus of man and awaken in him the act of seeing take the form of light vibrations that range in length between 390 $\mu\mu$ (violet) and 760 $\mu\mu$ (red) ($\mu\mu = 1/1,000,000$ mm.) [1] These are the stimuli in the narrowest sense, but it is common to apply the term also to the objects from which the vibrations are transmitted or reflected. A child acquires adjustments not so much to the light waves as to the sources from which they come: he comes to react not to brightness

---

[1] Shorter waves are found in the ultraviolet and the X-rays, and longer ones in the infra-red and radiant heat rays and the waves used in radio broadcasting. Man is sensitive to none of these, except to heat waves, which affect cutaneous receptors.

and to colors in themselves but to the milk bottle and the nurse's face.

In contrast to the effluvia of smell or the sound waves of hearing which can go around corners, a significant characteristic of light waves is that they are transmitted only in straight lines, even after they have been reflected or refracted. On this account, they serve as cues by which the active organism can accurately orient itself with reference to its spatial relations. Thus the receptor of sight is developed as an organ with its own delicate motor adjustments, so that sensitivity to fine differences in the direction and distance of stimulating sources may serve as the control for the subject's motor reactions in space.

The Receptors. The eye may well be compared to the photographic camera. In the latter there are necessary: (*A*) a lightproof box to shut out all rays but those from the object to be

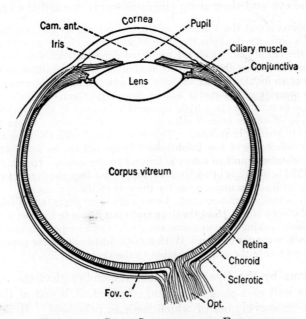

FIGURE 61. CROSS-SECTION OF THE EYEBALL

. The wall (*A*) is composed of three coats, the sclerotic, the choroid, and the innermost delicate retina. At the front the wall is transparent (the *cornea*). Behind it the circular window or *pupil* (*B*) is controlled by the blue or brown *iris* muscle (*C*). Light admitted through this window is focused by the *lens* (*D*) upon the retina (*E*) as upon a camera plate.

The lens is adjusted for near and far objects by the ciliary muscle. *Corpus vitreum*, the vitreous humor filling the main chamber, as the *aqueous humor* fills the anterior one, *Cam. ant.*

photographed; (*B*) an aperture through which the selected rays are admitted; (*C*) a diaphragm controlling the size of this aperture; (*D*) a lens to bring the admitted rays to a proper focus; (*E*) a sensitive plate upon which the focused rays are projected and in which they set up photochemical changes. These parts can be found in the eyeball as shown in Figure 61.

The innermost coat of the eyeball wall, the retina, is the receptive mechanism proper. It consists of three layers of cells. The layer that is sensitive to the action of light rays is made up of *rods* and *cones* and lies toward the periphery in such a way that the rays projected back through pupil and lens to the retina must pass through the other layers of cells before reaching the rods and cones. When light falls upon this last layer of cells, it sets up some chemical change, which in turn sets up a neural process, and in this manner afferent impulses are originated that pass out of the eye and then along the optic nerve toward the brain.

Some points about the anatomy of the eye explain certain peculiarities of vision. In ordinary daylight the objects seen most clearly are those in the center of the visual field which are projected upon the center of the retina at a spot where the cones are very great in number (about a million to a square one tenth of an inch). Under twilight or night conditions, however, objects a little to one side of the center will be more easily seen — as when a gazer finds it best to turn the eye a little to one side in order to see a very dim star — and these off-center stimuli fall upon areas of the retina where the rods are relatively greater in number. This is consistent with the view that sensitivity to differences of low brightnesses is limited to the rods, while that to high brightnesses and to colors is limited to the cones. In one region of the visual field the eye is blind (the *blind spot*), for here the layer of rods and cones is interrupted to make room for the exit of the optic nerve.

The fact is easily demonstrated. Draw a circle on paper, and a cross some 7 cm. to the right of it. Hold the drawing about a foot in front of a subject's right eye only, asking him to fixate the circle and to report to you whether the cross can or cannot be seen. With some adjustments of the paper a point will be found where the subject is blind to the cross.

Reactions by the Eye. We must remember that the eye is a motor, as well as a sensory, organ. Indeed, it is one of the most elaborate motor organs of which man is possessed. Besides the muscular iris, which regulates the amount of light to be admitted to the eye, and the ciliary muscle, which adjusts the lens for proper focusing, there remains to be noted the work of the six large *extrinsic muscles* on the outside of each eyeball, which rotate it in its socket. In binocular vision these muscles regulate the relative positions of the two eyeballs, so that a single stimulus will be projected on corresponding retinal points, drawing them inward if the object be near and returning them to parallel if it be far. But whether a man uses two eyes or one, the remarkable mobility with which his eyeball rolls about — glancing here, there, and everywhere, scanning print with jerked movements across the page, exploring a Grecian urn or a street car advertisement with veerings and shiftings that baffle all but a cinematograph — is, once mentioned, well enough recognized by the reader to call for no further elaboration.

Three Variables in Light Stimulation. Discrimination of one light stimulation from another may take any one of three different forms. Vibrations of light, like those of sound (cf. Figure 61), may vary as to *amplitude* or *intensity*, as to *length* or *frequency*, and as to *complexity* or *composition* (that is, number and character of component vibrations). (*A*) First, as to differences in the intensity of light. All human and animal organisms possessing eyes are able to distinguish light-dark or *brightness* differences, no matter what their other visual defects; and man must rely upon this difference solely under conditions of twilight illumination. All stimuli discriminated in terms of light-dark range from the high extreme of illumination, "white," to its opposite, "black." Seeing in terms of brightness differences is the principal part of seeing, as is shown by the satisfactoriness of most photographs and photoplays in which the absence of color is hardly noted at all. (*B*) Sensitivity to differences of wave length only, that is, color vision or the ability to distinguish *hues*, is more limited in several ways. Fewer animal species have demonstrated it; some human individuals show special disabilities (color blindness, to be discussed later); and the retinas of all individuals are insensitive to wave-length differences in certain areas (retinal zones, discussed later). (*C*) Discrimination of light stimuli in terms of the differences in their composition has not been so extensively explored, but it is certain that these differences in *saturation* of colors as seen have an important share in determining the esthetic reactions to such objects as paintings, natural scenery, houses, and dress goods. Light is called well saturated if the component vibrations are fairly homogeneous in their frequencies, poorly saturated if they are very heterogeneous; for example, light of 472 trillion vibrations per second with little admixture of other frequencies would be called a "pure" or "clear" or well-saturated "orange" and is colorful; whereas if it is mixed with vibrations of many other frequencies it approaches what would be called "gray" and is lacking in color or chroma. In Figure 62 is presented a much-used scheme for representing these three "directions" in which different stimuli of sight vary from one another.

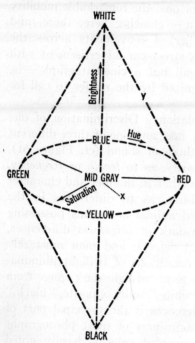

Some Special Phenomena of Color Vision. For half a century psychologists have given a great deal of attention in their experimental research to problems of sensitivity to the wave lengths of light, and certain phenomena of color vision have been determined in great detail. In this discussion space permits only brief mention of a few of these phenomena.

FIGURE 62. SCHEME FOR REPRESENTING THE THREE VARIABLES OF SIGHT

Differences of *hue* are represented as ranged about the periphery of the plane circle; differences in *saturation* as distances on radii out from the vertical core (neutral gray); differences of *brightness* (light-dark) as vertical distances above-below this plane of mid-brightness.

For illustrations, positions are assigned on this scheme to a poorly saturated orange of medium brightness (*x*) and a well-saturated pink (*y*).

If lights of two different wave lengths (two different colors) be projected upon the same retinal surface, a new excitation is there set up and the individual sees a new color. The usual technique for producing this *retinal fusion* [1] is with the color wheel, a spindle upon which are mounted interlapping paper or cardboard disks that are revolved so fast (at least forty times per second) that before excitation of the retina by one of them has subsided excitation by another is set up; the result is the same as

---

[1] This phenomenon must not be confused with that resulting from a mixing of the pigments themselves on a palette or in a bucket. For example, if blue paint and yellow paint be mixed in that physical manner, each absorbs some of the wave frequencies of light, reflecting the rest. What is left after this double absorption may be a green, instead of the gray that results from superposition of the two colors on the retina. The latter is a physiological phenomenon.

if the stimulations were simultaneous. An inertia of the retina is thus involved. (Figure 63.) Titchener has enunciated three laws of color fusion. (1) For every color there can be found another (*complementary*) which if "mixed" with the first in the right proportion will produce a gray. Thus a slightly purplish red when mixed with a slightly bluish green will excite the retina just as a gray would do. (2) The mixture of any two colors that are not complementaries will give an intermediate color, which varies in saturation with the nearness or remoteness of the two colors to each other in the wave-length series. A red and yellow revolved together produce the same retinal effect as would an original orange disk. (3) If two color mixtures which match each other are combined, the new combination will match either of the original mixtures.

FIGURE 63. COLOR WHEEL FOR MIX-ING COLORS

The disks are interlapped and mounted upon the shaft of the motor. For comparative purposes smaller disks may be combined at the same time as the larger. The instrument here illustrated has the additional advantage of permitting adjustment of the ratio between the disks while the wheel is in motion.

A striking phenomenon is that called *simultaneous contrast.* Any color stimulus falling upon a limited region of the retina tends to induce in an adjacent region an effect similar to that of its complement. Let a blue field be presented to the eye with a strip of gray alongside or across it: the retinal excitation induced by the gray strip will have an effect the same as that of the complementary of blue; that is, the gray will look yellowish. Gray on purple will appear yellowish green; a medium bright gray on dark green will appear a bright red; a blue strip on yellow will appear a more saturated blue.

After a long period of stimulation by a given brightness or color, the retina, when the stimulation is removed, is affected as if by the complementary brightness or color. This phenomenon is called *successive contrast,* and also is described as *negative after-imagery,* or better, negative after-excitation. After gazing at the lock on a window frame and then turning the eyes to a blank wall, a person is likely to "see" the visual pattern of the lock with the reverse arrangement of brightnesses; or after gazing at a red figure and turning to a gray background, the retina will be affected as if by the same figure except that it now appears as green.

But the first after-effect of retinal stimulation is a *positive after-excitation*. This is one essential of color fusion, as hinted above. It is demonstrated by whirling a lighted stick in a circle in a dark room, by gazing at an incandescent electric lamp for a few seconds and then turning it off, and so forth. A period of time is required after the removal of stimulation before the complete effect of the stimulation subsides.

Even the normal retina, as has been suggested, is not sensitive to all colors throughout its extent, but varies from differential sensitivity for all colors at the center, to that for none at the edge of the field of vision. This variation appears in concentric *retinal zones*.

Introspective Analysis of Light. It will be remembered that cutaneous sensations may be reduced to four elemental sensations, taste to four, and the like. We may ask, therefore, "Can all the 'sights' that one experiences be reduced to elemental sensations?" We find an answer in the work of introspective psychologists. The colors of the solar spectrum vary by fine degrees from red through orange, yellow, green, blue, and indigo to violet; and to these must be added the non-spectral purple. Careful scrutiny of these colors-as-seen leads to the judgment that some of them seem to partake of others (as orange seems to be reddish but also yellowish), but a few seem to be unique and irreducible, namely *red, yellow, green*, and *blue*. These are therefore called the psychologically elementary sensations of color. To them are added the two elementary sensations of brightness, *black* and *white*. All visual experiences are then said to be produced by the compounding or fusing of two or more of these elementary six.

Some Common Visual Defects. The most common eye troubles for which people consult their oculists turn out to be errors of refraction leading to difficulties in focusing. *Nearsightedness* is due to too long an eyeball (or too convex a lens), and *farsightedness* to too short an eyeball (or too flat a lens), so that with the ciliary muscles relaxed the light from distant objects is brought to a focus not on the retina but in front of it in the former case or back of it in the latter. Equally common is *astigmatism*, which is due to imperfect curvature of cornea or lens or eyeball, so that all the light rays being received from a single source point cannot be focused at one retinal point. Spectacles are lenses ground to correct these errors of light refraction; and their widespread use is evidence that such defects are common.

Poor eyesight, whatever the cause, should be recognized as early as possible. Many a child who had been having difficulties in his school work and is consequently rated backward or dull needs only reseating in his classroom or perhaps an oculist's examination and treatment to give him the opportunity to show what he really can do.

Color-blindness, on the other hand, is a disability possessed by less than 4 per cent of the male and less than ½ of 1 per cent of the female population, and not subject to change by treatment. The typical color-blind person is unable to distinguish two lights in terms of their red or their green components but is forced to rely upon their differences in brightness or in other color components. For example, purples and blue-greens are indistinguishable from blues; oranges and yellow-greens from yellow; and certain reds and greens from grays of identical brightness. There are other varieties of this defect. It may seem curious that these defects of vision were hardly recognized a hundred and fifty years ago, but we must remember that the objects environing a man vary by all gradations of brightness and that he can develop his reactions to them accordingly. Consider the readiness with which objects are identified in the usual uncolored photographs and motion pictures by these differences alone.

Theories of Color Vision. The above-described phenomena point to the fact that while physical light itself varies in its wave lengths by all gradations, the effects aroused in the retina and its nervous connections in man seem to be analyzable into a few elementary processes excited there. Many are the theories proposed and still being proposed, for the facts about color that must be accounted for are complex and contradictory. No single theory is completely satisfactory; and it would seem sensible here to mention only the two most famous ones. The *Young-Helmholtz* theory posited three kinds of receptive cells in the retina: one specially affected by light waves producing *red*, a second specially affected by *green*, a third by *blue*, but each responsive in some degree to all light waves. This has always been well regarded by physicists; and, after having been almost superseded by the Hering theory, it is now seemingly regaining favor, at least as the point of departure for new theories.

The *Hering* theory seems most in accord with facts and phenomena such as we have been presenting. It asserts that in the rods and cones are three distinct kinds of structures. One kind is set into chemical activity by green and by red light [1] in antagonistic ways (anabolic and catabolic, respectively); another is in similar manner made active by blue and by yellow light; and a third, by black and by white as well as by all the other colors.

SOME QUANTITATIVE PROBLEMS

Thresholds of Sensitivity.   Most of the problems about human sensitivity are originally of a qualitative character.   The following, for instance.   What kinds of stimulation are effective at the skin, or on the tongue, or on the periphery of the retina, or along the enteric canal?   If the olfactory membrane be exhausted for response to heliotrope, what other odors become ineffective at the same time?   What is the relationship between tones x and y that makes them more harmonious than tones x and z?   Does the after-excitation remaining from eye stimulation by a given wave length bear any special relation to the latter? The qualitative problems in any field of science tend, however, to become increasingly quantitative, increasingly a question of precisely and exactly how much.   And so it is with the above and similar queries.

Quantitative refinements of sensory problems date from 1860, when Fechner summarized elaborate investigations that he and others had been making.   In the first half of the nineteenth century it had become increasingly evident that the study of human nature could not be soundly prosecuted merely by the armchair method of comparing anecdotes and personal experiences, but that it must be closely linked with physics, physiology, and mathematics.   Accordingly, a few scientists addressed themselves to the measuring of certain phenomena in human nature, especially along the lines of reaction times and sensory thresholds.   The former has been given attention on earlier pages.   It is appropriate to discuss the latter here.

A receptor, like any other mechanism, has a certain amount of inertia; that is, it requires a certain stimulation to be awakened into activity.   A clock tick in an adjoining room may be too weak to excite the ear, a star too faint to affect the eye, a snowflake too light to excite the pressure receptors on the back of the hand, for they are all below the necessary intensity, or "below the threshold." Just what is the minimal intensity that a given stimulus must have

---

[1] The green selected by Hering would ordinarily be called a bluish green, and the red, a slightly purplish red.

in order to be sensed?   This is the question of the *stimulation threshold*.

The inertia of a receptor, like that of any other mechanism, is further revealed in its failure to react to infinitesimal gradations of intensity; when it is already in activity, it requires a certain increase of stimulation before it will be set into any increased activity.   An ear on hearing a large orchestra playing ensemble will not be sensitive to the increase of sound due to the adding of a single violin.   A tongue tasting coffee sweetened with three lumps of sugar will not be differently affected if a half-lump be added.   Just what is the minimal increase of intensity that a given stimulus must have in order to be sensed as "just perceptibly more"?   This is the question of the *difference threshold*.

Weber's Law.   While working on the difference threshold for the cutaneous and kinesthetic senses, Weber made the discovery of a significant relation between increases of stimulus and increases of receptor excitation (and increases of the experienced sensation).   This may be cast into the formula:

$$\frac{\Delta St}{St} = K$$

in which, Δ = "discriminable difference of," St = intensity of the stimulus, and K = a constant holding for a given stimulus (sight, hearing, etc.).   The law may be restated: *The increase of a stimulation necessary for the subject to discriminate it AS an increase bears a constant ratio to the total preceding stimulation.*   This law has been found to hold in various sense fields; and it furnishes us a ready explanation of some everyday phenomena.   The same star that is visible at night is invisible in the daytime: its own light is not enough, when added to that of the sun's, to be discriminable by the visual apparatus.   A voice is strong enough to be heard under conditions of quiet, but when it is added to the noise of a machine shop it forms an increment too slight to be discerned.   If a man is carrying a bucket weighing twenty pounds, an added half pound may make no difference to him, whereas if to a two-pound bucket the same half-pound addition is made, he will promptly react to the difference.   To be sensed *as* an increase, a stimulus must be increased relatively; a small original stimulus needs but little added, a large one, much.   This relative increase remains much the same for any one sense, but may be quite different in different ones, as the table shows.

VALUES OF K IN WEBER'S LAW

	COMMONLY ASSIGNED	LIMITS
Visual.................	1/100	1/65–1/195
Kinesthetic...........	1/40	1/20–1/100
Cutaneous: pressure...	1/20	1/10–1/30
Cutaneous: temperature	1/3	1/3–1/4
Auditory.............	1/5	1/3–1/8
Olfactory............	1/3	1/3–1/4
Gustatory...........	1/3	1/3–1/4

Exhaustive investigations given to Weber's Law have forced modifications of it as a general law.   (A) It holds principally for changes in intensity of stimulation, and not usually for other sorts of changes (such as a change in color or wave length).   (B) It holds well through the middle sections of intensity in the different senses, but not in the extremely high and extremely low intensities.   (C) It varies (to a small degree) with the individual, and within the same individual at different times and under different conditions.   Nevertheless, this principle, enunciated in 1831, deserves attention, as the first clear achievement in rendering psychology quantitative.

The Psychophysical Methods.[1]   The precise determination of a sensory threshold is by no means so easy a process as might be supposed.   It is necessary for both experimenter and subject to exercise particular care throughout long series of repetitions of some seemingly simple performance on the part of the subject. Also a definite and rather elaborate order of presentation of stimuli must be planned out in advance.

Suppose one were working to find the stimulation threshold of a sound.   In one series the stimulus is first presented at an intensity well above the threshold (easily heard) and by repeated changes reduced until it is well below the threshold (cannot be heard at all); then from the latter point the stimulus is increased in intensity back again to a point well above the threshold.   In both series of changes the subject is instructed to react positively as long as he can sense (hear) the stimulus and negatively as long as he cannot.   The two series must be repeated frequently.

---

[1] The reason for this name, being based on an outgrown metaphysics, need not detain us.   It is still universally employed — with no metaphysical implication.

Also, it is often well to reverse the order of stimulus changes within either series, for the purpose of checking such factors as the subject's expectancy of reaching the threshold and so making too prompt a report of it, or his continuance in a set manner of reacting and so making too late a report of it. Moreover, there are a number of incidental disturbing factors to be guarded against, so that all in all this is an exercise that will reward only the careful and the industrious investigator.

Again, suppose one were seeking to determine the difference threshold for kinesthesis. The experiment of the lifted weights would be used. (The description of this on p. 234 should be re-read now.)

It is not content so much as technique which has maintained interest for nearly a hundred years in these sensory threshold problems. These experiments have been particularly valuable in developing and refining statistical procedures. Whenever the question is that of determining *at just what point* in a series of changing values a certain phenomenon occurs, these methods are applicable. Moreover, despite the undramatic nature of these methods, a knowledge of them is valuable to the student who wishes to develop insight into the pitfalls of experimental procedure.

There are three most-used standard methods of threshold determination. One is the *Method of Average Error*, in which the subject (S) himself adjusts the Variable stimulus to make it apparently equal to the Standard stimulus, the amount of his errors from trial to trial being averaged and called the threshold. Examples: (*a*) S is to move a slide on the left arm of a horizontal (Galton) bar to make it look to him the same distance from the middle as is a standard slide on the right arm of the bar; (*b*) S is to adjust a rheostat so that the gray light at one ground glass window is apparently of the same brightness as that at another window.

The Method of Minimal Changes is one in which the experimenter (E) now manipulates the Variable stimulus, changing it gradually through all degrees until S reports that it apparently is just equal to the Standard stimulus; and the errors are averaged. Examples: (*a*) Little by little E slides the weight on a tuning fork to bring its tone nearer and nearer to that of another (Constant) tuning fork, S to judge just when they are identical; (*b*) E gradually increases the brightness of the darker of two windows.

In the *Method of Constant Stimuli* E has a definite number of definite values of the Variable. E pairs each in irregular order with the Standard stimulus, calls upon S to decide in each case whether the second-presented is greater than, equal to, or less than the Standard. Examples: (*a*) S may be asked to compare by "hefting" them weights of 88, 92, 96, 100, 104, 108 and 112 gr.

with a Standard weight of 100 gr.; (*b*) S may be asked to compare the sound
of forks varying .5, 1, 2, 3, 5, 8, 12, and 17 cycles below the Standard with the
Standard tuning fork.

A moment's consideration will make clear to the reader the necessity for
the development of statistical procedures in handling the results, especially
when the third-named method is employed. Suppose that a subject comparing weights with the 100 gr. Standard makes the following rather typical
judgments:

	Weights of the Variable			
	88 gr.	*92 gr.*	*96 gr.*	*100 gr.*
Judged "heavier" than the Standard	1 times	11 times	28 times	15 times
Judged "equal" to the Standard	8 "	24 "	40 "	67 "
Judged "lighter" than the Standard	91 "	65 "	32 "	18 "

Just where is his threshold!

A CONCLUDING VIEW OF RECEPTIVE PROCESSES

Let us now summarize the rôles played by the different classes
of receptors in the life economy in the light of the preliminary
descriptions and analyses of human and animal behavior we
have set forth in earlier chapters. The primary sources of human
and of subhuman behavior are to be found in the metabolic processes
occurring within the body and especially in the inadequate relations of external conditions to these processes. The *interoceptors*
are the sensitive organs most directly implicated here. Next,
the organism when it gets into action proceeds to make some
change in its environment. In this the *exteroceptors* act the part
of advance guards through which the specific characters of the
surroundings play upon the body and modify the directions of
movements. Further refinement of the movements is secured
through the co-ordinations made possible by the *proprioceptors*.

A simple illustration lies at hand in the behavior of a hungry
child. The empty stomach sets up interoceptive impulses which
initiate motion and locomotion: the child goes after food. The
direction in which he goes is determined by the smell or by the
sight of cookies or apples, the sight of doorways, and by other
exteroceptive stimulations. The maintaining of his general
bodily positions, and the effective reaching for and taking hold
of and eating of a cooky or an apple, depend upon his proprioceptive
organization.

REFERENCES

1. Cannon, W. B. Hunger and Thirst. In *Handbook of General Experimental Psychology* (Murchison, ed.). Clark Univ. Press, 1934.

2. Carlson, A. J. *The Control of Hunger in Health and Disease.* Univ. Chicago Press, 1916.

3. Dallenbach, K. M. The Temperature Spots and End-Organs. *Am. J. Psychol.*, 1927, **39**, 402–27.

4. Fletcher, H. Loudness, Pitch, and Timbre of Musical Tones and their Relation to Intensity, Frequency, and Overtone Structure. *J. Acoust. Soc. Amer.*, 1934, **6**, 56–69.

5. Gault, R. H. A Partial Analysis of the Effects of Tactual-Visual Stimulation of Spoken Language. *J. Franklin Inst.*, 1930, **209**, 437–58.

6. Goodfellow, L. D. Vibratory Sensitivity: its Present Status. *Psychol. Bull.*, 1934, **31**, 560–71.

7. Lickley, J. D. *The Nervous System.* Longmans, new ed., 1931. Chap. x.

8. Murchison, C. (ed.). *A Handbook of General Experimental Psychology.* Clark Univ. Press, 1934. Chaps. 4, 5, 13, 20.

9. Myers, C. S. *Text-Book of Experimental Psychology*, 2d ed. Longmans, 1911. Chaps. II–VIII.

10. Seashore, C. E., *et al. Studies in the Psychology of Music.* Vol. I: The Vibrato. Univ. Iowa, 1932.

11. Titchener, E. B. *A Text-Book of Psychology.* Macmillan, 1910. Pp. 59–224.

12. Titchener, E. B. *Experimental Psychology*, Macmillan, 1901. Vol. I, chaps. I–VI.

13. Wever, E. G., and Bray, C. W. Present Possibilities for Auditory Theory. *Psychol. Rev.*, 1930, **37**, 365–80.

14. Wever, E. G., and Bray, C. W. The Nature of Acoustic Response. *J. Exper. Psychol.*, 1930, **13**, 373–87.

On quantitative problems

15. Garrett, H. E. *Great Experiments in Psychology.* Chap. 12. Appleton-Century, 1930.

16. Guilford, J. P. *Psychometric Methods.* McGraw-Hill, 1936.

17. Myers, C. S. *Text-Book of Experimental Psychology.* 2d ed. Longmans, 1911. Chaps. XV, XVIII–XIX.

18. Titchener, E. B. *Experimental Psychology.* Vol. II, chaps. I and II. Macmillan, 1905.

CHAPTER X
NEURAL ORGANIZATION OF BEHAVIOR

INTRODUCTION

The General Importance of the Nervous System. In our attempts to comprehend the behavior of a person we shall be helped considerably if we have a general overview picture of the principal system by which he as an organism is integrated, and by which his actions are rendered consistent and serviceable. However excellent his motor organs and his sense organs, they will profit him nothing if he is not well equipped with connections for them. The muscles and glands of an idiot may not be greatly defective, and his eyes, ears, skin and muscular sense organs may be almost as good as those of the average person; but with his pitifully inadequate connecting mechanisms he remains nothing but a grimacing, twisting, monkey-like human body. A man can hardly boast of much nimbler fingers than the ape's, much better vocal parts than a parrot's, more acute distance vision than the eagle's, nor a keener sense of smell than the dog's; yet his capacities for surviving under complex or novel conditions by adapting himself to them or reshaping them to fit his own needs are enormously greater — just because his fingers and voice and feet, his eyes and nose and skin and muscle senses, are so much more richly interconnected.

THE NATURE OF NEURAL TRANSMISSION

Its General Character. We have seen that neural tissue furnishes the basis for interconnections within a person's body and therefore is behind the integrations of his behavior toward the world about him. In a "Western" motion picture the sight of the desperado (stimulation of eye) will arouse in the hero a split-second response of drawing and firing in a beautifully co-ordinated set of arm, wrist, and finger movements; and in an orchestral performance sight of baton and of musical notes, plus sounds of other instruments, can set up promptly in the player movements of fingers and hands on keyboard or strings which is the despair of the beginner. As the grocer "hefts" the sack he is filling, the sensory effect on muscle and skin receptors evokes the vocal response "ten pounds"; and the stenographer, to each variation of the voiced sounds to which she is attending, makes an appropriate manipulation of her writing fingers with a shading, hook, or line in her notebook. All such phenomena are dependent upon neural connections between stimulations and responses.

What is the character of these connections? In contrast with the transporting of materials from place to place in the lymph and blood stream we have here a transmission of energy-changes of the connecting medium itself. There is some transformation of the nature of the medium. The nerves are not tubes through which a substance is conveyed, but solid protoplasmic threads that propagate disturbances from end to end.

This energy-change should be thought of as a disturbance of equilibrium throughout the entire organism. In states of passivity an equilibrium has been struck, but any stimulus that is effective upsets this equilibrium at a receptive end, and the upset travels as a series of waves along the neural pathways to excite changes in the efferent or motor organs.

What, more precisely, is the nature of this propagated disturbance? In spite of the awe with which "nerve" and "brain" are popularly regarded, they are products of natural evolution in a natural world. They are protoplasm; and the only intelligent attitude is to seek out a more precise knowledge of their functions and structure.

About neural transmission some matters of physics and chemistry are now well known. A resting nerve is like any other tissue in that it consumes a certain amount of oxygen, gives off carbon dioxide, produces heat, and manifests electrical changes. When the nerve becomes active, these small physiological changes are increased in degree.

The disturbance that passes along neural tissue is not like the continuous flow of water in a pipe nor like the continuous flow of electricity in a simple conductor like a copper wire. Instead, it is more comparable to a stream of machine-gun bullets, a stream of interrupted firings that follow rapidly upon each other. Most important for the detection and study of these volleys of activity are the electrical changes or *action potentials*. We have dealt with the technique for their observation in connection with muscle tissue, on pp. 205 ff. We will confine ourselves, therefore, at this point to the fact that each neural impulse can be registered as a wave. If these waves are registered and measured as they pass along a nerve, we learn accurate details concerning the impulses themselves — their frequency, their intensity, and their complexity. We now turn to some of the facts discovered by this and other techniques.

Some Salient Characteristics. First and last, if a correct picture of nerve activity is to be had, it must be remembered that a nerve is a bundle of individual fibers (individual cells with elongated branches) and that its activity is a composite of the activities of the various fibers.

We are not to assume that the component fibers of a nerve are precisely alike. In fact, certain differences in the way they are activated are an important part of the story.

When a fiber is excited at all it is excited to its maximal degree.[1] This is known as the *all-or-none* principle. It is familiar enough in a general way, as in the fact that a given charge of gunpowder will explode with one specific amount of violence regardless of whether the agent that sets it off is a child's small match or a steel worker's acetylene welding torch.

Each fiber has its own *threshold of excitation*, that is, the minimum intensity that a stimulus must reach in order to call it into action at all. From this it is easy to understand that when a stimulus of a given physical intensity is applied to one end of a nerve, it may throw into action some but not all the component fibers, depending upon their thresholds.

Again, each fiber has its own *refractory phase*. Immediately after it has transmitted an impulse, a fiber will remain for a brief fraction of a second inexcitable and non-conductive. This is what gives to neural transmission its interrupted character (which has been already mentioned), and determines the *frequency* with which the successive impulses follow upon each other. And in different fibers there are different frequencies. One and the same stimulation applied to the end of a nerve trunk may arouse in the various fibers composing the trunk varying rates of rapid-fire conduction.

We are now prepared to answer a central question concerning the nerve-as-a-whole: In one and the same nerve how can there be

---

[1] The facts concerning neural transmission to be mentioned in this section have for the most part been obtained from special preparations in which the "stimulation" was in the form of mild electric shocks administered through electrodes attached to an end of an isolated fiber or set of fibers. The term "stimulation" is therefore to be understood in this special sense.

gradations of intensity in conduction if the all-or-none law holds true? In the life and behavior of men, it hardly needs stating that not only the quality or kind of a sensory stimulation or of a motor response is important, but also the degree or amount of it. It is often paramount in guiding a person's behavior when the same sound is heard loud or soft, the same sight is seen brightly or dimly, the same sort of taste or of smell, of touch or of kinesthesis appears strongly or weakly. Similarly on the motor side: the same movement or gesture or cry or word may be one thing when vigorously executed but quite another when weakly done. In neurological terms our question is posed: how, when a single fiber discharges completely or not at all, can varying degrees of intensity in one and the same stimulating condition set up varying intensities of neural transmission and so pass out to arouse varying degrees of vigor of response? The evidence points to a double answer. (1) The intensity of nerve activity is a matter of the *number of separate fibers* that are participating. The higher the strength of the exciting agent, the more the individual units that are thrown into activity by it. (2) The intensity of the disturbance has been found definitely to depend also upon the *frequency* of the impulses. In one and the same fiber, the higher the strength of the exciting agent, the more rapid will be the succession of impulses aroused by it.

The Physical Nature of the Neural Impulse. The membrane theory is the best of the several theories that have been advanced regarding the precise process that is occurring when a neural impulse passes. According to this theory, a nerve fiber is thought of as surrounded by a thin membrane with a difference of electrical potential existing between its outer and inner surfaces, being positive on the outside and negative on the inner (it is "polarized"). The neural disturbance or impulse is thought of as *a wave of temporary depolarization between these surfaces that passes along the length of the fiber.* In Figure 64, the potential differences (+ and −) of the passive nerve's membrane are shown reduced (depolarized, neither + nor −) at that point where the impulse is at a given instant. This depolarized condition propagates itself as follows: the neural tissue quickly recovers its equilibrium and restores its polarized state, but meanwhile in the next adjoining segment of the fiber (to the right in the figure) there is induced a similar depolarizing (through a local electric current represented by the arrowheads); and so the succession of upset-and-restored conditions moves progressively along.

Now, it will be well for us to bear in mind an incidental fact. Precisely the series of changes we have just described is to be found in some well-known inorganic phenomena. [18.] Suppose an iron wire that has been dipped in concentrated nitric acid just long enough to have started a corroding or oxidizing process is then placed in a weak nitric acid: the corroding process is

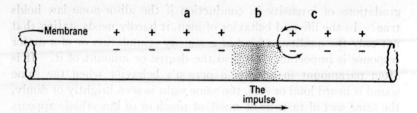

FIGURE 64. THE MEMBRANE THEORY OF NEURAL TRANSMISSION

In the resting state the outer membrane of a nerve is polarized: positive ions on outside and negative on inside. When the nerve is activated, the precise point where the impulse is at a given instant is depolarized (*b*). This sets up a local electric current (arrowheads) that is counter to the polarized condition in adjoining parts of the membrane (*c*) and so reduces it. At the same time the upset condition at *b* is being quickly recovered from, as has already occurred at *a*. This continuous succession of induced depolarization and spontaneous recovery moves as a rapid current down the fiber. (After Lillie.)

arrested and the iron remains bright and unaffected by the acid. But then let the wire be touched or tapped at one end: an oxidizing process will be set up again at this end, though for a very brief moment, and will sweep down the length of the wire at a very rapid rate, immediately followed by another arrest of the oxidizing. Let the wire be tapped again and it will again respond with another short-lived wave.

Chronaxie. In order to understand later discussions of nerve fibers, we must return to the question of how they are excited in the first place. It will be remembered that each fiber has its threshold, an intensity that must be reached or exceeded by any stimulus (exciting agent) if it is to excite the fiber. Now, it has been found that even for the same fiber this threshold will vary, depending upon the time during which the stimulus acts upon it. Up to a certain point, as the duration of stimulus is increased, the required intensity decreases; or, put otherwise, a weaker stimulus applied for a considerable time can excite the fiber to the same degree as a stronger stimulus applied more briefly. In Figure 65, this relationship is indicated by the slope of the line representing the excitation threshold.

A special way of formulating the relationship between intensity and duration has been worked out so that it can be used as an index of excitability in various tissues. First, the minimum strength of an electric current required to excite a given tissue if given an indefinite length of time is determined; this voltage is then doubled; and finally, the time required for this doubled strength of stimulus to excite activity is determined. This is called the *chronaxie* of that tissue. Chronaxie may then be defined as *the shortest duration*

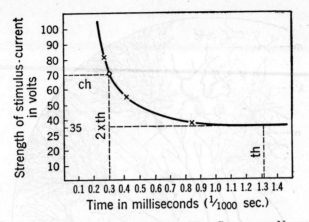

FIGURE 65. A TYPICAL STRENGTH-DURATION CURVE FOR NEURAL
EXCITATION

Illustrated from a nerve X.
Points may be found on the heavy line to indicate the intensity-threshold (i.e., just enough strength to excite this nerve X) for currents applied to it during different time-intervals. Examples: if operating for 0.27 ms. a current must be 80 volts; if for 0.4 ms., 56 volts; if for 0.8 ms., 37 volts. The threshold strength of current when allowed to operate for an indefinite time (th) is found to be 35 volts; this doubled = 70 volts; and the time-interval required for 70 volts to excite the nerve = 0.3 ms. Therefore the *chronaxie* for this nerve is 0.3 ms.

required of a stimulus that is double the threshold strength (of indefinite duration). It is represented by *ch* in Figure 65 [25].

One of the things that makes the notion of chronaxie of interest to psychology is the theory held by some that neural transmission from neuron to neuron and from neuron to muscle depends upon their having similar chronaxies: neuron *a* will succeed in activating neuron or muscle *b* when and only when their chronaxies are the same; and if they are different there is no excitation. Moreover, the chronaxie of a fiber changes from time to time.

The Neuron. We must pause in our study of functions to take better note of the essential structural elements involved. What *is* neural tissue? It is built out of individual cells, microscopic in size. In the differentiation of the multiplying cells in the body of the embryo the nerve cell becomes distinguishable from all others by its long branches. A great variety of neurons is to be found here and there throughout the nervous system, all with certain characteristics in common. (Cf. Figure 66.) First, each has a *cell body* which is the nutritive center of the cell. From this cell body run processes or branches of two sorts: the *axon*, frequently very long.

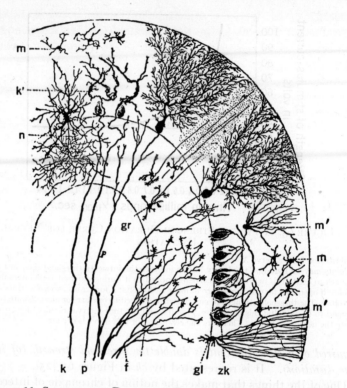

FIGURE 66. SOME OF THE DIFFERENT TYPES OF NEURONS TO BE FOUND
IN ONE REGION OF THE NERVOUS SYSTEM (THE CEREBELLAR CORTEX)

p, axon of a Purkinje cell, two of which are shown with their highly branched dendrites toward
the periphery of the figure; *m*, small stellate cells; *m′*, basket cells with their axons branching
about the bodies of Purkinje cells, as shown at *zk*; *n*, an association cell with short and much-
branched axon; *gr*, granule cells, with their long, straight axons; *f*, moss-like fibers; *k*, a climbing
cell fiber, terminating at *k′*; *gl*, neuroglia (not true nerve cells). (From Ladd and Woodworth,
Elements of Physiological Psychology, Scribner's, 1911; after Kölliker.)

and the *dendrites*. The axon is single, but it itself has branches; and
the dendrites, which may be in any number, are usually so ramified
as to present a tree-like appearance (hence their name). The two
sorts of branches have different functions based on a difference in
their structure. Impulses, in their passage through the cell, first
enter at some tip end of a dendrite, are then conducted along this
and through the cell body, and pass out along the axon and some one
of its branches to a tip end where they induce a change in an adjoining neural or muscular fiber. A most important feature to be

noticed is the richness of interconnections between numerous neurons that is furnished by the branchings of their axons and their dendrites. (Cf. Figure 67.) This, as we are to see later, is the very basis of the organization of behavior.

BASIC PRINCIPLES IN ORGANIZATION

The Problem Stated. Provided now with some comprehension of what neural activity is *per se*, we are ready to face a question confronting all students of the nervous basis of behavior. The way in which a person acts *changes* from time to time. This is strikingly true of John Doe as a baby compared with the same John Doe as a man. Consider his acts of eating, of handling such an object as a pencil, or of using his voice, at the one age and again later: his actions become remarkably altered with the years, and not only in respect to the particular motions he makes but also in respect to the stimulating circumstances under which he comes to make them. Through the years of his development (as we have seen in Chapter IV) maturing and learning conspire to remold his behavior. But his muscles and his sense organs have not been greatly changed; so we seek to know about the changes in his nervous system.

Again, even within a short quarter of an hour, John Doe's ways of acting may show a variety which is, on the face of it, puzzling enough. Toward one and the same office-boy or baseball pitcher or roommate he may show at first an attitude of approbation, only to shift a little later to a posture of challenge. In some instances the shift appears to grow out of a change in the externalities of the social situation: the other person may have done something to disappoint and irritate him. In other cases the shift may seem to be the external appearance of a change in John Doe's own internal condition: his digestion has gone wrong or he has had bad news from the stock market or he has been reminded somehow of an unpleasant incident of a month or a year ago. But regardless of whether the antecedents be extra- or intra-organic, there does occur a shift in the man's behavior that takes place within a few minutes. Here again, we are led to ask, what is happening in his nervous system?

But these long-time or short-time alterations in what a person does and in the way he does it involve another point. Note that a shift in the way a person acts is a shift *from* one and *toward* another given line of action. The primary fact, then, is this, that a person's behavior is always in some degree directed in some line or direction. On the physiological side, when a certain stimulus is received, the commotions it excites in the neural pathways do not travel in all directions and excite all the muscles in equal degree.

In a word, a person's activities seem at all times to be more or less directed, and the transmission of neural impulses is always more or less *channeled*.[1] It is this channeling and rechanneling that now presents itself as a problem to us.

In the preceding section we concerned ourselves exclusively with the nature of the impulses passing over a given nerve or nerve fiber. We must now enlarge the scope of our view to include the interconnecting of different nerves to form innumerable alternative pathways. Consider Figure 67. In that sketch are hinted a few of the ways in which neurons are laid in end-to-end relations throughout the nervous system, with special emphasis upon the alternative ways in which these relations are offered. For illustration, assume that a stream of impulses is excited at the receptive point R_2. What directions through the nervous system will it take: (1) over the synaptic junctions c and b and to effector E_1, (2) over synapses c and d to E_2, (3) over c and f to E_3, or (4) over c and h to E_4? What are the relations between each neuron and the next succeeding one that are the determining factors? Here we pass into the realm of physiological theories rather than physiological facts.

Theories of Selection of Pathways. Best known is the theory of *different synaptic resistances*. Where two neurons (axon of one and dendrite of other) lie in end-to-end connection (at a synapse), a resistance is offered there to the passage of impulses from neuron to neuron. These resistances, at various synapses, differ greatly in degree; and a volley of impulses will follow the line of least resistance. The differential existing between the synaptic resistances at b, d, f, and h (in Figure 67) is what determines whether the neural disturbances excited at R_2 will discharge finally into E_1, E_2, E_3, or E_4. The route which provides the lowest resistances will be the one followed. Putting it quite generally: what a person will do in a given situation all depends upon the differences of resistances at his synapses.

---

[1] By channeling we do not refer to single, local, and highly specific neural fibers to be found in a single anatomical place, but rather to great functional systems. For example: the fibers running from the touch end-organs to the brain ascend mostly in the ventral spinothalamic tracts, but some of them ascend in the dorsal funiculi, and at least the former include both crossed and uncrossed fibers. All these together may be considered as a channel. There is, then, recognition of the fact that a high amount of correlation exists between anatomy and function, but allowance is made for some variation in details.

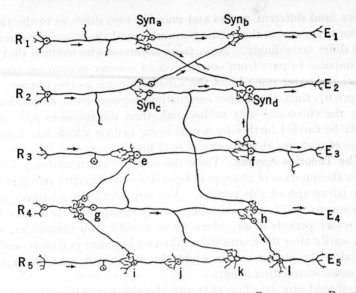

FIGURE 67. SHOWING MANY POSSIBILITIES OF CONNECTION BETWEEN
RECEPTORS AND EFFECTORS THROUGH MANY ALTERNATIVE
SYNAPTIC JUNCTION POINTS BETWEEN NEURONS
(Discussion in text.)

Simple though it is, much criticism has been directed against this
theory, and others have been advanced. One is the theory of
different nerve (and muscle) rhythms or frequencies. In an earlier
paragraph it was stated that each nerve fiber has its own refractory
period and frequency, that is, its own rhythm at which it will transmit impulses of a given intensity. The whole nerve, moreover, will
have its preferred frequencies of transmission based on those of its
component fibers. The theory before us assumes that, to awaken a
given nerve, a stream of impulses brought up to it by another nerve
must be of a certain corresponding rhythm. A disturbance of a
given frequency which is propagated over the neuron running from
R_2 will naturally pass on into that neuron which is most susceptible
to being excited at the same frequency (or a multiple or sub-mul-
tiple thereof). In a figurative sense, then, the channels that will be
taken by impulses in transit through the nervous system are those
channels that are most in tune with it and with each other.

Another latter-day theory is that of *similar and dissimilar chro-*
naxies. From a preceding paragraph it will be recalled that different

fibers (and different nerves and muscles, too) differ as to the time-factor necessary in the exciting stimulus, and that their chronaxies [1] will differ accordingly.   Now, there are those who contend that for an impulse to pass from one neuron to another neuron (or muscle fiber) the latter must be of the same chronaxie as the former.   In Figure 67, then, if the fiber conducting impulses from R_2 has, let us say, the chronaxie 0.27 millisecond, then the impulses will more likely be carried further by a next-lying neuron which has a chronaxie of 0.27 ms. than by one of 0.32 ms.

The Theories Applied. These theories of "which pathway" bear upon the question of changes in behavior — the matter raised in the first paragraph of this section.   For any condition whatever that operates to modify the resistances at any synapses, or to modify the refractory periods of any fibers, or to modify their chronaxies, will necessarily alter the routes to be taken by impulses in transit, and so will alter the precise way in which the person will react to one and the same stimulating agent.

It should now be plain that any theories concerning the way in which neural discharges take the routes they do lie at the base of most psychological problems. For one thing, the theories offer interpretations of "learning" and "habit" as well as of "maturation" and "development."   Further, they suggest interpretations of "attitude" and "attention," of "set" and "directing tendency," of "memory" and "recall," of "associations" and "thinking." Research in physiological laboratories may perhaps ultimately demonstrate the final truth of one of them, and the detailed working out of the contributing factors will ultimately be of great aid to the psychologist.

On the other hand, he whose primary interest is really in the behavior and experience of human beings as such, must lose no time in returning to the broader problems concerning the behavior of people.

SOME SIMPLER SEGMENTS OF BEHAVIOR:
THE SPINAL CORD

The Point of Approach.   Any case of human conduct is an enormously complex affair.   Take that of John Doe walking and

---

[1] It will be recalled that chronaxie is the time required for a stimulus of double the threshold intensity.

conversing with Richard Roe. "Conversing," yes. And we shall see later what an elaborately trained set of vocal habits and hearing habits conversation involves. But John Doe is walking, also, and doing other things. He is swinging a walking-stick. He is glancing at shop windows. He is smoking a cigar. He is breathing a bit heavily from his exertion. He is maintaining erect posture of head and trunk. He is considering the topic of the conversation — war in Europe. He is recalling a newspaper headline. Indeed, hardly any end could be found to the large and small aspects and segments of the total phenomenon we call, "John Doe taking a walk with Richard Roe." However, if we are to seek a scientific understanding of such a phenomenon as this, we must not leave it "in the large" but must approach it from different angles and analytically. It is the time-honored method in studying all natural phenomena to start with artificially simplified examples.

The Example of the Knee Jerk and Its Dependence upon Other Processes. If a person be seated so that a leg hangs free from the knee down, a smart tap administered just below the knee cap will elicit a prompt kick. A simple-looking act: simple enough to be called a reflex. Essentially it involves two neurons, an afferent running from the skin receptor to the spinal cord and an efferent which takes up the impulses there and passes them back out to the muscle that jerks the leg. Figure 68, $a - b$, shows the route schematically. As we describe it, however, this is an artificial abstraction from the facts. Back in the 1880's it was learned that this kick movement will be augmented if, at the time the blow is struck, another sensory stimulation such as a pressure on the finger or a sharp sound, be applied to the person simultaneously. To represent the neural base of this phenomenon, other lines appear in the figure, suggesting possible pathways of influence. (Lines c and d, lines e, f, g, h, and i.) The *spinal cord* is now revealed as playing a double rôle: (*a*) as furnishing immediate *connections between afferent and efferent* neurons involved in simple acts, and (*b*) as furnishing a highway in the form of *tracts of fibers that connect higher and lower afferent and efferent neurons at many different levels.* It also appears that the *brain* parts, too, play the latter rôle, though with more intricate connections involved.

But the intimate relationship between one segment and another of a total response is shown by further data on this "simple" knee jerk. The influence upon it by the extraneous stimulus at hand or

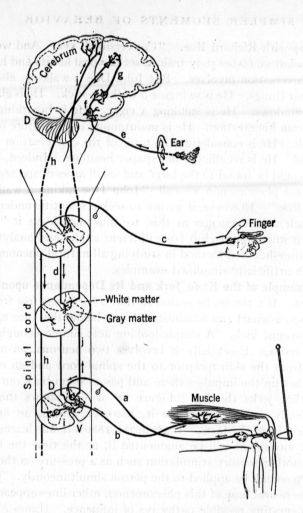

FIGURE 68. A SIMPLE REFLEX ARC AND ITS COMPLICATIONS

The knee jerk as a reflex involves neurons *a* and *b*, which are connected at one level of the cord.

The reflex act is influenced, however, by other neural processes, such as impulses from pressure on finger, conducted along the afferent fiber *c* and the descending fiber *d*; or by impulses from ear, passing along afferent fibers *e* and *f* to a relay point (thalamus) where *g* is excited and conducts to a place in the cortex of the cerebrum, at which point a descending fiber *h* transmits the impulses to the proper level of the cord to excite *b*.

Meanwhile the incoming afferent impulses on *a* also excite ascending fiber *j* to produce other less reflexive responses to the original stimulus, such as when the subject responds by saying "Now." (To avoid confusion, lines to represent the various more complicated responses are not added to the figure.)

Figure very incomplete. Relative proportions not preserved.

Each fiber represents very many of its kind.

V = ventral aspect, *D* = dorsal.

ear depends in a most surprising way upon the precise time interval between it and the tap stimulus. The re-enforcement is greatest when the two processes are practically simultaneous; if the incidental process precedes the tap on the knee by an interval of 0.4 seconds the re-enforcement amounts to nothing; with longer intervals between the stimuli re-enforcement changes to inhibition and the amount of kick is actually diminished below the normal; with one of 1 second the inhibiting influence tends to disappear; and after 1.7 seconds the kick ceases to be affected by the other process at all and is normal.

The very nicety of the relations found between the two variables — time interval and degree of *re-enforcement* or *inhibition* — is certainly arresting. Why, in the first place, should the transit of impulses aroused in a finger or in the ear influence a simple movement in a very different part of the body? Granting this influence, why should it be at times positive and at times negative? Why, finally, should this effect be so nicely graduated and dependent upon fine differences between time-intervals all of which are under 1.7 seconds? We must confess that we do not know the explanation in neural terms. We can only remain impressed with the delicate relationships that surround even the simple knee jerk.

A wider range of factors enters into the story. If the person is asleep, his knee jerk disappears, and even in a passive waking state it remains small; whereas if he is excited or irritated it becomes markedly increased. If he has just had flashed before him a word he dislikes, the kick is decreased. Even more generally, a daily rhythm is discoverable, for the amount of the reflex is lowest when the subject is just out of bed and at the close of an afternoon of standing and talking; it is highest just after breakfast and just after lunch. It seems, then, that *the knee jerk is increased and diminished by whatever increases and decreases the activity of the central nervous system as a whole.*

One point further. The knee jerk can be trained. It has been found that if either of the stimuli referred to above (a sound or a pressure on the finger) is repeatedly presented to an experimental subject just before the tap is delivered to the knee, eventually the mere presentation of the sound or the pressure *alone* without the tap will call out the knee jerk in a reflex-like way, that is, quite without any intention or even expectation of doing so on the subject's part.[1]

---

[1] This is the phenomenon of conditioning, to be given much attention on later pages.

From this examination of one simple segment isolated artificially we can conclude: *Any neural impulses passing through the nervous system may, under certain conditions, affect and be affected by any other impulses passing through. And to speak of a reflex is to speak of an artificial abstraction, useful but not complete, for even a single pathway is never active by itself.*

Some Simple Impairments Involving More Complex Processes. By this time we have come to recognize the significance of the spinal cord as an integrating avenue through which sensory and motor processes of different parts of the body are related. The impairments of these processes to be found in two well-known diseases are instructive. In the more serious cases of "infantile paralysis" the patient upon recovering from the disease itself finds himself incapable of carrying out certain activities that call for the use of certain muscles, especially those of the legs. The muscles themselves waste away. Now, post-mortem examinations of the spinal cord reveal destruction by the germs of the disease of many of the cell-bodies of the efferent nerves leaving the spinal cord at this level. (Cf. Figure 69, *A*.) Such lesions may be confined to a small region on one side the cord or may involve both sides for a great part of its length. What has happened is the destruction of an efferent channel.

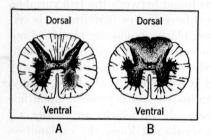

FIGURE 69. DESTRUCTIONS OF NEURAL TISSUE IN THE CORD ASSOCIATED WITH IMPAIRMENTS OF BEHAVIOR

A. A typical region found destroyed in *infantile paralysis.* The cell bodies of motor neurons in the left ventral horn being destroyed, movement of the muscles of the left side normally innervated by them is rendered impossible. (A motor paralysis.)

B. A region found destroyed in *locomotor ataxia.* Ascending afferent fibers in the dorsal part of the cord are destroyed. Afferent impulses aroused at moving muscles, tendons, and joints, cannot reach the brain to play their part in stimulating (controlling) muscular movement. (A sensory paralysis.)

(From Franz and Gordon, *Psychology.* McGraw-Hill, 1933.)

In locomotor ataxia a paralysis is again present, but in a different form. The patient finds it difficult to walk or to stand; and sometimes only by watching his foot can he lift it properly to mount a ladder. If told to close his eyes and touch his forefinger to his nose, the hand may fail utterly to find the nose. If he attempts to feed himself with eyes closed he is likely to spill his food on his clothing. What is wrong? Upon examination the patient may show ability to move his arms and legs to their fullest extent and vigorously, so that the impairment is not in the motor pathways. It is in the sensory, in the kinesthetic; and in fact, microscopic examination brings to light degeneration (due to disease germs) of ascending afferent fibers in the dorsal parts of the cord (Figure 69, *B*). With these afferent channels from the muscles interrupted, the patient has no incoming kinesthetic impulses to start and stop the moving muscles and so to control them. (Cf. discussion of this kinesthetic control of movement, pp. 233 f.)

In conclusion, we may say that a man is dependent especially upon his spinal cord not only for the central connections necessary to many of the simpler segments of his activity (reflexes), but also for the afferent and efferent functions involved in more complex kinds of activity as well.

The Structure of the Spinal Cord. Before leaving it, we should have a more definite anatomical description of the spinal cord. It is a long tube with greatly thickened walls, extending two thirds of the way down the inside of the vertebral column (Figure 70). Between the bony vertebrae spinal nerves emerge from the cord, coming off on each side by a ventral motor root and a dorsal sensory root. Two million fibers are said to make up these nerves.

In cross-section the cord presents a characteristic picture with its butterfly-shaped gray matter and the surrounding white. The gray matter is composed mainly of cell bodies. The white matter is composed of cell fibers, principally the axons with their whitish medullary sheaths, which are seen in cross-section as they run up and down the cord in "spinal tracts" or bundles.

MORE COMPLEX SEGMENTS OF BEHAVIOR: LOWER BRAIN PARTS

Special Types of Motor Co-ordinations Involved. When John Doe is walking and talking with Richard Roe, one of the obvious stages in the organization of his behavior is the process of maintaining his equilibrium. Each step occurs not as an independent operation but as the performance of one member of a team. Similarly, his use of his hands in manipulating his gloves and stick, and his vocal activities in speech, are additional samples of smoothly executed performances. These and other motor co-ordinations appear from experiments on animals to be dependent at least in part upon afferent-efferent connections in the *cerebellum*. When half of this organ has been experimentally removed, an animal may extend its paw to strike an object but miss it, and when it walks it is with a staggering gait. When all the organ has been excised, birds have lost ability to co-ordinate their movements sufficiently to fly, walk, or jump. Evidence of the same sort comes from human clinical

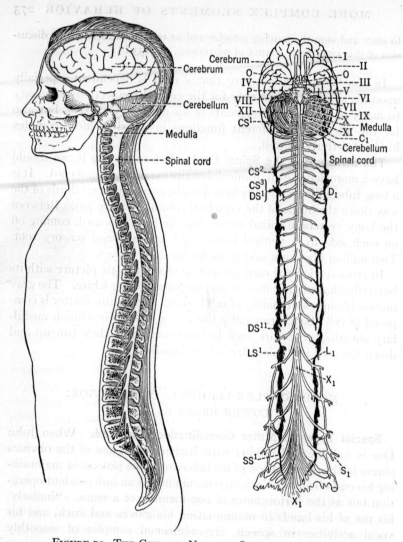

Cerebrum
Cerebrum
Cerebellum
Medulla
Spinal cord

Cerebrum — I
O — II
IV — O — III
P — V — VI
VIII — VII
XII — IX
CS^1 — X — Medulla
XI — C_1
Cerebellum
Spinal cord
CS^2 — D_1
CS^3
DS^1

DS^{11}
LS^1 — L_1
X_1
SS^1 — S_1
X_1

FIGURE 70. THE CENTRAL NERVOUS SYSTEM AS A WHOLE

On the left it is seen from the side in position in the vertebral column; on the right exposed and seen from the front. The 12 cranial nerves are designated by Roman numerals. The spinal nerves are designated in part: C_1, the first of the 8 cervical; D_1, the first of the 12 thoracic; L_1, the first of the 5 lumbar; S_1, the first of the 5 sacral; X_1 (lower figure), the coccygeal. Ganglia and connections of the autonomic division are shown in solid black: CS^1, CS^2, CS^3, superior, middle, and inferior cervical ganglia; DS^1–DS^{11}, thoracic ganglia; LS^1, the first lumbar ganglion; SS^1, the sacral ganglion.

cases. A patient suffering from cerebellar lesions may exhibit tremors, twitchings, and jerkings; his handwriting becomes mere scrawls; and his quavering voice cannot articulate a phrase like "Methodist Episcopal."

The cerebellum is that mass of corrugated tissue outgrowing from the brain stem just above and to the rear of the medulla. A cross-section view shows a mass of grayish tissue (made of layers of cell bodies and their branches) surrounding whitish tissue (composed of nerve fibers that run into and out of the white matter). Some of the neurons, especially the basket cells shown in Figure 66, have very richly branching axons, and thus appear to furnish an excellent basis for the co-ordinating of motor functions attributed to the cerebellum.

Vegetative Processes. Let us return to John Doe as he is walking and conversing with Richard Roe. We realize that certain visceral processes are going on steadily: he is breathing, his heart beat keeps up, his dinner is being digested, he is perspiring a little, and the like. These operations may strike the reader at first as being "purely physiological" and as having naught to do with the man's outward conduct nor with his inward experiences. Nothing could be more false. For one thing, they support and form a background for all his activity — a point that is perfectly obvious, since the man must remain alive. What is more, the afferent impulses arising from one's internal organs probably contribute an important share to his awareness of his own identity, his own self; for in pathological cases, anesthesias and other disorders of the viscera are often at the bottom of "feelings of alienation" and "feelings of lost identity."

The neural bases of the vegetative or life-maintaining functions involve more than the spinal cord. Many of the organs referred to — lungs, heart, throat, stomach, and numerous muscles and glands elsewhere — have afferent and efferent fibers running into the *medulla* and the *hypothalamus*. The former may be seen as a swollen part of the cord and in structure only a more complicated version of it. Its greater complexity furnishes the delicate and elaborate interconnections of incoming and outgoing nerve processes essential to the functioning of the organs. It is essential to the proper interrelations between organs, and between them and more overt behavior. The hypothalamus is a name applied collectively to several bodies [1] lying at the base of the thalamus and of the cerebrum.

---

[1] They include the optic chiasm, nervous part of the hypophysis (pituitary), infundibulum, mammillary bodies, and others.

Emotional Aspects of Behavior.   There are more dramatic ways in which these various physiological processes are of psychological importance.   Suppose, for instance, that the topic of the conversation has veered to something touching closely on the personal interests of John Doe and he becomes, as any observer will say, "angry."   What is involved in this "anger"?   Not only will his stride change, and his manual gestures and pitch of voice, but his breathing will be obviously heavier, his face flushed from an accelerated circulation.   If the observer could apply registering technique from the laboratory, he would discover profound changes of digestion, of perspiration, and numerous other "physiological" functions.   Doe himself, if he will stop to examine his own feelings now or in retrospect later, will realize that his "insides" are somehow working differently.

The evidences point to the hypothalamus as the most important site of those connections responsible for emotional changes in behavior.   They are of two principal kinds.   (1) Several different authorities have reported finding lesions in the hypothalamus on post-mortem examination of patients who had manifested strange deviations from the normal in their emotions only.   Some had lost all emotional expression on one side of the face without losing ability to move the same muscles voluntarily; some had become extremely apathetic, with a fatuous serenity of attitude and a complete indifference to insults and jibes.   On the other hand, there have been cases that showed over-reaction to the least emotional provocation, such as moderate warmth, tickling, or pricking, going off into long roars of laughter or into one weeping spell after another.   (2) More evidence pointing to the hypothalamus as the seat of the neural connections throwing the visceral and other emotional reactions into play has come from experimentation on animals.   Differing amounts of the brain in cats and dogs have been removed.   The result was that those animals that had been deprived of certain parts of the hypothalamus lost their capacity to make emotional reactions, while other animals in which those parts of the hypothalamus had been left intact after removal of other brain parts continued to manifest much their usual emotional behavior.

When closer analyses have been given to the clinical (on human subjects) and the experimental (on subhuman) evidence, more specific facts have come to light: (a) if the degeneration or injury affects the hypothalamus itself it impairs or even totally abolishes emotion.

whereas (*b*) if the degeneration or injury affects instead the neural pathways running down to the hypothalamus from the cerebrum, great exaggeration of emotion is the result. (Cf. the diagram in Figure 38, on p. 171.) Thus it seems to be pretty well established that while the hypothalamus furnishes pathways and interconnections that throw into play the visceral segments of a man's behavior, these processes are held in check by impulses discharging into the hypothalamus from the cerebral cortex. Injure the hypothalamus, and emotional behavior is reduced; injure the pathways of inhibitory impulses from the cortex or injure the cortex itself, and emotional behavior may run riot [1, 3].[1] This is a matter of high interest to psychologists. It supports the well-known view that the more primitive emotional aspect of a man's life is subject to domination and control by the more evolved and civilized intellectual side.

THE HIGHEST TYPES OF BEHAVIOR: THE CEREBRUM

Introduction. In our example of the behavior of John Doe, the segments and aspects so far described have been the more obvious, visible, and overt. In nearly all regards, moreover, they can be found about as well in lower mammals as in man. But the reader will properly protest: So far we have not really gotten to the more distinctively human capacities that John Doe can exercise. What other animal could talk with a friend about Manchukuo and Spain, about John Marshall and Disraeli, about heavy hydrogen or the star Aldebaran? Or — more modestly — what one would glance at shop windows mindful of the approach of Christmas; or casually remark of new vehicles passing, "The new Cadillac," or "The new Ford"; or debate subvocally with himself, "Dare I invite Roe home for dinner tonight?" These are higher capacities which from time immemorial have been called "reason" or "intellect." The modern psychologist would have some qualms about the use of these terms, for he would be mindful of the enormous rôle that the non-rational and irrational really play in anyone's life; yet he would accept them as limiting terms, that is, as describing unusually high degrees of functions that have more modest names, such as "perceiving," "recognizing," "abstracting," and other manifestations of "intelligence." In all of these the man is *adjusting himself to larger*

---

[1] The evidence presented is clinical and experimental. But little anatomical working-out has been given the neural fibers involved; hence, no detailed diagrams of them will be furnished in this book.

complexes and relationships between present situations and between physically absent or represented ones. This is far more than his reflex and emotional equipment would make possible alone. In these functions he quite outdistances even his nearest relatives among other animal forms. Looked at in another way, man's capacity *to readjust, to learn,* seems almost incommensurable with the capacities of other animals.

The neural basis for intelligent behavior is unquestionably the cerebrum. In certain types of feeble-mindedness the defect is clearly traceable to some deficiency in growth of these parts. In the microcephalic, for instance, an abnormally small cranium is indicative of a pitifully inadequate cerebrum; while in many other types post-mortem microscopic examinations have brought to light greatly inferior numbers of neurons in the most highly evolved layer (the "supra-granular") of the cortex. Again, it is well established that in some types of psychoses ("insanities") the deterioration in the patient's thinking and general behavior is associated with degeneration of these neurons through certain agencies such as old age, chronic alcoholic poisoning, or the germs of syphilis [2].

Support for this general view of cerebral functions comes also from experimental work on animal (vertebrate) brains, in which the capacity to learn and to remember is seriously affected by injuries to the cortex. (Cf., for example, Lashley's work, to be described below.)

The cerebrum, then, is the site of all those possibilities for interconnection that furnish the physical basis for a person to manifest learning and intelligence and all the more elaborate intellectual capacities that make him especially capable in fitting himself to his living conditions or in modifying them to fit him.

A way of regarding the cerebrum which may serve as a helpful key is to emphasize the enormous *complexity* of its *pathways* and of their synaptic *interconnections.* What does this mean for stimulus-response connection possibilities? Says Herrick:

"If a million cortical nerve cells were connected one with another in groups of only two neurons each in all possible combinations, the number of different patterns of interneuronic connection thus provided would be expressed by $10^{2,783,000}$." A staggering figure! But instead of a million neurons there are said to be 9,200,000,000. And instead of a grouping in two-neuron series we find that "Every neuron of the cerebral cortex is enmeshed in a tangle of very fine nerve fibers of great complexity, some of which come from very remote parts. It is probably safe to say that the majority of the cortical neurons are directly or indirectly connected with every cortical field. . . . The interconnections of these associational fibers form an anatomical mechanism which permits, during a train of cortical associations, numbers of different functional combinations of cortical neurons that far surpass any figures ever suggested by the astronomers in measuring the distances of stars."

Since man possesses such a means of connecting his receptors to his effectors, it is no wonder that he is enabled to perform his feats of extracting cube root, mastering Sanskrit and Chinese, carving the Lord's prayer on a pinhead, designing a new costume, directing a symphony, writing a history of Rome, superintending a steel mill employing five thousand men, or any other of the manifold operations that are so complex as to defy exhaustive explanation and therefore seem sometimes more than the action of mechanisms. But civilization and science have progressed by the exorcising of devils; and if earlier man began to obtain some useful control over harvests and seas and bodily disease by replacing demons with mechanisms, so man today can attain control of the human equation by seeking explanations in terms not of mystical powers hidden away in the brain, but of physical processes operating there and elsewhere.

Like all other parts of the central nervous system, the cerebrum is *an apparatus for making connections between afferent and efferent paths.* These connections may be devious and intricate, but they still are central connections for the outer neural fibers.

Gross Structure of the Cerebrum. The cerebrum overtops the whole nervous system, filling the bony cranium. (Cf. Figures 70 and 71.) It is partly divided by a deep *longitudinal fissure* into a right and a left *hemisphere* and these are joined by a broad band of white matter called the *corpus callosum.* The surface is much convoluted by fissures. The gray matter on the outside forms a "bark" or *cortex* of about three millimeters in thickness, and contains several layers of neurons and their fibers, of varying shapes and sizes, forming synaptic interconnections of inconceivable complexity. The large masses of white matter beneath the cortex are composed of great fibers (axons). These axons connect the cortex with lower centers of the nervous system, connect the two hemispheres, and connect the various parts of the cortex of the same hemisphere.

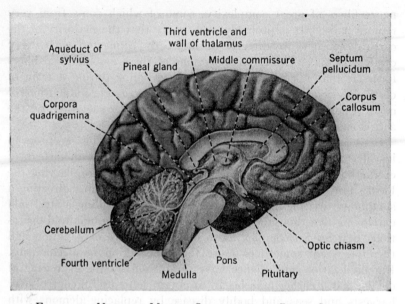

FIGURE 71. VERTICAL MEDIAN SECTION OF THE BRAIN, SHOWING
THE LEFT HALF

The cerebrum is the great convoluted mass filling more than half the picture. (Watson, J
B, *Psychology from the Standpoint of a Behaviorist.* J. B. Lippincott Company, 1929.)

Projection and Association Functions of the Cerebrum.   The
various receptors and effectors of the body are connected with the
cerebral cortex *via* the sensory and motor tracts of the cord and the
brain stem.   This implies that every given sense or motor organ is
in connection with some particular portion of the cortex.   What are
the facts?

It was a chance observation on a battlefield of the Franco-
Prussian War that started the careful experimental investigations of
this problem.   Fritsch, an army surgeon, happened to apply an
electric current to a surface of the exposed brain of a wounded
soldier, and noticed thereupon the twitchings of certain muscles.   At
once he and Hitzig took up laboratory research on similar phenomena in dogs, and they succeeded in demonstrating that certain
special areas of the cortex were in direct connection with certain
muscles of the opposite side of the body.   Very many succeeding
investigators have added to the facts; and today fairly consistent
views have been arrived at by different methods, so that a fair

amount of the surface of the cerebrum has been marked off into sensory and motor projection areas, that is, those general locations where afferent fibers from particular receptors first reach the cerebral cortex, and those where efferent fibers leave it to conduct to particular effectors. These are represented in Figure 72.

But we have not seen how these motor and these sensory projection centers are connected to each other in order to complete the transit of neural impulses from the receptors, in which they originate, out finally to the effectors.

The matter may be briefly introduced as follows. The general areas just in front of and just behind the fissure of Rolando are not purely motor and purely sensory, respectively, but are to be taken as forming a large *general sensory-and-motor area* [4, 6, 23], with what might be styled two poles, the anterior one being chiefly motor, the posterior one chiefly sensory. Connections of a fairly direct sort between afferent and efferent channels are thereby provided, making possible the simpler forms of human activity. But we must note two complications.

All parts of this area are connected to other parts of the cerebrum by *association* channels, which serve to increase the possible complexity of neural activity and hence of behavior. An enormous number of bundles of fibers have been made out in the white matter underlying the gray cortex which connects the two hemispheres, right and left, as well as the different cortical areas of the same hemisphere. These fibers seem to furnish the connecting links necessary for complicated behavior.

Besides the cutaneous and kinesthetic areas there are other *special sensory projection areas* that have been definitely localized — the visual, the auditory, and the olfactory. These are the parts of the cerebral cortex upon which the corresponding receptors are projected (in the photographer's or mathematician's meaning of this word). In the case of visual function, for instance, a quite definite point-to-point relation has been made out between different points on the retina and different points on the visual area of the cortex [16].

The Pseudo-Science of Phrenology. It is high time that the reader be warned. One of the pseudo-psychological "gold bricks" that continue to be sold in shady corners even after a century of scientific disproofs is the method of reading a person's character by feeling the bumps on his head. Phrenologists have mapped out the

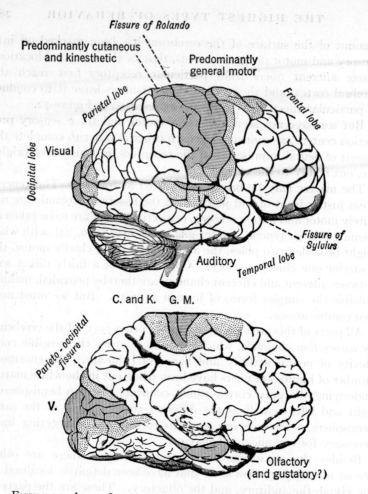

Fissure of Rolando

Predominantly cutaneous
and kinesthetic

Predominantly
general motor

Parietal lobe

Frontal lobe

Occipital lobe

Visual

Fissure of
Sylvius

Auditory   Temporal lobe

C. and K.   G. M.

Parieto - occipital
fissure

V.

Olfactory
(and gustatory?)

FIGURE 72. AREAS LOCALIZED AS THE CORTICAL TERMINATIONS OF
SENSORY AND MOTOR PROJECTION TRACTS

The upper figure shows the outer surface of the right hemisphere; the lower figure the mesial
surface of the left hemisphere. The sensory areas are marked by vertical shading, the motor
by horizontal shading. The doubtful or partially sensory and motor areas are dotted. The
association and unknown areas are unshaded. The surface of the hemisphere is roughly divided up by three fissures (Sylvian, Rolandic, parieto-occipital) into four lobes (frontal, parietal, occipital, temporal): which fissures and lobes help in specifying the precise localities of the
functions mentioned. It may be added that the longitudinal or median fissure is the one dividing the two hemispheres, and that the olfactory area is on the hippocampal lobe. (From
Pillsbury, *Fundamentals of Psychology*, after Campbell, Flechsig and Cushing. The Macmillan
Company, 1934.)

cranium into all sorts of regions under which are said to be localized in the brain such broad human traits as "mirthfulness," "benevolence," "tune," "imitation," "combativeness," "adhesiveness," "hope," "cautiousness," and so on.   If the subject has a skull prominence at a given point, then reference to the map is supposed to show the "character reader" that the person in question is strong in the corresponding trait.   But note the fallacies involved: (1) The shape of the skull is not a reliable index of the shape of the brain.   (2) The relative size of a brain part is no index of its functional capacity, which depends rather upon complexity.   (3) Most emphatically of all, such general and even vague human traits as those listed above are not centered in specific places in the cortex. It cannot be too vigorously insisted that *the only functions that have ever been definitely localized there are those directly involving the functioning of definite sensory or definite motor* organs in the body. In contemporary slang, phrenology is "the bunk," in spite of the cleverness of some of its practitioners, whose apparent success is really to be attributed to several other things.

The Cerebrum in More Complex Behavior.   In some preceding paragraphs we have seen that particular localized areas and points on the cerebral cortex are involved in specific sensory and specific motor functions.   But most human and infrahuman behavior is more complex than merely making simple responses to simple stimulations.   On the neurological side we find that the cerebrum is involved in a general way and as a whole organ; it is not a mere mosaic of distinct simple functions.

More important evidence has been developed by Lashley.   He was interested in determining to what extent an animal's learning of a habit is dependent upon its cerebrum.   He opened the cranium of white rats under deep anesthesia and destroyed some part of the cortical tissue — the locus and extent of the destruction in each case being ascertained later on by a microscopic examination of cross-sections made from the brain.   For illustration two cases are reproduced in Figure 73.   He so varied the injuries that in one or another animal every part of the cortex had been destroyed.   When each animal had fully recovered from the effects of the operation, Lashley tested its ability to learn its way through a maze [1] on repeated trials. Did losses of cerebral tissue have any effect on learning?   His results showed that there was a clear tendency for those animals having

[1] The general notion of a maze can be gathered from Figures 93 and 94 on pp. 367 and 368.

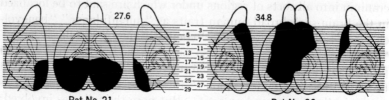

FIGURE 73. TYPICAL MAPS OF CEREBRAL DESTRUCTION

In each case the top number indicates the percentage of the cortex found destroyed upon a post mortem examination. The left portion of each figure shows the destruction (in black) as visible from the left side of the brain; the middle double-portion, the destruction as seen from above; the right portion, the same as seen from the right side.

The loci and the amounts of destruction were determined by: (a) making sections through the brain at the spacings numbered from *1* to *29*; (b) giving each section microscopic examination; (c) reconstructing the whole brain from the sectional examinations.

(From Lashley, K. S., *Brain Mechanisms and Intelligence.* Univ. Chicago Press, 1929. Plate III.)

great losses of cortex to be greatly retarded in their learning, and for those with lesser losses to be less retarded. The coefficient of correlation was high, + .86.

Another question naturally followed: Is the formation of a habit dependent upon certain particular parts of the cerebrum? From the microscopic examinations a map of the brain destruction was made out for each individual case. These maps were then grouped according to the general brain areas involved; then for each area the correlation was worked out between the amounts of destruction and the amounts of retardation. The coefficients, appearing in the second column of the accompanying table, run as high for one area as for another; and they show conclusively that a habit like the maze is as much dependent on one area as on another.

AREA INJURED	CORRELATION BETWEEN AMOUNT OF CEREBRAL INJURY AND AMOUNT OF RETARDATION IN LEARNING (ERRORS)	CORRELATION BETWEEN AMOUNT OF CEREBRAL INJURY AND AMOUNT OF RETARDATION IN RELEARNING (ERRORS) *
Frontal	.80	.51
Temporal	.80	.52
Occipital	.88	.38
Parietal	—	.82
All areas	.86	.59

* From Lashley, K. S. *Brain Mechanisms and Intelligence*, pp. 51, 61, 107. University of Chicago Press, 1929.

So much for learning: what about retaining? To answer this Lashley trained rats first, then operated upon them, and then tested their retention of the habit by measuring the amount of practice required to relearn it perfectly. Again the data showed a positive correlation (+ .59) between the amount of brain lost and the amount of habit lost. Further, another examination of area by area brought out a positive relationship in the case of each area between amount of destruction and amount of impairment. This appears in the third column of the table.

The conclusion pointed by these experiments of Lashley's is: *A habit like that of the maze is not dependent either for its learning or for its retention upon the neural connections in any specifically localized area of the brain but upon the total quantity of cerebral tissue that is intact.*

Experimental investigations of this type are multiplying nowadays. Varying conceptions of the precise way in which the cortex works are being set forth, under such names as "vicarious functioning," "mass action," "equipotentiality," and the like. The interested student will find here a field that, though over a century old, is still a pioneer field and a fascinating one. So far as we are here concerned, however, the following generalization must suffice:

Pathways through the central nervous system are not highly specific and fixed, but variable and plastic; and any set of neural impulses in transit will have their routing determined not only by local factors in the neurons and synapses directly involved, but also by more widespread conditions of the nervous system and even of the whole organism at the moment.

Electrical Potentials from the Brain. We must mention a phenomenon quite recently discovered. On earlier pages (especially 205 ff.) we have had occasion to refer to potentials that can be obtained from active muscular and neural tissues. Now, since the brain is a vast concentration of neural tissues we would naturally suppose that potentials would be set up there. Such is the case. When electrodes attached to occipital and frontal points of the head, for instance, are placed in circuit with exceedingly delicate registering apparatus, two or more rhythms of electrical discharge can be detected. These rhythms are disturbed when the resting subject is stimulated by a sound or light, when he is anxious or worried, when he does an arithmetic problem, when he falls asleep, and under other conditions. Research on this problem is too new to justify our speaking with much definiteness, but the possibilities are rather exciting. "Here is a key, fashioned by physiology out of radio. Has neurology a lock which the key can open?" [13, 19.]

CONCLUDING VIEW OF NEURAL FUNCTIONING

Our survey of the nervous system in this chapter has minimized anatomical details, which, if the reader be interested, can be found in any amount in numerous physiological and neurological texts. To place it in general perspective, let us trace again the analytic process by which we arrived at the study of the nervous system. Psychology, so we have said, is a study of behavior, that is, of how a person lives and moves under the life conditions in which he finds himself. This organism-environment interaction, however, is obviously dependent upon two sets of variables: the environmental conditions, social and non-social, and the variables of the person himself. If $B = f(PE)$, as we have previously had it formulated, then P and E each calls for scrutiny as a co-determiner of behavior. P, on his part, is an animate organism with certain tendencies to self-maintenance and adjustment; but, analyzed further, this is dependent upon his bodily organs and structures. The organs and structures most directly involved in adjustment are the receptors through which he is stimulated, the effectors by which he responds, and the system of interconnectives between the two. (Obviously enough, such things as one's blood corpuscles or the synovial membrane of his joints or the absorption of food chemicals through the walls of the small intestine — whatever their importance for his continuous body processes — have but negligible bearing upon how he is going to behave toward other people and things.)

It is appropriate, then, to gather up and generalize the substance of the present chapter as an answer to some such query as: How can we have a better understanding of psychological problems through what we have learned about the nervous system as a co-determiner of behavior?

From our survey we must now realize that the help of neurology to psychology is likely to be more in *general points of view* than detailed explanations of particular cases. Suppose, for instance, that a particular individual John Jones says, "The square of 6 is 36." The precise why and wherefore of this performance is not to be stated as the particular activity of a particular group of neurones at one particular locus in the brain. A methodological reason is that it is impossible at present to observe experimentally and control in fine detail the infinitesimal and infinitely complex neural impulses occurring in an actual case of human behavior. Our knowledge is indirect, as we have seen in preceding pages: it comes only from the post-mortem examination of the cases the clinician happens to run across or from the experimental examination of subhuman forms. In striking contrast to the detailed relations that are worked out between one's receptor equipment and his capacities to see and hear and otherwise discriminate the various aspects of the world in which he lives, knowledge of the nervous system throws light not on details, but on general characterizations of behavior.

(*A*) From our survey, we can see that the architecture of the nervous system determines the level or grade of behavior on which a person can act, the adequacy with which he can take care of himself. Comparisons of one animal with another, examination of pathological human cases, and operative procedure on animals, combine to furnish us with a general picture of how the character of a person's adjustments to his problems depends upon the integrity of the whole nervous system and upon the normal operation of some of its evolving parts.

(*B*) Through a review of available knowledge of neural process we have provided ourselves with some general principles of function and integration that will, if properly appreciated and employed, serve as explanatory keys in a number of problems of human conduct and thinking. In the expositions of psychological phenomena to follow, we shall not have space to return repeatedly to these fundamental neural principles; but the alert reader will be rewarded in both help and satisfaction by identifying the operation of such principles as "threshold," "refractory phase," "inhibition," "re-enforcement," and the like.

Finally: Our study of neural functioning would have been in vain had it not served to purge the reader of some lurking popular superstitions. The nervous system is not mysterious; nor is the cortex the residence of daemons. The brain is not even an independent agent, for it cannot initiate or instigate anything: it is but the switching-yard of trains of neural disturbances which were begun at receptive terminals and are propagated along the immensely complicated pathways toward effector terminals.

ORIENTATION

This completes a series of three chapters in which we have gone more directly and analytically to the study of some of the particular organs that are involved in the various forms of human behavior described previously and subsequently. After Chapter VII we paused in our study of man-as-a-whole to take special note of the ways in which his afferent, central, and efferent functions are carried on. We now return to our broader viewpoint.

REFERENCES

1. Bard, Philip. Emotion: The Neuro-Humoral Basis of Emotional Reactions. *Handbook of General Experimental Psychology* (Murchison, ed.). Clark Univ. Press, 1934.
2. Berry, R. J. A. *Brain and Mind*. Macmillan, 1928.
3. Cannon, W. B. The James-Lange Theory of Emotions. *Am. J. Psychol.*, 1927, **39**, 106–24.
4. Dusser de Barenne, J. G. Experimental Researches on Sensory Localization in the Cerebral Cortex of the Monkey (Macacus). *Proc. Roy. Soc., B.*, 1924, **96**, 272–91.
5. Evans, C. L. *Recent Advances in Physiology*. 4th ed. Blakiston, 1930, chaps. IX, X.
6. Foerster, O. The Motor Cortex in Man in the Light of Hughlings Jackson's Doctrines. *Brain*, 1936, **59**, 135–59.
7. Forbes, A. The Mechanism of Reaction. *Handbook of General Experimental Psychology* (Murchison, ed.). Clark Univ. Press, 1934.
8. Franz, S. I., and Gordon, K. *Psychology*. McGraw-Hill, 1933. Chapter on Nervous Structures and Functions.
9. Freeman, G. L. *Introduction to Physiological Psychology*. Ronald, 1934.
10. Herrick, C. J. *Brains of Rats and Men*. Univ. Chicago Press, 1926.
11. Herrick, C. J. *An Introduction to Neurology* (3d ed.). Saunders, 1922.
12. Howell, W. H. *Text-Book of Physiology* (13th ed.). Saunders, 1936.
13. Jasper, H. H., and Andrews, H. L. Human Brain Rhythms. *J. Gen. Psychol.*, 1936, **14**, 98–126.
14. Ladd, G. T., and Woodworth, R. S. *Elements of Physiological Psychology*. Scribners, 1911. Part I.
15. Lashley, K. S. Nervous Mechanisms in Learning. *Handbook of General Experimental Psychology* (Murchison, ed.). Clark Univ. Press, 1934.
16. Lashley, K. S. The Mechanism of Vision: VII and VIII. *J. Comp. Neurol.*, 1934, **59**, 341–73, **60**, 57–79.
17. Lickley, J. D. *The Nervous System* (new ed.). Longmans, 1931.
18. Lillie, R. S. *Protoplasmic Action and Nervous Action* (2d ed.). Univ. Chicago Press, 1932.
19. Loomis, A. L., Harvey, E. H., and Hobart, G. Electrical Potentials of the Human Brain. *J. Exper. Psychol.*, 1936, **19**, 249–79.

20. Maier, N. R. F., and Schneirla, T. C. *Principles of Animal Psychology.* McGraw-Hill, 1935.
21. Mettler, F. A. Cerebral Functions and Cortical Localization. *J. Genet. Psychol.*, 1935, **13**, 367–401.
22. Parker, G. H. *The Elementary Nervous System.* Lippincott, 1919.
23. Poliak, S. The Main Afferent Fiber Systems of the Cerebral Cortex in Primates. *Univ. Calif. Publ. in Anat.*, 1932, **2** (entire).
24. Schlosberg, H. A Study of the Conditioned Patellar Reflex. *J. Exper Psychol.*, 1928, **11**, 468–94.
25. Wilson, M. O. Chronaxie. *Psychol. Bull.*, 1935, **32**, 4–32.

CHAPTER XI

STATISTICAL METHODS

DESCRIBING A DISTRIBUTION

The Normal Curve. At the beginning of the nineteenth century Gauss and other astronomers, physicists, and mathematicians became interested in the fact that the variability of a scientific observer, that is, the number of errors (variations in his readings or estimates) he makes and the size of the errors, is calculable. Indeed this variation follows the same mathematical laws of frequency as do the laws of chance. This "normal law of error" was a manner of stating the relative frequency with which errors of different size are each likely to be made in the course of a series of observations. When the mathematical formulation is cast into a graphic form it assumes a bell-shaped curve. This curve, then, can be used to represent either (*A*) the occurrence of impersonal events due to chance (such as the results of flipping coins) or (*B*) the occurrence of variations in the performance of a human being under the same conditions.

The latter point is obviously of psychological importance, and in the treatment of massed data in a laboratory experiment, such a means of representing them visually is advantageous.

(*C*) Later it was discovered that the same laws of chance operate in the distribution in a population of many anatomical traits, such as the heights of French soldiers or the chest girths of Scottish soldiers, as well as of more distinctly psychological traits.

In Figure 74, we see how all these different manifestations of chance approximate a common bell-shaped type of curve, often called the Gaussian curve. In general it shows that the middle scores will occur the most frequently, but the extreme scores very rarely, and that the gradation of frequency from the middle scores to the extreme scores is not of the straight-line order but S-shaped like either side of the top of a bell.

What is Meant by "Chance"? In the tossing of a coin, what determines which face will lie upward when it has fallen to the table? Slight variations in the way the thumb and finger hold it, variations

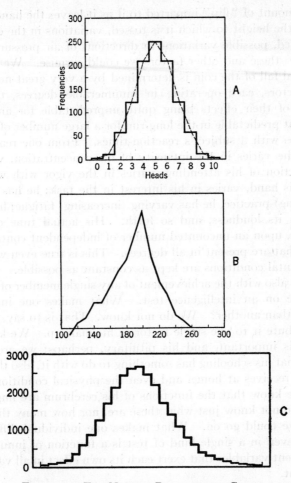

FIGURE 74. THE NORMAL DISTRIBUTION CURVE

A. A curve based on the data to be derived from a series of *chance physical events.* The vertical distances to the midpoints of each horizontal "step" represent the frequencies with which the various numbers of heads that are indicated on the base line, will occur in the course of 1024 tosses of ten coins. (These frequencies are represented mathematically by the coefficients in the expansion of $(a + b)^{10}$.) This figure is drawn both as a *column diagram* (in continuous line) and as a *frequency polygon* (in broken line).

B. A curve based on data obtained by *repeated measurements on the same individual* under conditions held as constant as possible. Vertical distances represent the frequencies with which the subject made reactions of each of the time-lengths shown in part on the base line in $\frac{1}{1000}$ second. This is drawn as a *frequency polygon.*

C. A curve based on data obtained from *single measurements on very many individuals.* Vertical distances represent the number of individual cases making each of thirty different scores (not indicated) on the Army Alpha group intelligence test; 25,200 cases in all. This is drawn as a *column diagram.*

in the amount of "flip" imparted to it as it leaves the hand, variations in the height to which it is tossed, variations in the direction
it is tossed, possible variations in directions of air pressure at the
instant — these and other factors we could surmise. We see that
the actual fall of the coin is determined by a very great number of
small factors, each operating in innumerable degrees, the joint
product of their effects being quite unpredictable for any given
throw but predictable in the long run for a large number of throws.

So it is with a subject's reaction-times. From one reaction to
another he varies in the intensity of his concentration, varies in
the direction of his attending, varies in the vigor with which he
moves his hand, varies in his interest in the task; he has varying
(increasing) practice, he has varying (increasing) fatigue; his signal
varies in its loudness, and so forth. His actual time depends,
therefore, upon an uncounted number of independent contributory
factors that are present in all degrees. This is true even when the
experimental conditions are kept as constant as possible.

So it is also with the achievement of any single member of a group
of people on an intelligence test. What makes one individual
brighter than another? We do not know. That is to say, we cannot attribute it to one single factor in his makeup. We know his
thyroid is important, and his pituitary, perhaps; we are pretty
certain that his schooling has something to do with it, also the treatment he receives at home, and even the physical condition of the
home; we know that the functions of his cerebrum are important,
but we do not know just what these are, nor how many there are;
and so we could go on. What makes one individual differ from
another even in a single kind of test is a function of innumerable
independent variables that exert each its own effect in all variations
of amount.

For mathematical reasons that we cannot go into,[1] the *composite
effect of innumerable factors working independently* to affect an event
is, in a large number of such events, expressed by the normal
distribution curve of which we have spoken above.

Let us look at some results of measurements of some physical
and psychological traits that were found in a psychology class of
77 men recently taught by the writer. See Figure 75.[2] It will be
seen that they all tend roughly to approximate the normal curve.

---

[1] These are best understood in terms of the expansion of the binomial in elementary algebra.
[2] The reader should compare also figures to be found on pp. 56, 352, 588, and 593.

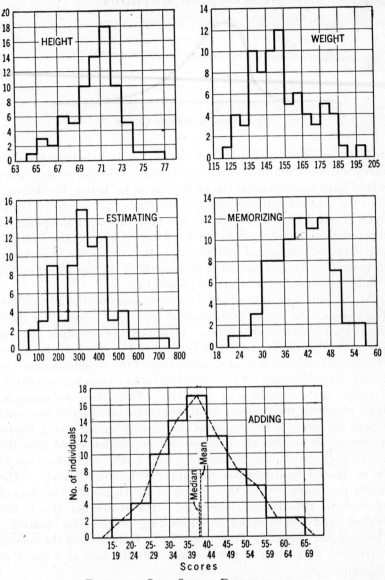

FIGURE 75. SOME SAMPLE DISTRIBUTIONS

A class of 77 male college students were given two physical and three psychological tests: —
(1) Height, in inches; (2) Weight, in pounds; (3) Memorizing, in number of ideas reproduced
after hearing a prose selection; (4) Estimating, in number of marbles guessed to be in a glass jar
seen (actual number 326); (5) Adding, in number of columns added in a given period of time.

A column diagram is drawn for the scores of each test. For the Adding test a frequency
polygon is also shown, as well as the location of certain measures to be described later.

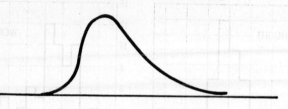

FIGURE 76. A SKEWED CURVE

It is reasonable to assume that had the class included ten times as many members, drawn from the same campus population, the curves would have approximated the normal curve far better, for this reason: the unusual and exceptional individuals that are to be found even in small groups will offset each other in larger samplings of a population, and also will be rendered less striking by the multiplication of the more usual individuals. Here we see the importance of getting as large a sampling as possible if we are to draw any reliable conclusions concerning a population.

At the same time, it would be an error to suppose that all distribution curves to be met in psychological work are Gaussian, for there are at least fourteen other types. Figure 76 represents one of them where the distribution is *skewed* because of the effect on the scores of some special factor that is more important in determining the group scores than any of the countless factors entering by chance. Consider the composition of any large college class, for example. If we measured the students for their general intelligence we would expect the range to be limited at the lower ("duller") end, for by no means all persons of an unselected population could pass the school work preliminary to that of college grade; while there would be no special limitation on the upper ("brighter") end. (The reader may have noticed that the curve for Height for the class of 77 students reveals some skewness. The reason for this is not evident, and would make an interesting problem for analysis.) However, the beginning student will find a knowledge of the normal curve and its general properties sufficient for him as a point of departure.

Measures of the Central Tendency. In all of the above distributions we have obtained measures of each individual, and we therefore know all there is to be known about this group so far as the quantitative measurement of this trait is concerned. It is impossible, however, to keep this great mass of data in mind, and we become lost in the details of the discrete scores.   For this reason we resort to statistical analysis and seek quantitative description which will accurately and simply express the general tenor of our results.

It has already been noted in the figures that there is a tendency for the individuals in the group to cluster around one point on the baseline; and the first step in the statistical description of a group is to obtain an expression which represents this clustering.   Thus the *central tendency* of the group is condensed into a simple figure and expressed by one of the three averages, the mean, the median, or the mode.

The *mean* is readily understood by the reader.   It is the total of the scores divided by the number of individuals in the group.   It is what is loosely called the average.   In the series, 28, 30, 34, 35, 36, 38, 42, 42, 48, the mean score would be 37.

The *median* is the middle score of the series of scores as they range from lowest to highest.   In the series just given, the median score would be 36.

The *mode* is the score made most frequently.   In the above case, it would be 42.

The use of any particular one of these depends upon the kind of data we have, and upon what we are interested in.   A haberdasher, for example, would not be interested in the mean or median-sized shirt that is worn, rather he would like to know the size shirt worn by most people — the modal shirt.   On the other hand, in measuring the learning of a group of subjects we find that on any given trial one or more subjects may make unusual scores, on account of a headache, a night of insomnia, or noises outside the laboratory. Since we are not interested in these exceptional cases but in the group as a whole, and since we are not studying the effect of insomnia or noise on learning, we use the median, a measure that will not be distorted by these aberrations.   Finally, a different measure would be used if we wished to gauge the batting strength of a baseball team.   Since all nine men bat almost equally often we must take into consideration the number of hits the team slugger as well as the "weak sister" will make; so we use the mean to characterize our ball club, for this average will best tell us how many hits the team as a whole can be expected to make in a certain number of times at bat.

We see, then, that all these measures of central tendency have certain characteristics peculiar to themselves, and in the treatment of our data we pick the measure whose particular characteristics will give us the most pertinent information about what we are interested in.

Grouping the Distribution.   Whenever the number of scores that have to be dealt with is very large, much labor is saved by grouping the scores into convenient *class-intervals* of, say, 3 or 5 or 10 points to the interval, depending upon the range of the whole group.   For example, on the Adding test given the class of 77 students (as described in an earlier paragraph) the scores ran as follows: 54, 29, 44, 53, 30, 41, 56, 46, and so on.   They were grouped for more convenient handling into the intervals of score shown in the table on page 297, 1st and 3d columns.   (This is easily done by first making out the intervals, then marking tallies in the appropriate ones as the respective scores are read off.)

From grouped scores the determination of the averages is some-what different.   In calculating the mean and the mode simply treat each score falling within a given interval as having the value of the midpoint of that interval.   Thus in the table of Adding scores, 2 cases are said to have scored 62.5, 2 cases 57.5, 6 cases 52.5, and so on. The rest of the computation of mean and mode should be easily made out from the table.

Finding the median of a grouped distribution involves an addi-tional detail of method.   When a middle score is one of several in the same interval, precisely what value is it given (how far up the interval)?   In the table for the Adding test, the middle case — the 39th — was found in the interval, scores 35–39, along with 16 others.   We assigned the bottom score-value of the interval, 35, to the 1st of these, and dividing the whole interval (5 score-points) into 17 steps (because there are 17 persons whose scores are in that interval), assigned 5/17 score-points to each case.   But when we reached the interval we had counted off 30 cases, leaving us 9 more to go.   The resulting operation is indicated in the table.

Measures of Variability.   Now, it is conceivable that two groups of individuals may make the same score, as a group, yet the scores of individuals of one group may vary more widely from the central tendency than do the scores of the individuals of the other group. For example, if group A makes the scores, 1, 2, 3, 4, 5, 6, 7, 8, 8, 9, 10, 11, 12, and 12, and group B the scores, 5, 5, 5, 6, 6, 7, 7, 7, 8, 8, 8, 8, 9, and 9, they would give the same mean (7) but would vary widely in their extremes.   What is needed then is an expression of the *variability* of the distribution. One form is the *mean deviation*, which is arrived at by finding the amounts of deviation of the respective scores from the central tendency, and averaging them. With grouped scores this means that for each interval we must find the amount of deviation of its midpoint from the central tendency, and multiply that by the number of cases within that interval. Then these products are summed and divided by the total number of cases. The process is illustrated in the table, using the mean to represent the central tendency — though the median and even the mode are sometimes used.

More common than the above as a description of group variability is the *standard deviation* (sigma, σ), a measure which places greater

SCORES ON AN ADDING TEST

CLASS INTERVALS	MIDPOINT*	FREQUENCY	F × MIDPT.	DEVIATION OF MIDPT. FROM MEAN	F × DEV.	F × DEV.²
60–64	62.5	2	125.	24.4	48.8	1190.72
55–59	57.5	2	115.	19.4	38.8	752.72
50–54	52.5	6	315.	14.4	86.4	1244.16
45–49	47.5	8	380.	9.4	75.2	706.88
40–44	42.5	12	510.	4.4	52.8	232.32
35–39	37.5	17	637.5	.6	10.2	6.12
30–34	32.5	14	455.	5.6	78.4	439.04
25–29	27.5	10	275.	10.6	106.0	1123.60
20–24	22.5	4	90.	15.6	62.4	973.44
15–19	17.5	2	35.	20.6	41.2	848.72
		77	2937.5		600.2	7517.72

Σ = "sum of." N = number of cases.

$$\text{Mean} = \frac{\Sigma F \times \text{Midp.}}{N} = \frac{2937.5}{77} = 38.1$$

$$\text{Median} = \left(\frac{N+1}{2} = 39\right) = 35 + \frac{5}{17} \times 9 = 37.6 \quad \text{Mode} = 37.5$$

$$\text{Mean deviation (from the mean)} = \frac{\Sigma F \times \text{Dev.}}{N} = \frac{600.2}{77} = 7.794$$

$$\text{Standard deviation (from the mean)} = \sqrt{\frac{\Sigma F \times \text{Dev.}^2}{N}} = \sqrt{\frac{7517.72}{77}} = 9.877$$

*When scores are interpreted as whole numbers only (example: "60" as "60" only and not as "60" ....60.99") the fraction ".5" should be dropped in this column.

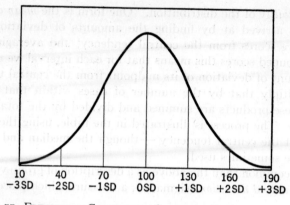

10   40   70   100   130   160   190
−3SD   −2SD   −1SD   0SD   +1SD   +2SD   +3SD

FIGURE 77. FREQUENCY CURVE WITH STANDARD DEVIATION AS A UNIT
OF MEASURE ON THE BASE LINE

The mean score of the distribution is 100 points, the standard deviation is 30 points. Note the area of the curve (i.e., number of individual cases) comprehended by 1, 2, and 3 S.D.'s, respectively, taken above and below the mean.

emphasis on the extreme variations.[1] It is very similar to the Average Deviation save that the process of squaring is introduced. It is obtained by squaring the individual deviations from the central tendency, averaging them, then extracting the square root. With grouped data of course one deals with the class-intervals instead of individual scores, squaring the deviation of the midpoint of each from the central tendency. This is also demonstrated in the table of Adding scores.

The arithmetical labor in the foregoing operations is lightened by short-cut methods in which means or medians are *guessed* and are then corrected to give the true ones. These methods are to be found in any handbook on statistical methods.

The standard deviation has another special utility. If a distribution is normal, and we mark off the value of the standard deviation as a distance to right and to left of the central tendency (the mean is generally used here), it is found that 68 per cent of the scores will be included between these two points. (See Figure 77.) Further, if we mark off distances of two standard deviations (2 S.D.'s) we include 96 per cent of the scores, and if we mark off 3 S.D., we include practically all of them, 99.7 per cent. Now, let us remind ourselves that the normal distribution represents the

---

[1] The student should note that in the measurement of dispersion the standard deviation is very helpful; for now we are not interested in how the measures tend to cluster around a central point, but rather in how they tend to vary from this point.

composite action of innumerable chance factors that determine the scores made by the various individuals. We can now utilize the standard deviation in a new way: since 3 S.D. includes practically the entire distribution of scores as produced by the chance factors, if any score is further from the central tendency than 3 S.D., the probability is great that it is produced by some other than the same chance factors, and the farther it is from the central tendency the greater this probability. In this way we know whether an individual score is *significantly different* from the group average.

In the same general manner, but with a little more mathematics, we can compare two groups to see whether a difference between their two central tendencies is a *reliable difference*.

CORRELATIONS

A Graphic Introduction. So much for measuring many individuals in regard to one performance. But it is often desirable to know about the relationship between the distributions of one performance and of another performance in the same group of individuals; as in such questions as: "Do ability in history and ability in arithmetic go together?" "Does weight of children indicate anything regarding their health?" The *coefficient of correlation* is a measure of the degree to which two series of scores go together.

A simple approach to the notion of correlation may be made graphically. Suppose twelve persons be measured in two performances, X and Y. Suppose that when laid out on a scale their respective scores on the two tests are as shown in Figure 78, A. John Doe makes the highest score on each test, Richard Roe makes the second highest, a third person makes third highest on both tests, and so on. It will be seen that from one performance to the other, the individual differences remain the same; so that, from the knowledge of an individual's position in one series, we could safely predict his position in the other. The correlation between the two series is then said to be a perfect positive one, and is represented by + 1.00. But now suppose the individuals' scores in the two performances are as shown in B, John Doe making the highest score on test X but a very low one on test Y, while Richard Roe makes high scores on both, and the other individuals change positions considerably. We then could not predict from knowledge of an individual's score on X how he would score on Y. The correlation

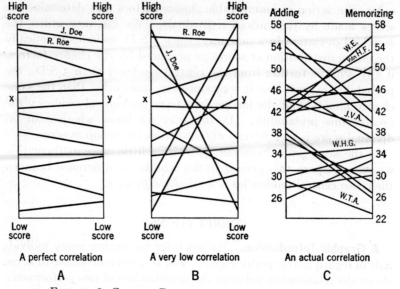

FIGURE 78. GRAPHIC REPRESENTATION OF CORRELATIONS

A and *B*, hypothetical; *C*, actual.

Each line represents an individual and connects his scores in two different distributions.

is then said to be very low, approaching zero or no-correlation, which is represented by 0.00. Inverse correlations are given negative signs.

Now, let us take an actual case, that of two of the tests applied to a college class as mentioned previously, limiting our treatment for simplicity's sake to the first twenty members. The scores (which are furnished numerically in the correlation table below) are here represented by points on two scales, for Adding and for Memorizing, as shown in Figure 78, *C*. It will be evident on inspection that we do not have a perfect correlation by any means, nor do we have an entire absence of correlation: prediction from one series to the other would be somewhat better than chance. But how much? What is needed is a more definite numerical index, a simple number by means of which the interrelationships of the two masses of data may be expressed.

The Rank-Difference Method. A simple form of the coefficient of correlation is based on ranking the scores. The individuals of the group are first ranked (1st, 2d, and so on) with respect to their scores on one trait, and then again ranked with respect to their scores on the other trait; and the difference in rank in the two series for each individual is the basis of calculation. The formula (Spearman's) employed is:

$$R = 1 - \frac{6 \, \Sigma \, D^2}{n(n^2 - 1)}$$

in which
  D = difference in the two rankings for each individual
  Σ = "sum of"
  n = number of individuals

This method is not recommended except for a small number of cases (under 30). It is not precise, for it fails to take account of the *amounts* of difference between individual scores in each distribution.

The Product-Moment Method. Much to be preferred is the method of determining the correlation between two distributions by taking account of the amount that each individual *deviates from his group mean* in each distribution. The formula (Pearson's) employed is:

$$r = \frac{\Sigma xy}{n \sigma_1 \, \sigma_2}$$

in which

  x = the respective individual deviations from the mean in one trait
  y = the respective individual deviations from the mean in the other trait
  σ_1 = standard deviation of the scores in one trait
  σ_2 = standard deviation of the scores in the other trait

Thus, the amount of correlation is "the sum of the products of each score in one trait by the same individual's score on the other, *over* the whole expression: the number of cases times the standard deviation of the scores in one trait times the standard deviation of the scores in the other trait."

The procedure is illustrated in the accompanying table where it is applied to the same group of 20 individuals as referred to in Figure 78, *C*, but using now the actual scores and their deviations from the group means.

The Interpretation of Correlation Coefficients. The correlation found above between Adding and Memorizing was +.59. For the

A CORRELATION SHEET

SUB-JECT	SCORE X (Adding)	SCORE Y Memorizing)	DEV. x	DEV. y	x^2	y^2	xy
1	54	40	13.8	1.6	190.4	2.6	22.1
2	29	23	−11.2	−15.4	125.4	237.2	172.5
3	44	39	3.8	.6	14.4	.4	2.3
4	53	49	12.8	10.6	163.4	112.4	135.7
5	30	34	−10.2	−4.4	104.0	19.4	44.9
6	41	50	.8	11.6	.6	134.6	9.3
7	56	42	15.8	3.6	249.6	13.0	56.7
8	46	45	5.8	6.6	33.6	43.6	38.3
9	38	26	−2.2	−12.4	4.8	153.8	27.3
10	39	27	−1.2	−11.4	1.4	130.0	13.7
11	31	31	−9.2	−7.4	84.6	54.8	68.1
12	47	37	6.8	−1.4	46.2	2.0	−9.5
13	44	46	3.8	7.6	14.4	57.8	28.9
14	42	56	1.8	17.6	3.2	309.8	31.7
15	26	33	−14.2	−5.4	201.6	29.2	76.7
16	37	29	−3.2	−9.4	10.2	88.4	30.1
17	44	53	3.8	14.6	14.4	213.2	55.5
18	34	35	−6.2	−3.4	38.4	11.6	21.1
19	28	30	−12.2	−8.4	148.8	70.6	102.5
20	42	44	1.8	5.6	3.2	31.4	10.1
	$\Sigma X = 805$ $MX = 40.2$	$\Sigma Y = 769$ $MY = 38.4$			$\Sigma x^2 =$ 1452.60	$\Sigma y^2 =$ 1715.80	$\Sigma xy =$ 938.00

$$\sigma_x = \sqrt{\frac{\Sigma x^2}{N}} = \sqrt{\frac{1452.6}{20}} = \sqrt{72.63} = 8.52$$

$$\sigma_y = \sqrt{\frac{\Sigma y^2}{N}} = \sqrt{\frac{1715.8}{20}} = \sqrt{85.79} = 9.26$$

$$r_{xy} = \frac{\Sigma xy}{N\sigma_x\sigma_y} = \frac{938}{20 \times 8.52 \times 9.26} = \frac{938}{1577.9} = .594$$

class as a whole it was +.39. The degree to which the class-members varied on each test as compared with how they varied on each of the others is shown in the table of *intercorrelations*.

INTERCORRELATION TABLE

	HEIGHT	WEIGHT	ADDING	MEMORIZING	ESTIMATING
Height	−	.60	.07	.12	−.06
Weight	.60	−	.18	−.02	.13
Adding	.07	.18	−	.39	.44
Memorizing	.12	−.02	.39	−	.21
Estimating	−.06	.13	.44	.21	−

One must not confuse a correlation coefficient with a simple percentage: he must not suppose that with a correlation of .44 he can predict with one half as much certainty as he can with a correlation of .88.   On the contrary, the *prediction value of a coefficient of correlation* drops away with accelerated speed as the coefficient reduces.   If between two tests, X and Y, a perfect correlation is obtained ($r = 1.00$), then we can predict with absolute accuracy what John Jones will score on Y from what he scored on X.   But if the r is reduced only to .86 the safety of predicting is reduced to 50 per cent — halfway between absolute certainty and the error we would be making if we assigned Jones the mean score of the group on Y.

We may think of a coefficient of correlation as the decimal fraction which informs us *what percentage of the causes that determine the scores of one variable also determine the scores of the other variable.* But it is only a preliminary piece of information.   The work of analysis of the actual relations involved is only just begun.[1]

Applications of Statistical Methods to Some Psychological Problems.   Having acquainted ourselves with the fundamentals of statistical methodology, we may now go forward to see how the applications of these techniques aid us in the solution of many psychological problems.   A few will be given in this chapter.   Others will come into our survey incidentally in other places.

INTERRELATIONS WITHIN THE INDIVIDUAL

Do Abilities Tend to Go Together?   For centuries men have speculated about the interrelationships of the different traits or abilities that go to make up a person.

In what respects are the various analyzable traits of a given individual related to each other, and to what extents?   Much research has of late years been devoted to determining the degree to which specified human behavior traits are correlated.   Does great capacity for remembering names and faces go with great capacity for recalling mathematical formulae?   If a child excels in arithmetic may we expect him to excel also in grammar?   If he can acutely distinguish differences in loudness may we expect him to be acute at discrimi-

---

[1] This point is illustrated by the curious finding someone made at the Brookings Institute that through a period of eight years the variations in the death rate in the obscure state of Hyderabad, in the center of India, were correlated highly (.86) with variations in the membership of the International Association of Machinists!

nating colors? Is a man who is cautious in his investments likely to be equally cautious in his political or religious convictions? Is the one who is very emotional in the sense of being quickly aroused to anger also going to be quickly aroused to grief, or to fear? The general trend of scientific findings gives but weak support to popular opinions on such questions as these.

Notions entertained by the layman concerning the makeup of human nature are likely to be in error in two diametrically opposite directions. On the one hand it is fairly certain that he will invest such terms as "memory," "school ability," "caution," and "emotionality" with a dignity and substance wholly unwarranted. A person — so the argument seems to run — who can recall names easily has "a good memory"; *ergo* he must be good at remembering figures and formulae. The fallacy apparently involved is, that when two or more forms of behavior may be described in a way involving the *same conventional name*, then those forms of behavior must be the operations of one and the same fundamental process or capacity. Now, statistical treatments of the results of psychological tests have exploded any such extreme conception, and have led to a more widespread recognition of some *specific* character in every distinguishable human function.

The other extreme toward which the layman's conception of human nature is likely to err is in the assumption that a high degree of capacity in one activity is likely to be offset by a low degree in a very different activity. A high-school boy, let us say, is quite inferior in his work on literary subjects: many of his friends will promptly conclude that he must then possess superior ability in mathematics, or, failing that, superior ability in manual training or in athletics. A man with highly trained discriminations ("taste") in music or in painting must — so many will think — be poor at anything demanding mechanical insight and skills. The child genius in intellect is popularly supposed to be underdeveloped in some other way. The fast worker is inaccurate. And so this balancing-up motive manifests itself in wide ranges of personal judgments. Whatever it is originally traceable to — whether to an exaggerated democratic tradition or what not — the tendency to think this way is strong. But, again, scientific findings are at variance with the popular assumption; for they point to the conclusion that, as Thorndike has put it, "*in original nature the rule is correlation, not compensation.*" This point is borne out by the fact that the intercorrelations of human abilities, while not running high, are overwhelmingly positive. High ability of one kind is likely to accompany high ability of another kind.

Introduction to the Problem of Factors. Today the question of interrelationships within the individual has become a deeper problem. If we are genuinely curious, we will not be content to know that abilities do (or do not) tend to go together: we want to know how these abilities are constituted. It would seem obvious that different talents are involved in, for instance, the ability to keep books for a business firm, to play a viola acceptably, to punt out-of-bounds near the goal line, and to design a coat or a dress that would be admired by one's friends, as well as dozens of other human achievements. Shall we then speak of bookkeeping ability, viola-playing ability, punting-out-of-bounds-near-goal-line ability, and so on, and assign to each a separate and complete ability which has no relationship to other abilities? Probably everyone would condemn this as too naïve. (1) Then, shall we conceive of these achievements as due to *one broad, general human capacity* that allows success in each and any line, so that the same person who shows high achievement in one way could — if he would — show high achievement in other ways? (2) Or, shall we assume that each achievement is due to some one of *several rather general sorts of capacity* but operating under specific conditions that call for specific abilities also: business ability which, operating in the bookkeeper's office, involves ability to write and "figure"; musical talent which, when devoted to the viola, demands also skillful fingering, a good "ear," and so on; football "stuff" that happens to be devoted at times to punting and so involves nice timing of the foot; a talent for domestic art that, when directed to costume-designing calls upon specific abilities to visualize, to cut accurately, to sew neatly, and the like? (3) Or again, shall we think of each of these achievements as due to a composite of *very many* ultra-simple and *specific* capacities and say that the form of the achievement depends upon the particular pattern of capacities which is called forth?

In the last ten or twenty years, psychology developed certain tools of research that give the questions an investigable concreteness, and offer some hope of solution. One of these kits of tools is the vast array of psychological tests now available. (A few are suggested in Figures 47 and 86). Another is the development of psychometric (that is, statistical) methods of handling test results.

In a general way, an investigation starts with the results of many tests that are combined and compared in a table of intercorrelations. For example, inspect the table furnished on p. 302. There we note a high correlation between Height and Weight scores, and we would conclude that there must be something in common in those two traits. Or, for a more psychological example, we see a fairly high correlation between Adding and Memorizing. Now, to what can this be due? Does it reveal a broad general human capacity operating in the two cases; or does it indicate an ability somewhat more restricted, such as the ability to work on symbolic school materials subvocally; or does it show simply very many specific abilities such as that of being able to hold and use a pencil, to listen, to sit erect, to read letters and figures, and so on and on?

Further, we note that Adding scores are also correlated to some extent with Estimating scores. Are we to infer from this that whatever abilities are common to Adding and Memorizing are involved also in Estimating? Or would it be better to assume that what are in common in Adding and Memorizing are different from what are in common in Adding and Estimating? But then we note that Estimating scores are correlated also with Memorizing scores. Does this justify us in concluding that the same abilities then run through all three of these kinds of performances?

It should now be clear that we cannot hope to get ahead by mere inspection of such tables. We must have recourse to more analytic methods.

The Tetrad Differences Method. Spearman made the curious observation that to the correlations between the scores of many different abilities a definite mathematical formula was applicable, the "tetrad difference." Let a, b, c, d represent sets of scores on four tests; and let r_{ab}, r_{cd}, etc., represent coefficients of correlation between the tests a and b, between the tests c and d, etc. Then the tetrad equation is written: $r_{ab}r_{cd} - r_{ad}r_{bc} = 0$. Now, by purely mathematical methods it has been determined that the intercorrelations of any four variables will satisfy the zero equation for the tetrad, if there is running through them all a common factor. Let us take an illustration of Spearman's application of this principle. Consider the accompanying table of correlation coefficients between four tests taken two at a time. Applying the tetrad difference method we have (using initials of the names of the tests for our subscripts) $r_{oc}r_{md} - r_{od}r_{cm} = .80 \times .18 - .30 \times .48 = 0$. Some common factor in these four test abilities is indicated by this zero value of the equation. This Spearman called "general ability" or "g," to distinguish it from the "specific abilities" or "s's" that vary from one test to another. This sample table of correlations, he would say, furnishes internal evidence

A TABLE OF INTERCORRELATIONS
To ILLUSTRATE APPLICATION OF THE TETRAD DIFFERENCE CRITERION

	OPPOSITES	COMPLETION	MEMORY	DISCRIM-INATION
Opposites	—	.80	.60	.30
Completion	.80	—	.48	.24
Memory	.60	.48	—	.18
Discrimination	.30	.24	.18	—

of a general ability operating along with the various specific abilities necessary for the particular operations of naming opposites, completing sentences, and the like.

The Claim for Group Factors. Spearman's principle has aroused a great amount of discussion, especially among the statistician-psychologists. The tetrad equation has not been universally accepted as proving the presence of g nor the non-presence of many abilities intermediate between it and the s's.[1] Some find, when they apply the tetrad method repeatedly and exhaustively to the various intercorrelations obtained from testing in different ways such functions as reading, arithmetic, memorizing, etc., that cross-relations appear between the results of certain sub-tests of these different functions, leading to the postulation of "group factors" called "verbal," "numerical," "spatial," "speed," and the like; that is, that in several but not all the tests a common "verbal" facility is required, in several but not all a common "numerical" facility, and so on [9].

The upshot of it all would appear to be the mathematical justification for assuming abilities that are not so general as to be operative in any and every intellectual operation but general enough to be operative in the several that deal with words, or that are based alike on speed, on brute retentiveness, on visual acuteness, and so on. What these statistical controversies concerning fundamental constitution of a person's intelligence seem to show is that a *hierarchy of capacities* exists. These capacities vary from the most particular and discrete, through more and more inclusive ones, to one or a very few capacities that are general and all-pervasive. For example, a person's ability for rapid adding may be thought of as a function of (a) facility in adding, especially; (b) a special aptitude with numbers; (c) a speedier rate of doing almost any work; (d) his general intelligence (as general as you please); and then still more specific or lower-order habits such as recognizing "6," "7," and other digits, holding pencil, proceeding up the column, knowing what "38 and 4" is, and so on.

Factor Analysis. Meanwhile a shift of interest to methodology has led to the development in the last few years of statistical methods

---

[1] The position is this: if there is a factor common to all tests, the equation must equal zero, but there are many other conditions which result in a zero equation.

aimed at explaining the many possible intercorrelations by a small number of factors. Conceivably we could set up tests for any and every form and manifestation of a person's abilities, but they would only swamp us with vast tables of intercorrelations derived therefrom. What we need is to see whether or not the intercorrelations can be compared and cross-compared to bring out a very limited number of human abilities that can be taken as involved in most human achievements. Statistical methods are being devised for treating the data in highly analytic ways, and it seems that there are but a few fundamental abilities involved in the very many performances measured [8, 9, 16]. Their exposition, however, is highly mathematical, and would be out of place here.

Suffice it to say that by these methods of factor analysis some results can already be stated. Thurstone, one of the leaders in this development, has found upon analysis of over fifty psychological tests applied to university students that we may conceive of intellectual performance as depending upon seven fundamental abilities: facility with numbers, verbal fluency, visualizing, memory, speed in perceiving, inductive ability, and deductive ability. Turning to the question of interests, he has similarly analyzed results on several thousands of tests of vocational interests, and has found the following: commercial, legal, athletic, academic, descriptive, biological, physical science, and art [14, 15].

A Dynamic View. To the foregoing should be added one point. The problems of factors referred to throughout this section of the chapter have been developed on the basis of a cross-sectional view of human nature. But in this book we have repeatedly recognized the importance of longitudinal views of the human personality. Today there are not lacking studies that call attention to changes and reorganizations in the fundamental abilities of the same individual. Changes occur as a result of age, as was found when the same tests were administered to the same children after a three-year interval. Changes are also produced when the children have been given special training. It seems clear that a more dynamic view of human performance will be worked out [1, 2].

INDIVIDUAL DIFFERENCES

Demands for Differential Psychology. "Possibly the greatest single achievement of the members of the American Psychological

Association is the establishment of the psychology of individual differences," said the President (Scott) of that organization in 1919. Much of the interest in human beings is in how they differ one from another. To the employment manager mankind in general is of no concern; his hiring and firing is of particular persons and his problem is always a question of "which ones." Is the new applicant X better fitted for a clerical or a mechanical job; has he the intelligence and the training for an advanced position or should he be at the bottom rung of the ladder; is he likely to work well with the cranky boss of department A or had he better be put with the more easy-mannered boss of B? From the applicant's point of view it is not an essentially different story. Not wanting to be the square peg in a round hole, he seeks advice and counsel as to just for what he — as one individual particular person — is best fitted. In educational psychology, too, the emphasis swings away from man as a type to the specific persons to be educated, as they vary in age, in sex, in intelligence, and the like. The college student does much of his thinking about himself and his fellow students in such terms as, " J is better able to work in the natural sciences than in literature," or "K is a poor student and would cut a poor figure in campus politics, but he made the college orchestra and the Monogram Club." The instructor grades his students — and the student grades his instructors. And if the reader will but stop to consider he will be struck with the exceedingly small amount of conversation about people that is about mankind in general, and the enormous amount given to the special peculiarities, even idiosyncrasies, of this person and that.

Differences, however, suggest common elements; and if the specific variations among members of the human race are to be understood, it is absolutely essential that that race be well understood in its more generic nature. General psychology, then, must come first to furnish a compass, if the student would later find his way about in differential psychology. Our first survey will therefore be somewhat like the zoologist's study of the starfish or the amphioxus or the salamander, which he must first understand generically by discovering its laws and principles as true of that type of natural object, before he can understand a particular starfish.

Sex Differences. When Doctor Samuel Johnson was asked, "Which is the more intelligent, man or woman?" he answered, "Which man? Which woman?" His perspicacity had led him to anticipate the findings of modern investigators of the question; for the many comparative studies of the two sexes by means of precise methods of examination have brought to light decidedly scanty evidence of any fundamental differences in their behavior that cannot be well explained as due to contrasts in their social environments. Popular opinion to the contrary notwithstanding, there are few if any differences in strictly psychological traits (ruling out the physiological) that are due to the biological difference. What differences that do obtain turn out to be social and cultural in their causation. We shall have more to say on this matter at various points and particularly in Chapter XX.

Samuel Johnson's remark was prophetic in a particularly interesting way. His words, "Which man? Which woman?" emphasize the fact that even if you did arrive at a conclusion you could assert concerning a whole sex, or any other large group of persons, you could not safely make the same assertion of any given particular person without some estimation of him himself. Let us take care to remember always that when we are dealing with a group of individuals, it is a group of *individuals*.

Age Differences. Investigations of individual variations due to age have been more fruitful. The whole structure of the intelligence examinations that have played so well-known a part in psychological applications to education, industry, and other fields during the last twenty years is built upon differentiations between the great mass of children of one given age and those of another age. This story will be told in Chapter XIII. More recently, the great output of research findings in the clinics for children during the past ten or fifteen years have shown how absorbingly interesting and practically important are the year-to-year changes in human behavior. This point has been elaborated in Chapter IV, and elsewhere as well. Are infant and man different in only a quantitative sense, the latter being simply larger? Or are the two separated by distinct and utterly different stages? Does the child change into man as a result of inner biological forces? Or does he change in consequence of his experiences?

Race Differences. Along with sex and age, there is no basis for sorting human specimens more commonly employed and more provocative of vigor and violence than that of race. Throughout history, it seems, these who are possessed of a different cast of countenance, shape of body, or manner of speech have been *ausländ-*

ische and barbarian to those in power; few peoples have shown the tolerance of the modern Frenchman or Russian.

A great number of comparative studies have been made by psychologists and anthropologists upon widely different races, such as the Whites, Negroes, Chinese and Japanese, American Indians, and many other peoples. We cannot attempt to summarize their results further than to point out to the reader that in just about every instance the outcome has given but scanty support to Everyman's assumption of great differences. Investigations of race differences are peculiarly subject to error on account of subtle disturbing factors that are difficult to control. Many errors are involved in the fact that many of the races have been tested on American soil. As an illustration in methodology, therefore, as well as for its concrete findings, we should take time here to summarize one well-controlled study.

We continue to hear nowadays much about the Nordics, who with the Alpines and Mediterraneans form what some anthropologists have held to be three true races of Europe. In physique the Nordic type is said to be long-headed, tall, and blond; the Alpine is round-headed, of medium stature, with brown hair and gray or light-brown eyes, while the Mediterranean type is long-headed, short, and very dark. A clean-cut investigation into the much-debated question of the relative intelligence of these "races" was conducted. Seven rural groups of boys in their tenth, eleventh, and twelfth years were examined in their native countries. Each boy was selected on the basis of his physical traits, so that the experimenter had three groups which were definitely Nordic, Alpine, or Mediterranean. He also examined three urban groups which had predominant ratios of each of the physical types respectively. In each of the ten groups there were 100 cases. The tests used were a battery of "performance tests" which did not depend upon the use of language on the part of either examiner or examinee. (See Figure 86.)

The results as summarized in the table are worth our inspection. (a) Note first the tremendous variability of individual scores within each group as represented by the range and the standard deviation. (b) Associated with that fact, note also the great amount of overlapping of group by group, in spite of the differences in mean scores. (c) Note how closely the three city groups — composed of three different predominating "races" — correspond. (d) Note that among the rural groups there is somewhat more correspondence between those of the same nation than between those of the same race. (e) And note especially that the three city groups are clearly superior to all the rural groups, regardless of racial composition in either case. So far as intelligence is validly tested by performance tests, then, we are led to this conclusion: there are no significant psychological differences between European races.

Again we say, it is not the group to which a person happens to belong which counts: it is himself.

PERFORMANCE SCORES BY EUROPEAN GROUPS *

	MEAN SCORE	RANGE	STANDARD DEVIATION
Paris	219.0	100–302	46.2
Hamburg	216.4	105–322	45.6
Rome	211.8	109–313	42.6
German Nordic	198.2	69–289	49.0
French Mediterranean	197.4	71–271	45.6
German Alpine	193.6	80–211	48.0
Italian Alpine	188.8	69–306	48.4
French Alpine	180.2	72–296	46.6
French Nordic	178.8	63–314	56.4
Italian Mediterranean	173.0	69–308	54.2

* From Klineberg, O. *Arch. Psychol.*, 1931, No. 132.

REFERENCES

1. Anastasi, A. The Influence of Specific Experience upon Mental Organization. *Genet. Psychol. Monog.*, 1936, **18**, No. 4.
2. Asch, S. E. A Study of Change in Mental Organization. *Arch. Psychol.*, 1936, No. 195.
3. Ellis, R. S. *The Psychology of Individual Differences.* Appleton, 1928.
4. Freeman, F. S. *Individual Differences.* Holt, 1934.
5. Garrett, H. E. *Statistics in Psychology and Education.* Longmans, 1926.
6. Garrett, H. E., and Anastasi, Anne. The Tetrad-Difference Criterion and the Measurement of Mental Traits. *Annals N.Y. Acad. Sci.*, 1932, **33**, 233–82.
7. Guilford, J. P. *Psychometric Methods.* McGraw-Hill, 1936.
8. Hotelling, H. Analysis of a Complex of Statistical Variables into Principal Components. *J. Educ. Psychol.*, 1933, **24**, 417–41, 498–520.
9. Kelley, T. L. *Crossroads in the Mind of Man: A Study of Differentiable Mental Abilities.* Stanford Univ. Press, 1928.

10. Klineberg, O. A Study of Psychological Differences Between "Racial" and National Groups in Europe. *Arch. Psychol.*, 1931, No. 132.

11. Morton, R. L. *Laboratory Exercises in Educational Statistics.* Silver, Burdett, 1928.

12. Spearman, C. *The Abilities of Man.* Macmillan, 1927.

13. Thorndike, E. L. *Educational Psychology.* Vol. III, part II: *Individual Differences and their Causes.* Teachers College, 1914.

14. Thurstone, L. L. Factorial Analysis of Vocational Interests (paper privately distributed by author). Abstract in *Psychol. Bull.*, 1935, **32**, 719.

15. Thurstone, L. L. The Isolation of Seven Primary Abilities. *Psychol. Bull.*, 1936, **33**, 780–81.

16. Thurstone, L. L., *The Vectors of Mind.* Univ. Chicago Press, 1935.

17. Walker, H. M. *Mathematics Essential for Elementary Statistics. A Self-Teaching Manual.* Holt, 1934.

CHAPTER XII

SET AND ATTENDING

GENERAL DESCRIPTIONS

The Determinants of Behavior in General. In most of the preceding chapters we have been dealing with man at pretty close quarters. It is time that we stood off and took account of things in a more general way. Let us look at a specimen of the genus Homo Sapiens as he lives his life of activity and thinking, and ask what are the conditions and factors that lead him to do as he does. Without unnecessary introductions and elaborations we will readily agree to two broad influences on man's behavior, and a third will then suggest itself.

Ontogenetically developed tendencies and capacities, habits and attitudes, the background of his past experience, make up a man's equipment at any given moment, and furnish him with his ways of acting as well as much of his why's. This material forms a substantial part of our survey. The story of this development affords us the biographical or long view of the man.

The particular stimuli actively playing upon a man, to release this, that, or the other reaction-tendency, habit, or attitude, also play their rôle in shaping his activity. We have given this direct sensory aspect of behavior a fairly thorough canvassing in Chapter IX.

But up to this point we have not paid direct attention to another general class of factors that influence behavior. A man's activity is organized about slowly generated and long-lasting reactions; and far from being a complicated jumping-jack, he is an organism whose activity, though varying in detail from moment to moment, still shows cores of continuity running through it all. What he does is influenced by the way in which he happens to be predisposed for the time being, that is, how he is *set*.

Examples from Daily Life. Instances of set are to be observed on every hand. The sprinter on his mark shows it in extreme degree as he awaits the signal of the pistol shot: a sudden sound of almost any sort or the sight of a quick movement in his vicinity may start him off. The skillful open-field runner on the football ground counts on the phenomenon of set on the part of a tackler:

he runs as if to pass directly within the latter's clutches and then at a nicely judged instant abruptly alters his course or momentarily arrests his progress; and the tackler caught unprepared for this new situation lunges ignominiously and harmlessly out of the way One more illustration from athletics is furnished by the batter upon whom is being used a change of pace: after watching and perhaps swinging at two or three fast balls, the movements become adjusted to this speed and he is likely to swing too fast on a slow pitch.

More subtle forms of predisposing adjustment are easily found. Let a person whistle or sing an air in a certain key, and, unless he be practiced in such shifts, it may be impossible for him to change to a very different key when he is halfway through and complete the melody without error. The popularity of the stories of O. Henry rested in part upon his cleverness in getting the reader well settled along one train of thought leading to one sort of outcome, and then toward the end introducing some novel turn to the tale that caught the reader off his guard. The common run of detective stories have employed this device to such an extreme that the sophisticated reader usually makes an early choice of the least · conspicuous and most harmless-appearing character as the ultimate villain. Many forms of laughter-evoking situations are those in which some sudden shift in the spectator's or auditor's general adjustment is excited by the appearance of some new angle on the situation.

In the emotional aspects of a person's behavior the part played by established sets, that is, "moods," is widely recognized and counted upon in a practical way. A salesman who learns that a certain prospective customer upon whom he is about to call has had a stroke of ill fortune earlier in the day does well to shift his call to another date, for it is a fair certainty that the customer will be predisposed to react to all overtures in a negative rather than a positive manner. Certain famous musical compositions, such as Tschaikowski's Sixth Symphony, are supposed to have been given their lugubrious and pathetic strains by the dominant mood of the given composer; and many a poem, such as Arnold's "Dover Beach," is in this same sense an "expression" or outcome of the emotional condition of the writer.

Examples from the Experimental Laboratory. The phenomenon of set has become well recognized by scientists. In experiments on *lifted weights* a blindfolded subject is presented two blocks of identical size and shape but of slightly different weights. He is instructed to "heft" each in turn once only with the same hand, and to make a verbal reaction by saying whether the second is "heavier" or "lighter" than the first. How is he able to judge which of the two weights is heavier when he is holding only one of them in his hand? It would seem to be that this judging is the setting up of a motor adjustment in the process of lifting the first weight, so that there is a tendency to expend the same amount of force when lifting again. Then when the second weight is lifted, it is said to be heavier or lighter according as it yields with difficulty or with ease to this particular expenditure of energy. The kinesthetic afferent impulses resulting from the movement and its resistance are the cues serving as stimuli to the vocal habits of saying "heavier" or "lighter." Discrimination of lifted weights is thus guided by a previous setting or adjusting of the "hefting" apparatus.[1]

The *reaction-time* experiment, which has already been described, brings out the importance of the subject's attitude in a somewhat similar manner. The reaction actually being measured is not simply the specific act (as releasing a key) given in response to the specific stimulus (as the click of a telegraph sounder): it includes wider segments of reaction that together form a "previously prepared adjustment." The point is convincingly brought out when the experimenter compares the results obtained with stimuli presented after the usual warning signal "ready" with the results from those stimuli given after no warning. The times of the reactions in the former case are decidedly the shorter.

Another form of laboratory study with a respectable history which clearly involves the phenomenon of set, is the *complication experiment*. A bell metronome is fitted with a cardboard arc marked off with scale divisions over which the pointed end of the oscillating pendulum arm may be seen to move. The metronome is set to a rate of one beat per second or faster, and the bell rings at a certain point in each oscillation. The subject being studied is asked to state how far the pointer has traveled when the bell rings. Now, if he is previously instructed to note especially the moving pointer, letting the sound of the bell take care of itself, the place on the arc where he will report the pointer's position simultaneously

[1] Possibly the reader supposes that the subject remembers what the first weight "seemed like" and then compares the second with this memory. Quite to the contrary. The subject makes no such deliberate comparison but experiences the second weight *immediately* as heavier or lighter.

with the bell sound will be found to be further out and beyond the place of actual physical coincidence, often as much as 6° or 8°. On the other hand, if he is previously instructed to be prepared to hear the bell and to bend his efforts more to that end than to watching the pointer, the place on the arc where he will report the pointer's position at the bell sound will be found to be not so far out as the place of actual coincidence, but short of it by perhaps 8° or 10°. The subject appears able more promptly to observe and to report that particular mode of stimulation for which he is set.

We cannot omit reference finally to the *word-association* experiment, for the importance of the previously established set of the subject is one of the most outstanding features of that work. The "control" of the controlled association tests consists essentially of some device whereby the subject is stimulated to set up a certain attitude determining his word responses in a certain direction. Previously instructed to react with nouns only, let us say, or with names of articles of food only, or with opposites only, the subject's word responses are accordingly selected or circumscribed in character. Under such controls his reactions are usually quicker than when uncontrolled or free.

HOW SETS INFLUENCE ACTIVITIES

Sets Predispose a Person to Continue an Activity. In the foregoing technical and non-technical examples, two characters or features may be discerned. One is brought out in the use of the German term *die Einstellung*. "Every continued activity arouses in the organism a tendency to persist in the same general type of activity, and a difficulty in changing over to very different activities." It is what is often called "preoccupation." Consider the example of the student who has difficulty in getting into a lesson that is to be studied, and must go through a "warming up" stage; but who, once he is well set, can work smoothly and in concentrated fashion. Let a roommate come into the room, and the student's answers to him will take the form of monosyllables and grunts. But if the roommate is not to be so easily ignored and continues the conversation, the student's participation therein becomes more complete, that is, he becomes more alert to the conversation. When the roommate leaves, and the lesson is again to be attacked, it is all too likely that the "warming up" process must be gone through all over again.

Class exercises testify to this phenomenon of set. It is clearly seen on a day of quizzes when, after thinking and writing for an hour or so on Elizabethan poetry, one must quickly adjust himself to thinking and writing on the integral calculus, and then perhaps to responding similarly to questions on the classification of and the symbols for the coal-tar derivatives, or on utilitarianism as a social philosophy. Many instructors confess that they cannot make the shift from lecturing to administrative duties to laboratory research problems and again to lecturing without losing much time in changing from one task to another.

So definite may be the nature of this act of getting set, and so narrow may be the range of the activities involved, that the load or inertia imposed upon the individual may be observable in his shifting from one to another particular form of activity, even when all are grouped under a single common head. This is shown in a simple experiment devised by the present writer. Several printed sheets of paper were used, upon each of which appeared one hundred simple arithmetic problems — twenty-five each in adding, subtracting, multiplying, and dividing. Two of the sheets presented all of the adding problems in a continuous row, then all the subtracting in a second row, and so forth. Two other sheets presented the hundred problems in a mixed order. The accompanying table shows samples of both kinds.

SAMPLES OF BLANKS FOR DEMONSTRATING SET IN RECALL

CONTINUOUS ORDER

$4 + 5 =$	$13 - 5 =$	$2 \times 8 =$	$12 \div 2 =$
$7 + 8 =$	$4 - 2 =$	$7 \times 9 =$	$28 \div 4 =$
$5 + 3 =$	$14 - 9 =$	$5 \times 8 =$	$8 \div 2 =$
$4 + 6 =$	$10 - 2 =$	$4 \times 7 =$	$20 \div 4 =$
$2 + 7 =$	$8 - 7 =$	$3 \times 8 =$	$15 \div 5 =$
		$8 \times 7 =$	$24 \div 3 =$
• • •	• • •	• • •	• • •

MIXED ORDER

$8 + 2 =$	$4 \times 7 =$	$9 + 9 =$	$6 \times 6 =$
$2 \times 6 =$	$8 - 3 =$	$24 \div 4 =$	$3 + 9 =$
$15 - 8 =$	$2 + 9 =$	$5 \times 5 =$	$9 \times 3 =$
$24 \div 3 =$	$21 \div 3 =$	$8 - 4 =$	$6 - 3 =$
$3 \times 4 =$	$5 \times 8 =$	$7 \div 1 =$	$16 \div 8 =$
$5 + 9 =$	$7 + 3 =$	$8 + 6 =$	• • •
• • •	• • •	• • •	

over again

The subject was instructed to jot down the answers to the problems as rapidly as possible and the time was taken for the completion of each sheet. Of the 69 individuals serving as subjects, 63 took less time for completing the continuous than for completing the mixed order of examples; the group averages being, respectively, 159.3 seconds and 181.7 seconds.[1] The recall of a specific habitual addition is more prompt when one has just been adding than when he has just been doing a variety of things. So with subtracting, with multiplying, with dividing.

Sets Direct New Subsequent Activities. Another phase of the phenomenon is observable when, in response to new stimuli, a new set is established, and this in turn determines the character of the activities that follow. A clear-cut case may be seen in a study of animal behavior. Hunter tested the ability of certain different species to react correctly after a delay. The ground plan of his apparatus appears in Figure 79. A subject introduced at R was trained to go to any of the boxes, $L, L, L,$ that might be lighted. Food found by the hungry animal in the lighted box furnished the positive incentive for learning, and a mild electric shock given before the unlighted doors furnished the negative. Once an animal was well trained to this habit, a complication was introduced. While it was held in restraint in the glass release box R, it was stimulated by a light

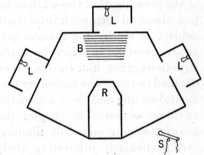

FIGURE 79. APPARATUS FOR THE STUDY OF DELAYED REACTIONS

R, release box, with glass front and sides; $L, L, L,$ boxes with small incandescent lamps visible through doorways situated equidistant from R; B, series of copper strips placed before each door, but here shown only before the middle one (the current is thrown on at the experimenter's switch, S).

that might appear in any one of the three boxes; and after the light was out it was released and allowed to seek its way to the correct box for food. The experimenter could vary the delay between turning out the light and releasing the animal; and, of course, he varied in random order the box to be lighted from trial to trial.

Hunter used among his subjects rats and dogs. These species

[1] It may be noted that the standard deviations of the means are not given here. In such an experiment we are not concerned with the effect on a group, but in the effect on individuals; and hence our data are not means but individual scores.

differed in the length of delay possible to a successful reaction; but the peculiar and interesting findings were in regard to what happened during the delay. A rat or a dog was able to proceed to the correct door oftener than chance would dictate only on the occasions when, during the delay in the release box, he had remained *oriented* (pointed) toward the door where light had been seen. The whole body or at least the head was turned toward the light while it was on, and this posture was maintained until the release from *R*, when he simply "followed his nose." Let this overt orientation be disturbed, however, and the animal on release was at a total loss. In other words, the body posture set the animal to go in a particular direction.

Experimental work with human subjects abounds in illustrations of the principle that the set determines the activity to follow; indeed just about all such work involves it in greater or lesser degree. The subject is set by the general arrangement of the apparatus and apparatus-room in which he is placed and in particular by the instructions given him by the experimenter; and the particular and detailed responses he makes are then largely a function of this experimental setting and these instructions. Of the experiments listed in an earlier section of this chapter, those on reaction-times and on word-associations are especially illuminating examples of the principle.

A particularly interesting analysis of the phenomenon has recently been made with the use of 5-letter anagrams. An experimental group of subjects had had training in solving twenty simple anagrams. Each of the anagrams had as its only solution a word associated with nature, but the subjects were not told this (example: "rokbo," which rearranged spells "brook"). Then they were given twenty ambiguous ones, each having several possible solutions of which a "nature-solution" was only one (example: "dacre" which spells either "cedar," "cared," or "raced"). A control group of subjects were also given the latter twenty ambiguous anagrams but without training on the preliminary series. When the work of the two groups on the ambiguous anagrams was compared, it was found that the experimental group turned in very many more "nature-solutions," as appears in Figure 80, *A*. Thus, by working through the "nature" anagrams they had established in themselves a tendency to look for "nature-solutions." Furthermore, the same result was obtained with other experimental and control groups who were given anagrams which had "eating-solutions," also unannounced to them.

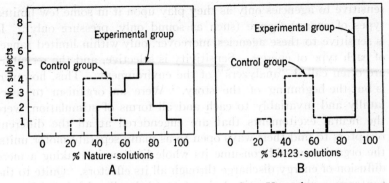

FIGURE 80. INFLUENCE OF ESTABLISHED SETS UPON ACTIVITIES

The frequency of percentages of the prescribed anagram solution made by the subjects with previously established set (experimental group) is compared in each case with those of control subjects.
In *A*, the set was to find "nature-solutions."
In *B*, the set was to find solutions by transposition of letters in a certain order.
(From Rees, H. J., and Israel, H. E.   *Psychol. Monog.*, 1935, **46**, no. 6.)

Had the experimental subjects caught on to the type of anagrams given them in the training and then deliberately set about looking for the same kind in the ambiguous set?   The answer to this is given by another phase of the same experiment.   Some other subjects were given a training series of simple anagrams in which the true word order of the letters of each one was transposed into the order 54123 (for example, "camel" was presented as "lecam").   After this a critical series of ambiguous anagrams was run, to see how many of the "54123-solutions" would be used.   The results of this group as compared with those of a control group of subjects are shown in Figure 80, *B*.   Now, the important thing is that of the 10 subjects in the experimental group, 6 had no idea that the various anagrams involved any regular order of arrangement, and only 1 of the remaining 4 detected the actual arrangement.   Thus it was demonstrated that an effective set can be established without the subject's knowledge of it and can operate quite automatically and unconsciously.

ATTENDING AS A FORM OF SET

Selectivity in All Behavior.   In Chapter IX it was noted that each one of the different receptors with which man is equipped is sensitive to agencies only as they play upon it in some few limited types of energy-change (such as sound only, pressure only). It is sensitive to these agencies, moreover, only within limited ranges of each type of energy. Sensitivity is selective, and the receptors are often called "analyzers" of the environment. This, however, is but the beginning of the story. Were an organism to react fatally and invariably to each and all forms of stimulation, were the neural excitements that are engendered at all the different receptors to find their ways open to as many separate motor units, the organism would consume its whole lifetime in making a mere diffusion of energy discharge through all its effectors. Quite to the contrary, a characteristic obvious enough in all animal and human behavior is its pointedness, its selectiveness. The conditions within the organism, then, determine that the organism will behave in a differentiating manner, at one time responding to this source of stimulation and at another responding to that.

When a person assumes a set that will facilitate his response to some particular stimulus or stimuli, that set goes by the name of attending or attention. Consider the military command of "Attention!" What is aroused on the soldier's part is a certain stance, a fixed position of arms and hands, a poise of head, even a certain directing of the eyeballs; and all of this posturing is designed to render the soldier more sensitive to the next commands heard and more prompt in their execution — and, by the same token, less sensitive and reactive to other stimuli, whether extra- or intra-organic. The dog at the rat hole displays an eager posturing, so intensified often that the hypertonicity of muscles passes over into visible trembling; the whole attitude of a *qui vive* rendering the dog ready in maximal degree to sense the victim and to pounce upon it.

Motor Components of Attending. Mach, after describing how complex musical sounds are analyzable by an attentive auditor into their elementary sounds, says of the process:

It is more than a figure of speech when one says that we "search" among the sounds. This hearkening search is very observably a bodily activity, just like attentive looking in the case of the eye. If, obeying the drift of physiology, we understand by attention nothing mystical, but a bodily disposition, it is most natural to seek it in the variable tension of the muscles of the ear. Just so, what common men call attentive looking reduces itself mainly to accommodating and setting of the optic axes.[1]

---

[1] Quoted by James, *Principles of Psychology*, i, n., p. 436.

For one thing, then, the act of paying attention is an act of (1) *adjusting the receptive mechanisms* for the better sensing of the necessary stimuli, and, negatively, for the exclusion of irrelevant stimuli. This phase of attending is so well recognized and so prominent a feature that in polite social relations a really indifferent listener may show a tilt of head and a fixity of gaze that will effectually simulate a complete and sincere concentration upon the speaker's words, when in reality he may actually be more sensitive to the sound of a familiar voice in the distance or he may be occupied with thought reactions of his own. It is an old device for the sophisticated high-school boy who is well prepared to recite on the day's lesson to turn his gaze out through a window of the classroom, so that the teacher, taking his overt adjustments as the measure of his implicit adjustments, will call upon him promptly in the hope of catching him napping.

In Chapter IX we found that receptors have effector mechanisms closely associated with them which aid in their receiving stimulation. The eye furnishes an excellent example, with its six different muscles rolling the eyeball about and pointing it toward the source of light, the ciliary muscle so accommodating the lens that the image projected on the retina will be clearly focused, and the *sphincter pupillae* controlling the aperture in a manner to provide the best illumination for seeing. So, in less complex ways, does the story read for the other receptors: contact stimulations of the skin awaken "feeling" or palpating; slight sounds cause a turning of the head; light odors evoke a whiffing; sapid liquids, a licking; poorly discriminated weights, a hefting; and so on. It has already been suggested in Chapter V that here is at least one of the organic bases for the behavior called "curiosity."

Support for these more local adjustments of receptors is furnished frequently in (2) *more widely distributed postural changes.* Leaning forward, turning the head and trunk and even the whole body about to orient toward the stimulus source, putting the hand to the ear or to shade the eye, are all familiar examples of the sort. Adjustments of this type are frequently found by delicate registering apparatus to be more common as well as more subtle than is ordinarily supposed. For instance, it has been demonstrated with an *automatograph* — which is really a scientific form of the common planchette or "ouija board." On a piece of heavy plate glass lay three metal balls and on them in turn rested a thin crystal-plate glass. To the latter was affixed a horizontal rod that carried a pointer which bore vertically upon a smoked surface lying at one side. When the finger-tips of a subject were rested upon the crystal-plate glass it was impossible to hold the apparatus perfectly still for more than a few seconds. The inevitable minimal movements that occurred were graphically recorded on the smoked surface. Three of the more striking tracings are reproduced in Figure 81. In each case the beginning of the tracing is marked with an *A*. In *I* is shown the tracing of a subject while he was calling out the names of a series of small patches of color displayed on a wall eight feet distant. The first row of colors was read downwards, the second upward, and the third downward again. In *II* is shown a tracing produced by a blindfolded subject while counting the audible strokes of a metronome which was transferred at intervals from corner to corner of the room. It stood originally at the rear left-hand corner and was transferred to the front left-hand corner, thence to the front right-hand corner, to the rear right-hand corner, and back to the rear left-hand corner. In *III* appears a record from the arm of a subject who had previously hidden a pocketknife and was now intently thinking of it. This involved a change in the direction of his attending, from the left to the right side of the room. Such clear results as these are not always obtained, but other experimenters have confirmed them in general.

Certain changes in (3) *respiratory* and *circulatory functions* also contribute to the more adequate receiving of stimuli. While these are not uniform and universal marked changes of some sort do occur when an individual shifts from a passive unconcentrated condition to an active concentrated attitude. Rapt attention is popularly said to be "breathless" attention. Several investigators have noted an accelerated pulse rate and accelerated breathing rate in the attentive person by using the sphygmograph, pneumograph, and like instruments. As to other variables (such as depth of breathing, blood pressure, blood volume) no consistent results have been obtained, for the results depend largely upon the types of attention stimuli employed.

There remain to be mentioned those (4) *diffuse muscular strains* that are an inalienable part of the picture of the attending person. These contribute to the total result of enhancing the stimuli in question negatively by serving to reduce the number of competing stimuli. "Attention" may be spelled as two words, "a tension."

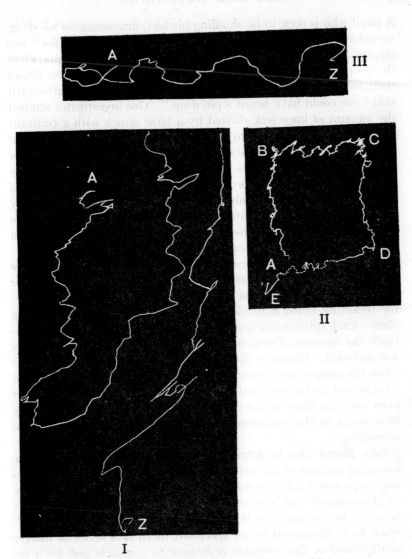

FIGURE 81. AUTOMATOGRAPH TRACINGS OF MINIMAL MOVEMENTS

    I. While reading vertical rows of colors.

    II. While counting the strokes of a metronome moved from corner to corner.

    III. While concentrating upon an object hidden on the right side of the room.

(From Jastrow, J., *Fact and Fable in Psychology*. Houghton Mifflin, 1900.)

A pupil who is seen to be shuffling his feet, drumming on his desk, stretching, and yawning is certain to be reprimanded for "not paying attention." In the tense moment of a melodrama when the people in the audience hang upon each whisper from the villain their overt bodily motions are so restrained that it is afterward said "one could have heard a pin drop." One investigator studied the amount of knee jerk elicited by a blow struck with a constant intensity and at a uniform rate, under two different attentional conditions. During "passive" periods the subjects sat as quietly as possible with their eyes closed; during "active" periods they were instructed to solve problems in arithmetic. With all of his subjects the results uniformly pointed to a greater muscular tonicity when they were in the latter attentional condition, the average amount of the knee jerk being nearly ten times larger than when they were in the former condition [15].

Another investigator arranged very delicate levers to rest over the principal muscles operating the right arm, left arm, right lower leg, and left lower leg. On the other end of each lever was a mirror reflecting (with magnification of 500 times) upon a traveling film. Each subject was given various instructions, and simultaneously the amount of muscular tension in each of the four members was recorded. Figure 82 shows what occurred in the arms and legs when the subject was attending to weak and loud sounds (A), and to expected and unexpected stimuli (B). It is clear from this that even such far-flung motor organs as those in the extremities play their parts in the organism's posturing when one is attending to something.

Sets Found also in Attending to Intra-Organic Stimuli. The foregoing analysis of the various component postures in a total attentive posture holds true not simply when the organism is attentive to extra-organic but also to intra-organic stimulations. A man's behavior is dominated so that most other activities are "silenced" when he is stimulated by an abscessed tooth or a series of hunger contractions or the excessive resistance to a muscle pull by a refractory door he is trying to open. The boy with a bad toothache is "inaccessible" to the sounds of playmates' voices and to the visual appeal of the story book. The hungry dog or child or man is often, in the extremity of his condition, apparently deaf and blind to all save food stimuli.

The Process of Attending may be Subjectively Observed. The

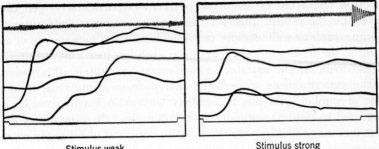

| Stimulus weak | Stimulus strong |

A. ATTENDING TO SOUND

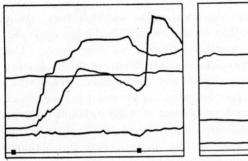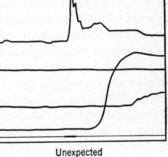

| Expected | Unexpected |

B. ATTENDING TO SHOCK

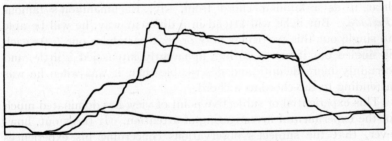

C. ATTENDING TO SUB-VOCAL ARITHMETIC

FIGURE 82. SOME MOTOR COMPONENTS OF ATTENDING POSTURES

Each line (except the topmost) is produced by tension of musculature that operates the right arm, the left arm, the right leg, or the left leg.

In *A*, the tension is greater and more widespread when one is attending to a weak stimulus (i.e., attending more "closely"). In *B*, the tension is greater when the person is expecting and waiting for the painful stimulus. In *C*, even in the case of so-called "mental" objects of thought, attending to them involves muscular posturing. (From Freeman, G. L., *J. Gen. Psychol.*, 1931, **5**, 479–494.)

selective character of attentive postures is particularly well observed by the person himself.   That to which he attends appears
to him *clearer* as well as more *intense*.   It is sometimes spoken of as
being at the *focus* while the rest of the situation (real and imagined)
is said to be at the *margin*.   For illustration, suppose the reader,
at the very moment of perusing this page, is stimulated by the
odor of smoke.   To this he is likely to remain inattentive: he is
long used to cigarette-smoking in his room, and the presence of the
odor now remains dimly in the hazy background of his experience.
It remains there, that is, until some peculiarity about the odor,
some other-than-usual quality of it, draws his attention (as we
commonly say it) away from the content of the book.   As the
odor becomes clearer under this scrutiny, he suddenly says, "Why,
that's not tobacco smoke, that's wood smoke!   Is the place on fire?"
Now occurs a complete transformation in his experience.   That
which had been focal, the argument and incidents of the book-story,
now recedes into dimness or "goes out" altogether.   That which
had been only marginal now becomes vivid; and the reader's experience is that of a rapid procession of highly definite sensory
and imaginal events — of flames, of smoke, of people shouting and
running, of an upheaval even within his own chest and abdomen
and tightenings of his whole musculature.

Or, for a less dramatic example, let the reader listen to a chord
struck on the piano while the keys are being held down.   He may
hear it as a familiar chord from, say, Rachmaninoff's famous
Prelude.   But if he will attend in a different way, he will be able
to single out this particular note or that particular one.   As each
is singled out it comes to him apparently intensified a little, and
certainly more definite and describable than it was when he was
attending to the chord as a chord.

This experiential or subjective point of view has dominated much
of the experimental investigating of attention.   It turns out, however, that the subject's observations concerning his experiences
parallel what his experimenter observes in his posturings and conduct, so that the findings and the general principles and laws of
attention can be pretty completely stated in objective terminology.
In this way the laws of attention can be made more obviously consistent with other observations on man, animal, social group, infant, or insane.   For simplicity's sake, therefore, we will continue
to treat attentive posturings mainly from the public or objective
point of view.

DETERMINING FACTORS

The Problem Stated. Granted that an individual at any moment is to some degree in a set of postures that limits and selects those things to which he is sensitive and reactive, the question arises, what are the conditions that determine *to which* things this posture is set up? Mr. X, seated in the street car, may be observed to be attentive at one moment to his newspaper, at another to the passing of a noisy truck, at another to the advertisement card overhead, again to the greeting of a friend, and still again to the conductor's call of a street name. Why these different directions of attending?

Suppose that a person is immersed in a book. The book and its print are not the only array of stimuli that are playing upon him. Just beyond the book and in the margin of the field of view stands a photograph on his desk. The light flickers a little. There is conversation in an adjoining room, and a blatant radio downstairs. An odor of cigarette smoke lingers in the air. The chair upon which he is seated is a hard one. One shoe presses a tender corn, and his collar, shrunk by the laundry, is a bit tight about his neck. A light draught of cold air reaches him at times from the open window. Nor are these exteroceptive stimuli all. He still has a lingering trace of that headache of the morning. His workout on the track or the drive from town has left him tired. Once in a while the dull hollowness in his stomach becomes acute with hunger pangs.

All this makes a common enough picture. But looked at in this analytic way, it is enlightening to see how many stimuli there are, each and every one competing in a fashion to arouse his reaction to it alone. Now our natural question is: Granted that the man does interrupt his reading to gaze at the photograph, or to listen in on that lively conversation, or to discard his hard chair for another, or to throw down the book and set out for the dining-room or a restaurant to assuage the hunger, what are the factors that gave that particular stimulus its advantage?

Objective Factors. Things and people undoubtedly have varying attention-getting values, depending upon certain attributes that they possess. Of these, *intensity* is at once to be recognized as of high importance. A loud noise or a blinding flash of light or a vigorously delivered slap on one's shoulder is a fairly reliable stimulus for forcing the subject to reset himself.   The ballyhoo man and the hawker, the automobile horn and the locomotive whistle, the brilliant electric sign and the lighthouse signal, the black newspaper headlines and the heavily inked advertisement of a fire sale, are all cases clearly in point.   Other things being equal, the more intense a stimulation, the more likely it is to attract attention.

Another attribute that is obviously effective is that of *extensity* or size.   Other things being equal, the larger a stimulus, the more likely it is to be noticed.   The principle was long ago hit upon by the advertisers: a full-page insertion is clearly preferable to a half-page or quarter-page, and a large signboard to a small one. The truth of this may even reach the point where the effectiveness of an advertisement may increase at a ratio greater than the size, and a full-page space be found to have much more than four times the attention-getting value of a quarter-page space.   In essence, this factor of size may be considered as only a subspecies under intensity.

A second subspecies of intensity is *duration* and *repetition*.   By successive repetition the effectiveness of a stimulus may be greatly strengthened.   An incident from the writer's experience will suggest others of the sort to the reader.   A man walking just ahead of the writer called across an avenue to a friend.   As the first call awakened no response, it was repeated, whereupon the friend turned, and hurriedly said, "Ah, Jones, I didn't hear you the first time!"   When, after reading in concentrated fashion for a while, one is at length forced to notice the drumming of a thoughtless person who has been making this sound all the while, he is being forced to notice a repeated stimulus which in itself was too small to evoke response.   The advertiser makes abundant use of this simple principle; in some businesses it is a deliberate policy never to stop the advertising for even a brief interval, but to keep up the insertions, however small.

A very different factor from that of intensity is involved in the fundamental biological principle that a *moving* object is far more likely to be noticed than a still one.   The beast of prey stalks its victim, often moving so slowly that it escapes observation until it has gotten within striking distance.   An insect crawling on the skin or under the resting hand will excite an attending attitude with an effectiveness out of all proportion to its size.   The flitting of a mouse across the periphery of the visual field will turn a dozing cat or dog into an alert and excited hunter. Derelicts cast up on a desert isle, upon sighting distant smoke or a sail, tear off their shirts, and, attaching them to long sticks, wave them vigorously back and forth, so that the ship's lookout may be sure to observe them. Many of the electric signs of a city's streets are operated by switching devices that flash the different lights in certain orders, producing illusions of motion that serve to attract attention from the passerby. Some experiments have made it clear that the waving of a red flag excites attentive attitudes in cattle not by virtue of the redness — white will serve even better — but by virtue of the motion imparted by the waving. Many a weak and helpless animal, on the other hand, has for one of its most effectual defenses a death feint, a "playing 'possum," which renders it so completely motionless that it may escape the notice of its dangerous enemy.

The factors of *change* and *contrast* are closely allied to that of movement. Undersea explorers say that when all other objects are moving uniformly under the influence of a water current it is the still object that attracts attention. The steadily ticking clock may receive no notice until it happens to stop, when the very cessation of the stimulation serves as a sufficient condition to arouse attention. The "protective mimicry" of the flatfish and the chameleon, of the mantid, the walking-stick, and the tree toad, which allows them so to resemble their usual backgrounds as to render them well-nigh invisible, is an obvious means of safety from a hunting foe. Differences of color (not a matter of intensity) are constantly employed in the painting of billboards and the printing of advertising pages. Differences of pitch are employed by the skillful speaker who holds attention by judicious changes from high- to low-pitched speech.

Subjective Factors. A living man or animal is not the mere sport of energy conditions external to himself. The conditions obtaining within have their own share in directing his orientations and posturings. This general truth is exemplified in that the organism's past experience operates in the form of acquired manners or directions of paying attention — what we may call *attention habits*. In the middle of the night the physician will often hear the telephone or the door bell although his wife will not; while on another night the wife will be awakened by the crying of one of the children but the husband will sleep peacefully on. A telegrapher often nods at his desk, but let his particular call signal come over the wire and he is quickly attentive. So, too, the well-trained nurse is able to sleep on her cot in the patient's room heedless of outside noises, until some turning movement of her patient arouses her at once.

Attention habits of a *negative* character — habits of disregarding — are of great importance to human efficiency. One eventually learns to sleep in spite of the noise of elevated trains near the window or of the wheels and trucks under the Pullman sleeper. The clicking of a dozen typewriters all assaulting the auditory mechanisms of the new clerk become with time decreasingly effective, until he has grown quite "negatively adapted" to them, and they no longer compete with the stimuli appropriate to his work. He may even grow so adapted that the sounds become "facilitating stimuli," actually furthering his proper work with ledger or dictaphone, so that during overtime hours when the office is quiet his work suffers.

All such habits of attending are functions of the *past* experience of the individual. But conditions of the *present* also have much to do with determining which way a man will attend and to what. A *motive* that happens for the time to be operating in the individual will tend to direct him toward those things connected with its satisfaction. On a simplified primitive plane the phenomenon is seen in the dog that is sorely driven by its thirst onward toward its habitual drinking place, and passes with scarcely a turn of the head any other dog standing invitingly ready for frisky play. The drive is so powerful as to establish for the present a right of way, all other stimuli becoming relatively less potent. Even the long-trained listening habits of a music lover will become "sidetracked" when fatigue becomes intensified by his standing in Carnegie Hall for an hour without support.

The same story holds often when both the motives in conflict are more elaborate than thirst or fatigue. A student who is usually attentive enough at his daily lectures will on some day be so preoccupied with a procession of thought reactions set going by an important letter he has opened just before class that throughout the hour his orientation toward his teacher will be frequently displaced by these processes. The writer was once approaching one of our greatest industrial centers on a train that from its track high on a hill across the river afforded a view of outlying parts of the city in all their smoke and muck and dirtiness. And it was the smoke and muck and dirtiness that he was noting — as on many another earlier approach by this route. On this occasion, however, it was at dusk, and it chanced that he was sharing a seat with an artist. The latter at his very first glimpse of the scene was carried away by the sight and spoke in terms of high appreciation: "Beautiful! Beautiful!" Thereupon the writer too became observant of many aspects and details of the setting that had previously quite escaped his notice: the sudden brilliant orange-red flashes of light from ovens of molten iron, the rays of the setting sun gilding the tops of domes and chimneys, and even in the murkiness itself a smoothing off of harsh details of buildings to furnish a background for an intricate patterning and repatterning of lines and masses, as structural steel and factory roofs intermingled in the panorama. With the motive changed, the subject was attentive to quite different aspects of the same objective situation.

SOME EXPERIMENTAL PROBLEMS

Span of Apprehending. Experimental interest in the problems of attention took definite form under Wundt, whose researches began in Leipzig about 1861 and were continued by such students as Cattell, Erdmann, and Dodge, and in later years by numerous investigators in Europe and America [4, 16].

One problem that has been given much working out is that concerning the span or scope of the attentive attitude: to how many stimuli can a person be attentively receptive at one and the same time? "If you throw a handful of marbles on the floor," Sir William Hamilton had said years earlier, "you will find it difficult to view at once more than six, or seven at most, without confusion; but if you group them into twos, or threes, or fives, you can comprehend as many groups as you can units." This is rough observation, yet one that has been shown by experiment to be not far from right. Investigations have taken two major forms.

In one form, a number of stimuli (dots, numbers, letters, and the like) are simultaneously presented visually to a subject, and he is instructed to respond by speaking the number of dots shown or reading aloud the letters or the words. To make sure that the presentation is psychologically simultaneous and allows of no change of posture on the subject's part during the presentation, an exposure apparatus, a *tachistoscope*, has been devised which will expose the stimulus material for one fifth of a second or less.   Several different styles of tachistoscopes have been in use, and certain basic specifications for their construction have been well recognized.   Figure 83 presents a design that is in common use. In a typical experiment the subject is presented a very few items at first, and, as he shows ability to reproduce them, the number presented at each exposure is gradually increased until a point is reached where he is definitely unable to name them all.   (In essence this is an application of the general technique employed in the determining of sensory thresholds, as described in Chapter IX.)

FIGURE 83. A TACHISTOSCOPE (NETSCHAJEFF'S MODEL)

The stimulus material to be exposed is placed in the holder *O* and swung to position behind the aperture *D*.   The arm *N* has previously been drawn up and held by hook *H* in a position between aperture and stimulus material, screening the latter from the subject's view through *D*.   When released at *H*, *N* drops by gravity and is replaced by the falling arm *F*. The stimulus material has then been exposed through *D* during the interval between the two screenings, the length of the interval being variable from 0 to 150 ms. by adjustments of the screw *V*.

Such results obtained in Wundt's laboratory have been generally confirmed.   The limit of separate stimuli that can be observed by one sense at one time has been fixed as no more than six.   But this one fact is of less interest and importance than another.   As Hamilton had remarked, the number of physically distinct details that can be noted may be made much greater if they be grouped into stimulus patterns to which the subject has habitual reactions in his repertoire.   Several dots, lines, and so forth, when grouped into the form of familiar pictures — a chair, a square, a domino nine-spot or a playing-card five-spot — become recognizable as total units, and the subject is enabled to attend to as many of these groups as he could individual elements.   Even more strikingly, as letters are combined into short words familiar to the subject, he can note as many of the words as he could disconnected letters.   He can take in even short sentences.   It is not the number of such items but the degree of organization that is the important thing.   This involves the phenomenon of "higher orders of habits" (to be treated *infra*, pp. 369 ff.)

Disparate Activities.   Much interest has always been taken in demonstrations of divided attentional attitudes.   Caesar and Napoleon are each said to have kept a dozen secretaries busy taking down as many different dispatches simultaneously.   A boy wonder plays fourteen chess games against as many opponents at one sitting.   A vaudeville performer adds great columns of figures, while he is answering questions that are hurled at him.   These and other examples have raised the problem, How many disparate (antagonistic) operations can one carry on simultaneously?   If the activities each requires pronounced concentration, then a person can concentrate upon only one at one and the same time.

Apparent contradictions are not difficult to explain.   (1) An individual frequently *oscillates* rapidly between one adjustment and another.   In the examples noted above this point is readily recognized.   The accomplished hostess shows a high capacity to shift from a conversation on her right hand to a lagging one on her left, resuscitating it sufficiently to allow her again to change and note what is transpiring farther down the table.   The orchestra conductor listens more to his wood-winds at one moment and more to his brasses or to his strings at the next.

(2) Carrying on one performance along with others is made easier in proportion to the degree to which it has become a highly routine and *habitual* performance.   The well-trained clerk can add long columns of figures with accuracy and dispatch even while he makes thinking reactions concerning procedure to be followed after the sum is obtained and jotted down.   Similarly, a pianist has no difficulty in playing a thoroughly learned musical number as he converses with a friend standing by.

(3) The case of the orchestra conductor suggests also that many performances can be carried forward abreast if they have become organized into habitual *patterns*.   Attending to an ensemble of musical sounds from ninety different instruments is not ninety different acts but one.   This is a familiar principle to the reader, as it is the same principle as that of attending to a large visual pattern of dots or letters.   It will be given other applications on later pages.

Many simple forms of experiments have been used to test ability to perform disparate activities simultaneously. A subject may be instructed to count the beats of a metronome while canceling certain letters from a printed sheet; to press a rubber bulb in groups of four and six pressures alternately while silently adding two-place numbers appearing on a printed sheet; to read a poem aloud while writing the letter *a* as rapidly as possible. Results of such tests may be interpreted in terms of the three foregoing principles.

In the laboratory of the University of North Carolina subjects were trained to carry on three very disparate motor performances simultaneously: (*a*) with the right hand, switching off electric lights that appeared in random order, (*b*) with the left, sorting blocks that were presented to the hand behind a screen, by dropping them through the proper holes, and (*c*) with the feet working an alternating two-pedal arrangement. At first the subjects showed great motor confusion and emotional excitement, but in the course of fifty daily trials they improved markedly in ability to maintain the three simultaneous operations, and the improve-ment was made at a rate conforming to the type of curve generally found for learning simple non-disparate acts. These subjects had organized three disparate habits into one habit.

Duration and Shifting. Movement and change of stimulus, as has been shown earlier in this chapter, are effective determinants of the direction of a person's attending. We may add that unless a stimulus changes *in some way* the organism will not be selectively oriented to it for long. Since the processes of the organism are not in a stationary equilibrium at any time, perpetuation of a delicately adjusted set for more than a few seconds at the most is out of the question. Attention shifts.

This is easily demonstrated by the use of "ambiguous figures." That of the staircase (Figure 84, *A*) is effective. The lines of the geometrical design correspond rather closely both (*a*) to the outline in perspective of a staircase as looked upon from above and also (*b*) to the outline in perspective of the under side of a staircase. For a subject who had never in his life been confronted with such a ledge-shaped formation, and who therefore had never developed habitual ways of reacting to it, it is doubtful if this design would appear more than the plane figure it actually is. But if he has the well-established habits of reactions of climbing steps and of hanging and stowing away things under steps, he is fairly certain to see this design as he would the outline of a staircase. Now, as he has two different but antagonistic ways of regarding the figure, it will be found that the subject will react to it for brief alternating periods as the symbol of a staircase-from-above and as the symbol of a staircase-from-below.

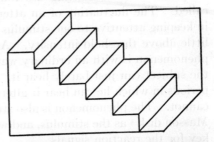

With training this alternation of attentive adjustments becomes increasingly regular and balanced. Suppose a rubber bulb be placed in his hand, pneumatically connected with a recording tambour, and he be instructed to press down on it when he sees the figure as a staircase-from-above, and to release it when he sees it in the reversed aspect. The kymograph tracing produced will show a fairly uniform oscillation between the two attitudes.

A subject will also find that by processes of thinking he can prolong his attentive adjustment to one way of regarding the figure only. Thus, in order to keep looking at it as a staircase-from-above he is aided by keeping in operation a series of congruous and allied reactions, such as saying to himself: "Suppose a stair runner laid on the steps — color green —

FIGURE 84. REVERSIBLE FIGURES

A, Schröder's staircase figure, illustrating reversible perspective.

B, Grecian urn figure, illustrating shifting of figure and background. This may also be inverted. (B from Franz, S. I., and Gordon, K., Psychology. McGraw-Hill, 1933.)

with an edging of red — flowery design — brass strips at outer edges of steps — ought to be a baseboard on that wall — where's the banister?" — and so forth.

Other ambiguous designs such as Figure 84, B, hardly require individual explanation, once the staircase design is understood. Essentially, the whole phenomenon is reducible to the competition of two antagonistic systematized sets of habits, each strongly built up in past experience. The success of either competitor depends upon relative fatigue, re-enforcing action-systems, and doubtless many other factors.

Special cases of shifting are found in *fluctuations*, as they are called. The fluctuating of an attentive set refers to the difficulty in keeping attentive to one stimulus at all when that stimulus is but little above threshold intensity. A simple means for studying the phenomenon is with an ordinary watch held at such a distance that the subject can just barely hear it. It will be found that there are periods in which he can hear it alternating with periods in which he cannot. The phenomenon is also studied in its visual form with the Masson disk [1] as the stimulus, and with a pneumatic bulb or electric key for the reaction signals.

The Effect of Distractions. It is a common notion that most forms of intense or fairly intense stimuli will interfere with concentrated work. Like all popular notions this one needed checking by experimental tryout. The results of several investigators agree in general, so that we will limit our description to one of their studies [9].

At a bank of ten different keys like those of a typewriter, a subject was put at work pressing the keys one at a time in an order determined by a stimulus-series appearing in a serial exposure apparatus (cf. Figure 140). The two pieces of apparatus were so wired that immediately upon each given reaction (pressure on a key) the next stimulus appeared. Each key was electrically connected with its own recording signal-marker to register each reaction, whether right or wrong; all keys were mounted on a delicate tambour pneumatically connected with a recording tambour to register the intensity of pressures by the fingers. A pneumograph secured the registering of breathing during the work. While the subject worked at the task of tapping the keys corresponding to the successively presented stimuli, a variety of auditory distractions were presented: a fire gong, a buzzer, phonograph music, and so on. The findings showed that although the initial effect of accompanying noise is to retard the speed of a task, the later effect is to accelerate it, even beyond the speed shown when no distraction

---

[1] The Masson disk is of white cardboard and bears a row of small black squares arranged in a line from center to circumference, so that when it is rotated on the shaft of a motor, it presents a row of concentric gray rings progressively brighter from the center outward. The subject fixates a ring he can barely make out, watches it steadily, and reports the interval in which it can and cannot be seen.

is present.   Nor was there any appreciable reduction of accuracy. What could be the explanation of this surprising result?   The records indicated two.   One was that greater energy was put forth (greater pressure on the keys) when a distracting noise intruded.   The other was that verbal articulations (shown in respirations) re-enforced the attitudinal set by enhancing the individual stimuli.   In summary, there is good evidence for the view that when encountering a difficulty in the shape of a distracting stimulus, the well-motivated organism becomes hyperactive, both by general increase of tonicity and by throwing into activity habitual types of behavior that will re-enforce the motivated line of action.   (The reader will recognize the essential principles of behavior enunciated in Chapter II.)   Put in another way, the self-regulating organism *compensates* by overconcentrating, by overmobilizing its strength. And this, so those suggest who have worked on the problem, is costly in the long run.

PHYSIOLOGICAL BASES

In this chapter we have treated a set as a phase of behavior.   We have made no attempt to describe this phenomenon in physiological terms, that is, as the function of specified particular organs or tissues.   In the face of great divergence of opinion among the physiologists themselves, it would be rash for us to set up a claim for any one single physiological description.   The part of wisdom is to content ourselves with a brief enumeration of various points that seem relevant to the general problem and let the reader who may have an interest in the matter follow up these leads.

Postural Activities in Effectors.   It has been stated in Chapter VIII that the striped muscle tissue can be thrown into the long-maintained contractions called *tonic* as well as into the short-lived contractions called *phasic*. When a person is set, this condition is often conceived as one involving the tonic states of musculature.   If that be true, what are some of the more precise conceptions of this phenomenon?   One of them is that most striped musculature is composed of *two different kinds of muscle tissue*, one kind producing quick contracting and the other slow.   The character of the action of the muscle as a whole is a resultant of the two [5].   Another view is that a striped muscle is supplied by *two kinds of efferent nerves*, one innervating it phasically and the other posturally [6].   A third view emphasizes a *difference in the neural centers* from which innervation is received by the muscle [17].   A fourth view ascribes the difference of motor reaction to a *difference in the sensory source* of the inflow of neural impulses from receptors to the centers [13]. Finally, there is authority for rejecting all these views and holding that the same neural and muscular structures are involved in both the phasic and the postural reactions [2].

In the activity of smooth musculature, also, a duality of function has been pointed out in relatively prompt and relatively slow-acting contractions. Even the relatively quicker contractions are, however, distinctly more sluggish than those of striped muscles, so that we should think of the activity of smooth musculature as contributing to the static or postural rather than to the kinetic or phasic aspects of the whole picture of the organism's behavior.

Neurological Principles. It is possible that certain types of set have their proper explanation in terms of the relations of the neural functions involved [14].

The determining effect of set may be reducible to the principles of *facilitation* and *inhibition* between action systems. When one stimulus or situation arouses a certain neural excitement leading to a reaction, this neural excitement will spread into other action systems and tends to re-enforce the activity of some and to inhibit the activity of others. A later stimulus which tends to arouse one of the facilitated systems will become effective, whereas a stimulus which tends to arouse inhibited systems will be ineffective.

Conclusion. The variety of physiological facts and theories just presented may serve us as a reminder that the phenomena themselves that have been included under the term used as the title of the present chapter may not be identical phenomena, and may not even be closely related in their true fundamental character. Resemblances noted in a general over-view may turn out to be specious. Taken together, the phenomena will, however, serve to remind the psychologist that what he has to deal with in the behavior of man are not simply the short-lived, quickly operating reactions to stimuli, but also the long-lived, slowly changing modifications of his gross adjustments.

REFERENCES

1. Evans, C. L.   *Recent Advances in Physiology*.   Blakiston, 1930.   Chap. XI.

2. Forbes, A.   Tonus in Skeletal Muscle in Relation to Sympathetic Innervation.   *Arch. Neurol. & Psychiat.*, 1929, **22,** 247–64.

3. Freeman, G. L.   The Spread of Neuro-Muscular Activity during Mental Work.   *J. Gen. Psychol.*, 1931, **5,** 479–94.

4. Glanville, A. D., and Dallenbach, K. M.   The Range of Attention.   *Am. J. Psychol.*, 1929, **41,** 207–36.

5. Hunt, J. R.   The Static and Kinetic Representations of the Efferent Nervous System in the Psycho-Motor Sphere.   In *Problems of Personality* (ed. by C. McF. Campbell *et al.*).   Harcourt, Brace, 1925.

6. Hunter, J. J.   The Sympathetic Innervation of Striated Muscle.   *Brit. Med. J.*, (I) 1925, 197–201, 251–56, 298–301, 350–53, 398–403.

7. Hunter, W. S. The Delayed Reaction in Animals and Children. *Beh. Monog.*, 1912, **2**, No. 6.

8. Jastrow, J. *Fact and Fable in Psychology.* Houghton Mifflin, 1900.

9. Morgan, J. J. B. The Overcoming of Distraction and Other Resistances. *Arch. Psychol.*, 1916, **5**, No. 35.

10. Myers, C. S. *Text-Book of Experimental Psychology.* 2 vols. Chap. 25. Longmans, 1911.

11. Rees, H. J., and Israel, H. E. An Investigation of the Establishment and Operation of Mental Sets. *Psychol. Monog.*, 1935, **46**, No. 6, 1–26.

12. Schulze, R. *Experimental Psychology* (trans. by Pintner, R.). Geo. Allen, 1912. Chap. VI.

13. Sherrington, C. S. Postural Activity in Muscle and Nerve. *Brain*, 1915, **38**, 191–234.

14. Sherrington, C. S. *The Integrative Action of the Nervous System.* Yale Univ. Press, 1906.

15. Tuttle, W. W. The Effect of Attention or Mental Activity on the Patellar Tendon Reflex. *J. Exper. Psychol.*, 1924, **7**, 401–20.

16. Whipple, G. M. *Manual of Mental and Physical Tests.* Warwick & York (2nd ed.), 1914. Chap. VII.

17. Wilson, S. A. K. The Old Motor System and the New. *Arch. Neurol. & Psychiat.*, 1924, **11**, 385–404.

CHAPTER XIII

INTELLIGENT BEHAVIOR

ITS NATURE

How Defined. Of all the psychological terms that have been encountered by the reader in conversations, in the popular magazines, and in the daily press, probably the most frequently heard is "intelligence."

Just what is this "intelligence"? First, let us not be misled by the form of the word: it is not a thing, not a substance. It refers to a quality or characteristic of a person's behavior. The present writer would recommend less use of the word "intelligence" and more use of modifiers such as "intelligent behavior," "intelligently," and so forth. It is an interesting fact that, although psychologists seem to be in fair agreement as to when it is proper to use the term and when not, they find it hard to define.

That the methods of examination get at some ability has been abundantly shown, even if *what* they get at remains in doubt. The ability can be isolated in fact if not in words. And, in any case, there is some point to the claim that "measurements should precede definition."

We will not go far astray if we adopt the statement that intelligence is *the ability to acquire and perfect through individual experience new and more efficient modes of adaptation.*

Measurements are by Tests. It has been said on an earlier page that one of the greatest achievements of modern psychology has been the building up of knowledge of individual differences. But the study of how individuals differ would have gotten nowhere in any definite way without the use of psychological tests. Tests have been devised for very many different kinds of human abilities — from such simple ones as the ability to distinguish colors or to make quick reactions or to grasp a handle with vigor, to such subtle or complex ones as the ability to condense and remember the meaning of a paragraph or to point out the fallacies in an argument.

It is of great importance for us to realize that there is nothing arbitrary, *a priori*, or easy about the way in which psychological tests are built up. Simple and even foolish as many a test may seem to the casual onlooker, its use is the outcome of labor and care. Let us review some cardinal steps in the construction of a good test. Suppose we desire a test of ability to drive a taxicab. (1) First, we would set up tentatively a *number and variety of possible tests,* many that on their face seem to resemble details of the taxi driver's job and many that do not, perhaps. Much would depend upon our ingenuity here. (2) Then by the slow process of experimentation we would determine whether any of these tests — or any combination of them — promised well. This would be the test of *validity.* Do the tests measure what they are set up to measure, we ask. (3) We would need, of course, some *criterion* of the ability in question. For instance, we might try out our tests upon men who have already demonstrated in a company's employ their relative success at the work. (4) We would want further to examine the *reliability* of the test, its consistency. This is measured by finding the degree of correlation between two halves of the test, or between the odd-numbered items and the even-numbered items, or between two different givings of the whole test. In all cases the question would be that of whether the individual differences of scores remain fairly constant: do both tests score Mr. A consistently very high while both score Mr. B fairly low? (5) Finally, we would find that just how the tests are to be *administered* and just how they are to be *scored* need to be worked out in detail and *standardized,* for many an error in one's score would be sure to result from different ways of giving the test and different ways of scoring it.

MEASUREMENTS OF INTELLIGENT BEHAVIOR

The Binet-Simon Scale. If you wish to know whether a boy, dog, monkey, or man is fairly intelligent and can learn, the most reliable way is not to accept hearsay, although that has its value, or to be satisfied with a photograph, but to set up a problem and see for yourself whether he can and does react in an intelligent manner.[1] If

---

[1] Pronouncing judgment as to people's intelligence merely on the basis of their appearance is common in daily life. Several careful studies have shown, however, that this is very unsafe. For example, consider the photographs in Figure 86 of four girls from the same orphanage. Let the reader try his own hand at estimating their relative intelligence by deciding which looks brightest, which next brightest, and so on to the dullest. The definitely determined I.Q.'s (cf. p. 348) are listed at the end of this chapter. Of twenty-five people who attempted to guess the right order, not one got it wholly correct. One experienced social worker, after making up his order of judgments, deliberately reversed the order — and the result was as nearly correct as any other that was submitted!

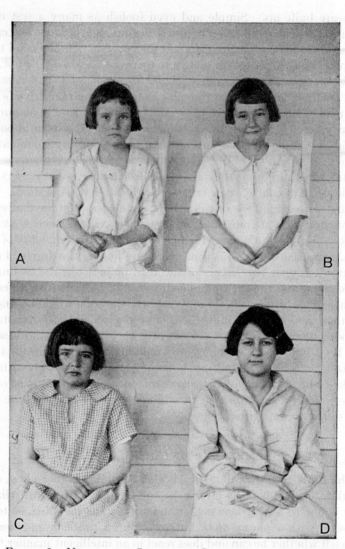

FIGURE 85. NORMAL AND SUBNORMAL GIRLS FROM AN ORPHANAGE

Is their facial and general appearance a reliable index for estimating their intelligence? See footnote in text. (Furnished by Dr. H. W. Crane.)

you wish, furthermore, to know *how* intelligent he is, you will be careful to determine the exact difficulty of the problem set. To judge of a reaction-capacity, provide the appropriate stimulating situation. In 1904 Binet and Simon set themselves the task of devising some accurate method of identifying the subnormal children needing special instruction in the Paris schools. The method of personal opinion based upon general observation was the only one in use and was not satisfactory. Among other things, what was needed was less impressionistic subjective judgment and more objective measurement. All available psychological tests as well as novel methods that Binet himself had been devising tentatively for some years were now reviewed, examined, and tried out.

It is important to understand that the method of selecting the tests was *empirical* and not *a priori*; that is, the tests were built up as the result of experimentation, rather than being constructed completely prior to the time they were tried out on subjects. The investigators tried great numbers of different tests upon some two hundred normal children ranging from three to fifteen years of age in order to find those tests which might differentiate children of different levels of intelligent behavior. For example, if a given test was successfully passed by two thirds to three fourths of the ten-year-olds but by a much smaller proportion of the nine-year-olds, it was set up as a suitable test of ten-year-old intelligence. By going over the results of work done by children of the different ages on the divers and sundry tests applied, it was possible to identify many tests as differentiating certain ages. Thus it is clear that the Binet-Simon tests were selected on the basis of actual objective results. They were not concocted in the privacy of a study: they were tests already (for the most part) in existence, and they were accepted and standardized only after they had been applied to many children.[1]

The peculiar contribution of Binet and Simon lay in their combining of tests into a system. For one thing, the tests were *varied* in nature. If situations are to be set for a child to test whether or not he can react intelligently in general, it is in fairness necessary that the situations be not of a single but of many different sorts. So, in the Binet-Simon series the subject may be asked to execute simple commands; to name familiar objects; to draw copies of designs; to give rhymes; to say what he would do in certain everyday situations

[1] This point is valid for psychological examinations in general. There is no disposition on the part of psychologists to fit mankind to their tests but rather to devise tests that may be fitted to mankind.

described; to give the meanings of words, and so forth. (See also the Stanford Revision list, given below.)

For another thing, the tests were *graded* and thus formed into a *scale*. Binet was the first explicitly to use the idea of arrangement of tests by ages. Having found that most normal children could pass certain tests at certain ages, Binet set up these tests for these ages; then when a new individual was examined, his capacity could be located in terms of age in the general population. A child who could pass those tests that had been passed by the great majority of eight-year-olds, but could not pass those that had been passed by the majority of nine-year-olds, was then called eight years old in intelligence or was given the "mental age" (M.A.) of eight. To say that Susie Smith has "eight-year-old intelligence" means nothing more mysterious or abstruse than that she is as intelligent as the normal eight-year-old. Examples of this grading of tests by ages may be found in certain problems that are repeated for different years. A four-year-old should be able to repeat correctly three digits spoken to him, an eight-year-old should repeat five, a fifteen-year-old should repeat seven. After observing a picture shown to him, a three-year-old should be able to enumerate objects in the picture, but a seven-year-old should be able to give a more connected description, while a fifteen-year-old should give interpretations.[1]

Still another characteristic was that the scale purported to get at *native* capacities, independent of special training. Of course, it would be idle to seek to measure some tendencies or capacities in a ten-year-old child that had never been affected by any experience. Every reaction system in his body has in some measure been excited at one time or another; and his behavior toward any situation is inevitably determined by habits already formed. The only way to bring out differences, then, in native capacity is to take children of a common environment (with equal opportunities to learn) and to measure the extent to which the respective individuals have profited by such opportunities. Has this child of three learned where his "nose" is, or his "mouth"? Has that one of twelve learned to use abstract words like "justice" or "charity"? If so, he gives that much evidence of at least normal capacity to learn.

Binet published scales of tests in 1905, 1908, and 1911. In the final form, the scale consisted of five tests for each age from three to sixteen (or "adult") inclusive, omitting years eleven, thirteen, and fourteen, and giving only four tests for the fourth year.

[1] These age values have been somewhat changed in American revisions.

American Revisions. The great value of the Binet-Simon arrangement in a scaled series was promptly grasped in America, and within four or five years several revisions and adaptations of the tests were published that made them more suitable to the American child living in an environment different from the French and speaking another language. Of these, one of the most successful is that arranged by Terman in 1916 and again in 1937, called the *Stanford Revision*. A list of the tests for some of the years included in that scale follows:

Year II (first half year) (6 tests, 1 month credit each)
  1. Fits blocks into holes of a form-board.
  2. Names six small objects shown him.
  3. Points to parts of the body of a doll: hair, mouth, etc.
  4. By imitation builds a tower of four blocks.
  5. Names objects in a picture.
  6. Obeys simple commands: "Give me the kitty," etc.
Year VI (6 tests, 2 months credit each)
  1. Vocabulary: gives meanings of words.
  2. By imitation strings beads in a certain order.
  3. Tells missing parts of mutilated pictures.
  4. Picks up requested number of blocks.
  5. Selects unlike picture from several.
  6. Traces a maze.
Year XIV (6 tests, 2 months credit each)
  1. Vocabulary.
  2. Discovers the rule followed in a series of paper-foldings.
  3. Points out absurdities in a picture.
  4. Ingenuity: tells how to measure out 3 pints using a 4-pint and a 9-pint can; etc.
  5. Directional orientation: "Suppose you were going west, then turn to your right...", etc.
  6. Meanings of abstract words.
Superior Adult, II (6 tests, 5 months credit each)
  1. Vocabulary.
  2. Finds three reasons for a statement given.
  3. Repeats digits.
  4. Gives meaning of a proverb.
  5. States how certain opposites are alike.
  6. Gives the thought of a prose passage.

The method of scoring the results on such a scale is simple enough: the subject is credited with all tests below a year group in which he passes all, and also with all tests above this point that he happens to pass. (The examiner usually begins with those of the year just below the subject's actual age.) By totaling "months" and "years" of test scores the "mental age" is determined.

The M.A., however, is an incomplete measure. As a child matures this may be expected to increase, and a more constant index is desirable. Stern proposed the use of a mental quotient. This was called by Terman an "intelligence quotient" (I.Q.), and it expresses the ratio of a child's mental age (M.A.) to his chronological age (C.A.) by a fraction: $I.Q. = \dfrac{M.A.}{C.A.}$ For example: if the value of the resulting fraction be around 100 per cent the child is rated normal (that is, he is about the equal of the average of his age); if it be 125 per cent, he is clearly supernormal (brighter than most of his own age); if it be only 70 per cent, he is subnormal. For the purpose of computing his I.Q. an adult's C.A. is assumed to be 16 years, on this scale, because very little improvement of test scores was obtained beyond this age. Terman suggests the following classification of intelligence quotients:

I.Q.	CLASSIFICATION
Above 140	"Near" genius or genius.
120–140	Very superior intelligence.
110–120	Superior intelligence.
90–110	Normal or average intelligence.
80–90	Dullness, rarely classifiable as feeble-mindedness.
70–80	Border-line deficiency, sometimes classifiable as dullness, often as feeble-mindedness.
50–70	Moron.
20–50	Imbecile.
0–20	Idiot.

Performance Examinations. The Binet type of examination in its various revisions involves the use of language, oral and written. In exceptional cases this may prove to be an insurmountable obstacle to employment of these revisions. They cannot be used for the testing of illiterates, of non-English-speaking immigrants, of the deaf, nor of those who are not illiterate and yet have inadequate opportunities.

The oldest and best known device is the "form board" devised by Séguin (Figure 86, *A*). A baseboard bears holes of varying geometrical shapes, into which the subject is to fit similarly shaped blocks, the time and errors in his procedure being recorded by the examiner. Numerous modifications of this block-fitting plan have been devised in various grades of difficulty. Another type of per-

FIGURE 86. SOME PERFORMANCE TESTS OF CAPACITY FOR
INTELLIGENT BEHAVIOR

A, Séguin's form board, Goddard's modification; *B*, Glueck's ship test; *C*, Healy's picture completion test, consisting of pictures of different incidents in a boy's day, a missing detail of each to be supplied from the blocks shown above; *D*, Pintner's manikin and feature profile tests.

formance test, "picture assembling," is patterned after the jig-saw puzzle, and consists of a dissected picture to be recombined into a whole by the subject. The ship test is an example (Figure 86, *B*). Combinations of the block-fitting and the picture-assembling devices appear in the picture completion tests, in which the subject is expected to fill in vacant spaces with picture blocks correctly chosen from a supply presented (as in *C*); in the manikin and feature-profile (*D*); and in other forms. A third type of performance test is the "cube-imitation" test. A row of four cubes is set before the subject, a fifth is tapped upon these four one at a time in one or another formal order, and the subject is handed the cube with signs to do likewise. His score depends upon the complexity of the tapping-orders that he is able to duplicate. With the use of pencil and paper other non-linguistic tasks may be arranged. The familiar pencil maze puzzle has been standardized for the purpose; and substitution and design-copying tests have been adapted. A scale for determining children's intelligence from their drawings is available.

The employment of all these devices to measure intelligent action in any reliable way calls for standardization in the extreme. The precise manner in which the apparatus is presented to the examinee, including the exact location of every little piece, and the unvarying form of the instructions to be conveyed by word or gesture — all must be standardized by the empirical method of trying out on large groups of children, before questions of scoring can be approached. Pintner and Paterson have drawn up a series of fifteen of these performance tests with standard instructions and norms of achievement for children of various ages.

Group Examinations.   The Binet and the performance types are individual examinations: they involve the testing of one subject at a time.   But conditions are sure to arise when the surveying of large masses of people is desirable.   Such an occasion appeared, for instance, upon America's entry into the war, when the rapid measurement of the troops at the camps was contemplated; and such conditions are encountered also whenever the psychological characteristics of a school population or of a group of applicants for work are the object of inquiry.   In these examinations each individual is supplied with a printed booklet containing a variety of tests, and his work upon these is timed and often verbally directed in part by the examiner in charge of the group.

The earliest complete form of group examination, that of Otis, consists of ten tests printed on ten separate pages.   Test 1 calls for the execution of simple and complex directions, as, "A certain letter is the second letter to the right of another letter [in the alphabet].   This other letter is the fifth letter to the left of R.   What is the 'certain letter' first mentioned?"   Test 2 calls for the selection of words that are the opposites of those in a given list; and Test 8 calls for the selection of words or designs similar to those shown in lists.   Test 3 requires the putting in order of disarranged sentences, and marking them true or false.   Test 4 requires the explanation of proverbs by selections from a list of explanations shown.   Test 5 is a list of problems in arithmetical thinking.   Test 6 shows diagrams of geometrical figures overlapping each other, and covered with numbers, and the examinee is to answer questions about them by jotting down the appropriate numbers.   Test 7 is a series of analogies, to be completed by underlining the appropriate word among several shown, as,

clothes: man — fur: (?) .....coat, animal, hair, skin, cloth.

Test 9 is a story with important words left out which the subject is to choose from a list printed at one side. Test 10 calls for a story to be read aloud by the examiner; questions about this are then read by the examinee and his answers are indicated by underlining in each case "yes," "no," or "didn't say." The answers to be given to all these tests are of the simplest possible sort: the jotting down of a letter, of a number, or the underlining of a word. Thus the mechanical part of the work is cut to a minimum.

For the testing *en masse* of large numbers of illiterates or of non-English-speaking subjects group examinations of a non-language nature have been devised. In these are presented printed mazes, substitution and cancellation tests, incomplete pictures, and so forth, such as are printed likewise in booklet form. The devising of group-scales, both language and non-language, has gone on apace; and today we are faced with almost too many rather than too few. The investigative problem now is, therefore, the critical refining and more adequate standardizing of those in existence.

Importance of the Technique in Testing. The psychological methods of measuring how intelligently a person will act are not foolproof instruments. They are no more reliable in the hands of the untrained or the careless than are the routine diagnostic devices of the physician. Too much stress cannot be laid on this point. For the unskilled to venture upon a program of wholesale testing is not only inaccurate and unscientific: it may be vicious. For the adequate employing of the more complicated tests, as in the Binet type for individuals, it is necessary that the examiner be conversant with the manifold subtle factors that may enter in to determine the ultimate performance of a human individual. Consider the intimate and detailed way in which a human subject's reactions are linked by original nature, and still more by habit, to the details of the stimulating environment, and it must be evident enough that only he who has been carefully trained, preferably in the psychological laboratory, can be relied upon to recognize and evaluate a large share of the details so important in test procedure. The subject may be uneasy about the examination; he may like or dislike the examiner; he may have a headache or be in need of glasses; sounds of voices through door or window may distract him.

SOME RESULTS AND APPLICATIONS

How are Degrees of Intelligence Distributed in a General Population? To evaluate properly a given person's intelligence rating it is important to know how he compares with the population of which he is a member. His I.Q. figure does indicate how he compares with the median of the population (which is taken as I.Q. 100); but that is all the I.Q. indicates definitely. Suppose, for instance, a person with an I.Q. of 128: he is clearly superior to the median of his age-population, but how much of the population he surpasses is not indicated, although it is often important to know this last relation. Terman has furnished tables of equivalents for I.Q. scores and percentages of population; but as they are detailed, we may satisfy ourselves in this place with a glance at the outcome of a quite recent nation-wide survey of all the Scottish children born in 1921. See Figure 87. We can note that the distribution of scores for either sex approximates the Gaussian curve of normal chance distribution (cf. *supra*, pp. 290 ff.). And we can see also that Terman's inferences from his own study hold good here — namely that (*a*) "there is no definite dividing line between normality and feeble-mindedness, or between normality and genius," and that (*b*) "the common opinion that extreme deviations below the median are more frequent than extreme deviations above the median seems to have no foundation in fact."

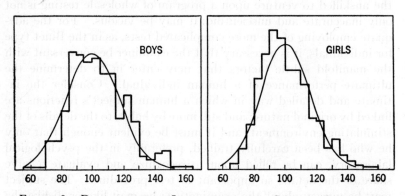

FIGURE 87. DISTRIBUTION OF INTELLIGENCE IN A GENERAL POPULATION

Column diagrams to show the distributions of Binet I.Q. scores for all Scottish children born in 1921 (numbering 44,210 boys and 43,288 girls). Distances on the horizontal = I.Q. scores in 5-point intervals; vertical distances = number of individuals making each score (absolute figures not furnished). These Binet scores were calculated from the children's scores on certain group tests, after comparing the Binet with the group test scores made by a sample of the same population (500 boys, 500 girls).

The curved lines represent theoretical normal chance distributions for the same means and SD's (for boys, *M* = 100, *SD* = 17; for girls, *M* = 100, *SD* = 16). (From Scottish Council for Research in Education, *The Intelligence of Scottish Children*. Univ. London Press, 1933.)

Does Intelligence Change with Age?   Blackstone, when writing his famous legal commentaries, said: "An idiot, or natural born fool, is one that hath no understanding from his nativity, and is therefore by law presumed never likely to attain any." Later psychological investigations have borne out substantially the wider implications of this dictum.   It is an exaggeration to say that "an I.Q. is an I.Q. and nothing can change it"; yet the latest researches in which the same children are given repeated measurements are continuing as did the earlier researches to show it to be a fact that the I.Q. of an individual remains surprisingly constant.   The practical value of this fact for predictions as to the future achievements possible for a given child are enormous, especially for the parent, the educator, and the vocational counsellor.

What of the age changes of *adults*?   To this question a less definite and less frequently verified return is available; and it will be well for us to have a look at one of the latest pieces of evidence.   Large blocks of people from many New England farms and villages were drawn together for free motion picture exhibits and "group questionnaires" (Army Alpha test) with some supplementary house-to-house testing.   On the basis of nearly twelve hundred cases, it was found that scores on Army Alpha showed a consistent increase with age up to about 16 years, a less rapid increase until 18 or 21, then a decline that by the age of 55 had receded to the 14-year level. Quite interesting it is, however, to find that the decline was not the same on all the eight sub-tests of the Alpha scale.   As Figure 88 shows, results on two sub-tests that depended in high degree on the subject's alertness show fairly rapid declines while results on two others that seem to involve more the use of one's organized knowledge show no decline at all.   The man of middle-life or later, then, shows *progressively less* "intelligence" than when he was in his later teens if we mean by the word, "*alertness*," though he may compensate for this slowing down by *more effective organization* of his mental capital.   (Cf. p. 436.)

Use of Intelligence Tests in the Schools.   The lockstep system of promotion of school children was destined inevitably to go by the board.   To advance a child grade by grade merely because he ages year by year may be well enough for many individuals, but it seriously hobbles and handicaps the boy or girl distinctly brighter than others of the same age and overstrains the one who is duller.   To be held back and assigned tasks too easy of execution breeds laziness or

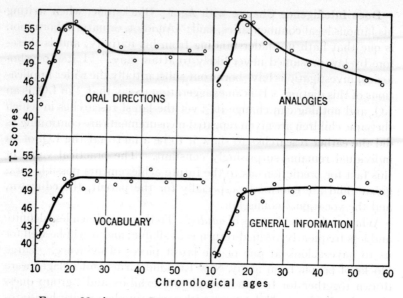

FIGURE 88. AGE AND PERFORMANCE ON DIFFERENT SUB-TESTS

Results on four sub-tests of Army Alpha with 1191 rural subjects between the ages of 10 and 60. Each dot represents the mean score of an age group (transmuted into "T-scores" to make them comparable). To these data best-fitting curves have been drawn. (From Jones, H. E., and Conrad, H. S., *Genet. Psychol. Monog.*, 1933, **13**, no. 3.)

restlessness, and not infrequently is found to be a root cause for misconduct in the schoolroom. On the other hand it is uneconomical of human effort and ability to promote those less educable than others of their age. If slow pupils are forced to attempt to keep abreast of pupils who learn more rapidly, they may take refuge in a defeatist attitude — a condition of lowered morale so reducing efficiency that it is to be avoided at all costs. Less mechanical systems of promotion, then, have become inevitable.

The revising and adapting to American conditions of the Binet-Simon scale for measuring a child's capacity to learn has been one of the greatest factors in this reorganizing of school promotion methods; and with the perfecting of the group scale, a device is put within reach of any school whereby all the children of all the grades can be measured within a few weeks or days by competent examiners. The use of such data for the *regrading* and *homogeneous grouping* of children has spread widely in the United States. Taken in conjunction with achievement in the school subjects, teachers' observations, and conditions of health, this is found to be an invaluable instrument for the administrator.

The theoretical expectation that a high score on a test for intelligence should indicate high educability in the school is well borne out by numerous studies of the relation between such scores of pupils and their grades in school or in subject-matter tests. A clear-cut illustration is furnished in report of a rearrangement of pupils in the VII-B grade of the Cleveland schools into six different groups on the basis of a group intelligence measurement, and a later measurement by standard tests of their abilities in school subjects. The accompanying table presents the data in abbreviated form. The brightest group (by intelligence test) exceeded the lowest group in arithmetic by approximately one and a half years of school progress, and in reading and in language by more than two years of progress.

MEDIAN CLASS SCORES BY INTELLIGENCE GROUPS

SCORES ON "ILLINOIS INTELLIGENCE TEST" *	MEDIAN SCORE *	MEDIAN AGE	SCORES ON "STONE ARITHMETIC TEST"	SCORES ON "MONROE READING TEST"		SCORES ON "CHARTERS LANGUAGE TEST"
				Comprehension	Rate	
82 and up..	86	12.7	7.0	32.3	133	21.1
72–82.....	75	12.8	6.6	26.8	133	18.8
67–72.....	69	13.1	6.1	23.8	133	16.7
62–67.....	65	13.2	5.1	23.6	115	15.8
52–62.....	56	13.3	5.1	21.5	115	14.0
Below 52 ..	48	13.7	4.6	18.0	101	13.8

* These are not I.Q.'s, but points on the "Illinois" scale.

The use of tests for differentiating pupils in terms of their native capacity to learn has had fully as much attention in colleges as in the lower schools. A substantial proportion of the colleges in the United States now administer group examinations to entering freshmen. In a few cases a certain grade on the test is necessary for admission to the college; but such complete reliance on the tests is unusual, and the results are commonly used as part of the data on the individual students to be available for more informal administrative purposes.

High agreements are here again found between scores on the tests and achievement in school work. At the University of North Carolina the scores of freshmen on the Otis examination one year predicted their relative standings in the case of each department of study for the freshman year, with correlation coefficients varying from + .32 to + .61.   Thirty-five universities and colleges have reported correlations between Army Alpha examination and class marks in general ranging from + .22 to + .66 [5].

Use of Intelligence Tests in Vocations.   It goes without saying that in some occupations, as public accounting, short-story writing, or practicing law, one is called upon for many more intelligent decisions than in others, such as pasting seals on packages, copying addresses, or dipping matches.   The measurement of intelligence has consequently been a problem of much concern with those interested in vocational placement.

There are a few cases where data obtained from intelligence testing have been correlated with occupational status.   The examination of army personnel brought to light differences in the men who were in different army occupations, ranging from the engineering and medical officers, who made the highest scores as a group, all the way down through nearly forty other occupations to the miners and the laborers, who made the lowest scores [16].   We shall not reproduce the scores here, for the various groups of men engaged in the same occupations in peace time might rank somewhat differently; and moreover, since the tests were mostly of the paper and pencil type, men in certain occupations (machinists, carpenters, etc.) were conceivably at a disadvantage as contrasted with those in other occupations (clerks, etc.).

The various occupations into which the alumni of a large college have gone have been compared with reference to the scores they had made on intelligence tests taken during their college years as well as the scholarship grades they had attained in their college courses. Those who later went into college teaching had scored highest in both regards, while those going into physical education work scored lowest in both [3].   But here other pitfalls beset.   The results obtained from the alumni of one school may not be applicable to alumni of other schools: the former may exert subtle influences leading the brightest students into teaching, or its admission standards to the physical education department may select a different type of entrant.   The distinct need here is for more and more thorough analyses of occupational groups and of the demands of particular jobs.   To the degree that this ideal is approached, vocational guidance on its negative side, at least, will become a more legitimate profession than it is today.   Once having determined by test John

Doe's capacity for acting in intelligent ways, the adviser can recommend that he stay out of this occupation as demanding more than his natural talents, or out of that because it demands too little. In either line he would become misfit, maladjusted. By the same token, employee selection will gain in reliability. With an accurate knowledge of the requirements for a vacant job all those applicants found by test not to have capacity for it can be promptly eliminated.

The negative or eliminative side has been emphasized by us for the reason that success in any line is dependent upon many other factors than intelligence — surely not a novel point for the reader. In the final examination at his military school Napoleon stood forty-second in his class. "Who," asks Swift, "were the forty-one above him?" Some kinds of work demand specific physical traits such as good eyesight, or a steady hand, or a not unpleasant appearance. Some demand emotional stability that will withstand shocks. Some call for great patience and persistence, others not at all. For certain occupations one must be a "good mixer." For others he must be of a "mechanical turn." And for many he must bring with him some equipment in special kinds of knowledge or skill. In every case the requirement in general intelligence is only one dimension of the whole; but even with ideally adequate knowledge of this, it will still be easier to predict failures than success.[1]

Social Importance of the Feeble-Minded. The topic of intelligence is by no means one of importance to the individual solely. Evidences have been accumulating for years that many of the evils of society are traceable in part to the incapacity of many people to make normal adjustments to the conditions of life. As Goddard says: "Every feeble-minded person is bound to be the victim of his environment because he has not intelligence and judgment and will-power enough to control that environment." Unable to compete with his fellows, he may submit passively — in which case he dies of starvation and disease, unless rescued by charity. Or, he may take things into his own hands — in which case he commits immoral or criminal acts. Examinations of the inmates of reformatories and prisons have led to estimates of deficiency in intelligence among criminals varying from 25 to 80 per cent. No reliable figures on alcoholism are available, but it is well known that feeble-mindedness is a potent factor in drunkenness. It is well known also that low

---

[1] On an earlier page (135) the importance of knowing a candidate's interests has been mentioned and a method of measuring them described.

intelligence is a factor in prostitution; intelligence surveys of houses of ill-fame, as well as of girl reformatories, produce figures ranging from 34 to 97 per cent deficient. Studies of truancy show from 51 to 80 per cent of truants to be defective. 36 per cent of the inmates of almshouses of New York have been found to be clearly feeble-minded; and others' estimates of paupers in general give higher ratios. Compare these figures with the estimated 2 to 5 per cent of feeble-mindedness in the general population and the importance of the whole matter to society and the State is obvious enough. What can be done about it? For one thing their *segregation* and care are the crying needs not only to protect society, but to protect themselves, and — since feeble-mindedness that is not due to accidents or disease is largely transmissible — to prevent further procreation of their kind.

This, however, is but one side of the picture. Careful co-operation, between placement offices of schools for the mentally defective and domestic or commercial employers, has brought about successful location of many a feeble-minded on a useful job. The world has always had need for its hewers of wood and drawers of water, and, it is sometimes argued, it always will. Jobs suitable for men and for women at mental age levels under 12 have been pointed out [1, 15].

All in all, it would seem that social planning must look to the substantial reduction in the number of feeble-minded to be brought into the world. For those who are born society must seek out the routine and menial jobs which still remain before the advancing machine.

Social Importance of the Gifted. What of those at the other end of the curve of distribution? What of the superior? The truth is that until recent years they have been neglected, except for biographies and anecdotes — and some popular superstitions. Now, however, the results of a few thorough investigations are available.

One thousand children all with I.Q.'s above 130 were studied by Terman. Taken as a group, they compared strikingly with the children of average intelligence of their own ages. In health and physique they were somewhat superior. They were more precocious, having shown earlier tendencies to walk, to talk, and to read, and were promoted faster in school. Their reading interests surpassed those of normal children both in quality and in quantity; the typical seven-year-old gifted child reads more books than any normal child under fifteen. In play they maintained their lead, for

they had many more play interests, more hobbies, more enthu-
siasms.   In moral traits they surpassed again in tests of trust-
worthiness, co-operativeness, honesty, and the like.   In emotional
stability they stood higher, showing less nervousness, less self-will
and egotism.   Socially they were leaders in many ways.   After a
lapse of seven years, these children were once again studied.   Again
they exhibited the same superiority, and again a superiority in
every way.

Other studies have all supported this one in this general finding:
*Gifted children do not tend to be one-sided in their abilities nor one-
sided in their interests.*   They do not show the compensation for
strength in one trait by weakness in another so expected in popular
opinion.   It is simply not true that they are more likely to be
sickly, or neurotic, or unsociable, or undependable, or in any other
way "freakish."   Indeed, it would furnish an interesting study in
psychology on its own account, to trace out the psychological bases
of popular misunderstanding along this line — exaggeration by
gossip, seeing what one is looking for, the democratic bias for equal-
ity, the human tendency to "balance off," and even a dash of prejudice, perhaps.

Something has been said above about the importance of re-group-
ing school children according to their abilities.   Into the question of
wider social programs for the gifted children we cannot here go.
But it may well be that most important is the creation of a sounder
attitude on the part of popular opinion, after which concrete programs, ways and means, may be confidently expected to develop.

Some Special Aptitude Measurements.   The rapid and impressive development of testing methods bearing on general intelligence
has had the natural effect of strengthening psychologists' interests
in seeking measuring rods for many other human traits, especially
those of vocational abilities.   We have space to name but two or
three.   Seashore has made exhaustive analyses of *musical* ability,
and has devised apparatus and methods for a standardized examination and measurement of the necessary component "talents" or
capacities.   Figure 89 shows a sample record.   The measuring of
some of these traits has been adapted to group testing through the
employment of phonograph disks.   These have been widely used,
especially by school supervisors of music.

An *art judgment* test [6] has been perfected which consists of 125
pages of pictures arranged in pairs, the two pictures of each pair

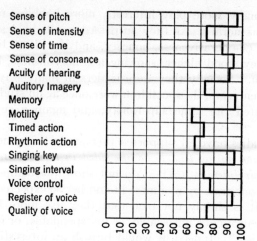

Sense of pitch
Sense of intensity
Sense of time
Sense of consonance
Acuity of hearing
Auditory Imagery
Memory
Motility
Timed action
Rhythmic action
Singing key
Singing interval
Voice control
Register of voice
Quality of voice

0 10 20 30 40 50 60 70 80 90 100

FIGURE 89. PSYCHOGRAPH OF A PERSON OF HIGH MUSICAL APTITUDES

The aptitudes are listed on the left. Scores by tests are expressed in terms of their compari-sons with scores found for the general population. This subject equaled or surpassed 98 per cent of the general population in discriminating pitches of tones; he equaled or surpassed 74 per cent in discriminating intensities; etc. (Seashore, C. E., *Psychology of Musical Talent*. By per-mission of the publishers, Silver, Burdett & Company, 1919.)

differing in only one respect. The subject is told in what respect they differ, and is instructed to decide which is the more artistic or the more pleasing.

Mechanical aptitudes may be tested with the Minnesota Mechan-ical Ability Tests which include a variety of such problems as intricate form boards, disassembled mechanical things as mouse-trap, monkey wrench, rod and clamp, coin clip, and problems in card-sorting, block-packing, and several paper and pencil language and non-language forms.

LOOKING AHEAD

This chapter has been devoted to the trait of intelligent adapta-tion in human beings as something that is measurable; and space has been given almost exclusively to the methods of the measure-ment rather than to the analysis of what is measured.

As we come to consider again what we mean when we call Mr. X intelligent we find our faces set at least in a general direction. We do not mean that X is very easily aroused emotionally, nor that he has an amiable disposition. We do not mean that his interests are high or are in any particular line. We do not mean that he is muscularly vigorous and strong, nor that he has excellent eyesight and hearing. On the other hand, when we call Mr. X intelligent we may mean that he learns rapidly and easily. We may mean that he remembers things well. We may mean that he can "see into" situations and can size up people. We may mean that he can reason effectively. These, the more intellectual or cognitive functions of man, lie before us for examination.

The I.Q.'s of the girls pictured in Figure 86 are: A, 90; B, 44; C, 98; D, 55. (Cf. footnote, p. 343.)

C A D B
A D C B

REFERENCES

1. Beckham, A. S. Minimum Intelligence Levels for Several Occupations. *Personnel J.*, 1930–31, **9**, 309–13.
2. Garrett, H. E., and Schneck, M. R. *Psychological Tests, Methods, and Results.* Harpers, 1933.
3. Hartson, L. D. Intelligence and Scholarship of Occupational Groups. *Personnel J.*, 1928–29, **7**, 281–85.
4. Jones, H. E., and Conrad, H. S. The Growth and Decline of Intelligence. *Genet. Psychol. Monog.*, 1933, **13**, No. 3.
5. Jordan, A. M. *Educational Psychology.* Holt (revised ed.), 1933.
6. Meier, N. C. *The Meier-Seashore Art Judgment Test.* Bur. Educ. Research, Univ. Iowa, 1929.
7. Miles, W. R., and Miles, C. C. The Correlation of Intelligence Scores and Chronological Age from Early to Late Maturity. *Am. J. Psychol.*, 1932, **44**, 44–78.
8. Paterson, D. G., *et al.* *Minnesota Mechanical Ability Tests.* Univ. Minnesota Press, 1930.
9. Pintner, R. *Intelligence Testing*, 2d ed. Holt, 1931.
10. Pintner, R., and Paterson, D. G. *A Scale of Performance Tests.* Appleton, 1917.
11. Seashore, C. E. *Psychology of Musical Talent.* Silver, Burdette, 1919.
12. Terman, L. M. *The Measurement of Intelligence.* Houghton Mifflin, 1916. *Measuring Intelligence.* Houghton Mifflin, 1937.
13. Terman, L. M., *et al.* *Genetic Studies of Genius*, esp. vol. I. Stanford Univ. Press, 1925.
14. Thorndike, E. L. *The Measurement of Intelligence.* Teachers College, 1927.
15. Vanuxem, M. Education of Feeble-Minded Women. *Teachers Coll. Contribs. to Educ.*, 1925, No. 174.
16. Yerkes, R. M. (ed.). *Psychological Examining in the United States Army, Memoirs Nat. Acad. Sci.*, 1921, **15**.

CHAPTER XIV

FUNDAMENTALS OF LEARNING

IMPORTANCE OF LEARNING IN HUMAN LIFE

Infant Compared with Man. The stork's eye view of the baby, as it has been called, certainly offers to an unimaginative observer little of hopeful interest. The infant is equipped with several physiological organ-systems of *visceral* types. Circulation has long been maintained through fetal stages; respiration was established promptly after birth; ingestion and digestion waited only upon the finding of nourishment; excretion through skin and through colon and bladder are not long delayed. This organism is vegetative, at least. But it cannot seek out its food nor open up an air hole when wrapped too snugly in its blanket nor abate the nuisance of a painful pin. Supplied in advance with crudely operating internal action mechanisms, it has yet to develop its overt reactions out of simple rudiments. We have seen this in Chapter IV.

Four years later the same child will have developed astonishing agility and some precision in his overt performances. He can run smoothly, toss a ball up into the air and sometimes catch it, can call out the conventionalized sound labels or names for all sorts of objects, animals, and persons, and what he himself cannot reach he can let you know he wants in rather definite and unambiguous terms. He is no adult, however. He may still be taking things because he wants them; he may maltreat the cat and bully the smaller boy who lives round the corner. "Conscience," "morality," "modesty," are yet hardly applicable to him, for it is still early to expect him to have put on very elaborate habitual attitudes toward general types of human situations. He is not yet well socialized. Esthetically he is a savage, for "loud" colors and banging noises may be his ideals of beauty. Ink-marks on paper and what he calls the "chicken-tracks" of the morning newspaper are utterly undecipherable. He has then a long way to travel, a great deal of making yet to undergo, before he can call himself a man.

But there is a positive side to the picture of infancy. The sprawling, helpless, random activity is furnishing the raw material for making the individual. Out of this inchoate behavior are to be organized in time such elaborate performances as driving an automobile, making out a bill of sale, delivering a sermon, planning an advertising campaign, instructing the maid how to prepare a new dish, or studying statistical returns and graphing a business cycle. No phenomena of human nature are more significant than the natural processes of learning. Let us study them to derive what principles we can. Under what general conditions does a person learn? What specific factors help and hinder? We may be sure that whatever salient principles or laws may be found will have their place in any art of human prediction and control.

Learning is Habit Building. It is hardly necessary to illustrate the all-pervasiveness of learning and its effects throughout the daily life of any person. Consider, for instance, the ubiquitous character of "habits." In common speech this term is used with primary reference to *overt* learned performances. Of such are throwing, dancing, handwriting, typewriting, speaking, singing, manners of eating, listening to music, and so on. The more technical uses of the word apply it also to implicit (internal, covert) forms of learned performances. There are the various employments of *silent speech* in "mental arithmetic," reading to one's self, telling one's self what one does not care to speak aloud. We shall have occasion to note the formation of habitual *emotional* reactions: a child's fear of "bugs" or of the dark, one man's love for his work, another's extreme self-esteem, still another's super-patriotism. Again, we shall note the organizing of habitual ways of *attending* as well as of *perceiving*: how one man notices the street-car advertisements while the other studies his fellow-man; how a husband may appraise analytically the wines served at a dinner while his wife makes appraisals equally critical of the gowns worn by guests. Still more general habits are the *attitudes* that reveal themselves in the man who shows consistent prejudices against those of alien races or who can be counted upon to explode whenever he hears mention of "communists," or who is for his town or his profession right or wrong. Habits then are of all sorts. There are movements observable in a person a block away. There are also those habits which are hidden away, private activities that may go on without detection by the keenest eye and which may be anything from a set of specific and nearly invariable motions in a handshake to such broad and inclusive manifestations as a general theory or point of view.

In an early chapter (Chapter II) emphasis was laid upon the concept of organismic adjustment as a key to human (and subhuman) behavior or psychology. In following chapters some of the developmental aspects of adjustive behavior have been brought to light: improvement therein has been found to be a result of (*a*) growth and maturing, and also of (*b*) exercise and practice, the two factors being sometimes rather bafflingly intertwined. Major attention was given to the former of these two in Chapter IV, and we shall now study the latter.

Let us recall the description of the adjustment process with the help of the diagram (Figure 90). A motivated person or other organism (1) upon encountering an obstruction or difficulty (2) shows excess and varied activity (3), until perchance one of his variant ways of acting happens to take him around his difficulty (4), and a more nearly optimal situation, or a goal, is obtained (5). It is now high time to observe an additional feature of much behavior of this sort. Upon the person's *again* encountering much the same difficulty the whole story tends to become a shorter one, for he tends to hit upon and utilize the appropriate solution (4) more readily and with less fuss and confusion. Put otherwise, upon repetition of the situation *on succeeding occasions* the individual's adjustment process shows *an increased directness and effectiveness, an economy of effort and of time.*[1] Our problem now is to study at close hand this improvement phenomenon.

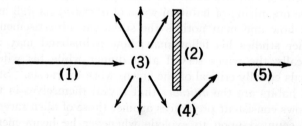

FIGURE 90. DIAGRAM OF ADJUSTIVE BEHAVIOR LEADING TO LEARNING

1, the organism is motivated to respond in the direction 5; when blocked, 2, it makes varied and excess reactions, 3, until by some reaction, 4, it surmounts the obstacle and is readjusted. On later occasions the organism is likely to meet the situation by making the successful response, 4, more and more directly.

---

[1] The reader will not confuse "learning" with other sorts of modification of behavior, such as "fatigue," which is a quite temporary loss of capacity to respond after continued exercise, and "sensory adaptation," which is a temporary "getting used to" a stimulus or situation so that it is no longer effective. The differentiating mark of true learning is, we may say, the test of time.

Plan of the Chapter. No topic of psychological discussion shows more angles and facets than does the problem of learning, both as to broad interpretations and as to detailed findings. Learning, embracing as it does so many phases of life, can be approached from different points of view. This has been true in a notable degree of experimental research on the general topic in different psychological laboratories. *Different ways of viewing the problem* of how learning occurs have led to very *different experimental attacks* and consequently to *different but supplementary results.* The appropriate thing then for us to do is to review these historically distinct lines of research, with the hope of arriving at final generalizations that will characterize the learning process as a whole.

Investigations on subhuman animal forms will figure somewhat largely in our reviews since the earlier experiments were conducted on them because they were simpler than the human forms.

EXPERIMENTS EMPHASIZING INTEGRATION OF PART-REACTIONS

Historically oldest of the experimental approaches to learning was that in which a person or animal was placed in a situation in which he had to learn to react appropriately to many more or less independent stimuli. It was not a situation in which he was able to see, hear, or otherwise apprehend a relationship among the parts; but the part-reactions awakened by these independent stimuli had to become integrated into a complete, smooth-running performance.

In Animal Habit-Forming

The Problem Box Method. The particular experimental problems first attacked grew out of some uncontrolled observations by English psychologists on how a dog came to unlatch the garden gate, a cat to ring a doorbell, or a terrier to await the rebound of a rubber ball thrown against a wall. Such performances, they said, are not to be taken as manifestations of wisdom or intuition or understanding, but simply as the result of previous experiences, in the course of which the various reactions of the animal somehow get organized into a complete performance but without any realization or understanding of it all on the part of the animal. It learns *merely by trial-and-error.*

This view of learning was taken into the laboratory and given experimental justification by Thorndike in America. He introduced the problem box. His method was to put a very hungry cat or dog into a box from which it could escape only by doing some simple act, such as pressing a lever, pulling at a loop of cord, or stepping on a platform. Food was placed outside the box to insure motivation, and the animal's behavior was then closely observed. A record was kept of the time the animal was in the box before it performed the necessary pressing or pulling or stepping. The general arrangement of the door and some of its fastenings, used one at a time, may be understood from Figure 91.

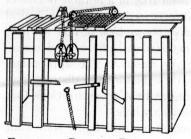

FIGURE 91. PROBLEM BOX USED BY THORNDIKE

(From *Psychol. Monog.*, 1898, **2**, no. 4.)

A learning curve was used to show changes in the amount of time taken by the animal in successive attempts to escape. In Figure 92 is reproduced a sample of Thorndike's curves. Distances on the abscissa represent the order of the trials, distances on the ordinate the amounts of time taken. The rate of decrease of time taken in successive trials is one measure of improvement in forming the habit of escape. From the more or less gradual and irregular slope of the curves Thorndike argued that the animals came to do things by accident rather than

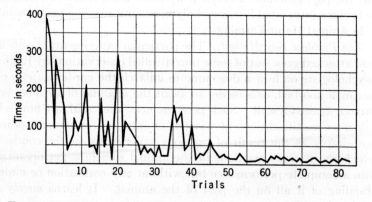

FIGURE 92. CURVE TO SHOW RATE OF LEARNING BY AN ANIMAL IN A PROBLEM BOX

(From Thorndike, *op. cit.*)

by anything like reasoning or understanding. This was certainly in accordance with his observation of their behavior.

When put into the box the cat would show evident signs of discomfort and of an impulse to escape from confinement. It tries to squeeze through any opening; it claws and bites at the bars or wire; it thrusts its paws out through any opening and claws at everything it reaches; it continues its efforts when it strikes anything loose and shaky; it may claw at things within the box.... The vigor with which it struggles is extraordinary. For eight or ten minutes it will claw and bite and squeeze incessantly.... The cat that is clawing all over the box in her impulsive struggle will probably claw the string or loop or button so as [accidentally] to open the door. And gradually all the other non-successful impulses will be stamped out and the particular impulse leading to the successful act will be stamped in ... until, after many trials, the cat will, when put in the box, immediately claw the button or loop in a definite way.... Cats would claw at the loop or button when the door was open.... Cats would paw at the place where a loop had been, though none was there. The reaction was not to a well-discriminated object, but to a vague situation, and any element of the situation may arouse the reaction.

The Maze Method. Another method used early for the analysis of habit formation in animals and destined to become one of the commonest of all laboratory instruments for studying learning, is the maze. Essentially a maze consists of complicated and alternative

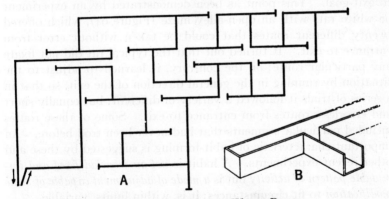

FIGURE 93. A MAZE FOR WHITE RATS

A. Ground plan of the series of pathways, T-choices, and blind alleys. *B.* Detail of construction at a T-choice.

Black curtains were hung in true and blind alleys at frequent intervals; and doors closing automatically behind the animal as it ran prevented retracings. An automatic electrical recording system, as well as an automatic table for introducing a rat at the start of the maze and receiving it at the end (neither apparatus shown here), eliminated the experimenter from the rat's situation. This maze proved to have a reliability (i.e., a correlation between the scores made on odd- and on even-numbered trials) of .987. (From Tolman, E. C., Tryon, R. C., and Jeffress, L. A., *Univ. Calif. Publ. in Psychol.*, 1929, 4, 99–112.)

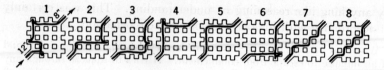

FIGURE 94. AN OPEN-ALLEY MAZE LEARNED AS A VARIABLE HABIT

The tracings are records of the first runs made by one subject. In five of these eight runs the
animal took routes that included segments that had not been taken before. (From Dashiell,
Comp. Psychol. Monog., 1930, **7**, no. 32.)

pathways and blind alleys among which the subject must learn to
find his way from starting point to goal (Figure 93). The progress
of his learning is rated in terms of the decrease in time taken and
in number of errors made (entrances into blind alleys, reversals in
the true path). As in all tests of learning, the subject must be
motivated; the typical condition for a lower form is hunger, with
food incentive at the goal point.

A further point in regard to the maze problem is that the various
twists and turns at different points are not learned separately in
piecemeal fashion and later hitched together, but become established
merely as incidental parts in the main habit of getting from entrance
to exit-goal. This point as been demonstrated by an experiment
on white rats with an open-alley maze (Figure 94), which offered
twenty different routes that could be taken without error from
entrance to exit. It turned out that the typical rat did not fixate.
any particular route; on the contrary, it learned to adjust to the
situation by running in the general direction of the exit, so that in
a series of trials it followed a variety of different, but equally short
and errorless, routes from entrance to exit. Some of these routes
included particular segments that had never been trod before. An
important characteristic of habit-forming is suggested by these and
other recent experiments. A habit is *not an ironclad fixed and im-
mutable pattern of activity* but is *a mode of adjustment capable of some
modification* to fit circumstances; it is, within limits, variable.

In Human Habit-Forming. Doubtless the reader will be inquiring: Does this same phase of learning — selection of the successful variants — hold for human learners as well? Adaptations of
the maze and of the problem box have been made for human subjects; but since an affirmative answer to this query appears in
studies of more elaborate processes which also exhibit some other
significant features, we will find the latter more interesting.

An early quantitative study of improvement in a human function is that of Bryan and Harter on *telegraphy*. Student telegraphers were tested each week on their rates of sending or receiving messages in the Morse code of dots and dashes, and their rates were plotted. Figure 95 shows some receiving curves that were typical. The subject was tested each week on (*a*) his rate of receiving letters not making words, (*b*) his rate of receiving letters making words but not sentences, (*c*) his rate of receiving letters in words and sentences. If we examine the curves closely we see that they check very well with the testimony of many experienced operators who had reported: "(*a*) At the outset one 'hustles for the letters.' (*b*) Later one is 'after words.' (*c*) The fair operator is not held so closely to words. He can take in several words at once, a phrase, or even a short sentence. (*d*) The real expert has all the details of the language with such automatic perfection that he gives them practically no attention at all," and in taking down the message he "prefers to keep six to ten or twelve words behind the instrument." As the experimenters conclude:

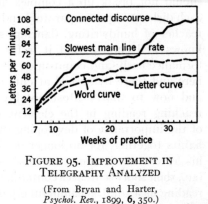

FIGURE 95. IMPROVEMENT IN TELEGRAPHY ANALYZED

(From Bryan and Harter, *Psychol. Rev.*, 1899, **6**, 350.)

All the facts point to the conclusion that the telegrapher must acquire, besides letter, syllable, and word habits, an array of higher language habits, associated with the combination of words in connected discourse. Mastery of the telegraphic language involves mastery of the habits of all orders ... a hierarchy.... *A hierarchy of habits* may be described in this way: (1) There is a certain number of habits which are elementary constituents of all the other habits within the hierarchy. (2) There are habits of a higher order which, embracing the lower as elements, are themselves in turn elements of higher habits, and so on. (3) A habit of any order, when thoroughly acquired, has ... psychological unity. The habits of lower order which are its elements tend to lose themselves in it, and it tends to lose itself in habits of higher order when it appears as an element therein.

It would be a mistake to assume that different levels of habits are organized one after the other: letters being learned first, then words, then phrases and sentences. The parallel rises of the three plotted curves correspond rather to the testimony of all operators that the letter-habit, the word-habit, and the higher-habit all show improvement *simultaneously*, if not equally; and from the earliest practice, they all gain fastest when practiced together in connected discourse.   In practical daily life it is a fairly general rule that one should not break up a complex act with the intention of drilling each dislocated part separately and reassembling them later.   Every teacher of handwriting, dancing, swimming, tennis, and even golf knows well enough that it is far better to tackle the whole per-formance early and count upon the elimination of inefficient moves here and there by special attention from time to time, now to this and now to that.   Most notably of all, the modern methods of teaching reading in the elementary school show this recognition of the importance of developing the simpler and the more complex habits together, for no longer does the child have first to learn all his letters one by one, then isolated words, "cat," "rat," "cow," etc., then short sentences containing these: from the first he practices reading as a total, meaningful organic kind of process.   (The reader will observe that this is really a confirmation of a point made earlier in reference to animal learning.)

The presence of these different levels of habits within one and the same total performance is easily enough demonstrated.   For example, *substitution* material was once used with two groups of subjects.   Each was provided with a code of the following type:

1	2	3	4	5	6	7	8	9	10
n	x	p	e	h	s	d	v	l	r

and was to write under each digit appearing on a large printed sheet the appropriate letter in the code.   While one group of subjects used the *same code throughout* the eighteen days of the experiment, the other group were given *a new code each day*.   We may say that the former group were to learn to substitute in-this-general-situa-tion but also to learn for permanent use one single letter for each digit, whereas the latter group learned to substitute in-this-general-situation but had to learn on each day the new specific letter for each digit.   Both practiced the same higher-level habit, then, but only the second group had to learn new lower-level habits.   As could easily be predicted, the rate of improvement by the latter group was a slower one.   When it came to a final test on a new code for both groups, however, the latter were better prepared for the shift and easily made the better score.   Perhaps they had all the while been developing a high-level habit in the form of a readiness-to-shift-from-code-to-code [11].

Before going on we should pause to remind ourselves that in learning such performances as telegraphing, typewriting, and substituting the human being is forced to work predominantly on the trial-and-error plane.   He must "hunt and peck," try this and that, over and over again, until in the course of an enormous number of repetitions his persistence will be rewarded by an increasing number of "hits" and a decreasing number of "misses," as the appropriate reactions become selected and established.

The Secondary Rôle of the Subject's Conscious Awareness. How, now, does this "selection" we have frequently referred to come about?   Does the practicing person attentively regard every detail of his own movements and upon recognizing the good and the bad bid the former be repeated and the latter dropped?   By no means.   As one experimenter writes: "A significant fact about learning typewriting is that all adaptations and short cuts in method were unconsciously made, that is, *fallen into by the learners quite unintentionally....* The learners suddenly noticed that they were doing certain parts of the work in a new and better way."   Consider a few scraps from his subject's reports "I have unconsciously learned to let my fingers remain on the last key struck.... This helps me greatly in locating the keys.   All I know about the way this new adaptation was made is that I unexpectedly noticed that I was letting my fingers remain on the keys.... As soon as I noticed it I recognized its advantage and tried purposely to adopt it, but found that I must more or less let it work itself out."   "The change was not premeditated in any sense.   I simply happened to notice that I was doing it this way and how much better it was, so purposely adopted it."   "All improvements in my method are unconsciously made" [7].

The same fact was quite clearly exhibited in subjects who were practicing the art of ball-tossing, in which they caught and threw one ball while the other was in the air.   "In avoiding errors," writes Swift, "there was adaptation to conditions apparently more organic than conscious, and often so delicate as to elude observation.   B, for example, found himself tossing high in order to have time to recover from a difficult situation, and at another time he caught himself putting his body into a more alert position by slightly raising himself on his toes.   Then he realized that he had been doing it for several days.   So far as he could determine *his consciousness had no originating part* in it.   All the subjects improved by hitting upon better ways of working without any further conscious selection than the general effort to succeed" [32].

The Importance of Motivation in Learning. This, however, is not to say that the subject's attitude, intentions, and interest are unimportant.   Indeed it is a cardinal principle that if there are to be "trials" and "errors" and "successes" the subject must *try.*

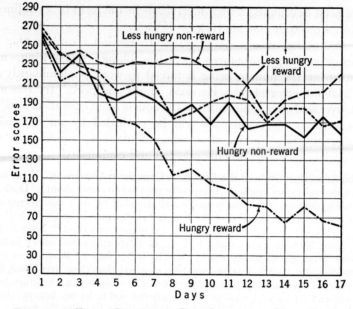

FIGURE 96. ERROR CURVES FOR RATS LEARNING A MAZE UNDER
DIFFERENT CONDITIONS OF MOTIVATION

"Hungry reward" animals: no feeding until maze run completed, then full rations.
"Hungry non-reward" animals: no feeding before run nor after.
"Less hungry reward" animals: part rations before run, remainder after.
"Less hungry non-reward" animals: part rations before run, none after.
    The organic condition of hunger is of primary importance (to get the subject going); and the
attainment of a goal or reward is also important for the selection of the more adjustive responses
to take place on ensuing trials. (From Tolman and Honzik, *Univ. of California Publ. in Psychol.*,
1930, **4**, 246; also in Tolman, *op. cit.*)

must be active.   Excellent illustrations of this fact are afforded in
the animal experiments; and we should take time for one.   Figure
96 tells the story clearly.   A double condition of motivation must
be provided.   An organic "drive" must be operating, else the rats
will not exert themselves, will not try in the first place; and an external "incentive" must be present, else they will not come to select
and fixate certain pathways out of the total lot because none are
"adaptive" or "successful."

    Every teacher knows this to be true of her child subjects — that
they must show some kind of inner urgings and must receive some
kind of encouragement of personal or impersonal nature.   If experimental verification be desired it is to be found in abundance.
For example, college students were given protracted series of trials

to improve their work in (*a*) writing *a*'s, (*b*) canceling letters, (*c*) substituting letters for digits, and (*d*) multiplying silently two two-place numbers.   The subjects were divided into two groups, one as a "motivated" and the other as a "control" group, their rôles being reversed on the tenth trial while the experiments were still in progress.   The members of each motivated group were led to take interest and make effort by counting and recording their own scores, by constant verbal assurances of the possibilities of their improvement, by instructions to be on the alert for anything that might come to light to facilitate their learning; while those of the control group were told to pay no attention whatever to the scores made or to the rate of improvement.   The resulting data showed that the motivated groups in all experiments made rapid and continuous gains in both amount and accuracy, in decided contrast to the work of the same subjects when acting as control groups on the same tests.   Results from one of the experiments are shown in Figure 97.   But the arousal of interest and effort was found not to have equal effect on the work of different individuals.   It became apparent that this attitude made for improvement only as it led the subject to discover for himself the *more efficient means and methods*.

For one thing, we can see that the devices resorted to by these experimenters were calculated to set up and maintain the *emotional* condition that would best support intensive work, "confidence," "interest in making good scores," and the like.   This is a general

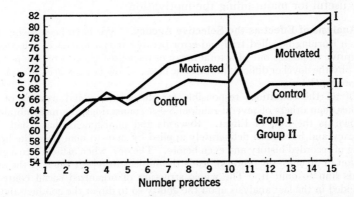

FIGURE 97. IMPROVEMENT IN WRITING *a*'s WITH AND WITHOUT SPECIAL INCENTIVES

(From Book and Norvell, *Ped. Sem.*, 1922, **29**.)

principle applicable to all kinds of work, whether improvement is or is not involved. In the second place, these devices were calculated to direct the subject's *attending* toward the variations in his mode of attack so that there might be a more prompt and alert recognizing and selecting of adaptive variants — a facilitating of these fundamental processes involved in learning. Two main things, then, on the part of the subject's condition and attitude are to be guarded: the emotional and the attentional.

In general — although not invariably — the emotions or moods most favorable to work of any sort will be those favorable to acquiring new habits. "It is intense effort that educates," said Bryan and Harter; but Swift found rather that "steady and calm intensity counts for progress." In advance of highly definite and detailed knowledge, but in the light of observations in and out of the psychological laboratory, we may hold that, for learning, optimal emotional reactions are (1) those that involve some but not too great excitement and (2) those of the sthenic rather than asthenic type ("ambition," "confidence," "liking the work," "wanting to beat others," and so on, rather than "discouragement," "staleness," and the like). Many are the tricks of the trade that are useful here. A few suggestions are offering prizes, stimulating rivalry by division of a group into sections, assuring the learner that he is doing well, that he can do still better on the next few trials, and promising rewards rather than punishments. The resourceful and intelligent learner or teacher will find no lack of devices that are useful for maintaining the motivation.

Analysis of Effect as the Selective Agency. We have been seeing that much learning is called trial-and-error because it is a matter of selection of adaptive responses out of a total array of responses aroused on the person's part by the novel or difficult problem he faces. Now *just how does this selecting come about?*

Of all the conditions responsible for the selecting and fixating of one rather than others of several random $S \rightarrow R$ connections, the most notable is known as the Law of Effect. Rewards and punishments have had their efficacy and have been deliberately applied by man to man from the beginning of recorded history and even before. The one, when attached to a given action (a given $S \rightarrow R$ process), leads the subject to repeat the act; the other leads him to omit it. The whole structure of organized social control is founded in the last analysis upon the ability so to direct the conduct and the resulting habits of individuals. The effectiveness of these factors in the control of what a person learns to do from infancy up is so universally evident as to call for little special illustration here. Food, confinement, flogging, gold medals, cookies, scolding, bruised hands and heads — of such does much of the guidance of life consist. As a general principle of observation there is no denying the Law of Effect.

Suppose we try to dig to the roots of the matter. For this we shall have need of a concept that has been mentioned in earlier connections (pp. 119, 271) and is to be given in more detail in the next section of the present chapter, that of "conditioning." Briefly stated it is: "If an indifferent stimulus be present many times along with one that is already arousing a given response, the indifferent stimulus may acquire potency to arouse that response when presented alone." We will need also to remind ourselves of the concepts of "re-enforcement" and "inhibition" of one reaction by another (p. 271).

Let us consider a classical example from Lloyd Morgan. To some chicks he tossed cinnabar caterpillars, conspicuously marked with rings of black and yellow, and distasteful to chicks. These were seized at once, but dropped again uninjured. The chicks wiped their bills and seldom touched the caterpillars a second time. The cinnabar larvæ were then removed, and later in the day thrown in again. Some of the chicks pecked at them once, but soon they were left alone. The next day, when a caterpillar was again thrown in one chick ran for it, but, checking himself, refused to touch it and wiped his bill. Another seized it and dropped it at once. A third was seen to approach a caterpillar that was crawling along, then to sound the danger note and make off. The mechanisms of conditioning are not hard to discern here. S (worm seen) arouses the R (pecking); but the latter action sets up the S (worm tasted) which arouses the R (dropping, wiping bill, and so forth); and the original S becomes conditioned to the latter R, thus inhibiting the antagonistic former R. The chick has learned to give a negative or avoiding response upon sight of a cinnabar caterpillar and not to give a positive approaching response.

How, let us ask now, does a reward operate? In the baby this process, too, can be observed. Let us spy upon him on the occasion of his first acquaintance with a milk bottle (or when older with a piece of an orange or candy). The stage is set for a simple learning process. The S (bottle or orange seen and touched) will provoke the R (clasping and mouthing); then a new S (tasting) appears and arouses the R (feeding); whereupon the latter R may be expected to become conditioned to the former S. Sight of bottle or food now directly excites the positive feeding reaction and its allied reactions, clasping and mouthing.

To one and the same infant, then, the hot radiator has functioned as a punishment, the bottle or food as a reward. The former, by leading to the fixation of negative reactions, led to the elimination of the antagonistic positive ones. The latter led to the fixation of positive reactions. Or, to put it in another way: the punishment incurred in the former R led to its elimination; the reward obtained by the latter R led to its fixation.

Now let us put the gist of the last few paragraphs into a nutshell. *If to a situation S_1 a given R_1 is made which brings about a condition that stimulates an ANTAGONISTIC R_2 that has right of way, the original S_1 becomes conditioned to R_2 and thus INHIBITS R_1. On the other hand, if to a situation S_1 a given R_1 is made which brings about a condition that stimulates an ALLIED R_3, the original S_1 becomes conditioned to R_3 and thus RE-ENFORCES R_1.*

In passing let us recognize that many of the reactions eliminated in time are not such as bring about punishment and the $R's$ which are antagonistic thereto. Many false moves of the human hand in learning to write or the human voice in memorizing, many wasted movements in reversals and blind alleys by the maze-running animal, may not be of that sort. They may become "neglected," disused by reason of the selection and fixation of the efficient and adaptive $R's$ — and in this sense they may be "inhibited" by "antagonistic" $R's$. Interpreted broadly, the statement in the preceding paragraph may be used to cover this variety of elimination.[1]

While we are speaking of these excessive $R's$, it should be pointed out that almost never are all of them eliminated from a habit that is being formed. Industrial psychologists have, through their employment of the cinematograph in motion study, discovered that almost any expert workman with years of experience behind him has all the while carried along with him various superfluous motions in his work. One such study of bricklaying procedure led to retraining that resulted in a reduction of the motions made from 18 to 5, at the same time increasing the output from 120 to 350 bricks per hour (Gilbreth). So, too, with occupations involving more implicit reactions. The president of a prominent university cannot rid himself of habits of attending to minute and unimportant details, such as the manner of parking motor cars on the campus; and the dean of a well-known college is unable to delegate to a subordinate the laborious computation of grade averages of prospective Phi Beta Kappa candidates. The present writer once had a class of forty school superintendents and high-school principals and teachers, each of whom, for from fifteen to thirty years, had been adding and teaching pupils to add. Yet, when given a five-minute test in adding, which was repeated for a total of nineteen days, making in all just one hour and thirty-five minutes of practice, these "seasoned" adders improved their speed by fifty-five per cent, with no loss in accuracy. They testified to many devices hit upon and many superfluous methods eliminated. That was fifteen years ago: probably by this time most of them have backslidden to their more easy-going and "good-enough" methods.

Different Types of Trial-and-Error. Throughout this section of the present chapter the idea of random behavior, expressed in different ways, has been invoked repeatedly. In all likelihood the

---

[1] The writer believes that it may still be debatable whether even such "excessive" $R's$ are not separated by degree rather than by kind from the punishment-earning $R's$. Such seems one possible inference from Kuo's experiment in which rats were found to eliminate earliest those turns leading to electric shock, next those leading to confinement, and last those leading into excessively long alleys to food.

reader has had some qualms and misgivings. Can it really be, he would ask, that trial-and-error is qualitatively identical, one and the same kind of behavior, with all subjects and at all times? Surely, he will claim, the trials made by a paramecium, a frog, and a man will not be really the same; and even in the same person they will differ vastly in character at different times, as when he is drowning, when he is hungry, when suffering toothache, when in a helpless rage.

A particularly relevant and convincing experiment on the question was conducted by Hamilton when he devised a procedure for bringing to light *qualitatively different sorts or types of trial-and-error* efforts, and *with different human and sub-human* subjects. The floor plan of his "quadruple choice" apparatus is reproduced in Figure 98. (It was built in various sizes.) The subject was admitted at *Ent.*, and upon advancing to point *O* found himself equidistant from four swinging exit doors, *1, 2, 3, 4*. Three of these doors were locked, and the subject had to find the unlocked one to reach his food or other reward. On the next trial that door was locked, and some other was unlocked; and so on for a series of trials, no door being unlocked on two successive trials. Now, the order of unlocking was settled by chance so that not even the cleverest genius could "catch on" to it; and thus the subject, whoever or whatever he might be, was forced to resort to some kind of searching or try, try again.

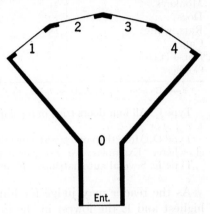

FIGURE 98. THE QUADRUPLE CHOICE APPARATUS

(Explanation in text.) (From Hamilton, G. V., *J. Anim. Behav.*, 1911, **1**, 33–66.)

It was the *kinds* of searching used that form the heart of the story. Hamilton classified them into five types, as follows:

Type A: The three inferentially possible doors tried once each, the previously unlocked door being avoided. Examples (assuming *2* to have been unlocked last trial): *3–4–1* or *1–3–4*.

Type B: All four doors tried, once each, in irregular order. Examples: *3–4–2–1* or *4–2–1–3*.

DIFFERENT TYPES OF TRIAL-AND-ERROR IN DIFFERENT SUBJECTS *

SUBJECTS	DISTRIBUTION OF REACTIONS IN PERCENTAGES				
	A	B	C	D	E
Human Adults.........	76	20	2	2	0
Children (3–12 y.)	34	3	30	25	8
Infant (1 case)...	16	5	19	26	34
Monkeys...............	21	23	20	29	7
Dogs..................	12	22	0	34	32
Rats, white............	15	5	11	19	50
Cats..................	9	20	4	27	40
Horse (1 case)..........	8	4	2	24	62
Gophers...............	7	2	2	8	81

* From Hamilton, G. V., *J. Anim. Behav.*, 1911, **1**, 33–66, and *Behav. Monog.*, 1916. **3**, No. 13.

Type C: All four doors tried in regular order R to L or L to R.   Examples: *1–2–3–4* or *4–3–2–1*.

Type D: More than one try at same door, though with an intervening trial elsewhere.   Examples: *1–2–3–1–4* or *4–3–4–3–2–1*.

Type E: Several automatisms.   Examples: *1–1–2–3–4* or *3–4–4–4–1–2*.

As the reader may judge for himself, A would appear to be the highest and E the lowest in the intelligence scale.   Now compare the frequencies with which different kinds of subjects revealed these different levels of searching, as presented in the table.   It becomes apparent immediately that the sort of try, try again behavior that appears when an organism is maladjusted will depend upon what kind of organism it is, upon its mental development, and will vary by degrees from the stupid repetitious pushing against the same door to a process of rational inference.

The type of behavior varies for the same individual, too.   One's effectiveness in trial reactions suffers reduction when he is worked up emotionally.   This has been aptly shown by an extension of the above experiment.   College students, after being put through a control series similar to those above described, were then tested again in the same apparatus but under conditions arousing high degrees of emotional excitement.   From the moment of arriving at *O* until escaping through the one unlocked door, they were subjected to (*a*) a shower, (*b*) electric shocks applied to the feet, or (*c*) the loud noise of an automobile horn.   All three of these stimuli con-tinued to have their exciting effect throughout the series.   The results, as appearing in the second table, are eloquent.   Emotion clearly has a disorganizing effect upon the individual's responses,

DIFFERENT TYPES OF TRIAL-AND-ERROR IN DIFFERENT STATES OF
THE SAME SUBJECTS *

CONDITIONS OF THE SUBJECTS	DISTRIBUTION OF REACTIONS IN PERCENTAGES				
	A	B	C	D	E
Normal, "control"........	60	29	10	0	1
Emotional excitement.....	16	14	10	3	57

* From Patrick, J. R., *J. Comp. Psychol.*, 1934, **18**, 1–22, 153–95.

and the level of his trial-and-error behavior is reduced to that of
much lower animal species.   More generally, *different types of trial-
and-error are shown by the same individual in different conditions and
situations.*

EXPERIMENTS EMPHASIZING SPECIFIC REACTIONS TO SPECIFIC STIMULI

The Experiments of Pavlov.   Another way of envisaging the
facts of human learning has had its origin in laboratories in Russia.
Everyone knows, of course, that when a small boy smells food saliva
is secreted in excess amounts — his "mouth waters."   This is easy
to understand as a glandular reflex action.   But his mouth will
water also when he and his playmates are describing their favorite
pies and puddings.   And the same response is excitable, especially
in adults, by yet more insubstantial and non-nourishing stimuli:
as the reader can doubtless observe in himself as he merely reads or
talks about the act of eating and about the process of salivary flow.
The phenomenon of mouth-watering at smell, taste, or sight of
food is observable in other organisms as well, and the Russian
physiologist, Pavlov, set himself to an experimental study of its
occurrence in the dog.   An incision was made through the dog's
cheek or chin, the end of one of the salivary ducts was carried
through to the outside, and over the opening of the duct a small
glass bulb was hermetically sealed.   (Cf. Figure 99.)   From the
bulb led two tubes, one permitting the drawing off of the collected
saliva after an observation was completed, the other connecting with
a horizontal glass manometer filled with a colored liquid.   As saliva
flowed into the bulb the air in the tube displaced the colored liquid
along a scale graduated in 1/100 cc. divisions.

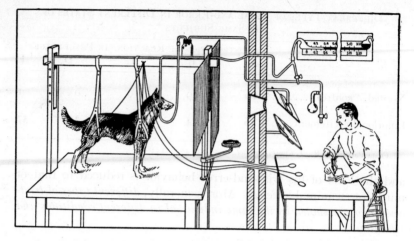

FIGURE 99. PAVLOV'S ARRANGEMENT FOR A SALIVARY CONDITIONED
REFLEX IN THE DOG

In this figure the incidental stimuli to be employed are tactual, at shoulder and hip, and are under control at the experimenter's table. (From Pavlov, *Lectures on Conditioned Reflexes*, International Publishers, 1928.)

The dog was first trained to stand quietly in a room soundproof and free from all distracting stimuli, by being fed (in some of the experiments) from a dish swung around in front of him under the control of the experimenter. The experimenter sat in another room with electric or pneumatic control of all other stimuli to be presented, and through periscopic lenses and mirrors was able to observe by eye the general behavior of the animal.

The procedure of conditioning or formal training was as follows (with variations). With the dog alert and attentive to the usual food source some extraneous stimulation was given him before the food appeared — sound of a metronome, of a buzzer or bell, pressure or irritant applied to the skin, a flash of light, or other stimulus to which the dog did not make a salivary response, however much he might prick up his ears or show tension in neck and leg muscles or change his breathing or make other negligible responses. Shortly after this incidental or "conditioned" stimulus was started, the original or "unconditioned" stimulus of food was presented, whereupon the animal of course made the usual eating responses, including a copious flowing of saliva. On frequent repetitions of the situation, however, with the sound or contact or light presented each

time just before or along with the food, it came about that eventually the former developed potency to arouse the salivary response when given alone.   The general principle suggested by this finding is: *A stimulus arousing a particular response may come to arouse another response if the stimulus is presented many times along with the stimulus to the second response.*   The phenomenon is schematically shown in Figure 100, in terms of the familiar S $\longrightarrow$ R symbols.   Let S_A represent the adequate or original stimulus evoking reflexly the glandular reaction R_G.   Let S_I represent one of the many incidental physical conditions (as sound of a bell) present along with the original stimulus, but tending to arouse, say, a pricking of the ears or some heightening of tonicity of neck muscles.   If S_I be presented with sufficient frequency along

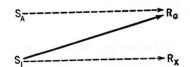

FIGURE 100.   DIAGRAM OF THE CONDITIONING PROCESS
(Explanation in text.)

with S_A, eventually S_I when presented alone will then excite R_G; and a conditioned response will have been formed, as represented by the continuous line. S_I is then a substitute stimulus to R_G; and R_G is a substitute response to S_I.

Other Experimentation with Conditioning.   While Pavlov was at work in Leningrad, another eminent Russian, Bekhterev, was studying essentially the same phenomenon at Moscow, though called by him "association reflexes," and involving *muscular* reflexes in *man*.   He took for his original stimulus-response the retraction of the foot to an electric shock, and for his incidental stimulus-response the general and mild reaction — which did not include retraction of the foot — to the sound of a bell.   He found that after repeated combined stimulations of bell sound and shock the subject became trained to the point where the bell sound alone was sufficient to produce foot-withdrawal.   Successful conditioning required from 1 to 11 experimental sessions, each session including 100–150 trials; and the first appearance of the conditioned response ordinarily was not made until after at least 200 or 300 trials.

Many other kinds of reactions in man have been demonstrated as subject to conditioning.   A few of the more different ones may be briefly mentioned, so that we may note their variety.   The salivary *glandular* response in human beings has been studied especially in the child (Krasnogorski; Winsor).   The saliva was caught in a vessel held by suction over the normal opening of the duct, and drained through a tube leading from the mouth.   The *withdrawal* from shock of *hand* instead of foot was worked on by Bekhterev, and in America (after Watson) it has become almost a standardized procedure, in which variations of the finger electrode are used as shown in Figure 101.   The

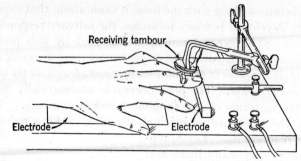

Receiving tambour

Electrode   Electrode

Secondary of inductorium

FIGURE 101. WATSON'S ARRANGEMENT FOR A MOTOR CONDITIONED
REFLEX IN MAN

A large electrode is placed under the hand, and a small electrode under the finger. When the key, in the experimenter's room, is pressed down by the operator the secondary current from the inductorium passes between the electrodes through the finger, causing a reflex jerking up of the latter. Over the back of the finger is mounted a tambour (rubber-faced air chamber) which is in pneumatic connection with a recording tambour operating a marker on a kymograph drum. The closing of the circuit and the presentation of the incidental stimulus are also recorded on the kymograph by markers operating electrically or pneumatically. Thus a graphic record of shock stimulus, of incidental stimulus, and of reaction are graphically recorded. (From Watson, J. B., *Psychol. Rev.*, 1916, **23**, 105.)

reflex *winking* of the *eyelid* to a puff of air on the eyeball, to a threatened blow, to cutaneous pain, or to a snapping sound has been conditioned to other stimuli such as a previously neutral sound or light (Figure 102). The *breathing* apparatus, always a sensitive index of motor conditions of the body, has not only been found relatively easy to hitch to new substitute stimuli, so that the substitutes come to excite greater amount and greater irregularity in the breathing, but has also been found frequently present along with other reactions to complicate the picture. (Cf. Figure 103.) Still other types of responses will be mentioned in succeeding paragraphs.

A Caution Concerning Interpretations. The reader may profit by a warning. From the foregoing descriptions of the conditioning process he may yet carry away an inadequate notion of it. Let us return to Pavlov's original experiment. After training, we saw, a dog's salivary reaction would appear in response not only to food stimuli, but even to such an artificially provided stimulus as the sound of a bell. How are we to account for this? The reader is likely to fall back on a popular explanation and say that, when the dog hears the bell, he remembers that bell and food went together and so reacts to the former as to the latter — just as the hungry boarder on hearing the dinner gong is likely to say to himself, "The bell; that's dinner; let's go and eat." To apply this interpretation

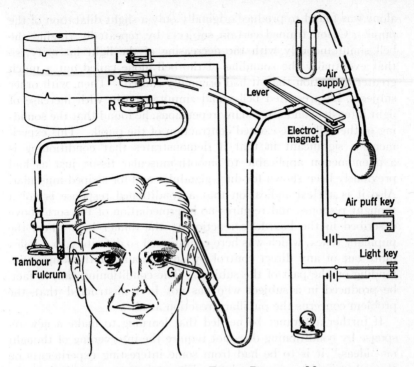

FIGURE 102. THE AIR-PUFF EYELID-RESPONSE METHOD

For the *unconditioned stimulus,* a puff of air from the air supply is delivered to the cornea of the left eye through a glass tube. This is automatically recorded on the revolving drum by the tambour *P.* The puff is controlled at the experimenter's key, which operates an electromagnet and a lever that releases air through the tube.

For the *conditioned stimulus,* a light is flashed when the light key is closed. This is recorded by the signal marker *L.*

The *response* measured is the winking of the eye. A fine wire balanced on a fulcrum is attached at one end to the eyelid and at the other to the rubber membrane of a receiving tambour. This is in pneumatic connection with a recording tambour *R,* which thus records the response. (An alternative method of recording the response is with an artificial paper eyelash that crosses a beam of light playing on traveling sensitized paper.)

(Adapted and combined from photographs kindly furnished by Dr. C. L. Hull and Dr. D. G. Marquis, and from a description in Bernstein, A. L., *J. Gen. Psychol.,* 1934, **10**, 173-97.)

to the phenomenon of conditioning, however, would be utterly false: once an S —→ R connection has been made by conditioning, it is not one mediated by any thinking process, it is direct.

An excellent clinching of this point is afforded in Cason's experimental study of the pupillary reflex. As is well known, increase or decrease of the intensity of light falling upon the retina respectively excites contraction or dilatation of the pupil. The sound of a bell alone was found to produce originally only a slight dilatation of the pupil. Cason trained certain subjects by repeatedly ringing the bell simultaneously with the decreasing of the light intensity, so that eventually the sounding of the bell alone called out a much greater dilatation than it had originally caused. Then, with other subjects, he presented bell-sound simultaneously with increase of light intensity; and after many repetitions, he found that the sounding of the bell alone excited contraction of the pupil. This experiment is significant in that it demonstrates that conditioning is a phenomenon applicable to smooth-muscular tissue just as had previously been shown for duct-glandular and for striped-muscular. Also it is a clear indication that a conditioned response is not a thought response and requires no intermediation of the sort above described in the boarder's reaction to the dinner bell. For, the pupillary reflex, which was here conditioned so definitely, is a reflex quite out of any direct control by any amount of thinking or intending on the part of the subject. The conditioning can, in fact, be produced in a subject who has not been instructed that the problem concerns the pupillary reaction at all.

If further assurance be needed that learning to make a new response by conditioning does not require the intervening of thought or "ideas," it is to be had from some interesting experiments on the galvanic skin response [18]. Electrodes were attached to the foot of infants who were only three to nine months old, and it was found that a galvanic skin response (G.S.R.) could be elicited by a tactual stimulation akin to tickling applied to the arm. Then along with this tactual stimulation the infant was presented a tapping sound or a dull-glowing lamp which originally had excited only interested exploratory eye-movements or smiling and chuckling with no G.S.R. at all: after a sufficient number of such combinations the tapping alone or the glow alone was sufficient to set up the G.S.R. If one bears in mind the character of the G.S.R. this result becomes interesting in several ways: it was a demonstration of conditioning of emotional processes; it was successfully performed on young babies; it involved a reflex process of which even the adult subject is never directly aware and, for these reasons, it was clear evidence of the independence of conditioning from any ideas or thought control or conscious intentions.

Some Special Phenomena and Principles. So far we have but touched on the general fact of the conditioned response (C.R.). Out of the very abundance of researches by Pavlov and the many Russian workers inspired by him, an impressive series of special points has been developed. Many of these points have been confirmed in America by work on the foot-withdrawal reflex in sheep [21]; and some of them have had intensive examination in human subjects by other Americans. These principles form the bulk of current discussions of conditioning by psychologists; and they will be found to have importance in our understanding not alone of learning but also of human behavior in general. Their peculiar interest and value lie in their highly analytic biological character. We shall not have space for much more than a listing of the more significant ones.

In the process of formation, a C.R. usually appears irregularly and then in increasing degrees of frequency and of intensity, so that *learning curves* can be plotted to show the gradual building up of the process. There are exceptional cases, however, in which the C.R. appears to have been suddenly established definitely at one time.

The C.R. in its early stages is aroused by *general* and *non-specific stimuli*. In one investigation [3], along with a shock stimulus applied to the wrist that aroused a G.S.R., a tapping stimulus was applied to the shoulder, until the subject was trained to the point where the shoulder-tapping served as an effective substitute stimulus. After this was well established it was found that the same sort of tactile stimulus would be effective if applied at the small of the back, on the thigh, or on the calf of the leg, though it decreased in degrees of effectiveness with remoteness from the point originally conditioned. The conclusion follows that the C.R. was really established not simply to a tactual stimulus at one particular local point on the shoulder but to that general sort of tactual stimulus applied to the skin generally. Taken in conjunction with studies on dogs, this experiment leads to the broad statement that any C.R. in its early stages is a response *to a general type of stimulation*. Analogues of this principle abound in everyday life: if snapped at by one dog, a child fears all dogs; one who has learned a musical tune in one key perceives the same tune in another key; to recognize the word "cat" the letters need not be of one specific size or type-face. This point will turn out to have considerable theoretical value for us.

It is of great practical importance to the experimenter to bear

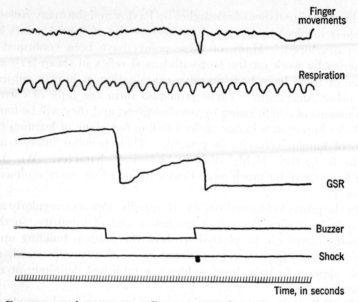

FIGURE 103. ANTICIPATORY CHARACTER IN SOME COMPONENTS OF A
CONDITIONED RESPONSE

The response to a buzzer sounding for 30 seconds before being accompanied by a shock to the
finger.   Note that on this the third presentation of buzzer-followed-by-shock a disturbance
of respiration and a sudden alteration of skin resistance occur at the first appearance of the
buzzer, even though the finger jerk does not occur until the shock (*i.e.*, the latter is not yet conditioned).   (From Liddell, H. S., "The Conditioned Reflex," in *Comparative Psychology* (Moss,
ed.), Prentice-Hall.)

in mind that to get the simple-appearing results ordinarily described
for the C.R., the experimenter is compelled to *isolate* his subjects
from all extraneous stimulus sources, and must train him to remain
in a state of alert quiet.   The subject may be truthfully said to be
responding to the whole environment, but the environment is now
artificially simplified on one localized reaction element alone.

On the motor side, also, the simplicity of the C.R. has been much
exaggerated.   In reality, there is in the beginning *a diffusion of the
reaction.*   This is rather clearly shown in Figure 103, in which the
effect of the conditioned stimulus, a buzzer, is seen not only in
finger movement but also in change of breathing and in the G.S.R.
And who knows how many other participating reaction segments
might be brought to light out of the total conditioned response if
still other instrumentation were employed?

The conditioning phenomenon is usually studied with reference to the narrowest and simplest movements, reflexes; yet the evidence seems to indicate that what goes by the name of conditioned reflex is not a true reflex. At least it is *different from the original reflex* for which it acts as a substitute. Its latent time (time required for getting into action) is longer and is more like that of a simple voluntary reaction (*supra*, p. 45) [5, 16]. It may be different qualitatively, also, as in the cases where a stroking of the sole of the foot produced an unconditioned toe reaction of flexion, whereas a buzzer sound that had become a substitute stimulus elicited a conditioned toe reaction of extension [31].

In the presentation of the two kinds of stimuli, positive results in training seem to depend upon the presentation of the new incidental stimulus *preceding* or *simultaneously with* the original stimulus, never subsequent to it. Thus, if we plan to train a subject to make a flexion movement of the left arm whenever he hears a buzzer, we should sound the buzzer ahead of or along with the sending of the induction shock. In this connection we should take note of a fact of weighty import for a final understanding of the biological nature of the C.R. Conditioned salivary, winking, respiratory, galvanic, and other responses come to appear at moments *in advance* of the unconditioned stimuli to which they originally responded. It therefore seems that the substitute stimulus functions as a *sign* or *signal* or warning, and that the substitute response is much like a *preparatory kind of behavior* in which the organism gets itself ready to avoid a noxious or to welcome a favorable change in its situation.

C.R.'s are formed that are not only excitatory but *inhibitory* in their action. Several types of inhibition were worked out by Pavlov and have been found also in human subjects. (1) When a C.R. is frequently repeated without ever any renewed coupling with the original stimulus (no re-enforcement), it may appear to lose its conditioned effect, to undergo *extinction*. This is not a true "wearing out," however, for after a rest period of a day or week or even more it will spontaneously reappear and in strength. (2) What is more, this "extinguished" state is often set aside by some new extraneous stimulus that appears to release the reflex from a kind of inhibition. In other words, we have an example of inhibition of an inhibition, or *disinhibition*.

A good example of both (1) and (2) is found in an experiment on college students. A G.S.R. was first conditioned to a previously neutral faint light which had frequently accompanied a shock. Then the conditioned light stimulus was repeatedly presented alone until the G.S.R. weakened and "died out." But then a raucous buzzer was sounded, with the effect of reinstating the G.S.R. somewhat. It, too, was "extinguished" by repeated presentation of the light alone; but after an interval of time it spontaneously reappeared. The accompanying tabulation may make this story clearer.

SOME STAGES IN EXTINCTION AND DISINHIBITION *

Stimuli Used in Practice	Eventual Result on the G.S.R. to Light	Phenomenon Illustrated
Shock + light	+	Formation of C.R. to light
Light (repeatedly)	o	Extinction of C.R. to light
Light + buzzer	+	Disinhibition of C.R. to light by buzzer
Light (repeatedly) (interval)	o	Extinction of C.R to light
Light	+	Spontaneous recovery of C.R. to light

* Based on Switzer, *J. Gen. Psychol.*, 1933, **9.**

(3) A third kind of inhibition is to be found in the process of *differentiation*, in which the non-specific and general nature of the stimulus when first conditioned becomes more and more narrowed and refined upon continued training. This phenomenon was exploited early by the first American psychologists to work with conditioning. A reflex retraction of the hand after being conditioned to a red light is likely to appear also at sight of a green one; but if the shock be used only when the red is shown and never with the green, the retraction to the latter will die out. A retraction conditioned to a tone of 256 cycles per sec. will appear also at a sound differing from it by only 6 cycles; but after frequent shocking with the former and never with the latter, the hand will be trained to respond to the former only.

Still other phenomena of conditioning seem to depend upon some kind of time-recording in the animal or human. If in the training series a constant interval be introduced between the incidental stimulus and the normal adequate one, the responses will finally come to appear at that same interval of time following the incidental stimulus and in the absence of the adequate one. This delay phenomenon can be made to appear either at a constant interval after the beginning of an incidental stimulus that continues and is overlapped by the adequate one (the *delayed* or *retarded* C.R.), or at an interval after the cessation of a short-lived stimulus that does not continue (the *trace* C.R.).

Now for a final principle. From one C.R. a *secondary* C.R. can be formed by accompanying a newly effective stimulus with a second neutral one. For example: a human subject that had been trained to withdraw the hand at a tactile stimulation formerly coupled with an electric shock was further conditioned to a metronome-ticking after the latter had accompanied the tactile but without the shock. In other words, the metronome became substituted for the tactile S, as the latter had already become substituted for the shock. Conditioning without re-enforcement beyond this *second order* to a *third order* and higher orders has not been highly successful.

Some Broader Applications. Illustrations of how the principle of the conditioned response operates on more complex levels of behavior are to be furnished on many pages through the remainder of the present book. In this place we may, by way of anticipation, briefly note a few instances taken from daily life.[1] (*A*) At the slam of the gate to their corral, the chickens come running. (*B*) At the sounds, "Here, Gyp!" the dog dozing on the front lawn jumps to his feet and heads around the house for the back door, where he finds the cook ready to offer him a bone. (*C*) At sight of master-carrying-gun the quiet house dog changes at once into a vibrant impatient hunter. (*D*) A child under the writer's observation, who had heard others cry "hot" when he was near a steam radiator by which he was slightly burned, always drew back at hearing that word wherever he might be.

Consider cases of emotional behavior. (*E*) A boy was given examination and treatment before and after tonsilectomy by a white-coated shiny-instrument-wielding physician: for a year and more thereafter he was terrorized by the very sight of a barber wearing his white coat and manipulating his nickeled clippers and scissors. (*F*) This fear reaction was eventually overcome by a barber who set a bowl of goldfish near the child, directing his highly interested attention to them, and saying "fish," meanwhile working upon the boy's hair unobtrusively and casually. (*G*) Later the child, upon hearing "fish" or "haircut" or "Dayton's" (the barber's shop) spoken aloud would smile, and with a hand describe circular gestures with rising and falling vocal inflection (mimetic of the swimming of the goldfish). (*H*) A college student relates that once he greatly enjoyed Chopin's Marche Funèbre, but that ever since he heard it played in a certain naval hospital whenever the body of an unfortunate sailor was being removed for burial, he has been unable to react to it with anything but extreme depression. (*I*) In the early stages of the World War there appeared some harrowing newspaper accounts of atrocities in the city of Louvain, and many a reader was so stirred by this that as a consequence he could not for many weeks thereafter see or hear the word "Louvain" without again becoming emotional. So it is with the human reactions to many words and other symbols that have become emotionally loaded, such as "liberty," "mother," "God," "communists."

---

[1] The reader would do well to analyze these cases into appropriate S's and R's, and their respective connections, after the manner of Figure 100.

Nor is the matter essentially different when the responses acquired are of less emotional and more "intellectual" types. (*J*) A common procedure in teaching a child to read is to point out to him some printed word, as C A T, at the same time pronouncing the word aloud, in the expectation that, as he has already learned to speak such a word upon hearing it, he will now be able to substitute the new visual for the familiar auditory stimulus, and so be enabled to read the print. (*K*) The remembering of a melody, of musical notes in a serial arrangement, is based upon earlier neural changes in which the vocal production of each successive note was conditioned to the auditory or to the proprioceptive afferent impulses of the note produced just before it. (*L*) The clerk in his office soon becomes so habituated to the sounds of the clicking typewriters and adding machines that, should all abruptly cease, concentration on the job before him might be rendered extremely difficult: his reactions have become conditioned in part to these sounds.

EXPERIMENTS EMPHASIZING TOTAL-REACTIONS TO TOTAL-SITUATIONS

In these experiments the situations are such that the particular specific reactions and the particular stimuli are of secondary importance. The subject must learn to react not to independent stimuli but to some relation among them. One particular reaction may be as effective as another, provided the end-result is the same; and one specific item of the situation may be substituted for another, provided only it bears the same relationship to the total situation as does the original one.

"Roundabout" Experiments. The German psychologist, Köhler, has done some of the most interesting work on animal learning, and it has great significance for the understanding of human beings. (Somewhat similar observations had been described earlier by others, especially Yerkes.) In general, a properly motivated (hungry) animal was placed in a situation in which an incentive (food) was present but was blocked off or out of reach of the animal by any direct movements, but accessible if some roundabout or indirect way was resorted to.

First, for his method of detour. Hens were barred off from their food by a fence with an L and an opening a short distance back on the L (Figure 104, *A*). "They keep rushing up against the obstruc-

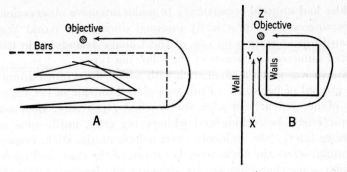

FIGURE 104. ROUNDABOUT BEHAVIOR

A, Behavior of a hen before taking detour necessary to reach an objective seen through the bars. *B*, Behavior of a dog taking the necessary detour at once. (From Köhler, W., *Mentality of Apes*, Harcourt, Brace, 1925.)

tion when they see their objective in front of them through a wire fence, rush from one side to the other all a-fluster, and do not fare any better, even when they are familiar with the obstruction . . . and the greater part of the circuitous route." Contrast with this the behavior of a dog (in *B*). A dog is brought into the blind alley from direction *X* to the point *Y*, and food is put down at *Z* on the other side of the rail. The dog "sees it, seems to hesitate a moment, then in a second turns at an angle of 180 degrees, and is already on the run in a smooth curve, without any interruption, out of the blind alley, round the fence to the new food." Note that though the first part of the correct run, when the dog is headed away from the lure, is physically or geometrically a "going away" it has become psychologically a "going toward." It is an indirect sort of reaction. It will be seen that something of the same indirectness characterizes the more complicated cases now to be described.

Tool-using. Laying hold of and manipulating one object in order to affect another has always been regarded as an evidence of high mental development. Man has been called "the animal that can make and use tools"; and much has been made of the point that it is by the fashioning and employing of instruments that he has radically changed his conditions of existence. In some contemporary Russian work on the cultural development of the child, his attempts to manipulate objects as means for attaining objectives are made the basis for the genetic study. But can man be fairly claimed to be the only animal to use instruments in any way?

Köhler had unusual opportunity to make intensive observations on chimpanzees while practically interned during the World War at an anthropoid station on one of the Canary Islands.   He has reported numerous occasions of the following types.

Nueva was given a small stick with which she scraped around on the ground of her cage.   Fruit was placed outside of her cage just out of her reach.   In vain she reached repeatedly, then set up characteristic beseeching and whimpering cries, until, some seven minutes later, "she suddenly casts a look at the stick, ceases her moaning, seizes the stick, stretches it out of the cage, and succeeds, though somewhat clumsily, in drawing the banana within arm's length."   Two days later, deprived of her stick when food was again placed out of reach, she tried to pull it toward her with rags, with straws, and with her drinking bowl.   Still more striking are the following cases.

(a) Sultan, having had his attention drawn to food out of reach, "approaches the bars, glances outside, the next moment turns round, goes straight to the tree, seizes a thin, slender branch, breaks it off with a sharp jerk, runs back to the bars, and attains his objective . . . one single quick chain of action."   (b) Sultan, being allowed to play with two sticks of different size so that the end of one can be just fitted into the end of the other, "first of all squats indifferently . . . then he gets up, picks up the two sticks . . . and plays carelessly with them. . . . He pushes the thinner one a little way into the opening of the thicker, jumps up and is already on the run toward the railings . . . and begins to draw a banana towards him with the double stick."

Building.   Erecting structures to be used as the means of getting at a lure is a form of activity having something of the same psychological character.   Köhler has described several varieties, such as that shown in Figure 105.   Fruit was hung quite out of an animal's reach, and the animal was forced to adopt special methods for securing it.   In the initial test, the food objective was nailed to the roof and a wooden box was left standing some distance away.

All six apes vainly endeavored to reach their objective by leaping up from the ground.   Sultan soon relinquished this attempt, paced restlessly up and down, suddenly stood still in front of the box, seized it, tipped it hastily straight towards the objective, but began to climb upon it at a (horizontal) distance of half a meter, and springing upwards with all his force, tore down the banana . . .; from the momentary pause before the box to the first bite into the banana, only a few seconds elapsed, a perfectly continuous action after the first hesitation.

FIGURE 105. CHIMPANZEE REACHING FOR FOOD, COMBINING
BOX-STACKING AND TOOL-USING

(From Köhler, W., *Mentality of Apes*, Harcourt, Brace, 1925.)

On a later date two boxes were left handy.

The objective is placed very high up, the two boxes not very far away from each other and about four meters away from the objective; all other means of reaching it have been taken away. Sultan drags the bigger of the two boxes towards the objective, puts it just underneath, gets up on it, and looking upwards, makes ready to jump, but does not jump; gets down, seizes the other box, and pulling it behind him, gallops about the room, making his usual noise, kicking against the walls and showing his uneasiness in every other possible way. He certainly did not seize the second box to put it on the first; it merely helps him to give vent to his temper. But all of a sudden his behavior changes completely; he stops making a noise, pulls his box from quite a distance right up to the other one, and stands it upright on it. He mounts the somewhat shaky construction.[1]

The persistent pursuit of the objective involves variations of procedure that are not merely repertoire reactions appearing in more or less random fashion as the expression of exploratory excitement, but are directed explicitly at the boxes while at the same time the original set is maintained toward the ultimate objective, the food.   From Köhler's descriptive account it is apparent that some of the skill in manipulating sticks, strings, blankets, boxes, and the like was developed by the familiar trials-and-errors.   But there was a wide latitude of variation in the sizes, shapes, and placings of the objects.   Most important, there was an abruptness with which on the original occasion the animal's behavior became all at once reoriented and systematized about the getting-or-fixing-stick-and-reaching-out-and-scraping-food-inward or the placing-of-box-on-box-and-climbing-upon-them-and-reaching-toward-fruit.   This suddenness bespeaks a mode of behavior definitely different from that of a cat in a problem box or a rat in a maze.   Is it totally different? Not if we bear in mind that the ape chances upon this "insight," happens in the course of his random and sometimes wild activity to get into a position where he seems to see some connection between the unreachable food and the object lying handy.   At the same time, there is here surely some degree of perceiving of the *relation of means to objective*, some grasping, if only upon seeing them in a line, of a *connection* of stick-and-banana or box-and-banana, a seeing of each as part of a *configuration* or *Gestalt*.

Three points, then, are to be remembered concerning the learning process.   (1) A learning process may be more or less *suddenly* terminated, the adjustment abruptly completed.   (2) This all-at-

[1] Köhler, W.   *The Mentality of Apes*.   Harcourt, Brace, 1925.

once solution of the difficulty involves *adjustment to a relationship* within the whole field. (3) This relationship is crucial because it is a relation between the incentive or objective and some tool or instrument serving as a *means*.

The Methods Applied to Children. The same types of problem situations as set by Köhler and Yerkes were not long in being applied in the observation of human children. Let us note an individual study of each of some forty nursery school children [2]. In Problem I the experimenter had the child enter a room in which hung a toy just out of reach. The question was whether and how the child would hit upon the possibility of using a block placed near-by, or of stacking two blocks, or making some similar adaptive response according to the setting. In Problem II the child found himself in a play pen with the toy incentive outside and beyond reach but with a stick or broom or two halves of a fishing rod lying at hand. Somewhat similar modifications of the problem situations were adopted in other work on children, and also in experiments on feeble-minded children of nine or ten years of age but with the tested intelligence of only two- or three-year-olds [9, 23, 1]. From the various series of studies on chimpanzees, on normal children of two or three years, and on imbeciles of about equal mental age, some interesting comparisons have appeared.

In one respect, all three kinds of subjects tended to be alike. They all showed some measure of exploratory behavior at first when they espied the objective but could not obtain it by merely reaching for it: the try, try again type of activity appeared. Sooner or later, however, in the typical cases, they all hit upon the mode of getting the lure in a more or less abrupt manner after apparently *perceiving its crucial relationship to other things* in the environment.

Some Special Characteristics of Human Insightful Adjustment. Some differences, however, came to light. It will be more easy to appreciate these if we consider excerpts from the experimenters' records of the children.

Girl, 40 months old. Problem II-A (toy outside, stick on floor).
First trial. Subject handled the stick and talked about it before instructions were completed and then dropped it, trying to climb out of the pen to get objective; tried to reach objective by leaning over the top of pen, by stretching for it between the bars; sought an exit, repeating over and over, "I can't get birdie"; asked Experimenter to move objective closer; stepped on stick, looked down at it, and began to walk around. Subject picked up stick, banged with it on the wall, and threw it down; looked around and again

tried to reach objective as before and by pushing her legs out between the bars. Subject appeared tired, and trial was terminated.

Second trial. Subject stretched for objective through the spaces, first with right hand and then with left, shouting, "Today, I can get him"; tried to climb out and again reached through the spaces. Subject stepped on stick, *pounced down on it,* and used it for obtaining objective, which she had inside the pen in a short time. Repeated the performance for fun.

Same child. Problem II-B *(broom replacing stick on floor).*

First trial. Subject picked up broom at once and swept objective in deftly.

Here not only was the solution hit upon all-at-once and completely, but also it was transferred to a new situation. Once a child (normal or feeble-minded) had caught on to the solution of one situation, he usually lost little time in transferring the essential principle to a second situation varying from the first only in details. This was graphically shown in time "learning curves" for similar problems, the curves being much steeper for children than had been found in the case of chimpanzees [6]. The reader will find that this ability to *transpose* or transfer from old to new situations is a quite fundamental and central characteristic in the more effective kinds of behavior, and it increases strikingly with increase of "intelligence."

The foregoing case displays a complete insight gained; but the occurrence of *partial insights* was frequently noted in the children. For example:

Boy, 34 months. Problem I-A. *Second trial.* Subject appeared much interested in the suspended airplane; examined it from every angle, at a distance of 12 feet, asking many questions as, "Who put it on the light? How does it go?" His eyes traveled in the direction of the block several times. Subject slowly approached objective, with many glances at block en route. (All his movements were tentative as though he were not quite willing to commit himself.)

Boy, 32 months. Problem II-C (necessary long stick lying outside pen but reachable with a short stick lying inside). Subject tried to reach airplane with short stick and then tried to climb out; made one attempt to reach long stick and then, aiming at objective, threw the short stick out at it, not viciously, but merely to establish contact with objective, it would seem. Experimenter casually replaced the stick. Subject pleaded, "May I have the other stick?" pointing excitedly at long stick; threw short stick out at long stick, and Experimenter once more returned it to the pen. Subject reached the long stick with short one and then reached objective with the former.

In such cases as these, two characteristics of human behavior appear to mark it off strikingly from that of subhuman forms. For one thing, the child used much *verbalization,* talking to himself and talking to the experimenter. ("I can't get birdie"; "She's tied to the light?" "It's too far away," and the like); and it is likely that such talking was a help to the child in refining his problems and his procedures.[1] A related capacity is that of responding to the words of others — to profit by instructions — though not well shown in this study since the child was put on his own resources.

Equally striking is the degree to which the children attempted to *utilize social aids*. Direct verbal requests ("You swing the dolly"; "May I have the other stick?"), indirect seeking of guidance (glancing at E's face before continuing with a new method), and emotional appeals (whimpering or crying) — many and sundry such incidental social items are found through the running accounts.

Boy, 42 months. Problem I-A. Second trial. Subject tried to reach objective with both hands, repeating, "I can't reach it"; came to Experimenter, repeating this chant, almost with a sob. Receiving no assistance, Subject began to cry, and trial was terminated with the promise that Subject should have another opportunity to reach objective.

Finally with the children, other types of *emotional response* and general *personality characteristics* were often of importance in aiding or hindering the solution.

Developmental Aspects. We must not exaggerate the degree to which children employ the more insightful methods. As a matter of fact, some careful investigators, when working with children of pre-school age, have been able to turn up only slight evidence of their using much more than the hit-or-miss methods. The bearing of the evidence is that the configurational types of problem solving manifest themselves in early childhood somewhat sporadically and sketchily. Much depends upon the individual children involved and even more upon the problems that they face. What we plainly need now is the genetic perspective. From our earlier acquaintances with developmental studies (Chapter IV) we may confidently expect to find evidences of modes of procedure based upon more and more insight as children mature. This we have already seen hinted, indeed, in Hamilton's study (*supra*, pp. 377 ff.); and the theoretical deduction seems so sound that doubtless we can safely content ourselves here with the mention of only one experimental demonstration of it.

Animal psychologists, for over thirty years, have employed a

---

[1] This important function of language as a means of self-stimulation is still more clearly brought out elsewhere. (Cf. pp. 528 ff.)

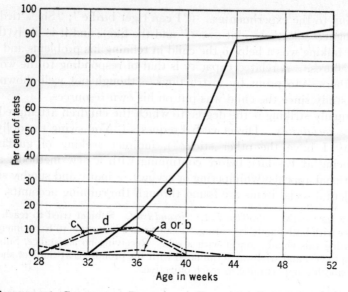

FIGURE 106. CHANGES IN PERCEPTUAL TYPE WITH INCREASES IN AGE

The string-pulling test. At each age, the frequency of appearance of each of the types described in the text is shown in terms of the percentage of test presentations in which it was clearly observed. The connecting lines exhibit the kind of changes from age to age in the frequencies of the respective types. (From Richardson, H. M., *Genet. Psychol. Monog.*, 1932, **12**, nos 3–4, 270.)

"string-pulling" technique for testing the ability to perceive and use means that lead to ends. Food is placed out of reach, and a string tied to it is laid with the other end within the subject's reach. An adaptation of this method was made at the Yale Developmental Clinic to the study of human infants at different stages of maturity. The baby, seated behind a grill, was made interested in a toy, such as a squeaking rubber cat, a gaily colored doll, or a yellow wooden duck, and a string attached to it was laid with one end where he could grasp it by reaching through the grill. Taken at the age of twenty-eight weeks and tested every fourth week until a year old, the infants showed a definite development in their adaptive behavior. On the basis of differences in the baby's total manner of "looking" and handling, the experimenter inferred five types of perceptual attitude that represented different levels of infant maturity:

a. Interest in the string rather than in the lure.

b. Interest in the lure and accidental contact with the string.

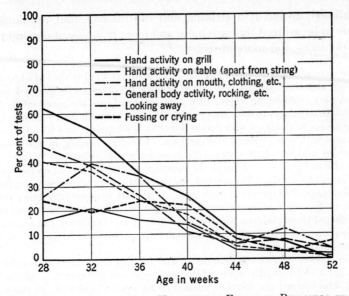

FIGURE 107. DROPPING OUT OF UNADAPTIVE FORMS OF BEHAVIOR WITH INCREASE IN AGE

The string-pulling test. At each age, the frequency of appearance of each of the kinds of unadaptive behavior is shown in terms of the percentage of test presentations in which it was observed. (From Richardson, H. M., *Genet. Psychol. Monog.*, 1932, **12**, nos. 3-4, 246.)

   c. Awareness of both string and lure, but no utilization of string.

   d. Experimentation, moving the hand and watching the result.

   e. Definite utilizing of string to bring in the lure.

In Figure 106 the story of the age changes in these perceptual attitudes is graphically told: the *e* type became clearly established *by the forty-fourth week*, so that by this age the babies *were showing insight*, were definitely "structuring the (simple) situation," *were perceiving and utilizing a crucial relationship within the field presented*.[1] On the eliminative side of this development, we may note in Figure 107 that with increasing age and with higher levels of perception went a progressive decrease in hand and body activities of the more random and distracted sorts.

   There is, then, *increase in the insightful form of problem solution with increase in age*, even in this first year of life. We may confidently expect the story to be continued, and through the years of

---

[1] That this development is one of maturation and not one of practice or learning should be evident from considerations that have been advanced in Chapter IV, as well as from the fact that the tests were given once only at four-week intervals.

childhood to find it a striking and central fact that relationships come to be utilized that are more and more complex, more and more subtle, more and more abstract.

An example of relationship of the more abstract kind is that of *opposition;* and an experimental demonstration of how it comes to be grasped by the developing child ought to give us a glimpse ahead into the more subtle types of human capacity, to offer us a connecting link between man's simpler forms of behavior as dealings with concrete physical situations and his more subtle dealings with non-physical abstractions.   Children ranging in age from five to seven and one half years were questioned individually: "What is the opposite of 'good'?" "What is the opposite of 'big'?" and so on for twenty-five more test words.   As expected, the percentages of children showing knowledge of opposites increased with age.   But what is more interesting for the present discussion is the answer to the question: What was the nature of the learning of those children who did not know at the beginning the meaning of opposition and who learned it through instruction (which was in the form of completed examples)?

The answer is brief and definite.   After making one correct response in the test list a child usually made all correct responses thereafter.   All the subjects who learned the relation seemed to hit upon it suddenly, *to grasp it all at once,* by a sudden acquisition of insight.   There was no gradual fixation of right responses and gradual elimination of wrong, such as is so striking in the acquisition of some of the acts of skill we have noted in an earlier section of the present chapter.   It is going too far to say that the children in the course of learning did not make trials and errors, but the trial and error did not result in improvement.   It was only after this period that the learning suddenly appeared completely [20].

SUMMARY AND GENERALIZATIONS

The Three Types of Research are Supplementary.   It is now time to stop and take stock.   From the many experiments cited under the three classifications we ought to be able to deduce some principles common to all.

By way of summary, let us repeat that there are three major kinds of learning experiments: (1) those emphasizing the integration of part-reactions, usually, though sometimes misleadingly, called "trial-and-error" experiments; (2) those emphasizing specific reactions to specific stimuli, usually called "conditioned response" experiments; (3) and those emphasizing total-reactions to total-situations, usually referred to as "configurational" experiments.

Let us attempt to see how well the experiments hang together when the differences of experimental procedure are taken into consideration.   We shall not have space here to go into detailed analysis of the studies, but a few of the cardinal principles may be presented [12].

Some Important Principles Common to All Experiments.

(a) *The subject must be motivated.*   This has been emphasized in our description of the "trial-and-error" studies (I); and it is obvious enough in the use of lures in the configurational studies (III). Upon inspection we find it in the conditioned-response studies (II), too; for the human or the dog has to be in a state of "alert readiness," and the reflexes that are conditioned have to be biologically important ones, as in feeding or as in defensive withdrawal from pain.

(b) *The main motive encounters some obstruction.*   The hungry or otherwise motivated animal or person in maze or problem box is restrained by the enclosure; and the beginner in telegraphy is delayed by his ignorance from achieving his ambition of becoming an operator on the line (I).   Similarly the subject's desire was thwarted (III) by the out-of-reach character of banana or toy or other lure that is hung too high or that lies too far outside the bars of one's enclosure.   In the conditioning situation the subject is restrained, often by straps and holders, from escaping the punishment or from laying hold of the food at once (II).

(c) *Hyperactivity is aroused, great energy appears.*   This and the following principle should be quite obvious in all three researches as we have described them.

(d) *The responses are multiple and varied.*

(e) *The stimuli to which one is to react are in some kind of relation* or setting.   The turns of a maze, or the letters of a language, are to be learned in their relationships (I).   The particular signal in conditioning may be a pattern of lines, a sequence of tones, a certain rhythm, and the like (II).   This is most emphatically brought out in the configurational problems (III).

(f) *The most important relation is that between the objective and a means to be found.*   This, while being implied in principles (a) and (b), is worth special emphasis.   Learning is the discovery or development of means-to-end.

(g) *Some selection process occurs.*   In each case there appears eventually a successful response to which the subject comes to restrict his activity. Out of the more or less random responses of the rat in the maze or the typist at his machine (I), or of the dog or man showing excitement and widespread activity when unable to avoid shock or obtain food at once (II), or of the ape or child running about the enclosure and talking and handling this and that when he finds a lure out of immediate reach — in each case the activity gets narrowed down.

(*h*) *These ultimately selected responses originally occur "by accident."* The subject cannot predict in advance what response is the one to be made, but he must hit upon it, whether suddenly or gradually.

(*i*) *The effects of the responses are crucial in the selection.* To be selected, the "right" response must bring about relief of the subject's tensions, must remove the obstruction to his motivated behavior.

(*j*) *The rate of learning varies in degree from gradual to abrupt.* Learning curves can be drawn for all: there is no sharp demarcation line between the extremely slow improvement rate in crude trial-and-error (as illustrated by a young child first practicing handling a spoon or writing the letter *a*) and the extremely sudden improvement in simple insight (as illustrated by the same child "spotting" a chair as a means to reach the jam jar or "seeing" the answer to a riddle).

ORIENTATION

These principles are in essence only elaborations of the conception of learning as a phenomenon of organismic adjustment to environment. Our survey of the yieldings of typical experimental researches, to which so many of the pages of this chapter have been devoted, should have enriched this conception and provided us with an equipment in the fundamentals of learning. They have also pointed the way ahead for our inquiries into the more subtle forms of human adjustment, by suggesting in advance many of the problems that are to be attacked — the nature and rôle of "*perceiving*," of "*social*" and "*verbal behavior*," of "*generalizing*," and of "*thinking*." There is no more helpful approach to each of these problems than from the notion of the learning and readjusting organism which in its higher evolved stages has developed these more elaborate capacities.

For the immediate present, however, there remain unanswered a great number of detail questions about learning, both practical and theoretical. To these the following chapter is to be devoted.

REFERENCES

1. Aldrich, C. G., and Doll, E. A. Problem Solving Among Idiots. *J. Comp. Psychol.*, 1931, **12**, 137–69; and *J. Soc. Psychol.*, 1931, **2**, 306–36.

2. Alpert, A. The Solving of Problem-Situations by Preschool Children. *Teach. Coll. Contrib.'s to Educ.*, 1928, No. 323.

3. Bass, M. J., and Hull, C. L. The Irradiation of a Tactile Conditioned Reflex in Man. *J. Comp. Psychol.*, 1934, **17**, 47–66.

4. Bechterev, V. M. *General Principles of Human Reflexology.* International Publishers, 1928.

5. Bernstein, A. L. Temporal Factors in the Formation of Conditioned Eyelid Reactions in Human Subjects. *J. Gen. Psychol.*, 1934, **10**, 173–97.

6. Bingham, H. C. Chimpanzee Translocation by Means of Boxes. *Comp. Psychol. Monog.*, 1929, **5**, No. 25.

7. Book, W. F. *The Psychology of Skill.* Gregg Publishing Co., 1925.

8. Book, W. F., and Norvell, L. The Will to Learn. *Ped. Sem.*, 1922, **29**, 305–62.

9. Brainard, P. P. The Mentality of a Child Compared with That of Apes. *J. Genet. Psychol.*, 1930, **37**, 268–93.

10. Cason, H. The Conditioned Pupillary Reaction. *J. Exper. Psychol.*, 1922, **5**, 108–46.

11. Dashiell, J. F. An Experimental Isolation of Higher Level Habits. *J. Exper. Psychol.*, 1924, **7**, 391–97.

12. Dashiell, J. F. A Survey and Synthesis of Learning Theories. *Psychol. Bull.*, 1935, **32**, 261–75.

13. Garvey, C. R. A Study of Conditioned Respiratory Changes. *J. Exp. Psychol.*, 1933, **16**, 471–503.

14. Guthrie, E. R. Association as a Function of Time Interval. *Psychol. Rev.*, 1933, **40**, 355–67.

15. Hamilton, G. V. A Study of Trial and Error Reactions in Mammals. *J. Anim. Behav.*, 1911, **1**, 33–66. Perseverance Reactions in Primates and Rodents. *Behav. Monog.*, 1916, **3**, No. 13.

16. Hilgard, E. R. Conditioned Eyelid Reactions to a Light Stimulus Based on the Reflex Wink to Sound. *Psychol. Monog.*, 1931, **12**, No. 1.

17. Hull, C. L. Learning: II. The Factor of the Conditioned Reflex. *A Handbook of General Experimental Psychology* (Murchison, ed.). Clark Univ. Press, 1934.

18. Jones, H. E. The Retention of Conditioned Emotional Reactions in Infancy. *J. Genet. Psychol.*, 1930, **37**, 485–98.

19. Köhler, W. *The Mentality of Apes.* Harcourt, Brace, 1925.

20. Kreezer, G., and Dallenbach, K. M. Learning the Relation of Opposition. *Am. J. Psychol.*, 1929, **41**, 432–41.

21. Liddell, H. S. The Conditioned Reflex, in *Comparative Psychology* (Moss, ed.). Prentice-Hall, 1934.

22. Luria, A. R.   The Problem of the Cultural Behavior of the Child.   *J. Genet. Psychol.*, 1928, **35**, 493–506.

23. Matheson, E.   A Study of Problem Solving Behavior in Preschool Children.   *Ch. Devel.*, 1931, **2**, 242–71.

24. Patrick, J. R.   Studies in Rational Behavior and Emotional Excitement: II. The Effect of Emotional Excitement on Rational Behavior in Human Subjects.   *J. Comp. Psychol.*, 1934, **18**, 153–95.

25. Pavlov, I. P.   *Conditioned Reflexes.*   Oxford Univ. Press: Humphrey Milford, 1927.

26. Pavlov, I. P.   *Lectures on Conditioned Reflexes.*   International Publishers, 1928.

27. Razran, G. H. S.   Conditioned Responses in Children.   A Behavioral and Quantitative Review of Experimental Studies.   *Arch. Psychol.*, 1933, No. 148.

28. Razran, G. H. S.   Conditioned Withdrawal Responses with Shock as the Conditioning Stimulus in Adult Human Subjects.   *Psychol. Bull.*, 1934, **31**, 111–43.

29. Razran, G. H. S., and Warden, C. J.   The Sensory Capacities of the Dog as Studied by the Conditioned Reflex Method (Russian Schools).   *Psychol. Bull.*, 1929, **26**, 202–22.

30. Richardson, H. M.   The Growth of Adaptive Behavior in Infants: An Experimental Study at Seven Age Levels.   *Genet. Psychol. Monog.*, 1932, **12**, 195–359.

31. Shipley, W. C.   Conditioning the Human Plantar Reflex.   *J. Exper. Psychol.*, 1932, **15**, 422–26.

32. Swift, E. J.   Studies in the Psychology and Physiology of Learning.   *Am. J. Psychol.*, 1903, **14**, 201–51.

33. Switzer, St. C. A.   Disinhibition of the Conditioned Galvanic Skin Response.   *J. Gen. Psychol.*, 1933, **9**, 77–100.

34. Thorndike, E. L.   Animal Intelligence.   *Psychol. Monog.*, 1898, **2**, No. 4.

35. Tolman, E. C.   *Purposive Behavior in Animals and Men.*   Century, 1932.

36. Watson, J. B.   The Place of the Conditioned Reflex in Psychology.   *Psychol. Rev.*, 1916, **23**, 89–116.

37. Wever, E. G.   The Upper Limit of Hearing in the Cat.   *J. Comp. Psychol.*, 1930, **10**, 221–33.

38. Wolfle, H. M.   Conditioning as a Function of the Interval between the Conditioned and the Original Stimulus.   *J. Gen. Psychol.*, 1932, **7**, 80–103.

39. Yerkes, R. M.   The Mental Life of Monkeys and Apes: a Study of Ideational Behavior.   *Behav. Monog.*, 1916, **3**, No. 12.   The Mind of a Gorilla.   *Genet. Psychol. Monog.*, 1927, **2**, No. 1.

CHAPTER XV
CONDITIONS OF LEARNING

INTRODUCTION

"Habit" and "Memory." In popular speech the words "habit" and "memory" are used as if connoting two quite different human functions. In a general way, habit is used to refer to an act or series of acts of non-verbal sort that involve some movements of the skeletal and/or visceral musculature like bicycling or using knife, fork, and spoon; while memory has been applied to the acquiring and retaining of words and other implicit and explicit symbols, and of conscious experiences. Habit is the modification and improvement of overt behavior; memory, the acquisition of new modes of activity in which muscular action is at a minimum. But though both words have survived in technical psychology, the distinction must not be overworked. Many an act of motor skill has been learned with the aid of verbal cues and instruction furnished by another or by oneself (examples: golf, automobile driving, using a calculating machine); and there is hardly any activity of remembering that is not based on some kind of muscular movements, if only of the vocal apparatus (examples: calling a man's name, taking an examination, testifying in court). What is more, the facts and findings concerning "memories" hold with equal weight for "habits," and *vice versa*. In the present discussion, therefore, this verbal distinction will be largely ignored.

Four Problems in Learning. The various questions we will want to ask about learning fall conveniently into four groups. They correspond to roughly marked stages in the whole process of learning. It is obvious that when we say any reaction has been learned, it must have been first *acquired* at some past time, recent or remote, and that it does or can function again at a later time. It has been acquired and can be *recalled*. But what of the meantime? Many hours, days, or years may elapse between the earlier occasion, when the reaction was first aroused and fixated, and the later date when it is rearoused. Clearly, the reaction as a reaction-possibility has somehow been *retained* through the interval. It has been potentially there. Finally, at the moment of its later recall the reaction may be rearoused faithfully enough in itself, but it may appear in a novel instead of in its usual setting; so that the question arises as to whether it is correctly *recognized*. Our inquiries will revolve about Acquiring, Retaining, Recalling, and Recognizing, respectively. At each stage there are many things that the inquiring student would like to know.

ACQUIRING

The Curve of Acquiring. How shall we measure a person's learning? The primary point of attack will be: how rapidly does he learn; and to measure this we must adopt units. For the known variable it is customary to take specified and controlled amounts of practice, usually stated in terms of length of practice period and number of periods. For the unknown variable, to be tabled and plotted against the known variable, usually either or both of two criteria are employed: speed, stated in terms of either amount of work per unit of time, or amount of time per unit of work; and accuracy, stated in terms of the number of errors made, or of the general scoring of the character of the work done. (In plotting graphically, the known variable is always indicated by distance from O on the horizontal or x axis; the unknown by distances on the vertical or y axis.) Some sample curves are shown in Figures 93, 96, and 109. Note that the scoring methods used determine whether the curve is a rising or a falling one.

It will be noted that most of the curves show a *negative acceleration*, a slowing down in the rate of improvement, that is, as the number of trials increases the amount acquired per trial decreases. These studies have been almost exclusively on overt functions or functions in some single type of work. Thorndike, who has given a thorough analysis of learning curves, has the following to say on the point:

Negative acceleration of any great amount is far from being a general rule of learning. On the contrary, it may well be that there are some functions, such as amount of knowledge of history ... or of fiscal statistics, where, by any justifiable score for "amount of knowledge," the rate of improvement in hour after hour of practice would rise, giving a pronounced *positive* acceleration.   Each item of information may, in such cases, make the acquisition of other items easier.[1]

A characteristic of the learning curves which the reader has already noticed is their irregular, saw-toothed appearance.   These irregularities may be long or short.   The short-time *fluctuations* represent the fact that the efficiency of a performance is affected by all sorts of factors: distraction by extraneous stimuli, changes in the learner's interest and effort, changes in his practice methods, altered physiological condition and health, and the like.   The reader can easily add a dozen other factors that would be important here if he bears in mind changes in the external environment, changes in the subject's intraorganic condition, and changes in his attitude toward the work.   Anything, we may safely say, that bears upon the efficiency of a person at a given time would have a helpful or hindering effect upon his progress in acquiring knowledge or skill.

Prolonged irregularities, if they tend to a "dead level" that is terminated later by a change indicating improvement, have been called *plateaus*, and have been the subject of much discussion — probably more than they deserve, since they cannot be found in all learning records. (It can be said in summary that such periods of neither improvement nor loss, followed by later improvement, are due to such temporarily lasting factors as the mechanizing of a lower order of habits before the appearance of a higher order; relaxation in the subject's interest and effort; a changing of his methods of learning.   There is nothing mysterious or inevitable about a plateau: it is simply a function of the facilitating and inhibiting forces and factors at work in the subjects who are learning.)

Some Principles of Economy in Acquiring.   Our knowledge of factors that help and hinder in learning has reached respectable proportions, thanks to the work of many experimental investigators, especially in Germany and America.   Ebbinghaus initiated the studies of this type in 1885 with his monograph, "*Ueber das Gedächtniss.*" His technique was so remarkable and his findings were in many ways so well verified by later workers that in the following pages we will accord him the lead.   Instead of thinking of a person's "memory" as a faculty or agency to be treated only in armchair discourses, he saw it as a natural function investigable by natural-science method.

[1] *Educational Psychology*, vol. II, p. 257.

We all know of what this method consists: an attempt is made to keep constant the mass of conditions which have proven themselves causally connected with a certain result; one of these conditions is isolated from the rest and varied in a way that can be numerically described; then the accompanying change on the side of the effect is ascertained by measurement or computation.

Two fundamental and insurmountable difficulties seem, however, to oppose a transfer of this method to the investigation of the causal relations of mental events. . . . How are we to keep even approximately constant the bewildering mass of causal conditions which . . . almost completely elude our control, and which, moreover, are subject to endless and incessant change?   In the second place, by what possible means are we to measure numerically the mental processes which flit by so quickly and which on introspection are so hard to analyze?

The kind of performance he selected was memorizing, or, in common parlance, "learning by heart," in which the learner reads material over and over until he can make a perfect reproduction of it unaided, the total time spent in reading (at uniform rate) furnishing the score. (For the material to be learned, he sought to eliminate chance disturbing factors and also to provide units of measure by devising nonsense syllables (each a vowel placed between two consonants), these drawn by chance as "from a hat" and then combined into series of various lengths.   Each syllable series was to be learned as a whole, so that the subject could repeat it all verbatim.

Ebbinghaus had no apparatus, which makes his procedure all the more important.   Using himself as the subject and drawing his materials quite in chance order, he established most constant possible experimental conditions throughout the learning: (1) The separate series were always read through completely from beginning to end.   (2) The reading and the reciting of a series took place at a constant rate set by a metronome making 150 strokes per minute.   (3) After the learning of each series a uniform pause of 15 seconds was made.   (4) Associations of syllables with mnemotechnic devices were avoided.   (5) Concentration of attitude on the task was maintained as far as possible.   (6) Care was taken that the objective conditions of life during the period of the tests were so controlled as to eliminate too great irregularities.

Ebbinghaus employed the Savings method for testing.[1]   The

---

[1] Several other methods of memorizing and testing have been employed by different investigators. Cf. Whipple [22], pp. 151-52.

number of repetitions necessary to enable a subject to make one complete reproduction of the series was noted; and after an interval of time the series might be relearned and the time saved in the relearning noted.

Since Ebbinghaus, various models of apparatus have been devised by later investigators to provide more objectively standardized presentation of the stimuli in their serial orders. It can readily be appreciated that a precise timing of the duration of each exposure is important. One of the better known models is shown in Figure 140, on p. 556.

(1) For the relearning of a 12-syllable series at a given date, Ebbinghaus found that 38 repetitions distributed over the 3 days just preceding was as effective as 68 repetitions made on the one immediately preceding. (The conclusion drawn from this, that *distributed learning* is more effective than *massed learning* has been amply borne out by other studies.) Starch found that improvement in the test of substituting numbers for letters according to a key came at different rates, varying in accordance with the amount of practice distribution. This is shown in more detail in

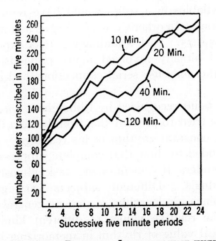

FIGURE 108. DIFFERENT RATES OF IMPROVEMENT WITH DIFFERENT DISTRIBUTIONS OF LEARNING

10 min. curve = group working 10 min. twice a day.
20 " " = " " 20 " once " "
40 " " = " " 40 " every other day.
120 " " = " " 120 " at one time.
(Starch, D., *Jour. Educ. Psychol.*, 1912, **3**, 209–213.)

Figure 108. From a great number of such researches, we may consider it well established that, in the learning of practically any kind of habit, economy is found by spacing the practice with time intervals instead of attempting to get it completely formed all at one sitting. This is one of the reasons why "cramming" has always been looked upon as a good enough method to prepare for certain mechanical types of quizzes, perhaps, but surely a bad one for anything like permanent retention. The question as to whether it is more advisable for college courses to meet three or five times weekly involves this point, but also others. So too, with the problem of length of study period. A complicating point is the fact that the postural set or *Einstellung* exerts an important influence on the response of a person to material that calls for much thinking activity. It may often be more advisable, therefore, to continue study for some time, once the student has gotten well set.

(2) To determine the relative rates at which *rote and meaningful material* could be memorized, Ebbinghaus used stanzas of Byron's *Don Juan*. He found that each stanza (consisting of 80 syllables) required an average of less than 9 repetitions, whereas that number of nonsense syllables in a series would have required between 70 and 80 repetitions. In other words, expressed as a ratio — meaningful : nonsense = 9 : 75. Such a finding was to be expected : the meaningful material already involved many previously formed serial habits, while the nonsense serial connections had all to be formed *de novo*.

(3) Another point recognized by Ebbinghaus was the importance *of rhythm*. He tried to prevent this from being a disturbing factor by adopting a constant rhythm in his readings. Experiments by others have tended to show that complete suppression of rhythmic vocalization renders the memorizing task almost impossible for certain individuals. Different subjects vary greatly in their rhythmic tendencies in learning, so that no general rule can be laid down as to the relative values of different kinds of groupings; but the practical value of rhythm in memorizing has always been obvious enough — or at least ever since young children rehearsing to "speak a piece" have fallen into the "sing-song" manner.

(4) *Reciting* — that is, attempt at reproducing — is of quite considerable effectiveness. One investigator who was practicing on nonsense syllable series tried out twelve different combina-

tions of readings and prompted recitings, as shown in table below:

READ-INGS	RECIT-INGS	READ-INGS	RECIT-INGS	READ-INGS	RECIT-INGS	READ-INGS	RECIT-INGS
6	0	6	5	6	10	6	15
11	0	11	5	11	10	11	15
16	0	16	5	16	10		
21	0						

Of these he found the most economical method to be the combination of 6 readings with 15 recitations. The meaning of this seems to be that an active attitude on the part of the subject aids rapid acquiring [11].

A caution. The foregoing principles or so-called laws of economical learning frequently call for liberal interpreting and applying. It should be borne in mind that they are derived under laboratory conditions, and that they deal for the most part with language rather than manual or other habits, and frequently with only special types of the former.

They are, moreover, for the most part objective, as referring directly to the nature of the material or to the formal and mechanical arrangements of the practice. But — as we have already noted in connection with the fourth point — fully as important is the attitude of the subject who is doing the learning.

Importance of the Subject's Motivation and Attitude. After his reading of Chapters V and XII, it is a familiar enough point to the reader that the way in which a person acts in any particular instance is a function not only of his environment, and of his more overt manner of attack, but also of his motivation and the degree to which and the direction in which he is oriented and mobilized *at the time.* Letting O stand for a subject's organic conditions of motivation and of set, we may revise our familiar formula to read: $S \times O \longrightarrow R$. It is now in order for the student to inquire: What, on the basis of the available evidence, are the conditions of the subject himself that one should control in order to facilitate the acquisition of knowledge and habits?

((1) Attending to the material is not enough; it must be attending with the *intent to learn* it.) As said above, an active attitude is demanded: the learner must "go after it!")

(2) What is at first a curious scientific finding re-enforces this emphasis upon the subject's being active in his learning. In different experiments, one on the memorizing of series of nonsense syllables and words, the other on the running of a stylus maze, it has been clearly brought out that if the subject exerts a continuous *muscular tension* by pressure on a dynamometer or a stylus, his learning is greatly facilitated in either case. Apparently, a mild increase of muscular tonicity serves to keep the learner "on his toes," and in this *active attitude* he is more alert.

This principle simply cannot be overemphasized for the average student. His reading of a book has only a fraction of its value if done in a passive manner: he should actively attack it, address questions to it, ask himself questions about it. Summer fiction, "movies," and other forms of entertainment contribute their share to the breeding of passive habits of attending — although an alive thinker can profit by such things without letting his wits slumber.[1]

(3) A dozen or more investigators have measured the effect upon grade school, high school, and college students of their *knowing the results* of their practice from time to time; and the results are almost unanimously favorable. There is little to be said in favor of mere blind practice. We may ascribe this effect to the facts (a) that the learner by knowing how he is getting on is enabled to check on his right and his wrong procedures and so more rapidly select the one and eliminate the other, and (b) that the rises and falls in his score serve as stimuli to emotional responses of reinforcing character.

(4) The value of *physical rewards and punishments* has been assumed throughout human history — especially the latter. In all ages the ferrule and the cane have had their honored place near to the schoolmaster's hand, as instruments not merely to inform the learner of his errors, but to inflict pain. Is there scientific warrant for this? Investigations of the question have usually taken the form of administering electric shocks whenever the practicing subject made errors. It is a uniform finding that unless the punishment be extremely severe, it serves to reduce errors by setting up an attitude of caution. But — and again everyday

---

[1] Not long ago one of the writer's beginning students who had been dismally failing in his efforts to keep abreast of the work, hit upon the device of continually asking himself questions about the topics of his reading, then conscientiously consulting his books for the answers. It was not long before he was among the leaders of his class.

experience is vindicated — when too severe, the punishment is disruptive in effect. Something like "neurotic" results may be produced, in which the person grows excessively emotional in an unbalanced way: weeping or swearing or tearing at the apparatus. This can be seen to be a practical problem of importance.

(5) *Praise and reproof* soon become substitutes for corporal reward and punishment with human beings; and experimental checking of the effect of encouraging and discouraging comments on school pupils' work tends to verify the commonly practiced notion: both praise and reproof were of value in facilitating the learning [6]. This has to be practiced within limits, however, for when fictitiously high and fictitiously low scores were reported back to the learner, the former accelerated his work but the latter slowed him down [18]; and, indeed, the realization that one is hopelessly unable to meet the (fictitiously established) pace has been found to produce emotional upsets of worry or disgust, expressed in cynical laughing or hearty swearing [10]. As has been brought out in other connections in Chapters VI and VII, the physiological nature of such emotional responses as these is such as to prepare the organism for vigorous overt plunges into action, not for the refined verbal and manual manipulations and dexterities called for in most learning exercises.

(6) Furthermore, the *emotional reaction* aroused by the *learning material* itself must be recognized. For instance, in an experiment in which nonsense syllables were memorized in pairs, when the paired syllables were such that they suggested words with salacious or sacrilegious meanings (as in *gad-dem*) the average number of repetitions needed for learning increased from 7.6 to 14.6, and the next day, the average number of syllables that could be recalled dropped from a normal 12.8 to only 8.0 [2]. Something like a repression of forbidden tendencies appeared.

Interrelations between Habits. Given one habit learned, what will be its effect upon the learning of another habit? Theoretically we can predict that the former may facilitate the latter, may inhibit it, or may have no effect.

(*A*) The conception of the first relationship mentioned has had a history. From the early modern days down to the recent past, schoolmen had made much of the disciplinary value of certain studies, holding that the training in habits of reading Latin and Greek or of handling mathematical formulae had general value:

that such training increased his "general power of observation," his "general reasoning power," making possible a *transference of the training* to any other activity the student might later take up. This theory of the "formal discipline" value of an education in rigorous subjects like the classics and the calculus was naturally in contrast with the view that education is valuable for the content obtained — for the ability to read, to cipher, to know human history and the world of nature, on their own account. No other topic of psychology as applied to education has received the amount of attention devoted to this.

The present-day critical treatments of the question date from 1901, and an epoch-making series of experiments by Thorndike and Woodworth. They briefly tested the ability of subjects to estimate areas, lengths of lines, and weights (the original test series). Then they gave the subjects prolonged practice and training in estimating somewhat different areas, lines, and weights (the training series), and finally they briefly tested them again on the areas, lines, and weights of the first test (the final test series). In a similar way they examined the training effect of perceiving words containing certain letters upon the tested perception of words containing certain other letters. The results can be briefly summarized: in all these tests most subjects did show some improvement in final test over original test, but it was surprisingly slight.[1] From this and other studies of the question, Thorndike concluded that a change in one human function alters any other function only in so far as the two have common or *identical components.*

"Components" must be understood broadly. They include

---

[1] Even some of that may have been due, as Thorndike later pointed out, to whatever practice the subjects had received in the original test; and in later years it is recognized as important to have a group of "control" subjects take the final test *without* having had the intervening training. Thus:

	ORIGINAL TEST	TRAINING SERIES	FINAL TEST
Experimental group	Activity A (one sitting)	Activity B (prolonged practice)	Activity A (one sitting)
Control group	Activity A (one sitting)	No practice	Activity A (one sitting)

If the two groups have been equated on the basis of their original test scores, then the difference in their final test scores furnishes the scientific evidence on the transfer question at issue. This use of a control group is important to note. It illustrates the modern scientist's emphasis upon "controls" of all sorts, that is, methods of holding constant all variables but the one in question.

(*a*) details of stimulus-content (such as letters and words, the figures and the additions and subtractions and fractions, the detailed "facts" learned in history and geography, all of which "carry over" from subject to subject and to outside activities); (*b*) identical habits of special procedure (such as making allowances for a constant error in judging, memorizing with a certain constant rhythm, ignoring distractions, using a dictionary, and the like); (*c*) acts of generalization (as, grasping a principle or a rule or law and applying it to another problem or field); and even (*d*) ideals or attitudes (such as being neat in one's papers, keeping an open-minded attitude, getting down to work). In other words, the beneficial effect of any educational subject upon any other subjects or upon one's after-school activities resides not in any magical potency of the subject-matter itself, nor in any effect upon one's "faculty" of memory-in-general or attention-in-general or reasoning-power-in-general. It resides only in those habits of responding in this or that identifiable way to this or that detail, aspect, or configuration that may be *a common feature of both situations.*

(*B*) One habit that is learned may not, after all, have a positive effect on the learning of another: it may have a neutral effect, or even a negative effect. There is, for instance, the well-known phenomenon of *interference.* Münsterberg noted that if he changed his watch from the left vest pocket where it was usually carried to the right trousers' pocket, he made a number of false movements when he wished to know the time, although he could soon get habituated to the new reaching reactions required; but, on returning the watch to its original left vest pocket, he again made a few false movements. Everyday illustrations of interference abound. What man, on changing from a sailor straw hat to a soft felt in the early fall, has not found himself fumbling at the wrong place when he had occasion to lift his hat — only to experience the opposite difficulty when changing back in the spring?

It is a general finding that the interferences that seem striking when one or both habits are in their initial stages of formation tend to disappear as the habits become well integrated. This point is well exemplified in the rule that forbids a student to begin his study of two foreign languages in the same year.

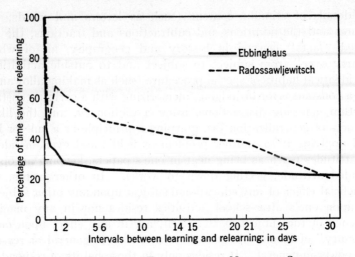

FIGURE 109. CURVES OF FORGETTING OF NONSENSE SYLLABLES

RETAINING

Introduction. Once a habit has been acquired, what about its permanence? Forgetting is an all too familiar process, and everyone can probably make very hazy estimates concerning the processes and factors involved. But here, fully as much as in the discussion of Acquiring, we must depend upon scientific evidences.

The Rate of Forgetting. Working with his series of nonsense syllables Ebbinghaus found that the process of forgetting occurred in a definitely measurable way. His results are graphed in Figure 109, along with those of a later investigator.

The reader is doubtless asking himself whether these curves of retaining can be of universal validity and can be true for all kinds of habits. Surely we do not forget how to swim, jump, speak English, or give a friend's name as rapidly as this! The world would be at sixes and sevens if the grocer remembered no better than this the prices on his commodities in stock, or the postman his mail route, the physician his standard prescriptions, or the mother her own child.

As a matter of fact, experimental support is not lacking for a more optimistic conception of human capacities. Conservation of practice effect on a manual habit was once tested on subjects who had been trained in tossing two balls with one hand, one ball being caught and thrown while the other was in the air. Average scores of ten trials daily for forty-two days in the original acquisition experiments are shown on the left of Figure 110.[1] Then once per month for five months thereafter tests for retention were made with results as shown by the points connected with dotted lines. One and a third years after the last monthly test, with no intervening practice, a retest was made. Finally, four and a fourth years after this a test of retention in the form of a few days of relearning resulted in the acquisition curve shown at the extreme right, which is to be compared with the original acquisition curve at the extreme left.

How are we to account for the differences in the retaining value of this, that, and the other $S \longrightarrow R$ function? We know the following to be apparent enough in everyday life: people do not forget the movements and strokes of swimming, tennis, or dancing, in anything approaching the degree to which they may very easily forget the foreign language studied in high school, the names of people met years previously at an afternoon tea, or a schedule of trains used months before. One suggestion has been that it is a

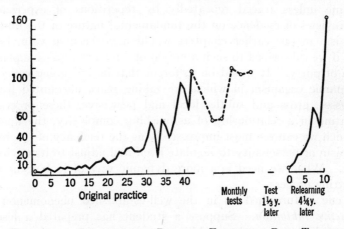

FIGURE 110. RETENTION OF PRACTICE EFFECTS IN BALL TOSSING

(Swift, E. J., *Amer. J. Psychol.*, 1903, **14**, 204 ff.; 1905, **16**, 132; and *Psychol. Bull.*, 1910, **7**, 18.)

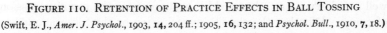

[1] This curve of acquisition is seen to be of the positive acceleration type. This is due to the arrangement of trials; each trial consisting of continued throwing until a failure to catch. Had each trial consisted of a constant number of throws, the curve would have been one showing negative acceleration — as Peterson proved by experimental retrial.

question primarily of number of repetitions given. In the experiments in ball-tossing the muscular movements involved in keeping the two balls going were repeated many thousands of times in the 42 days of practice. With this immense amount of repetition and overlearning it is no wonder that the bonds persisted. If one were to take a poem involving 46 words or 46 ideas and practice saying it for 60 days, and then after a year and a half relearn it, the results might be similar to those obtained in ball tossing.

A clincher on this question has been brought forward in the results of a careful comparative study of the rate of forgetting skill in maze-running and memory of nonsense syllables when given equivalent amounts of practice: neither type of proficiency was retained better than the other [9].

Dynamic Nature of the Forgetting Process. What *is* this forgetting? The curves show only the results, not what is going on. It is the traditional popular and scientific view that forgetting is some kind of "fading out": that the newborn child is a blank tablet upon which the writing stylus of experience makes its impressions, and that these impressions gradually disappear with the passing of time unless traced repeatedly by repetitions of experience. The reviews of evidence on the fundamental nature of the human organism in our earlier chapters would have been in vain, however, if we subscribed to such a notion of a man as a passive plastic lump of putty. It would be to forget that he is a going concern, a dynamic organism in which are taking place uncounted living processes, gross and subtle, local and pervasive, these processes operating in a relationship of astonishing complexity, the upshot of which we can see most impressively as the tendency of the total organism or personality to regulate itself and adjust to its environment. What we need is a more dynamic way of looking at the forgetting process.

A cue is furnished us in the well-established phenomenon of *retroactive inhibition.* Suppose a student has prepared a lesson well or a lawyer has rehearsed his argument for the morning session of court. Whether the classroom recitation or the forensic address is to be well recalled tomorrow will depend not simply on how well it has been acquired but also upon what other activities the person will have participated in meanwhile. Experimentally, suppose the following two learning programs to be compared.

ORIGINAL PRACTICE ⟶ ACTIVITY OF ANOTHER KIND ⟶ TEST OF RETENTION
(For example, mem-   (For example, memo-   (For example, Ger-
orizing a German-   rizing pictures, work-   man-English vocab-
English vocabulary)   ing sums, taking an   ulary)
                         intelligence test, fig-
                         uring statistical cor-
                         relations)

ORIGINAL PRACTICE ⟶   REST   ⟶ TEST OF RETENTION
(For example, as above)   (For example, as above)

The many careful researches on this subject leave us in no doubt: what one will retain over an interval of interpolated activity will show impairment as compared with what he will retain over an interval of rest. This difference, moreover, will vary in its magnitude with differences in the nature of the interpolated work or rest, retention being best of all after an interval of sleep.

The point of it all, for us at this time, is that what is responsible for the loss of a learned function is clearly not a passive fading away on its own part, but some active interference with it, an *inhibition of it by other functions that are going on.*

Not only are those "other functions" dynamic in character, but also the original learning process. When a child or adult is practicing he is an active participant, not a passive recipient. This was clearly implied in a preceding section of this chapter, and in the concluding section of the preceding chapter.

Nowhere has this been brought out more neatly than in a famous experiment in Lewin's laboratory. A number of learners were assigned tasks such as printing names, sketching, and assembling puzzles. In some cases the subjects were interrupted before completing their tasks, while in others they were allowed to complete them; and a test of retention was given after each. In 26 out of 32 subjects better memory for the uncompleted tasks was definitely shown, one subject doing six times as well on them. The learning process, it seems, set up a *tension*, a determining tendency *to completion of the activity*, which remained unresolved when interrupted; and the better memory of the interrupted subjects may be thought of as an expression of this tendency in them to complete the learning task.

Forgetting, in a word, is not a passive fading out but is a phase of the subject's active life.

Is a Habit Once Acquired Ever Lost? It is interesting to ask whether or not a habit once acquired is ever entirely lost. Evidences against any such total forgetting seem to come from different sources. The accelerated form of curves for the *reacquiring of old habits* is in point. Outside the laboratory, too, this is to be seen in the surprisingly short time often taken by an adult to relearn some of his high school or college subjects which he supposed he had entirely lost. Consider the experiment in which selections of Greek drama were read aloud to an infant daily, with changes of selections every three months, from the age of 15 months to 3 years. When the boy was 8½ years old he was set to learning these passages as well as new equal-length passages of similar material. The surprising result was that in every case the selections to which he had been exposed in his infancy were now learned (relearned) considerably faster than were any of the new ones [4].

A second way in which an apparent forgetting may not be a real and total loss is manifested in the way the training that a person has once had helps almost mysteriously *in learning new tasks*. The fretful freshman may wonder why he has so many required courses to take in subjects of which he is certain to forget the major part in the course of two or three years. But it is almost a certainty that those thousand-and-one bits of habits once acquired will continue to exert their influence in determining his point of view, his "background," his *Anschauung*, to a degree distinctly noticeable and important. Indeed, this kind of transfer is the very essence of culture.

Finally, we must not neglect the abnormal cases of unusual *recall under special conditions*. In the hypnotic stage of sleeping, for instance, old "forgotten" habits have frequently been evoked by the operator. The crystal-gazer may after steady eye-fixation be thrown into a condition in which weak, poorly formed habits are relatively more potent. The anesthetic hand of an hysterical subject may be able to write down old things once learned but no longer recalled by the less dramatic processes of vocal reactions. (Cf. cases given on pp. 151 f. above.) So much for evidences on one side of the question: evidences on the other side would, like most forms of negative evidence, be somewhat inconclusive. In view of the fact, however, that it will remain forever impossible to test out a man's ability to recall every little $S \rightarrow R$ that has been hit upon in his past thirty years, the question may be called "academic" and so dismissed.

REPRODUCING

Reproducing is a Way of Reacting. The measure of retention is recall, and the value of a person's learning inheres in his capacity to set at work again segments of behavior established formerly. If recalling be an act, it cannot be an unstimulated response any more than an effect can be uncaused, but it must have its initial excitation in some extra- or intra-organic event or condition. Suppose a person finds himself repeating "Ich weiss nicht was soll es bedeuten." This may be due to his having seen or heard the word "Heine" or even "Heinrich"; or he may have heard a snatch of Silcher's music, or only a certain tapped rhythm; or he may have heard the Rhine mentioned, or "mermaid" or "siren." The name of an instructor, who once read the poem aloud or sang it in its musical arrangement, may have been heard or may have been pronounced by the subject himself in his soliloquy; or someone with the instructor's cast of eye may have passed on the street. Or again, a revival of the particular emotional mood in which the poem had formerly been read might now effect a revival of the poem itself. The speaking of the sentence has, in short, been a part of so many and so subtle events that the precise stimulation evoking its recall may be beyond detection.

The stimuli to recalled reactions, then, are many and fall into many types. *Socially produced stimuli* are common — the words of the dinner-table conversation provide a potent and rich supply of stimuli to many a spoken or unspoken "that reminds me." There are the *physical stimuli* of the world about: a certain type of headgear, a familiar train whistle, the string on one's finger (a placed "reminder"), a calendar seen, the pressures on foot and hand of pedals and steering wheel, moonlight on water — each of them likely to excite some old response conditioned to it. Then there are the *organic and emotional conditions*; such as the hunger that causes Arctic explorers to be musing continually — whether awake or asleep — about bountiful tables that they have formerly seen. Again, there is the reawakening of old reactions by stimulations *via* auditory and kinesthetic pathways from the *subject's own words, gestures, and bodily postures*. The following is an example of this last. The writer's ten-year-old son, who had been a great "fan" in attendance at university athletic events, was once being shown how to tie a better four-in-hand, when he cried, "Wait a minute, wait a minute, let me!" The rhythm of this speech rearoused some well-integrated cheering activities frequently performed in concert in the bleachers; and he stepped over to the mirror, calling over the above words to the tempo and beat of a college cheer, accompanied by motions of a cheer leader, and finishing up with a drawn-out "Wait — wait — wait."

There is no recalling, then, without some kind of present stimulus. Or, to turn this statement into a more practical form, if you want a person (yourself, for instance) to recall a former activity of his, you should supply an appropriate stimulus — one that is, or contains an element that is, connected to that activity by previous experience.

It is a Phase of Adjustive Behavior. The whole truth is not yet told when we speak of a man's recalling as reacting. He is indeed so active in this reacting that he makes, in a sense, contributions of his own. The unintended falsification of memory at the very moment of recall is a well-recognized phenomenon in everyday life — and one not limited to the witness stand, nor to children, either.

One technique for getting this phenomenon under closer scrutiny is to have a subject who has been "exposed" to a situation or story attempt to reproduce it several times after different intervals, and then to compare his successive accounts for any definite trends therein. Students in an English university read a tale from American Indian folklore; then at various intervals (ranging from fifteen minutes to ten years) they attempted several reproductions [1]. The experimenter made no quantitative counting of details lost, but was interested rather in a qualitative analysis of what happens to the material in the recalling. He did notice a true forgetting in the simplification of the stories by dropping out proper names, definite numbers, and the like. But he observed at the same time some tendency to elaborate the story by transforming some items into more familiar ones or by inventing and inserting new ones. What we should especially note, now, is that what was particularly well retained was the subject's reactions to the general plan, scheme, form, order, arrangement of it all, and that omissions were mostly of items unessential to this general form, while inventions and transformations were usually quite in harmony with it. Of this we are assured by the evidence: when a person is originally reacting to a (story) situation, he is reacting not simply to its details in piecemeal fashion but also to the whole general pattern or configuration; and when recalling that experience *he recalls it primarily as a general pattern or configuration*, and his errors are errors in harmony with it. Indeed, the distortion of recalled details to fit the general scheme often proceeded to the point of naïve rationalizations in which definite reasons were furnished by the subject for new items he had unwittingly introduced.

From the above it is clear also that recalling is not mere reproducing, it is *a dynamic process of adjustment* that the individual is making *to some problem* at the time, one in which his *personal interest is enlisted.*

Some Objective Determinants of Recall.   The richness of human experience is such that any sight, sound, or other stimulus may be capable of arousing any of several very different reactions.   It is a commonplace that the one appropriate response to an automobile horn, to a request for a loan, or to a proposal of marriage will have to be determined by many coincident and qualifying circumstances: who it is, where it happens, and when.   And so it is with the re-exciting of an old habit: the one of the reactions formerly coupled to the stimulus which will now be called forth depends upon many things.

For over a century, certain factors, "secondary laws of association," have been considered as some of the conditions that determine which of many possible responses is the one most likely to be reinstated.   These secondary associations, which were originally the fruit of everyday observation, have since been corroborated in the laboratory.   They are as follows.   *Other things being equal:*

(The S.R. connection or series of connections most frequently exercised is the one most apt to be operative later (the law of *Frequency*).) Of the various faces seen in pictures or in life the child or man is most likely to react with recognition to the one he has seen oftenest.) The right rather than the wrong way of spelling "occasion," of writing the product of "11 times 12," of speaking the lines of a play depends for its proper selection and especially its fixation upon this law of Frequency.

(The most recently used function is the one most apt to be re-aroused later (the law of *Recency*).) The student does special reviewing just before his examination.   The lawyer concentrates on his brief just before a case is to be called.   One can repeat in full a conversation of yesterday, whereas one of a year ago is repeated only by snatches or not at all.   A pianist who is asked to play a certain composition may protest that it has been too long since he last played it.

(The first S.R. function used is most easily reinstated later (the law of *Primacy*).) One is often able to give a better account of the happenings during his first day in college or his first day in the new business office, remembers better his first medical case, his first ocean voyage.

The function first organized with the greatest intensity is the one most likely to reappear later (the law of *Intensity*). Every teacher knows that a pupil's overt and implicit reactions that are made attentively have a greater recall value than those performed in a perfunctory manner. To this end the teacher may adopt various devices for enhancing the stimuli: raising the voice, lowering it, using diagrams, using red chalk, and so on. The learner on his own part may employ various ways of intensifying the original stimulation, such as taking a concentrated attitude toward the lecture, book, or experiment. Emotionalizing the reaction to a stimulus seems likewise in some instances to improve its readiness on later recall; and a sub-law might not be out of place: "that connection formed with more emotional re-enforcement is more likely to be arousable later." For months after a child's death the parents may be quickly and excessively reactive to any situation containing elements in common with earlier experiences with the child. The lovelorn is excitable by stimuli in any way conditioned by or associated with the sight and sound of his loved one, at times to the well-nigh total exclusion of any other kind of behavior.

These four classic laws have been experimentally confirmed repeatedly, but in their general forms as they have been stated above; and the very generality of the terms "frequency," "recency," and the others ought to lend some interest to an investigation as to what might be the effect on recall of different *degrees* or different *kinds* of frequency, of recency, of primacy, and of intensity [7]. An experimenter read aloud to groups of college students a biographical sketch of a fictitious character containing seventy items; and they were immediately to try to reproduce it. (In changing from group to group he arranged the particular items in different orders, to control the factor of differences in their content.) Some of the items were given the advantage of frequency by being repeated either immediately or later in the recital. Some of them were intensified by such devices as remarking immediately after, "Did you notice that?" or saying in advance, "Now get this"; or they were accompanied by a gesture or a banged fist, or were given in a louder voice or slower voice or a pause. The first three items of each reading had the advantage of primacy, of course, and the last three of recency.

The clearest presentation of the results of these exercises would be by showing some of the final tabulated data. In the table results for all groups are reproduced.   The scores are turned into percentages.   The frequency of recall of the items falling in the middle part of the biography and having no reinforcement by repetition nor intensification is represented by 100 per cent.   The reader will note by casting his eye down the columns that all but one of the particular methods of applying the four laws did strengthen the recall above the normal standard.   He will also note interesting and important differences in the effect of variations within

ADVANTAGES FOR RECALL OF PRIMACY, RECENCY, FREQUENCY,
AND INTENSITY
(No. of cases 253)

Middle neutral (normal)	100%
Primacy	
1st item	175
2nd item	163
3rd item	135
Recency	
68th item	123
69th item	119
70th (last) item	128
Frequency	
2 concentrated repetitions	
10th and 10th	116
60th and 60th	139
2 distributed repetitions	
35th and 40th	162
11th and 60th	139
3 repetitions	197
4 repetitions	246
5 repetitions	315
Intensity	
"Did you notice that?"	154
Slow	79
Bang	115
Gesture	118
Loud	126
Pause	143
"Now get this"	191

each of the four; for example, the very first statement had advantage over the next to the first, that the next to the first had an advantage over the second from the first; 5 repetitions led to better recalling than 4; a verbal warning preceding an item had more effect than one following it — and others.

Incidentally, we should note that this study illustrates neatly the second great office of the experimental method in the advancement of knowledge: not only does it check and verify everyday observations, but it goes on to work out the detailed conditions, the qualifying circumstances. Instead merely of following up popular experience, it goes on ahead.

Identity of setting and context. Research leads us to add another law to these well-known ones. In the animal laboratories, after a white rat has learned to run a maze successfully, a change

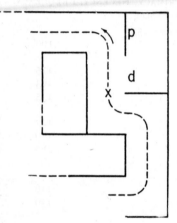

has been made in some detail of its general environment — a light or sound from a new direction, the appearance of a spectator, the mere turning of the maze about on its pedestal so that directions are changed, or the alteration of some detail within the maze that is not really an alteration in the true path being learned (cf. Figure 111). Changes like these will produce a poorer reinstatement of the running. Approaches to the same general problem have been made in the human laboratories. Memorized material can be recalled most completely if the general surroundings be the same as on the occasions of original acquisition: if learned in a certain laboratory room it is not so well recalled outdoors as in the laboratory, and *vice versa* [15]. Even the absence of a per-

FIGURE 111. DOOR OF CUL-DE-SAC CHANGED, PRODUCING HESITANT BEHAVIOR

A group of white rats had just been trained in daily runs to the point where they had learned the whole maze (shown in part), running the true path (dotted line) without hitch or hesitation. At this point the writer shifted the partition section *p* over to *d* where the *cul-de-sac* entrance had always been, leaving the entrance now at *p*. On the next run eight of the ten animals came to a full stop at the point *x*, then without error continued their true course on to the exit.

vading odor that had been present during learning has been shown to have an unfavorable effect on the attempt to recall. Similarly for the narrower environmental conditions more usually called context. In one research word-pairs were learned by the paired-associates method, using cards bearing in smaller type other words not concerned in the learning. When these incidental words were changed it became more difficult to recall the essential word-pairs.   Similarly, when faces and names were learned in pairs from picture postcards, a change in this postcard background for the faces reduced the subject's ability to recall the names to go with them [13].

But there is another phase of the matter of considerable practical importance.   The incidental details of an animal maze setting can be systematically varied from trial to trial throughout the learning stages — maze rotated, lights and shadows interchanged, a maze wall panel changed, direction of a sound shifted, and the like.   The animals so trained will *not* show evidence of a disturbance when tested later for reproduction of the habit under unusual conditions [14].   The matter is simple enough to understand if we write it as *S*'s and *R*'s.   If a given *R* be practiced always in the presence of a given situation of *S*'s, then it is likely to become conditioned to some degree to all of the component *S*'s.   Then, (1) in order that a given habit or memory be best reproduced at a later time, that reproducing should be assisted by having present as many as possible of the original circumstances (*S*'s).   (2) If future recall of the function *R* is likely to be desired under widely different sets of circumstances (*S*'s), then the unessential details of the learning situation should be carefully varied during the learning.[1]

Subjective Determinants are Important.   Closely related to objective context is the subject's *set*.   Out of all his learned repertoire, just which *R* a person is likely to revive on a given occasion depends upon what he is set for, what "determining tendency" may be uppermost, what he is expecting.

Place before a number of school children the problem

$$\begin{array}{r} 36 \\ \underline{17} \end{array}$$

and simply ask them to "do" it, and you are fairly sure to get three very different responses: 53, 19, and 612.   Each is a correct enough answer which has been drilled as the *R* to such *S*'s.   Each, however, was acquired in a certain context of material, when the pupil was doing a certain kind of thing and was thereby set to continue that kind of thing.   The reactions leading to the answer 53, for instance, were originally acquired when adding happened

[1] The reader will be able to see how this point is supported by points presented elsewhere, especially on pp. 386, 559 f.

to be the order of the day. If a teacher, then, would test whether a pupil can multiply the two numbers 36 and 17, it is not sufficient to place these two visual patterns before him. He must be prepared to multiply — either by being given the verbal signal "multiply this," or by being occupied previously with multiplying — so that when he addresses these new figures he is primed, oriented, set in the right direction.

Important in a person's set is his mood, and this is indeed an important determinant as to which old habits will reassert themselves. The Dead March from *Saul*, Chopin's Funeral March, the last movement of Tschaikowsky's Sixth Symphony, come more readily from the fingers or the throat of the musician who is steeped in sorrow than would Anitra's Dance, March of the Sardar, or the Eroica. So, too, the man who is in love is more likely to be heard repeating snatches of lyrical, springtime verse than words remembered from some more solemn epic. Such illustrations remind us that the emotional segments of the whole motor attitude are there and are operative. Emotional congruity is a determining factor in recalling.

Experimental results confirm these general observations of the strong influence of a person's present attitude upon the rearousal of his habits. Subjects were once provided with printed lists of skeleton words with missing letters to be supplied. Some of the lists were headed with a statement that "the following are names of familiar fruits," or "of American authors," or "of domestic animals." Other lists were not described further than as miscellaneous nouns. The exact time required for each person to complete each list was noted, and a comparison was drawn between the average time for the classified and for the unclassified lists. For every one of the 28 individuals the average for the classified was found to be shorter than for the unclassified, the group averages being, respectively, 36 sec. and 1 min. 15 sec. The establishing of a set in some particular direction, as in that of naming fruits, or authors, or animals, not only dictated which previously acquired response would be reproduced but also facilitated its reproduction [16]. An experiment devised by the writer to show similar results has been described on other pages (pp. 318 f.). A preliminary orientation or set, we may conclude, aids definitely in recall.

The Scientific Study of Testimony. So important are the subjective determinants in recall that it has always furnished a most serious practical problem in the psychology of testimony.   Not only is the average man subject to errors, but even the trained reporter may frequently betray his own limitations either in the observing or in the recalling of an event.

Consider the following case.   On a certain date all the New York newspapers agreed in reporting that Alexander Kerensky had been slapped in the face by a young woman on the stage of the Century Theater.   But their descriptions varied as follows:

> *The World:* "Slashed him viciously across the cheek with her gloves."
> *The News:* "Struck him on the left cheek with the bouquet."
> *The American:* "Dropped her flowers and slapped him in the face with her gloves."
> *The Times:* "Slapped his face vigorously with her gloves three times."
> *The Herald Tribune:* "Beat him on the face and head . . . a half-dozen blows."
> *The Evening World:* "Struck him across the face several times."
> *The Daily Mirror:* "Struck him a single time."
> *The Evening Post:* "Vigorously and accurately slapped him."

Nearly forty years ago, Stern initiated research on the reliability of report by using two kinds of *Aussage* or testimony experiments. In one, a picture of a scene or of an occurrence was placed before a subject who was told to observe it; and later his ability to recall was tested.   The picture that was used most frequently was one of a room containing the simple furniture of a peasant's cottage — table, stools, bed, cradle — with a man and a boy eating at a table and a woman standing and serving.   In a cradle was a baby, with a doll on the floor and a dog near by.   Other things to be seen were dishes on the table, a vacant chair by the woman, clock and pictures on the wall, a window with curtains and shade and holding a plant, etc.   Many objects were strongly colored [17].

For another type of experiment Stern devised what has come to be known as the "dramatic incident" method.   In one case he says: "my lecture was interrupted by the entrance of a gentleman who spoke with me and took a book from the bookcase, the performance having been exactly studied beforehand in all its details.   The members of the seminar gave but little attention to what was going on.   A week later they were required to report upon what had taken place."   As frequently used by scores of teachers since, the event may contain much action, sound, and fury, so that the effect of distracting and emotion-arousing elements of the situation may be observed.

The many investigators of testimony agree that the more immature the subject the more unreliable the report. For one thing, his suggestibility is greater. A young child on the witness stand, we can be assured, is of exceedingly doubtful value to any court. Other factors that enter in to distort testimony are a low level of general intelligence, the subject's emotional attitudes, the emotion-exciting character of the event in question, and the nature of the questions in the examination and the cross examination. These are but a few of many psychological points about human fallibility that, as experimentally demonstrable and measurable facts, are bound to be increasingly recognized in the legal process of presumably seeking the truth about an event that is in question.

Some Special Difficulties in Recalling.   A man who has never shown distress when seeking to rearouse an old reaction is as fortunate as he is rare. It seems to be the portion of humanity that sometimes when occasion arises for the prompt using of a certain part of a man's former equipment, that part stubbornly refuses to be recalled. On his first night the budding actor may hear the cue for the thoroughly rehearsed speech that he has learned by heart, and yet be able only to stutter and shiver before the sea of upturned faces. The overanxious young host or hostess upon presenting an old friend to a different circle of acquaintances may of a sudden be seized with an unaccountable forgetting of the old friend's name, though he has spoken it readily enough dozens and hundreds of times.

What can be the cause of such irregularities in human performance? In the case of the actor it is fairly obvious that emotional complications are at the root of the difficulty. We have already seen that many grosser emotional reactions operate to block the smooth-running activities of more delicate and elaborate reaction mechanisms. The more primitive and lower-center processes, taking their right of way, inhibit later acquired and higher-center processes. *Intense emotion*, particularly if it be of the fear type, will then block attempts to recall such delicately organized activities as the language responses — will render negative the effects of stimuli to them. Anxiety over an examination has been known often to render an otherwise well-informed person partially helpless, so that he will set down answers which on cooler reflection he easily knows to have been wrong.

In the same class with these recognizable emotional blockings is the less dramatic *interference by antagonistic habits.* Skillful speakers are known to be overcome with confusion when a certain phrase just uttered has the power to start them off on two different lines of serial reaction, and the set and context are not sufficient to determine the recalling of one alone. The difficulty observed in introductions, mentioned in an earlier paragraph, is of this type also. Let a person start asking himself, "Now let's see, shall I be able to speak each name properly or shan't I?" — and this question is given so undue an amount of his attending that the easy-running naming reactions become displaced (inhibited). The trouble then is in allowing too many antagonistic stimuli to be operative.

> The centipede was happy quite until the toad in fun
> Said, "Pray, which leg comes after which?"
> This raised her doubts to such a pitch
> She fell distracted in the ditch,
> Unable now to run.

Another form of failure in recall has been stressed by the psycho-pathologists. In cases when a subject may be unable to recall a name, or a number, analysis of his past life and the conditions under which the desired reaction was once acquired or with which it has later been conditioned may bring to light a somewhat more complicated causal explanation. Suppose a scene, a story, a form of socially forbidden behavior, to be of a strong emotional character such as to arouse an avoidance reaction by the subject. By conditioning, the avoidance or repression may come to function as the regular R to any S that may have been in any way connected with the original avoided situation. The substitute R has become the habitual way of dealing with such occasions. The original R has been forgotten, or, as the psychoanalysts prefer to say, "*repressed.*" We may well recall the cases of forgetting by repression given on pp. 151 f.

RECOGNIZING[1]

As a Test of Memory. The degree to which a particular learned mode of reaction has been retained up to a given time may be

---

[1] Properly speaking, Recognizing is a phase of Reproducing, but as some special studies have been directed to this phase alone, and as one may at times recall without recognizing, we may follow the precedent of treating it as involving a fourth set of problems.

tested by the method of recognition. A series of stimuli (for example, nonsense syllables, digits, geometrical designs, etc.) once presented to the subject for memorizing are subsequently presented again in conjunction with other stimuli to see how many of the first series he can identify in the second. It is a universal result of experiments that the subject can recognize many items that he has been unable to reproduce by direct recall. So too in everyday life. Thousands are the musical airs, the passages of prose or poetry, the names of acquaintances that one can identify promptly as such and such upon hearing or seeing them, but few are those that he can resurrect without special and elaborate aids. The unhappy public speaker searching for his word would recognize it instantly were someone only to whisper it to him.

Ability to recognize correctly is another aspect of memory that is important from a legal standpoint. The identification of suspects by injured parties or by incidental witnesses is at times taken as sufficient evidence for conviction; and it is unfortunate that the authorities take too little account of the errors so easily committed. For instance, to have a witness identify by indicating whether a single person or a single thing presented before him is the one in question is little more than worthless on account of the powerful suggestive effect, and whenever possible he should be called upon to pick out the man or object from a group of similar persons or things.

Incomplete Recognizing Analyzed. Essentially, to recognize an object or situation is simply to react to that stimulus pattern in an habitual way. Rover is recognizing his master when he runs to meet him, fawns, jumps up for a petting. The cat that responds promptly to the call "Kitty, kitty, kitty!" is recognizing those vocal sounds. Similarly we train children to "know" spoken and written words, to be able to share in musical airs heard, to name correctly kinds of trees, and animals, and maps. The animals momentarily arrested in their run through the slightly changed maze referred to in Figure 111 were manifesting incomplete recognition, since the co-operating stimuli to the elaborate serial habit of maze-running were not completely present and active in their usual way.

There is a phenomenon playing a dramatic part in fiction as well as in everyday life that goes by the name of "paramnesia." A man in a situation absolutely new to him — and one that he can assure you is new — may yet manifest (or at least may describe to you) impulses to act as if he were in an old environment, as if he were quite accustomed and habituated to it all.   Yet he has never been here before.

> But there's a tree — of many, one —
> A single field which I have looked upon:
> Both of them speak of something that is gone.

How then explain?   Such occurrences turn out to be cases in which identical components are the crucial items.   To be concrete, assume

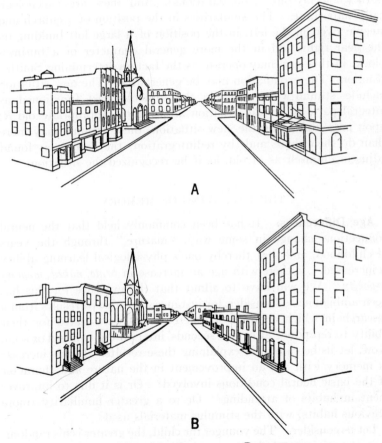

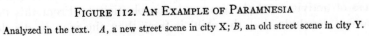

FIGURE 112. AN EXAMPLE OF PARAMNESIA

Analyzed in the text.   *A*, a new street scene in city X; *B*, an old street scene in city Y.

that Mr. Smith upon facing a street vista in city X, sketched in Figure 112, *A*, is strangely moved to act as if in an old environment. He partially recognizes the scene spread before him, although complete knowledge of his personal history is conclusive on the point: he has never been within a hundred miles of this city X before. A careful canvassing of his past life may, however, bring out the fact that at one time he was often in the foreground of the scene in city Y sketched in Figure 112, *B*. Now, to be sure, the majority of the items present differ in the two scenes, but there are a few in common; and also there are some general relationships common to both whole lay-outs (configurations). And these are psychologically important. The similarities in the position of a church and steeple over on the left, in the position of a large loft building on the near right, and in the more general character of a business block, in this case may operate as the factors determining Smith's reaction. The explanation may be generalized. The new situation includes stimuli which have in the subject's past functioned as integral parts of an old situation arousing the appropriate old *R*; upon presentation of the new situation, these stimuli may more than do their share and (by redintegration) the subject is found adjusting himself as of old, as if he recognized the situation.

THE IMPROVING OF MEMORY

Age Differences. It has been commonly held that the neural connections change in some way, "mature," through the years of childhood, and that thereby one's physiological learning ability is increased. Is there with age an increase in *brute, naked, memory capacity*? We will have to admit that the evidence for this has been ambiguous. Consider, for instance, the table of results from a research in which children of different ages were tested for their ability to reproduce after five seconds' interval digits heard or seen. Now, let us be careful in explaining these results. Is this increase in memory with age an improvement in the nature and character of the basic neural conditions involved? Or is it due to improvement in habits of attending? Or to a greater familiarity (more previous habits) with the stimulus materials used?

Let us consider. The younger the child, the greater is his randomness of activity and the greater is his plasticity. From this fact we can conclude that the child is freer than the man to develop

DEVELOPMENT OF MEMORY FOR DIGITS (SMEDLEY)

AVERAGE AGE		PER CENT REPRODUCED	
YEARS	MONTHS	AUDITORY	VISUAL
7	8	36.4	35.2
8	8	44.6	42.8
9	6	45.0	47.4
10	5	49.4	54.6
11	6	55.4	64.7
12	6	55.7	72.3
13	7	57.9	76.8
14	6	66.2	80.5
15	6	65.6	78.2
16	6	66.9	81.3
17	6	65.5	84.1
18	5	67.2	77.5
19	5	70.0	85.3

and learn in many new directions; he is less prejudiced and committed; he can take up a very new activity and learn it with less interference from pre-established habits.   American parents in a long sojourn abroad have difficulty in ever mastering a radically new language, while their children pick up the speech habits of the new environment with astonishing readiness.   The former have too many and too deeply grooved English-speaking habits that constitute interfering ways of naming this thing and that thing.   They tend to react as did the North Country squire who protested against the Frenchman's calling bread *pain*, "when it really is bread, you know."   It is a case of habit interference.

If we turn to the acquisition of new habits that are built upon, rather than counter to, old habits, the child is at a disadvantage. A seven- or eight-year-old would be enormously handicapped in attempting to master stenography, to learn algebra, to understand Malthus or Marx.   On the other hand, if the habit to be acquired has little in common with any already learned, and so presents small possibility of either interference or transference, little difference between the child and the adult is to be expected.

For one thing, then, age differences in learning and memory are a matter of *the relationship of old and new habits*.   It is a question of the degree to which the individual is already habitualized.

The above question of the ability of the child as compared with that of the adult has had much attention for many years.   But

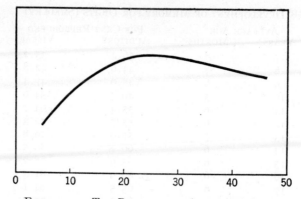

FIGURE 113. THE RELATION OF AGE TO LEARNING

A curve drawn to represent the learning ability of persons of varying ages. (From Thorndike, E. L., *et al.*, *Adult Learning*, Macmillan, 1928, 127.)

what of the adult as he grows older?   It is a common assumption that his learning and remembering abilities decline rapidly during middle life and on into old age.   Thorndike has obtained results on the basis of some very extended researches with a variety of rote and logical memory materials; these appear in Figure 113. Through childhood as far as about 16 years there was found a very rapid increase in capacity, then a very little increase that reaches a level around 30, then a gradual decline to 45, where capacity is approximately that of age 16.   Some findings by the Miles [12] are not different for the same ages, though they found somewhat sharper declines from 50 to 90.   Their results would seem to support Thorndike in the practical conclusion that "in general, nobody under 45 should restrain himself from trying to learn anything because of a belief or fear that he is too old to be able to learn it."   The important things are his motivation and his stock of habits.

Artificial Mnemonic Systems.   Everyone is familiar with certain simple artificial devices that aid in recall: "Thirty days hath September"; "Wash Ad Jeff Mad"; the medical students' "On Old Olympus'"; rhythmical emphases; picking off the initial letters of an array of names or terms and forcing them into a familiar word — such methods are legion, and serve their purposes well.   It is o'ershooting the mark, however, to carry the procedure to the point of the usual mnemotechnic system.   Let a sample taken from one now on sale serve as illustration. Assign a figure to each consonant sound, or *vice versa.* Thus:

let the equivalent of *1* be *t, th,* or *d*

2	*l*
3	*r*
4	*m*
5	*n*
6	*j, sh, g,* or *ch*
7	*k, c g,* or *q*
8	*p* or *b*
9	*f* or *v*
0	*s, ç,* or *z*

Given a number to remember, the forgetful man is bidden to consider the consonant equivalents of the respective digits, then ingeniously to interpolate vowels to make an easily recalled word or phrase more or less appropriate to the number. Take a simple case: suppose one has great difficulty recalling his friend's telephone number, which is 6505. One is supposed to be helped by the fact that perhaps the friend's name is Johnson, or that he is a lover of songs (*chanson*), or maybe that he raises jinseng (!); for such a keyword is so much easier to remember than the number. This is only a first lesson, however. For the rest, Meumann says:

"Mnemonic aids employ a jumbled medley of the most heterogeneous aids to memory which cannot fail to confuse one by their unsystematic arrangement. At one time, they rely upon similarities of sound; at another, upon logical relations — which are usually falsely stated; at another, they have recourse to memory of locality; at another, they bring in a complicated substitution of other letters or numbers, and the like." [1]

It is idle to say that such systems do no good. Many a man has purchased one and, by his own testimony at least, profited much. But the profit has accrued not from the employment of the devices themselves as much as from the interest and energy and attention put into the matter of watching how one does his learning, the active attitude enlisted. If a given course of mnemotechnics costing ten dollars profits a man, the same course bought for twenty would profit him still more.

Sound Memory Training. What is to be recommended as rational training? Memory capacity is not "the memory" which, like a biceps muscle, can be strengthened by repetitious exercise.

[1] Stephen Leacock suggests the following: "The best illustration ... is the series of the names of the Presidents of the United States in order of office. ... Take the first link in the chain. We want to remember that after Washington came Adams. ... We connect with the word Washington anything that it suggests, and then something that that suggests, and so on till we happen to get to Adams —

Washington evidently suggests washing.
Washing evidently suggests laundry.
Laundry evidently suggests the Chinese.
The Chinese evidently suggest missionaries.
Missionaries evidently suggest the Bible.
The Bible begins with Adam.

How ridiculously simple!"

Improvement must come by training in the *ways* of learning, the technique. If formal memory training is to be advocated in the schools, let it not be the study of this or that particular subject in which disciplinary potencies are thought peculiarly to reside, but instruction and guidance in the best methods of studying. Here there is nothing to be added to the principles already enumerated and discussed in this chapter. Many of the points made, for example, on the Acquiring of habits and on the Recalling of habits, have been put forward not simply as scientific facts or laws but also as rules of economy and utility; and the student eager and conscientious and persistent in adapting them to his individual needs will be abundantly rewarded.[1] But there is no short cut, no royal road.

REFERENCES

1. Bartlett, F. C. *Remembering.* Cambridge Univ. Press, 1932.
2. Bills, A. G. *General Experimental Psychology.* Longmans, 1934. Part III.
3. Bruce, R. W. Conditions of Transfer of Training. *J. Exper. Psychol.,* 1933, **16,** 343–61.
4. Burtt, H. E. An Experimental Study of Early Childhood Memory. *J. Genet. Psychol.,* 1932, **40,** 287–95.
5. Ebbinghaus, H. *Memory* (trans. by Ruger and Bussenius). Teachers Coll., Columbia Univ., 1913.
6. Hurlock, E. B. An Evaluation of Certain Incentives Used in School Work. *J. Educ. Psychol.,* 1925, **16,** 145–59.
7. Jersild, A. Primacy, Recency, Frequency, and Vividness. *J. Exper. Psychol.,* 1929, **12,** 58–70.
8. Jersild, A., and Melton, A. W. The Comparative Retention Values of Maze Habits and of Nonsense Syllables. *J. Exper. Psychol.,* 1929, **12,** 392–414.
9. McGeoch, J. A. Reviews of literature on learning in *Psychol. Bull.,* annually, 1927 to 1934.
10. McKinney, F. Certain Emotional Factors in Learning and Efficiency. *J. Gen. Psychol.,* 1933, **9,** 101–16.
11. Meumann, E. *The Psychology of Learning* (trans. by Baird). Appleton, 1913.
12. Miles, W. R., and Miles, C. C. The Correlation of Intelligence Scores and Chronological Age from Early to Late Maturity. *Am. J. Psychol.,* 1932, **44,** 44–78.

---

[1] And if proof of this general assertion should be demanded, it, too, can be furnished [23].

13. Pan, S.   The Influence of Context upon Learning and Recall.   *J. Exper. Psychol.*, 1926, **9**, 468–91.
14. Patrick, J. R., and Anderson, A. C.   The Effect of Incidental Stimuli on Maze Learning with the White Rat.   *J. Comp. Psychol.*, 1930, **10**, 295–307.
15. Smith, S., and Guthrie, E. R.   *General Psychology in Terms of Behavior*, chap. III.   Appleton, 1921.
16. Starch, D.   *Experiments and Exercises in Educational Psychology*.   Macmillan (3d ed.), 1930.
17. Stern, C. and W.   *Erinnerung, Aussage, und Lüge*.   Leipzig: Barth, 1909.
18. Sullivan, E. B.   Attitude in Relation to Learning.   *Psychol. Monog.*, 1927, **36**, No. 169.
19. Thorndike, E. L.   *Adult Learning*.   Macmillan, 1928.
20. Thorndike, E. L.   *Educational Psychology*.   *II. Psychology of Learning*.   Teachers Coll., Columbia Univ., 1913.
21. Thorndike, E. L., and Woodworth, R. S.   The Influence of Improvement in One Mental Function upon the Efficiency of Other Functions.   *Psychol. Rev.*, 1901, **8**, 247–61, 384–95, 553–64.
22. Whipple, G. M.   *Manual of Mental and Physical Tests*, 2d ed.   Warwick and York, 1915.   II, tests 31, 32, 38, 39.
23. Woodrow, H.   The Effect of Type of Training upon Transference.   *J. Educ. Psychol.*, 1927, **18**, 160–71.

CHAPTER XVI
PERCEIVING

THE GENERAL NATURE OF PERCEPTUAL RESPONSES

Their Importance. Man's sensitivity to specific stimuli is of importance in the life of activity that is his. It is essential, of course, that he be affected by the changes in pressures and temperatures and lights and sounds that are occurring about him. But there is another aspect to stimulation that we must now examine. The chauffeur or the locomotive engineer should be affected differently by a red light from the way in which he is affected by a green one. He should be able to react to the one by a prompt applying of the brakes and to the other by an increase of speed. What is more, he should not confuse this red light with *any* red light, should not execute the hasty stopping performance when he sees a red star near the horizon, or a red lamp in an advertising display, even though it resembles the traffic signal closely. His adequate seeing of the light and adequate resulting behavior depend upon his seeing it as a red danger signal. Note that to the eye there is nothing inherently dangerous about the red beam. A passenger from Tibet or from Timbuctoo would not be excited by, or might not even attend to, that little spot of brightness. And the driver or engineer himself, in his childhood days, would have given no more attention to such a spot than to the many other spots and lines and masses in the visible field.

It has always been a central theme in psychological as well as popular literature that a person's reactions to stimuli are seldom if ever reactions to them as individual stimuli but to something more inclusive. Sounds are listened to, not as sounds, but as music, as human voices, as the cows a-calling, as wedding bells a-ringing.

Black marks on a white background are treated not as just so many black marks on white but as signs or cues: arrange them in one pattern on a street sign and the approaching human traffic turns in one direction; arrange them in another and the oncoming people turn into another avenue or may halt altogether. Two college students are standing at the foot of a staircase, when one of them is heard to utter a sound, "Squup." How the other was to perceive this strange stimulus became apparent when the students with one accord turned and ascended the stairs.   Stimuli act upon the human being, then, not only in their capacity as physical energies physically measurable one by one, but also as inciters to activity in ways not to be fathomed by any amount of painstaking analysis of the stimuli alone.

To put the last point into more abstract biological terms: *the process of adjustive behavior is immensely facilitated when the organism is able to respond perceptually to the physical energies playing upon it.* So much for the general biological setting; the question now on our hands is, what, on closer inspection, is meant by "to respond perceptually"?

Some Familiar Examples.   In several places through preceding chapters of this book attention has been specially directed to cases of behavior that were far more than reactions to separate details of stimulation.   References to a few of them may be counted on to start us off.

Yerkes, Köhler, and Bingham, and others working with apes, and Alpert, Matheson, and others with young children, have brought out dramatically enough the way in which an organism in its restive casting about to correct some want or lack in its situation will oftentimes hit upon a new structuring of it, an *insight*, as it is called, into the relationships of different elements therein.   A stick or a box would come to be reacted to not as stick or box merely but as an instrument with which to reach the inconveniently placed fruit — a stick-(or box-) leading-to-fruit.   The animal or child's success depended, then, upon his adjusting to a *relationship* [1] within the whole field, one of *means-and-objective*.   He had to perceive this relationship.

In other cases we have seen that readjustment by learning was a more drawn-out story of developing ways of perceiving.   Subjects studying telegraphy achieved only gradually the abilities to react to larger and larger groupings of dots and dashes; but by dint of much perseverance and perspiration they did get their reactions organized into higher and higher *combinations* or *patterns*.   It goes with-

---

[1] Here and elsewhere throughout our treatment the words "relation" and "relationship," as well as synonyms to be used occasionally, are not to be taken in too narrow a sense.   We shall not debate the metaphysical status of "relation," whether it be constituted by "its terms," is constitutive of them, or is external to them, nor the physiological-metaphysical status of *Gestalten* and *Gestaltqualitäten*.   Whether a pure relation as such can be, like the grin of the Cheshire cat, an object of human perception, is perhaps not appropriately decided in a book of this type.   Here and elsewhere we shall use the word "relation" always with the assumption that there are things related.   Cf. also note, p. 444, *infra*.

out saying that the first-grader's learning to read and write, the
freshman's learning to understand his French instructor's speech,
and any and all forms of language-learning are but other illustrations of this cardinal principle.

Further Examples from Childhood. What this general phenomenon boils down to is happily shown in Köhler's famous critical
choice experiment on fowls, chimpanzees, and a child. Two
stimuli, *b* a lighter and *c* a darker one, were placed before the
subject, in various positions; and the subject was trained by the
feeding method to choose the lighter, *b*, invariably. Then this pair
of stimuli was replaced by another pair, *a* and *b*, *a* being still lighter
than *b*. In the majority of cases the *a* stimulus was chosen. The
original training had been, then, a training of the positive reactions
not precisely to *b* as a certain absolute amount of brightness but to
it as the *lighter-of-two;* and the subject was *reacting* not to either
stimulus *per se* but *to the relation or ratio between them.*[1]

It is implied in the foregoing pages that reacting to relations is at
the very core of perceptual and indeed of intellectual capacity.
And with so simple an introduction as is afforded in the immediately
preceding paragraph, it would seem worth while to follow up the
critical choice technique, especially as applied to children.

In one case a number of different variations of the procedure were
tried out with children ranging from one to three and one half years
in age [16]. Two two-inch boxes were placed on a table before the
child, one red, one yellow. As the child looked on, a toy was hidden
beneath one, a screen was interposed a few seconds and removed,
and then he was allowed to choose a box, which he did by reaching
for the box covering the toy. After this preliminary training had
been established, a critical test was set in which the arrangement of
boxes was changed and the subject was not shown the hiding of the
toy. This was done in order to see whether the child would take
the box that was similar to the originally correct one in respect to
color, in respect to its position relative to the other box (on the right
or left of it), or in respect to its position relative to the subject (in
the same spot before him). (Cf. Figure 114, *A.*) It turned out
that the very youngest subjects reached mostly for the box that had
the same *position relative to the other box*, and paid little attention to
its *color* or to its *position relative to himself*. With increasing age

---

[1] In some researches it has been shown that some animal and child subjects on the critical trial
will choose the identical absolute stimulus (*b* in the above case); but it is enough for our purposes
to see that they *can* make the relative type of choice.

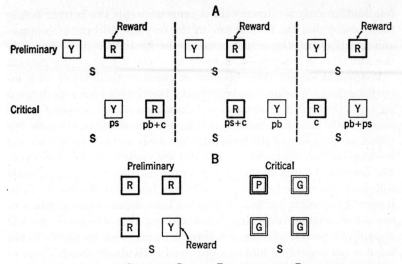

FIGURE 114. CRITICAL CHOICE REACTIONS BY CHILDREN

A. Three different procedures are shown. In each case, the upper row indicates how the two boxes were placed before the child (seated at *s*) for preliminary training in locating the toy under the box of red *color*, located to the right of the *other box*, and to the *subject's* near right.

In each case, the lower row indicates how the boxes were arranged for the critical trial, to see which relative character of the rewarded box the child would follow: color (*c*), position relative to the other box (*pb*), or position relative to the subject himself (*ps*).

B. On the left is shown the arrangement of boxes for the preliminary training in locating the toy under the box-of-different-color and located at the subject's near right. On the right, the arrangement for the critical trial, to see which cue he would follow: different-color or position. (Adapted from Miller, N. E., *J. Genet. Psychol.*, 1934, **44.**)

the color cue came to be used more and more until it became the leading one; while with increase in the distance between the boxes, the position relative to the subject assumed importance. All three kinds of cues served for one subject or another, however, which shows us a few of the variety of purely relative stimulus-characters which the young child can perceive.

But more subtle cues were also found effective, as illustrated by a sample in another series. Four boxes were placed in the form of a square, three being red and one yellow. After the child had learned to reach invariably for the yellow box for his toy, he was tested with three green and one purple box. (Cf. Figure 114, *B*.) Would he choose the box of different color? The results gave a strong affirmative answer: 68 per cent of the younger children and fully 92 per cent of the older chose it, as contrasted with the 25 per cent who would be expected by chance to do so. Here the capacity to respond to a relationship only is shown with a vengeance, for the correct box in the training and the correct one in the test had nothing in common as regards either the actual color or the spatial position, but only the abstract-seeming point of being *any-color-different-from-the-rest*.

We would expect this capacity of children to develop with increasing age. The present writer recalls from his own experience a little girl of the first grade who was drawing a man. Starting with a profile with nose and mouth to the left she drew in the one eye visible on that side of the face, but then went on to draw in a second eye also on that same side. How did she come to make that error? The answer is found in the well-accepted dictum that a young child will draw not what her eye actually sees but what she knows to be there. Proceeding backward from her later drawing performance to her act of original observing, we would say that whenever she was regarding a person who happened to be turned with his profile to her she was not regarding him as a one-eyed individual. Such a way of noticing him probably never had occurred to her. She had long before developed *habits* of dealing with people as whole persons, not as half-shells, and *to react to a few stimuli as if to whole patterns of stimuli of which they were only a part*, a point we will treat further on a later page.

Summarizing the interpretations of the several illustrations that have been given, we can say that development in the child's perceptual ability is revealed in his greater grasp not only of details-within-a-whole but also of larger and more complex wholes. Development, we see again, is a story of organization, that is, of the differentiation of parts and at the same time of incorporating them into more adequate wholes.

ANALYSIS OF THE PERCEIVING PROCESS

Some Characteristics. That it is the relationships and not the particular items related that is the crucial thing to which a person reacts, is one of the emphatic claims of the vigorous contemporary school of *Gestalt* psychologists [1]; and a few of their outstanding principles deserve our consideration, and will serve to start our analytic treatment.

---

[1] As a matter of fact, members of that school sometimes insist that "relations" are not equivalent to *Gestalten* since a "relation" implies "related things" or "relata" that are prior to and independent of the relation. For simplicity's sake we shall not labor the point beyond asserting that in this book no such discrete atomistic bits, no such things-in-themselves are assumed. Cf. note p. 441, *supra*.

The whole pattern to which a person reacts, being independent of the absolute character of the stimulus-detail, is *transposable*. This has been exhibited in the studies by the critical choice method described above, as where the same relation of different-color was identified even when transposed to a different setting. It is easily shown from everyday examples. When a person has learned the air of "Yankee Doodle" or of Tschaikowski's "Andante Cantabile," he is able to recognize it regardless of the key in which he hears it produced and regardless of the instrument on which it is played, and even, within limits, regardless of the tempo. Through truly great variations of the sounds actually produced, the pattern remains the same. Though different in a physical sense, they are *equivalent* psychologically. So with rhythms. A waltz is identifiable as such, whether it be the "Waltz of the Flowers," "The Blue Danube," or the latest dance number. The pattern, that is, the time relations of the notes, is unaltered. As a matter of fact, this attribute of transposability furnishes the central interest in the more dignified forms of musical composition. In a sonata or a symphony a certain *motif* once announced by, let us say, the first violins, is taken up by the woodwinds and in a different key, then is sounded by the French horns, then is given over to the 'cellos, and is perhaps resumed by the violins now to the accompaniment of the full orchestra. In some of these transpositions the air may actually have been inverted. The important point, of course, is that the trained listener can follow this melodic fragment through all these embellishments, transpositions, and shifts of absolute pitches, loudnesses, and tempos, and it is from these relationships that he derives the heart of his enjoyment.

Perceptual recognitions are frequently *sudden*. Every reader is familiar with this fact, especially in the hidden-picture puzzles which form the stock illustration. He may stare at such a puzzle in vain for many seconds or even minutes until, quite suddenly, the elephant emerges from the background, not eye, then ear, then head, then trunk, but "all at once and nothing first." This, we will readily recall, was a striking point about the insightful problem-solving by apes and children, and also about the way in which one learns to grasp an abstract relation, such as "the opposite of" (*supra*, p. 400).

The way in which a perceptual recognition often "clicks" into place is a phenomenon that is familiar on still higher levels of human behavior, where one is dealing with other than physically present stimuli. It is seen in the mathematical student when, after much fruitless stressing and straining, he suddenly gets the "lay" of his problem and sets to applying his stock of manipulations. It is seen in the inspiration of the musical composer, the inventor, the literary or scientific writer, an event so fittingly called *the "aha!" phenomenon*. And it is seen in anyone at the instant he "catches on" to a joke.

1. Some Primary Configural (Relational) Tendencies. Not content with merely stating the general fact that perceiving is dealing with stimuli in patterns, nor merely describing these, we are moved to ask the question "Why?" Are there any conditions or factors which determine to which kind of patterning a person will react on a given occasion?

It is the contention of many, particularly of the *Gestalt* school, that the patterns of stimuli to which a person is responsive are not, in their simpler forms at least, the results of the person's experiences, but are simply "given" him. They are due to *the organizing functions of sense-organ or nervous system or of the bodily organism generally*. In everyday phrases: it is "just natural" to see or hear or otherwise perceive certain kinds of totals; the baby does, anybody does, in spite of himself. Wertheimer has blazed the trail for this conception; and he has pointed out some interesting principles at work.

Suppose, he says in effect, an organism is facing a row of dots like those in Figure 115, *A*. It will treat them not as so many individual items but as a row. Suppose then some of these items be absent, as in *B*. Inevitably the organism will perceive the row as broken up into the groups ab/de/gh and not as broken into a/bd/eg/h. The *nearness* of stimulus details, then, is one thing that directs the way the organism patterns them. Similarly for audition: if a succession of taps be heard with alternating short and long intervals between them, they will group themselves (nearness in time).

Suppose, however, the row be constituted of different characters, as in Figure *C*. Now the items automatically group themselves ab/cd/ef/gh. Or better, suppose they be arranged in several rows as in *D*. Now they fall into vertical arrays, the rows giving place to columns. The same phenomenon appears with auditory stimuli when an unbroken succession of taps is sounded, alternating singly or in pairs or in threes between loud and soft taps: the organism is so

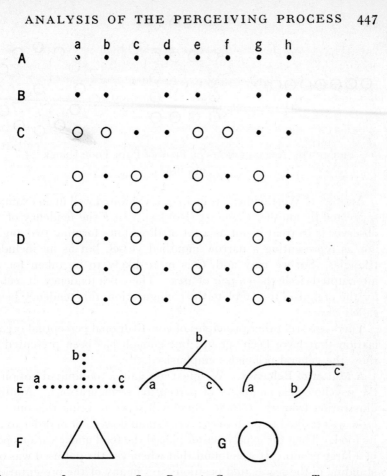

FIGURE 115. ILLUSTRATING SOME PRIMARY CONFIGURATIONAL TENDENCIES
Described and analyzed in the text. (After Wertheimer.)

constituted that it will inevitably group them in these rhythms. The *similarity* factor, then, is another basis of organization.

Further, suppose that the items in the first and third rows of *D* be moving toward the right while those in the second and fourth are moving toward the left. The columns will now give place to rows, as the subject would regard them. This *common fate* of certain items tends to segregate them into new constellations.

The dots or lines in Figure *E* group themselves as ac/b. This is called the principle of *continuity*, for it seems that with the *a* segment the *c* segment is more continuous than is the *b* segment.

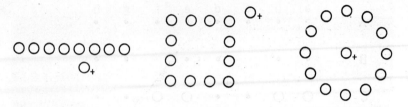

FIGURE 116. ARRANGEMENTS OF FLOWER POTS, FOOD UNDER "+"

(After Hertz.)

Another of Wertheimer's principles is exhibited well in an example suggested by another *Gestalt*ist (Koffka). In *F* the tendency of an observer is to treat it not as a set of three lines forming two angles nor as representing a narrow mouthed vessel, but as an included triangle. So, we may add, *G* is more likely to be taken for an interrupted circle than a pair of arcs. There is a tendency, it seems, for the organism to complete the configuration, this tendency being called *closure*.[1]

There are still other principles of constitutional perceptual organization that have been set up; but enough has been presented to show the general principles emphasized.

A Matter of Behavior. We must not gain a too-limited notion of the psychological character of perceptual configurations. Another illustration from the *Gestalt* school will serve to bring this out. A crow was trained to push over a very small flower pot in order to get its food. Then the experimenter placed the food under various pots of a large group. It was found that whenever the pot used was one standing in the segregated position "+" in any of the presentations shown in Figure 116 the bird had no difficulty in going to it directly; but if the pot used was any of the others, the bird was forced into random searching. Incidentally, this case of the bird will serve as a hint that the principles of perceptual configuration in the preceding paragraphs apply *not simply* to perceiving as *consciously experienced and verbally reported*, but also to perceiving as an *objectively investigable process*.

In the second place, the structuring of the crow's perceptual field is most intimately *bound up with its overt responses*. Configurations are not simply configurations seen, heard, tasted, smelled, or

---

[1] By analogy, explanation through closure has been extended to apply also to other ways in which incomplete systems seek equilibrium; and would be applied to the wide range of phenomena we have preferred to call adjustive behavior, the organism completing its adjustment.

FIGURE 117. THE EFFECT OF OLD HABITS IN REACTING TO LIGHTS
AND SHADOWS
(C. H. Stoelting Co.)

touched by an organism that is playing the part of a passive spectator or auditor or observer. [22]

2. The Important Rôle of Habit. So far the emphasis has been on
primary structurings in perceiving. However, the reader has
probably had some qualms. Is not the perceiver's past history to
be taken into account? Most assuredly it is.

This is vividly brought out if the reader will turn to Figure 117.
With the picture held so that the word "LEHIGH" is easily read,
let him observe the larger light-and-dark areas, which are roughly
circular in shape: what are they seen to be? Let him also regard the
small light-and-dark spots: what "are" they? Next, invert the
picture so that the word is upside down. What are the larger light-
and-dark areas now seen to be? And how do the small spots appear?
Here we have one and the same figure producing totally different

effects upon the observer merely by the rotation of 180 degrees, effects easily observable to another person when the reactions take verbal form in such words as "dents," "rivet heads," "bulges."

What can be the explanation of this difference in the two ways in which this picture affects the observer? It must be sought in terms of his experience, that is, his habits. In early childhood he chanced upon certain ways of responding to lights and shadows. In his experience light usually came from above and shadows were cast accordingly. Gradually circumstances compelled him to learn the difference between the light and the shadow of the convex and concave surface, until he developed consistent tendencies to place his hand *upon* the one and reach his hand *into* the other. Not that he ever was aware of this. It was a mode of behaving that became established unconsciously and without any intention on his part.

The rôle of habits can be readily recognized in the following incident. The writer sounded before a class a series of four musical notes, with the announcement that they constituted the beginning of a well-known air. Many of the students promptly recognized in these notes the beginning of the refrain of the "Banana Song," a popular jazz number of the day; others, however, reported that they heard them as the opening of the "Hallelujah Chorus." The mere juxtaposition of two such totally different types of music is startling enough. We may ask, how can we explain such widely diverse forms of recognition? It is clear that in either case the four notes operated to arouse in the auditor a serial habit, of which they were the first segments. But again, why were two such different habits aroused in different auditors? An answer to this particular question is to be found in our third point, to be presented later.

A few other illustrations, now. Whether a given stimulus will arouse one or another meaning-reaction depends upon what the subject's experiences have been. Certain native Australians, upon first seeing a book, called it a "mussel," since that was the only object with a hinge-like opening with which they had ever dealt, and they had never had to do with printed marks. Indians of the Mississippi Valley called their first horses and cows "big-dogs," "pull-dogs," "milk-dogs." To show how stubbornly the well-formed verbal habits manifest their strength, read aloud to a friend the following passage by Gertrude Stein, asking him to disregard utterly the sense of the words, attending simply to the sounds as sounds. This passage has been described by one who is an enthusiast about impressionistic writing as "so exquisitely rhythmical and cadenced, that when read aloud and received as pure sound, it is like a kind of sensuous music." Does the reader find that his hearer succeeds in thus throwing aside his old word-meaning habits of perceiving?

It is a gnarled division, that which is not any obstruction, and the forgotten swelling is certainly attracting. It is attracting the whiter division, it is not sinking to be growing, it is not darkening to be disappearing, it is not aged to be annoying. There cannot be sighing. This is this bliss.

Experimental Examples. The factor of one's experience as an influence on how he will perceive sensory data came out clearly in the course of a research conducted by the reproduction method. Fourteen geometrical designs were shown in serial order in the

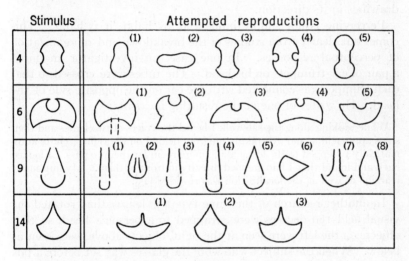

FIGURE 118. EFFECT OF PAST EXPERIENCE (VERBALIZED) UPON PERCEIVING

At the left appear some of the stimulus-designs.

To the right appear some attempts of different subjects at reproducing them from memory, the subjects having named the original stimulus-designs after familiar objects. These names were:

No. 4: (1) woman's torso; (2) footprint; (3) dumbbell; (4) violin; (5) dumbbell.

No. 6: (1) battle axe (dotted lines to show handle); (2) maid's collar or apron; (3) Napoleon's hat; (4) helmet; (5) dress shield.

No. 9: (1) club; (2) electric light bulb; (3) hairpin; (4) end of ball bat with label around it; (5) loaded doll (with lead in base to bob up when pushed over); (6) sector; (7) druggist's pestle; (8) light bulb.

No. 14: (1) meat chopper; (2) boy's top; (3) basket.

(From Gibson, J. J., *J. Exper. Psychol.*, 1929, **12**.)

Ranschburg exposure device. (Cf. Figure 140, p. 556.) The series was repeatedly presented until the subject was able by drawings to reproduce the fourteen in approximately the original order. It was soon noted that the subject's reproductions varied from the original forms by certain characteristic changes, which tended to become firmly established in spite of new showings of the originals. For instance, in Figure 118 we see on the left hand a few of the original figures presented, and to the right of each some individual variations in the attempts to reproduce it, variations clearly influenced by the various S's manners of perceiving. These manners of perceiving were — by the S's own verbal testimony — influenced by their previous experiences with objects. A design was perceived as resembling some particular object; then in reproducing the design the S was influenced by the object-name and distorted his drawings in its direction.

Perceiving is not simply influenced by habit, it *is* habit. This comes out clearly from studies of the breakdown and reorganization of perceptual responses. In one case, an investigator mounted a pair of ear-trumpets on his head. The tubes were crossed so that each trumpet was connected with the ear on the opposite side of the head. He writes of one of the resulting incidents:

While walking along the sidewalk I heard the voices of two ladies and their steps approaching and overtaking me from behind on the right. Quite automatically I stepped to the left making more room for them to pass. I looked back and found that I had stepped directly in front of them. My automatic reaction as well as the localization was reversed [25].

In another research of the same type [5], lenses that rotated the visual field 180 degrees were strapped to a person's head, so that objects on the left were seen at the right, objects above were seen as below. When the subject who wore the glasses was set before a box of pigeonholes bearing numbers and was given a set of cards for sorting into the correct holes, he was unable to "see" the proper locations; for example, a hole actually located high-and-to-the-left was perceived and reacted to as if it were low-and-to-the-right. So many were the mistakes that it took considerably longer to complete the sorting of the pack than when not wearing the lenses. However, with repetition of the task, each subject learned rapidly how to locate the pigeonholes by properly co-ordinating sight and hand movement. The plotted data furnished a graph that was typical of trial-and-error learning.

We are led to conclude from such evidences that *the way in which a person perceives a stimulus-complex depends in part upon his habitual responses.* Perceiving a thing as right-side-up, or upside down, or over-to-the-left or right, depends upon the way the perceiving person is used to reacting. The "real" thing is whatever he has adequate reactions toward.

Analysis of How a Perceiving Habit is Formed. To observe a perceptual mode of response in its original formation let us consider in a theoretical way how a child learns to recognize a stick of peppermint candy when it is held before his eyes. The sight of a red-and-white-striped thing (S_{vis} in Figure 119) may be sufficient to evoke the act of reaching out toward it. At contact of the fingers with the object the cutaneous and kinesthetic stimulations induce a "feeling" or palpating reaction, together with the reaction of bringing the object to the mouth. Once it is there, the object serves to stimulate smell and taste receptors in a way to produce an eating response involving many muscular and glandular effectors. Now it is easy to see that the stage is set for a conditioning process. Let the situation be repeated, with the visual, cutaneous, olfactory, and gustatory stimuli presented simultaneously or in close succession, and the eating response, to which only the olfactory and gustatory were the originally adequate stimuli, can be eventually elicited by the incidental stimulus, the visual. Thereafter, the mere sight of the red-and-white-striped cylinder, or even a piece of wood similarly colored, will excite excess flow of saliva, licking movements of the tongue, sucking of the lips, not to mention characteristic actions of face, hand, and trunk. At this stage, the peppermint candy is not simply a seen thing evoking random behavior: it now evokes specific behavior, *it is a good-to-eat thing.* And as a good-to-eat thing it serves to determine the next phases of the child's behavior.

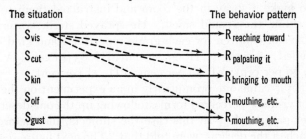

FIGURE 119. DIAGRAM TO REPRESENT CONDITIONING AS INVOLVED IN THE FORMING OF A PERCEPTUAL RESPONSE

This example is not limited to the visual stimuli alone. The smell, the taste, or the touch of the candy come to serve as well to incite the whole redintegrated process of handling and mouthing. The candy is then appropriately recognized after any of several kinds of stimulation.

3. The Importance of the Subject's Set. The manner in which a man perceives a thing, person, or situation is influenced not only by his long-established habits, but by the set into which he has just been thrown. The art of the ventriloquist was founded upon this principle. Voices would never be taken for voices from the basement or from the garret, if the audience were not led to expect them from such directions. In another way the writer was struck with the force of the general principle in connection with a performance of marionettes or puppets. Many of the audience knew in advance that at the conclusion of the performance the manager of the entertainment would step into view on the toylike stage and present a striking contrast to the marionettes; yet, so adapted had they become to the size of the figures through the hour or more of the play that when the manager finally stepped forward on the puppet stage, he was greeted with exclamations of surprise at his hugeness.

All puns and many other types of humor depend for their effect upon a sudden shift in the set of the auditor, as the reader can verify for himself with examples from the humor columns in any popular magazine or newspaper. When the impatient lover on the station platform rushes up to greet and embrace a perfect stranger, the psychological interpretation is equally simple.

Experimental evidence for these general assertions is easy enough to obtain. Some years ago Small demonstrated it simply but clearly with school children. He placed labeled perfume bottles on the teacher's desk, and, taking an atomizer, told the pupils he was about to make a spray in the room and instructed them to report what perfume they could smell. He sprayed sterile water. The percentages of children for each grade reporting some kind of odor was: Grade I, 98 per cent; II, 95 per cent; III, 83 per cent; IV, 76 per cent; V, 70 per cent; VI, 50 per cent; VII, 23 per cent.

The factor came out prominently in an experiment on the reproducing of visually perceived forms, following up the one described in an earlier paragraph. In this case the subjects, just before being shown each of the designs, were told that "The next figure resembles a ――" In this place for one group of subjects one object-name

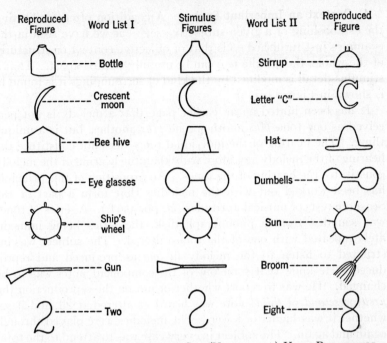

Reproduced Figure	Word List I	Stimulus Figures	Word List II	Reproduced Figure
	Bottle		Stirrup	
	Crescent moon		Letter "C"	
	Bee hive		Hat	
	Eye glasses		Dumbells	
	Ship's wheel		Sun	
	Gun		Broom	
	Two		Eight	

FIGURE 120. EFFECT OF PRESENT SET (VERBALIZED) UPON PERCEIVING

In the middle column appear some of the stimulus-designs. To the left and right appear some attempts at reproducing them from memory, the subjects having heard announced in each case the name of some familiar object which the stimulus-design was said to resemble. Differences in the drawn reproductions for each stimulus are to be attributed to differences in the subjects' sets established by the different names announced. (From Carmichael, Hogan, and Walter, *J. Exper. Psychol.*, 1932, 15.)

would be supplied, for another group another object-name. What was the effect of hearing the word upon the person's way of regarding the design? A clear answer appears in our Figure 120. In the case of the first design, for instance, when a subject had been thrown into a bottle-regarding set, this way of perceiving and reproducing the stimulus was distorted in the direction of a bottle, but when a stirrup-regarding set had been awakened, he perceived the figure in a very different way.

This reminds us of that famous dialogue in *Hamlet.*

Hamlet. Do you see yonder cloud that's almost in shape of a camel?
Polonius. By the mass, and 'tis like a camel, indeed.
Hamlet. Methinks it is like a weasel.
Polonius. It is back'd like a weasel.
Hamlet. Or like a whale?
Polonius. Very like a whale.

4. Context an Important Factor. A condition often facilitating the establishing of a given subjective set — as we have seen in the examples just furnished — is that of objective context or structure-of-the-whole, though the two can be usefully treated apart. That a stimulus-detail is modified by the kind of surroundings it is found in is shown in Figure 121.

It has been hinted on an earlier page that a melody is not perceived as one tone *plus* another tone *plus* another, but is a unique thing. The hearing of the individual tones does not constitute the hearing of the melody any more truly than the hearing of the melody constitutes the hearing of the tones. An exposition of this principle has been worked out with the melodies that form a part of the Seashore tests of musical aptitudes (cf. pp. 359 f.). A series of tones was sounded from a phonograph disk, the series being immediately repeated with one of the tones altered. The subject was instructed to listen to the melody *in toto* as produced and reproduced. He knew that some one of the component notes was to be changed. He was to report whether or not on the reproduction the *first* (or *second* or *third*) note was heard as altered at all, and if so, whether it was higher or lower. The melodies were played through again and again. The subject in every case was to attend to the total melody but to report whether the specified tone was heard as altered, if ever so slightly (and regardless of whether it was one known to be the objectively altered one). There were strong dynamic effects produced upon the way one heard the objectively unaltered tones by his hearing the objectively altered ones. In every length of melody except the longest, where the effect was negligible, the former tones were heard on the average as if shifted in the same direction as the changes in the latter [10]. In more general terms: when one tone in a melody is objectively raised or lowered the human auditor is likely to perceive all the other tones as changed slightly in the same direction.

The psychological character of a given tone is thus dependent in a degree upon the patterns of relationship in which it is found. Now for a bit of evidence secured by a very different technique, conditioning. Three human subjects were trained to the point of a clear differentiation; that is, to the point where they made the C.R. (retraction of hand) upon hearing a given note (formerly accompanied by electric shock), and did not make that R. to other notes. Upon further testing, it was found that the R. was not aroused by

FIGURE 121. THE INFLUENCE OF CONTEXT

Cover the right side of the picture and ask some one to estimate the size of the fish. Cover the left side and ask him to estimate again. What determines the estimating of size in each case? (From Bennett, H. E. *Psychology and Self-Development.* Ginn & Co., 1923.)

that same critical tone *when* presented as one member of a familiar old tune, of a chord, or of an arpeggio.[1] One of the best records is reproduced in the table, which reports the successive stimuli that were used and the appearance or non-appearance of the reflex to each [12].

From this last-mentioned study there are some valuable morals to be drawn. The very fact that the technique used was that of

RESPONSES TO A DIFFERENTIATED STIMULUS

PART OF A RECORD OF A SUBJECT PREVIOUSLY TRAINED TO REACT TO NOTE NO. 7 AND NOT TO OTHER NOTES. POSITIVE (CONDITIONED) RESPONSE IS INDI-CATED BY "P," NO RESPONSE BY "N," ARPEGGIO BY "A," OTHER TONES BY NUMBERS.

Stimulus:	7	Mel-ody	5+7	7+9	A	A	A	A	A	A	A	8	7	A
Response:	p	n	n	n	n	n	n	n	n	n	n	n	p	n

conditioning is another reminder that we *must not interpret perceiving* as a *consciously experienced process only* nor as a *passively receptive phase* of life. These points become all the more impressive when we find that the demonstration bears a close resemblance to some ob-tained in Russian physiological laboratories in the conditioning of the dog.[2]

Minimal Cues. The response called "perceptual" depends, as we have seen, upon the presence of certain stimuli or stimulus-relations that have come to arouse the whole response. It is import-ant for us to bear in mind that frequently — if not as a rule — these *cues* or signs are *difficult to identify.* The perceiving person himself is notoriously unable to tell in most cases just what it is that makes him recognize or estimate a situation as he does. This is easily demonstrated in a well-known experimental exercise on the localiza-tion of sounds. The blindfolded subject is seated in a "sound-cage,"[3] the experimenter produces a light clicking sound from time to time at points equidistant from a point midway between his ears but in varying directions, and the subject is instructed to "localize"

---

[1] An arpeggio is a chord the notes of which are played in rapid succession instead of simultane-ously.

[2] We may be pardoned for pointing a still more general moral. To the student who is curious about the different "schools" of psychological interpretation, it ought to be refreshing to find a principle of Wertheimer's to be demonstrated well with Pavlov's technique.

[3] A sound-cage consists of a set of metal arcs attached to the back of the subject's chair, and so pivoted that a telephone diaphragm borne at one end and connected electrically with a switch in the experimenter's hand can be placed accurately at any point in an imaginary sphere encircling the subject's head.

— that is, to point toward, the source of each sound. Errors of as much as 180 degrees are not uncommon. Note that in no case can the subject tell just how it is that he localizes a given sound as from such and such a direction; he is at a loss to specify what the characteristics of the sound are, by which he was directed; he cannot by analysis identify the cues. The sound "just came from that direction" and that is all there is to be said. Objective control and variation of the conditions of the experiment, however, throw light upon the matter. By comparing the subject's correct and incorrect localizations it can be demonstrated that the physical differences in the sound as it falls upon the right and upon the left ear cause the difference in his reaction. These differences may be in the time of reception, in the timbre, in the intensity, in the cycle-phase, or in the complexity of the tone. They are differences that the subject cannot directly detect, yet they guide his localizing.

The importance of these obscure stimulus-cues in determining a reaction has long been recognized by those who work with animal subjects, particularly the dog, the horse, the monkey, and the ape. Dogs were once being tested for their ability to choose the correct one of two paths to a food box simply on the basis of the pitch difference between the tones of electrically operated tuning-forks. The animals were to turn right if a c fork was sounded and left if the e fork. They showed a remarkable facility in learning this discrimination; but the experimenter was not long in discovering that they failed utterly when he absented himself and operated his devices from an adjoining room. Plainly they were being guided by him, or better, by very slight movements he would unwittingly make as he watched them work. This explanation he checked by noting that he could lead a dog to change its direction by turning his head, catching his breath, or shifting from one foot to another [13]. It has been stated on excellent authority [3] that the truly surprising ability of the Berlin police dogs to pick out the guilty man from a lineup is to be explained by the dogs' delicate sensitiveness to the slightest movements of the detectives (who often have strong suspicions fixed on someone in the lineup) or of the guilty person (whose betrayal of himself by uncontrollable not-easily-perceptible motions is not hard to understand if we but remember the situation he is facing, his knowledge of guilt, the sight of the alert dog, etc.).

Some horses at Elberfeld were once greatly celebrated for their feats in tapping out sums, square roots of numbers, and the like, when such problems were posted on a board in front of them; yet when no one was present who knew the problem or the answer, the animals failed.   Evidently, in the course of tapping out their "answers," these acutely impressionable animals were prompted or checked by the unintentional gestural or vocal responses of the person knowing the correct solution.

The performances of certain human "wonders" are of the same order.   The "mind-reader" may announce one or another fantastic explanation of his ability to "tell what you are thinking about." But his true cues are really his consultant's slight gestures and changes of facial expression — a complex and subtle ensemble of fine muscle reactions — if not, indeed, certain words uttered by the subject which serve to correct and direct the vague trial-and-error talking of the mind-reader.   *Mind-reading is muscle-reading.*   In a similar way the intelligent salesman perceives that it is time to close his interview. Something about the movements of the auditor's eyes, or the fingering of his blotter, or his way of sitting backward in his chair, or glancing at his papers or at his office force — something, though he cannot say just what it is, tells the salesman that it is time for him to go.   Most of the so-called "sizing-up" of one man by another is a complex reaction to many obscure stimuli, which are not at all catalogued or weighted but simply enter into the total mass of stimulation and help to determine the general impression.   It is the operation of such minimal cues that often leads to the intuition or what is colloquially called the "hunch," and gives some basis to the claim that even a guess has a certain value.

Symbolic Cues.   If there is one thing most outstanding in the life of mankind it is surely this: that far from being limited to the here and now their world is extended to include past history and future time, mythology and fairy tales, China and the Antipodes, and even other planets and suns and the vast interstellar spaces.   With all such remote things man can deal.   Or rather, with their representations he can deal.   No living man, of course, has ever seen Cortez, though he can roundly condemn that freebooter and plunderer; no child really ever hopes to see or hear Snow Fair or Hansel and Gretel or even supposes that they ever were in flesh; the temple of the Lamas and the snowy peaks of Everest are not ever to be seen by most of us; and the new planet Pluto was discovered mathematically by scientists before they ever saw it.   How has such an extension of his world been rendered possible to man?   In a word, it is by *symbols.*

We may define a symbol as *an object or a response that becomes a representative substitute for some other object, response, or situation*; it is reacted to directly, but only in this recognized relationship of sign-and-thing-signified.   The sign may in fact be something utterly distinct in all sensory qualities from that for which it stands.   The printed word "ORANGE" cannot be eaten, but it can throw the child reader into preparatory attitudes appropriate to that for which it is a sign.   What is more, in this case reacting to the black-marks-on-white is not reacting to some larger whole of which they are a part, as would be the case in recognizing a motor car by its noise or a burning pudding by its odor or an orange by the feel of it in a Christmas stocking.   The child is responding to something with which the pattern of black marks has been artificially associated and for which it then has come to function as a substitute.   It is not a full and complete substitute, to be treated exactly as the original object or situation would be treated; it is always handled as in-relation-to that other.   "Words," Hobbes puts it, "are wise men's counters, they do but reckon by them; but they are the money of fools."   But even money is only symbolic material, until it becomes sought after by the miser on its own account purely, for its touch and sight and grateful clinking sounds.

Dealing with symbols, or symbolic behavior, as we may call it, develops characteristically under *social* conditions, and has both the active and the receptive aspects.   As communicative relationships between man and man evolve beyond the level of brute cries and ejaculations and pushings and shovings, and as co-operative attacks upon third objects are hit upon, the ability to deal with things not in their first intention but as instruments or signs of other things becomes of first importance.   Now man can signal to fellow-man, concerning something the first can observe or has observed, so that the latter, taking the word or gesture or other signal for the fact or thing itself, can behave appropriately thereto.   A *symbolic response* by one is perceived as a *symbolic stimulus* by the other.

The advantages are obvious.   The printed symbol "ORANGE" is in a more convenient form than the visible, odorous, palpable, piece of fruit; it may, so to speak, be packed away in a smaller space; it is not liable to chemical disintegration and is replaceable if lost. In like manner, the interchange of commodities, of wealth, of real estate is made possible between men seated in offices remote from the material itself.   The stock speculator can handle sugar, millions of pounds of it, buying it with thousands of dollars and selling it for thousands of dollars — and all with merely a ticker tape and a telephone.   If symbols have become the chief means of economic exchange between man and man, they have also become the great means of interstimulation and response in other ways, making possible the highly organized society peculiar to *Homo sapiens.*

We must postpone further analysis of symbolic behavior and genetic aspects of its development to the special treatments of Social Behavior and of Language.   Meanwhile, let us note here that in this *capacity to perceive symbols* we find only *an extension of* the fundamental *capacity to be affected by and responsive to relationships,* in this case the relation of the-sign-and-the-signified.

ILLUSORY RESPONSES

Introduction.   To err is human, and to be misled by appearances, equally so.   Man's life is one in which he is continually forced to handle and respond to things, people, and happenings upon very slight and partial stimulation from them; and, furthermore, even his manner of responding to quite rich and adequate stimuli varies much under the influence of context and pre-established set.   It is only to be expected, therefore, that oftentimes his particular perceivings may lead him astray.   Everyone is subject to illusions.[1]

Optical Illusions.   Probably the most famous of illusions is that produced by the Müller-Lyer design (Figure 122, *A*).   The two base lines are of equal length, but with the attachment of small inward-turned and outward-turned lines at their ends they are taken to be of unequal length.   Many variations of this illusion have been devised.   Another well-known misleading design is that of Poggendorff (*B*), in which the continuity of a line is interrupted by laying across it at an angle strips of narrow width.   The reader will readily discover what effect is given to the character of the line as a stimulus. There is the Zöllner figure (*C*), in which the value of lines as indicators of direction is made misleading by the introduction of cross-hatching; the lines are originally drawn parallel.   What is the nature of the observer's error here?   An interesting error is that in the illusion of ring segments (*D*): the two arcs or areas are drawn with lines of exactly equal length, but the misleading effect of the spatial

---

[1] This term is not to be confused with "delusion" which is used to refer to a false judgment or belief, nor with "hallucination," which refers to apparently perceiving when there is no corresponding extra-organic stimulus at all.

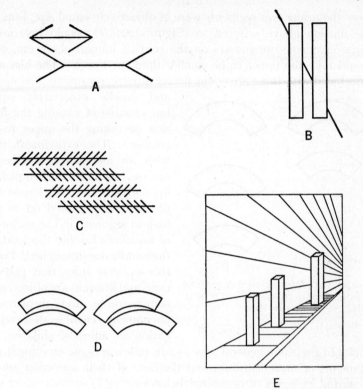

FIGURE 122. SOME OPTICAL ILLUSIONS

A, Müller-Lyer; *B*, Poggendorff; *C*, Zöllner; *D*, ring segments; *E*, perspective.

relation of one to the other is apparent. Another is the misleading perspective effect of converging lines lying adjacent to equal areas and lines (*E*). The inquiring student can find at least a dozen different theories advanced by psychologists to explain the Müller-Lyer, and other, illusory forms of perceiving.

An Animal's Illusion. By this time the reader should realize well that illusions are not to be looked upon as essentially mysterious. For example, let us consider a case of illusion in a subhuman species. Révész succeeded in training a hen to peck for grains always from the smaller of two areas, whether they were two circles, two squares, two triangles, two oblong rectangles, or the two arcs shown in Figure 123, *A*. When this habit was well established, the hen was offered grain on the three areas in *B* used in the spatial arrangement shown.

Now the upper two segments were of objectively equal size, but, by the illusion above referred to (Figure 122, *D*), would invariably cause erroneous judgments on the part of human observers, who would take the upper to be smaller than the lower. The hen was thus faced with three areas, the nearer objectively smaller, the upper

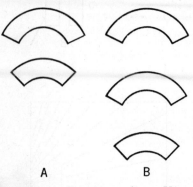

A   **B**

FIGURE 123. DESIGNS OF AREAS USED BY RÉVÉSZ IN HIS STUDY OF OPTICAL ILLUSIONS IN THE HEN

(Révész, G., *Brit. J. Psychol.*, 1924, **14**.)

and middle objectively equal but capable of causing the illusion of taking the upper to be smaller. The experiment met with an astonishing degree of success. As a rule the hen picked up the grain from the lowest figure first, then passed on to the highest segment, in the majority of instances leaving the food on the middle one untouched. From this we may infer that perceptions and illusions are objectively demonstrable and measurable phenomena, capable of investigation in animals, children, or adults in the same general way as are reflex actions, emotional excitement, or maze-learning; and the laws of their operation are to be stated in terms of organized behavior.

The Proof-Reader's Illusion. In learning to read language one learns to react to larger and larger patterns of stimuli, as we have seen (pp. 369 ff.). Once these large higher-order habits are organized, they tend to be arousable by various particular stimuli forming a usual and frequent part of the whole stimulus-pattern. It follous, then that a word-perceiving act should often be arouseable when not all detials of that word are actully stimulating" The printed word may be misspelled, by omission or insertion or transposition of letters, or in other ways; spacing may be superfluous or omitted; punctuation marks may be improperly introduced or left out. But the reader, set for the meanings and silently speaking whole words in response to the few cues that do fall upon the center of his retina, reads confidently on with hardly an interference or trip on account of the printer's errors. In one of the preceding sentences seven different errors are intentionally left standing: how many of them attracted the reader's attention? In the effort to print books perfectly proof-readers are employed whose chief duty it is to scan the page and keep set to respond to all printer's errors. Yet so inveterate are a reader's habits of responding not piecemeal but to patterns of stimuli that even the professional proof-reader has his illusions. Not even the most experienced can inspect printed sheets with one hundred per cent accuracy.

The Phi-Phenomenon. One more illusion deserves our attention both because of its common occurrence and because of its importance to recent psychological history.

The enormous success of moving pictures is based upon their power to arouse an illusory perceiving of action. The screen, although actually in darkness many times per second, is able to stimulate the audience much as do the continuous movements of actors in person — arousing and holding attentive postures, touching off emotional tendencies, exciting thinking behavior. The situation presented is discontinuous and the observers are not actually looking at objects in motion; but the successive pictures obtained by instantaneous photography follow each other so rapidly, while their actual movement in this succession before the projector is being concealed by a shutter, that the same responses are elicited as though the scenes of things and people were actually moving.

This phenomenon has long been familiar to the laboratory worker. Since 1912, however, it has assumed a new importance in the psychological world on account of a closer analysis given it and an interpretation which marks that year as the beginning of the *Gestalt* movement. Wertheimer set up the phenomenon in question as follows. Two black lines were shown on a white background in rapid succession, the first vertical, the second horizontal, as in

FIGURE 124. THE PHI-PHENOMENON
(After Wertheimer.)

Figure 124, *a* and *b*. If a fairly long interval of time, say 150 milliseconds (thousandths of a second), be allowed between the two flashes, the two lines will be perceived successively as *a* then *b*. If the interval be cut extremely short, to around 20 ms., then the two lines will be seen simultaneously and forming a right angle. If, however, the interval be adjusted between these two lengths, at somewhere about 60 — 90 ms., then still a third manner of perceiving is aroused: the vertical *a* line will be seen to move over to the horizontal *b* line in a sweeping motion, as indicated by the arrow in *c*. This Wertheimer has called the phi-phenomenon.

Space forbids our telling in detail all of the intensive analysis of this event which has been conducted. One analysis employing illuminated slits on black lines has brought out the fact that other conditions than (1) time-intervals determine whether the phi-type of perception is aroused. They are (2) the spatial distance between the slits, and (3) their brightness. These three are intimately interdependent so that as one is varied one or both the others must be changed also if the phi effect is to be preserved. Some fascinating varieties in this effect itself have been produced. Under certain conditions the subject can be made to see one line pass behind the other, or one to pass to the other and back again, or one to pass in the opposite of the usual direction, and so on. The phenomenon has been produced by tactual stimulation also, the subject perceiving the movement on the skin, or, in a curious variant of the experiment, perceiving a movement from the first-touched spot up into the air and in a bow over to the other spot.

More important for general theory is the conclusion to which we are led: *The perceived movement is not made up of separately perceived lines* a *and* b *or of these and intervening lines: it is a unique and indivisible event.*

The Causes of Illusory Responses. The foregoing survey of the illustrations of misperceiving and their analyses offers us a basis for a generalization. In all cases of illusion we can find one or more of the following causal factors responsible: long-established and *deep-rooted habits* of response; the person's *present set*, posture, expectation; the *context* in which the stimulus is found; and, occasionally, *peculiarities of the sense-organs.*

SPECIAL EXPERIMENTAL PROBLEMS

Spatial Relations. None of the problems of human behavior have been so extensively examined in experimental laboratories as the problems of perceiving, and the studies of space perception have easily led in number. When the stimulations from an agent provoke a person or animal to turn directly toward it, or to treat it as something large or something small, or something near at hand or far away, what is it about these stimulations that is the determining thing?

First, to stake out the field: It is clear that the stimulations can affect man through various receptors — cutaneous, auditory, kinesthetic (indirectly), static (indirectly), and visual. Second, a moment's attention to the character of what we call space suggests that stimuli may vary in three regards, the *direction* from which they are received, the *extent or size* of the stimulating agent considered at right angles to the direction of the stimulating effect, and the *distance or depth* of the stimulus in the third dimension.

Cutaneous perceptions of space have been examined largely by determining the distribution of pressure end-organs over the body (mentioned in Chapter IX), and they have concerned the direction and the extent of the stimuli applied.

Auditory space has been studied by the sound cage technique for measuring subjects' ability to localize sounds as to their direction and as to their distance away.   This has already been touched on in this chapter.

Kinesthetic afferent impulses returning from one's moving limbs, head, eyeballs, and so forth, play a most important part in the control of his movements in space, a part generally recognized as primary to all others.   They have received little investigation, however, if we except the lifted-weight method of determining sensory thresholds and the value of k for Fechner's law.   (Cf. Chapter IX.)

Static stimulations have had more attention, due in some measure to the interest therein fostered by the aviation service, where it was supposed that "once a poor balancer always a poor balancer" until psychological experiments on training recruits proved that notion false.   Subjects with closed eyes in a revolving chair showed complex compensatory movements.   For instance, as the chair began to move to the subject's left with accelerated speed the eyeballs could be seen (through the closed lids) to drift to the right then to be jerked ahead at intervals; the musculature of the trunk, arms, and neck showed increased tension in resisting the torsion being given the body; and the subject reported his judgment that he was revolving leftward.   After a given speed of rotation was maintained for some seconds the objective evidences of "being turned leftward" disappeared, and the subject reported "standing still." Upon the speed being suddenly reduced, just the opposite compensatory movements of the eyeballs and body appeared and the subject reported "turning to the right."   There have been some interesting complications of these effects, but we cannot go into them.

Along with the kinesthetic, the *visual* mode of stimulation is most important and most used by man in the guidance of his movements in space.   The retina of the eye is so refined that when two points of light are separated by only 1 or 1½ minutes angular distance they can be discriminated as two points. Add to this the astonishing delicacy of the various muscles of the eye, and it is easy to see that localizing the directions and gauging the extents of objects presented to vision should be quite acute.

Cues to Visual Perceiving in the Third Dimension. A favorite problem for psychological analysis arises from the fact that a man can make adequate responses to objects seen at various distances. Consider that the retina is essentially a two-dimensional, although curved, surface, and that differences of physical distance in stimulus-objects cannot be directly projected upon this, since distance lies in the third dimension. How, then, can an object which stimulates the retina at a given set of points on this two-dimensional surface be reacted to as near and as far? In Figure 125, it is shown that so far as the retina itself is concerned there can be *no difference in the area stimulated* by objects 1 and 2, though one is much farther from the retina than the other. If they are to be distinguished, some other stimulus-characters must be present for the organism to use in learning to react to them as near and far. What are these cues?

The infant seated upon the floor and busying himself with building-blocks has opportunities to form adequate visual-motor co-ordinations toward the different blocks as they variously stimulate his retina. The principles of learning as we have already studied them are involved here. An object lying low in his field of vision, for instance, is one for which he must learn not to reach out too far. It is pretty sure to be near him, down in front of him. If one block partly obscures another he learns to reach around or knock away the former to get the latter. If he has been playing with blocks of a uniform size, he learns to make more effort to reach one that stimulates a relatively smaller area of his retina. Thus various cues to the distances of objects are learned — not in the

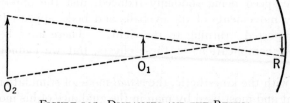

FIGURE 125. DISTANCES AND THE RETINA

The projection of light on the sensitive plate of the eye from objects of different sizes but at different distances may be identical.

verbal or in the memorized sense but as a part of that equipment of fundamental sensori-motor habits upon which higher co-ordinations depend. "I can remember," wrote Helmholtz in his *Physiological Optics*, "as a child passing by the spire of the garrison church in Potsdam and seeing people on the balustrade, whom I took to be dolls. I asked my mother to take them down for me, believing she could do this by merely reaching up with her hands. I remember the incident so well, because it was this mistake which taught me the law of perspective, that is, the diminution of size with distance."

We may now canvass the different visual cues to which have become attached these near-reaching and far-reaching responses and the vast number of refinements and substitutions observable in the developing individual's spatial orientations. (1) Relative *height* in the visual field, (2) *interposition* of one object before another, and (3) *apparent size*, are three aspects already mentioned. (4) *Clearness* is another: an object appearing as a dim, vague mass is taken to be further away than one with a clear-cut, distinctly detailed figure. This is a principle of "aerial perspective." Another cue in this same class is that of (5) *color*: light waves transmitted through a long distance of atmosphere, especially if it is hazy, are so affected that the original clear values are distorted; trees that are green when near at hand appear to be bluish on a distant mountain. In the example analyzed in Figure 117 the principle of (6) *lights and shadows* was found to be involved. The adequate handling of objects in terms of their depth and solidity is especially dependent upon usualness and normality of shading. Again, when the seeing organism moves through space, on a tricycle or on a railroad train, or when he merely moves the head from side to side in the gesture of negation, the relative positions of the eye with reference to objects seen are altered decidedly. The moon, or even a distant tree or house, will continue to stimulate the retina from a given direction while objects nearer the person enter, move across, and leave his field of vision. (7) *Apparent motion* (change of direction of stimulation) is, then, another cue to adaptations to objects both near and far. All of the foregoing seven principles are used in those arts that seek to produce the same effects as visible scenes: painting, the stage, photography in motion picture studios. To clarify his understanding of these principles the reader himself might draw a picture designed to imitate a three-dimensional scene with its trees and houses indicated at varying distances. The explanation of the "flatness" of

Egyptian sculpture and painting lies in the fact that the artists failed to use these principles.

The eye is not merely a receiving organ, as was noted in Chapter IX: it is equipped with muscles by which it can accurately adjust itself to differences in the distance of the sources of stimulation. (8) The *focussing* of the lens, which allows definition of the image (in the photographer's sense), varies for objects within about fifty feet of a person; and, as a function of the ciliary muscle, this gives rise to afferent kinesthetic impulses to which spatial reactions can become attached. The same may be said for kinesthetic impulses arising from (9) the *convergence-divergence* of the eyeballs in binocular vision. The six muscles attached to each of the two balls co-operatively produce in varying degrees a certain turning-in of the eyes so that the stimulations from the objects, whether near or far, will fall upon the centers of both retinae. In binocular vision another cue is provided. Owing to their different positions in the head, the two eyes "take" different pictures of the object being looked at, the one from a position a little to the right, the other from a little to the left. Consequently, when a solid object, such as a book, a pencil, or a tree-trunk, is being regarded it presents to one eye a view of the front and a little around the right side, to the other it shows the front and a little around the left side; and, as cameras placed a short distance apart will have their films exposed to slightly different aspects of the same object, so with the eyes and their retinae. The amount of overlapping of the two views varies with the distance, up to a mile or more. (10) The *double images* produced in this way furnish a cue of great reliability for the finer afferent controlling of behavior in space.

Doubtless the reader is surprised to find all these factors analyzed out of the visual perceiving of depth. He had seldom if ever been aware of them in his own perceiving. Precisely so. They illustrate most happily the participation of minimal cues in normal perception — cues to which responses became attached more and more accurately back in his early infancy.

Temporal Relations. The living organism must adjust itself not only to things "in space" but to things "in time"; it must be able to time its own reactions adequately to seize the prey, or to dodge the blow. Man's life, in its complexity of organization, has forced upon him elaborate conditionings of his behavior to many sorts of time factors. Dressing, fixing the furnace, catching the 7:49 for the city, getting to work at the desk, stopping for lunch, returning to the office, and all the round of the day's and night's routine, are based upon nice adjustments of a man's personal habits in point of time. To be sure, much of this is controlled by repeated references to standard time indicators, clocks, watches, and factory whistles, which are attuned to the movements of celestial bodies (the most constant of phenomena); but even so, without some ability to "beat time" himself a man would be fatally handicapped. In special interests, as in music, the perception of time intervals is necessarily extremely delicate, and it is one of the objectives of special training.

Experimental investigations have brought to light the fact that of all of the kinds of stimulation that affect man, it is in the auditory field that he is most capable of perceiving time differences. Two methods of investigation of acuity in perceiving intervals are in common use. In the first, two strokes of a telegraph sounder, which is wired in circuit with the experimenter's key, announce the original interval, and the subject with his own key tries to reproduce it. The strokes of both E's and S's keys are electrically recorded by signal markers on a kymograph drum, upon which also some time indicator, such as a tuning fork, a signal marker in circuit with pendulum or metronome, or a Jaquet chronometer, traces a standard reference time line, with its absolute divisions. In the other method two intervals are announced to the subject, who is asked to indicate verbally or otherwise whether the second interval is the longer or the shorter. Accurate control of the presentations can be obtained with the disk-and-arm type of apparatus.

If one stimulus be followed closely enough by another they will operate as one stimulation; if the sequence be delayed more and more, a discontinuity in stimulation appears, and the organism can react to the "two-ness." As short an interval as 10 ms. is discriminable by hearing. It has been found that there is a human tendency to overestimate short intervals of time, and to underestimate longer ones, the "indifference interval" lying at about six hundred ms. In daily life many errors of time estimation have become familiar, the degree and direction of error varying with the length of the interval and also with the "filling." There is a marked difference in estimating the lengths of a busy and a tedious day, also of time spent on liked as compared with disliked tasks.

What, now, are the cues operative in time perceiving? If we neglect sunrises, mill whistles, clocks, and other external guides, we must seek the occurrences to which activity is timed in terms of intraorganic changes. This is shown with especial certainty in the surprising ability of some people to tell the precise hour, by day or by night, without any deliberate computation, and also in the ability of many to awaken exactly at a given hour, without — so they say — any loss in depth of sleep. Consider also cases of visceral anesthesia as described on page 238. Now, certain physiological processes have well known rhythms, respiration, heart-beat, digestion, striped muscle phasic changes, and so on; and evidence is accumulating that more profound and more general chemical processes in the body furnish rhythms that are independent of exteroceptive stimulations [11]. (1) Is the ability of the body to respond appropriately to a given interval traceable to some kind of quantitative summating of such rhythms, so that when a certain number have occurred the total effect serves as the stimulus? We know that a person's judgment of certain intervals is modified by the amount of muscular and visceral strain maintained, as in prolonged orientation and waiting, and the resultant afferent restimulation. (2) Is the time-perceiving ability in general due to some qualitative changes in organic conditions, which operate as the stimulus? [1] There may be other cues; it is still much of a problem.

Perceiving in Reading. Of peculiar interest to the student is that type of perceiving he employs much of the day and every day, reading. It is an exceedingly complex process, as the years of training in school eloquently testify, even if we neglect its highly symbolic nature and view it on its motor side. If we stand directly behind one who is reading and observe one of his eyeballs by reflection in a small mirror held just below it, we will note that the eye moves from left to right not with a steady sweep but with alternating jerks and pauses, swinging back from the extreme right to the extreme left to start the next line of reading. During the actual moving of the eye nothing can be distinctly registered on the retina and anything like reading is quite impossible; so that the eye's work as a receptor is done during the fixation-pauses. This peculiarity of the eye-movements in reading was first discovered in 1879 and has been abundantly examined and confirmed since. With refinement of apparatus (such as that diagrammed in Figure 126) detailed facts and principles have been brought to light that have been useful for testing and for making diagnoses of readers and for prescribing proper kinds of printing.

[1] Compare the method described by Plautus:
"When I was young, no time-piece Rome supplied,
But every fellow had his own — inside;
A trusty horologe, that — rain or shine —
Ne'er failed to warn him of the hour — to dine."

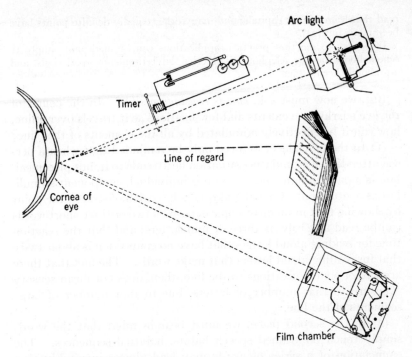

FIGURE 126. A METHOD OF RECORDING EYE-MOVEMENTS IN READING

An arc light projects a light beam through a blue lens that filters out all but the actinic (chemically active) rays (to avoid stimulating the subject). These are projected upon the cornea of the eye, and thence reflected through a focussing lens upon a moving photographic film housed in a dark chamber. Right-left movements of the eyeball produce right-left deflections of the light beam on the film. A signal marker operated by an electrically maintained tuning fork (50-cycle) interrupts the light beam so that it is registered upon the film as a series of dots each of the time value of 1/50 sec. On the moving film eye-fixations show as a vertical row of dots, eye-movements as dashes to right or left. In the figure is suggested a record representing three fixations and two rightward movements.

The film records can be related to the printed matter as follows. The reader first fixates in turn upon a dot placed just above the first letter in the first line and another just above the last letter, producing two guide marks on the film. When finished, the whole film record can be enlarged to the precise dimension of the printed line, and the successive eye-fixations accurately located thereon. (Dodge technique modified by Schmidt, Gray, and others in Judd's laboratory; here freely adapted.)

A general way of stating some of the findings is that the fixations vary around 5 or 6 for lines the length of those in the present book (100 mm.) if the reading matter is easy, but more if it is difficult; that the number of words seen per pause averages about 2; that the eye does not sweep from very beginning to very end of line, but leaves "indentations." Hue, it has been shown, has little effect on legibility, the important thing being brightness contrast between the type and its background; words in lower case are more readily read than words in all capitals; and many other equally definite points have been made out [21].

It is easy to see that practical applications can be made not simply to school books but to telephone directories, advertisements, road signs, and automobile license tags.

But, we now must ask, *how is reading possible?*   In the course of the eye's jerky movements and few fixations as it travels over a line, how can it be effectively stimulated by all the elements of that line?

(1) In the first place, we need only be reminded that when a person attends to a stimulating situation he attends to it, not piecemeal, but as a pattern or a whole — not as individual, component stimuli, but as a situation.   Cattell and others have demonstrated the point by showing that in tachistoscopic exposures two or three short words can be read as easily as three or four letters; and that the reaction time for reading aloud letters that have no connection is about twice that for reading aloud letters that make words.   The fact that there are five or six eye-fixations to the line, then, does not mean sensory exposure to that number of letters, but to that number of large segments of the line.

(2) In the second place, we must bear in mind that the words simply touch off trained speech habits, habitual sequences.   The enunciation of a series of words may lead almost inevitably to a certain concluding phrase: "Senator Sorghum will not again run...."   "Of the people, by the ..."   "Virtue is its ..."   "There ought to be a law ..."   "The land of the free and the home ..." In reading, the visual patterns of the printed page touch off speech habits which supplement visual stimuli.

(3) But the reader is not merely a bundle of habits.   He is a going concern.   Perhaps he is in the midst of a story, and eagerly anticipating later developments: the stimuli from the printed page serve now as hardly more than "stop" and "go" signs for his pellmell progress, or better, signposts of direction which give him the cue to turn down this avenue or that of his prospective thinking.   This activity of the reader takes a hop-skip-jump form in glancing down a newspaper column.   Who reads every word?   Whole sentences, whole paragraphs are skipped, and yet the informed reader, recognizing this phrase and that one for symbols of large organizations of his experience (high-order habits), is able to integrate the whole account into a sufficiently connected story, a story in the perusal of which he was truly half reader, half teller.

Esthetic Perceiving. One aspect of the perceptual responses we have been discussing through the chapter has been frequently neglected: their *valuing* character. Things, persons, situations, occurrences to which man is reactive are for him values — "good" or "bad" — and much of the story of learning to perceive things correctly is a story of learning to value them correctly. In human society this is especially true; and a man is judged and treated by others in accordance not only with the skill he displays in handling things about him but also with his ways of liking and disliking. Much of human conversation — especially mere gossip — turns upon judgments of another's judgments. Does he prefer jazz and chromos? Is he content with a shabby dwelling? Does he prefer winning his point to learning the truth? Does he vote the straight Republican ticket? Does he uncover as the flag goes by? Is he given to flashy or to subdued colors of dress? Does he laugh at only the broad, slapstick type of humor? Now, all such attributions are ways of describing, directly or by implication, a person's perceiving tendencies; and we must here recognize the fact that perceptual reactions have often directly to do with esthetic, ethical, logical, and other standards of worth.

For sample analysis let us take the first-named type of perceiving. Consider a man before a picture. His overt reactions are negligible, his emotional responses not intense; he does nothing with the picture as a physical mass or bulk, neither fondling, stealing, nor trampling it; he (apparently) merely turns his eyes upon it for some minutes, then passes on. This is by no means a dramatic performance; yet, if we could get overt vocal reactions from him and possibly measures of his slight emotional changes, long years of training in perceiving and evaluating would be evidenced. He perceives it as a true Matisse or Sorolla or just a copy; as in the classical, impressionistic, or futurist manner; as balanced or unbalanced in composition; as showing good or bad draughtsmanship on the hands, and so forth. The performance might conceivably lead to certain types of conduct such as glowing reference to the picture at the dinner table or an inquiry as to whether it was purchasable.

Man's appreciation of the beautiful is subject to objective study and analysis as truly as any other natural phenomenon. Even quantitative investigations are possible. To be sure, a person's reaction to a work of Rembrandt, Milton, Chopin, or Praxiteles is not yet subject to detailed psychological description; and the experimentalist must limit himself to modest beginnings with colors, lines, rhythm beats, or tonal combinations. But this is also true of the scientific study of any complex phenomenon.

Experimental methods in esthetics have usually taken either of two simple procedures — the method of Order of Merit or the method of Paired Comparisons (already referred to on p. 134). If the esthetic value of a given art object is to be determined, show it or sound it along with another or others, and then note the directions and amounts of preferences. For, by the very nature of it, the artistic properties of an object are not something to be determined by examining the object itself but by noting the human reactions to it. The above methods and their variants have seen application in a fair number of experimental researches. For the most part these have dealt with pictures, musical compositions, and poems; and they have taken the typical experimental form of analyzing the complex subject-matter into simpler parts: iambic versus trochaic rhythms, balanced versus unbalanced masses, complementary versus non-complementary color combinations, the curve versus the straight line — these are typical. One famous discovery was Fechner's. Of many shapes of rectangle shown, his observers showed a consistent preference for the "golden section," in which the two dimensions of the figure are in the ratio 21/34 or approximately .62. The great importance of habituation in esthetic perceiving has in more recent years been brought out by the fact that training can modify to a high degree and permanently one's likings for dissonances as versus consonances and also for different endings or resolutions [6]. But the yield has not been heavy, nor has it thrown much light upon human perceiving in general. Considering the universal interest in beauty, and also the simplicity of the technique and procedure demanded, this is as surprising as it is regrettable.

THE PLACE OF PERCEIVING IN THE LIFE ECONOMY

Handicaps of Poor Perceiving. What does it profit a man (or other animal) to be able to respond to the things about him perceptually? He makes responses to environmental stimuli, and to intra-organic stimuli. But if he were allowed only a capacity to respond to them in their first intension, so to speak, merely as physico-chemical energies which excite his receptors, his activity would be limited to a primitive array of simple reactions to what is explicitly and immediately present. In infancy, he might, like a clam, make some invariable defensive movement when a shadow falls upon the sense organs; but he could not learn to open his mouth if the shadow were cast by an approaching nurse, to laugh and "pat" if it were made by Scottie's bulk, or years later to reach forward, pull down, finger and inspect the object when a light stimulation strikes him after being reflected from the back of a new book. A similar limitation of man's possible reactions to sounds as physical sounds only would debar him from more than a turn of the head or a meaningless, distraught behavior in the presence of symphonic music, of a friend's voice, or the whistle of an approaching locomotive.

The disabilities entailed by an incapacity to build up and use perceptual reactions may be glimpsed by considering the case of profound idiocy. Let the reader remember that idiots cannot adjust themselves adequately to their living conditions. If left alone, they would in many cases promptly die. When they are able to feed themselves they may eat anything and everything including refuse from the garbage pail. The seeing or hearing or smelling of something that has been repeatedly an agent of pain may not function for them as a pain signal at all. Many do not learn to respond to certain interoceptive stimulations, and fail to attend to the calls of nature. An oscillating object such as a swing excites no anticipatory behavior, as they "walk right into trouble." The same feeding attendant who has thrice daily entered their field of vision may not excite their salivary and gastric glands or their facial and vocal muscles — he is but a visibly moving mass. In fine, although the idiot of low mentality has eyes to see and ears to hear and may in general be receptive to all the usual modes of external and internal stimulation, his responses are not habits appropriately adjusted to the whole objects and whole situations in his world. The raw stimuli fail to touch off any of the larger organizations of activity.

Looking Forward. In the present chapter we have given more direct attention than we have hitherto to the fact that human beings concern themselves not with isolated and abstracted stimulus details but with whole objects, persons, situations, and facts; and we have turned our efforts in the direction of analyzing the controlling factors and the detailed problems involved. And now, having clarified the notion of reacting-to-relationships, we are well equipped and accoutered to advance and come to grips with the higher thought processes. In unraveling them we shall find ourselves dealing again with relationships and especially those of symbolic character. Thinking has, in fact, frequently been characterized as "manipulations of symbols."

However, in that attack we will be greatly re-enforced by a better knowledge of the social situations out of which symbolic behavior evolves, so that we will do well to devote our next two chapters to a survey of psychological problems in social life, and especially in language. Meanwhile there are several problems in those fields that are interesting and important on their own account.

REFERENCES

1. Brown, W.   The Judgment of Difference.   *Univ. Calif. Publ. Psychol.*, 1910, **1**, No. 1.
2. Carmichael, L., Hogan, H. F., and Walter, A. A.   An Experimental Study of the Effect of Language on the Reproduction of Visually Perceived Form.   *J. Exper. Psychol.*, 1932, **15**, 73–86.
3. Craig, W.   The Dog as a Detective.   *Scient. Mo.*, 1924, **18**, 38–47.
4. Dunlap, K.   *Habits, Their Making and Unmaking.*   Liveright, 1932.
5. Ewert, P. H.   A Study of the Effect of Inverted Retinal Stimulation upon Spatially Coördinated Behavior.   *Genet. Psychol. Monog.*, 1930, **7**, Nos. 3 and 4.
6. Farnsworth, P. R.   Papers on ending preferences.   *Am. J. Psychol.*, 1925, **36**, 394–400; 1926, **37**, 116–22, 237–41; *J. Comp. Psychol.*, 1926, **6**, 95–102; *Genet. Psychol. Monog.*, 1934, **15**, No. 1.
7. Gibson, J. J.   The Reproduction of Visually Perceived Forms.   *J. Exper. Psychol.*, 1929, **12**, 1–39.
8. Goodenough, F. L.   *Measurement of Intelligence by Drawings.*   World Book Co., 1926.
9. Gordon, K.   *Esthetics.*   Henry Holt, 1909.
10. Guilford, J. P., and Hilton, R. A.   Some Configurational Properties of Short Musical Melodies.   *J. Exper. Psychol.*, 1933, **16**, 32–54.   Guilford, J. P., and Nelson, H. M.   Changes in the Pitch of Tones when Melodies are Repeated.   *J. Exper. Psychol.*, 1936, **19**, 193–203.
11. Hoagland, H.   The Physiological Control of Judgments of Duration: Evidence for a Chemical Clock.   *J. Gen. Psychol.*, 1933, **9**, 267–87.
12. Humphrey, G.   The Effect of Sequences of Indifferent Stimuli on a Reaction of the Conditioned Response Type.   *J. Abnor. & Soc. Psychol.*, 1927, **22**, 194–212.
13. Johnson, H. M.   Audition and Habit Formation in the Dog.   *Behav. Monog.*, 1913, **2**, No. 8.

14. Köhler, W.   *Gestalt Psychology*.   Liveright, 1929 (especially chaps. v, vi, x).

15. Leeper, R., and Leeper, D. O.   An Experimental Study of Equivalent Stimulation in Human Learning.   *J. Gen. Psychol.*, 1932, **6**, 344–76.

16. Miller, N. E.   The Perception of Children: a Genetic Study Employing the Critical Choice Delayed Reaction.   *J. Genet. Psychol.*, 1934, **44**, 321–39.

17. Moore, H. T.   The Genetic Aspect of Consonance and Dissonance.   *Psychol. Monog.*, 1914, **17**, No. 73.

18. Révész, G.   Experiments on Animal Space Perception.   *Brit. J. Psychol.*, 1924, **14**, 387–414.

19. Russell, J. T.   Depth Discrimination in the Rat.   *J. Genet. Psychol.*, 1932, **40**, 136–59.

20. Starch, D.   *Experiments and Exercises in Educational Psychology*.   Macmillan (3d ed.), 1930.

21. Tinker, M. A.   Experimental Study of Reading.   *Psychol. Bull.*, 1934, **31**, 98–110.

22. Washburn, M. F.   Gestalt Psychology and Motor Psychology.   *Am. J. Psychol.*, 1926, **37**, 515–20.

23. Wertheimer, M.   Untersuchungen zur Lehre von der Gestalt.   *Psychol. Forschung.*, 1923, **4**, 301–50.

24. Wertheimer, M.   Zu dem Problem der Unterscheidung von Einzelinhalt und Teil.   *Zeitsch. f. Psychol. u. Physiol. d. Sinnesorgane*, 1933, **129**, 353–57.

25. Young, P. T.   Auditory Localization with Acoustical Transposition of the Ears.   *J. Exper. Psychol.*, 1928, **11**, 399–429.

CHAPTER XVII
SOCIAL BEHAVIOR

INTRODUCTION

Man's Life is Essentially Social. Up to the present point in this book the man we have been describing has, for convenience of discussion, been isolated from the complexities of the society of which he is a part. Except for an incidental qualification and an occasional reference, we have neglected to give attention to the contribution that social environment has furnished to making the man. This contribution has been enormous. In the discussion of native reactions and their training into habitual forms of reaction, the incitements, checks, and controls administered by nurses, parents, neighbors, and others, have been touched on to some extent. But the modifications and directions administered by social agencies are also of fundamental importance in the building-up of behavior which arises from perception and thinking. At this point, then, let us make good our comparative neglect of the social factors in the description of man's nature and behavior by giving them special attention.

The life of a man is that of a person among persons. The world in which he lives is a world of human beings as truly as it is a world of inanimate and impersonal objects. As a newborn infant, he is placed in a crib, is nursed, and tended by another human being. Through childhood and youth he is a constant object of solicitude to his parents and other adults, and a frequent object of favorable or unfavorable treatment at the hands of childish and youthful associates. As an adult, he gradually assumes obligations toward the people about him, in his own family, in the family he acquires, in his church or lodge, his profession or business, in his town and state. So constantly present and constantly sensed is this social aspect of his environing conditions that even in childhood the major portion of his interests and aims is cast in terms of his relation to others; and throughout life the stresses or strains, the episodes of maladjustment, are but the difficulties in adapting to these other human agents.

The values of life, too, certainly assume predominantly social forms. Not only do they include the individual's satisfaction in the approbation or the envy or occasionally the fear manifested by others toward him as an individual; they include also the actual seeking of the welfare of others as much as, or even more than, the welfare of oneself. In many a subhuman form the biological principle of "regulation," or "adjustment," becomes extended to include more than the one organism to be regulated or adjusted. In human life, likewise, this extension of the sphere of interested reference is striking. Educating one's children, purchasing life insurance, carrying home the pay envelope, contributing to the community chest, and similar prosaic actions are primarily motivated by some kind of interest in others as truly as the noble interests in posterity of the Roman statesmen, or as the dramatic readiness for patriotic suicide of the Japanese.

SOCIAL PERCEIVING

The Perceiving of Social Cues. In Chapter XVI it was stated without elaboration that one of the most important capacities of a person is his ability to "size up" or "see into" a social situation that involves people and their attitudes — or his "knowing the thing to do." The lack of a fair amount of this ability usually makes a person both noticeable and unpopular among his fellows. If a man is blunt, he speaks of things that make his audience gasp; if he is tactless, he talks or acts to the injury of his friend; if he proves to be the object of amusement or ridicule, he unwittingly smirks his satisfaction over the effect he is making, and fails to observe the glances exchanged in his presence or the silence with which he is greeted: a woman's raising of her lorgnette or a man's irrelevant humming do not serve to abash him.[1] When he does rightly recognize the attitude of his fellows and seeks to guide his own conduct accordingly, what are the signs to be noted? What are the cues to social perceiving? In response to precisely what stimuli is he adjusting himself when he "does the right thing"?

The Perceiving of Facial Reaction Patterns. One of the more obvious cues is that composite of visible stimuli called facial expression. If our subject is holding a telephone conversation, the quickness with which he perceives his friend's speech in all of its

[1] The writer recalls a glaring instance: an otherwise intelligent professional man took his family to a formal church wedding, and as his child babbled during the ceremonies the proud father grinned appreciatively into the faces that were turned around at him in consternation.

allusions is appreciably lessened by his inability to see and watch
the friend's face and the reactions thereon.   Many a phrase may be
misunderstood in its more delicate implications; and it behooves
the man at the other end of the wire to make his sentences short and
his meanings obvious.   A good share of the interest maintained by
an audience in a motion-picture show is traceable to the perceiving
of sets and changes in the facial reactions of the actors and actresses
portrayed upon the screen.   The effectiveness of our most famous
comedians, for instance, depends not alone on cleverness of incidents
or on the actors' grosser performances of running, falling, or fighting,
but also to a considerable extent on the subtler changes of their
physiognomic reactions, as the situations in which they find themselves prove new and unexpected.   Indeed the way in which one
perceives the whole pictured scene is largely determined by the way
he reacts to the facial behavior of the actors.   Of course a man's
appropriate "seeing" of the screen dramas depends upon his everyday experience (habits) in reacting to the aspects of faces about him
— as these aspects have become substituted for the weals and woes,
the feedings, the pummelings, the ticklings, the strokings, the
pinchings which they originally accompanied.   The pattern on
another's face is now a substitute stimulus.

Research on the perceiving of facial expressions has been conducted mainly with photographs or sketches showing a person posed
in a variety of facial attitudes, or with mechanical models.   The
subjects of the experiment were usually instructed to observe a given
picture or model and to name the total emotional reaction of which
the given visible segments form a part.[1]   In most experimental
studies the judgments asked from the subjects were "free," in a few
they were selected by the subjects from a list supplied.

A general finding in such studies is that people have less ability
to guess or judge the original intended emotions from pictures than
might have been expected — for a reason that will appear later.
Some success is shown with subtle combinations like half-crying and
half-laughing, or midway between jest and earnest; but the easiest
to judge are the coarser types, notably laughter, pain, anger, fear,
hatred.   As we would expect, the ability to judge or recognize

---

[1] The reader will recall that in Chapter VII it was explained that the names applied in common speech to emotional behavior in its varying phases ("love," "anger," "grief," "suspicion," and the rest) are not to be considered as names for the visceral reaction-patterns of a man in any consistent way, but rather as convenient labels for viscerally re-enforced overt behavior patterns that have social significance and so come to be recognized and distinguished by his fellowmen.

specific kinds of emotional behavior from pictures is one varying greatly from individual to individual; and, since this is apparently not correlated with powers of perceptual observation in general, it is presumably a function of the interests of the subject. The more social person, for instance, falls into habits of watching faces and adjusting his behavior accordingly.

A finding that possesses special interest is that subjects would react to training in analyzing. For a key the various conventionally assumed components of the different types of expression was given them (for example, that the eyes are partly closed in "grief" or "pleasure" but wide open in "amazement," "fear," or "anger"; that the mouth is lowered in "grief," opened wide in "amazement" or "fear," slightly elevated in "disgust"; and the like). This training improved considerably the skill of those subjects who were originally poor at the judging of the total facial expressions, but it did not help much those subjects who were originally more successful [1, 7]. In other words, *a highly inverse correlation* was obtained between *initial skill in judging* and *improvability through study of the individual features.*

There is evidence bearing in the same general direction in a more recent study [6]. Drawing copies were made from photographs of poses made by an actor; they were then cut horizontally into three parts, the eyes, eyebrows, and forehead, the nose and cheeks, the mouth and chin; and segments from different pictures were recombined in various composites. (Cf. Figure 127.) These composite pictures were judged by many observers who assigned emotion-names to them. The experimenter then made an exhaustive quantitative analysis of these judgments to see how much the various facial muscles were involved in the poses that were frequently judged as "sneering," as "hate," as "gloating," and so on. What he found was that while most muscular details were the same in the various pictures commonly judged as one emotion, some apparently great variations appeared, but these were dominated by the characteristic pattern created by the others. In his own words, "The *significance of a given muscular involvement* is not constant, but is *relative to the rest of the pattern.*"

From this and the preceding studies, the generalization suggests itself that here, as in other matters, the way a person judges or perceives a thing seems to be a question of how he reacts, not to this detail plus that detail, but to the *toute ensemble*, the whole pattern

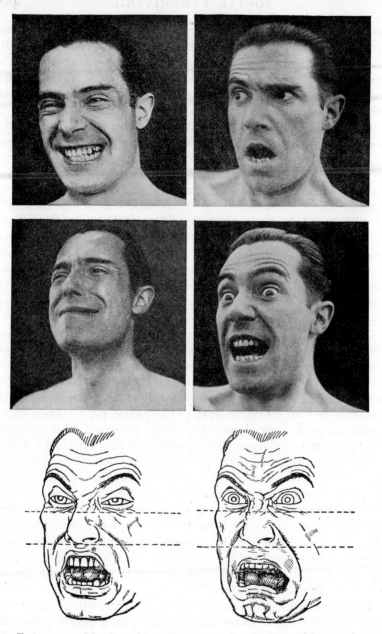

FIGURE 127. MATERIALS FOR JUDGING FACIAL REACTION PATTERNS

See note on page 485.

as such. Incidentally, a practical question may be touched on in this connection. When judges are rating contestants at baby shows, livestock exhibits, diving contests, dog shows, or jam and jelly exhibits they usually try to analyze each one in terms of certain "points"; but it is almost a certainty that the general impression will subtly affect them; for, as Thorndike found in the case of personnel ratings in the army psychological service, the "halo effect," while subtle, is considerable. A judge's rating of a man X on one trait is affected by his ratings of him on other traits and by the general impression he has formed of him.

The studies mentioned in preceding paragraphs were made on adults; what about children and their capacity to size up other persons' facial expressions? One investigation has demonstrated the great variability among children in their capacity to perceive facial expressions from pictures, and — what is perhaps more interesting — a general improvement in this capacity with increasing age (Gates). The present writer obtained somewhat similar results with children, employing a different method: instead of showing a picture and asking the child to name the emotion, a concrete situation was verbally described in simple terms, and for this he was to choose the appropriate picture from a set presented.

We do well to remember that a facial expression is but a part and detail of a more inclusive reaction. There are two ways in which this is true.

(1) It is obvious that the facial pattern as pictured at any instant is but an integral part of the whole attitude of the person in that momentary cross-section, and so is intimately and complexly involved not only with his vasomotor, pilomotor, and respiratory changes, but also with his vocal responses and with the gestures and attitudes of his whole body.

This has received indirect verification in a study of gesture patterns [3]. Subjects were furnished full-length photographs of an actor posed to represent nine different emotional postures, in different degrees of mutilation: (A) some complete, (B) some with the faces blocked out, (C) some showing head and shoulders only with the faces blocked out, (D) some showing torsos and arms only, and (E) some showing hips and legs only. The subjects scored higher in matching the poses with the emotions intended by the actor when they were using the A sets than when using any of the other sets. The facial expression throws light on gesture, with which it is so commonly bound up in everyday life.

(2) The momentary view of a man's face is an artificial abstraction from the on-going dynamic process of his behavior which in real life is reacted to as a whole by the other-man. For example, two smiles, which are "snapped"

Note to Figure 127, on page 484.

Four are shown of the forty-six original photographs used. The photographs were copied in ink; and these drawings were cut horizontally and recombined, for the analysis of particular features. Two of the composite drawings are shown. (From Frois-Wittmann, J., *J. Exper. Psychol.*, 1930, **13,** 149.)

at certain instants may seem identical, but actually they may be readily distinguishable by any observer who has opportunity to note their beginnings, completions, and vanishings. Someone has suggested the use of the motion picture for getting at the recognizability of facial changes in process, and this is a recommendation that is of obvious value; but to date no advantage seems to have been taken of it.

THE INFLUENCE OF SOCIAL SITUATIONS UPON THE INDIVIDUAL

The Present Need for Emphasis on Social Psychology. The remark has often been made that man's scientific and technological discoveries and knowledge in regard to physical and biological nature have been carried very far beyond his knowledge of himself. Today, as never before, we have become conscious of the Machine; and it is almost a commonplace assertion that the woes and ills of our Western civilization are due in large part to a too-rapid development of mechanical discovery and invention and a too-slow development of knowledge about ourselves. "Was Europe a success?" queries a recent writer. The answer is "Yes" and "No"; "Yes" if measured by advance in control of the material world, "No" if measured on a scale of social (especially political and economic) achievements. The world is certainly out of joint. It is high time, then, that scientists turned to a more intensive study of psychological and social phenomena, applying to them, not theories only nor general observations, but the experimental techniques that have proved so fruitful and epoch-making in other fields.

It would seem that the handwriting on the wall has been read especially by the psychologists of Russia and of Germany. In Russia, in addition to the already existing universities and technical schools, there have been established over eight hundred institutes to investigate the basic psychological problems of human behavior in society. In Germany, the vast majority of original papers presented now at sessions of psychological societies have been devoted to analyses of social psychological problems. It is true that in both cases the investigators are not motivated purely by interest in knowledge *per se* but are working in behalf of the political aims of the Soviet and of *Der Führer*; yet the fact remains that they are at work. In America, too, some beginnings have been made.

The reader will probably be incredulous at first. What kinds of approaches can be made to the study of society that can possibly be scientific and experimental, he will ask. But the matter is not so baffling if he will remind himself that, after all, man-in-the-mass is really *men*-in-the-mass, and that the behavior of each of these men is a matter of his stimulation and response.

Social Behavior is Analyzable into Interstimulating and Responding. The behavior of a man in a social situation is not essentially different from his behavior in the presence of non-living things only. The difference is that the behavior is more complicated. In place of one sensitive and behaving organism, adjusting itself to its environment and adjusting its environment to itself, we have two or more sensitive and behaving organisms, forced by conditions to be sensitive to each other and to behave toward each other. Nothing new is added — no new force, no new mechanism. Figure 128 shows a schematic analysis of this psychological interaction between different organisms. Let us start with an audible or visible move on A's part. We will suppose that, as a wink or a sneer, a curt word or an amicable wave of the hand, it will suffice to stimulate B to some sort of reciprocal demonstration, such as a smile returned to the wink or a head-toss of *hauteur* to the sneer, a soft answer to allay the wrath or a wave of the hand to return the salutation. Air or ether vibrations act upon B's receptors r_1, and neural impulses *via* centers c arouse to action certain effectors e_1. But now the plot thickens. B's smile or toss of head, his mild words or friendly wave,

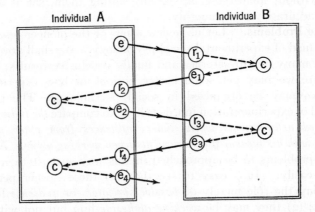

FIGURE 128. A SCHEMATIC ANALYSIS OF RECIPROCAL STIMULATING
AND RESPONDING

The broken lines represent general neural channels or general
functions rather than single pathways and simple reflex arcs.

may stimulate A to further overtures. Activity of B's effectors of face, throat, hand, and so on, e_1, are heard or seen by A, as air or ether waves excite r_2, and arouse some more or less appropriate reaction in turn at e_2. Further interchange of such hand, eye, face, or voice signals add no really new features to the actions in progress.

A few additional illustrations may assist us. In a flirtation, each individual puts the best foot forward, with sufficient tentativeness. A's advances are made first and are hardly noticeable for their casualness; then, if B's reactions be not of an unfavorable tenor, A later advances with more boldness; but always the bits of conduct of each principal serve in turn as cues to the other. The writer once observed two not over-pugnacious men facing each other in the center of an excited and urgent Bowery crowd. When one, on being prodded from behind, lowered more darkly and advanced ever so little, the other grew visibly more tense and belligerent; then, when either relaxed a bit from his strain of fist-clenched vigilance, the other was fairly sure to follow suit. Hostile act provoked hostile act, but a sign of relenting awoke relenting. Incidentally, it is important to remember that in this general description of social interstimulation and response "minimal stimuli" are generally involved. In dancing, the leader may be largely unaware of the slight changes in his movement of right or left hand or of the body generally, yet these serve as sufficient cues to his partner so that, without identifying or verbally noting them, she is able to follow accurately and smoothly.

Some Problems.[1] Let us review a few of the pioneer researches in this field of experimental social psychology. We shall not expect to find many definite studies and finally conclusive results; but at any rate we may get some better notions of how experimental inquiries may be organized in social psychology. The general method of experimentation in this field is, to compare *the individual's measured achievements when under influences from other persons present with his measured achievements when working alone.* A number of problems to be approached in this way suggest themselves rather easily. It is easy to see that (1) these "other persons" may play the rôle merely of *passive spectators* or *audience* for the subject; (2) they may be *working alongside* him but not with any particular reference to him; (3) they may be *contestants* against him

---

[1] The material of the following section is adapted from the author's chapter in *A Handbook of Social Psychology*, where most of the studies to be referred to here are listed [5].

in that work; (4) they may verbally seek to affect his work with *remarks about him* or what he is doing; (5) they may co-operate with him by *interchange of ideas*. In all these situations their influence upon him may be due (6) to sheer numbers or *majority* or (7) to personal *prestige* or (8) to other forms of *suggestion* in general. Each of these describes a relationship common enough in daily life so that any findings obtained ought to have promise of wider social usefulness.

1. **The Effect of Spectators or Auditors upon the Individual's Work.** The phenomenon of stage-fright has always been well recognized. The frequently "rattling" effect of having others present and attending upon one's own behavior is an everyday observation. On the other hand are those numerous occasions in which the opposite type of phenomenon appears. There is, for instance, the case of a certain famous public speaker who when first placed before a radio microphone cried, "But where's the audience?" and refused to proceed until a physically present and visible audience could be assembled for him quickly.

Experimental studies on this problem have not produced consistent results. In one study, where each subject worked on paper-and-pencil tests, the presence of spectators had the effect of *reducing the accuracy* of his work while *increasing his speed;* and this is probably the type of result to be most generally expected. However, there are studies in which the presence of auditors or spectators (*A*) increased the individual's accuracy in a manual task that called for close attention and accurate hand movements, (*B*) decreased the speed in block-assembling work, (*C*) slowed down the responses of a majority of the subjects and also reduced their range and quality, in a free word-association test.

2. **The Effect of Co-workers upon the Individual's Work.** It has been observed that, even when little or no occasion is allowed for the setting-up of a rivaling or an imitative attitude, the mere presence of others beside X who is at work on something — provided those others are not distracting to him — will often exert a favorable speeding-up effect on X's performing. Allport arranged an experiment with adults in which they were given the same tests under two different sets of conditions: at one they sat working as solitary individuals in separate rooms, at another they were working together in a group seated about a common table. To reduce rivalry to a minimum, all comparisons of achievement and discussions of

results were prohibited, and the subjects were further assured that their results would not be compared afterward. Tests were given in free chain word-association, letter cancellation, attention to a reversible figure, multiplication, and written argumentation to disprove an assertion. With a distinct majority of the subjects the results showed a facilitation or *speeding-up* of the reactions in all tests when work was done with the group as compared with the work done when alone. This increase in quantity, however, was generally accompanied by a *decrease in quality* so far as the responses were of the thinking type. The same result has been obtained in a German factory situation where skill in the manual operations of shoemaking was demanded.

This "social facilitation" fails to appear, however, with tasks of the unskilled heavy muscular type. In a series of measurements of the amount of work done at rope-pulling, it was learned that the output of the average individual of a group decreases by 10 per cent with each additional worker. This result seems to support a dictum of the efficiency expert, Taylor, that to put more than four men together at this kind of shared work is uneconomical.

We can conclude that, apparently, whether the sharing of a task with co-workers is to have a facilitating or an inhibiting effect *depends* in large part *upon the precise character of the task*.

One substantial discovery is to be noted. Working together seems to affect favorably the activities of the poorer individuals much more than that of the better. An important "*levelling*" influence then is seen. This is true of groups in which rivalry is a potent factor, too, for the poorer individuals seem stimulated to better achievements by the presence of the better, whereas the better are not stimulated by the poorer and may even be retarded. We turn next to rivalry.

3. **The Effect of Competition upon the Individual's Work.** It is said that the Shah of Persia, when attending the English Derby, showed only profound boredom. He commented wearily, "Everybody knows that one horse can run faster than another horse: what does it matter which one?" This is in accordance with the view that much of the competitive character of the life we know is purely Occidental. It is the result of traditions and customs of aggression that have had their part in molding the personality of each individual child. From the time he enters the nursery he has been encouraged to win prizes against others, and to seek higher school

grades and places on the teams or in the play, so that competition of one sort or another becomes almost a *sine qua non* of any indoor or outdoor sport, and he develops a rugged individualism in his economic and political gospel. But, regardless of its genesis, the motive is powerful. As we have hinted before, it is likely to creep in insidiously in any sort of social situation one may try to set up.

To isolate this factor of rivalry experimentally, subjects were once employed on a task of printing with rubber stamps. They worked under three different instructions. At one time they worked non-competitively without any comparison of scores; at another time they competed actively with each other as individuals; and at a third they competed as groups. The *individual* competition attitude made for *increased speed* but *decreased quality* over that of non-competition; and the *group*-competition attitude made for still further increased speed without, however, definite change in quality.

That group rivalry furnishes more motivation than individual rivalry, as in this case, is not to be expected always — or usually, perhaps. The reverse was found true, in fact, in an experiment in which the subjects worked on a substitution test and a test of comprehension of reading.

Surely here is a problem of stupendous social importance. Loyalties founded upon some compromise of the individual person's aggressiveness for the sake of the advantage of his group against other groups can be named *ad infinitum*: honor among thieves, codes of practice among business organizations, non-repudiation of gambler's debts, agreements on limitation of planted acreage, teamwork on the athletic field, citizenship as membership of one's own ward or city or state, patriotism, *esprit de corps*. The difficulties of instilling the spirit are great; the difficulties of maintaining it are greater, as witness the private infringements of public economic agreements, political graft, and other forms of secret "chiseling." On the contrary side, the group spirit often comes to assume an overweening importance; and in its name projects of aggression, as war, will gather impetus regardless of the welfare of any single individual at all. Loyalty expressed as the ratio of *inter-group competitiveness to inter-individual competitiveness* is an exceedingly variable and unstable quality.

For one thing it has been demonstrated that the more general family and neighborhood environment is exceedingly important; for in a community of laborers' children where co-operativeness was low, it grew lower with age. In a community of children of higher status and closer interaction where co-operativeness was high, it grew higher with age, which shows social influence of a still wider kind.

4. The Effect of Social Encouragement and Discouragement upon the Individual's Work. A trial was once made on college athletes to see whether a man's strength, already exerted at his "best," could be still further increased by coaching. While each man was at work on machines the coach urged him persistently to work harder, in this way producing a marked increase in the output, sometimes as much as 50 per cent. But this is not news to the athlete nor to the fan. In other phases of social life as well, the same phenomena is observable: in industry and business where increasing productiveness of labor is a desideratum; in school-work where the teacher is concerned with the application of the pupil to his learning tasks; above all, in the training of the habits of the child in the home. In fact, many a writer on psychology or ethics or sociology places sensitivity to social praise and blame as perhaps the most important single factor in social control. It is the more disappointing, then, that so few experimentalists have chosen to bring their methods to the exploration of this phenomenon; and that of those few, none concerned with adult subjects seems worthy of mention here.

The best-known investigation has been made on school children in their performances on certain group intelligence tests [10]. After taking the tests in the usual manner, the children were given them again a week later, some after having been highly complimented, some after having been severely reproached, and the others under the original normal conditions. Comparisons of the changes from the first to the second test for the three different groups brought out the conclusion that praise and reproof are effective incentives in producing *better* work (in accuracy mainly, though involving speed also); and that they are of about equal value, except that the effectiveness of reproof declines decidedly if continually applied. It seems, moreover, that the effectiveness of praise and reproof is greater with the older children and with the brighter ones. Most likely, we are not to suppose that the specific emotional effects of these two social influences are identical, but only that the outcome of the emotional excitement is an increased motivation (at least temporarily) in both cases.

5. The Effect of Group Discussion on the Individual's Reactions.

If susceptibility to encouragement and discouragement by others be one of the great modes of social control of the individual, an equally potent avenue is that of verbal discussion.   Yet while the former has been in evidence through all savage and civilized life, the latter is a later product of societal evolution and is to be seen at its best in the more civilized settings.   In fact, freedom of discussion — of assemblage, of speech, of the press — is a closely guarded right which liberal-minded people regard as the basis of all rights. And while the praise-and-blame type of influence inevitably causes conservatism, open controversy may, and usually does, cause changes.

The relationship between the individual person and his group is a more complicated one now.   Whereas his own reactions and attitudes may have negligible importance in making up the ap-proval-disapproval attitude of his whole group on any particular question or toward any particular person, his own contribution in discussion is actively or tacitly solicited, is for a brief moment at least set before the attention of every other individual and has its day in court.   This becomes a matter of weighty import when we regard the unusual individual, who with his original and novel ideas may make opportunity for the whole assemblage to consider and adopt plans and procedures that would never have occurred to the prosaic average men.

In this division of the field of experimental social psychology we may accord the lead to Bekhterev, who worked upon kindergarten children, teachers, and medical students.   In general, his program was to present the stimulus material to subjects, to have them make and record their reactions individually, then to present these individual responses before the group-as-a-whole for discussion, and finally to call for a second reaction and recording from everyone. Differences between the first and second sets of recorded reactions were then naturally attributed to the effect of the discussion.

The psychological functions he tested were such as: judging the time interval between two taps upon the desk; observing and recall-ing the details of pictures; making ethical judgments about a picture of a boy getting a beating; thinking up a suitable memorial to a poet. The results that he obtained consistently showed that group discus-sion improved the individual's reactions both as to *quantity of details* and as to *level of thought and judgment*.

The point seems simple enough.   If each individual has at hand not only his own earlier responses but also others furnished by associates in discussion, it is no wonder that he has a better chance of making a decision more objectively accurate and more considered. His range of choice has been increased.

This leaves out the argument factor. In a discussion group is most advance made by the mere *presentation of different viewpoints* or by the *pro and con arguments about them*? This question received a direct experimental approach when a large college class was given the problem of estimating the number of beans in a glass bottle, before and after being detailed into sections. Sections A and C were each made up of individuals varying widely in their original guesses; Section B was, without their knowing it, made up of individuals not varying much in their original guesses; and those in Section D merely made two estimates without any intervening discussion. The results condensed in the table indicate some fairly safe deductions. When

EFFECT OF KNOWLEDGE OF DIVERSITY OF OPINIONS

	SECTION A (WIDE RANGE OF ORIGINAL GUESSES)	SECTION B (NARROW RANGE OF ORIGINAL GUESSES)	SECTION C (WIDE RANGE OF ORIGINAL GUESSES)	SECTION D (NO DISCUSSION)
No. individuals improving their judgments	20/26	12/24	17/23	16/28
Mean deviation reduced	60%	17%	40%	4%

individuals enter into a discussion knowing of great diversity of others' opinions, a much greater proportion of them improve their estimates than when without this knowledge. (A and C *vs.* B and D.) And again, knowledge of the diversity of others' opinions makes for increase in *typicality* of opinion; that is, reduction of individual difference within the group — the "leveling" effect that has been referred to before.

In the foregoing research the argument process in the group work seemed negligible in its effect. There may be many reasons for this: debate is likely to arouse the rivalry attitude and so to intrench the debater in his original position; the persons doing most of the talking may not be doing most of the thinking; and for other reasons the discussion may not proceed on strictly logical and intellectual lines. Nevertheless, the experience of humankind with deliberative assemblies has been on the whole distinctly favorable to advance; so that what is needed from the scientific angle would seem to be more analytic procedures in the study of experimentally-set-up discussions.

6-7. The Effect of Majority and of Expert Opinion upon the Individual's Reactions. In just about all the situations in which an individual is influenced by other persons, there are two general classes of variables. One variable which runs through the experiments we have reviewed in preceding sections is the *quantitative* one of size or *number*. A group of two people, one of ten, one of a hundred, and one of a thousand, are notoriously different factors to be reckoned with — whether they be spectators, co-workers, competitors, or what-not. A second variable that may be even more profoundly important is the *qualitative* one of personnel. The degree of likeness or difference between the individual concerned and the persons influencing him is all-important.

To put the two general points made above into more specific form, we may recognize the fact that the individual person often shows, wittingly or unwittingly, deference to the attitudes and opinions of a *majority* and to those of persons enjoying *prestige*. Call the first the democratic motive in its naïve form and the latter the aristocratic motive, if you will; but they are both of unquestionable weight, whether in the formal establishment and exercise of public authority or in the implicit and subtle relations of any person toward any personal situation.

Some experimental attempts at unraveling these two factors in the influence of the group on the individual have been made. The general procedure has been first to present to the individual subjects materials on which each was to record his personal judgment; then later these materials were re-presented, (1) with no additional information — the "control" to see what changes would occur without any special social condition, (2) with accompanying information as to what the majority of the group had voted, and (3) with information as to what opinions well-qualified authorities or experts hold. The weight of the "majority" factor and of the "prestige" factor could then be derived from the number of individuals who reversed their own judgments after (2) and after (3) respectively.

The table furnishes us the results from two studies of the kind. From the upper half of the table it appears that both the influences are weighty, and that they are especially weighty where it is a question of speech or morals but less in questions of musical preference. We often hear expressions of the greater individualism asserted by

EFFECT OF MAJORITY AND EXPERT OPINION

NUMBER OF REVERSALS OF JUDGMENT ON RE-TEST OF THEIR PREFERENCES (MOORE)

	LINGUISTIC CHOICES	ETHICAL CHOICES	MUSICAL CHOICES
Normal or chance	13%	10%	25%
With knowledge of majority judgments	62%	50%	48%
With knowledge of expert judgments	48%	48%	46%

NUMBER OF REVERSALS OF JUDGMENT ON RE-TEST CONCERNING PUBLIC QUESTIONS (MARPLE)

	HIGH SCHOOL SUBJECTS	COLLEGE SUBJECTS	ADULT SUBJECTS
Normal or chance	17%	16%	14%
With knowledge of majority judgments	64%	55%	40%
With knowledge of expert judgments	51%	45%	34%

the average man in esthetic matters, "Well, I know what I like!" From the lower half of the table it appears that decreasing susceptibility to these influences goes with increasing maturity; and also that the influence of the majority is somewhat heavier than is that of the expert. Many "morals" can be drawn, and many needed and useful refinements of the experimental inquiry can be pointed out; but space forbids. That, anyhow, is the province and privilege of the intelligent reader.

8. The Effect of Suggestion upon the Individual's Reactions. One fundamental fact underlies all the phenomena of this section: One person is influenceable by others in non-logical ways. That is, he is "suggestible." Our inquiry concerning inter-individual influences might very properly, then, turn to the question of the nature of this fundamental susceptibility.

"Suggestion" as a scientific topic has been revived recently as a result of the investigations of Hull and his students. Figure 129 presents the essentials of some of their procedures. A subject, uninformed of the objective of the experiment, would be asked to see "how still he could stand." Without his knowledge, a hooked pin caught in his coat collar communicated his actual body swayings to a recording drum. In one series, a subject was (apparently acci-

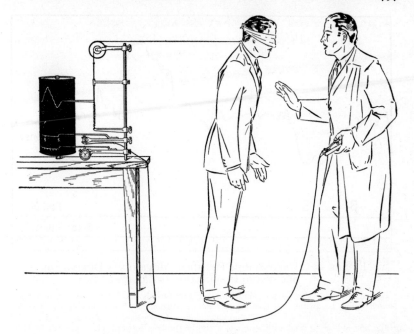

FIGURE 129. UNCONSCIOUS POSTURAL MOVEMENTS DURING SUGGESTION
OF MOVEMENT

A blindfolded subject is being told by the experimenter that he is falling forward.   Without
his knowledge backward-forward swayings of his body are communicated to a delicately hung
pointer tracing a record line on a revolving drum.   Also on the drum are indicated the time
(bottom line) and the spoken signals (middle line).   The recording apparatus appears on larger
scale than the human figures. (From Hull, C. L., *Hypnosis and Suggestibility*. Appleton-
Century, 1933.)

dentally) allowed to *watch another "subject"* go through a test of
trying hard to reach an object in front of him: in typical cases the
recording pointer would produce a clear rise in its tracing, showing
clearly that the unsuspecting subject had unconsciously mimicked
these forward-reaching movements.   In another series, the subject,
blindfolded, would *hear the experimenter saying* to him: "Now you
begin to feel yourself falling forward.   Now you are falling forward.
Now a little more.   More ——" and so continually.   The most
characteristic reaction was the subject's gradually swaying forward,
with occasional reversals, until he was off his balance and was
caught by the experimenter.   In still another series, the blindfolded
subject would be instructed to *imagine* himself bending backward,
then to imagine himself bending forward; in both of which cases

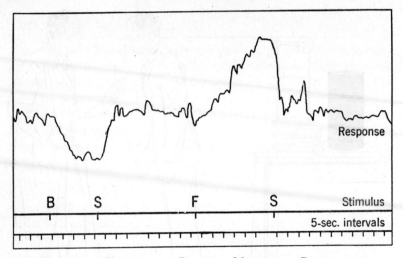

FIGURE 130. UNCONSCIOUS POSTURAL MOVEMENTS DURING THE
SUGGESTED IMAGINATION OF POSTURE

Record of a subject in the position shown in Figure 129 who has been instructed to imagine himself falling backward, and then falling forward.   Signals: *B*, "imagine falling backward," *F*, "imagine falling forward," *S S*, "stop imagining."   Upper line, actual body position, a fall in the line indicating backward swaying, a rise in the line, forward swaying.   (From Hull, C. L., *Hypnosis and Suggestibility*.   Appleton-Century, 1933.)

the pointer registered actual swayings of his body.   (Cf. Figure 130.)

These are the results of the investigations conducted by Hull: (*A*) that the "empathic" tendency of an individual to mimic or share in the behavior of others is a *genuinely unintentional* one; (*B*) that the *words* of others addressed to him have a profound and *genuine* effect *even unconsciously* to himself; (*C*) and that in "*imagining*" he is really *stimulating himself* just as the sight of another or the words from another would stimulate him.   The first two principles have obvious importance in relation to the phenomena described in this section of the chapter.   We will find the third principle exceedingly helpful later.

SOCIAL ATTITUDES

A considerable portion of latter-day work in the psychology of man in his social relations involves the study of attitudes and opinions on social problems.   The reader is referred to treatments of these in Chapters V and XX.

THE DEVELOPMENT OF SOCIAL BEHAVIOR IN CHILDHOOD

Introduction. Is Homo Sapiens a social animal by very nature, or does he only become so by virtue of the environment in which he grows up? Was Grotius correct in holding that there is an involuntary impulse that compels men to seek communion and association with fellow-men, or was Hobbes nearer the truth in claiming that in a state of nature every man's hand would be raised against his neighbor? These philosophical tenets have been quoted for centuries; but uncontrolled reflections on human beings plus strong *a-priori* preferences do not result in sound knowledge.

What are the findings of more scientific investigations? A final and definitive answer is not returnable. But the question posed is probably all too simple. To ask, "Is man by inborn nature social or anti-social?" is to assume too sharp a division, first, between "social" and "anti-social," and again between "inborn" and "acquired" nature. In Chapters III and IV we have seen that it is more profitable to map out actual processes of development than to seek overly precise answers to such questions.

The Infant's Early Reactions to Adults. The first social contacts of a baby are, of course, with adults — nurse, parents, older brothers or sisters, visitors. What is the character of its behavior toward them? Observations and the application of standardized baby tests were made on over a hundred cases by Charlotte Bühler and others in Vienna. A summary of their findings will give us an orientation.

The newborn infant seemed to be in a "pre-social" period of his life. He was pacified by an adult's soothing voice; but he was pacified just as well by any other sounds experimentally provided. The important thing, so it seemed, was not the human factor in particular but merely the sound factor. Nor was the newborn found to be any more social in response to other babies. He might cry when another one cried; but even when this did occur, it could be duplicated precisely by sounding in the baby's presence various noisy laboratory instruments: he would cry to them, too.

Sometime during the second month, however, some differentiation between his human and his non-human stimuli did seem to develop, for now he began to respond to the human voice with a smile that refused to appear at the mere sounds of bells or musical instruments, however sweet-toned, or to shining objects, however colorful. The social was becoming distinguished from the non-social.

Furthermore, the infant's capacity to differentiate among the social stimuli themselves became evident. At first the smile response had been given regardless of the particular mien and bearing of the adult. Both smiling expressions and angry ones, both the soft, kindly, speaking tones and the harsh scolding ones, both gentle inviting gestures and abrupt threatening ones, had elicited the infant's smiling. By the sixth or seventh month, however, the infant often assumed the very facial expression that he saw on the adult, and his general bodily behavior became appropriate thereto. The response was differential. In another way this was shown: strangers no longer could arouse the same reactions as did familiar faces: they now were strangers.

By the time the baby was a year old this differential reacting to the two kinds of adult facial patterns, the smiling and the frowning, apparently lapsed, but only apparently. It was not a reversion to the earlier stage. When the baby gave back smiles for the adult's frown, it seemed now that the make-believe glowering and threatening (seen often enough in his experience by this time) were responded to distinctly as play stimuli. He might cloud up at first, but in a moment he would break into a radiant smile.

In summary: as the infant develops through his first year of life, his behavior toward adults shows *increasing differentiations among his stimuli* — the social from the non-social, the friendly from the unfriendly, the familiar from the unfamiliar, the make-believe from the real.

The Infant's Reactions to Infants. Let us continue with the Vienna investigations. Two infants of near the same age, varying from six to ten months, would be placed in the same crib facing each other with a toy between them or given to one of them. Usually the two would pay no attention to each other unless their glances happened to meet or they happened to come into physical contact. Not until the second half-year did one child seem to attract another's attention, first by cooing or touching him, then by pulling him or snatching him or obstructing his movements.

Between six and eighteen months some interesting individual differences were found making their appearance. Three general patterns or types of behavior began to emerge [4]. The *socially*

---

[1] The reader will bear in mind that when the term "types" is used in describing people, the types set forth are usually to be thought of as limiting concepts, as extremes, between which many individual cases may be expected to fall, and are not hard-and-fast, black-and-white, all-or-none divisions. See pp. 583 ff.

blind infant usually paid little attention to another, even to the point of taking toys and moving about just as if he were not there at all. His primary interest was in the physical objects, not in the social. The *socially dependent* individual by contrast was frequently highly sensitive to the other's presence and apparently awaited his reactions. His characteristic behavior was dependent on the presence of the other. He might display himself before the other, and smile in triumph if he overcame him in some way, or, by the same token, be downcast if he was himself overcome. The *socially independent* child was still different. Though attentive to the other and responsive to him he was ordinarily neither intimidated nor inspired. He willingly played with him or not, as the occasion might make convenient. He might ward him off when necessary, but he never became aggressive. The presence of another never seemed to embarrass him nor to throw him out of his orbit.

Now, it is asserted that these types were found to occur independently of such factors as the child's home conditions, his nationality, his previous social contacts, and the like; and the investigator concludes that they are primary and independent of environmental conditions. As yet we have no evidence as to what produces these different types or as to what conditions in the child's physiological make-up led to their formation. If we regard them from another angle, such descriptions read not unlike classifications of older children and adults. The reader can easily find illustrations among his acquaintances; and we naturally begin to inquire concerning the permanence or the transience of social behavior patterns.

An experimental study that bears on this question was one in which various nursery school and pre-school children were introduced as individuals into small, already formed groups. During five-minute intervals of careful observation the experimenter noted such points as the child's shifts of attention, his initiating or responding to contacts with others, the amount of vocalization he did, and the like [16]. The typical behavior of a "new" child at first showed much alert but inactive watching of the others, then some exploring of the objects seen around the room, and then finally talking with other children. But individual variations appeared. Some never emerged from the frozen observation attitude; a few cried; and one lad trotted into the room saying nonchalantly, "Hello, boys and girls!"

Each child was observed again as he joined another new group at varying intervals from eight months to four years later. The striking finding was that, while a greater ease and freedom in the presence of strangers came usually with greater maturity and experience, still *the different types of social behavior* originally noted in the different individuals *remained essentially the same.* The solitary child, the follower, the ascendant leader, the timid and unself-confident, the impulsive outgoer — each remained much the same kind of child in his reactions toward his companions.

Other researches bring out trends in the same direction, but reveal at the same time some of the dangers and difficulties in drawing conclusions. In one well-controlled set of studies, children were observed in a nursery school and then a year later in kindergartens. During many five-minute observation periods there were recorded the number of five-second intervals during which each child was seen to manifest one or another kind of social reaction. Correlations were then computed between the records of individuals while in nursery school and while in kindergarten. Some of them are furnished in the accompanying table. We see that most of these

CORRELATIONS IN SOCIAL ACTIVITIES BY CHILDREN AT DIFFERENT
AGES (NURSERY SCHOOL AND KINDERGARTEN) [1]

ACTIVITIES OBSERVED	ρ
Talking to persons	.19
Talking to self	.40
Physical contacts with others initiated by oneself	−.11
Physical contacts received from others	.35
Laughter	.11

coefficients are low, but that the tendency is to the positive side; and they suggest at least a small degree of conformity between a young child's behavior toward his fellows this year and last. They borrow impressiveness if we take note of the fact that in the change from one school to the other there were changes in the personnel of the total group in which each child found himself, and further, that a child's specific reactions on either occasion were largely a function of the particular situation and of the particular individuals surrounding him.

Therefore, we are led to conclude that there is some evidence that *aspects of one's social makeup become established very early indeed,* and *they tend to remain more or less constant and characteristic of the individual.*

[1] From Jersild, A. T. The Constancy of Certain Behavior Patterns in Young Children. *Amer. J. Psychol.*, 1933, **45**, 125–29.

THE DEVELOPMENT OF SOCIAL BEHAVIOR IN OTHER ANIMAL FORMS

Our scientific ideal, of course, would be to set up experiments involving long-time experimental control, that is, with this or that factor studied intensively throughout a lifetime. Unfortunately for science, this obviously cannot be done with human beings. We cannot lock them up or rigidly prescribe every detail of their living and control every incident of their social contacts. Lower animals, then, must be used. Several investigators have already been at work here [2, 8, 12, 13]; and, although their experiments are by no means complete, they do indicate important possibilities for extended study. To be sure, the subjects would not be human beings; but it is reasonable to suppose that the most fundamental principles of social organization in human life would be manifested in subhuman life in some degree.

THE INDIVIDUAL'S UTILIZING OF SOCIAL SITUATIONS

Reaction-Getting Habits. In our frequent returns to the fundamental concept of the organism's adjustments to, and of, its environment, we have not usually characterized its environment in particular. But the fact is that the individual lives among other human beings, so that the problems of his life are problems of adaptation to these others and by means of them. We have already noted the fact that children, when facing difficult problems, set up experimentally, often call upon other people for aid in getting the suspended ball or the barred-off doll (pp. 396 f.); and the elaboration of this in later childhood and adult life is one of the central features of the socializing of the individual. But let us first look to its phylogenetic antecedents.

When Köhler's apes were seeking the out-of-reach banana, he sometimes observed one of them to push or pull him or the keeper over to a position under the lure so that it might climb him and so reach the latter. The man was treated like a box. This is hardly social behavior yet.

Bekhterev tells the story of a pigeon he once observed, which, "flying round a horse's head, at first frightened the horse by the whirring of its wings and thus made him spill grain from his nose bag. Led by this casual experience, it repeated the trick several times and for the same purpose." The pigeon was plainly utilizing the horse. But it was not using him as a mere physical object: it was *getting reactions out of him, reactions useful to itself.* It had developed a *reaction-getting habit.*

Along with this consider a description of a rather common chimpanzee mother-baby relationship. At first, the mother controls her young by physical force, drawing it suddenly back from danger and clasping it to her breast, vocalizing excitedly meanwhile. After many repetitions of this, the baby learns to leap into its mother's arms, at first when her hand is extended to seize it, and later at a mere gesture on her part suggestive of the seizing movement, or at a slight squeal [15]. The mother has gotten social control of her baby now, by the mere device of eliciting desired responses from it. She uses it as a reactive organism for her own end — an end that is, to be sure, concerned with the good of the baby in this case, but still an end or adjustment of hers.

Here we can with profit return to our diagram of the adjustive sort of behavior (Figure 7, p. 35), but with an amplification to include the fact that much successful adjustment is through social stimulation and response. (Cf. Figure 131.) Let *1* again represent the on-going activity of our original subject *A*, and let *3* again indicate the encountering of some difficulty or hitch (*2*) and *A*'s consequent excited and exploratory behavior. Now, let the reaction *4* be such as to stimulate another person or animal *B* to make the response *4–b*, a response that in one way or another removes the

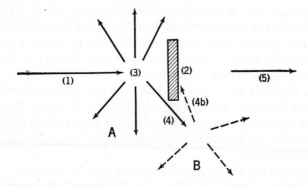

FIGURE 131. DIAGRAM OF TYPICAL ANIMAL BEHAVIOR IN WHICH STIMULATION OF ANOTHER ANIMAL AND ITS REACTIONS FURNISH THE "WAY OUT"

(Compare with Figure 7.)

hitch or difficulty (in the above examples: horse spilling oats, baby chimp leaping to its mother). Then we can represent the satisfaction of the original motive again as 5. Instead of avoiding or removing the obstacle himself, subject A stimulates subject B, who removes it. It is an adjustive process in exactly the same sense as before, except that the intermediation of a social reactive object is now involved.

This sort of phenomenon is to be seen constantly in human society. Some of the more dramatic illustrations that present themselves to the clinical psychologist are appropriate here. Take the following cases: the adult who "has her way" when facing ugly situations by the habitual device of copiously weeping or hysterically fainting or screaming and scolding; the confirmed toady ingratiating himself and fawning; the persistent bulldozer and bluff, and the four-year-old child who develops the reaction of vomiting as his habitual way out of disliked assignments. One and all, they have found how to "get that way" by the familiar process of trial-and-error. Once upon a time, finding themselves in a difficulty and reacting this way and that, they chanced to do something (to weep or faint or scold, to fawn or bluff, or even to vomit) that aroused from people near them just the kind of behavior that removed the disliked restraint. They didn't *have* to go to school, to give up the coveted toy, or to eat the cereal. And the rest is merely the story of fixation of this successful way of adjustment as a tool or weapon to be used on all such obnoxious occasions.

Learning to Make Abbreviated Social Stimuli. In the case of the chimpanzee mother referred to above, it was to be noted that she developed control over her young merely by a gesture or a warning cry. Another illustration from animal psychology will re-enforce the point and give us a further hint as well. In over fifty species of birds, from sparrow and canary to flamingo and gray goose, it has been observed that there obtains a definite order of precedence between any two individuals, a definite "peck-right" [14]. Bird A can peck or threaten to peck bird B without being pecked in return. The "right" is ordinarily determined after one encounter. On that occasion A has inflicted pain on B; whereupon occurs a change in B's neuromotor organization that is simple enough. The situation in which B's cutaneous receptors were receiving the intense pain stimulation, thus arousing his own withdrawal movements, included also such incidental stimuli as the sight of A's ruffled feathers, high-held head, or reddening face and eyes, and the sound of his pugnacious squawking. It is easy to see that on later occasions the re-presentations of A's ruffled feathers or angry squawk will become potent to excite the complete act of withdrawal by B. Henceforth, whenever B's proximity furnishes any obstruction to A's progress, A need only ruffle up or give one warning squawk to control B's responses satisfactorily.

A relationship of this sort often furnishes the psychological basis of a whole social order. To continue with the case of the birds: A pecks B, B submits to A but pecks C, C pecks D, and so on; furnishing a pretty complete hierarchy. Curious anomalies often appear, however; as where A pecks B, and B pecks C, but C in his turn can peck A. We need not go into the explanations of this latter exception, but the whole picture serves to show well how a social group can derive a definite structuring from the building up of these interindividual stimulations and responses carried no further than the merest gesture and vocal sound.

Of course, it is in the human that we would expect to find and do find the most elaborate developments of social control through abbreviated reactions. And they can be traced to early years. Preyer found his infant son turning away his head when he had had enough of feeding, and then later shaking his head in the same general manner when a negative response was aroused to any presentation or demonstration by another person. Similarly, what began as an actual pushing away of things he disliked evolved into the more refined head and arm gesture of rejection that we see in older children and adults to wave other people aside or indicate to them, "No!"

When a boy draws back his hand and threatens a younger brother, or when he cries aloud and gets attention from friendly quarters, or reaches toward the ground and so sets a dog in fleeing retreat, we cannot fail to see that he has picked up, or learned, the trick of letting an abbreviated reaction do duty for a complete one in socially stimulating others. Given a drive and an environment which does not satisfy that drive until a change is produced by the action of another person B, and the response aroused from the subject A will be only an abridged one. B has previously learned to perceive social cues, that is, to recognize the whole reaction from this partial act of A and will readjust his behavior accordingly, and A will have hit upon and fixated this device by trial and error as an adequate adjustment on *his* part when the whole situation arises. The mere

ANALYSES OF ABBREVIATED RESPONSES SERVING AS EFFECTIVE SOCIAL STIMULI

ACTIVITY OR TENDENCY IN A (SERVING AS INTERNAL S)	OBJECTIVE SITUATION OR S, INCLUDING B	ORIGINAL COMPLETE R BY A	EFFECTIVE ABBREVIATED R BY A	R BY B FURTHERING (OR HINDERING) THE ORIGINAL ACTIVITY OR TENDENCY IN A
Defensive or aggressive	Dog	Reaching down, picking up stone, throwing and hitting B	Reaching toward ground	Fleeing
Defensive or aggressive	Another person	Angrily striking and beating, with vocal and facial accompaniments	Clenching fist (or growling, or frowning)	Withdrawing (or attacking)
Disapproving	"Naughty child"	Striking or shaking B	Shaking finger	Ceasing "naughty" conduct
Aggressive disapproving	Animal or person trespassing	Giving chase to and striking	Stamping feet a few times	Retreating
Friendly	Chum	Taking hold of and drawing along	Beckoning with pulling motion of hand	Approaching
Amatory (in M sex)	Member of opposite (F) sex	Smiling, approaching, and embracing	Quizzical glance	Returning glance or smiling (or avoiding glance or frowning)
Amatory (in F sex)	Member of opposite (M) sex	Retreating and resisting	Coy glance	Approaching (or ignoring)
Hurrying	Person in the path	Pushing B bodily aside	Waving hand sidewise	Stepping aside

threat to act thus and so is now the selected and fixated line of activity with him. A few typical concrete examples are offered in schematic form in the table. The reader will readily see that all sorts of variations in the statement of each S and each R are to be allowed, and many can be easily supplied by him.

It is by the medium of language, however, that the most potent, most delicate, and most versatile forms of social influence are made possible. The use of language is so important that we shall devote a special chapter to its presentation.

REFERENCES

1. Allport, F. H. *Social Psychology.* Houghton Mifflin, 1924.
2. Bayroff, A. G. The Experimental Social Behavior of Animals. *J. Comp. Psychol.*, 1936, **21**, 67–81.
3. Blake, W. H. A Preliminary Study of the Interpretation of Bodily Expression. *Teachers Coll. Contribs. to Educ.*, 1933, No. 574.
4. Bühler, Ch. The Social Behavior of Children. Chap. 9 in *Handbook of Child Psychology* (Murchison, ed.). Clark Univ. Press, 1933.
5. Dashiell, J. F. Experimental Studies of the Influence of Social Situations on the Behavior of Individual Human Adults. Chap. 23 of *Handbook of Social Psychology* (Murchison, ed.). Clark Univ. Press, 1935.
6. Frois-Wittmann, J. The Judgment of Facial Expression. *J. Exper. Psychol.*, 1930, **13**, 113–51.
7. Guilford, J. P. An Experiment in Learning to Read Facial Expression. *J. Abnor. & Soc. Psychol.*, 1929, **24**, 191–202.
8. Harlow, H. F. Social Behavior of Primates. *J. Comp. Psychol.*, 1933, **16**, 171–85.
9. Hull, C. L. *Hypnosis and Suggestibility: an Experimental Approach.* Appleton-Century, 1933.
10. Hurlock, E. B. The Effect of Incentives upon the Constancy of the I.Q. *Ped. Sem.*, 1925, **32**, 422–34.
11. Jersild, A. T. The Constancy of Certain Behavior Patterns in Young Children. *Amer. J. Psychol.*, 1933, **45**, 125–29.
12. Kuo, Z. Y. The Genesis of the Cat's Responses to the Rat. *J. Comp. Psychol.*, 1930, **11**, 1–35.
13. Pattie, F. The Gregarious Behavior of Normal Chicks and Chicks Hatched in Isolation. *J. Comp. Psychol.*, 1936, **21**, 161–78.
14. Schjelderup-Ebbe, Th. Social Behavior of Birds, Chap. 20 in *Handbook of Social Psychology* (Murchison, ed.). Clark Univ. Press, 1935.
15. Tinklepaugh, O. L. "Social Psychology of Animals." Chap. 14 in *Comparative Psychology* (Moss, ed.). Prentice-Hall, 1934.
16. Washburn, R. W. "A Scheme for Grading the Reactions of Children in a New Social Situation." *J. Genet. Psychol.*, 1932, **40**, 84–99.

CHAPTER XVIII
LANGUAGE HABITS

THEIR GENERAL IMPORTANCE

Anthropological Importance of Speech. For our consideration speech is by far the most important of all the reciprocal stimulations. From an anthropological standpoint its advantage in social communication is obvious. When we view mankind living in the mass and note the external evidences of man's development in civilization and culture, it becomes clear that these monuments to human achievement are a result of co-operative endeavors made possible not so much through gestural signs, facial posturings, inarticulate cries, or any other type of personal communication as through speech. A common speaking means of intercommunication is necessary before there can develop refinements in the activity of the integral members of a group and the nicety of the personal adjustments of man to man, which are necessary for men to accomplish anything really worth while in concert. Let communication be destroyed, and any work dependent upon such close co-ordinations becomes a Tower of Babel. The organization of peoples into an Aztec empire or a Soudanese kingdom would be practically impossible with deaf-mutes. It would be almost inconceivable for speechless peoples to carve a totem pole with its dependence upon magico-religious practices or to erect pyramids like those of Maya or of Egypt. Moreover, speechless peoples could not develop such cultural products as systems of counting, the preserving of a tribal history, and so on. Language, then, has made possible cultural achievements in their more complex forms.

As a matter of convenience it is also apparent that speech has had a distinct everyday advantage over other modes of signaling; for in the majority of social activities — tramping, weaving, planting — the hands and feet and eyes are likely to be importantly occupied, and a man's face is often necessarily averted from his companions. Sound, then, becomes the most convenient medium, for it will even pass around corners and bodies. The vocal apparatus becomes the most available signaler, and practically no activity, not even eating, excludes the use of speech. Whatever be their occupation, the members of a group remain possessed of an excellent signaling device in vocal sounds.

Psychological Importance of Speech. "Man is the talking animal." For decades language has been recognized by psychologists of many different schools as intimately and subtly linked with man's most delicate and elaborate forms of activity. We shall take abundant occasion to expand this conception.

For the present it may suffice to notice how early and how dominating is the employment of language habits. A baby's demonstration of ability to talk, that is, to speak a word or two with symbolic significance, is an event as eagerly awaited as his learning to walk. Normally it occurs around the thirteenth or fifteenth month, although it may not be easily observed owing to the difficulty in making sure whether the baby is doing any more than merely babbling or making a general vocal response without any specific relation between it and some particular thing. In childhood and maturity language maintains a principal place in a person's equipment. A surprisingly large part of a man's or woman's life involves speaking or listening to speech, writing or reading. It would indeed be difficult to describe a full day's program for a normal man with complete elimination of any language activities. An oculist's proscription of any reading whatever, combined with a laryngologist's ban against any speaking at all, would succeed in giving a thoroughly miserable time to a patient who was otherwise well. Such a man is free to engage in very few actions. We may pity the army draftee who, when asked by his comrade who had just received a letter if he could "read writin'," had to answer, "No, I can't even read readin'!" But, at least, his experiences since childhood had equipped him with adequate habits in hearing and speaking.

To understand better the peculiar character of language and certain other forms of social behavior, we must turn to the analysis of symbolic stimuli and responses. Let the reader be warned that no single character of human life and conduct is of more psychological significance than this. It is a key essential to the interpretation of all the more complicated social relations as well as all higher thought life of man.

LANGUAGE AND OTHER SYMBOLIC SOCIAL BEHAVIOR [1]

Introduction. We have now to note the development of a phase of socially stimulating behavior of first importance. So far, our examples and analyses have, for the most part, concerned reactions by B to A's stimuli in which B's behavior has more or less direct reference to A and A's actions. But in much human intercommunication the activity of B has nothing to do with A directly. *It has to do with a third object.*

When the student at luncheon or dinner enters into vocal or gestural conversation, by far the larger number of the sounds and movements he makes will be to arouse on the part of his right-hand or left-hand neighbor not responses to him personally and directly so much as toward other things: "Please pass the salt," "Have we ice cream for dessert?", "Did you hear the concert last night?" and the like. So, too, at the stadium: any vocal signals between bleacherites above the level of "Down in front!" is likely to amount to references, favorable and derogatory, about human beings out on the field, not the immediate parties to the conversation. So, too, in the classroom: the vocal and other demonstrations of instructor or of student are far more elaborate than the mere physical give-and-take of two individuals, for their remarks and notes have abundant signification to third objects of discourse. An intercollegiate debate differs strikingly from a boxing or wrestling match in this same regard: whereas the man in the ring makes overt movements toward his adversary and responds more or less effectively to that adversary's overt movements, the debater is not concerned to make direct actions upon the other disputant at all nor to ward off threats of his bodily approach. Instead, he is making sounds and motions that refer his opponent and his audience to third objects and events, objects and events that may actually be thousands of miles distant or hundreds of years away or even entirely fictitious; and it is respecting those objects and events that his opponent must in his turn make appropriate response. "Is the war party in Japan the dominant element?" "Was Old World culture transported across the southern Atlantic to form the basis of the ancient Inca and Maya civilizations?" "Will the next war be one of extermination of populations?" "Was Hamlet mad?"

[1] The reader should not fail to refresh his knowledge of symbolic behavior by reading again pp. 460 ff.

As the reader will readily appreciate, new dimensions have now been added to the life and activities of men. No longer are they limited to the here and now, but transcend space and time.

There is no mystery here, however, and no essential departure from the proposition that psychology is a matter of organismic behavior analyzable into stimuli and responses. Let us try an analysis in these terms. Let a stimulus X, which does not directly affect person B, stimulate A (S_a) to make a communicating or signaling response (R_a) to B; then this may operate as a stimulus (S_b) to the latter person, and excite in him a reaction (R_b) appropriate to the unsensed X. Let us fill in concrete details.

Huckleberry Finn (A) appears in the alley, and, under the stimulating conditions of weather and habit and a possible sight (S_a) of the old swimming hole (X), holds aloft two fingers (R_a), to which (S_b) Tom Sawyer's prompt response (R_b) of "goin' swim-min'" is the answer. Or, on another day, Tom may signal with a crook of a thumb the imminence of Auntie, and his chum will disappear (Figure 132). A lecturer (A) has occasion to point (R_a) to a map that he sees (S_a); thereby directing the attentive postures (R_b)

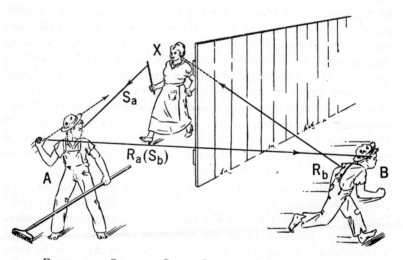

FIGURE 132. SYMBOLIC SOCIAL STIMULUS AROUSES REACTION
TO ABSENT OBJECT

Tom (A) signals by hand gesture (R_a) in direction of Auntie (X), who is invisible to Huckleberry (B); and the latter reacts to this signal stimulus (S_b) by retreating (R_b) from this "absent stimulus" (X).

of his audience (B) toward the map (X). Or, a stranger (X) appears in Batouala's camp, and by the latter's drumming (R_a), his tribesmen for miles around (B) are prepared (R_b) for this new turn of events.

In each of the cases the stimuli are symbolic. Two fingers can in no conceivable way be a derivative or abbreviation of swimming or of the hole. A jerked thumb bears no likeness to and may never have been formerly spatially connected with Tom's aunt. The lecturer's extension of arm has nothing especially in common with a map. The thump-a-thump of the mid-African's drum in no way sounds like a stranger.

There is another aspect of the problem. The object or event referred to may be one not actually in the direct environment of the person oriented to it. For instance, Tom Sawyer is probably not in sight of the pool or of people going in that direction. Tom's aunt may be doing her scowling behind a fence or a kitchen door out of Huckleberry's sight. The lecturer's map may be on a side wall visible to the auditor only after rotation in his seat. Batouala's distant tribesmen may not be able to see or hear the stranger. Yet in each episode under these circumstances the party of the second part is led to make an adjustment to a stimulus that was an indirect stimulus.

Methods of Signaling. The anthropologists, in their study of man and the genesis of his social organizations, have laid emphasis upon the earlier and simpler forms of human culture and relationships. They have been wont to describe several distinct methods by which one individual person has gotten into (S and R) communication with others by the utilization of symbols. For one thing, there is the *whistling* of messages. In many parts of Africa explorers have noted "conversation" in the form of whistling from some distance. The arrival of one visitor was announced by relays in this way to an official forty miles away. There is the *drumming* of messages, again in Africa. Every white man takes his drummer, and officials moving up or down stream have their drummers to announce their mission to the natives along shore.

Rude forms of reciprocal stimulation take the form of *marks made on objects*. Some Australian tribes convey messages from place to place by means of notched "message sticks," the notches being often decipherable only by sender and recipient. North American Indian tribes sketched rude pictures which varied greatly in the literalness with which they conveyed meanings. A drawing of a land-tortoise could mean a tortoise or it could mean dry land; a kingfisher could denote a bird of that species or a chief who happened to bear the name of a bird. (The meaning of a stimulus, as we saw in the Chapter on Perceiving, depends in part upon its context.)

The employing of *facial* reaction patterns has already been dealt with in the present book. That it should have been hit upon and fixated as a device in controlling others is small wonder. It forms a striking and readily observed part of total emotional reactions, and, since emotional behavior generally concerns other people, this device is likely to obtain and hold their attention. Then, too, the facial patterns are determined by numerous combinations of many muscular bundles and so are capable of a very great variety of significations.

To *gestural* signals, also, we have already had occasions to refer, although in no systematic way. The anthropologists have emphasized the part played by fingers, hands, arms, head, and trunk as signs used in social communication the world over. Bring together folk from Tibet and from Timbuctoo, from Bolivia and Bengal, and they will be able to establish some basis of communication by means of the simpler gestures and facial expressions. The doughboy in Paris, wholly untrained in the conventional system of vocal signals known as the French language, could nevertheless make his simpler wants known by his manipulations of shoulders, hands, and face. The American Indians developed gestural signs to a high degree, owing no doubt to their nomadic life and to the great variety of vocal language met among their different tribes. In fact, some of their communication was by this sign language only and had no substitutes in vocal sounds. Many of the signs were used in an identical way from the Gulf of Mexico to Hudson Bay. These same signs are employed by deaf-mutes in civilized society; so that once when a small company of Ute Indians were brought to converse with a number of students in the National Deaf-Mute College at Washington, there was a surprising degree of common understanding. Some of the obvious signs usually used by the Red Man are readily understood. "Riding," for example, is signaled by making a pair of legs of two fingers of one hand and placing them astride a finger of the other hand. "Raining" is signified by dropping the fingers from a partly closed hand; "fearing" by placing the hands on the lower ribs; "sleeping" by leaning a heavy head against the open hand: "candle" by holding a forefinger straight up and puffing at its tip.

Gesture language has, of course, been used by other peoples than the American Indians; and it is even said that the massacre of foreigners in the "Sicilian Vespers" revolt of 1282 was plotted throughout the island, even to the precise day and hour, without the use of a single spoken syllable. A fine example of the modern

Neapolitan sign language is shown in a plate of De Jorio's, reproduced in Figure 133.

> "Action is eloquence, and the eyes of the ignorant
> More learned than the ears."

The Pre-eminence of Word Signals. As was pointed out in
our first section, speech has tremendous advantages over other
modes of interstimulation, by reason of the physical properties
of sound conduction and the independence of the vocal mechanism
from nearly all occupations in which a communicating person is
likely to be engaged. Moreover, vocal sounds can be combined
in an enormous variety of patterns. Speaking is developed and
elaborated as a mode of behavior precisely because it affords a
highly convenient and a highly modifiable mode of signaling.
Like facial expression, gesture, cries, drawing, and drumming,
it is a method by which the perceiving acts of John Smith can be
aroused also in others even when they are out of direct touch with
the thing perceived and are stimulated only by the signal from
Smith. The word "kangaroo!" passed along from the original
speaker who espied the animal, becomes an adequate stimulus to
arouse his fellow hunters to much the same responses as if they, too,
had directly seen it. It is a symbol. The vocal sounds now stand
for and represent the animal, not, in this case, by resembling it but
by their capacity to initiate the same sort of behavior in various
people. As we shall see in the language development of the child,
the throat-and-head sounds have become a substitute stimulus by
conditioning.

Now, let the sounds uttered be the Australian equivalents for
"kangaroo over on the left" or "big kangaroo over on the left and
he's facing this way," and the control of the fellow hunters' perceptual and overt behavior becomes still more detailed and complete.
Thus the manifold refinements of language enter into the story to
make this mode of signaling more and more effective in controlling
the other man's behavior: words are grouped together, with some
modifying others; words are inflected to produce fine variations of
stimulus; different orders of words are established in the sentence,
for the same purpose; words are compounded; and so forth. We
may leave further study of these phenomena to the comparative
philologists; but if we bear in mind the incidents and accidents of
the geographical and social conditions under which each variation

FIGURE 133. AN EXAMPLE OF NEAPOLITAN GESTURE LANGUAGE

See note on page 517.

appeared and was selected and fixated, there is no wonder in the fact that today there are said to be a thousand different spoken languages in use, no one being immediately intelligible to the speakers of another.

The Highly Symbolic Character of Word Signals. The manner in which one person stimulates another often takes the form of setting up stimuli to which the other person has already learned to react as though they actually were something else totally different in all its attributes, so that the stimulus has become for these two people, at least, a wholly artificial and conventional sign. This has been shown in some detail with regard to gestural language. Its fullest flowering, however, is seen in verbal language. Suppose that one's neighbor says to him: "Sehn Sie das Pferd." This succession of voiced sounds may be received merely as such; but if the auditor understands a little German, he will be stimulated to a new attentive posture directed toward an object in the environment. Now the connection between voiced sound and the particular way that the hearer acts because of it, or the connection between the voiced sound and the particular object in the environment named, is largely arbitrary. The series of sounds, "Regardez ce cheval!" or the series, "Look at that horse!" would perform the same functions as the sounds first mentioned — assuming the hearer's possession of the necessary habits of perceiving. The sounds used in either case constitute a set of symbols.

The artificiality of most word symbols is further shown by the variety of signification with which almost any one of them may come to be used. "Mill" at one time does duty for a small hand device; at another, for a large factory; at others, for a monetary unit, for a pugilistic encounter, for a process of cutting fine grooves on a metal edge. "Race," again, may signify a watercourse, a

Note to Figure 133, page 516.
"*The Homecoming of the Bride.*" She enters in tender mien, her pendent arms indicating soft yielding, the right hand holding a handkerchief ready in case of overpowering emotion. She is followed by a male member of the family, whose joyful face is turned toward supposed by-standers, right hand pointing to the new acquisition, left making the "sign of horns" meaning "may evil eyes never have power over her." The friend who supports her with the right arm, brings her left hand into the sign of *beautiful* — "See what a beauty she is!" (found also among Dakota and other Indians). The mother-in-law greets the bride by making with the right hand a sign of ancient origin (found on Greek vases) meaning in this instance an invocation against evil, while with the left she makes a sign of the maternity to be hoped for. The hunchback, a familiar clown figure, dances to please the company, snapping his fingers, and making a sign of the left hand meaning *joy* (also appearing on Etruscan vases and on Pompeian paintings). — The gestures of the remaining figures are equally significant in detail. (From Mallery, *1st Report, Bur. Ethnol.*, 1881.)

competition, a slot for ball bearings, a division of mankind, a flavor of wine.

The precise nature of a symbol may be better appreciated from the following case related by the deaf-blind Helen Keller.

"The morning after my teacher came she led me into her room and gave me a doll. . . . When I had played with it a little while, Miss Sullivan slowly spelled into my hand the word 'd-o-l-l.' I was at once interested in this finger play and tried to imitate it. . . . Running downstairs to my mother I held up my hand and made the letters for doll. I did not know that I was spelling a word or even that words existed; I was simply making my fingers go in monkey-like imitation. . . .

[One day my teacher and I] "walked down the path to the well-house, attracted by the fragrance of the honeysuckle with which it was covered. Some one was drawing water and my teacher placed my hand under the spout. As the cool stream gushed over one hand she spelled into the other the word *water*, first slowly, then rapidly. I stood still, my whole attention fixed upon the motions of her fingers. Suddenly I felt a misty consciousness as of something forgotten — a thrill of returning thought; and somehow the mystery of language was revealed to me. I knew then that "w-a-t-e-r" meant the wonderful cool something that was flowing over my hand. That living word awakened my soul, gave it light, hope, joy, set it free! There were barriers still, it is true, but barriers that could in time be swept away." [1]

Other Forms of Language. If space allowed, it would be interesting to review the historical rise of other signaling methods that developed from speech. Written language has been, of course, of incalculable importance in the life of civilized men of all times. By writing down his "talk" an individual can effectively communicate with others in distant parts and in coming ages. The development of written language is usually said to have had three stages. (1) First came the *pictographic*, in which the inscribed character is some sort of pictorial representation of the thing being referred to. There was no relationship between such writing and the *sounds* one made in oral speech when referring to the same object. (2) In time, these pictures became more and more simplified and *schematic*, more and more conventionalized and looking less like the object or relationships symbolized (*hieroglyphic*). Hearing among the Peruvians was early represented by the picture of a man with very large ears; then by only a head with large ears; and later by large ears only; until finally the schematic lines lost their obvious picture character entirely, and were only conventional strokes. Such characters are familiar to us in modern Chinese (some appear in Figure 141). (3) These hieroglyphics came also to stand for the sounds made in the vocal naming of the objects. They became *phonetic*. They were not essentially different in psychological character from the modern rebus or the modern game of charades: a picture of an object or action (as a "bee" for the verb "be," an "inn" for the preposition "in," or an "eye" for the pronoun of the same sound) standing for the sound of the name applied to it and not for the object at all. (4) Eventually, with a vocal language developing on its own account,

[1] Helen Keller, *The Story of My Life*. Houghton Mifflin.

the written language underwent a change of the greatest conceivable importance when it became entirely phonetic. All its characters were then reduced to the representations of sound elements and an *alphabetic* array of consonants and vowels was produced.

The elements of the written languages with which we are familiar are not direct symbols of the things meant. They are, rather, symbols of the vocal sounds made when the things are referred to in speech. In the preceding sentence, for instance, not a word as a pattern of marks even remotely looks like that to which it refers, but each depends upon its ability to arouse a speech reaction formerly learned in connection with it. It would be interesting also to make a survey of the evolution of number systems and number notations — through the Roman, in which quantities were indicated by fingers and thumbs in their *I*'s, *V*'s, and so forth, to the Arabic and decimal system permitting the astonishing elaboration we find in higher mathematics.

But enough has been presented for the reader to see that in the evolution of written means of social interstimulation some familiar psychological processes have been at work. Throughout this development there has been a tendency to simplify to the mere rudiments that are necessary. There has been a constant standardizing or conventionalizing of the signals (a species of Social Conforming). And there has been evident the human capacity and propensity to get away from the limitations of concrete particulars by Abstracting and Generalizing common aspects for more independent and universal use. We are to examine the last capacity in more detail in the following chapters.

A GENETIC APPROACH

Do Lower Animals Use Symbols? Any child knows that the domestic cat shows a disappointing inability to react to certain gestures that point. Be it ever so hungry, and ever so whining and attentive to its mistress, it will be utterly unable to follow the direction of her arm or finger pointing to the saucer of milk behind a corner. The outstretched member is simply a stretched-out member, it is not a pointer. Let the mistress stand gazing fixedly in a certain direction: the animal would never look in that direction likewise. The dog and other domestic animals are similarly insensitive to any very definite pointing stimuli. To be sure, a poor beginning can be made by the dog trained to chase the thrown ball or stone: it may be excited to an initial start-off when the master's arm describes a swinging movement of pointing character. This, however, is far from an ability to follow out with the eye and head the specific line of pointing of an outstretched finger or a jerked head.

Lubbock in his famous work with ants in the 1880's found those active and gregarious creatures communicating in an effective way, but the limitations in the effectiveness are worth considering. He noted that an ant that had found a pile of larvae or of food would hasten back to the nest and would come out again leading hosts of his fellows to the pile, which they would immediately load on themselves for transport back to the nest. At first, this behavior looked like some kind of signaling with symbols. But when Lubbock restrained the particular individual that had found the pile so that it could not leave the nest to lead its mates, the excited hosts of ants would not run to the pile but in all directions from the nest. Clearly, the finder had not communicated to them the location of the treasure, had not "told" them where it was. As for the fact that there *was* a treasure, that did not need signaling, for — as other naturalists have observed — the finder ant returns in some excitement and its excited turnings about are enough to generate excitement in its mates. It is likely also that the odor of the find, clinging to the finder's body, had its own effect on the other ants. There is no evidence that anything was definitely *signified*, pointed at, described, told about. In other words, if, after the finder ants had returned to their nests, the other ants had been able to run out to the larvae or food in anything like a directed manner, there would have been evidence of symbolic communication, but hardly otherwise.

When we come to the anthropoids we find a few scattered entries on the positive side of the account. Köhler has told how if the keeper suddenly shows signs of terror and fixes his gaze at a given spot as if possessed, the whole black company of apes will stare at the same spot. Better evidence of symbol recognition appeared when chimpanzees learned to use poker chips as tokens with which to obtain food from a specially improvised vending machine [22]. They learned to seize and use any white token, which when put into the machine produced a grape, but not to bother with brass ones, which would bring forth nothing. Later, when blue tokens were found which would bring two grapes each, these were seized first in preference to the white ones. Still better, in a later experiment they learned when they were hungry to pick out the black tokens, which alone produced food, but when thirsty to use the yellow ones, which produced water. Even when they were forced to work a heavy lever for the tokens and were not allowed to "spend" them at once in the vending machine, they would hold on to them for as long as five hours or more. The tokens, it is clear, had become true substitutes for food, and not in the sense of simple conditioned stimuli, either, but in the full sense of symbols that represented, indicated, pointed to the ultimate reward. This symbolic significance was strikingly demonstrated in the animal which when proffered a white token would make the same lip-smacking movements she ordinarily made when she saw a grape.

The Infant's Repertoire of Vocal Sounds. The learning of language, as with the learning of activities generally, starts from a capital of acts and tendencies already on hand. Our first question, then, is: What is the infant's original equipment in sound production? It is by no means complete, of course, on the first day of life; and the problem becomes that of the times of initial emergence of the different sounds.

The first vocal sound of the infant is the birth cry. Speculative thinkers have called it various things from *himmlische Musik* to a wail of protest against being ushered into this world of sin; but as scientists we shall be content to describe it as the vocal part of the first act of drawing breath. The cry is purely reflex action, possibly excited by pain stimulation by the air newly drawn into the lungs.

During the first few months the crying of the infant becomes differentiated — or at least becomes more easily discriminable by attendants. Preyer and others have noted the wail of hunger, the monotonous cry of sleepiness, the sharp loud cry of rage, the high-pitched yell of pain, and the crow of delight. These are reactions of the (*A*) *emotional* order, forming parts of innate patterns of response. Their arousal is mainly but not wholly by intraorganic conditions.

With increasing frequency other vocal sounds come to be made by the baby, especially if he is healthy; these are sounds of a more (*B*) *random and playful type*. Again the source of stimulation is principally intraorganic, and such babblings and cooings are often called "spontaneous" reactions. The organs of speech are a new-found toy. Now, however, the reactions are not made to such specific stimulating conditions as are those mentioned in the preceding paragraph, nor do they have their places in organized action-patterns. As mere energy overflow through motor outlets not forming a part of definite reaction circuits, they take many forms of laryngeal, epiglottic, lingual, labial, and palatal adjustments.

During the first month the sounds that are made are mostly *vowel: â, ōō, ă,* and so forth, and they may be heard both on inspiration and on expiration. Some observers report next the appearance of *nasal-gutturals* such as *ngâ, ng-gng, mgm.* Finally appear the distinctly *consonant* sounds. Of these, *p, b, d, m,* and *k* are by all observers reported among the first to be heard, and *l* and *r* among the last. These points are of interest for two considerations. The last two sounds are apparently most difficult of precise enunciation in a given language when they are attempted by an adult who is a stranger to that language. Because the group including *p, b, d,* and *m* comprises the earliest distinct consonant sounds, these determine the character of the first syllables spoken by the infant: *da, ma, pa, ba.* It is no accident, then, that the first words that the child comes to use are variations of the polysyllables, *da-da, ma-ma-ma, pa-pa, ba-ba-ba-ba.*

In short, the newborn baby does not present a full armament of vocal sounds; and he must await the processes of his organic maturing. It is a developmental matter. This is suggested in the accompanying table which summarizes Gesell and Thompson's findings of some of the vocal and related items of behavior in infants observed in their clinic. For each of the bits of behavior listed at the left, the percentage of the infants who manifested it at each successive age-stage is shown in a figure. For example, cooing appeared in none of their infants at 4 weeks of age, in 3 per cent of them at 6 weeks, in 42 per cent at 8 weeks, in 88 per cent at 12 weeks, and in 76 per cent at 16 weeks. At the last age the vocalizing of *ma* or *mu* emerges and grows in frequency for a while.

"The number of sounds that ultimately find a place . . . is astonishing. One cannot fail to hear all the vowels and consonants, diphthongs, aspirates, sub-vocals, nasals, German umlauts and tongue trills, French throaty trills and grunts, and even the Welch *l.* Then these syllables are rehearsed in grotesque mixtures" [1].

Learning Vocal Habits. The repertoire of sounds that become available to the infant from time to time furnish the raw material for his building-up of certain habits of vocal reactions which are adaptive in character. It is a matter of common observation that babies, even before they are able to use words as such, are able to satisfy their wants through the medium of one or another sort of vocal sound. The crying reaction, if it invariably brings the too-

The Maturing of Vocal Behavior [1]

Behavior Items	Weeks of Age														
	4	6	8	12	16	20	24	28	32	36	40	44	48	52	56
1. Face brightens..	40	**68**	..	..	..										
2. Chuckles.......	0	0	36	42	24										
3. Smiles..........	22	**65**	**96**	**100**	**100**										
4. Laughs.........	0	0	7	31	**88**										
5. No vocalization heard........	45	31	21	15	28										
6. Vocalizes small throaty noises.	**84**	**72**	3	4	4										
7. Vocalizes ah-uh-eh....	40	**96**	**82**	**96**	**67**										
8. Coos...........	0	3	42	**88**	**76**										
9. Blows bubbles...	0	0	3	42	44										
10. Gurgles........	0	0	10	42	**56**										
11. Vocalizes da....					0	7	7	18	**59**	**64**	**63**	**62**	**69**	**67**	**59**
12. Vocalizes ma or mu..........					5	11	26	43	47	**51**	**60**	**52**	**60**	**64**	**64**
13. Two syl., 2nd rep. first, ma-ma, ba-ba, etc.....					14	11	7	25	**66**	**70**	**80**	**83**	**86**	**79**	**91**
14. Makes "d" sound					0	7	22	21	**66**	**64**	**69**	**62**	**88**	**67**	**73**
15. Makes "m" sound........					5	11	26	43	47	**58**	**63**	**55**	**60**	**64**	**64**
16. Makes "ē" sound (at end of word)........					0	4	7	7	16	12	14	35	46	48	**64**
17. Makes "b" sound					9	4	15	14	22	24	32	41	32	**57**	**64**
18. Says no word ...					**100**	**100**	**100**	**93**	**88**	**79**	**66**	31	23	12	5
19. Says one word or more........							0	7	12	21	34	**69**	**77**	**88**	**95**
20. Says two words or more..........							0	4	0	3	3	28	34	**67**	**86**
21. Says three words or more......											0	10	26	40	**68**
22. Says four words or more.......											0	7	9	26	36

All percentages over 50 are set in boldface type.

[1] From Gesell, A., and Thompson, H., *Infant Behavior; Its Genesis and Growth.* McGraw-Hill, 1934.

indulgent nurse and parents on the run, will become selected and
fixated as an easy "way out": this will then appear in any and every
situation that is uncomfortable, no matter how slight the degree
of discomfort or how advisable it be to leave the baby alone. He
will cry when left by himself, when in the dark, when another child
happens to possess a toy he is interested in, when anything desired
is out of reach or out of sight. Such crying is one side of the
"spoiled" child's habitual makeup. Even articulated words may
have this routine and mechanical character. Not long ago the
writer noticed that a child of two years, who was playing with her
older sisters some distance from home and mother, mechanically
murmured "mamma" in protest whenever she was imposed upon
by the other children.

In the light of the discussion in the preceding chapter, we can
see how this acquiring of a vocal habit is the learning of a mode of
social stimulation, of reaction-getting. It is, for the child, only one
of several possible reactions, yet, through the stimulated ministrations of others, it brings about a satisfactory adjustment, and
therefore becomes selected and fixated as the habitual response
to be made under the given set of circumstances. When "mamma"
herself is brought by the uttering of that word or by a cry or a coo,
we need not suppose that the presence of the mother is necessarily
the objective of the activity, but rather that the uttering, crying,
or cooing is a "way out."

These vocal reactions need not be words as yet. A child who
was once observed by the writer made a single type of vocal reaction
(a persistent ăăăăă with rising and falling inflection) do duty in a
variety of situations, for instance, when he showed a new fruit-
painted plate to guests and then proceeded to mimic eating the
fruit and offering it to the guests; when he wanted a tray replaced
upon a high buffet; and on other occasions when the arousing of the
adults' attention was an important segment of the behavior.
So with many other forms of vocal sounds. They all come to partake of the nature of signaling responses. They are not exclusively
human responses. Yerkes and Learned have included, in their
long list of vocal sounds made by two chimpanzees, some that
appear to be socially stimulating habits; and when a pet dog
"speaks" for his supper, it is to be similarly interpreted.

Learning to React to Words as Stimuli. Meanwhile the infant
is learning also to make appropriate responses to verbal signals

made by others. As is repeatedly observed, his understanding of — reacting appropriately to — simple words in the spoken language of adults precedes by some time his ability to make and use such sounds himself. Most of the infant vocabularies furnished in psychological literature are confined to the word-reactions made; but the present writer can supply lists of words to which a child made the right response with eye, face, hands, and body, several months in advance of his even attempting to articulate his reactions. Thus the hearing vocabulary is acquired much in advance of the speaking vocabulary. For example, at nine months of age, "Give me bite" elicited the child's movements of offering the speaker the food in hand; at ten months, "horse," "bottle," "berries," aroused attending postures toward the objects named; at twelve months, the commands "wink," "shut your eyes," "take this to . . .," "brush hair," and at fourteen months, the words "powder your face," "smell," "hide your eyes," "knock on door," and so on, were responded to correctly. In all these cases the ability to act appropriately appeared six to twelve months previous to the ability to say the words. The same thing has been observed systematically by another, who reports that long before his son could pronounce a word, he knew the meanings of (could appropriately react to) 152 words and phrases [1].

The process of learning to suit the action to the other person's word is a simple matter for us to analyze. We need only bear in mind the principle of conditioning. Assume that the child has learned to exchange kiss for kiss; then let the mother or father say "kiss" several times simultaneously with the act of kissing the child; and finally substitute the word for the action. It is a sufficiently strong stimulus to arouse the child's kissing and is not essentially different from the substitution of a bell sound for the food to arouse a dog's salivary reflex. Let "bottle" be clearly enunciated with each feeding, or "kitty" with each presentation of a cat, and the stage is clearly set for the child's conditioning of his eating and his stroking behavior to those words when heard alone. This phenomenon has indeed already been described and analyzed under the topic of Perceiving.

Learning to Speak Words. When the child has learned to recognize words and to behave appropriately in response to them, how does he come to make such verbal sounds himself? There was a time when such a question was answered, as it seemed, simply and easily, by invoking the term "imitation": the baby merely imitates the words heard, it was explained. But "imitation" as an explanatory concept has been discredited. If babies did have a tendency to imitate all the sounds and words heard about them, the wonder would be not how quickly they acquire speaking vocabularies but how slowly, for during month after month the babblings of the baby resemble in no way the sounds that are spoken to it. We must keep in mind the fact that the human individual is a dynamic affair, furnishing not only its own store of energies but also its own avenues and types of energy-expression. Some one has remarked that the baby does not imitate the adults but the adults imitate the baby, and this has an element of truth.

How does the vocal repertoire of an infant become made over into word-speaking habits? Let it be borne in mind that vocal reactions are reactions in the same sense as are blinking the eye, grasping by the fingers, kicking, or wiggling the toe; and it will not be hard to see that habits of speech are built up as are habits of any other types.

(I) For one thing it may be thought of as a case of *trial-and-error learning*. It is a story of *random articulation, with selection and fixation of correct speech-patterns when they are hit upon*. When the baby first chances to sound "da-da," the action is hailed as a real achievement by the social environment of fond and admiring relatives. As a matter of fact, the infant "just happened" to make those sounds; it was making other sounds as well. But if every occurrence of this particular reaction is accompanied by pettings and applause, it is easy to suppose that the essential conditions are provided for a selecting and fixating of the "da-da" or "daddy" reaction. So with the developing of certain other well-integrated sound-patterns: "mamma," "bye-bye," "kitty," "baby," "ball," and the rest. These sounds come to be made more and more especially in certain situations and in connection with bodily efforts to handle certain things. Let the random sounding of "ball" or of "doll" or of "papa" be frequently accompanied by the appearance and approach of certain highly stimulating objects, and the stage is set for the selection and fixation of these very responses. The writer has watched nurse-girls withhold food or toys until the infant charge made some stumbling approach to "berry" or "doll" or "box." Thus the social environment, by granting or withholding the objective sought by the child, provides

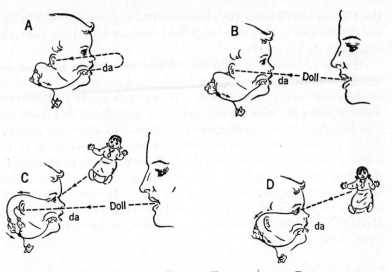

FIGURE 134. THE CIRCULAR-REFLEX THEORY OF THE DEVELOPMENT
OF LANGUAGE HABITS

A. Random articulation of syllables; then fixation of them as circular responses by conditioning. When the baby articulates a syllable, for example, *da*, he is receiving auditory stimulation from the sound he makes at the same time that he is receiving kinesthetic stimulation from his vocal apparatus. In time the auditory stimulus of hearing *da* spoken by himself evokes the motor response of saying *da*: a circular reflex is formed. The very sound of the syllable leads to his saying it over and over.

B. Sound of *da* articulated by another becomes substitute for sound of *da* articulated by himself. Another person, by repeating some of the baby's own syllables, can get him to say them again in response to that other person's voice. This is the so-called "imitation."

C and *D.* Sight of object frequently accompanying sound of *da* becomes stimulus for articulation of the syllable. A doll, having been presented frequently at the same time that the syllable *da* is articulated by another person, the baby's response now becomes conditioned to this new stimulus; and eventually he comes to say *da* whenever that doll is seen. He is now said to "name" the doll.

(From Allport, F. H., *Social Psychology*, Houghton Mifflin, 1924.)

the positive or negative incentives in his trial-and-error efforts at a talking control over things around him.

The syllables *ma* and *da* (or *pa* or *fa*) are the roots of the words signifying "mother" and "father," respectively, in English, French, German, Latin, Greek, and Sanskrit; yet the Chilians say *papa* for "mother" and the Georgians say *mama* for "father," and among various peoples the sound *dada* may signify "father," "cousin," or "nurse." Whatever meaning a given pattern of sounds happens to have in the vernacular of a group will determine the meaning built up by the infant: *papa* will, when enunciated by an English baby, bring the father running, but when sounded by the Chilian it will bring the mother.   The former baby will in time use the device thus hit upon when he is seeking his father, the latter when seeking his mother.

(II) An additional explanation of how the infant, after merely making sounds, comes to speak words has been advanced in terms of the *conditioning* experiments.   Allport has made a clear statement of this view with an illustration as reproduced in Figure 134. The principle of the circular reflex — a reflex in which the response serves to renew the stimulus and so leads to a repetition of the same response — is a well-established one; and it is abundantly shown in infantile "lalling," the reiteration of *muh-muh-muh-muh, bup-bup-bup, goo-goo-goo-goo*, and the like.   In fact, many of the infant's words are of this double-syllable character — the fixation of these repetitive articulations — as seen in *bow-wow, choo-choo* train, *papa*, and *mama*.

SELF-STIMULATION

Introduction.   In the first general section of the present chapter we have had opportunity to realize the significance to life in human society of the capacity to make symbolic responses that will serve in turn as symbolic stimuli to one's fellow.   Society otherwise would never have evolved beyond the level of swarms and flocks and herds.   But the fact was also hinted that the individual man by reason of his symbolizing ability is able to transcend the limitations of the immediate here and now.   That is a high-sounding assertion.

First and foremost, it is of profound importance that the reader grasp the notion that a person can stimulate himself.   An excellent scientific introduction to this point is afforded by some interesting details of a learning experiment conducted on children and apes. A subject was given the problem of learning always to choose (in order to get food) that one of two boxes that had on it a figure with a cross in the center and not a half-moon or circle or triangle or other negative stimulus.   (See Figure 135.)   Both the chimpanzees and the two-year-old children learned to make the correct discrimination after long series of trials.   But what interests us is the *way* they learned it, or rather, helped themselves to learn it. The chimpanzees, after a hundred or so poor trials, were seen to bring their faces up very close to the figures on the boxes and

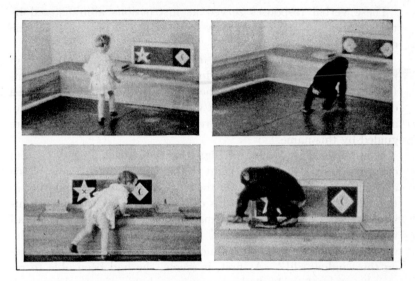

FIGURE 135. SELF-STIMULATION IN A DISCRIMINATION PROBLEM

In order to obtain food, child or chimpanzee was to learn always to choose that one of two boxes that bore a small cross in the center of the figure (the positions of correct and negative boxes being exchanged in irregular order). Both the children and the chimpanzees developed means of stimulating or signaling to themselves as an aid in the discriminating (described in text). (From Gellermann, L. Form Discrimination in Chimpanzees and Two-Year-Old Children, *J. Genet. Psychol.*, 1933, **42**, 3–27, 28–50.)

then to trace the outline of the figures with the back side of their crooked fingers or even with the tips of their forefingers. Then, soon after they showed this sort of behavior, they succeeded in mastering the problem. What shall we make of this? It is the reasonable thing to follow the experimenter and assign to this tracing behavior a definite symbolic significance, and, we would add, a self-stimulating significance. When facing this problem, an ape, finding it difficult to master the difference between a food-less box and the food box merely by the visual characters thereon, would follow the outlines with his hand and thus give himself kinesthetic stimulations in terms of which the choice was more easily made. The young children used this tracing method much as did the apes; but they went them one step better. Before the correct figure they would be heard finally saying, "Yes, yes, yes," and before the negative ones, "No, no, no," this utterance followed by the appropriate taking or leaving. In the experimenter's words,

"These verbal responses served as instructions administered by the children *to themselves* on how to react to the particular stimuli concerned."

Another effective laboratory example has already been met in the experiment on the reproducing of visually perceived forms (above, pp. 451 ff., 454 ff.). There the subject upon looking at a design *named* it to himself as "a violin," "an anvil," and the like; and his subsequent attempts to reproduce the original design were guided by this name.

Some Everyday Modes of Signaling to Oneself. A case from everyday human life was brought to the writer's attention in which a reaction was made that was then to serve as self-stimulation in the field of memory. One of his colleagues had occasion to ask his wife for her scissors. For a moment she was unable to recall where they had been left; then, stretching out her left arm sideways and backward, she announced suddenly, "Why, I left them on the window sill!" At first, it seems, she had been able to remember only that she had previously laid the scissors down with a certain arm-movement; then on executing the same movement again she set up kinesthetic afferent currents that rearoused the whole situation-response. Other illustrations of the general point abound on every hand. A string on the finger of the absent-minded man has been deliberately placed there by him as a means of stimulating himself later. The musician often finds it convenient to beat time with his foot, the rhythmic responses of that member helping to direct the tempo of fingers or voice.

Facial reaction patterns as well as bodily posturings and gestures perform this self-stimulating function at later ages as well. A girl's rehearsals of coyness before her mirror and a boy's empty-handed attitudinizing as a great baseball pitcher are terminated abruptly upon the sound of a footstep: such use of social reactions is here really private in character. The functioning in general is the same, except that now the stimulating individual and the responding individual happen to be combined in one and the same human body.

As another variety of self-stimulation consider the girl who is busily at work at her typewriter, when the buzzer sounds summoning her for dictation. She may not stop the typing *instanter*: she may continue to the end of the sentence or of the page. But in the meanwhile she has maintained an orientation set up at sound of the buzzer — a slight turn of head or of feet toward her employer's door, a raising of eyebrows or lifting of chin — and this postural reaction eventually becomes a directive stimulus which is effective the moment a pause in her typing is reached.

Self-signaling with drawings is an activity clearly in point. A map may be sketched for oneself and not for the eyes of another person at all. It may be a memorandum for the future locating of treasure that has been hidden or for the completion of an automobile tour.

It is in the use of language, however, that we can find the most effective and refined modes of self-control. Private uses of written language exhibit this well. The broker on 'change makes a few scratches on his pad so that later he can follow up the deal he has just made. At the ball or dance a man marks on his card early in the evening so that later, as the various dance numbers are announced, he can, by reference to those marks, be guided to the proper partners. "Sug peas porterh 2#" a busy man may scribble on a card as he leaves the house to go to the grocer's; or, "meetg bd direct PS&W 4 Tues" he may write upon his desk pad. In both cases he is providing signals to stimulate himself later.

Oral language is used to serve this same *memorandum* function. The chauffeur repeats to himself the words heard at the filling station: "Where car track turns keep straight on one block, then turn left two, then right one, then to third house on right," and at appropriate moments he suits the actions to the words. The novice at bridge repeatedly tells himself such things as "First look for a king lead," so that, when his turn may come to play the first card, the quiet rehearsal of this speech will serve as a directing stimulation. The engineer or the pharmacist memorizes his formulae and the law student his definitions and rules in order that, as later occasion may demand, each can say these over again and so have his behavior adequately regulated.

Aside from this memorandum-furnishing function of private speech that is previously memorized, there is the enormously significant rôle played by *talking to oneself in the carrying forward* of a more or less *continuous train of behavior*. This is well illustrated in simple arithmetical computation. When a school child first adds his column of figures he often articulates as explicitly and fully as, "6 and 4 are 10, 10 and 7 more are 17, 17 and 5 are 22, 22 and 9 are 31. So the total is 31!" As each particular vocal act is performed, the precise character of the response is a stimulus partly determining the next response, that one the next, and so on.

A more complicated form of the same procedure is to be found in the *soliloquy*. In the course of a man's talking to himself, the words spoken provide stimulations which do not determine his subsequent language reactions alone, as in the case of continuous adding; they do more. They often arouse nascent reactions of a visceral and somatic nature.[1] It is easy to see that much of the speaking in a monologue is of largely habitual character — word order in sentences, superficial transitions from one word or phrase to another, and other manners of speaking now well automatized by repeated use. Once some of the words are spoken, however, they operate *via* auditory and kinesthetic afferent neural pathways as potent stimuli to perceptual readjustments from time to time — so that in the course of a short soliloquy the speaker is thrown into a succession of different attitudes awakened (as a result of established habits) by the auditory and kinesthetic afferent impulses arising from the articulation of the words he is uttering. The most dramatic point in Hamlet's famous soliloquy exhibits this:

> To die; to sleep;
> No more; and by a sleep to say we end
> The heart-ache and the thousand natural shocks
> That flesh is heir to. 'Tis a consummation
> Devoutly to be wish'd. To die; to sleep; —
> *To sleep? Perchance to dream!* Ay, there's the rub;
> For in that sleep of death what dreams may come,
> When we have shuffled off this mortal coil,
> Must give us pause . . .

The first of these lines may well have been uttered in a fairly straight-away and smooth-running fashion. The whole set of the speaker is of a single type continuously maintained; and the language spoken — with apologies to Shakespeare! — is of routine enough sort for a character supposedly equipped with such a vocabulary of word- and phrase-habits. But when Hamlet has uttered the phrase "to sleep," its frequent associate, "to dream," is

---

[1] That words can do just this — can serve as effective (conditioned) stimuli to emotional behavior — is apparent at once upon examination. This is traceable back to the original learning to perceive word symbols in childhood. Often one prefers to say or write "abattoir" rather than "slaughterhouse" or "shambles," although all refer to the same thing: the difference is in their values as emotion-arousing stimuli. The arts of the poet, of the prose writer, of the orator, of the lecturer. depend in varying degrees upon their ability to choose verbal signals that will nicely call out from the reader or auditor just the emotional responses sought

next aroused, and this in turn acts as a stimulus to the exciting of a new perceptual set, and word-associations congruous therewith. These new words now show startlingly different emotion-arousing value, and the soliloquizer proceeds on a new series of speech reactions.[1]

Abbreviation of Speech to Implicit Forms. When one talks to himself, the conditions of his social environment are often such as to lead him to hit upon a more and more restrained and reduced manner of speaking. When learning to read, his vocal reactions are loud and pronounced, but with increasing facility he is encouraged by others to read more quietly. His voice is disturbing to other pupils at work or to other readers about the family table. It would be an unsocial act to shout his lesson as did the pupils of the traditional Chinese memorizing schools. From loud speech he learns perforce to shift to *sotto voce*, later on to whispering, still later to inaudible throat, tongue, and lip movements, and finally he may reach that stage of speaking in which all of his reading reactions are both silent and invisible. Few people do reach the last, however, as the student can verify for himself by watching readers in libraries and street cars. These stages, by the way, are not well marked, but go along more or less together. Time and circumstance as well as the nature of the material to be read may dictate whether one shall read aloud, quietly, or silently.

Our illustration from arithmetic will serve us again here. At one extreme we have the child from the third or fourth grade adding with obvious difficulty and slowly, voicing the names of the successive sums attained. At the other is the expert clerk so practiced in the performance that we can observe scarcely any signs of his work other than the vertical excursions of eye and finger and the jotting down of the final result. Between these two lies the vast majority of human beings for whom the casting up of a short column of one-place numbers is easy enough. But, when confronted with a long list of figures running into the millions or even with a score-pad of a substantial evening's play, they resort to whisperings and even to counting aloud with accompanying tappings of pencil and noddings of head.

---

[1] This explanation may seem a bit complicated. The difficulty is that so many of the principles of serial habits, of set, of perceiving, are concentrated in this example. It is not a simple one. But the writer is confident that any reader familiar with the principles developed in earlier chapters of this book can work his way through a natural scientific explanation of this dramatic human incident along the lines suggested. And it should be clearer still after our analysis of Thinking.

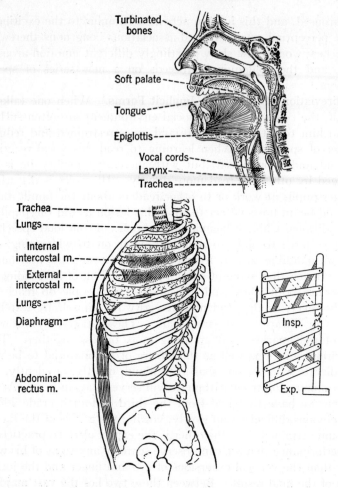

Turbinated
bones

Soft palate

Tongue

Epiglottis

Vocal cords
Larynx
Trachea

Trachea
Lungs
Internal
intercostal m.
External
intercostal m.
Lungs
Diaphragm

Insp.

Abdominal
rectus m.

Exp.

FIGURE 136. THE SPEECH APPARATUS

I. *Inspiration.* The external intercostal muscles contract, pulling the ribs, which are hinged at the vertebrae, upward and outward (as shown in the mechanical model); and the great dia-phragm muscle contracts, lowering its dome. In this manner the cubic contents of the chest are increased, and air is drawn in through the trachea, mouth, and nose.

II. *Expiration.* The internal intercostals contract, pulling the ribs downward and inward (see mechanical model); and the muscles of the abdominal wall contract, pressing the contents of the abdomen against the diaphragm, which is now relaxed upward. Thus the cubic contents of the chest are decreased; and air is forced up through the trachea, mouth, and nose.

In the production of small speech-units (syllables) expiration is principally the result of quick ballistic movements of the external intercostals; while in the "breath groups" of several syllables (phrases) expiration is principally the work of the abdominal muscles.

Voiced *tone* is given to air in expiration when the two elastic vocal cords are drawn together, constricting the air passage upward through the larynx. The air sets the cords (which act like

Now it should not be forgotten that when speech has been reduced in intensity to an implicit degree, it is still speech. Much mystery has been needlessly attached to the speaking that may be going on in a person silently. Just because it is inaudible and invisible to an attentive neighbor we need not jump to the conclusion that some new non-physical process of some new non-material entity is at work. Calling it a "psychic" process, or a working of "the mind," only adds to our problems. It explains nothing.

The reality and actuality of motor responses that have become implicit, such as gesturing or speaking, is really so cardinal a point in our understanding of higher processes that we may well postpone it for separate and fuller treatment than space would allow here.

SOME DISORDERS OF LANGUAGE FUNCTION

Introduction. In preceding sections of this chapter we have seen that the language functions are of absolutely fundamental importance to the human being both in his social relationships and in his individual private behavior. Perhaps no other physiological loss — not blindness nor deafness, lameness nor paralysis — would easily compare with the total impairment of one's language mechanisms. They are, therefore, of primary concern to us.

They are of exceedingly great interest, also, by reason of the fact of their very great complexity. Learning to say "cat" — and mean it — is an achievement possible only to humans, and involves the teamed and integrated co-operation of a vast range of mechanisms. It furnishes us with the highest type of integration of almost the entire organism, in which motor structures that ordinarily subserve divers and different functions now operate together as a beautifully unified whole. Figure 136 shows the grosser details of the mechanisms.

---

reeds in a musical instrument) into vibration, and these in turn impart their vibrations to the expelled air. The *pitch* of the voice is dependent upon the degrees of nearness and of tension in the vocal cords, which are adjusted by some nineteen different muscles. *Resonance* is furnished by the chest cavity and by many cavities and chambers in the head. *Consonant* sounds arise from friction of the breath with different mouth parts: with the lips for the sounds of *b*, *p*, *w;* the lips and teeth for *v* and *f;* the teeth alone for *s*, *z*, *j;* the forepart of the tongue for *d*, *t*, *l;* the middle or sides of the tongue for *g*, *k*, *qu*, *r*, *x;* and tongue and teeth for *th* and *sh.* The nasal consonants are produced with all expiration through the nose but with lips and tongue co-operating — in *m*, *n*, and *ngh*. The consonants of other languages than English require still other adjustments.

Stuttering. An affliction of speech that seems to be in nearly all cases psychological in character, and that occurs in at least I per cent of the population, is that of stuttering. The reader is doubtless acquainted with some of the symptoms of this disorder. Frequently the victim is given to a repetitious sounding of some of his consonants or syllables or words. Sometimes he shows a blocking or excessive delay between his words or phrases. (This latter form is sometimes termed "stammering," but the distinction is probably not important.) Superficially, the condition may be easily described as a lack or loss of teamwork or timed integration of the various mechanisms of speech. Perhaps the expiration movements of thoracic and of abdominal muscles are diametrically opposed; perhaps expiration is interrupted by short inspiratory movements; there may be tremors of lips or of jaw or of the abdominal musculature; there may be pronounced spasms in the larger breathing muscles or in finer muscles of articulation; or it may be any of a dozen other types of poor integration of the whole speaking equipment.

The more fundamental nature of stuttering is not so easy to state. In fact today there are several rival theories in the field; and, when making a first approach to the topic, it seems wisest not to commit ourselves but to get acquainted with those interpretations advanced by the more authoritative spokesmen.

Theories of Stuttering.

(a) *A bad motor habit.* This conception is simple enough: the child picked up a wrong way of speaking, perhaps after hearing it in a relative or playmate, and what he needs is only retraining in the correct way. Rehearsals of material with plenty of attention on the patient's part to the details of his articulation and breathing are a part of the program of correction (Russell, Dunlap).

(b) *An emotional habit.* A stutterer can often talk better alone than when with others, when calm than when excited, when he is attentive to something quite objective and impersonal and others present are not by look or word reminding him of his usual difficulty. The overemotional child may stutter simply because he is at a given moment excited and "rattled" (and who does not a little then!); then other people by look or word direct attention to this phenomenon, making him acutely self-directed in his thinking, and a vicious circle becomes established. Stuttering makes him self-conscious, which makes him stutter. Plainly, the way to help is to get his interests and his attention directed elsewhere. At the same time, there must be established a more self-confident general attitude as well as a general habit of taking things calmly (Blanton, Fletcher).

(c) *An emotional conflict.* The disturbances of a person's speech may be symptomatic of a conflict among his less observable motivational tendencies. A boy, terribly frightened by an encounter with a dog, began to stutter the next day, and continued to show this impediment for years until the original occasion was described and analyzed for him, after which his speech began to improve. (The reader should bring this interpretation into harmony with the phenomena of repression set forth in an earlier chapter, pp. 151 ff.) The psychoanalysts have carried the notion further, basing each particular disorder upon some particular complex, especially one of erotic character (Coriat).

(d) *Imperfect cerebral dominance.* Movements of the right half of the body are controlled most immediately by impulses from the left half of the cerebrum, and *vice versa.* The speech functions seem to be centered on the same side as are those of the preferred hand or foot: in right-handed persons in the left hemisphere, in left-handed, in the right. Now, suppose a left-handed child, whose speech centers have already become established in the right hemisphere, be forced to practice his handwriting, eating, throwing, and other uni-manual movements with his right hand and so with his left hemisphere. His cerebral functions will then be uncertainly divided. The hemisphere which originally served as a locus for the connections of oral speech now no longer dominates the other one, and a lack of integration of the delicate neural mechanisms will produce a disordered speech (Travis). [18]

It is well that we are not forced to choose from among these interpretations. Evidences can be found for each. Two considerations may be advanced. (1) It is possible that stuttering arises out of distinctly different causes in different individuals. (2) It is more than likely that these interpretations overlap a great deal; for example, a forced change of handedness (d) may set up emotional stress and strain (b) even to the point of severe conflict (c); a child that has fallen into the easy habit of "imitating" a stuttering adult in the home or neighborhood (a) is certainly likely to be laughed at in school (b).

A warning note should be added for practical reasons. The very lack of a finally accepted scientific explanation of stuttering has encouraged the development of all sorts of schools of treatment, some motived by the soundest of clinical aims, others profiteering at the expense of desperate victims. There are many who can testify to having studied in several of the latter "cures," all advocating different pet methods and all making money.

Aphasia. A totally different class of language defects from the foregoing are those in which the symbolizing function of language, the very heart of it, suffers impairment. Head, an acknowledged authority on this subject, found upon examination of British

World War soldiers who had gunshot wounds in the head that many of them revealed *disorders in symbolic formulation and expression.* These referred in particular to language and did not involve any loss of general intelligence [7]. A few of the observations on his cases will help us to grasp the meaning of his phrase.

Some of Head's war patients showed primarily a defective word-formation or inability to find the words necessary for ordinary conversation, so that any thinking process based on fluent use of words was affected. "Yesterday," said one, "I had diff-ulty in remembering what you do with a skull tri . . . tre . . . trephine." Another spoke of the "the claration of war by the Ollies." One patient, upon being asked about his education, was able to convey largely by gestures that he had reached the sixth standard at age of twelve. He added, "Then was going," and, lifting his left hand in the air, "you see?" The physician said, "To a higher school," and he answered "Yes. He something here," pointing to his chest, "he died." When asked, "Your father died?" he replied, "Yes. Not enough me go there," and raised both hands. He was asked, "Not enough money to go to a higher school?" and assented "Yes, yes."

Some of the patients got their words fairly well but showed a lack of that perfect balance and rhythm and phrasing that make discourse comprehensible: their speech was jargon. They would talk extremely rapidly, rushing over their mistakes in the expectation of being understood. There was also a disconnectedness in much of their discourse. One wrote quite spontaneously: "I am going to London seeing a Doctor. In the night the darkness is very funny. The weather is good for the corn and not now spoiled." But he could not read a word he had written, and, when asked what it was about, replied, "I can't, I know, I suppose in time, not now, funny thing why." Another one, asked about his wound, answered, "When I woke straight in bed, I couldn't say it. I knew what it was, but couldn't say it. I couldn't say, France nobody was; but I couldn't say it."

A third variety of aphasia differed from the preceding in that so far as words were used they were enunciated accurately and united into coherent phrases, but the patients had trouble with their significances, meanings, references. Some could match a knife by selecting another knife from an assortment of articles, but they could not name it, nor even pick it out when named by the physician. One patient was shown two cards, one bearing the word MATCHES, the other WATCH, only the first of these objects being among an assortment on the table. He pointed to the matches; then, holding up the latter card he said "nothing here." "This one is here" [pointing to the matches], the other there is nothing." He moved his eyes around the room as if seeking something, and added, "When I look at that big one [a wall clock] that helps me." Still another could not name any colors but identified them by roundabout expressions. *Black* — "that is the dead"; *red* — holding his red lapel, "Where the staff have it"; *blue* — pointing to blue band on his arm, "this is this"; *green* — pointing to trees "that is up there"; *white* — took hold of white coat; *yellow* — touching his khaki tie, "this one, karktoo."

A fourth class included difficulties in comprehending discourse in large wholes, when patients missed the sense not of the individual words or phrases but of the whole argument or story, and showed want of recognition of the relative significances of the parts.   The difficulty appeared typically in trying to understand a picture or a joke.   It is well represented by a soldier who had been a gardener.   When he looked at a political cartoon of a man riding a cow over which stood the description, "Mayor's curious steed," he said: "That's a man riding on a colt . . . no, it isn't, sir, it looks more like a cow . . . or a young cow . . . no, it isn't . . . heifer, sir . . . Major . . . no, the Mayor curse sted . . . the Mayor curious stid.   It's something you don't see every day, that stid . . . I should think myself they are going to show that animal; it's uncommon, that stid."   Simple arithmetical operations were troublesome to these cases.   One of them started all his adding and subtracting from the left-hand side of the example and worked to the right; then, upon discovering he was wrong, could not make the correction at once but only after much pondering.   It was not the detailed significances of the numbers that was at fault, but rather the general conception of the acts of adding and subtracting.[1]

It is hoped that with these cases of impairment before him the reader will see by contrast what the *normal process of symbolizing* involves.   Briefly, it is *setting up some substitute name or designation or sign or formulation for an object, relation, or situation,* and *reacting to this name or sign or formulation as if to that which it signifies.*   For example, the symbolizing power had been lost by the patient who could match a knife with another one but who could not give it a name nor pick out one in response to the name. In our $S \rightarrow R$ terms, he had lost the capacity to make a symbolic R (naming) to the sight of the object and to make an appropriate overt R to the symbolic S (name) when furnished by another.

A Forward Look.   As we have seen in our anthropological and genetic surveys in the present chapter, a truly enormous amount of social life is carried on through stimulating others with symbols and reacting in turn to the symbols of others.   But we have also seen that communion with oneself, self-guidance and self-control, are made possible by the use of symbolic stimuli and responses of more or less implicit degrees.   It is to the phenomena of a human organism directing himself by providing his own stimuli that we now turn.

---

[1] These varieties that have been described were called by Head *verbal, syntactical, nominal* and *semantic* types, respectively; but this differentiation seems to rest on a logical analysis more than on a psychological one [21].

REFERENCES

1. Bean, C. H.   An Unusual Opportunity to Investigate the Psychology of Language.   *J. Genet. Psychol.*, 1932, **40,** 181–202.

2. Bloomfield, L.   *Language.*   Holt, 1933.

3. Bühler, K.   *Mental Development of the Child.*   Harcourt, Brace, 1930.

4. De Laguna, G. A.   *Speech, Its Function and Development.*   Yale Univ. Press, 1927.

5. Esper, E. A.   Language.   Chap. 11 in *Handbook of Social Psychology* (Murchison, ed.).   Clark Univ. Press, 1935.

6. Fletcher, J. M.   An Experimental Study of Stuttering.   *Amer. J. Psychol.*, 1914, **25,** 201–55.

7. Head, H.   *Aphasia and Kindred Disorders of Speech.*   2 v.   Macmillan, 1926.

8. Hudgins, C. V.   A Comparative Study of the Speech Coordinations of Deaf and Normal Subjects.   *J. Genet. Psychol.*, 1934, **44,** 3–48.

9. Jesperson, O.   *Language.*   Holt, 1924.

10. McCarthy, D.   Language Development.   Chap. 8 in *Handbook of Child Psychology* (Murchison, ed.).   Clark Univ. Press, 1933.

11. McCarthy, D.   *The Language Development of the Preschool Child.*   Univ. Minnesota Press, 1930.

12. Mallery, G.   Picture-Writing of the American Indians.   *Tenth Annual Report*, Bureau of Ethnology, 1893, 1–822.

13. Mallery, G.   Sign Language Among North American Indians.   *First Annual Report*, Bureau of Ethnology, 1881, 269–552.

14. Mott, F. W.   *The Brain and the Voice in Speech and Song.*   Harpers, 1910.

15. Sapir, E.   *Language: An Introduction to the Study of Speech.*   Harcourt, Brace, 1921.

16. Shirley, M.   *The First Two Years: A Study of Twenty-Five Babies. II. Intellectual Development.*   Univ. Minnesota Press, 1933.

17. Smith, M. E.   An Investigation of the Development of the Sentence and the Extent of Vocabulary in Young Children.   *Univ. Iowa Stud. Child Welfare*, 1926, **3,** No. 5.

18. Travis, L. E.   Speech Pathology.   Chap. 16 in *Handbook of Child Psychology* (Murchison, ed.), 2d ed.   Clark Univ. Press, 1933.

19. *Twenty-Eighth Yearbook of the National Society for the Study of Education* (1929).

20. Vossler, K.   *The Spirit of Language in Civilization* (trans. by O. Oesler).   Kegan Paul, 1932.

21. Weisenburg, T., and McBride, K. E.   *Aphasia. A Clinical and Psychological Study.*   Commonwealth Fund, 1935.

22. Wolfe, J. B.   Effectiveness of Token-Rewards for Chimpanzees.   *Comp. Psychol. Monog.*, 1936, **12,** No. 60.

CHAPTER XIX

THINKING

THINKING IDENTIFIED

Necessity the Mother of Thinking. Man has been known for ages as the thinking animal. There are other traits that may differentiate Homo Sapiens from the other genera and phyla. The capacity for language (for using vocal sounds symbolically) is a noticeable distinction. The using of tools is largely, though not completely, man's peculiar privilege. Laughing is a trait of human-kind only. His far greater capacity to learn has been duly boasted. But the most striking differentia offered is that he can think far more adequately and effectively than can other forms of life.

Now, as a means of man's adapting himself to his environment and of adapting the environment to him, this has been of paramount biological importance. When other animals run into obstacles, they usually set to work with some fixed manner of response. If that be unavailing they usually fall back upon an exploratory trying-out of the other reactions they may have in their repertoire. A member of the human genus, however, is not so dependent upon the direct exciting of overt reactions. He is not likely to kick and squeal, pull and tug, run to and fro; he will "stop to think it over"; he will "sit down to consider." The upshot of the matter usually is that he will be able to handle the situation far more adequately and effectively — and far more economically of effort, too. Necessity, they say, is the mother of invention; it is equally true to say that it is the mother of thinking. One thinks, characteristically, when he meets an obstacle. It is a response aroused in situations of difficulty. Then it is that he will "sit up and take notice." To describe the thought-provoking situation more narrowly: it is a situation with which the individual has no established way of dealing practically, and into which he is unable to get a prompt insight; but at the same time it is one to which he does not make his trial-and-error reactions in an overt manner. This failure to make overt reactions may be due to a variety of conditions; for example, the situation may include social conditions which inhibit conduct, or the situation may have primary bearing upon future conduct and not upon the present.

There are still in the air some faint echoings of an ancient conception — that the processes of thought, of a pure reason, are somewhat supermundane processes that have little or naught to do with base animal needs and raw material things. *Ratio in vacuo.* But the nineteenth century's recognition of the fundamentally biological character of man has led to the explosion of this conception. Today it is inconceivable that thinking is a performance that goes on spontaneously and irresponsibly in a person, out of any contact with his wants and needs, as a pure luxury which follows no laws of nature but only "laws of thought." In the world of living things including the kicking, loving, fearing, desiring, hating, ever-active and ever-exploring mankind, such a notion of thought is anomalous in the extreme. Man is

> Endowed perhaps with genius from the gods,
> But apt to take his temper from his dinner.

Let the reader not consider that thinking, then, is anything but a phenomenon of natural science, a biological event. It can be given a natural scientific analysis and description.

Thinking as Indirect Reacting. When a man is thinking, what is he doing? Surely he is doing *something*. The photographic or sculptured picture of a thinking person may be one of great immobility; he may, like Rodin's figure, be sitting still with chin on hand and elbow on knee. But the pose is not mistaken by any human observer for a comparatively inert state like sleep. Any intelligent five-year-old child knows that something is going on inside this man.

For one thing, when a person is thinking he is making some kind of indirect or mediate reaction upon the object or situation with which he is confronted. When one thinks about yesterday's meal or one's absent friend, it is easy to see that the thinking is going on in the absence of the physical object of the thought. So, the indirect response that is called thinking is a response that may go on when the object of the response is not present.

But there is a second application of this word "indirect" in connection with thinking. The indirect response may be in the presence of the thing. Consider the behavior of a child or animal which actively and overtly deals with such a thing as a puzzle-box.

It manipulates the box with the hands or paws and shouts or cries at it. Now consider the action of a man who looks at the puzzle-box hard, puts his hands in his pockets, scratches his head perhaps, and "ponders." He may even close his eyes, but something is still going on in that man. He is treating that thing in a fashion, acting in regard to it, dealing with it, and yet not in any overt way. One trait of the thinking response, we see, is that it is a kind of behavior that is indirect. It may go on in the absence of the thing toward which it is directed. Or, if the thinking takes place in the presence of the object, the behavior does not consist of direct practical contacts with it.

In coming to closer grips with the problem of the nature of thinking let us employ again the general principle that psychological phenomena which are complex in the human adult may be strategically approached in the child and in the lower animals, where their manifestations will be simpler and their experimental control easier.

Delayed Reaction Experiments. If you want to know whether an animal can think about a thing, see if it can react to it when the thing itself is absent. Such in substance was the principle of the method applied in Hunter's investigations with the "delayed reaction" method. Much of this experiment has been described on pp. 319 ff. and in Figure 79. Let us take up the story where it was left at the conclusion of that earlier account. It will be recalled that a rat or a dog could be trained so that, upon release from the glass box R, it would go directly to that one of the three possible food boxes, L, L, L, which had been lighted a short interval of time earlier but was now dark. This was explained by the fact that the animal had kept some part of its body or head pointing the way it had been turned while the light was stimulating it; and upon being released it merely moved in the direction in which it was thus oriented.

But with other subjects more complicated behavior was observed. Raccoons [1] showed ability to go to the correct box upon being released, even when no part of the body had remained "pointed" during the delay interval. Also children who were tested with apparatus of the same general plan, and who were distracted during their delays by means of stories, the drawing of pictures, and gifts of candy, reacted with a high degree of success after much longer intervals.

---

[1] Other experimenters later have observed it also in rat and dog in other types of apparatus.

How are we to explain the ability of the raccoons and the children to turn to the correct box when it is not lighted and there is no objective cue offered? Cues of *some* kind must have been retained by these subjects (or at least kept ready for rearousal) during the delay; and if the experimenter could observe none, they must have been intra-organic in character. Now, in the case of the children we might say that the cue was of the language memorandum type described in a preceding chapter; but raccoons are not known to use anything remotely resembling human speech reactions, and, moreover, Hunter later found that an infant of thirteen months, who had not yet learned to make language sounds,

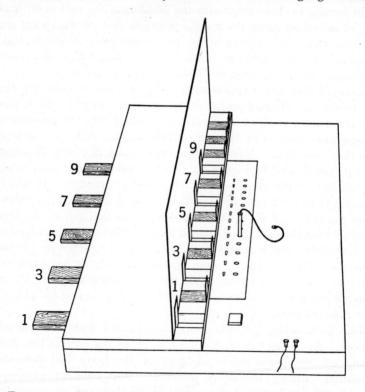

FIGURE 137. MULTIPLE CHOICE APPARATUS, ARRANGED FOR HUMAN
SUBJECTS

Keys, *1, 3, 5, 7, 9*, are presented to the subject, who sits at left. When he presses a wrong key the miniature lamp of corresponding number is flashed for the experimenter; when he presses the correct key a buzzer is sounded, by connection established through the plug-in (at key *5* in case shown). (Yerkes.)

was able to react successfully after delay and distractions. Whatever the precise physical nature of these intra-organic cues may or may not be, at any rate they played a *symbolic* function. The actual light-in-certain-box was represented, symbolized by some internal processes.

Multiple Choice Experiments. Yerkes's multiple choice method of research in animal and human psychology may help us. A special technique was developed for the study of complex choosing-behavior and applied to crows, pigs, monkeys, rats, psychopathic human subjects, and school children. A problem was set which could be solved only by the perceiving of a certain constant relation existing within a series of different situations. (Cf. Figure 137.) For example, if the problem that was set be the choice of the first key at right, the first setting might be the keys 7, 8, 9, pushed forward and so presented to the subject at one time, with 9 to be chosen; the next might be 3, 4, 5, 6, 7 forward, with 7 to be chosen; the third, 4 and 5, with 5 to be chosen. In this way any of several possible kinds of spatial relations could be arbitrarily taken as the one to be learned by the subject, and each could be presented in a great variety of settings. Some of the relations or problems suggested by Yerkes for different subjects are: (*a*) first key at right, (*b*) second at left, (*c*) alternately first at right and first at left, (*d*) middle key, (*e*) third at right, (*f*) progressively right end to left end, one by one.

The solution of the more difficult problems (solved only by human subjects) imposes upon the subject the task of discriminating and abstracting to a high degree, in a manner, in fact, practically inconceivable except as involving some thinking. What is the nature of this thinking activity? Subjects working for the writer were found largely to be using *verbal reactions to stimulate and guide themselves.* To take an example — one subject when given the setting of keys, 3, 4, 5, chanced to sound the buzzer on key 4: promptly he said to himself silently, "Aha, middle one!" When the next setting, 1, 3, 5, 7, 9, was presented, he spoke the formula to himself again, and this vocal response now acted as a stimulus so that he pressed key 5. But this was incorrect, so he was again thrown back upon trial-and-error behavior, finally "buzzing" at number 3. He was at a loss for a formulation on this trial. On the following one, 2, 5, 8, 11, he chanced, after an error or two, upon the correct key in 5, and, suddenly analyzing the situation in a new way, said to himself, "second from left." His reactions to subsequent settings established the correctness of this cue-phrase.

Language, however, is by no means the only kind of reaction by which one can signal to himself. For instance, on the problem (*c*) some subjects certainly got the correct cue in terms of right-left oscillatory movements of the hand or of the head, and it is possible that they or others may have used a slightly wagging tongue. A few such movements were visible to the experimenter. (Refined instrumentation to bring out any minimal movement present was not resorted to, but would unquestionably be worth trying.)

In the two preceding experiments we have noted the value to the organism of its being able to bring symbolic processes — for example, language — to bear upon a problematic situation. One other research from the field of comparative psychology will serve to direct our attention more explicitly to another feature.

Experiments on Combining Past Experiences. Maier used white rats and gave each animal two separate kinds of experiences or training. The rat was allowed to become familiar with a table top (see Figure 138) on which were a high wall, a box with two openings, and food. It was also trained to run the maze correctly from start to finish. Then a test was given: the food on the table was shut off from the animal at *X* by a wire screen. After a certain amount of active running about on the half of the table

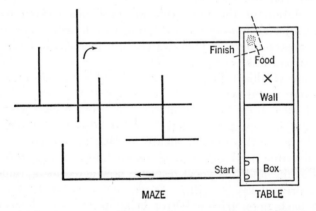

FIGURE 138. APPARATUS FOR TESTING ABILITY TO COMBINE SEPARATE EXPERIENCES (MODES OF BEHAVIOR) INTO A NEW ADJUSTIVE WHOLE RESPONSE

(From Maier, N. R. F. *Comp. Psychol. Monog.*, 1929, 6, No. 29.)

top where the food could be seen and smelled, the animal would abruptly scale the wall, make directly for the nearer hole of the box, go out the farther hole on to the maze, and rapidly run the true path around to the food. The animal apparently *combined two separate previously established types of behavior ((a)* on table top and (*b*) in maze) *to make a new form of response* in order to solve the difficulty and overcome the obstruction to its motivated activity [17].

Children ranging in age from three and one-half to eight years were given much the same sort of test. A full-sized swastika-shaped maze was used with booths or small rooms at the ends of the four runways. After having become familiar with the runways and four end-booths (experience I), each child was conducted on the outside to one of these end-booths and allowed to place a penny in a toy there to play a tune (experience II). For the test, he was then conducted blindfold around the outside to some other booth, where he was given another penny to go find the toy and start the music again. His ability to go without error through the maze to the booth where the music toy was standing, was taken as indication that he could combine his two types of earlier experience ((*a*) knowing his way about in the maze and (*b*) knowledge that the music box was in a certain booth of the maze) into a newly integrated response. As it turned out, children below six years did not show much capacity for this. Younger children do readily learn to make responses to associated stimuli when both are given to them together and at the same time (for example, as in learning to speak the names of objects, to respond to the dinner gong, and so on through the thousands of habits so early acquired). We must conclude, therefore, that there exists a developmental stage from merely associative learning to rational learning [15].

When this same technique was also adapted to college students, again it was demonstrated that some recombining of old experiences into a novel organization is a central principle in rational solutions [16].

One thing that we must not overlook is the *abruptness* with which the recombination usually occurs. We are prepared for this by the latter part of Chapter XIV.

Experiments on Articulated Acts of Thinking. Now let us conclude this preliminary scouting survey with an expedition directly into the field of adult human thinking. Already one

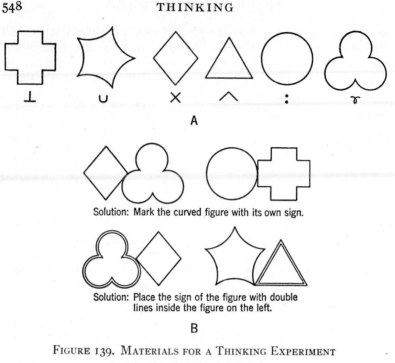

Solution: Mark the curved figure with its own sign.

Solution: Place the sign of the figure with double
lines inside the figure on the left.

B

FIGURE 139. MATERIALS FOR A THINKING EXPERIMENT

A. The six basic designs and their signs.
B. Two of the many problems set.
(From Heidbreder, E. *Arch. Psychol.*, 1924, no. 73.)

well-known experiment has been described on an early page (pp. 33 ff.). It is worth rereading here. In that experiment complicated manual manipulations were demanded, however; and we will now want to see how a subject thinks when the particular muscular co-ordinations are insignificant and more implicit cues are called into play.

In an experiment with subjects of college age, Heidbreder used tasks that were novel although they utilized simple materials. Each subject first learned to write within each of six designs a particular small symbol or sign for it. They are shown in Figure 139, A. He was then shown a card bearing two or more such designs with no particular instructions, and he proceeded to write on the card some one of the signs, in the general manner he had learned. As soon as he had marked a card he was asked: "Tell me everything that 'went on in your mind' from the time you saw the card to the time you marked it"; and a verbatim record was kept of these reports. Then the subject was told whether his response was right or wrong. Another trial followed with a somewhat similar combination of other designs, to be marked on the same principle; and so on through a series, until the subject had hit upon the correct response, could state the rule, and marked several cards accordingly. A new series was then begun. Two such series, with their principles of solution, are furnished in Figure 139, *B*.

What was the way in which a person attacked such problems? A sample subject's report given at one juncture was as follows:

First I noticed the double lines and thought that ought to have something to do with it, but I noticed that one of the double figures was marked and the other wasn't, so I didn't get anything out of that. Then I started thinking about curves and noticed that both marked ones were curved, but I knew it wouldn't be just marking the curve because we've had that and that would be too easy. Besides that didn't do anything with the double lines and I felt that they ought to come in somewhere. Then I noticed that one of the curves was marked with the sign of the other figure and all of a sudden I thought that if the curve had double lines you gave it its own sign and if not you gave it the sign of the other figure. That's the way I marked this one; but I'm not awfully sure that's right because now I see that both marked ones are on the left, so it might be marking the ones on the left. Oh! Always put the sign of the double figure inside the one on the left — or maybe inside the one that's curved. This one that I've marked will bring that out because I marked the curve and it's on the right. I mean it will show whether it's the curved figure or left figure that gets the mark. I'm pretty sure you use the mark of the double figure.

Reports of this sort furnished excellent confirmation of the experimenter's objective scores and time records. From the two together she characterized in the following way the thinking behavior that went on. The subject actively threw himself into the task, trying one or another hypothesis, each response being a specific enterprise of his, based upon his past experience and the present problem. If his action turned out to have been correct he would repeat, whereas if it was incorrect he would change his hypothesis and try another. Here we can discern *trial-and-error* behavior, but on the level of *implicit* (frequently verbal) responses, each hypothesis being a kind of trial. But we can also see more than blind trying: we can see the emerging from time to time of *new ways of formulating general principles*.

Furthermore, objective records and subjective reports make it clear that in his thinking the subject (*a*) would break up his material into parts and react to these discrete parts — an *analytic* procedure, and at the same time he (*b*) would bring different parts of situations together — a *synthetic* procedure. Both analysis and synthesis, then, were used as the subject would bring to bear on a new situation many reactions acquired in other series or in other parts of the same series.

Well, I noticed the little red star and didn't think it would be there for nothing. And the old principle I learned for this arrangement was marking the figure with curved lines. So I put the star in the figure with curved lines because that would use both.

And here again comes out that cardinal principle of thinking: the combining of separate experiences (in the case quoted, one old, one new) to form a new organized response.

VARIETIES OF THINKING RESPONSES

Two Extremes. So many are the different ways in which a person manifests thinking responses, so many are the types of situations arousing them, and so complicated are the contributing factors in each case, that a complete canvassing of the different modes and orders of thinking is quite beyond the scope of this book. Nevertheless, the mention of a few will serve to exhibit something of the variety that must be recognized.

The most *routine* type of thought sequences is shown in the mere repetition of well-learned chains of implicit responses. Going silently over a familiar air from the opera; recalling to oneself the formula for computing a circle's area from its radius; calling up all sorts of rules, principles, formulae, definitions, tables, literary passages — such serial reactions need no analysis here. Thinking of this sort is excited by particular needs in uncomplicated situations; and appears often with apparent irrelevance to objective conditions, as a sort of energy-manifestation. Such a simple meaning is implied in a frequent popular use of the word "thinking." It needs no special elaboration now, for in many places throughout our survey processes of this character have been referred to. The word-association technique, for instance, furnishes an excellent approach to it. When the associations are "free," the word-responses that appear in answer to the word-stimulus received reveal something of the thought-habits of the subject, the main tracks and the particular switchings along which his trains of thought are likely to take their courses.

The least routine thinking is done when one is *reasoning*. This behavior is aroused in a complicated situation which calls for some characterization or formulation by which the individual may be guided, and this formulation is not easily arrived at.   Reasoning is thinking in its most explicit, its most articulated form.   (Cf. examples, pp. 33 f., 549 f.)

The Principal Stages in Reasoning.   A complete act of reasoning would, according to Dewey's famous analysis [3], include five steps.   Not that all five always appear distinctly, but that they are at least implied.

1. *Maladjustment.*   Some crux or difficulty obstructs the motivated person.   It may be a practical problem, like a stoppage in a waste-pipe, a distant city that must be reached by some one of several routes or an error in the day's balance sheet, the soil of a field that demands special treatment if a crop is to be had, or a party that must be given for one's house guests of the coming week. The difficulty may be a theoretical question, like that of the real murderer in a detective story one is reading, like that of why Grimms' Fairy Tales always present stepmothers in unkindly light (to the sorrow of real stepmothers throughout Germany), like the question of the authorship of the Apocrypha or the causes of the World War, or like the problem of boundaries to the universe.

2. *Diagnosis.*   The difficulty is located and defined by discrimination and insight.   Precisely what is the source of the trouble? The man who buys the bottle of "patent medicine" because he is "not feeling well" is on much the same level of diagnosing as the college girl who failed in chemistry and admitted to her counselor that she did not know whether the trouble lay with her laboratory work, her notebook, her reading of the text, or her understanding of the lectures.   A first requirement in a good reasoner is an ability to discern and go to the heart of the matter.   As has been said before in these pages, when one is facing a situation that is urgent he must face the difficulty in as clear-eyed a manner as possible.   He must try to locate the crux of the matter, and as precisely and narrowly as he can.   The physician calls this diagnosing; but the lawyer, too, must do it for his client, and the business man for himself and his partners.   Ability to "put one's finger on the sore spot," to go to the root of the matter, is the first intelligent step toward a solution.

3. *Hypothesis.* To any but the most stupid of people, various suggestions, guesses, conjectures, will occur in the form of nascent or tentative activities that may promise to solve the difficulty. Tentative formulations or concepts appear in the cogitations of a lawyer, an engineer, a physician, a manufacturer, a tradesman, or a chef. "Is this a case of ... or a case of ... ?" Now, this phase of reasoning is more or less adventurous. The step is taken not as a directly determined consequent of the immediately preceding (as when one says "34" after "27 and 7"), but is a trial, a "flyer." This "inductive leap," as the logicians call it, depends not upon a person's logical consecutiveness in thinking but upon his fertility, his spontaneous and irresponsible-seeming originality. On the other hand, simply because the "new idea" or "hunch" or "inspiration" seems often to pop up uncaused by the immediately preceding train of thinking, we are not to assume that it is uncaused. It is, of course, a function of the particular individual, and arises somehow from the deeper groundwork of his habits and attitudes which have longer histories than this particular episode. What controls its arousal now? That is an interesting question; and the whole problem of inspiration is fascinating enough to warrant our awarding it a special treatment to itself in a later chapter.

4. *Deductions.* Once a suggestion about one's difficulty and how it may be solved has occurred to a man, he will — unless he is of that snap-judgment sort of person who goes off half-cocked and at any tangent — examine the suggestion carefully. His inspirations may come to him best in irresponsible fury but he must check them in critical phlegm. He must follow out their bearings, must deduce their consequences. "*If* I do this, then what will happen?" "*If* this be the real fact, then what about x and y and z?"

Here is the point where the formalized logic of the philosopher has its application. His syllogism is a device for explicitly setting forth the involved concepts and their relations so that their cogency may be directly ascertained. Compare the two following:

(*A*) Bubbles are appearing on this liquid in my test tube.

> When sulphuric acid is poured on copper, bubbles will appear on the surface.

> Therefore, the contents of my test tube are sulphuric acid and copper.

(*B*) All animals having jointed dorsal columns are vertebrates.
This specimen has a jointed dorsal column.
Therefore, this specimen is a vertebrate.

For a clear-cut example of deductive reasoning in which each step is seen to follow clearly upon its predecessors, the reader should turn to geometry and its succession of propositions.

5. *Observations or Experiments.* The purely subjective checking up on an hypothesis by deduction often needs the support of objective checking up by trying it out, either literally or by watching for further instances to see if it will fit them. Does it square with the observed facts?

Finally, at the conclusion of his thinking, the thinker is ready for action again; and if his interpretation or solution has stood the tests of *consistency* in step 4, and of *validity* in step 5, this will become his cue for further conduct or for further thought-work.

Other Varieties of Thinking Responses. Between these two extremes of routine repetition on the one hand and of logical reasoning on the other, there lie, of course, all degrees of difference. There is the free *thought-play* of the person who is resting or indulging in activity uncontrolled by any exigencies. In this, one specific response follows another with a minimum of influence from emotional or attentional sets and a minimum of habit. The fancies indulged in by the young child, the "mind-wandering" of the peasant seated with a pipeful of tobacco at the evening fireside, the inconsequentiality of drowsiness, all exemplify this. Here is the source, too, of much of the fancifulness of poetry, music, and other types of constructive free play.

More nearly resembling full reasoning but still lacking important checks is *autistic* thinking. A person who is maladjusted to his situation may set up implicit trial-and-error processes, and in time chance upon such a way of formulating his difficulties as to satisfy the motives impelling him, but because this is done without adequate control by social perceptions, he gets out of touch with actualities. It is all very well for the poverty-stricken man to talk to himself about what he would do if he had millions, or for a Cinderella to plan elopements with her prince; but in such cases mental health depends upon not losing the capacity to perceive correctly and to recognize that such thought-about situations are not really actual situations.

Up to this point we have been considering how a man thinks,

with particular emphasis upon the manner and the order of his thinking. A persistent question of another kind has doubtless been pressing itself upon the reader. What *are* these processes of his thinking? What are his "thoughts," "ideas," "concepts"? What is the "stuff" of his thinking?

THE DEVELOPMENT OF CONCEPTS

In Childhood. Two children walking along a country road at night were startled by a peculiar whitish thing rushing at them with low whistlings and cracklings. They had just turned to flee when one of them, recognizing something about the object as familiar, cried out: "Oh, pshaw! It's nothing but a newspaper in the wind!" That settled it: newspapers were familiar to them. In like manner the problems a person meets in life are in most cases problems calling for some insight, some perceiving of them in such a way as to rearouse habits which will furnish the meaning or cue leading to effective readjustments in those cases. These are concepts.

This practical and utilitarian basis for the organization of knowledge is brought out in a pat way by the examination of children's generalized responses as shown in a vocabulary test. The younger and less sophisticated the child, the more he shows that his reactions to discriminated aspects of things are motived by his interests and desires. Things are originally attended to for the sake of their possible usefulness to him, and are referred to in terms of action and use. Only as he learns that the composition and structure of a thing are often to be taken into account in getting it under control does he come to attend more and more to those aspects. This alteration of emphasis with age is readily observed by inspection of the accompanying table, which presents the verbal reactions given to the same verbal stimuli on the part of children of different ages.

An Experimental Development of Concepts. A young child finds himself in a certain situation, reacts to it by approach, and hears it called "dog." After an indeterminate intervening period he finds himself in a somewhat different situation, and hears that called "dog." Later he finds himself in a somewhat different situation still, and hears that called "dog" also. Thus the process continues. The "dog" experiences appear at irregular intervals. The appearances are thus unanticipated. They appear with no obvious label

DEVELOPMENT OF GENERALIZED REACTIONS IN CHILDREN

	PHILIP — 7 YRS.	MARY — 9 YRS.	BILLY — 11 YRS.	GEORGE — 13 YRS.	CHAUNCEY — 15 YRS.
I. Definitions: "What does this word mean, —; what is —?"					
Bread	You eat bread	You eat it	Dough that is cooked	Thing we eat; made of wheat	Mixture flour, water, yeast & baking powder; subjected to heat
Clock	Clock ticks	Tell time by it	We keep time by	Timepiece	Something to tell time with
Horse	Horse runs	You ride a horse	Domestic animal	Large animal	Animal used as draught animal
Automobile	Ride in it	You ride in it	A machine	Gasoline vehicle	A conveyance drawn by its own power
Hard	Work hard	Harden the clay	Something you think you can hardly do	Extreme from soft	Unyielding
II. Similars: "How are these two things alike?"					
Iron and silver	Hard to break	(don't know)	Dug out of ground	Both metals	Both metals or elements
Table and chair	Sit in c. eat on t.	(don't know)	Use them in kitchen	Made of same material	Both furniture
III. Differences: "What is the difference between —?"					
Water and ice	I. melts, w. leaks	Ice is hard	I. is w. frozen	I. is frozen w.	W. is fluid, i. is solid

as to their essential nature. This precipitates at each new appearance a more or less acute *problem* as to the proper reaction. Meantime the intervals between the "dog" experiences are filled with all sorts of other absorbing experiences which are contributing to the formation of other concepts. At length the time arrives when the child has a "meaning" for the word "dog." Upon examination this meaning is found to be actually a characteristic more or less common to all dogs and not common to cats, dolls, and teddy-bears. But to the child the process of arriving at this meaning or concept has been largely unconscious. He has never said to himself, "Lo! I shall proceed to discover the characteristics common to all dogs but not enjoyed by cats and teddy-bears." The formation of the concept has never been an end deliberately sought for itself. It has always been the means to an end — the supremely absorbing task of physical and social reaction and adjustment.

Hull sought to duplicate these conditions in a well-controlled experiment. An exposure apparatus was used somewhat like the model shown in Figure 140. For the stimuli the Chinese characters shown in Figure 141 were drawn on cards and mounted in twelve separate series on the revolving drum of the apparatus, the series or packs being numbered from I to XII. As a given pack of cards (let us say, Pack I) was presented serially to the subject, the experimenter pronounced the syllable (the "word" in the figure) that corresponded to the character on each card; and the subject repeated it after him, striving to learn the series to a point where he could repeat the word ahead of the experimenter. When

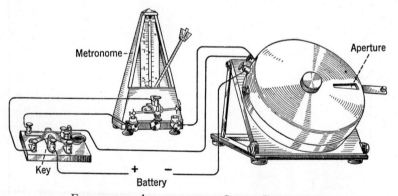

FIGURE 140. APPARATUS FOR SERIAL EXPOSURES

Syllables, words, or other materials are inscribed on a circular card mounted just under the cover of the drum upon a central axis, and by rotation of the card are brought one at a time under the aperture. The rotations of the axis are controlled by two ratchets, one of which is operated electromagnetically by the interruptions of an electric circuit. The interruptions are kept regular by a metronome. By means of the ratchets each exposure is a "still," and the change from one to the next is produced by a quick jump. This is the Ranschburg model.

		Pack											
Word	Con-cept	I	II	III	IV	V	VI	VII	VIII	IX	X	XI	XII
A	oo												
B	yer												
C	li												
D	ta												
E	deg												
F	ling												
G	hui												
H	chun												
I	vo												
J	na												
K	nez												
L	fid												

(Series, left margin)

FIGURE 141. CHINESE CHARACTERS USED AS MATERIAL FOR STUDYING THE FORMING OF GENERALIZED RESPONSES TO ABSTRACTED STIMULI

Each word, "oo," "yer," etc., is the name for a simple "concept" or "radical" which is used as a component of the many complex characters shown in a horizontal row to the right of it. Inspection will reveal these embedded radicals (the first, named "oo," looks a bit like a check mark with two misplaced commas; it is to be found in the left-hand part of each complex character in the first horizontal row). In each pack of cards (shown in vertical row) there is included one character to contain each radical. Throughout the twelve packs, then, each radical will have been involved twelve times in as many different characters. (From Hull, C. L. *Psychol. Monog.*, 1920, **28**, no. 123.)

one pack or series had been learned, the next was taken up. Now, with the several different series of characters the same twelve "words" were used, but in different orders. Further, it will be seen by inspecting the horizontal rows in the figure that the same twelve "concepts" or "radicals" were embedded in the characters of the different series. The subject was not informed of this; and the outcome of the experiment depended upon his hitting upon them quite incidentally in the course of his memory exercises. So far for the first six series of packs (I to VI), in which learning was the thing demanded.

The latter six packs (VII to XII) were used to test whether the subject had incidentally *abstracted* the radicals and had *generalized* his reaction to them, that is, whether he could note them in new

situations.   Three exposures were given of each test "pack" and
the subject was encouraged to guess at them freely.   Whenever
he could give the correct word for a character it was taken as evidence that he had hit upon a discriminating of the particular radical
or concept embedded in certain characters and could name it.

Some Practical Questions.   The results obtained from this
experiment threw light upon some questions of a practical nature.

(1) "From simple to complex" has been the counsel given to
teachers for generations.   The teacher is told that he should use
simple situations first and more complex later when he introduces
pupils to new experiences and new materials with a view to developing in them abstracted and generalized ways of recognizing
things.   Hull tested this principle experimentally with the use
of his Chinese characters.   Some of the radicals (A to F for some
subjects) were shown in simpler characters in the first series and
then in increasingly complex characters; the others (G to L) were
shown in characters first complex, then simpler and simpler.   The
results showed that the former radicals were not easier for a person
to learn to single out and to name; and the time-honored rule hit
upon in everyday practical life was given no experimental support.
Probably the rule is too general as it is usually stated, and whether
it applies or not may depend upon the kind of material that is to
be learned.

(2) In developing generalized ways of responding to conditions
about him a person is enormously aided by the assistance of his
fellow men in the form of ready-isolated and ready-formulated abstractions.   They are a part of the knowledge of his class, family,
or race.   The shoemaking apprentice is called to attend definitely
to this and that detail of cutting, stitching, or nailing, and is furnished with verbal stimuli that will serve to generalize and render
universally applicable the particular details of technique pointed
out.   "Always hold the sole piece so, then take your hammer and
——"   The cook is frequently falling back on the formulated language signals of printed recipes that represent the accumulated
learnings of others.   "The foundation for common sauces is the
roux.   This is butter and flour worked together and thinned out
slowly with milk or water."   The school child is given outright
some verbal description of "passive voice," and then in several
examples is encouraged to pick out cases.   Left to himself he would
probably not discover this detail of human speech in a lifetime.

The saving of time in learning these abstractions is unquestionably great. There has long been a suspicion, however, that their value is less than that of those developed by the individual in the course of his own private experiences. Present well-chosen situations, the teacher is bidden, and let the child himself learn to pick out the essential detail you wish him to discriminate. *"Learn to do by doing,* not by seeking theoretical information from books," says the practical workman. Hull attacked this problem also in his experiment. He had some of the Chinese radicals or concepts presented by themselves and the other radicals presented as usual embedded within the characters. He found that neither method of presentation had a distinct advantage in preparing the subject to identify the radicals in later characters. The most effective procedure of all was to show the detail in its concrete settings in the characters, but in such a way (in red) that it would be specially attended to. Again it would seem to us that general rules like these two must be applied with caution, for they are likely to be too broad and general for uncritical use in a particular case.

Anyway, the reader will agree that these are not final answers on these practical questions. One experiment must be amplified by very many others with carefully selected variations in setting and in technique before science can say to the experienced practical man, "Here you are correct; there, in error."

(3) Another principle which deserves to be mentioned here, though not attacked experimentally, is the one made emphatic by James in his *Law of Dissociation by Varying Concomitants.* Suppose you wish to help a person to respond selectively to one certain color, dimension, tone, time, or other aspect of a situation. You must see to it that the aspect appears now in one combination and now in another. If a and b always and invariably appeared together as stimuli to a certain organism, and always in their same relative intensities, the organism would continue to react to a and b as to one thing. The failure of either to stimulate it alone would render impossible the forging of more specific a-reactions or b-reactions. This principle has had practical application in thousands of ways. Does a teacher wish to train a child to perceive the quality of "sphericity"? Let her give him marbles, balls, oranges, and globes to observe, all alike in being spheres but different as to colors, textures, sizes, uses, and so forth. Is he to be taught to recognize and use the numerical relation of "four"? Let him be given four

apples, four matches, four leaves, four children; let him draw four lines, hold up four fingers, make four swings in succession. The Sterns tell of a child of four years who when asked by his grandfather, "How many fingers have I?" responded, "I don't know, I can only count on my own fingers." He had not abstracted the "four fingers" from the particular setting of his own hand.

Knowledge a Hierarchy of Generalized Reaction Habits. It should now be clear that one of the main purposes of education, the imparting of information, is the building-up of concepts. Observation of a person's behavior further reveals that these are built up in hierarchical forms. "A science," runs an old definition, "is organized knowledge reduced to a system." The subject-matter of fields of study are so organized into minor and major principles, sub-topics and topics, particular facts and general laws, that to the student it must often seem as though getting the skeleton or architecture of the study were more than half the task. A simple case is afforded by mathematics. To know arithmetic one must be able not only to identify numerals, but also to add, subtract, multiply, and divide them; to treat these four fundamental processes again as applicable to both whole numbers and fractions, then to decimals, then even to unknown quantities. But in further mathematical study lines and areas and their transformations must be dealt with; later these are linked up with the numerical operations. And so on through the higher phases. Furthermore, as with mathematics, so in some degree with any field of knowledge.

THE NATURE OF AN IDEATIONAL ACTIVITY

Introduction. We come now to still closer grips with a persistent problem. When asked what a person thinks with, almost any man you meet will readily say, "With ideas." Here is a term that has had a most chequered career, and even today there is no agreement as to what it means. "Even in technical usage the term is used loosely and popularly for plan or project, general notion, fantasy, belief or opinion, or for something contrasted with fact and reality" [5].

To examine narrowly into the nature of an ideational process (as it is better called) we shall invoke both objective and subjective approaches.

THE NATURE OF AN IDEATIONAL ACTIVITY 561

The Essential Process is an "$S \rightarrow$ implicit R $(S) \rightarrow R$" Function.
In all cases it is apparent that when one thinks about a thing his
reactions toward it, whatever they are, are not direct reactions.
He does not engage in direct and actual manipulation of the thing
of which he is thinking. The object or person may be present or
may be absent, but in either case the first move of the thinker is
not an overt dealing with it, but an indirect dealing. This indirectness is plain enough where the use of tools is involved; that is,
where the subject makes some of his direct behavior toward the
tool instead of toward the object. Indirectness, moreover, is the
only way in which we can conceive of successful behavior when
the subject acts without the use of tools. When a raccoon, in a
delayed-reaction box, or when a person of our acquaintance shows
that he has in some manner been thinking previously about the
situation, person, or thing he is now overtly addressing, we are
forced to the assumption that he is doing something when he is
thinking about it. This is plausible enough. It will be recalled
that the animals which reacted successfully after delay, but on a
lower level of behavior than the raccoons, had maintained a general
body or head orientation or set. That was what they had been
doing during delay. Similarly, the raccoon and the child were
doing something during the delay.

In these different cases the only satisfying description of what
goes on in the organism is in terms of *responses that are set up and
that serve in turn as stimuli. Implicit reactions now operate as cues.*
As a formula it would read, "$S \rightarrow$ implicit R $(S) \rightarrow R$." And this
is no new notion. Emotion, we have seen, is an intra-organic
reaction of a sort that in turn influences and determines overt
behavior. Attending is primarily a response that prepares for
and facilitates overt reactions of particular sorts. In the process
of perception, the subject is thrown by some aspect of a situation
into some anticipatory set (largely implicit) that orients him for a
certain type of conduct with reference to that situation. In
thinking, then, a situation arouses some implicit reaction and
that reaction in turn arouses a new implicit reaction, until sooner
or later the implicit reaction arouses overt behavior.

An illuminating reference is to the treatment of self-stimulation
(pp. 528 ff.). We have seen in that connection that a person can
make a response that stimulates *himself*, and then be affected by
his reaction as a new stimulus to himself, just as he can react to

another person's reaction (cf. Figure 128). Language is another illustration of self-stimulation. Some previously cited illustrations are worth keeping in mind here, especially (*a*) using a silently spoken word or phrase as a memorandum, (*b*) soliloquizing or thinking aloud just as if in verbal interchange with a second person, (*c*) thought-work in adding. The last-named will reward fuller analysis now.

Suppose a person not adept at the task be adding the columns of figures to the left. Starting up the right-hand column, he will be talking to himself after this manner: "9 and 4 is 13. 13 and 8 is 21." Now, how does he come to say that "21"? It is not a response to any such figure on the page. Nor is it simply concocted irresponsibly by the person. It is a response to (*a*) the previously enunciated "13" and to (*b*) the visible "8." If he had not previously made the "13" response he would not now make the "21" response. In brief, the man's *response* "13" now serves as a *stimulus* to *himself* which excites (along with an exteroceptive stimulus, "8") the next following response. He is responding to his own response.

56
73
18
34
69
―

Thinking during addition operates under a high degree of support and control from exteroceptive cues. It ought to be easy for the reader to broaden the illustration to apply to thinking performances where exteroceptive cues are at a minimum or wholly absent.

Imagery in General. If we shift our avenue of approach and inquire as to the nature of ideational processes from the viewpoint of the thinker himself, we shall find that the trains of thought as he experiences them are substantially a matter of imagery. Here is a term that has played a tremendous part in the history of psychology. It is especially important in the psychology which deals with the contemplation of one's own experiences. The meaning of "image" is familiar enough. One can "hear" a movement in Beethoven's Sixth Symphony when no music is physically present to him; he can "see" Greenland's icy mountains or India's coral strands while he is singing in his church; he can "smell" a New Orleans French market or a San Francisco or Gloucester waterfront; and he can re-present to himself what his arm muscles and his finger tips "feel" like when he is rapidly typewriting. This representative function of imaging, it is clear, is too common and everyday a phenomenon to need further identification.

So common is the experiencing of imagery that it is not surprising to find that many psychologists have in earlier centuries supposed it to be the necessary raw and finished material of ideational activity. In the early 1880's, however, we can see signs of a shaking faith. It was then that Galton published the results of his questionnaire addressed to people in many walks of life. "Think of some definite object," he instructed them. "Suppose it is your breakfast-table as you sat down to it this morning, and consider carefully the picture that rises before your mind's eye.

"1. *Illumination.* Is the image dim or fairly clear? Is its brightness comparable to that of the actual scene?

"2. *Definition.* Are all the objects well defined at the same time, or is the place of sharpest definition at any one moment more contracted than it is in a real scene?

"3. *Coloring.* Are the colors of the china, of the toast, breadcrust, mustard, meat, parsley, or whatever may have been on the table, quite distinct and natural?"

Galton found to his astonishment that the great majority of men of science in England and France protested that they had no such imagery at all.

My own conclusion [he says] is that an over-ready perception of sharp mental pictures is antagonistic to the acquirement of habits of highly generalized and abstract thought, especially when the steps of reasoning are carried on by words as symbols, and that if the faculty of seeing the pictures was ever possessed by men who think hard, it is very apt to be lost by disuse. The highest minds are probably those in which it is not lost, but subordinated, and is ready for use on suitable occasions. I am, however, bound to say, that the missing faculty seems to be replaced so serviceably by other modes of conception, chiefly, I believe, connected with the incipient motor sense, not of the eyeballs only but of the muscles generally, that men who declare themselves entirely deficient in the power of seeing mental pictures can nevertheless give lifelike descriptions of what they have seen, and can otherwise express themselves as if they were gifted with a vivid visual imagination. They can also become painters of the rank of Royal Academicians.

The Value of Imagery to Thinking is Challenged. Since Galton's work there have been many other signs of disaffection, especially in the studies of Binet, Woodworth, and the Würzburg school. Contemporary experimental studies bring out such facts as these: (a) the imagery employed by a thinker is for the most part irrelevant to the material being thought about and on occasion may even hinder the direct trend of thought [1]; (b) individuals especially gifted in the ability to form images have no advantage over others inferior in this regard when geometrical problems are assigned them [2].

The work of a group of psychologists at Würzburg is of special importance [6, 18, 22, 23]. They, too, found imagery to be far less important to thinking tasks than was once supposed.[1] In one experiment the subject was given the task of judging which of two lifted weights was the heavier. He would report that while he did have sensory and imaginal experiences in connection with the weights he could not thus account for his judgment. He did not retain the kinesthetic image of the first weight and compare it with the kinesthetic sensation or image of the second weight. The judging simply occurred, the decision was ready; and the subject had *no experiences of any imaginal or other processes that determined it.*

But they did report certain positive findings of another character. In one experiment on word-association the subject was instructed to react with a word that was a superordinate of the stimulus word (as, "horse" — "quadruped"; "orange" — "fruit"). After a few correct responses had been given, the subject would find himself reacting to later stimuli with words of the correct logical relationship *without any more reminding himself or even being aware of the particular relationship being used.* After he had been set toward a certain goal (*Aufgabe*), this set continued to operate as a determiner of his responses. This was what came to be called a "*directive tendency.*" It might also have been called "selective tendency," for it operates often by rejecting or accepting, by shutting off or releasing this and that particular ideational activity as it occurs, so that it determines the direction of the following activities. The reader will find this to have been a striking feature of the subject's verbal behavior cited on page 549.

The Central Importance of Directive Tendencies in Thinking.

[1] The reader can easily verify this point for himself. Let him answer as quickly as possible each of the questions listed below. After each answer is given, let him recall whether he had imaginal sounds, sights, or other such representative content *between* the reading of the question and the instant of the answer (not afterward).
  1. Was Confucius a Roman general?
  2. Is red a color?
  3. In what year did Columbus discover America?
  4. Do you like cranberry sauce with your turkey?
  5. What is your name?
  6. Is happiness desirable?

Or again, let the reader bear in mind the way in which a process of recalling often occurs: no recall; a frantic effort and "search" for the item; giving up the quest and turning to something else; casual appearance now of the item desired.

When a person is making overt efforts to surmount an obstacle, he may be showing trial-and-error behavior in many different directions, yet he remains persistently oriented. We have discussed this phenomenon of set in Chapter XII. Likewise, the procedure of a subject who is thinking may veer this way and that, yet it reveals *a persistent tendency that dominates the whole performance.* This is clear from examples furnished earlier in the chapter. Subjects working on the multiple choice experiments tried one key and another, but all for the sake of reaching the single solution. Subjects marking the designs on cards tried this, that, and another plan of marking them — but all was done simply to get the thing solved. In everyday life it is the one who can keep thinking consistently toward the desired end who is the effective thinker. Of what avail is it in the knottier problems of life to be able to manifest insight and to have at hand an ample stock of "knowledge" but to be unable to keep working on the problem attacked? Thinking of the more effective sorts is *nachdenken,* "thinking toward" an objective.

Once a man is oriented in a given direction, the maintenance of these thought reactions has been known to intrude upon such behavior as would be more fitting in his immediate physical and social environment; the preoccupied man may step into mud puddles, lift his hat when saluting mere males, hold aloft his walking stick when it begins to rain, or do any of the thousand and one inappropriate acts that are attributed to absent-minded men. Sometimes the orientation or set may be so profound that it persists through all sorts of distracting situations, as in the case of a man who returns again and again to the original unsettled topic of conversation after he and his friends have discussed a dozen other matters. Once he has become set for the original problem, this thoroughgoing set is not entirely disrupted by the occurrence of more superficial vocal, gestural, or manual reactions meanwhile.

The importance of a directive tendency in thinking is especially well appreciated when it is conspicuously absent, as revealed in the following verbatim account of the talk of a manic patient:

Now I want to be a nice accommodating patient; anything from sewing on a button, mending a net, or scrubbing the floor, or making a bed. I am a jack-of-all trades and master of none!... Oh, I am quite a talker; I work for a New York talking-machine company. You are a physician, but I don't

think you are much of a lawyer, are you? I demand that you send for a lawyer! I want him to take evidence. . . . I will make somebody sweat! I worked
by the sweat of my brow! [Notices money on the table.] A quarter; twenty-
five cents. In God we trust; United States of America; Army and Navy
forever! [1]

Here, whatever consistencies of direction there are in the talk are
weak and are easily displaced by reactions to distracting exteroceptive stimuli or by smooth-running but irrelevant habits of
particular word sequences.

The same defects appear in drawings furnished by some psy-
chotics. Starting off, let us say, with the outline of a horse, the
patient may suddenly shift to sketching a ghost, then a mouse;
he scribbles his initials or a number or two; he draws two eyes
nowhere in particular; covers it all with characters looking like
Greek, though he knows no Greek; and maybe ends the process
with a hint of earrings without ears, or a snatch of syllables.

The same defects are observable again in the free activity of
both the hands and the voice of the young child. Unpracticed
as he is in the exercise of thinking, he is notoriously distractible
by almost any sort of intruding sound or sight. He fails to inhibit
tendencies to follow almost any habitual chain reaction that is
partially set up.

THINKING CONSIDERED PHYSIOLOGICALLY

Introduction. Thus far we have identified thinking as occurring
in an organism when it meets difficulties and strives to surmount
them by a rational procedure. The difficulty confronting the
subject excites in him some implicit response or series of responses
which eventually serve to excite some overt forms of conduct. This
outward conduct is thus not directly aroused by the situation,
but it is intermediated by the thinking reactions which finally
serve as its directing cue. These intra-organic motor activities
operate as substitute stimuli replacing the original extra-organic
ones.

Now precisely what mechanisms are operating? When thinking
is going on, *what* is going on?

The Intracerebral View. "A man thinks with his brain. The
brain is the seat of thought." This view is shared alike by the

---

[1] Reprinted by permission from *Manual of Psychiatry* by A. J. Rosanoff, published by John Wiley
& Sons, Inc.

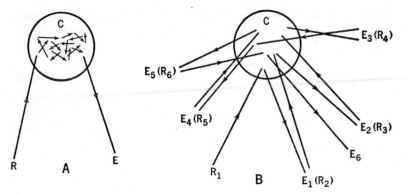

FIGURE 142. DIAGRAMS TO REPRESENT (*A*) THE INTRACEREBRAL VIEW AND (*B*) THE PERIPHERAL VIEW OF THE RELATION OF THE CEREBRAL CORTEX TO THE NEURAL IMPULSES OPERATING IN THINKING ACTIVITY

R, R, receptors; *E, E,* effectors; *C,* cerebral cortex. Note that in (*B*), *C* has the important function of determining over which pathways the impulses from the receptors go.

schoolboy and the traditional psychologist.   According to this conception, the bodily mechanism that is at work when one thinks consists of one or more neural impulses from receptors (*R* in Figure 142, *A*) which reach some area of the cortex (*C*).   Then, instead of passing more or less immediately to some motor organs, these impulses shift along association fibers to another cortical area, thence to another, and so on.   A series of impulses is set up which travels back and forth, here, there, and elsewhere.   The activity all goes on between innumerable cortical centers, and the whole field of operation is comprised within the cerebrum.   Thinking, according to this view, may be called a complication, refinement, prolongation, elaboration, of the central segment of the whole reaction arc.   The simpler human activities involve fairly close and immediate connections between afferent and efferent pathways and may include the simplest reflexes; but in more complex acts, the central associative phases become more and more important, until in deliberative thinking these central connections are found to be indefinitely complicated.

What ground is there for this view?   What is the actual status of cerebral localization today?   At the best we have some definite knowledge of how specific sensory and specific motor peripheral organs are projected upon certain areas of the cortex; but no localization can be claimed for any functions other than those connected with specific bodily organs. At least, we have frequent reminders by Lashley, Franz, and others that the cerebrum acts as a whole in the more complicated behaviors, and that brain-mapping is commonly carried too far.

The Peripheral View. In the peripheral interpretation of thinking, the associative pathways serve merely as connectors between peripheral tracts. These connectors are subject to an enormous amount of modification by the joining and disjoining of simultaneously and successively operating central connections. In other words, the emphasis here is upon whole arcs. (Cf. Figure 142, *B*.)

Note that the peripheral view does not deny that the central organs play a leading rôle. It is there that connections are made, are strengthened and weakened; it is there that whole teams of arcs are integrated and disintegrated. It is through the central organs that the influences of postural responses upon phasic responses, of postural on postural, or of phasic on phasic are in a large measure produced. With this view, the differential resistances at manifold synaptic connections or the chronaxies of the neurons remain the heart of behavior. First and last, however, they are points of connection between arcs.

This description of the physical side of the process of thinking in terms of the interplay of entire sensori-motor circuits instead of merely the central segments thereof possesses the advantage of fitting in with our view of thinking as behavior that is set up by a difficult situation and that takes the economical form of trial-and-error reactions which are made indirectly and implicitly.

What Effectors are Involved? **(A) Language Mechanisms.** If we adopt the peripheral view, our next question follows naturally: what peripheral organs are the operating ones? If a man thinks not with his brain but with his whole body, what mechanisms are most intimately involved? First of all let us remind ourselves that thinking involves the perceiving of a situation that leads to the setting-up of some implicit motor response, which is in turn to serve as a sensory cue either to an overt response or to new implicit responses that ultimately will arouse the overt response. What we seek to identify, then, are the effectors that can react in a manner which will furnish implicit intra-organic cues.

That the speech mechanisms are the thinking mechanisms *par excellence* has long been recognized by many psychologists and laymen alike. *"Thinking is restrained speaking and acting,"* said Bain a half-century ago. *"A thought is a word or an act in a nascent state . . . a commencement of muscular activity,"* said Ribot with equal insight. Writers of more philosophical interests have often said as much — if not always so accurately. "It troubles me greatly to find that I can never acknowledge, discover or prove any truth except by using in my mind words or other signs. . . . If these characters were absent, we should never think or reason distinctly" (Leibniz). "Thinking and speaking are so entirely one that we can only distinguish them as internal and external" (Schleiermacher). "Without language it is impossible to conceive philosophical, nay, even any human consciousness" (Schelling). "We think in names" (Hegel). "Reasoning, the principal subject of logic, takes place usually by means of words, and in all complicated cases can take place in no other way" (J. S. Mill). Literary men, too, have made the same point. "The word is not the dress of thought, but its very incarnation" (Wordsworth). "If I do not speak I cannot think" (Daudet).

These statements, let us note, are by men who have been stimulated in large part by reading and have found their outlet in writing. They have not done their thinking in terms of pipe-fitting or cabinet-making, careful motoring, skillful boxing, communicating with deaf-mutes or with savages of unknown tongues. The possibility remains that men working in occupations like the latter have many of their nascent and their short-circuited responses based upon quite other effector organs than those of speech. Symbolic reactions are not limited to language mechanisms.

(B) Other Striped Musculature. Recently there has been reported a series of researches that forcefully directs attention to the striped musculature, and in general gives comfort and support to the peripheral view of the bodily mechanisms in thinking [13]. In brief it is an application of the action potential technique [1] to the musculature which was presumably involved in or related to ideational processes. The subjects had been given prolonged training in how to relax their whole bodily musculature while lying on a couch in a darkened sound-proof room. For these experiments two telegraph clicks were used. At one the subject was to begin a prescribed muscular activity, at the other to cease and

[1] For this technique see the description on pp. 205 ff., *supra.* In the experiments here referred to, a string galvanometer with great amplification was used, producing a sensitivity to changes of a millionth of a volt. These changes were photographically recorded.

immediately relax any tension that was present. Then the patterns
of action potentials so obtained were compared with the patterns
obtained when the subject only imagined performing the acts.
(1) For instance, the subject was instructed to imagine bending his
right arm. It was found that currents which were set up from
electrodes placed at biceps muscle and at elbow of the right arm
were similar in kind to those appearing when the arm was actually
bent. On the other hand when the subject was instructed to
imagine bending some other member (left arm or foot) no current
was registered from the right arm. (2) When the subject was instructed actually to look upward, the action potentials set up from
electrodes attached near the eyeball muscles produced the record
shown in Figure 143, 1; and when the subject was instructed to
imagine the Eiffel Tower in Paris, the potentials were recorded as
in 2. (3) When his instruction was to look from left to right, the
record was as shown in 3; and when it was merely to recall the
morning's newspaper, it was as in 4. The evidence is pretty conclusive that when a person imagines movements of his own he
goes through these movements in a minute degree, and if he imagines
some outer object he makes (in minute degree) the very movements he would if he were attending to the object itself. This is
experimental confirmation of older theories that "images" are not
some unique mental stuff but simply the experiencing of minute
motor adjustments and readjustments of the body.

From another source comes some further interesting evidence concerning the participation of striped musculature in thinking activity.
Action potentials were obtained from the finger-muscles of deaf-
mutes while asleep at times when no finger movements were visible
to the observer. If awakened at such times the subjects would
report that they had been dreaming, whereas if they were awakened
at times when no action potentials appeared, they reported no
dreaming [19]. Evidently, then, deaf-mutes do their dreaming with
their fingers — and dreaming is a kind of thinking during sleep.

(C) **Visceral Mechanisms.** We need only to be reminded that
thinking does not proceed in a vacuum, is not unmotivated, to
realize that the total physiology of thinking might be said to
involve also visceral mechanisms of response. For more than a
quarter-century, many laboratory studies have had as their aim
the detection of those respiratory, circulatory, electrical, and
other changes that occur when a person is thinking. Amid many

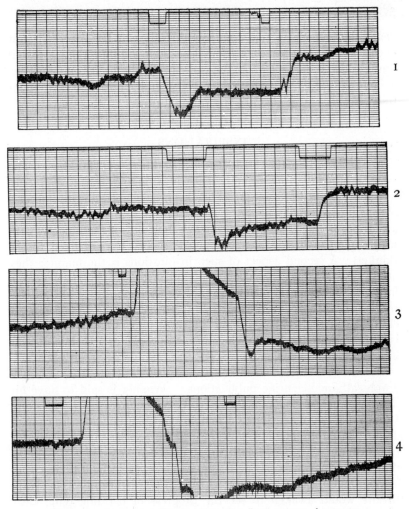

FIGURE 143. ACTION POTENTIALS AND IDEATIONAL ACTIVITY

1. Photographic record of potential differences *during eye-movement of looking upward.* Electrodes of platinum, covered with cotton moistened with NaCl, were placed one above the right orbital ridge, the other to the right of the external corner of the right eye. Vertical lines indicate time intervals of one-fifth second. The subject had been instructed, "When the signal comes, look upward." Previous to this sound, the eyes had been quiet, as shown by the horizontal tracing of the string shadow.

2. *During visual imagining.* Conditions the same as for 1; but the subject had here been instructed, "When the signal comes, imagine the Eiffel Tower in Paris." Note the resemblance between 1 and 2.

3. *During eye-movement of looking left to right.* Conditions the same. Subject was instructed, "When the signal comes, look toward the right."

4. *During visual recollecting.* Conditions the same. Subject instructed, "When the signal comes, recall this morning's newspaper." Note the resemblance between 3 and 4.

(From Jacobson, E. "Electrical Measurements of Neuromuscular States During Mental Activities. III." *Amer. J. Physiol.*, 1930, **95**, 694–712.)

conflicting reports a few common threads can be discerned; but even these scanty generalizations lose their appropriateness to our quest when it is seen that they are probably to be explained as evidences simply of general tenseness and emotional excitement fully as well as evidences of the rational processes themselves.

INSPIRATIONS

A Special Phenomenon in the Third Stage of Thinking. The most profoundly interesting aspect of thinking is the degree to which originality of hypothesis has been developed and the process of inspiration made fertile. A feature that has received much attention is the *sudden, unexpected,* bolt-out-of-the-blue way in which many a happy idea, theme, or theory has occurred to the thinker. A second aspect of such inspirations is the manner they often have of appearing when the subject is *in a relaxed condition* in which his attention, if he be awake, is on quite other and extraneous matters. A third is the spontaneous and *out-of-nowhere* character of their emergence, so that not uncommonly the thinker is almost convinced of their authorship and origination outside himself, that he is being "inspired" in the mystical sense.

Illustrations by the score can be gleaned from literary, biographical, and scientific publications.[1] Wagner is said to have hit upon a principal theme in the overture to *Das Reingold* in his sleep. In one of the most famous instances, Coleridge awoke from a dream with the complete structure of his *Kubla Khan* ready for transcribing. Masefield tells us of his poem *The Woman Speaks* that it appeared in a fading dream, "engraven in high relief on an oblong metal plate, from which I wrote it down." Charlotte Brontë would awaken to see the progress of her tale lying clear and bright before her, its incidents being even more distinct and vivid than her physical surroundings.

The eminent French mathematician Poincaré has written that his mathematical discoveries were often in the nature of an "apparent, sudden illumination" when he was crossing the Boulevard, when he lay awake from effects of black coffee, when he was about to step into his carriage, and on like occasions when work had been

---

[1] Our illustrations will be drawn from fields in which highly original ideas often appear, but it is to be remembered that the phenomenon is one of daily occurrence in the course of everyday business and domestic life. It appears in the multitudinous little hunches, guesses, and conjectures that are a part of one's daily living.

given up. Another mathematician, Hamilton, made his great discovery of the quaternions while walking with Lady Hamilton "as they came up to Brougham Bridge near Dublin."

Inventors have written of their inspirations.

I have waked out of sound sleep with a new idea. Sometimes when I am dressing or shaving or tying a shoestring. Sometimes after hours or days of sweating over the drafting table. But most often when my mind is fresh and rested and free from worry or care and when I am approaching a new subject so that I am thinking in qualitative terms.

I studied the problem, read all I could find pertaining to it, tested experimentally all the ideas that came to me, and sooner or later the right solution would flash on my mind often at the moment of awakening in the morning after a sound sleep [21].

Scientists, too, have testified to having helpful "hunches," which, following long periods of concentrated study, come into consciousness at a time when they are not consciously working on the problems [20].

Creative Work is Not Pure Inspiration. From these accounts one might gather that the process of creating is simply an irresponsible business of waiting for the inspiration to come, like the ignorant man who, having heard the "call to preach," asserted that all he would have to do would be to "open his mouth and let the Lord fill it with the message." As an antidote to this romantic notion let us be reminded by creative thinkers themselves. Interviews with many French poets and novelists bring out the fact that all of them when hoping to do a piece of creative production first enrich their verbal equipment, look up everything available in the field to be entered, and saturate themselves in the subject-matter they are to work up [4].

Hear a literary genius, Poe:

Most writers — poets in especial ... would positively shudder at letting the public take a peep behind the scenes, at the elaborate and vacillating crudities of thought — at the true purpose seized only at the last moment — at the innumerable glimpses of idea that arrived not at the maturity of full view — at the fully matured fancies discarded in despair as unmanageable, at the cautious selections and rejections — at the painful erasures and interpolations [see Figure 144] — in a word, at the wheels and pinions — the tackle for scene-shifting — the step-ladders and demon-traps — the cock's feathers, the red paint and the black patches which in ninety-nine cases out of the hundred constitute the properties of the literary actor.

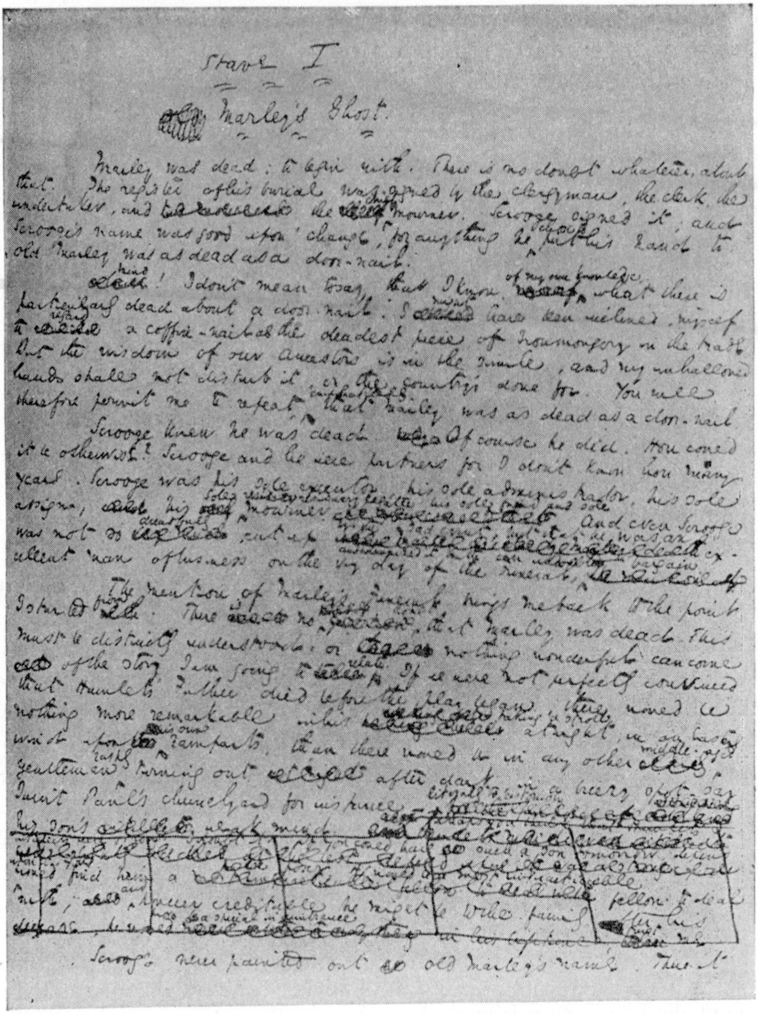

Stave I

Marley's Ghost.

Marley was dead: to begin with. There is no doubt whatever about that. The register of his burial was signed by the clergyman, the clerk, the undertaker, and the chief mourner. Scrooge signed it. And Scrooge's name was good upon 'Change, for anything he chose to put his hand to. Old Marley was as dead as a door-nail.

Mind! I don't mean to say, that I know, of my own knowledge, what there is particularly dead about a door-nail. I might have been inclined, myself, to regard a coffin-nail as the deadest piece of ironmongery in the trade. But the wisdom of our ancestors is in the simile, and my unhallowed hands shall not disturb it, or the country's done for. You will therefore permit me to repeat, emphatically, that Marley was as dead as a door-nail.

Scrooge knew he was dead? Of course he did. How could it be otherwise? Scrooge and he were partners for I don't know how many years. Scrooge was his sole executor, his sole administrator, his sole assign, his sole residuary legatee, his sole friend and sole mourner. And even Scrooge was not so dreadfully cut up by the sad event, but that he was an excellent man of business on the very day of the funeral, and solemnised it with an undoubted bargain.

The mention of Marley's funeral brings me back to the point I started from. There is no doubt that Marley was dead. This must be distinctly understood, or nothing wonderful can come of the story I am going to relate. If we were not perfectly convinced that Hamlet's Father died before the play began, there would be nothing more remarkable in his taking a stroll at night, in an easterly wind, upon his own ramparts, than there would be in any other middle-aged gentleman rashly turning out after dark in a breezy spot—say Saint Paul's Churchyard for instance—literally to astonish his son's weak mind.

Scrooge never painted out old Marley's name. There it

FIGURE 144. FACSIMILE OF A PAGE FROM DICKENS'S MANUSCRIPT, SHOWING THE TRIAL-AND-ERROR CHARACTER OF HIS THINKING WHILE AT WORK ON *A Christmas Carol*

And now, an inventor:

With few exceptions my inventions have been cold-blooded attempts to solve a problem presented in the course of my business. The first step is to give this problem and the proposed methods of meeting it a ruthless "third degree."

Scientific Explanations. We must keep our feet on *terra firma* in other respects. In a paragraph above three characteristics of the extreme forms of inspiration have been set forth. Let us have another look at these from our psychological background.

The "hunch" or inspiration may come suddenly, we said. For this phenomenon we should be prepared. In several places in the survey made in this book (especially the treatments of Learning and of Perception) our attention has been caught by the sudden-ness with which many an insight is gained. This sudden acquisition of insight is shown in the imagining or verbal formulating of absent objects just as it is in the perception of physically present objects.

Again, we said that the happy suggestion frequently bobs up when one is not consciously occupied with the problem but is doing anything else, or nothing at all. Now, we have seen in our treatment of Memory that successful recall is dependent upon an absence of interfering associations set up by excessive concentration on the recalling. Again, the experience of everyone that he is "fresher" in the morning is explainable by a lapsing of the thought-sets of the night before which had been keeping his thinking too "determined." In states of relaxation, and notoriously in dreams, the removal of prosaic and sober inhibitions is witnessed by a re-freshing freedom of one's fancy.

Thirdly, we remarked the apparent independence of the inspira-tion of the subject himself. He is, it often seems, quite passive; and the idea enters as if from without — as if from a Muse. It need only be urged: who has the inspiration? Coleridge's dream-delivered "Kubla Khan" came to Coleridge, not to Newton nor Wagner nor Whitman; and indeed the sources of that remarkable poem have been traced back by thorough research to twenty-five years of his reading and travel experiences [14]. Similarly, the physician does not experience insights into legal tangles nor the lawyer into engineering projects. Inspirations, in fine, come from the thinker himself.

One further consideration now seems demanded. How is it possible that the relevant idea should come when the thinker is not consciously thinking about the matter at all? Such a question, however, could be asked only by one who had not been with us in the treatment of many points and topics throughout the present book. It has been shown often that performance — whether of overt muscular, of verbal, or of thinking order — appears at the appropriate time without any specific beckoning. A suddenly demanded act of dodging a missile, a response on a word-association test, a recall of appropriate answers to a quiz — these, so far as the subject's awareness is concerned, just appear. And, as in the final emergence, so in the incubation: rational processes commonly go on without the person's being aware of them.

SUMMARY

A Definition of Thinking. If we gather together salient points that have appeared in various sections of this chapter, we are ready to formulate a statement of what "thinking" is. With slight modification of the wording we will find the definition furnished in Warren's *Dictionary of Psychology* a succinct summary of much of our treatment. When a person is thinking, it reads in substance, he is following *a course of ideational activity, symbolic in character, initiated by a problem or task he is facing, showing some trial-and-error but under the directing influence of his problem-set, and leading ultimately to a conclusion or solution.* We add a point or two. His *ideational activities are ways of symbolizing or formulating generalizations of his past experiences (concepts)* which, by furnishing *more adequate ways of viewing the situation as a whole,* further a more appropriate way of responding to it. His thinking is best understood as a *direct outgrowth of his intercommunications with others and his soliloquies,* only that now he is *stimulating and responding to himself in an implicit manner.*

When we consider the enormous economy of effort and of life and the enormous increase in precision that thoughtful behavior affords, we are prepared to believe that thinking is indeed "the most powerful tool for progress that humanity possesses."

REFERENCES

1. Betts, G. H. The Distribution and Functions of Mental Imagery. *Teach. Coll. Contribs. to Educ.,* 1909, No. 26.
2. Bowers, H. The Rôle of Visual Imagery in Reasoning. *Brit. J. Psychol.,* 1935, **25,** 436–46.
3. Dewey, J. *How We Think.* Heath, 1910.

4. Downey, J. *Creative Imagination.* Harcourt, Brace, 1929.

5. English, H. B. *A Student's Dictionary of Psychological Terms.* Harpers, 1934.

6. Fearing, F. The Experimental Study of Attitude, Meaning, etc. *Methods in Social Science.* Univ. Chicago Press, 1931.

7. Galton, F. *Inquiries into Human Faculty.* Dutton, 1883.

8. Heidbreder, E. An Experimental Study of Thinking. *Arch. Psychol.,* 1924, No. 73.

9. Hull, C. L. Quantitative Aspects of the Evolution of Concepts. *Psychol. Monog.,* 1920, **28,** No. 123.

10. Hunter, W. S. The Delayed Reaction in Animals and Children. *Beh. Monog.,* 1912, **2,** No. 6.

11. Hunter, W. S. The Delayed Reaction in a Child. *Psychol. Rev.,* 1917, **24,** 74–87.

12. Hutchinson, E. D. Materials for the Study of Creative Thinking. *Psychol. Bull.,* 1931, **28,** 392–410.

13. Jacobson, E. Electrophysiology of Mental Activities. *Am. J. Psychol.,* 1932, **44,** 677–94. Electrical Measurements of Neuromuscular States During Mental Activities. *Am. J. Physiol.,* 1930, **91,** 567–608; **94,** 22–34; **95,** 694–712; **95,** 703–12; 1931, **96,** 115–21; **96,** 122–25; **97,** 200–09.

14. Lowes, J. L. *The Road to Xanadu.* Houghton Mifflin, 1927.

15. Maier, N. R. F. Reasoning in Children. *J. Comp. Psychol.,* 1936, **21,** 357–66.

16. Maier, N. R. F. Reasoning in Humans. *J. Comp. Psychol.,* 1930, **10,** 115–243; 1931, **12,** 181–94.

17. Maier, N. R. F. Reasoning in White Rats. *Comp. Psychol. Monog.,* 1929, **6,** No. 29.

18. Marbe, K. *Experimentell-psychologische Untersuchungen über das Urteil.* Leipzig; Engelmann, 1901.

19. Max, L. W. An Experimental Study of the Motor Theory of Consciousness: III. *J. Comp. Psychol.,* 1935, **19,** 469–86.

20. Platt, W., and Baker, R. A. The Relation of the Scientific Hunch to Research. *J. Chem. Educ.,* 1931, **8,** Pt. 2, 1969–2002.

21. Rossman, J. *The Psychology of the Inventor.* Inventors Publ. Co., 1931.

22. Titchener, E. B. *Lectures on the Experimental Psychology of the Thought Processes.* Macmillan, 1909.

23. Watt, H. J. Experimentelle Beiträge zu einer Theorie des Denkens. *Arch. f. d. ges. Psychol.,* 1905, **4,** 283–436.

24. Wilkins, M. C. The Effect of Changed Material on Ability to Do Formal Syllogistic Reasoning. *Arch. Psychol.,* 1928, **16,** No. 102.

25. Woodworth, Robert S., and Sells, Saul B. An Atmosphere Effect in Formal Syllogistic Reasoning. *J. Exper. Psychol.,* 1935, **18,** 451–60.

26. Yerkes, R. M. Methods of Exhibiting Reactive Tendencies Characteristic of Ontogenetic and Phylogenetic Stages. *J. Anim. Beh.,* 1917, **7,** 11–28.

CHAPTER XX

PERSONALITY

PERSONALITY DEFINED

Man-as-a-Whole. We must return to the view of man-as-a-whole with which we started. In the course of our survey we have from time to time watched him from one angle and then from another, and each time we took first a general view then made a closer examination. Frequently we have had warning that each of these partial views was itself an abstraction from the rich dynamic facts of organismic behavior. We have been frequently reminded that man's behavior arises from the interlocking interdependence of functions that makes of a person not a set of organs but one organism, and not an assortment of acts but an active life.

Man Viewed Socially. The term "personality" has a further connotation. It refers to the ways in which a man-as-a-whole presents himself to his fellow men. The word seems to have derived from the Latin "persona," meaning the actor's mask which was chosen and worn to indicate the character that was to be played. (The same root word survives in the *"dramatis personae"* on one's theater program.) Hence "personality" may be taken to refer to the rôle one plays in life's drama, in which "all the world's a stage, and all its men and women merely players." The mask had a double importance. It indicated the type of conduct that might be expected from the actor. It also served as a stimulus to other actors. Accordingly, it is interesting to find that "personality" involves the full duality of meaning for a psychological fact; it is that which characterizes a person as both a socially reactive and a socially stimulating agency.

This social meaning of personality has warrant in its popular usages. When asked for a letter about X's personality, an acquaintance of his is likely to write somewhat after the following fashion: that X is co-operative, truthful, optimistic, a bit impulsive in his movements, prone to snap judgments, can "take criticism standing up," is a driver of himself as well as of others, "catches on" quickly, is well informed in a general way, makes a rather clean-cut appearance, and is a little diffident in his address. All of this has become apparent in his past relations to other people about him, and is prognostic of his future relations toward people he may meet. It is true that not every one of these characteristics is developed originally in social settings nor is every one manifested only in such settings, but each characteristic derives its significant and useful meaning when applied to his life and dealings with his fellow men.

Conception of Man as Behaving Consistently. Throughout all the uses of the term "personality," whether technical or popular, there runs one kind of logical assumption: that there is some degree of consistency in his conduct and thinking. This is the really empirical and investigable expression of the semimystical notion of a personality as something that diffuses through and permeates all that a man does, and that is revealed by degrees through his actions and his words.

This consistency is expected of one whether he be looked at cross-sectionally or longitudinally. After he has been observed to act thus and so under a few sets of circumstances, his acquaintances entertain fairly definite expectations of him when they find him under a new set of circumstances, so that if he fails to fit the expectation they are taken by surprise. "I wouldn't have expected that of him," is the way their surprise is often phrased. But the man is also supposed to be much the same sort of individual he was two years ago, or as we knew him to be when a child. A core of continuity is expected to be maintained through the changes of his growth and his experiences. "He isn't the fellow he used to be" is a verbal expression of bewilderment on the part of his fellow-man that illustrates this point in a negative way.

A man's personality, we may conclude, *is the total picture of his organized behavior, especially as it can be characterized by his fellow men in a consistent way.*

THE PROBLEM OF PERSONALITY TYPES

The Problem Stated. A first expression of interest in any subject-matter appears in attempts to classify it. So, both technically and popularly, the classification of human beings is as old as any intelligent interest in understanding them at all. It is a device of very great economy, for if one can say that the liquid in this bottle belongs to the class, H_2SO_4, he can predict its action on other solids and liquids and hence has control of it. It might be supposed, analogously, that if one could determine the class or type to which Mr. John Doe belongs, he then could proceed with complete assurance to treat him and talk to him according to the detailed characteristics of that type. He is a Republican, let us say; therefore he is sure to have this very attitude on the sugar tariff and that very one on higher taxation of surplus corporation profits. Or, he is a man slow to anger; therefore we can rest assured that he wouldn't threaten a harmlessly barking dog any more than he would reprimand a dilatory restaurant waiter. And so the process goes on: upon observing certain bits of A's behavior we assign him to a class; then we deduce from that class what his other actions and attitudes are likely to be.

We must recognize the fact that in many of its applications to human beings this logic is fraught with grave dangers. Efforts to divide human beings into a set number of neatly divided piles are reminiscent of that express agent who tried to fit the subleties of biological nature into the few swivel-chair classifications in the tariff schedule of his company. He was overheard to remark: "Now, let's see: cats is 'dogs' and guinea pigs is 'dogs,' but I suppose this here turtle must be an 'insect.'"

It will clarify the issue if we look at the question statistically. In Chapter XI we saw that in nearly all psychological dimensions, the individuals of any large, normal, unselected population distribute themselves in a quantitative way represented by various approximations to the so-called Gaussian curve. But now if a population is really divisible into, say, two types with respect of a given psychological trait, then the curve of distribution will be bimodal. This is shown in Figure 145.

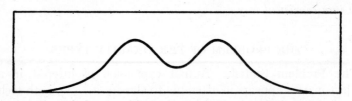

FIGURE 145. BIMODAL DISTRIBUTION CHARACTERISTIC OF A POPULATION ASSUMED TO CONTAIN TWO TYPES OF PEOPLE

Compare with the normal distributions in Figure 75, page 293.

But before going further into questions of logic and methodology let us look at certain typological systems.

Kretschmer: Morphological Types.   In 1921 the German psychiatrist Kretschmer set forth the claim that by determining certain indices of the bodily dimensions of a person we can assign him to a certain physical type and then safely conclude therefrom as to his general temperamental makeup. He classed his patients into two original types: the *pyknic*, displaying a broad head, a long trunk and short legs, narrow shoulders and broad hips, and abundant flesh; and the *asthenic*, having a long head, a short trunk and long legs, narrow shoulders and hips, and very little fat.   A sub-group of the asthenic he named the *athletic*, with a fairly long head, more symmetrical development of trunk and legs, broad shoulders and narrow hips, and much muscle; and then it was found necessary to have a *dysplastic* type, including cases not fitting into any of the three mentioned.   Kretschmer's classification started from observations he had made on his psychotic patients.

On the psychological side he emphasized the difference between the first two especially.   The long slender asthenics were those patients who were inclined to seclusiveness, to withdrawing into themselves.   The rotund pyknics were those more inclined to the emotional ups and downs — alternating in a circular way between being on the heights and in the depths.   The former is an outstanding mark of a type of psychosis (insanity) we shall present later as dementia praecox; the latter, of manic-depressive psychosis. It is true that a few psychiatrists have found their patients falling into Kretschmer's types according as they reveal one or another condition of behavior disorder.   In normal unselected populations, however, no success has attended efforts to find clear divisions as demanded by the theory. This is in spite of the fact that popular impressions support this assumption, as when Shakespeare has Caesar say:

> 'Let me have men about me that are fat,
> Sleek-headed men and such as sleep o' nights.
> Yond Cassius has a lean and hungry look,
> He thinks too much: such men are dangerous."

Jung: Introversion-Extroversion Types.   Quite the best known of modern typologies is that of the Swiss psychiatrist Jung, who suggested that men can be classed as either *extroverts or introverts*. The former are those whose interests are directed mostly toward the world about them, especially social life and activities broadly speaking; while the introverts are interested more in themselves and their own emotional experiences and trains of thinking.   The former are more objectively interested, we might say, the latter more subjectively.   The contrast is somewhat that which is implied by the words "the man of action" and "the man of thought."

One will find a fair amount of agreement among psychologists that there is some such distinction between personalities as suggested by Jung's terms, though different psychologists differ in their emphases. Some emphasize the direction of a person's interest, some the expressing or the inhibiting of his emotions, and others the amount of his social participation. There are a half-dozen tests of introversion-extroversion in the field gotten up by assembling questions that were supposed in advance to be differentiating; but results of their use have been disappointing, for in only one study has there been a trace of bimodality found in the distributions of the individuals examined. The individuals do not seem to fall neatly into the two types.

It would seem easy to classify some historic characters: the Roosevelts, Napoleons, and Elizabeths would fall clearly into a different pile from that in which the Kants, Darwins, Poes, and MacDowells would be found; yet where would be placed the Jeffersons, Franklins, Lincolns, and perhaps the majority of geniuses as well as common folk? A middle class of "ambiverts" has become a recognized necessity, to include those who fall somewhere between the extremes. This class turns out to be so much the largest that when all data are thrown together no bimodality in the population appears. The types as distinct types vanish. This fact appears clearly in the results of a typical study as furnished in the accompanying table.

A DISTRIBUTION OF COLLEGE STUDENTS RESULTING FROM AN APPLICATION OF A TEST FOR INTROVERSION-EXTROVERSION [1]

CLASS INTERVALS OF SCORE		FREQUENCY
20	24 (highly introverted)	1
15	19	7
10	14	14
5	9	31
0	4	62
−1	−5	70
−6	−10	108
−11	−15	85
−16	−20	106
−21	−25	66
−26	−30	35
−31	−35	9
−36	−40	5
−41	−45 (highly extroverted)	1

$N = 600$ cases

[1] From Heidbreder, E. Measuring Introversion and Extroversion. *J. Abn. & Soc. Psychol.*, 1926, 21, 124.

Jung himself, by the way, had been driven to the setting up of sub-types under each of his two main types.   From different considerations, other reinterpretations have been suggested.   Statistical (factor) analyses have been made of the question-items selected as the best ones from a number of different introversion-extroversion tests.   These have been tried out on new subjects, and the conclusion has been that such tests get at not a single personality-factor to be called introversion-extroversion but a list of as many as eighteen different factors.[1]   Most important of these were: (*a*) a tendency to shrink from the environment, (*b*) an emotional sensitiveness to the environment, (*c*) impulsiveness, and (*d*) interest in oneself [12].
Some sample items used in the test were:

Do you prefer to work with others rather than alone?   (Yes — No)
Do you like to speak in public?
Are your feelings rather easily hurt?
Have you ever kept a personal diary of your own accord?
Do you like to confide in others?
Do you like work which requires considerable attention to details?
Do you like to change from one type of work to another frequently?

What is the general upshot of these critical attempts to make use of Jung's psychological types?   If, as someone has facetiously remarked, "there are two types of people in the world, those who divide everybody into types and those who do not," then we are clearly warned not to enroll ourselves among those of the former brotherhood.   Instead of abstracting some attribute of human nature and then dividing people into two groups as being fundamentally marked and determined throughout their behavior by presence or absence of that character, the part of wisdom is to inquire whether the abstracted attribute *is descriptive of this or that reaction* of Mr. *X*, and *in what degree*.

This is the treatment more generally accorded "introversion-extroversion" by critical psychologists in America today.   It is a way of describing simply one trend-in-behavior, one trait.

Restatement of the Problem of Types; Conclusion. From our survey of some well-known examples, we should be able to see now two underlying assumptions in a type-theory of human personalities.

(1) One is that there is *a certain especially revealing key trait* or characteristic which is so central and basic in the organization of

[1] For this term see above, pp. 305 ff.

any man-as-a-whole that once we know John Doe in that trait, we will know him in all.   Something like this kind of thinking is familiar enough to us: Alexander's ambition, Jesus' humility, Washington's sagacity, Lincoln's humanitarianism, Theodore Roosevelt's strenuousness.   These are one-trait characterizations that, like thumbnail sketches, serve as complete portraits.   And, for an analogy, any cartoonist shows amusing ability in spotting and playing up a facial detail that when exaggerated seems to identify his character more patly than all the rest of his features taken together.   These, of course, are not perfect parallels of typology, for the salient item is not systematically used for all subjects: they are not all classified, for example, as ambitious-unambitious.

(2) The other underlying assumption in a typology is that with respect to the key trait mentioned, individual *persons will tend to fall into more or less distinct groups* (types).   Even when more than two types are included in the scheme each type is differentiated from each other type by the either-or dichotomy in respect to at least one characteristic.

This way of thinking, too, is familiar enough.   Morally people are good or bad; modernistic interiors are beautiful or ugly; lamb chops are expensive or cheap; this book is interesting or dull.   It seems to require discipline for us to learn to judge and describe in degrees and gradations.

Now, how are these two assumptions of a typology to be tested?   (1) The first assumption calls for verification as follows.   If a particular trait is claimed to be a key to the whole individual, then the claim must stand up against examination into interrelations of the trait with other traits and patterns of traits.   Is it found to hang together with them so frequently as to furnish presumption of a causal interconnection with other traits?   We can best take up this kind of investigation in our following section.   (2) The second assumption of a typology demands checking to determine whether in empirically studied populations the individuals do as a matter of fact fall into distinct groups.   We have already had the answer hinted: bimodal distributions have practically never been found except in some cases of psychotic patients who were studied under clinical conditions that fell short of full experimental controls. *What are offered as the names of types of whole personalities might better be considered as names for extremes of particular traits or variables.*

The German-Swiss Non-Statistical View.   It is only fair that the theoretical background for much of the typological psychology be at least acknowledged.   The statistical considerations we have been urging would be styled typically American by the major proportion of German and Swiss psychologists and psychiatrists. From their viewpoint the fruitful way to investigate personality lies in the intensive examination of a very few individual subjects so as to determine the general pattern or style of behavior for each.   We dare not hastily decry this claim.   We have seen in our study of Perceiving that the adequate recognition and appreciation of a given thing, person, or situation, is often achieved through abrupt insight.   Perception is a configural performance.   So, it is claimed, a true understanding of another person is not obtained by mechanically adding up his scores on a number of tests.   You must get him as you would a picture or a tune — as a unique unity.   This is sound enough.   One important reminder, however, is in point.   Consider the clinical practitioner in psychology and in medicine: he must size up and understand each of his patients in just this way; but it must be remembered that he has not become a skillful practitioner by merely exercising hunches through the years.   On the contrary, he has gone and continues to go through rigorous training in the details of symptoms and the details of processes.   In essentially similar manner, we must say that skill in grasping the meaning of whole arrays of the manifestations of an individual's personality is not furthered by looking at the whole man only.

Illustrated in the Rorschach Ink-Blot Test.   This qualitative and subjective approach to the understanding of the personality is well shown in a test that is showing surprising promise as a diagnostic aid.   Everyone knows how an irregular mass like a cloud or a blot of ink on paper may be perceived in an inexhaustible variety of ways.   Printed ink blots have long been used in a modest way in psychological laboratories as a method of studying perception.   But it was the Swiss psychiatrist Rorschach who saw also that many of the profounder characteristics of his patients were revealed by their manners of "seeing" such objects.   He devised a standardized set of ten blots, some in black and gray, some with colors added; and he worked out an elaborate scoring method for tabulating the different ways in which different patients responded to the test.   He checked these with the case histories, and announced close agreements.

In administering the test the experimenter characterizes in four principal respects the way in which the subject looks at each blot: (1) Does he regard it as-a-whole or does he see details primarily?   (2) Is his way of regarding it determined more by its form, by its arousal of kinesthesis, or by its color?

(3) As to content, does he note animals, human beings, plants, non-living objects, or landscapes? (4) Are the responses original or common? This looks at first like a simple recording process. But under each of the heads are subdivisions and weightings; and all the data are placed in a special tabular form. The clinician is supposed to inspect this carefully. He is *not* to add up the results or to treat them otherwise quantitatively. He is to inspect the results much as he would a picture, and from the inspection he is to get the true picture of the subject as a unified personality — his emotional temperament, his expressive movements, interests, talents, occupational tendencies, and even his philosophy of life. That is quite a broad claim! The Rorschach test is found to be extremely useful to the clinician, but throughout it is thoroughly inexact and its administration is an unstandardized art [32].

THE PROBLEM OF PERSONALITY TRAITS

A Sample Trait: Ascendance-Submission. As was stated above, what have been offered as names of whole personality types are better considered as names of particular characteristics that vary from individual to individual, that is, personality variables or traits. In this way, Jung's "introversion-extroversion," for instance, is reinterpreted as just *one aspect of their behavior in which people differ from each other in a continuous way.* For further classification of the matter let us now use another trait study.

When people meet, what often happens is that certain ones come to play the more dominant rôle while the others play the more submissive. Is this characteristic of dominating (ascendance) or following (submission) one single general and consistent fact about an individual? The same girl who had been a belle and dictator of her "crowd" in a small town, when trying to hold down a minor job in New York astonished an old friend by her timorous manners and subdued speech. One and the same man bosses his section gang, is no hand at disciplining his children, may be ready on occasion to offer ideas to his own boss, and is dutifully respectful to the priest. In animal behavior the same thing is observed. As was noted in Chapter XVII, a hen A might be able regularly to peck hen B with impunity, and B peck C, but A might be unable to peck C. From such instances we are prepared to find that a trait like ascendance-submission is a fairly specific thing. That is, an individual is ascendant, say, not in all situations but only in certain ones; and when he is called by either term it must mean that the degrees of ascendance and of submission he has displayed in many personal situations have been averaged and have been found over-balanced in one direction or the other. A verbal approximation to this has been constructed by G. W. and F. H. Allport [1]. A number of specific and real situations from everyday life are described, and the subject is instructed to indicate what his usual behavior in such situations would be. The following items are fair samples:

1. At church, a lecture, or an entertainment, if you arrive after the program has commenced and find that there are people standing but also that there are front seats available which might be secured without "piggishness" or discourtesy, but with considerable conspicuousness, do you take the seats?

Habitually.............
Occasionally............
Never................

2. When you see someone in a public place or crowd whom you think you have met or known, do you inquire of him whether you have met before?

Sometimes.............
Rarely................
Never................

This test and a revision of it [4] have turned out to be distinctly useful in vocational guidance, employment, and personnel work generally. A distribution of scores on this test is shown in Figure 146.

The Questionnaire-Inventory Method. Emotional Stability. After America had entered the World War a questionnaire was drawn up by Woodworth for the purpose of diagnosing the ability of individual soldiers to withstand the stress and strain of life in military camp and trenches. This "psychoneurotic inventory," as it has come to be known, was built up after a scrutiny of the many kinds of symptoms shown by soldiers who had had difficulty in adjusting themselves to their trying conditions. Some sample items will reveal the nature of the test.

Do you have nightmares?	Yes	No
Do ideas run through your head so that you cannot sleep?	Yes	No
Have your employers generally treated you right?	Yes	No
Are you ever bothered by a feeling that things are not real?	Yes	No
Can you do good work while people are looking on?	Yes	No
Did you ever have the habit of biting your fingernails?	Yes	No
Do you feel sad or low-spirited most of the time?	Yes	No
Did you ever have dyspepsia?	Yes	No
Has any of your family been a drunkard?	Yes	No

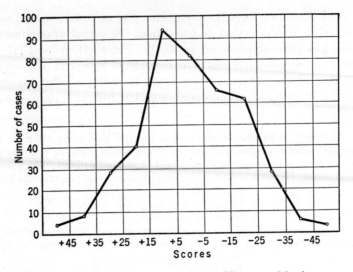

FIGURE 146. DISTRIBUTION OF 400 CASES (COLLEGE MEN) ON THE
ASCENDANCE-SUBMISSION TEST

Note the unimodal distribution resembling the Gaussian curve.
(From Allport, G. W. *J. Abn. and Soc. Psychol.*, 1928, **23**, 129.)

Simple and superficial as such questions may strike the reader, when adequately administered they are penetrating.

In the history of methods for the preliminary study of an individual or a group for possible neurotic conditions, the Woodworth test is a milestone. There have been revisions of it arranged for children, for juvenile delinquents, for college students, and others; and its usefulness as a general method is attested by the fact that several adaptations have been made in the form of other inventories that have proved to be highly useful.

One of these is Thurstone's [31] for the detection of incipient neurotic conditions in college freshmen. It may be of some interest to the reader to know that at the time of its first application to freshmen entering the University of Chicago some group differences appeared. More neurotic average scores were obtained by the non-fraternity-pledges than by pledges, by the women than by the men, and by students of better scholarship than by those of poorer; and very slightly greater scores were made by the Jewish students.

Another much used adaptation of the inventory form is that of Bernreuter. He arranged four ways of scoring the answers on his sheets in order to bring to light six different personality-variables: (1) neurotic tendency, (2) self-sufficiency, (3) introversion-extroversion, (4) dominance-submission, (5) self-confidence, and (6) sociability. Here is an interesting feature. When scored in different "directions" by applying different sets of grades or "weights," one and the same set of answers yields information on six different personality variables. This fact is interesting evidence that the variables or traits are *not different sections or compartments* of the individual but are *different ways of looking at each behavior-act* as it bears on the individual's adjustments.

The Rating Scale Method. The Personal Inventory technique calls, as we have seen, for statements about himself by the person in question. It is peculiarly valuable for eliciting statements from the persons themselves about facts not otherwise obtainable concerning their implicit and subjective processes, such as feelings of unreality, dreams, worries. Another technique has been elaborated for obtaining data on how a person comports himself in relation to his fellows, the Rating Scale. The information is gathered from his acquaintances in a standardized manner; hence it is concerned not with what he says he does, but with what others say he does. Rating scales have been much exploited in several practical fields: in the Army for getting information about officers, in industrial and commercial firms for the selection and study of employees, in teachers' and other employment bureaus for fitting square pegs to square holes, on college campuses for assisting the individual student to meet his problems. In the later scales there is a clear shift from trait-names and trait-descriptions to particular types of behavior that are described more in verbs than in adjectives: it is *what the individual observably does* that is wanted, not inferences as to what qualities he possesses. For another thing, there is increasing emphasis upon *quantifying* the statements, putting them into degrees. In the scale reproduced on the following page both these advances are shown, along with another device of considerable importance. That is the "behaviorgram," or supporting instances in the nature of *narratives of fact*, which, aside from their importance as data on the record are highly important in focussing the attention of the rater upon actual behavior-in-situations [7].

Simple and easy as such an instrument at first appears, the rating scale requires trained skill and much judgment in the original construction; the raters, too, need to exercise great care, not to rate good friends unduly high and not to let their general impressions of the person prejudice their judgments on particular questions (the "halo effect").

The Life-Situation Test Method. Honesty. Of course, as we have remarked before, the ideal method of surveying a personality

Name of student..................................

A. How are you and others affected by his appearance and manner?

Avoided by others	Tolerated by others	Liked by others	Well liked by others	Sought by others	No opportunity to observe

Please record here instances that support your judgment.

B. Does he need constant prodding or does he go ahead with his work without being told?

Needs much prodding in doing ordinary assignments	Needs occasional prodding	Does ordinary assignments of his own accord	Completes suggested supplementary work	Seeks and sets for himself additional tasks

Please record here instances that support your judgment.

C. Does he get others to do what he wishes?

Probably unable to lead his fellows	Lets others take lead	Sometimes leads in minor affairs	Sometimes leads in important affairs	Displays marked ability to lead his fellows; makes things go

Please record here instances that support your judgment.

D. How does he control his emotions?

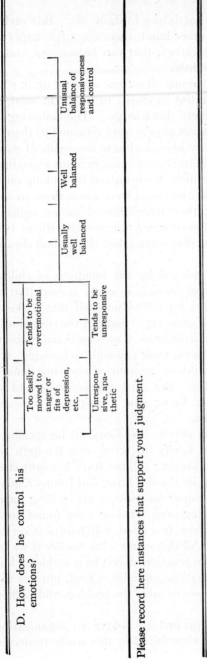

Too easily moved to anger or fits of depression, etc.	Tends to be overemotional	Usually well balanced	Well balanced	Unusual balance of responsiveness and control
Unresponsive, apathetic	Tends to be unresponsive			

Please record here instances that support your judgment.

E. Has he a program with definite purposes in terms of which he distributes his time and energy?

Aimless trifler	Aims just to "get by"	Has vaguely formed objectives	Directs energies effectively with fairly definite program	Engrossed in realizing well-formulated objectives

Please record here instances that support your judgment.

would be to record his actual activities in daily life.   But such an ideal is impossible.   On the other hand, there are a few important classes of human behavior-situations that can be *sampled*, such as honest behavior in school children.

In one series of studies [14] actual situations were set up in which children were given opportunities to cheat, to lie, or to steal, apparently without the examiners' knowledge.   The following are examples.   The children's answer papers were returned to them for (apparently original) scoring by keys, and note was made of papers handed in the second time with improved answers; some exceedingly difficult puzzles that could be dishonestly solved by looking on the bottom or by lifting pieces off the board were given them to solve in a quite insufficient time; they were allowed to use coins for counters in puzzles, these to be returned apparently without being counted by the experimenters; they were asked if they had cheated, etc.

The amount of honesty displayed by the hundreds of children tested varied with a number of factors, so many indeed that the distribution of the total scores for individuals fell into a skewed Gaussian form, as appears in Figure 147.   Some of the contributing factors were: The children's intelligence, their emotional stability, occupational level of their fathers, their cultural background, relationship of teachers to the children, amount of cheating done by their friends and by classmates.   But such correlations are of less significance to us if we want to know what a trait like "honesty" *is* than are two other outcomes.

(1) Honesty or its opposite, deceit, was found to be specific to the situation.   John X might falsify his score on a strength test but not for a moment think of keeping a dime; Ruth Y might cheat on her arithmetic paper but not lie about it later; and Jimmy Z might even cheat on his arithmetic paper but not on his spelling paper. The motives for cheating, lying, and stealing were found to be certainly complex.   Most children, in a word, will deceive in certain situations and not in others.   All this seems a bit simpler if we but bear in mind that when a person practices deceit he is making a kind of adjustment to a difficult situation; an indirect kind, but one that in his limited experience promises to solve the problem and perhaps has solved it in the past.

(2) Those children who happened to belong to organizations purporting to teach character were found in this study to deceive

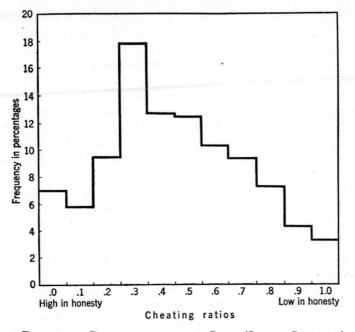

FIGURE 147. DISTRIBUTION OF 2443 CASES (SCHOOL CHILDREN)
ON HONESTY TESTS

The cheating ratio = the ratio between the number of cheatings and the chances to cheat. Each child was measured on ten tests.   (Based on data from Hartshorne and May.   From Jones, V., *Children's Morals*, *Handbook of Child Psychology*.   Clark Univ. Press, 1933.)

about as often as those who did not belong.   Those attending Sunday school regularly cheated about as much as those rarely or never attending.   It is clear from this drift in the data that verbal training by precept and maxim had had little or no effect on overt conduct; and that if we seek to train a child in honesty we must train him to honest ways.

This brings us to a central problem as to the constitution of personality.   Is a trait only a characteristic that we find we can apply to several of a person's acts, or can it be reasonably thought of as some sort of more general determiner of conduct?   Some have held to the former notion.   But these investigators were working on children.   Accordingly, (1) the specificity of "honesty" — its holding only for specific behavior-situations — may be reinterpreted as due to the immaturity of the subjects: they had not surmounted the plateau (cf. p. 407) where such specific habits get combined into

more inclusive forms of response.   The immaturity of the children
may furnish a key also to (2) the discrepancy between honest words
and honest actions.   With it is bound up the persistent problem of
verbalism in training in any line, and the downright necessity of
training verbal and performance reactions together, so that the
one will link up with and control the other.

Personality Traits as Hierarchical and Often Dynamic.   There
need be no mystery at all about the notion of broader traits which
function as determiners of particular kinds of conduct.   Consider
some pertinent facts already included in our survey of general
psychology.   In our chapter on the Bases of Motivation we have
seen that a person may be possessed of attitudes toward very general
public problems which determine how he responds to more specific
statements of opinion.   In our treatment of Postural Responses
we have noted the way particular forms of response are directed in
large part by the way a person happens to be set.   In our chapter on
Learning we have seen how even overt motor performances like
operating a typewriter depend upon a hierarchical organization of
skills in which more inclusive higher-level habits dominate and
partially determine lower-level habits.   In the treatment of Perceiving we have noted that the way a person regards details of
objects, words, and other things is subject to the influence of how
he regards the total pattern.

In the same way, we may seriously consider personality trait-
names as not merely descriptive categories, convenient adjectives,
but as referring to (A) actual *stages in the integrative organization
of a person's behavior-tendencies.*   Moreover, while the trait-names
often refer primarily to *abilities*, they may also be names for (B)
*active determining factors in behavior which play dynamic rather than
purely static rôles.*   We now take up convincing illustrations of these
points.   The hierarchical nature of human character and how it is
constituted of behavior tendencies of more-inclusive and less-
inclusive scope (A) is to be illustrated in the following pages by the
trait of masculinity-femininity.   The highly dynamic and determining nature of much of a person's organization (B) is then to be illustrated by personal attitudes toward the values of life.

Masculinity-Femininity.   Up to the present, the picture of the
typically masculine or the typically feminine individual has been
constructed principally by novelists and parlor conversationalists.
It has been enormously oversimplified and stereotyped by motion-

picture directors.   Only today have we at hand a scientifically constructed instrument for measurement of differences between the sexes.   And only in recent times has any data on the subject been gained from small populations.   Terman and Miles assembled thousands of test items and tried them out on men and women groups.   Those items reacted to in one way predominantly by the one or by the other sex were retained and then organized into a test. This is made up of several exercises, most of which are in their general character familiar to the reader: questions on interests, questions on judgments of right and wrong, word-associations, and so on.   Evidence that the test is based upon genuine differences in men and women is presented in the accompanying table, where it can be seen that in their test scores the men and the women groups show very little overlapping.

We are now moved to ask: What other characteristics, if any, were found peculiar to the one or the other sex?   Is the M–F score dependent upon an isolated trait or is it tied up with other traits? After the test had been applied to many groups of people along with standard tests of other traits, some generalizations emerged.   Masculinity was found correlated with scores for extroversion, femininity with introversion, especially in college men.   High-scholarship men were more feminine, low-scholarship men more masculine.   Some interesting occupational differences suggest the value of this test for vocational prognosis, as for instance in the cases of engineers who made high masculinity scores, and of office workers who made high femininity scores.   One of the most definite trends was that associated with age: through childhood and early teens both sexes make more M scores, then throughout maturity steadily increasing F scores.

The males evinced a distinctive interest in exploit and adventure, in outdoor and physically strenuous occupations, in machinery and tools, and in business and commerce.   On the other hand, the females of our groups evinced a distinctive interest in domestic affairs and in esthetic objects and occupations, as well as occupations more directly ministrative, particularly to the young, the helpless, the distressed.   The males directly or indirectly manifested the greater self-assertion and aggressiveness, and more roughness of manners, language, and sentiments.   The females expressed themselves as more compassionate and sympathetic, more timid, more fastidious and esthetically sensitive, more emotional in general (or

DISTRIBUTION OF SCORES ON THE M–F TEST*

SCORE \ SEX	MALE	FEMALE
+201–220		
+181–200	6	
+161–180	4	
+141–160	14	
+121–140	36	
+101–120	42	
+ 81–100	72	
+ 61– 80	95	
+ 41– 60	101	5
+ 21– 40	78	18
+ 1– 20	60	30
− 0– 19	51	50
− 20– 39	32	76
− 40– 59	6	104
− 60– 79	6	103
− 80– 99	1	117
−100–119		85
−120–139		58
−140–159		32
−160–179		12
−180–199		5
−200–219		1
N	604	696
M	+52.58	−70.65
S.D.	49.93	47.51
S.D.M	2.03	1.80

* From Terman, L. M., and Miles, C. C. *Sex and Personality.* McGraw-Hill, 1936.

High positive scores indicate extreme masculinity; high negative scores indicate extreme femininity.   The mean score for males is +52.58, and for females, −70.65.   The standard deviations are high; but even so, the ranges overlap but little.

at least more expressive of emotion), and they were severer moralists.

The authors conclude:

Masculinity and femininity are important aspects of human personality. They are not to be thought of as lending to it merely a superficial coloring and flavor; rather they are one of a small number of cores around which the structure of personality gradually takes shape.   The masculine-feminine contrast is probably as deeply grounded, whether by nature or by nurture, as any other which human temperament presents.

Valuing Attitudes. Certainly among the most important factors in the organization of a man's character and personality are his interests and values. His standard of values has probably more to do with how he is regarded by his fellows and where he finds his friends than have any of the personality traits we have so far considered. In the history of human culture the primitive acceptance-rejection acts and attitudes toward "good" and "bad" in vague and general ways have come to be differentiated reactions to situations as ethically good or bad, esthetically good or bad (beautiful or ugly), intellectually good or bad (true or false), economically good or bad, and so forth. Different human societies have been marked by the preponderance of some of these classes: the esthetic and intellectual in Athenian Greece, the political in Rome, the religious in mediaeval Europe, the economic and political in modern Europe, the ethical in Scottish and other Northern peoples, and so on. Individual men, too, are marked in history quite as much by their major values as in any other way.

This many-sidedness of the evaluating attitude of man reveals itself in another way. When looking at a wedding ring, for instance, one may regard it as made of fourteen-carat gold (theoretical or factual), as worth probably twenty-five dollars on the market (economic), as a badge of love and loyalty (social), as a symbol of rights and duties (political), as an emblem having sacred significance (religious), or as an object that with the modern engraving is more glittering than rings in the older style (esthetic).

A method has been designed [33] for determining the relative strength within an individual of these six classes of valuing attitudes.[1] It consists of questions to which answers are demanded, as in the two following illustrations with arbitrary answers written in.

The main object of scientific research should be the discovery of   (a)   (b)
pure truth rather than its practical applications.
(a) Yes; (b) No.   3   o
[answers numbered according to relative importance]
If you should marry do you prefer a wife who ——
    ..4..can achieve social prestige, commanding admiration from others;
    ..1..likes to stay home and keep house;
    ..2..is fundamentally spiritual in her attitude toward life;
    ..3..is gifted along artistic lines.
[answers numbered in order of preference]

---

[1] The scale was suggested by the classification by Spranger in his *Types of Men*, but does not follow his theoretical and speculative tenets.

This test has brought to light some interesting differences between sexes, between people of different occupations, between students at different colleges, and between students of differing cultural backgrounds; and it has checked well with tests of newspaper reading, with examinees' statements of qualities attributed to ideal persons, and their statements of qualities attributed to leaders [8].

Taken together, the results obtained with this test appear to demonstrate clearly that these six classes of values stand for attitudinal traits in a person which are *generalized dynamic dispositions* that direct the kinds of responses he is likely to make to varied situations in daily life.

PERSONALITY CONSISTENCY IN DEVELOPMENT

Do Individual Differences in Personality Remain Constant? Early in the present chapter it was said that the problem of human personality involves problems of man's consistency both in cross-section and longitudinally. We have devoted space in preceding sections to the former: let us turn to the latter.

In very many ways the problem of problems in human psychology is whether John Doe remains John Doe in the many aspects he presents to the world and remains consistently different from Richard Roe. All hopes of predicting what he can do or will do rest finally on that basis. All the structuring of social life — industrial, political, fraternal, religious, professional — presuppose a high minimum of stability in the day to day and year to year conduct and attitudes of individual people, so that each can "bank on" the other. (When an individual becomes too troublesomely variable and unpredictable he is likely to be rated "insane.")

Unfortunately, little scientific research has been done directly on this problem of *the consistency of individual differences through varying ages*; and we are quite on the pioneer border where everyday observations by the layman are the principal source of our opinions and impressions. It will be appropriate, therefore, for the present writer simply to indicate in what general directions the reader might first look if he should be interested in the topic.

In the exploitation of intelligence tests and the determination of I.Q.'s, a central assumption well supported by fact is that the intelligence differences between different children remain remarkably constant under fairly stable environmental circumstances (cf. *supra* pp. 353.)

Observations of the social activities of young children taken at intervals have tended to show some persistence of individual differences (cf. *supra* pp. 501 ff.), but perhaps not as much as we would have expected — owing probably to insufficient variety of situations in which the child's behavior was recorded [18].

The same can be said of their emotional responses when as infants they are subjected individually to the strangeness and the handling involved in measurement and test situations [3, 27]. Studies of twins, especially of identical twins, have emphasized the stability of individual traits (cf. *supra* pp. 66 ff.) [10].

Careful records of juvenile delinquents show a high percentage of them who, in spite of strong efforts at their reformation, become recidivists (repeaters), although environmental conditions do have demonstrable weight [11, 15].

An exhaustive study of geniuses shows that as a group they remain apart from the garden variety of human beings from childhood into maturity [28].

Studies of behavior in adolescents tend to show only limited consistency in their traits of ascendance-submission and extroversion-introversion [22, 25].

All in all, the popular assumption that individuals do remain characteristically different is likely to be borne out; but the evidences from scientifically controlled observations are meager and not consistent throughout. We are in the dark on one point especially: in which respects is it most true that "the child is father of the man" — in his intellectual, social, motor, or emotional traits, in traits of physique, or in his interests? The literature of general biography, of course, furnishes us inexhaustible materials, but with dishearteningly little information about all relevant contributing factors. Furthermore it entices the reader into the uncontrolled judgments so undesirably displayed by some psychoanalytic biographers. There is, also, some clinical material, in spite of the changing populations which prevent the same patient from being treated by the same consultant for any term of years. But where judgments are made on the basis of this clinical material, it suffers grievously in lack of adequate scientific safeguards on various counts.

CULTURAL DETERMINANTS OF PERSONALITY

The Principle Stated. We must admit the possibility that at least a fraction of the stability to be found in the organization of each individual is attributable to a stable environment in which he has been living. This carries us back to a previous question: what are the known effects of environmental controls on personality manifestations? If one's personality is, as we have defined it, a matter of his being both socially stimulating and socially reactive, it is reasonable to suppose that his social surroundings have had much to do with its building-up.

One way of schematizing this importance to the individual of his membership in social groups is that used in the new topological [1] psychology. (Consider Figure 148.) There the makeup of the two individuals is shown as determined in some degree by their membership in certain social groups. The author of the book from which Figure 148 is taken states at length that a person's pattern of traits is chiefly determined by the groups in which he has membership.

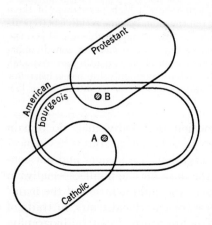

FIGURE 148. A TOPOLOGICAL REPRE-
SENTATION OF MEMBERSHIP IN
GROUPS AS DETERMINING PERSON-
ALITIES

Individuals *A* and *B*, by virtue of their membership in the groups *American* and *bourgeois*, would be similar in their attitudes and behavior; but by virtue of their membership in the *Catholic* and the *Protestant* groups, respectively, they would be different in their attitudes and behavior in many situations. (After Brown, J. F. *Psychology and the Social Order.* McGraw-Hill, 1936.)

Differential Effects of Divergent Cultures in New Guinea. The point just mentioned is being much emphasized by anthropologists today. Their view is clearly (if perhaps extremely) represented in a recent study on the primitive peoples on the island of New Guinea [21]. In the course of a two years' expedition to that island exhaustive observations had been made of three primitive tribes there, and brought to light what to the layman must be a most striking fact. The mountain-dwelling Arapesh people — both men and women — reveal a personality that may be called predominantly "feminine." Despite differences in occupation, both sexes are passive and unaggressive, co-operative and responsive to the needs of the young and the

---

[1] Topology is that branch of geometry which investigates the properties of figures which remain unchanged through continuous one-to-one transformations. Example: Suppose on a piece of rubber two dots be drawn one within and one without a circle, and the circle and both dots within a square; then regardless of how the rubber be stretched to distort the measurable relations, the general relationships (inclusion and the like) between dots, circle and square will remain unchanged.

weak, and are preoccupied with their personal affairs. For them, if life is an adventure it is an adventure in growing things — children, pigs, yams, cocoanuts. They are interested in faithfully and carefully tending their charges until happy retirement in middle age. The river-dwelling Mundugumor, in perfect contrast, have standardized the behavior of both men and women as actively "masculine." Gay, hard, arrogant cannibals, they care little for human life. The men hunt their head-trophies among women, children, and weakly males. The women are almost equally careless of the young, the elderly, and the sickly. In contrast to both the other tribes as well as to our own culture, the lake-dwelling Tchambuli present both the "masculine" and the "feminine" patterns of temperament but reversed as between the sexes. Every man is an artist in some line; he is concerned much with his rôle in society, showing little responsibility and much emotional and economic dependence upon women. The women are the fishers and managers, looking after the men and boys with solicitude. In courtship, too, they play the active rôle.

The malleability of human temperament and whole personality, revealed so strikingly for masculinity-femininity, has been the subject-matter of other anthropological studies of primitive tribes in which other sides of human nature have been taken for the starting point [5].

Differential Effects of Different Levels of Culture in American Mountain Folk. We have just seen how the encouraging-discouraging elements of one's surrounding culture can profoundly determine the temperamental pattern of his personality. It can determine its general breadth and richness, also. A wide range of traits is likely to be developed in a social organization where variety of experiences is provided — contacts with many persons, handling many materials and instruments of use, encountering problems and difficulties. This was found, for example, by comparison of four different communities of English and Scotch-Irish ancestry in the Blue Ridge Mountain section [26].

In C. Hollow, cut off almost completely from the currents of American life, the inhabitants live in scattered, mud-plastered log huts. They have neither cattle nor chickens, and tend only small cabbage and corn patches. Their food is strictly of the hog-and-hominy sort. No general road leads to the outside world nor is there any system of communication between cabins. No church nor local government nor other common meeting-place affords contacts. In R. Hollow, to take the one at the other extreme of the four, is found a more substantial compact community. The cabins are substantially built and much better furnished. The cultivated patches are almost farms, and there is a fair amount of cash in circulation among the people. Food is more varied. A public road and daily mail service connect with the outside world. A seven-months' school term, ability to read newspapers and to order from mail order catalogs, furnish indirect avenues of contact with the world. The men and women are more friendly to each other, as well as to strangers. Even some social stratification is setting in.

Children of these four communities when examined by several intelligence tests showed a consistent increase in score from C. Hollow to R. Hollow. But what interests us more at present are the differences in their general modes of behavior, especially social and emotional. To take the two extreme cases, again, the children of R. Hollow as compared with those of C. Hollow showed a greater variety of interests, and quicker apprehension of novel ideas. They adjusted themselves more readily to strangers, were more critical of other children, were more interested in matters of social prestige, and displayed more definite attitudes on matters of morals and propriety. Their worries were different: the C. children worried only about food and clothing, storms, and cold, while the R. children worried about their school grades, and about personal matters such as the attitudes of others toward themselves. In a word, those children who had a greater variety of social conditions and contacts developed personality-traits more varied in character and more flexibility or adaptability.

SOME PRONOUNCED DEVIATIONS IN PERSONALITY ORGANIZATION

Abnormal = A-normal. The distribution of any sizable population in almost any respect trails off into the extremes where relatively few individual cases are found. This oft-repeated principle needs one more repetition. It is essential in gaining the only adequate perspective for understanding those people who deviate so far from the populational mean in certain respects as to earn them the names "psychoneurotic" (or "neurotic") and "psychotic." They are "even as you and I," and differ only by the exaggeration and pervasiveness of some traits which lead to the restructuring of many others, and to the development of *maladjusted* personality-patterns that happen to be of particular concern to their fellowmen. To present even the best-known varieties in anything like adequacy would itself require a volume: here we will have space only for a few thumbnail sketches.

Let it not be forgotten that in the case of each sketch we are portraying an "ideal" or abstract kind of person. What we have had to say in earlier parts of this chapter about the fluidity of types applies here, too. The reader will not let himself be misled by names into assuming that neurotic and psychotic people can be neatly classified and pigeonholed as of this or that disease type. Each has his individuality.

A word as to "causes." It must be remembered that one's hereditary and congenital factors, his physical disease history, his habits of thinking and conduct, the particular degrees of seriousness of each crisis he faces — these and other multiple factors determine his behavior. Therefore, when we make suggestions of interpretation they are suggestions.

The Hysterical Personality. We have referred to cases of this variety of behavior on previous pages. (See pp. 142 f.) The hysterical character is marked by a few outstanding traits. He (or more commonly, she) is extremely *unstable*. When he is seriously thwarted he is most likely to go into some sort of emotional blow-up; and there may be weeping or screaming or swearing, especially if a good audience be on hand. In some cases the instability and disorder may be revealed by a sort of dissociation or disorganization that takes the form of bodily symptoms so closely resembling a true physical ailment as to deceive for a time even practical diagnosticians. The patient meanwhile is usually unaware of the psychogenic (that is, experience-produced rather than physiologically caused) character of the symptoms. (The discussion on pp. 144 f. should be reread.)

It is because he is so suggestible that the hysterical person comes to display the bodily disorders of which he has heard. It is also the reason why some special borderline forms of behavior can be easily induced in him: automatic writing, in which the writing hand unknown to the patient holds the pencil and scribbles meaningful or meaningless phrases and sentences across the page; hypnosis, in which the patient shows an extreme narrowing of attention and an (almost) unquestioning compliance with the notions suggested by the clinician; somnambulisms, in which he goes on quests in a dream-like way, and other forms.

Another mark of the hysteric is his (her) extreme *egoism*. All roads lead to himself; he takes everything personally. Being in very fact a "spoiled child" he will do almost anything to gain his selfish ends.

The Psychasthenic Personality. Cases of this variety are furnished on earlier pages (151 f., 156 f.) The psychasthenic person is marked by morbid *anxiety*.

> She is troubled with thick-coming fancies
> That keep her from her rest.   —

This may take manifold expressions. The little uneasinesses to which the common run of mankind is given at times — a tantalizing worry whether one has left his automobile locked though he is really sure that he has; the fear of a student that maybe he did cheat on that quiz though he has no memory of doing so; the constantly returning desire to touch a lighted match to the hay in the barn or to cast oneself in front of the oncoming express; the strong impulsion to keep counting the number of cement blocks in the pavement as one walks — such things appear in gross exaggerations. One patient has the tormenting obsession that he has committed the unpardonable sin. Others have phobias (morbid fears) of open places, of crowds, of small places, of dirt, or of germ contamination by everything touched. Still others are obsessed by morbid compulsions to steal even unneeded and otherwise unwanted articles, to see fires blaze up and hence to set them, or to go through certain countings of numbers, and the like.

We cannot go further into the causation of psychasthenia or "anxiety neurosis" than to suggest the interpretation that it has basis in some emotional frustrations that have not been faced and solved.

The preceding personality patterns are called forms of *psycho-neuroses*. In contradistinction, the clinician speaks of the graver forms of deviation as *psychoses* (in popular language, "insanities"). The distinction is one of social adjustment: while persons falling into the former classes may be great inconveniences to others, those of the latter are so completely unable to adjust to the conditions of life among their fellow-men that they must be specially cared for.

Only a few of the many varieties of psychotic patterns can be mentioned here.

The Manic-Depressive Personality.   The manic-depressive psychosis is characterized essentially by morbid exaggeration of the "ups and downs" of reaction in thinking, in overt activity, and in emotion.   In the manic or excited phase, the patient is exalted and on the heights or irritable and quarrelsome or erotically a nuisance. He may display a "flight of ideas" (cf. example on pp. 565 f.) in rapid and unconnected speech.   He may become quite active overtly, too, breaking up the furniture, somersaulting, and howling.

When the depressed phase is on him the picture is reversed.   He falls into a dull stupor, and as he sits in a corner by himself, contracted almost into a ball, he furnishes the picture of one overwhelmed by profoundly unpleasant emotions.   His speech comes slowly and almost inaudibly.   He may now be beset by hypochondriacal convictions of serious diseases within his frame, or by tormenting accusations of blame toward himself.

One interpretation of this disorder is psychogenic.   It seems that the patient, unable to resolve certain serious personal difficulties, adopts either or alternately both of two tactics.   By growing excessively active he in a way forgets his problems: by his very busyness he gives himself no time for thinking of them — a morbidly extreme and complicated manner of "whistling in the dark."   On the other hand, he may be "licked"; the problems that beset him will not be denied, and overwhelmed, he withdraws into a contemplation of his own moral turpitude.

The Dementia Praecox Personality.   Of all the disorders of behavior this is much the most common; and it is to be found developing in individuals on college campuses as elsewhere, for the late teens and twenties is the period of highest incidence.   Dementia praecox is not characterized simply, for it has many variations. The name signifies a *premature intellectual deterioration*, and to this should be added *emotional* deterioration as well.   In its simple form, a patient who as a child had perhaps the usual amount of promise begins in his middle teens or later to slow down.   He grows listless, inattentive, lazy, is easily tired out, is the victim of insomnia and often of fleeting delusions and hallucinations.   "Silly" is an adjective excellently describing much of his behavior.   His thinking grows incoherent, as evidenced in his verbal expression.   His emotional deterioration may show a split between his intellectual functions (so far as they are retained) and his emotional reactions: he cries when he should be glad, or simpers in a silly fashion upon losing his home and property. It takes also the common form of a dulling and deadening: he merely smiles where formerly he laughed aloud, or he becomes utterly callous and apathetic.

A condition often complicating the picture of the dementia praecox patient is the development of *paranoid* trends. Mild delusions appear. He financed Henry Ford, who is owner of the Bass Clef Society; he invented "eenie, meenie, minie, moe"; or he is the new Messiah and will (actually) preach for you by the hour; or he is hounded and persecuted by enemies, by telephones, by mirrors, by voices.

A more dramatic though infrequent complication of the picture is to be seen in the *catatonic* seizures. A patient's motor performances may show a negativistic contrariness in which he does nothing he is asked to do (but may do the opposite), and may grow absolutely mute and take no notice of anything or anybody. In some cases a "waxy flexibility" appears: he will assume and maintain for long minutes or even hours peculiar positions in which his head and limbs are placed by the clinician. On the other hand, the motor activity may show excitement in mild and silly grimacing and attitudinizing, or may assume dangerous proportions in breaking windows, arson, murder, suicide — but these are infrequent occurrences.

When a disease is so diversified in nature, theories of its causes are likely to be complex. However, a definite trend of the day is to emphasize certain psychological factors as central. A case is often traced back in the individual's history to a persistent habit of "crawling into one's hole and pulling the hole in after," that is, to the dangerous method of meeting frustrations of one's motives by withdrawing from social contacts completely, and thus becoming so "shut in" that one gets more and more out of touch with the actualities of life. Therefore, a major emphasis of mental hygiene today is to counteract such specious methods of problem solving.

The two preceding forms of psychotic behavior are among those that are psychogenic in causation, that is, are *functional* disorders. Several kinds, however, have definite *organic* bases in structural changes of the body. Since they have psychological effects of some interest we must notice two or three of them.

The Paretic Patient. When syphilis germs happen to direct their destroying attacks upon the cerebrum, their destruction of highly important interconnecting tissues there plays havoc with the man's behavior. Paresis is typically a disorder that affects men, often apparently sound and prosperous ones in middle life. It can be described briefly as *progressive deterioration in all phases*. At the zenith of his mental and physical powers, a man may gradually become a votary of every form of vice, and if not understood and put under care will waste his family's wealth and astonish both his social and his business acquaintances with his conduct. Not least striking are the very extreme delusions often shown: his wealth is not in the millions but in the quadrillions, he has children all over the world, or he fashioned the moon with his own hands. At first, besides the eccentricities just mentioned the clinician will note particular definite sensory and motor disturbances: inability to enunciate such words as "hippopotamus" or "Methodist Episcopal," to write a legible hand, to sew on buttons, and the like. As the patient grows worse he becomes fat instead of fit, stupid instead of active, and along with other muscles those of the face lose their tone and grow flabby and expressionless. After he is bed-ridden his dementia becomes profound, his emaciation exaggerated, he lapses into coma, and he is little more than a bulk of living flesh before death occurs.

Treatment of this degenerative disease is being developed; but that is too far afield for us.

The Sufferer from Involutional Melancholia. At the time of the menopause in women, between the age-years 45 and 50, one of life's critical periods is reached. It is critical psychologically because the atrophying of certain endocrines disturbs the chemical equilibrium of the organism. It is critical psychologically for a double reason. The disturbance of chemical balance itself directly sets up characteristic emotional states, predominantly those of depression, and the individual is possessed of "free-floating fear" (as Freud picturesquely names it); that is, subject to arousal by this, that, or the other incident in the form of causeless anxiety and even self-accusatory states. A second reason for the crisis is more purely psychological. The woman now must face the fact that old age (technically) is definitely arrived and her womanhood a thing of the past; and this is a severe test of emotional balance.

It is no wonder, then, that the general character of a woman's behavior may now change in such a degree as to astonish her family.

She affects gay costumes as if she were again in her twenties, and shows an interest in frivolous matters quite beneath her erstwhile dignity. But not for long: as the endocrine system restores its own equilibrium, and as the woman through long habit as much as through assimilating the difficulty comes to look at life more serenely, melancholic moods and the regressions to earlier days grow infrequent and disappear. She is readjusted.

REFERENCES

1. Allport, G. W. A Test for Ascendance-Submission. *J. Abn. & Soc. Psychol.*, 1928, **23,** 118–36.
2. Arkin, E. The Problem of the Stability of the Human Organism. *J. Genet. Psychol.*, 1933, **42,** 228–36.
3. Bayley, N. A Study of the Crying of Infants during Mental and Physical Tests. *J. Genet. Psychol.*, 1932, **40,** 306–29.
4. Beckman, R. O. Ascendance-Submission Test — Revised. *Personn. J.*, 1933, **11,** 387–92.
5. Benedict, R. *Patterns of Culture.* Houghton Mifflin, 1934.
6. Bleuler, E. *Textbook of Psychiatry* (trans. by Brill). Macmillan, 1924.
7. Bradshaw, F. F. Revising Rating Techniques. *Personn. J.*, 1931, **10,** 232–45.
8. Cantril, H., and Allport, G. W. Recent Applications of the Study of Values. *J. Abn. & Soc. Psychol.*, 1933, **28,** 259–73.
9. Flanagan, J. C. *Factor Analysis in the Study of Personality.* Stanford Univ. Press, 1935.
10. Gesell, A. Some Observations of Developmental Stability. *Psychol. Monog.*, 1936, **47,** 35–46.
11. Glueck, S., and Glueck, E. T. *One Thousand Juvenile Delinquents.* Harvard Univ. Press, 1934.
12. Guilford, J. P., and Guilford, R. B. An Analysis of the Factors in a Typical Test of Introversion-Extroversion. *J. Abn. & Soc. Psychol.,* 1934, **28,** 377–99.
13. Gulick, W. V. *Mental Diseases.* Mosby, 1918.
14. Hartshorne, H., and May, M. A. *Studies in Deceit.* Macmillan, 1928.
15. Healy, W., and Bronner, A. F. *Delinquents and Criminals, their Making and Unmaking.* Macmillan, 1926.
16. Heidbreder, E. Measuring Introversion and Extroversion. *J. Abn. & Soc. Psychol.*, 1926, **21,** 120–34.
17. Henderson, D. K., and Gillespie, R. D. *A Textbook of Psychiatry.* Oxford Univ. Press (3d ed.), 1932.
18. Jersild, A. T. *Child Psychology.* Prentice-Hall, 1933. Chap. XI.
19. Jung, C. J. *Psychological Types* (trans.). Harcourt, Brace, 1923.

20. Kretschmer, E. *Physique and Character* (trans.). Harcourt, Brace, 1925.

21. Mead, M. *Sex and Temperament in Three Primitive Societies.* Morrow, 1935.

22. Newcomb, T. M. The Consistency of Certain Extrovert-Introvert Behavior Patterns in 51 Problem Boys. *Teachers Coll. Contribs. to Educ.*, 1929, No. 382.

23. Pillsbury, W. B. *An Elementary Psychology of the Abnormal.* McGraw-Hill, 1932.

24. Rosanoff, A. J. *Manual of Psychiatry.* Wiley (6th ed.), 1927.

25. Schuler, E. A. A Study of the Consistency of Dominant and Submissive Behavior in Adolescent Boys. *J. Genet. Psychol.*, 1935, **46**, 403–32.

26. Sherman, M., and Henry, T. R. *Hollow Folk.* Crowell, 1933.

27. Shirley, M. M. *The First Two Years.* Vol. III: Personality Manifestations. Univ. Minn. Press, 1933.

28. Terman, L. M., and Burks, B. The Gifted Child. Chap. 19 in *Handbook of Child Psychology* (Murchison, ed.), 2d ed. Clark Univ. Press, 1933.

29. Terman, L. M., and Miles, C. C. *Sex and Personality.* McGraw-Hill, 1936.

30. Thurstone, L. L. A Multiple Factor Study of Vocational Interests. *Personn. J.*, 1931, **10**, 198–205.

31. Thurstone, L. L. A Neurotic Inventory. *J. Soc. Psychol.*, 1930, **1**, 3–30.

32. Vernon, P. E. The Rorschach Ink-Blot Test. *Brit. J. Med. Psychol.*, 1933, **13**, 89–118, 179–205, 271–95.

33. Vernon, P. E., and Allport, G. W. A Test for Personal Values. *J. Abn. & Soc. Psychol.*, 1931, **26**, 231–48.

34. White, W. A. *Outlines of Psychiatry.* Nerve & Ment. Dis. Publ. Co (13th ed.), 1932.

CHAPTER XXI
CONDITIONS OF EFFICIENCY

INTRODUCTION

EFFICIENCY is a word of first importance in contemporary American life, not only as it is applied to machinery and tools, accounting systems, and sales devices, but to the human factor as well. We have already observed in the exposition of some of the principles of Motivation that many psychological processes make for or against a man's fitness for his work and for activities in general. These we need not rehearse. It has also been an undercurrent or assumption in the discussion that man's fitness depends likewise more upon distinctly physiological than upon distinctly psychological conditions; and these physiological conditions in turn depend upon his regimen of living or upon environmental influences that operate upon him not as specific stimuli but as more general physical-chemical conditioners.

FATIGUE

The Nature of Fatigue. In everyday life there is no more common set of phenomena than the many different forms of what goes by the name of "fatigue." There are numerous kinds of "being tired": one may be tired after a long run or after hours of heavy-lifting work; one may be tired from a long automobile or train trip on which he did little but sit on some well-cushioned seats; he may report being tired after a long afternoon of reading in his easy chair; or he may tire of the sound of his neighbor's radio, just as the orphanage children do of corn mush; and a neurasthenic is tired all the time. Clearly this word, and even the more technical one, fatigue, is variously used; and upon examination it becomes painfully apparent that a disentangling, standardizing, and relabeling of the various meanings are very much to be desired. Even in the narrower technical usage of "fatigue" — *the reduction of capacity to do voluntary muscular work in consequence of long-continued work of the same kind* — the term is still somewhat ambiguous, since different structures may be affected

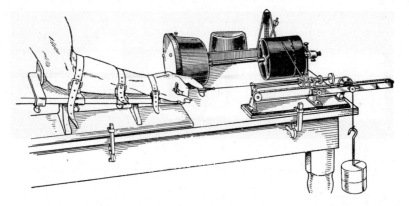

FIGURE 149. MOSSO'S ERGOGRAPH

The middle finger in a stirrup pulls against a free-hanging weight, the other fingers and the arm being confined to permit isolation of the muscle to be fatigued. As the finger alternately draws and releases the sliding carriage to which the weight is slung by a pulley, a pointer attached to the carriage records its excursions on the revolving smoked drum of a kymograph driven by clockwork. Contractions are made at regular intervals to the sound beat of a metronome. The smoked paper when removed from the kymograph shows graphically the work done by the isolated muscle throughout the task. (Cf. Figure 150.) (By permission of the C. H. Stoelting Co.)

at different times. The precise locus of fatigue may appear in some cases (1) to be the muscle itself; in others (2) to lie at the end-plate junction of efferent nerve and muscle; or again (3) to be at the nerve centers in the central nervous system. It is probable that with persistently maintained work each of these three places is in turn affected, but in an order the reverse of that given. If we consider (1), the muscle, alone, we find that there are rival conceptions of the basic nature of a condition of muscle fatigue: whether it be due to (a) depletion of stored energy in the muscle, or to (b) an accumulation of waste products, or to (c) the production of toxins in the blood. Finally there is, of course, the fatigue caused by change of attitude, loss of interest which is commonly called "boredom," and which is not associated with a change in any particular physiological mechanism.

The phenomenon of fatigue in a simple form has been extensively studied with Mosso's ergograph (Figure 149). Figure 150 shows some ergograph tracings made in the author's laboratory. On the left is a record of repeated pulls on a 2-kilogram weight. Here are shown the onset of "fatigue," and the progressive decrement in work on the part of the muscle to a point at which it loses ability to

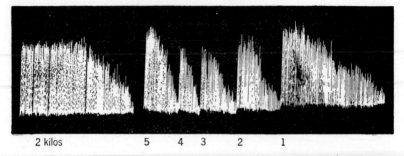

FIGURE 150. KYMOGRAPH TRACINGS MADE ON A MOSSO ERGOGRAPH

The tracing on the left is a record of repeated pulls against a 2-kilogram weight. The composite tracing on the right is a record of repeated pulls against a load decreased in amount at intervals. When the muscle appeared "fatigued" for a given weight, reduction of the load led to apparent renewal of contracting power: shown for reduction of 5-kilogram weight to 4 kilograms, then to 3, to 2, to 1.

contract. But total inability to move a given weight does not signify complete loss of the contracting power of the muscle. If the load be reduced the muscle may show an apparent renewal of work capacity, as shown in this case by the successively renewed contractions when the weight was changed from 5 kilos to 4, then to 3, to 2, and to 1. (The reader might well ask himself: Which of the loci of fatigue changes mentioned in the preceding paragraph (1), (2), or (3), would seem to fit best this rather common finding?) A number of interesting facts are revealed by this technique. The work done can be accurately recorded and measured, not only for each pull but for a whole working period; and the time relations also can be accurately shown. The part of the body doing the work can be limited to a very small muscle-group, making it difficult for other muscles near and far to participate in the performance and so to shift the principal burden irregularly from one to another part of the body, which so commonly happens in any ordinary course of work.

The psychological and physiological nature of fatigue is naturally of great importance from even the most practical viewpoint. Studies of human efficiency in the factory and elsewhere in the process of economic production have given rise to the latter-day profession of psychotechnologists, which is thus far flourishing more in Germany and in England than in America. Attention has been given for the most part to efficiency problems in their more readily measured forms, in the repetitive activities of manual workers. Less has been done with the "white-collar" jobs, and especially with work calling for the higher levels of thinking as in the work of the student and in the professions. But a beginning must be made; and where substantial advances have been gained in reference to the simpler forms of occupations, we are at least furnished with bases for considering the more complex forms.

From the many factors that tend to hasten or delay fatigue, we will select two for discussion in the limited space at our disposal.

Working Hours. During the Great War, the British munition factories were being pushed to the maximum rate of production. Through patriotic as well as wage motives the workers were induced to stay at their jobs for unusually long hours. It became evident, however, that on a Tuesday morning they would start out at a slower pace than on Monday morning, on Wednesday at a slower pace than on Tuesday, and so on through the week. It was finally decided to try shortening the total number of working hours. In one factory the working week of the men was cut from 58.2 hours to 50.6, a reduction of 13 per cent; this resulted in increasing the hourly output by 39 per cent, the total weekly output by 21 per cent. The working week of the women was cut from 66 to 48.6 hours. As a result the hourly output increased by 68 per cent and the total output by 15 per cent. Two factors, it seems, were involved: the direct physiological effect of length of work, and the psychological tendency of the workers *to save themselves* against the long hours ahead of them. (The latter implies no deliberate restraint, but is an expression of the tendency of any worker to adjust himself to the known length of the working period) [3].

The conclusion to which these and many other lines of evidence that could be cited seem clearly to hint is that *increases in the length of working hours beyond a certain optimal point bring diminishing returns hour by hour* and may even *reduce the total return* of the whole day.

Rest Pauses. Some results of an early Italian investigation [15] employing the ergographic technique set an interesting practical and theoretical problem. It was found that if a subject were put to work pulling a weight of 6 kilograms, (*a*) when only 2 seconds were allowed for rest after each contraction he would be completely unable to move the finger after about 1 minute, and would need a 2-hour rest to return to his full former efficiency. (*b*) When he was compelled to work at the same rate for only ½ minute, he would need but half an hour for return to full efficiency. Finally, (*c*) when he was allowed a 10-second rest after each contraction, he could continue this sort of work indefinitely with no evidences whatever of fatigue. Now if these findings be applicable to a day's work of approximately 8 hours, the three methods would result in the following respective total outputs (allowing 2 seconds for each contraction): (*a*) 120 contractions; (*b*) 240; (*c*) 2400. The data are recapitulated in the table. This is eloquent testimony of a logical sort drawn from a laboratory source as to the central importance of introducing rest pauses in work.

EFFECT ON OUTPUT OF LENGTH AND FREQUENCY OF PAUSES

LENGTH OF PAUSE FOLLOWING EACH CONTRACTION	TOTAL LENGTH OF "SPELLS" OF WORK	No. CONTRACTIONS MADE PER "SPELL"	TIME REQUIRED FOR RECUPERATION	THEORETICAL OUTPUT (No. CONTRACTIONS) IN 8-HR. DAY
2 sec.	1 min.	30	2 hrs.	120
2 "	½ "	15	½ hr.	240
10 "	continuous		0	2400

Observations in actual industrial situations have pointed in the same direction. In an English shoe factory heavy double presses were used that required two girls as operators. If the usual plan were followed whereby the two girls worked continuously throughout the working day, the weekly output of the plant was 42 gross in a 46-hour week. But if three girls were put to each press and worked 40 minutes and rested 20, in rotation, the weekly output was increased to 49 gross in a 30-hour week. Significant, too, was the testimony of all the operatives that their health had improved and a day's work no longer left them tired out [14].

And now for a much-celebrated American case. Taylor, the father of "scientific management," studied the working habits of laborers handling pig iron. The work consisted of lifting a pig weighing 92 pounds, carrying it up an inclined plane, and dropping it upon a freight car. He found that the daily average amount of iron loaded per man was 12½ tons. By instituting regular pauses, directing each man to sit down and rest after handling 20 pigs (and incidentally improving the methods of handling through "motion study"), Taylor was able to increase the daily average per man to 47½ tons — and with decreased fatigue at the end of the day. As he explained it: "Throughout the time that a man is under a heavy load the tissues of his arm muscles are in process of degeneration, and frequent periods of rest are required in order that the blood may have a chance to restore these tissues to their normal condition." With the proper pauses, the fatigue effects were continually being corrected about as fast as they were set up.

Illustrations of the same principle could be multiplied easily, and from a wide range of human work-activities. Let us consider some of the points involved. From several studies the generalization seems warranted that, in the course of uninterrupted activity, *fatigue occurs at a rate with a positive acceleration*: the longer one keeps at the work the more rapidly do the fatigue effects appear.

A practical problem is to discover just when a pause should be introduced. No concrete or explicit recommendation can be made, naturally, since with different kinds of activity different rates of fatigue will appear. A safe generalization would be: Find that length of working time after which *a drop in production first begins to appear*, and insert the pause there.

This is complicated somewhat by a distinctly psychological factor. In several types of industry the anticipation of the pause makes for improved output just before it is due to occur. In one case individuals were occupied in adding digits morning and afternoon. On certain days a mid-morning and a mid-afternoon pause were introduced. The workers' output on these days was greater than their output on the days when no pauses were allowed, not only in the periods following the pauses but also in the periods preceding the pauses [27]. Thus, not only the physiological rest during the pause but also the *psychological anticipation* of it made for increased efficiency.

This matter of pauses is one of prime importance to the student, to the houseworker, and to the man of affairs. There can be no doubt whatever that a mid-morning and mid-afternoon pause means much to a person's fitness for work. In an English study a 12-minute rest pause was introduced in the middle of a 2-hour stretch of work which consisted of doing arithmetic problems without pencil and paper [3]. The gains in achievement with different methods of filling the rest pause were:

Walking	2%
Tea	3%
Music	4%
Sitting, talking, smoking	8%
Complete relaxation in easy chair	9%

To this could be added another effective method — the refreshing and restoring benefits to be obtained by a very brief nap at mid-day. A brief loss of consciousness (and the general relaxation of musculature over the body) turns a dull afternoon into an alert morning.

Some Subjective Aspects of Fatigue. Without explicitly making a point of it we have confined our discussions so far to fatigue in its objective meaning — "decreased ability to work in consequence of work." We must now repair our omission of the subjective aspect by analyzing the state of "feeling tired."

One broad statement can be made at once. *A person's experience of feeling tired is not a valid indicator of his ability to work.* It is indeed the fact that in certain stages of tiredness he may actually do far better work, whether it be heavy labor or thinking. It seems that the toxins when produced in certain amounts affect the neural centers and probably the endocrine and other systems in a way to increase one's general excitement; and this status of heightened energizing leads to the throwing of greater power into the work and a longer continuance of it. Surely the reader can furnish his own testimony to this general phenomenon of accomplishing surprising things when he had been feeling "done." It is also of a piece with the accelerated tempo at which one lives and works during the first stage following an energy-depletion, such as loss of sleep — a compensatory phenomenon. One should bear in mind, however, the fact that this heightened level of work in the first stage of fatigue often turns out to be a "temporary extravagance in the expenditure of energy, the organism living recklessly, as it were, on its capital" [19].

A famous case that illustrates the remarkable power to do work if incidental feelings be neglected is that in which a person subvocally multiplied four-place numbers by four-place numbers without the use of paper and pencil for figuring, working continuously from 11 A.M. to 11 P.M. on four successive days [1]. The average time for solving the first four examples on each of the four days was 5.5 minutes, that for solving the last four examples, 11.7 minutes. (If the reader will try to multiply a three-place number by a two-place number — a vastly easier task! — without aid of pencil, he will appreciate much better the nature and the implications of this experiment.)

Conversely, it not infrequently happens that an experience of freshness and avidity is misleading and is based upon a condition of actually decreased productivity. This state is not unlike a certain stage in alcoholic poisoning, when a man's emotional expansiveness ill consorts with his actual clumsiness and ineptitude.

It is a fact, of course, that the subjective state of an individual — the way he feels — is a function not only of his general physiological state (muscular, neural, endocrinal, and so on) but also of his preceding thinking processes. Anticipation of the end of a job is a thing we have already noted as important. Contrariwise, the *monotony* of an endless, inexorable, and unremitting repetition of the same little set of motions hour after hour becomes for some people a restraint and frustration that has serious consequences not only for the job output but for the nervous and mental health of the workman. Much concern over this is to be found throughout the critical literature written by industrial experts as well as by literary observers. We need not expand the theme.

The discrepancy between objective output and subjective experience is well shown in an experiment with a task involving clear thinking, namely, completing sentences by inserting appropriate words. In the experiment the work was continued for 5½ hours, and this total period was divided into 15 units. No pause was allowed between units except one of 10 minutes between the 14th and 15th. At the beginning and end of each unit of work each subject rated his feelings on a scale of seven degrees. Figure 151 shows the data. The curve of feeling fell steadily until the 10-minute pause, and fell again after the last unit, in spite of the fact

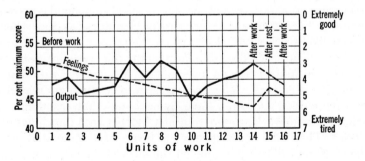

FIGURE 151. RELATION BETWEEN FEELINGS AND OUTPUT

Distances on the base-line indicate the units of work into which the whole was divided. The left-hand vertical scale indicates the output score (as a percentage of the maximum possible), the right-hand scale, the seven grades of feeling. A pause of 10 minutes was inserted after the 14th unit. (From Poffenberger, A. T., *Applied Psychology*, Appleton-Century, 1927.)

that the curve of production held steady and even rose.   The experimenter noted in the course of the work that the subjects manifested weariness, irritability, restlessness, outbreaks of profanity, and even scattered threats of quitting (in spite of a high rate of pay).   It may be added that on experiments involving day-to-day learning the writer has almost invariably found that the subjects' daily testimony as to their degrees of interest was no index of how well they actually were performing.

So-called "Mental" Work.   The reader will notice that in many cases cited the work that is measured is of some predominantly manual type.   The chief reason for this is that such work can be easily measured.   We are not to assume any distinct line of demarcation between "mental" and "muscular" work.   If we rename these more accurately "verbal" and "manual," the distinction appears clearly fine-drawn, for many occupations involve both kinds of activity.   And, in point of fact, the very same principles of work and fatigue apply to many jobs of the verbal type just as they do to heavier manual or muscular labor.[1]

It would seem that if any distinction is to be drawn, it should be between the more repetitive and the more creative sorts of work. This is a distinction that any student can find in his own activities. And, if a general statement may be hazarded, it is that the psychotechnical principles that have been derived to date are primarily applicable to the repetitive activities of shop and of office, of mill and of counting-house.   Their applicability to activities such as writing a theme for an English class, solving a problem in calculus, or making a qualitative analysis of a chemical compound is extremely limited.   For instance, if a rest pause be introduced as per a schedule, it is as likely as not to fall just when the thinker is immersed in his problem, has succeeded in reawakening his relevant sources of knowledge, and is hot on the trail of his quarry, with hunches beginning to emerge.   There would seem to be abundant reason why creative workers so often have living hours that scandalize their neighbors who work at more routine tasks between punchings of the clock.   They may apply themselves feverishly all day and most of the night and repeat the same on the morrow; then, when a task is finished, an answer obtained, or a thesis worked out, they may drop away into hours and days of seeming idleness.

[1] For a thorough critical analysis of work and fatigue in the more ideational activities, Thorndike should be consulted [25].

To what extent, then, the reader should apply to his own case the principles of psychotechnics cannot be decided with a simple formula. He should realize that the most important thing practically is not this or that particular plan, but his own attitude of inquiry and criticism addressed to his own working program.

Overwork versus Overworry. It is a fact of immense practical and personal importance that in most instances what has been described as "nervous breakdown" is a result not of excessive work but of excessive worry. In the first place such breakdowns occur much less often among the workmen who are forced to heavy labor than among "white-collar" workers and professional and business men on higher economic levels. It is true that the laborer's health may be undermined by too long hours; but the ill-health takes the form of general weakness and greater susceptibility to systemic infectional diseases. The source of "nervous breakdown" must accordingly be sought outside the working muscles and neural connections. In a very few cases it is diagnosed simply as infections at tonsils or teeth or other foci; and in other cases the endocrine system has been seriously unbalanced. But the most important inducing condition is that of prolonged worry and emotional stress, sometimes incidental to the work itself, sometimes set up by extraneous problems in a person's private life.

Neurasthenia, often classed with psychasthenia and hysteria (pp. 603 f.) as a major psychoneurosis, is a form of breakdown. A neurasthenic patient shows exhaustion of his strength. Tired all the time, he loses weight, and is a victim of insomnia and despondency, which serve only to increase his anxieties and so complete the vicious circle.

The principle underlying the theme of the preceding paragraphs may be more widely applied. The deleterious effect of an agency may not be directed primarily at an individual's working apparatus, in the strict sense, but at his emotional apparatus. This we will see demonstrated again.

OTHER PHYSIOLOGICAL CONDITIONS

Sleep. Of all the conditions making for human efficiency sleep is by all odds the most important. It is the one most necessary to normal metabolic activity, and the one most neglected on college campuses. Experimental animals deprived of any sleep whatever die within a very few days, no matter how well they may be fed, watered, and housed. Since the physiologists are not agreed as to what constitutes the essential nature of sleeping, it would "be foolish to be wise" on that question. We will therefore content ourselves with the view that it is a period of cessation of nearly all overt muscular activities and of nearly all sensory functions. It differs in depth just as waking life differs in vividness and intensity, to form the other half of a continuous scale.

What are the psychological effects of the loss of a considerable amount of sleep? Experiments have taken the form of abstention from sleep for fifty, sixty, or more hours, with tests administered before, during, and after. The results of such researches at first seem puzzling. On a wide variety of psychological tests (color naming, canceling, computing, aiming, steadiness, etc.) no impairment has usually been found even in subjects deprived of sleep for sixty hours. No one who has worked with men in this condition can fail to be impressed with their ability to perform well on such tasks.

A significant thing, however, is to be noted. The sleepless subjects do fall down when it comes to tasks demanding persistent and *sustained attention*. They may be able, say, to name a hundred color patches with normal speed and accuracy, but they cannot do so with a thousand, which they can do when fresh. They may be as skillful in parking an automobile as anyone else, but on a long driving trip they would tend to lapse into sleep. In the same connection, another obvious thing is to be considered. Whatever their objective achievement scores, all subjects show or report vivid and impressive *illness symptoms* of other sorts: "buzzing in the head," burning eyes, and headache, head feeling "musty," being dazed, feeling "almost dead," and the like; and their general deportment becomes irritable and "nervous," or else silly. They feel almost "tight," and laugh at anything. How can the test results showing only slight impairment in specific short tasks be reconciled with failure in sustained tasks and with these general bodily symptoms of disorganization? One key to the problem may be found in the phenomenon of *compensation*. The dull weight imposed upon a man's activities by his sleepiness operates, as any other impediment is likely to do, to arouse in him extra effort to overcome it. And because of its costliness, the extra effort cannot be maintained. This principle is supported by some evidence on the physiological side. It has been found that the energy consumed (as measured by metabolic rate) during an arithmetic task was something like three times as great with subjects who had lost only two hours of sleep as with those who had lost none: the excess muscular effort put forth in keeping oriented to the task was costly.

Another characteristic of the sleep-deprived person is his *sluggishness in shifting his set* from task to task or even item to item.   It is difficult to redirect his activity.   Once started on a given line he can hardly be drawn from it.   This behavior may at first seem to contradict the point made above; but there it was stated that it is the excess effort that is short-lived, rather than a general orientation. Now, this sluggishness in turning from one task to another has been strikingly found in other experimentally induced conditions of impairment: deprivation of oxygen with aviation candidates, alcoholic poisoning, excessive fatigue.   And it is a noticeable feature in life outside the laboratory: the alcoholized person is not easily diverted; the goggle-eyed child does not want to move or go to bed; the student working on into the night finds himself more and more reluctant to quit and seek his rest, though he may well know he is slowing down.

Exactly how much sleep makes for highest efficiency it is impossible to say, for individuals differ in the depth of their sleeping. We know that the value of sleep is a function of its depth multiplied by its length.   This is shown when after long hours of vigil a person ordinarily can "catch up" with a much shorter sleep if it is undisturbed and profound.

Finally, sleeping has many elements of the *habitual*.   One can learn to sleep only at certain times — or at any time by merely lying down and closing his eyes; he can learn to sleep only in certain places on certain kinds of beds — or in any place.   Tomes of advice have been written telling one how to fall asleep, and the methods recommended — counting sheep, stroking one arm, taking a hot bath — are countless.   The writer would recommend two peripheral devices especially: eliminate sensory stimuli as far as possible, and relax all possible muscles — open the hands, drop the jaw, and "look over" the body to see if there is tenseness in a muscle group anywhere [11].

Among the current health fads are several that prescribe the *position in which a person should sleep*.   All such prescriptions seem to be *a priori* deductions from the position of the heart, shape of the shoulder girdle, and the like; and apparently none are based on evidence.   Evidence that does bear on the question has been

FIGURE 152. SUCCESSIVE POSTURES ASSUMED BY A SLEEPER

(From Johnson, H. M., Swan, T. H., and Weigand, G. E. *J. Amer. Med. Assoc.*, 1930, **94,** 2058–2062.)

accumulated by Johnson and his associates, based upon the changes of posture that occur in the course of normal sleep.   The subject of Johnson's experiment slept on a bed which had under it a recording pen writing on a continuous traveling paper strip, the pen being so attached by a cord to a sensitive coil in the bedspring that any gross movement of the sleeper's body produced a shift in the inscribed line.   There was also a motion-picture camera electrically wired with the above apparatus so as to take a picture each time the sleeper changed position.   Figure 152 presents a short sample series.   The sleeper does not lie like a log throughout the night. On the contrary, typical healthy subjects change from one gross position to another between 20 and 45 times in the course of a typical eight-hour night, each of these stirs being separated from the next by at least 2½ minutes.   The muscles, the skin, and other parts of the body grow fatigued in any one long-continued position, and each shift of the posture provides a change, a specialized rest.

Alcohol.   Safe generalizations on the subject of alcohol and its effect on human efficiency are not easily made, and for two reasons in particular.   Susceptibility varies from individual to individual in a way that is baffling.   The effect of different amounts on any one individual is likewise surprisingly different.   Because of their failure adequately to control certain factors, most of the experimental studies have helped very little in clearing up the great confusion on the general subject that is to be found in popular discourse.   A principal error is that of "suggestion": a subject, if he knows when he is and when he is not taking the dose, will expect himself to perform differently in the two cases, and this expectation serves to induce or influence the very behavior supposed to be in question. In such a welter of conflicting opinions and discordant findings we will do well to limit ourselves to the evidence from two of the best-accepted pieces of research.

One experiment was concerned more with the simpler motor phenomena [4].   Some of the findings appear in the table.   A glance at them will reveal a fact that is at variance with one strong popular opinion: alcohol proves to be a *depressant*, at least of the functions measured, reducing either the strength or the quickness of an action.

INFLUENCE OF ALCOHOL ON SIMPLE MOTOR REACTIONS

	PER CENT
Latent time of the knee jerk increased	10
Thickening of the quadriceps muscle decreased	46
Protective eyelid reflex, latent time increased	7
Extent of eyelid movement decreased	19
Eye reactions, latent time increased	5
Speed of eye movements decreased	11
Sensitivity to electric stimulation decreased	14
Speed of finger movements (tapping) decreased	9

Another study was devoted to more complicated processes such as are tapped with some well-known psychological tests [7].   Six men were given a battery of tests at half-hour intervals before and at similar intervals after a noon drinking of genuine beer of three different strengths, and similarly on other days when the beer contained no alcohol.   The subjects were unaware of the differences in the beers.   (One man was a total abstainer, one a regular drinker,

and the others occasional drinkers.)   The results of drinking the beer
with alcoholic content may be briefly summarized as follows: [1]

Hand steadiness........decreased	Naming opposites..........slower
Hand-eye co-ordinations....poorer	Adding..................slower
Tapping.................slower	Learning substitutes........slower
Color-naming.............slower	Memory, paired associates ..slower

Again the depressing effect of alcohol is shown, and this time on
distinctly psychological performances.

These results are reinforced by those of another study [17] in
which the effects of alcohol were as follows:

Pulse rate.............increased	Visual acuity............less keen
Skin temperature........increased	Finger movement..........slower
Patellar reflex..........decreased	Eye-hand co-ordination.....poorer
Eyelid reflex..............slower	Typewriting, errors......increased
Eye reaction time.........slower	Typewriting, speed.........slower
Word reaction time........slower	Using code...............slower

From everyday observations of people we would be warranted in
asking for an interpretation of such results as these.   Do not light
doses of alcohol excite rather than depress, increase rather than di-
minish?   Does not many a man testify sincerely to the supporting
effect of a small drink?   The fact is that popular experience and the
laboratory data are not really in conflict.   The *depressing effects at
first concern the very highest inhibitory functions*, and as these dampers
are removed the emotional functions are released.   The result is increased experience of well-being, good fellowship, freedom from
timidity before a crowd, increased confidence in one's own powers —
a condition that on further poisoning passes into an emotional
exaggeration in sentimental weeping or absurd anger, gesticulations,
and much loud talk.   *In vino veritas* has only this much truth in it.
When a person is in this alcoholized condition it is only in some
special senses that we can speak of his increased efficiency.   There is
an apparent increase from the point of view of the man's feelings,
and an increase in any other way only in the negative sense of the
removal of inhibitions.

Caffeine.   Caffeine is the active principle in coffee, tea, and certain
proprietary drinks, which are taken the world over for increasing
one's fitness.   The best evidence bearing on the effect of caffeine is

---

[1] Most of these tests the reader will recognize by name. Apparatus for a few have been shown in Figure 47.

the following well-controlled experiment. For a 40-day period subjects were given capsules, on some days containing caffeine in different amounts and on others a milk sugar of similar appearance. The contents of each day's capsule were unknown both to the subjects and to the assistants serving as their examiners. The subjects were given several times daily a battery of tests. A comparison of scores made by all subjects after different-sized doses on the caffeine days and on those of the caffeineless days led to some fairly definite conclusions. These are summarized in the table. The effect upon simpler motor performances (Tests 1, 2, 9) tended to be one of

EFFECTS OF CAFFEINE

+ = increase	o = no effect	— = decrease	
TEST	SMALL DOSES	MEDIUM DOSES	LARGE DOSES
1. Tapping	+	+	+
2. Complicated tapping	+	o	—
3. Typewriting			
(a) Speed	+	o	—
(b) Errors	—	—	—
4. Color naming	+	+	+
5. Naming opposites	+	+	+
6. Adding	+	+	+
7. Discrimination reaction time	—	o	+
8. Cancellation	—	?	+
9. Steadiness	?	—	—

stimulation. On the more definitely psychological functions (3, 4, 5, 6, 7, 8) the effect was stimulating, with a few exceptions for certain sizes of dose. In general, then, *caffeine makes for heightened efficiency*, at least in the period immediately following the dose. An interesting and important incidental fact is that in no case was there a secondary reaction of let-down [6].

It remains to be said that caffeine is clearly *habit-forming*, that is, he who uses it frequently comes to depend upon it, as witness the numbers of people who experience headaches, dizziness, and other discomforts when denied their usual dose.

Tobacco. The question of the effect of tobacco upon a man's work is today a football being booted about by rival interests in a game that knows few rules. While they were under the ban of certain reforming organizations cigarettes — otherwise known then as "coffin nails" — were in many states not sold to minors under legal penalty; and even yet they are not used by women as freely as by men in certain sections of the country, a faint taint of iniquity

still adhering to them.   Since the World War, however, an un-
paralleled orgy of advertising has been devoted to them in which
nonsensical and even false claims have been dressed in the garb of
untempered and fulsome language.   Where does the truth lie?   We
may surmise offhand that it lies in neither extreme position.

As for scientific evidence there is little that is available.   To be
sure, a host of investigators here and there have followed such
procedures as that of comparing the scholarship or the athletic
records of smokers and non-smokers, but where does the tobacco
"come in"?   Is it cause, effect, symptom, or accident?

One experiment seems to have been conducted with an adequate
appreciation of the checks and controls that need to be employed.
In all studies of the effects of drugs a disturbing factor of very great
importance has been the subject's knowledge of when he is and
when he is not being administered the drug, and the resulting operation of suggestion (q.v., pp. 496 ff.).   This has been particularly
difficult to eliminate in the case of tobacco smoking.   In the
experiment referred to, however, the following check was devised.
The subjects were blindfolded and were allowed to suppose that
tobacco would be smoked on each occasion.   On the tobacco days
a full pipeful of tobacco was placed in their mouths, while on the
tobaccoless days they were given pipes of exactly the same shape,
empty of tobacco, but with an electric heating-coil that warmed the
air drawn into the mouth from the pipe.   While puffing on the latter
they smelled tobacco smoke in the room produced by the experimenter.   This control was effective.   In fact, in one case a confirmed smoker with the warm-air pipe in his mouth went through the
motions of blowing smoke rings.

A battery of tests was run before the "smoking," just after a 25-
minute "smoke," and at two approximately half-hour intervals
later.   The data obtained are summarized in the accompanying
table.   As the reader can see, no single conclusion as to the effect of
tobacco smoking upon the more strictly psychological functions can
be drawn from this study.   (A) Different psychological functions
were differently affected.   (B) They were affected sometimes in
opposite ways depending upon whether the subjects were habituated
to smoking.   (C) Where definite increases or decreases are indicated,
the original figures have but low reliability.   We are left to conclude
either that the technique of experimentation is not adequately perfected to reveal the true effects of smoking, or (more probably) that

EFFECT OF TOBACCO SMOKING ON EFFICIENCY

+ = gain in efficiency on tobacco, as compared with no-tobacco days.
0 = no decided change.
− = loss in efficiency.

FUNCTION TESTED:		NON-SMOKERS			HABITUAL SMOKERS		
		test 1	2	3	test 1	2	3
Pulse	(increased)	+	+	+	+	+	+
Tremor of hand	(increased)	−	−	−	−	−	−
Tapping		0	0	0	0	0	0
Muscular fatigue	(decreased)	+	+	+	+	0	0
Cancelling of A's, speed		0	0	0	0	0	0
Cancelling of A's, accuracy		0	0	0	0	+	+
Reading reaction-time		+	+?	+	+	+?	+
Learning reaction-time		+	+	+	+	+	+
Adding, speed		−	−	−	+	+	+
Adding, accuracy		−?	−	−?	0	0	0
Memory span		−	−	−	−	−	−
Rote learning		−	0	0	−	0	0

tobacco smoking has little if any definite and consistent effect upon psychological functions.

It may be in order to add that besides whatever physiological and psychological effect the tobacco has as a drug, some of the motivation to smoking possibly lies in the pleasure derived from cigarettes, cigars, pipes, and even chewing-tobacco as something to be handled and mouthed.

Sidelights on Some Mystical States.   A curious chapter in the history of psychological phenomena is the recurrence of certain abnormal episodes that are brought about by employing some of the very methods known to weaken and destroy efficiency in normal behavior.   We refer to the hallucinatory phenomena ("visions") which are more or less deliberately secured by fatigue (as in the whirling dervishes), by fasting (often for "forty days and forty nights"), by prolonged sleepless vigils ("watching"), and by flagellations and other self-tortures [12].

It may be argued that in many religious cults these often extraordinarily rigorous practices have a double motivation.   The well-known one is, of course, the desire to mortify the flesh and to exalt the spirit by expressing one's indifference to base clay.   The other is the wish to experience the mystical visions.   We must remember that these are of all sorts; and only rarely do they contain any truly inspirational element or ethical content.   For the most part these hallucinatory phenomena are on about the same level and subject to the same interpretation as what is popularly called "a good drunk." In other words, when a fanatic, after subjecting himself for hours and days to one of these exhausting techniques, develops hallucinations and compulsions, he is disorganized in the same general way as he would be if his system were subjected to a powerful drug (alcohol, mescal, opium, hashish, and the rest).

Doctor Oliver Wendell Holmes has furnished a brilliant example:

I once inhaled a pretty full dose of ether, with the determination to put on record, at the earliest moment of regaining consciousness, the thought I should find uppermost in my mind. The mighty music of the triumphal march into nothingness reverberated through my brain, and filled me with a sense of infinite possibilities, which made me an archangel for the moment. The veil of eternity was lifted. The one great truth which underlies all human experience and is the key to all the mysteries that philosophy has sought in vain to solve, flashed upon me in a sudden revelation. Henceforth all was clear: a few words had lifted my intelligence to the level of the knowledge of the cherubim. As my natural condition returned, I remembered my resolution; and, staggering to my desk, I wrote, in ill-shaped, straggling characters, the all embracing truth still glimmering in my consciousness. The words were these (children may smile; the wise will ponder): "A strong smell of turpentine prevails throughout." [1]

ENVIRONMENTAL CONDITIONS

Noise. In recent years some of the largest cities have conducted anti-noise campaigns, partly because noises are a nuisance (that is, are reacted to unfavorably as noises), partly also because they are supposed to reduce fitness for work. On the latter question scientific investigation has strangely lagged, both in factory and in laboratory. Undoubtedly one reason for this is the rapidity with which a workman subjected to noise becomes adapted to it. This is a well-known fact. In shipyards and steel mills the noise is such as almost to deafen visitors, yet a workman after a very few days is acclimatized and suffers no inconvenience. Families living in apartments abutting on elevated railways, with trains noisily whirling by every few minutes, live apparently normal lives as they eat, read, converse, sleep with no obvious disturbance. But the true nature of this adaptive process is not well known.

There is some evidence to indicate that it involves an active *compensatory putting forth of extra effort.* In this connection Morgan's experiment described on pages 338 f. is a classic one.

The available information gathered from experiences in commercial and industrial houses may be summarized as follows.

Loud noises that are continuous have an adverse effect upon the output of a small proportion of manual workers, and on a larger proportion of office workers. Irregular and startling noises have pronounced disturbing and irritating effects upon all types of workers. Even where noise has no effect

[1] From *Autocrat of the Breakfast Table.* Houghton Mifflin Company.

on output or on health in a measurable degree, the strong possibility remains that it leads to increased expenditures of energy and thus contributes to earlier fatigue [27].

Presumably the same generalizations apply to the environment of the student. Arguing by analogy it is to be expected that radios and phonographs will tax a student's energy supply no matter how well adapted to them he may become. Since many noises cannot be removed, however, the problem arises as to how most efficiently to compensate for the energy drain.

Ventilation. Oxygen, as every child knows, is essential to life, and the more lively and active the organism the more oxygen it will require. This is a commonplace. Yet there are certain details and qualifying facts that need to be considered. Two lines of laboratory research furnish the scientific viewpoint on the matter.

During the World War a routine part of the examination of candidates for the American aviation service was a test of the candidates' capacity to continue normal operations under conditions of depleted oxygen supply, which is one of the conditions encountered in flying at high altitudes. The laboratory arrangement was for the examinee, while at work on a variety of tests, to breathe from a supply tank air that had already been passed through his lungs or was artificially diluted, continuing until there were definite signs of impending collapse and fainting. A variety of tests were assigned him: sensory (difference thresholds in vision, audition, and pressure); motor performance (steadiness, tapping, and the like); memory (repeating digits, locating lamps flashed on and off); and attention (throwing switches to turn off lights that flashed on in irregular order, adding, card sorting). As to the motor performances the most obvious effect of the depleted oxygen supply was the production of muscular tremors and jerky movements that were unco-ordinated and too vigorous. The effect on the way in which subjects attended proved to be a loss in their alertness, in their ability to shift attention rapidly from task to task (a condition we have seen to be true of subjects deprived of sleep); and in the last stages, an inability to concentrate even on the simplest task unless they were shouted at insistently. There were, finally, peculiar emotional manifestations: some subjects flew into a rage and tried to "take it out on" the apparatus, others grew silly, smirking and winking at apparatus and experimenter, or even laughing uncontrollably. (Compare with what we have said of the effects of alcohol.)

In a general way, then, very serious reduction of a man's energy supply of oxygen leads to a breakdown of his behavior, a *disintegration*, in which the *higher inhibitory and higher shifting functions are lost first*, to be followed by deterioration of simpler and simpler functions [2].

Ventilation is more than a matter of sufficient oxygen. The air in which one works and breathes has a certain temperature, a certain humidity or moisture, and a certain amount of circulation; and variations in these characteristics should be investigated.

This has been rather thoroughly done in a research project sponsored by the New York State Commission on Ventilation [26]. The subjects of the investigation worked in an airtight room in which the air could be experimentally controlled as to oxygen content, temperature, humidity, and circulation. For work of the heavy muscular type the men lifted heavy dumbbells. At a temperature of 86° F. and a humidity of 80 per cent they accomplished 28 per cent less total work than at 68° F. and 50 per cent humidity. Or again, taking their output in 68° F. fresh air as 100 per cent, their output under other changes were: in 68° F. stagnant air, 91 per cent; in 75 °F. fresh air, 85 per cent; and in 75° F. stagnant air, 77 per cent. This is definite testimony to the importance of oxygen content, temperature, and humidity, if the work to be done is of a muscular type.

When work of the thinking type is in question the results of the Commission's investigation are much more surprising. When tested with some well-known psychological tests of thinking efficiency no reliable differences appeared in the workers' accomplishments under considerable variations of the atmosphere. Some typical data are selected from the report and presented in the accompanying table. As the report concludes: With the forms of work listed and the lengths of period that were used, when a person "is urged to do his best he does as much, and does it as well, and

PSYCHOLOGICAL TEST SCORES UNDER DIFFERENT ATMOSPHERIC CONDITIONS

	68° F., 50% HUMIDITY FRESH AIR	86° F., 80% HUMIDITY, SAME AIR RECIRCULATED
Naming colors	49	49
Naming opposites	53	55
Cancelling	101	102
Adding	74	76
Multiplying	57	57

improves as rapidly, in a hot, humid, stale, and stagnant air condition ... as under an optimal condition."

What can such results mean? For the industrial manager they indicate the importance of conditioning the air of his factory. For the student and other "brain workers" they indicate that so far as his subjective experiences of comfort and discomfort go, the *atmosphere is an important item in his motivation but not in his capacity.* His diminished inclination to work in hot weather is not to be taken for inability to work. These are the facts. What "morals" are to be drawn from them we cannot consider here. In any case, the reader here, as throughout any presentation of psychological or other scientific data, must be expected to use his own judgment in making his own applications.

Time of Day. Dawn is the hour of hope, when a new day begins. Twilight is the time for sentiment and peaceful contemplation, of retrospect through the hours and the years. Midnight is the witching hour, as also the time for wild parties, thuggery, and rascality generally. High noon means activity, the height of life and life's affairs. To such associative fancies humankind is addicted, and for the substantial and obvious reason that at these hours the kinds of activity mentioned are usually in process. There is nothing "natural" or biologically appropriate about them. So with the hours of work. No doubt because daylight and darkness are convenient or inconvenient for this or that activity, it has become customary to arrange the twenty-four hours in certain conventional programs. Then, when the working day has become well established, certain fairly consistent fluctuations of efficiency have been noted, and the conclusion has been hastily drawn that those fluctuations are affected by the times of day when they occur. The "10 o'clock slump" and especially the "dull drag" at 3.30 and 4 o'clock are proverbial. But what have those clock hours to do with it?

An investigation of the question was conducted by having subjects conform to certain varied programs of eating, working, resting, and sleeping, and then by measuring their energy expenditures in terms of losses of body weight. To measure the loss the subject was asked to lie on a cot that formed one "pan" of a large balance sensitive to one tenth gram; his body weight was then measured at regular intervals through the twenty-four hours. The results obtained show quite clearly that the energy-expenditure curve

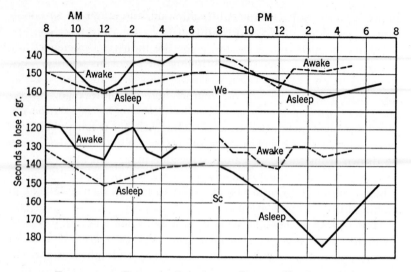

FIGURE 153. DIURNAL COURSES OF ENERGY EXPENDITURE

We, Sc, the subjects.

Continuous line, the awake-in-day régime; *broken line,* the awake-in-night régime.   (From Freeman, G. L. *Diurnal Variations in Performance and Energy Expenditure.* Northwestern Univ. Press, 1935.)

throughout the day is dependent upon the times of eating, of working, of resting, and of sleeping.   For instance, when two subjects were put on a day régime and again on a night régime their curves of metabolic activity (weight loss) were strikingly similar for the two régimes regardless of the fact that one occurred in the day and the other at night.   This point is shown graphically in Figure 153.   To express the point of the experiment in a more general manner: *a person's achievements at various times of the day are not a function of the astronomical day nor of some biological rhythm determined by it, but of* **his** *"day":* his time of arising, his time of eating lunch, and the rest of his program.

Some less scientific but relevant evidence is contributed by industry showing that the nature of production by night shifts is directly comparable to that of daytime shifts.   And from the individual workman's point of view night work can be adapted to quickly, so that it may be as normal as daytime work.   (The difficulty for the night worker is principally that of getting his sleep under proper circumstances.)

Finally, we can draw a parallel from animal behavior.   Surely it would be supposed that the rat has its own special diurnal rhythm with a great burst of activity in the night. A careful investigation of the matter, employing the activity cage shown in Figure 22, and changes in the hour of daily feeding brought to light the fact that while the animals continued to run slightly more at night than in daytime, the period of their greatest activity was in the hour or two just preceding the time for the regular feeding, no matter at which particular hour of the clock that had been established [23].

CONCLUDING STATEMENT

In the present chapter we have canvassed a few of the many external conditions that bear upon the effectiveness of a person's work with hand or brain. The conclusions drawn from scientific studies are not meant to serve as practical prescriptions. They are laid before the reader for his serious consideration and for his thoughtful adaptation to the concrete practicalities of everyday life.

REFERENCES

1. Arai, T. Mental Fatigue. *Teach. Coll. Contr. to Educ.*, 1912, No. 54.
2. Bagby, E. The Psychological Effects of Oxygen Deprivation. *J. Comp. Psychol.*, 1921, **1**, 97–113.
3. Burtt, H. E. *Psychology and Industrial Efficiency.* Appleton, 1929.
4. Dodge, R., and Benedict, F. G. *Psychological Effects of Alcohol.* Carnegie Inst. Wash., 1915.
5. Freeman, G. L. *Diurnal Variations in Performance and Energy Expenditure.* Northwestern Univ. Press, 1935.
6. Hollingworth, H. L. The Influence of Caffeine on Mental and Motor Efficiency. *Arch. Psychol.*, 1912, No. 22.
7. Hollingworth, H. L. The Influence of Alcohol. *J. Abn. & Soc. Psychol.*, 1923–24, **18**, 204–37, 311–33.
8. Hollingworth, H. L. Variations in Efficiency During the Working Day. *Psychol. Rev.*, 1914, **21**, 473–91.
9. Hull, C. L. The Influence of Tobacco Smoking on Mental and Motor Efficiency. *Psychol. Monog.*, 1924, **33**, No. 150.
10. Hull, C. L. The Influence of Caffeine and Other Factors on Certain Phenomena of Rote Learning. *J. Gen. Psychol.*, 1935, **13**, 249–74.
11. Jacobson, E. *You Must Relax.* McGraw-Hill, 1934.
12. Johnson, H. M. The Real Meaning of Fatigue. *J. Nat. Inst. Indus. Psychol.*, 1929, **4**, 433–45; also in *Harpers*, 1929, **158**, 186–93.

13. Johnson, H. M., Swan, T. H., and Weigand, G. E. In What Positions do Healthy People Sleep? *J. Am. Med. Assoc.*, 1930, **94**, 2058–62.

14. Loveday, J. An Experiment with Rest Pauses. *Report Indust. Fatigue Res. Bd.*, No. 10.

15. Maggiora, A. Les Lois de la Fatigue Étudiées Dans les Muscles de l'Homme. *Arch. Italiennes de Biologie*, 1890, **13**, 187–241.

16. Manzer, C. W. An Experimental Investigation of Rest Pauses. *Arch. Psychol.*, 1927, No. 90.

17. Miles, W. R. *Alcohol and Human Efficiency.* Carnegie Inst. Wash., 1924, No. 333.

18. Muscio, B. *Lectures on Industrial Psychology.* Dutton, 1919.

19. Myers, C. S. *Mind and Work.* Putnam, 1921.

20. Poffenberger, A. T. *Applied Psychology.* Appleton, 1927.

21. Robinson, E. S., and Robinson, F. R. Effects of Loss of Sleep. *J. Exper. Psychol.*, 1922, **5**, 93–100.

22. Schulze, R. *Experimental Psychology and Pedagogy* (trans. by Pintner, R.). Geo. Allen, 1912. Chaps. XI, XII.

23. Shirley, M. Studies in Activity. *J. Comp. Psychol.*, 1928, **8**, 159–95.

24. Taylor, F. W. *The Principles of Scientific Management.* Harpers, 1915.

25. Thorndike, E. L. *Educational Psychology. Vol. III, Part I: Mental Work and Fatigue.* Teachers Coll., 1914.

26. Thorndike, E. L., *et al.* Ventilation. *Report of N.Y. State Commission on Ventilation.* Dutton, 1923.

27. Welch, H. J., and Miles, G. H. *Industrial Psychology in Practice.* Pitman, 1932.

CHAPTER XXII
CONCLUDING ORIENTATION

SPECIAL FIELDS OF PSYCHOLOGY

THE survey presented in this book has been a survey of *general* psychology. As a mere introduction to the application of scientific methodology we have had to touch on only those problems of most general significance. But the reader who may have found his interest whetted will be inquiring, in a slang phrase of the day, "Where do we go from here?" Or, in case he brought to the study of psychology a special interest of his own, he will be wanting to follow it through. General Psychology, we may say, is the study of the *typical, normal, human, adult individual*. These words now suggest, by contrast, a few of the special fields to which the reader will presumably go if he continues his study of psychology.

One of these fields is concerned with the psychological differences between men. The last twenty years have witnessed a remarkable development of interest in *individual differences*, starting with the work of Galton and Cattell, which has been elaborated and critically standardized by Pearson, Thorndike, and a host of others. The movement has swept on increasingly until today it is an open question whether the original investigations in the psychological field are concerned more with man in the generic sense or with the differences between man and man. Not unconnected with this development is the remarkably rapid evolution of the *mental testing* technique and program, which has of late years so largely interested the public. Binet is the father of this movement. For these differences, however, we have little time in an introductory presentation. The beginning reader should first become acquainted with man-in-general, and with the principles that operate in determining his general nature. With this as his groundwork he will be in a favorable position to mark out variations from one individual to another. We have limited our study to the typical man.

Another branching of psychological interest has been in the direction of the *abnormal*. Mankind has always been curious about the unusual, in whatever field, and the strange behavior of certain individuals has aroused perennial interest in the study of abnormal forms of personal behavior, such as the various types of psycho-neurosis, psychosis (or insanity), and feeble-mindedness. Also, the appearance of special defects of sight or hearing, of speech or of writing, is always of practical concern. The work of the major investigators of these human deviations — Janet, Kraepelin, Freud, Kempf, and others — has yielded principles profoundly important to psychology, normal as well as abnormal. When certain conditions of human life become disproportionately influential in their effects upon an individual's conduct, these conditions are then most easily identified. The analysis of manifold types of disordered behavior has served to throw into relief processes at work not only in unbalanced but also in normal persons, and the knowledge of these processes is proving to be invaluable for explanatory purposes.

Animal psychology forms another branch of the general field. Interest in the how and why of animal conduct is widespread; and many are the anecdotes related by hunter, horse lover, and dog fancier to prove that some animal has acted in certain ways which according to the narrator showed advanced powers of intelligence. In such cases the interesting psychology may be not that of the animal but that of the narrator. The scientifically conducted study of animal behavior as inborn and as acquired has been another exceedingly fruitful source of principles of psychology in general. Thorndike, Yerkes, Watson, and Köhler have been important contributors in this field.

As in the observation of animals, so in that of children there is a great advantage in dealing with subject matter on a more primitive plane than that used in the observation of adult man. *Child* psychology, after falling into some disrepute twenty-five years ago, owing to the superficial investigations of the "child study" workers, is now becoming re-established as a legitimate scientific discipline by such workers as Ch. Bühler, Goodenough, Shirley, Terman, and Gesell.

It is a common observation that a person behaves differently in different groups. His behavior is not the same in a large group as in a small one; nor is it the same at a social gathering as at morning chapel. He is the same animal organism in both cases and answers to the same name; the striking differences in behavior must be socially determined. Ever-pressing economic and social problems have awakened people to the need of reliable, certain knowledge of *social* psychology, knowledge that will some day furnish the first principles for applied sciences of politics. Promising beginnings have been made — but as has been said by Allport, one of the leading authorities on social psychology, the first need for the beginning reader is to understand the conduct of the individual person.

And now for mention of some of the fields of the *application* of psychological facts or psychological methods.

Educational problems, being problems quite distinctly and obviously problems of human nature, have for decades been studied by psychologists; and this is unquestionably the largest field of applied psychology. What is the true conception of childhood? How does learning go on, especially in certain scholastic activities? How can learning be best facilitated? How shall progress in school work be measured? These are a few of the questions that naturally arise with any teacher or educator; and on each of them a voluminous literature is to be found.

In the *industrial and business* fields the human factors have become recognized as needing study on their own account. Human beings are not adequately conceived of as mere machines — so industrialists themselves are coming to realize. No one knows this better than the man whose duty it is to hire and discharge employees, and his concern is with methods of interviewing and testing and properly fitting the worker to the job. Maintaining a man's fitness for work is another important objective. The worker — and especially his boss — must know at least some first principles here. How to create a marked demand, how to "put across" a commodity by advertising, is an obviously practical problem that deals with human beings as prospects.

In the courtroom as well as in his consultations the lawyer is dealing with people. In fact, it is the troubles and misunderstandings arising between them that is his concern. What is reliable evidence? When is a man "responsible"? Is the system of twelve jurors as poor a method of determining fact and reaching judgment as some critics maintain? Can we tell when a man is lying? How does a judge proceed in his deliberations? *Legal* psychology is somewhat backward in its development, as compared with other applied fields, but the problems here that cry out for more scientific analysis are legion.

In conclusion it may be said that if the reader's interest is in any field that in any way involves human beings, he is likely to find relevant and helpful material in the facts which psychology has already accumulated; and he is quite certain to find the psychologist's (that is, the scientist's) attitude toward people a solvent of many difficulties.

THE PSYCHOLOGICAL VIEWPOINT RESTATED

Throughout this book man has been treated as an object of scientific investigation, with a view to determining what cause-effect relationships obtain in his life. "Human nature" has been viewed not only as "human" but as "nature," as a natural object involved in natural events. In concluding this survey, let it be said again that this is not claimed to be the only legitimate and proper way of regarding man. Human beings are to be valued; and the items and incidents of their surroundings that contribute to their living are to be regarded as weals and woes. Just as the accurate knowledge of details of chemical properties and processes does not in any way invalidate nor displace personal interests in foods as things good-to-eat, and as the precise formulation of physiological laws and principles does not conflict with a desire for health, so likewise an increasingly exact science of the laws of human behavior does not challenge any values to be placed upon human personalities and their behavior. Rather, as in the other two cases mentioned, science should materially further such interests by providing the bases for practical techniques — techniques to be employed in the service of securing those things valued by man.

The natural science method is non-moral; and to psychology as such "goods" and "bads" are irrelevant. But for ethics of the future there is being built a solid foundation in the fundamentals of psychological science. As we obtain increasingly adequate data and laws as to why this juvenile delinquent or that adult recidivist, this public benefactor or that private distributor of blessings, conducts himself as he does, then we shall be equipped in increasingly adequate ways to set into operation just those forces that contribute to the making of approved types of character and conduct and not those forces that work toward an opposite result.

The same interpretation applies to all the other valuational aspects of life. The determination of the details of stimuli that arouse esthetic types of response, for example, in no way invalidates nor challenges artistic endeavor and artistic appreciation. It should, in fact, support and further them. To adapt a phrase from Santayana: the true philosophy looks to science for its view of the facts and to the happiness of men on earth for its ideal.

As the nineteenth century was notable for the unprecedented advance in man's control of his non-personal environment through the technological application of the physical and biological sciences, it may be fairly anticipated that the twentieth century will become remarkable for the development of psychotechnology. The "pure" science of psychology, though still in its swaddling clothes, is today being rapidly expanded in many directions, and — what is more important — is being built upon more solid and certain foundations. And as the fundamental principles and formulae of this science become determined with increasing degrees of accuracy, technological applications are sure to follow. Already trends of practical usefulness are becoming evident, as a steadily growing host of investigators are engaged in working out the applications of the laws of human behavior to the fields of medicine, education, industry, commerce, and law. That "man may become master of his fate" is a phrase invested now with new and fruitful meaning.

REFERENCES

Some general treatments and introductions to each field.

Individual Differences.
Ellis, R. S. *The Psychology of Individual Differences.* Appleton, 1928.
Freeman, F. S. *Individual Differences.* Holt, 1934.
Thorndike, E. L. *Educational Psychology*, vol. III. Teachers Coll., 1914.

Intelligence Testing.
Pintner, R. *Intelligence Testing*, 2d ed. Holt, 1931.
Terman, L. M. *The Measurement of Intelligence.* Houghton Mifflin, 1916. *Measuring Intelligence.* Houghton Mifflin, 1937.

Abnormal Psychology.
Bagby, E. *The Psychology of Personality.* Holt, 1928.
Morgan, J. J. B. *The Psychology of Abnormal People.* Longmans, 1928.
Pillsbury, W. B. *An Elementary Psychology of the Abnormal.* McGraw-Hill, 1932.
Shaffer, L. F. *The Psychology of Adjustment.* Houghton Mifflin, 1936.
Wallin, J. E. W. *Personality Maladjustments and Mental Hygiene.* McGraw-Hill, 1935.

Animal Psychology.

Maier, N. R. F., and Schneirla, T. C. *Principles of Animal Psychology.* McGraw-Hill, 1935.

Munn, N. L. *An Introduction to Animal Psychology.* Houghton Mifflin, 1933.

Warden, C. J., Jenkins, T. N., and Warner, L. H. *Introduction to Comparative Psychology.* Ronald, 1934.

Child Psychology.

Cole, L. *Psychology of Adolescence.* Farrar and Rinehart, 1936.

Gesell, A., and Thompson, H. *Infant Behavior.* McGraw-Hill, 1934.

Goodenough, F. L. *Developmental Psychology.* Appleton-Century, 1934.

Social Psychology.

Allport, F. H. *Social Psychology.* Houghton Mifflin, 1924.

Brown, J. F. *Psychology and the Social Order.* McGraw-Hill, 1936.

LaPiere, R. T., and Farnsworth, P. R. *Social Psychology.* McGraw-Hill, 1936.

Educational Psychology.

Jordan, A. M. *Educational Psychology.* Rev. ed. Holt, 1933.

Sandiford, P. *Educational Psychology.* Longmans, 1928.

Thorndike, E. L. *Educational Psychology: Briefer Course.* Teachers College, 1914.

Trow, W. C. *Educational Psychology.* Houghton Mifflin, 1931.

Applied Psychology.

Burtt, H. E. *Principles of Employment Psychology.* Houghton Mifflin, 1926.

Griffith, C. R. *An Introduction to Applied Psychology.* Macmillan, 1934

Poffenberger, A. T. *Applied Psychology.* Appleton, 1927.

Viteles, M. S. *Industrial Psychology.* Norton, 1932.

Legal Psychology.

Burtt, H. E. *Legal Psychology.* Prentice-Hall, 1931.

McCarthy, D. G. *Psychology for the Lawyer.* Prentice-Hall, 1929.

INDEX

ing, 412; work of, distinguished from mental, 618

Muscles, skeletal, function of, in emotion, 165; changes of, in emotion, 181, 182; effect of anterior pituitary lobe on, 218

Muscles, smooth, 207–210; rôle of, 207, 208; distribution and function of, 208–210; cardiac, 210; contraction of, 216; minute structure of, 210; sphincter, 210; effect of posterior lobe on, 218; static and postural activities of, 340

Muscles, striped, defined, 103 *n.*; as source of drives, 110; distribution and arrangement of, 196–198; contraction of, 198–202; minute structure of, 198, 199; tonic contractions of, 201, 202; co-ordination of, 203; involved in thinking, 569, 570. *See also* Muscles, skeletal

Music, tests of aptitude in, 359, 360

Mutations, in natural selection, 57

Mystical states; effect of, on efficiency, 627, 628

Myxedema, 215, 216

Natural selection, 54–56; Darwinian theory of, 54; five steps in, 54–55; mutations in, 57

Nausea, 239

Nearsightedness, 250

Necessity, the mother of thinking, 541, 542

Nerves, afferent, 200; effect of ductless glands on, 221, 222; efferent, two kinds of, 339

Nervous system, integration of, 213; general importance of, 258; general view of, 286; psychological significance of, 286, 287

Nest-building, as stimulus to behavior-patterns, 118

Neural excitation, strength-duration curve for, 263

Neural organization, of behavior, 258–288; basic principles of, 265–268. *See also* Behavior

Neural transmission, nature of, 258–265; general character of, 258–260; salient characteristics of, 260–262; chronaxie, 262, 263; neuron, 263, 264

Neurons, described, 263–265; types of, 264; number of, 278

Neurosis, as outgrowth of behavior crises, 143–145

New Guinea, anthropological study of, 600, 601

New York State Commission on Ventilation, research by, 630, 631

Newborn, studies of behavior of, 81–84; mass activity in, 83; specific movements of, 83; external stimulation of, 83, 84; adjustive behavior in, 84–86; vegetative processes in, 86

Noises, distinguished from tones, 243; effect of, on efficiency, 628, 629

North Carolina, University of, attention experiments at, 336; examination scores in, 355, 356

Noyes, A. P., example of hysteria from, 143

Observation, or experiments, as final stage in reasoning, 553

Obstruction, method of, for attention measurement, 132–134

Occupation, learning of an, 1

Olfactometer, 230, 231

Ontogenetic development, of emotion, 172–179

Opposition, insight into meaning of, 400

Order of merit, method of, 134; in esthetics, 476

Organism, as biological concept, 38, 39

Organismic and reflexological views, of embryonic development, 78

Organization, as factor in perceiving, 446

Organ-systems, visceral, 362

Oscillation, in disparate attention activities, 335

Oscillograph, cathode ray, 207

Otis, A. S., group tests devised by, 350, 351

Overt behavior, 42, 43

Overtones, 243

Oxytricha, experiment in behavior of, 28, 29

Pain, 239

Paired comparisons, method of, 134; in esthetics, 476

Pancreas, 220, 221

Paramnesia, 432–434

Parathyroid glands, 216

Paresis, 606, 607

Part-reactions, integration of, 365–378; in animal habit-forming, 365–368; in human habit-forming, 368–371; effect as selective agency in, 374–376; trial-and-error in, 376–378

Patrick, J. R., types of trial-and-error, 379

Patterns, of discrete movements, 74; control of, 76, 77; total, of responses in emotion, 190; of disparate attention activities, 335

Pavlov, I. P., as advocate of reflexology, 74; experiments in salivary flow and